C# 8.0 and .NET Core 3.0 – Modern Cross-Platform Development

Fourth Edition

Build applications with C#, .NET Core, Entity Framework Core, ASP.NET Core, and ML.NET using Visual Studio Code

Mark J. Price

BIRMINGHAM - MUMBAI

C# 8.0 and .NET Core 3.0 – Modern Cross-Platform Development
Fourth Edition

Acquisition Editor: Ben Renow-Clarke
Acquisition Editor – Peer Reviews: Suresh Jain
Content Development Editor: Ian Hough
Project Editor: Radhika Atitkar
Technical Editor: Aniket Shetty
Proofreader: Safis Editing
Indexer: Rekha Nair
Presentation Designer: Sandip Tadge

First published: March 2016
Second edition: March 2017
Third edition: November 2017
Fourth edition: October 2019

Production reference: 3311219

Published by Packt Publishing Ltd.
Livery Place
35 Livery Street
Birmingham B3 2PB, UK.

ISBN 978-1-78847-812-0

www.packt.com

Packt>

`packt.com`

Subscribe to our online digital library for full access to over 7,000 books and videos, as well as industry leading tools to help you plan your personal development and advance your career. For more information, please visit our website.

Why subscribe?

- Spend less time learning and more time coding with practical eBooks and Videos from over 4,000 industry professionals
- Learn better with Skill Plans built especially for you
- Get a free eBook or video every month
- Fully searchable for easy access to vital information
- Copy and paste, print, and bookmark content

Did you know that Packt offers eBook versions of every book published, with PDF and ePub files available? You can upgrade to the eBook version at `www.Packt.com` and as a print book customer, you are entitled to a discount on the eBook copy. Get in touch with us at `customercare@packtpub.com` for more details.

At `www.Packt.com`, you can also read a collection of free technical articles, sign up for a range of free newsletters, and receive exclusive discounts and offers on Packt books and eBooks.

Contributors

About the author

Mark J. Price is a Microsoft Specialist: Programming in C# and Architecting Microsoft Azure Solutions, with more than 20 years of educational and programming experience.

Microsoft
C E R T I F I E D
Solutions Developer

App Builder

Microsoft
Specialist

Programming in C#

epn
Episerver CMS
Certified Developer

Since 1993, Mark has passed more than 80 Microsoft programming exams and specializes in preparing others to pass them too. His students range from professionals with decades of experience to 16-year-old apprentices with none. He successfully guides all of them by combining educational skills with real-world experience in consulting and developing systems for enterprises worldwide.

Between 2001 and 2003, Mark was employed full-time to write official courseware for Microsoft in Redmond, USA. His team wrote the first training courses for C# while it was still an early alpha version. While with Microsoft, he taught "train-the-trainer" classes to get Microsoft Certified Trainers up to speed on C# and .NET.

Currently, Mark creates and delivers training courses for Episerver's Digital Experience Platform, the best .NET CMS for Digital Marketing and E-commerce.

In 2010, Mark studied for a Postgraduate Certificate in Education (PGCE). He taught GCSE and A-Level mathematics in two London secondary schools. He holds a Computer Science BSc. Hons. degree from the University of Bristol, UK.

Thank you to my parents, Pamela and Ian, for raising me to be polite, hardworking, and curious about the world. Thank you to my sisters, Emily and Juliet, for loving me despite being their awkward older brother. Thank you to my friends and colleagues who inspire me technically and creatively. Lastly, thanks to all the students I have taught over the years for motivating me to be the best teacher that I can be.

About the reviewer

Damir Arh has many years of experience with software development and maintenance; from complex enterprise software projects to modern consumer oriented mobile applications. Although he has worked with a wide spectrum of different languages, his favorite language remains C#. In his drive towards better development processes, he is a proponent of test-driven development, continuous integration, and continuous deployment. He shares his knowledge by speaking at local user groups and conferences, blogging, and writing articles. He has received the prestigious Microsoft MVP award for developer technologies 7 times in a row. In his spare time, he's always on the move: hiking, geocaching, running, and rock climbing.

I'd like to thank my family and friends for their patience and understanding during the weekends and evenings I spent on my computer to help make this book better for everyone.

Table of Contents

Preface

There are C# books that are thousands of pages long that aim to be comprehensive references to the C# programming language and the .NET Framework.

This book is different. It is concise and aims to be a brisk, fun read that is packed with practical hands-on walkthroughs of each subject. The breadth of the overarching narrative comes at the cost of some depth, but you will find many signposts to explore further if you wish. This book is simultaneously a step-by-step guide to learning modern C# proven practices using cross-platform .NET and a brief introduction to the main types of applications that can be built with them. This book is best for beginners to C# and .NET, or programmers who have worked with C# in the past but feel left behind by the changes in the past few years. If you already have experience with C# 5.0 or later, then in the first topic of *Chapter 2, Speaking C#*, you can review tables of the new language features and jump straight to them. If you already have experience with .NET Core 1.0 or later, then in the first topic of *Chapter 7, Understanding and Packaging .NET Types*, you can review tables of the new platform features and jump straight to them.

I will point out the cool corners and gotchas of C# and .NET, so you can impress colleagues and get productive fast. Rather than slowing down and boring some readers by explaining every little thing, I will assume that you are smart enough to Google an explanation for topics that are related but not necessary to include in a beginner-to-intermediate guide.

You can download solutions for the step-by-step guided tasks and exercises from the following GitHub repository. If you don't know how, then I provide instructions on how to do this using Visual Studio Code at the end of *Chapter 1, Hello, C#! Welcome, .NET!*

```
https://github.com/markjprice/cs8dotnetcore3
```

What this book covers

Chapter 1, Hello, C#! Welcome, .NET!, is about setting up your development environment and using Visual Studio Code to create the simplest application possible with C# and .NET. You will learn how to write and compile code on any of the supported operating systems: Windows, macOS, and Linux variants. You will also learn the best places to look for help.

Chapter 2, Speaking C#, introduces the versions of C# and has tables of which version introduced new features, and then explains the grammar and vocabulary that you will use every day to write the source code for your applications. In particular, you will learn how to declare and work with variables of different types, and about the big change in C# 8.0 with the introduction of nullable reference types.

Chapter 3, Controlling Flow and Converting Types, covers using operators to perform simple actions on variables including comparisons, writing code that makes decisions, repeats a block of statements, and converts between types. It also covers writing code defensively to handle errors when they inevitably occur.

Chapter 4, Writing, Debugging, and Testing Functions, is about following the **Don't Repeat Yourself** (DRY) principle by writing reusable functions. You will also learn how to use debugging tools to track down and remove bugs, monitoring your code while it executes to diagnose problems, and rigorously testing your code to remove bugs and ensure stability and reliability before it gets deployed into production.

Chapter 5, Building Your Own Types with Object-Oriented Programming, discusses all the different categories of members that a type can have, including fields to store data and methods to perform actions. You will use OOP concepts, such as aggregation and encapsulation. You will learn language features such as tuple syntax support and out variables, and default literals and inferred tuple names.

Chapter 6, Implementing Interfaces and Inheriting Classes, explains deriving new types from existing ones using **object-oriented programming** (OOP). You will learn how to define operators and local functions, delegates and events, how to implement interfaces about base and derived classes, how to override a type member, how to use polymorphism, how to create extension methods, and how to cast between classes in an inheritance hierarchy.

Chapter 7, Understanding and Packaging .NET Types, introduces the versions of .NET Core and has tables of which version introduced new features, then presents .NET Core types that are compliant with .NET Standard, and how they relate to C#. You will learn how to deploy and package your own apps and libraries.

Chapter 8, Working with Common .NET Types, discusses the types that allow your code to perform common practical tasks, such as manipulating numbers and text, storing items in collections, and implementing internationalization.

Chapter 9, Working with Files, Streams, and Serialization, talks about interacting with the filesystem, reading and writing to files and streams, text encoding, and serialization formats like JSON and XML.

Chapter 10, Protecting Your Data and Applications, is about protecting your data from being viewed by malicious users using encryption and from being manipulated or corrupted using hashing and signing. You will also learn about authentication and authorization to protect applications from unauthorized users.

Chapter 11, Working with Databases Using Entity Framework Core, explains reading and writing to databases, such as Microsoft SQL Server and SQLite, using the **object-relational mapping (ORM)** technology named Entity Framework Core.

Chapter 12, Querying and Manipulating Data Using LINQ, teaches you **Language INtegrated Queries (LINQ)** — language extensions that add the ability to work with sequences of items and filter, sort, and project them into different outputs.

Chapter 13, Improving Performance and Scalability Using Multitasking, discusses allowing multiple actions to occur at the same time to improve performance, scalability, and user productivity. You will learn about the async Main feature and how to use types in the System.Diagnostics namespace to monitor your code to measure performance and efficiency.

Chapter 14, Practical Applications of C# and .NET, introduces you to the types of cross-platform applications that can be built using C# and .NET.

Chapter 15, Building Websites Using ASP.NET Core Razor Pages, is about learning the basics of building websites with a modern HTTP architecture on the server-side using ASP.NET Core. You will learn how to implement the ASP.NET Core feature known as Razor Pages, which simplifies creating dynamic web pages for small websites.

Chapter 16, Building Websites Using the Model-View-Controller Pattern, is about learning how to build large, complex websites in a way that is easy to unit test and manage with teams of programmers using ASP.NET Core MVC. You will learn about startup configuration, authentication, routes, models, views, and controllers.

Chapter 17, Building Websites Using a Content Management System, explains how a web **Content Management System (CMS)** can enable developers to rapidly build websites with a customizable administration user interface that non-technical users can use to create and manage their own content. As an example, you will learn about a simple open source .NET Core-based one named Piranha CMS.

Chapter 18, Building and Consuming Web Services, explains building backend REST architecture web services using ASP.NET Core Web API and how to properly consume them using factory-instantiated HTTP clients.

Chapter 19, Building Intelligent Apps Using Machine Learning, introduces you to Microsoft's open source ML.NET package of machine learning algorithms, which can be used to embed adaptive intelligence into any cross-platform .NET app, such as a digital commerce website that provides product recommendations for visitors to add to their shopping cart.

Chapter 20, Building Windows Desktop Apps, is the first of two chapters about topics that go beyond what is achievable using cross-platform .NET Core and Visual Studio Code. This chapter introduces you to how .NET Core 3.0 and its Windows Desktop Pack enable Windows Forms and WPF apps to benefit from running on .NET Core. You will then learn the basics of XAML, which can be used to define the user interface for a graphical app for **Windows Presentation Foundation (WPF)** or the **Universal Windows Platform (UWP)**. You will apply principles and features of Fluent Design to light up a UWP app. The apps for this chapter must be built using Visual Studio 2019 on Windows 10.

Chapter 21, Building Cross-Platform Mobile Apps Using Xamarin.Forms, introduces you to taking C# mobile by building a cross-platform app for iOS and Android. The app for this chapter will be built using Visual Studio 2019 for Mac on macOS.

Appendix, Answers to the Test Your Knowledge Questions, has the answers to the test questions at the end of each chapter. You can read this appendix at `https://static.packt-cdn.com/downloads/9781788478120_Appendix_Answers_to_the_Test_Your_Knowledge_Questions.pdf`.

What you need for this book

You can develop and deploy C# and .NET Core apps using Visual Studio Code on many platforms, including Windows, macOS, and many varieties of Linux. An operating system that supports Visual Studio Code and an internet connection is all you need to complete Chapters 1 to 19.

You will need Windows 10 to build the apps in *Chapter 20, Building Windows Desktop Apps*.

You will need macOS to build the apps in *Chapter 21, Building Cross-Platform Mobile Apps Using Xamarin.Forms*, because you must have macOS and Xcode to compile iOS apps.

Conventions

In this book, you will find a number of text styles that distinguish between different kinds of information. Here are some examples of these styles and an explanation of their meaning.

Code words in text, database table names, folder names, filenames, file extensions, pathnames, dummy URLs, user input, and Twitter handles are shown as follows: "The `Controllers`, `Models`, and `Views` folders contain ASP.NET Core classes and the `.cshtml` files for execution on the server."

A block of code is set as follows:

```
// storing items at index positions
names[0] = "Kate";
names[1] = "Jack";
names[2] = "Rebecca";
names[3] = "Tom";
```

When we wish to draw your attention to a particular part of a code block, the relevant lines or items are set in bold:

```
// storing items at index positions
names[0] = "Kate";
names[1] = "Jack";
names[2] = "Rebecca";
names[3] = "Tom";
```

Any command-line input or output is written as follows:

```
dotnet new console
```

New terms and important words are shown in **bold**. Words that you see on the screen, for example, in menus or dialog boxes, appear in the text like this: "Clicking on the **Next** button moves you to the next screen."

More Information: Links to external sources of further reading appear in a box like this.

Good Practice: Recommendations for how to program like an expert appear like this.

Reader feedback

Feedback from our readers is always welcome. Let us know what you think about this book—what you liked or disliked. Reader feedback is important for us as it helps us develop titles that you will really get the most out of.

To send us general feedback, simply email feedback@packtpub.com, and mention the book's title in the subject of your message.

If there is a topic that you have expertise in and you are interested in either writing or contributing to a book, see our author guide at www.packtpub.com/authors.

Customer support

Now that you are the proud owner of a Packt book, we have a number of things to help you to get the most from your purchase.

Downloading the example code

You can download the example code files for this book from your account at http://www.packtpub.com. If you purchased this book elsewhere, you can visit http://www.packtpub.com/support and register to have the files emailed directly to you.

You can download the code files by following these steps:

1. Log in or register to our website using your email address and password.
2. Hover the mouse pointer on the SUPPORT tab at the top.
3. Click on Code Downloads & Errata.
4. Enter the name of the book in the Search box.
5. Select the book for which you're looking to download the code files.
6. Choose from the drop-down menu where you purchased this book from.
7. Click on Code Download.

Once the file is downloaded, please make sure that you unzip or extract the folder using the latest version of:

- WinRAR / 7-Zip for Windows
- Zipeg / iZip / UnRarX for Mac
- 7-Zip / PeaZip for Linux

The code bundle for the book is also hosted on GitHub at https://github.com/PacktPublishing/CSharp-8.0-and-.NET-Core-3.0-Modern-Cross-Platform-Development-Fourth-Edition. We also have other code bundles from our rich catalog of books and videos available at https://github.com/PacktPublishing/. Check them out!

Downloading the color images of this book

We also provide you with a PDF file that has color images of the screenshots/diagrams used in this book. The color images will help you better understand the changes in the output.

You can download this file from `https://static.packt-cdn.com/downloads/9781788478120_ColorImages.pdf`.

Get in touch

Feedback from our readers is always welcome.

General feedback: If you have questions about any aspect of this book, mention the book title in the subject of your message and email us at `customercare@packtpub.com`.

Errata: Although we have taken every care to ensure the accuracy of our content, mistakes do happen. If you have found a mistake in this book we would be grateful if you would report this to us. Please visit, `www.packtpub.com/support/errata`, selecting your book, clicking on the Errata Submission Form link, and entering the details.

Piracy: If you come across any illegal copies of our works in any form on the Internet, we would be grateful if you would provide us with the location address or website name. Please contact us at `copyright@packt.com` with a link to the material.

If you are interested in becoming an author: If there is a topic that you have expertise in and you are interested in either writing or contributing to a book, please visit `authors.packtpub.com`.

Reviews

Please leave a review. Once you have read and used this book, why not leave a review on the site that you purchased it from? Potential readers can then see and use your unbiased opinion to make purchase decisions, we at Packt can understand what you think about our products, and our authors can see your feedback on their book. Thank you!

For more information about Packt, please visit `packt.com`.

Chapter 01

Hello, C#! Welcome, .NET!

In this first chapter, the goals are setting up your development environment, understanding the similarities and differences between .NET Core, .NET Framework, and .NET Standard, and then creating the simplest application possible with C# and .NET Core using Microsoft's Visual Studio Code.

After this first chapter, this book can be divided into three parts: first, the grammar and vocabulary of the C# language; second, the types available in .NET Core for building app features; and third, examples of common cross-platform apps you can build using C# and .NET. The last two chapters are about two types of application that can be built with C# but the first is not cross-platform and the second does not use .NET Core yet so they should be considered bonus chapters.

Most people learn complex topics best by imitation and repetition rather than reading a detailed explanation of the theory; therefore I will not overload you with detailed explanations of every step throughout this book. The idea is to get you to write some code, build an application from that code, and then for you to see it run.

You don't need to know all the nitty-gritty details immediately. That will be something that comes with time as you build your own apps and go beyond what any book can teach you.

In the words of Samuel Johnson, author of the English dictionary in 1755, I have committed "a few wild blunders, and risible absurdities, from which no work of such multiplicity is free." I take sole responsibility for these and hope you appreciate the challenge of my attempt to *lash the wind* by writing this book about rapidly evolving technologies like C# and .NET Core, and the apps that you can build with them.

This first chapter covers the following topics:

- Setting up your development environment
- Understanding .NET
- Building console apps using Visual Studio Code
- Downloading solution code from a GitHub repository
- Looking for help

Setting up your development environment

Before you start programming, you'll need a code editor for C#. Microsoft has a family of code editors and **Integrated Development Environments (IDEs)**, which include:

- Visual Studio Code
- Visual Studio 2019
- Visual Studio 2019 for Mac

Using Visual Studio Code for cross-platform development

The most modern and lightweight code editor to choose, and the only one from Microsoft that is cross-platform, is Microsoft Visual Studio Code. It is able to run on all common operating systems, including Windows, macOS, and many varieties of Linux, including **Red Hat Enterprise Linux (RHEL)** and Ubuntu.

Visual Studio Code is a good choice for modern cross-platform development because it has an extensive and growing set of extensions to support many languages beyond C#, and being cross-platform and lightweight it can be installed on all platforms that your apps will be deployed to for quick bug fixes and so on.

Using Visual Studio Code means a developer can use a cross-platform code editor to developer cross-platform apps. Therefore, I have chosen to use Visual Studio Code for all but the last two chapters for this book, because they need special features not available in Visual Studio Code for building Windows and mobile apps.

More Information: You can read about Microsoft's plans for Visual Studio Code at the following link: `https://github.com/Microsoft/vscode/wiki/Roadmap`.

If you prefer to use Visual Studio 2019 or Visual Studio for Mac instead of Visual Studio Code, then of course you can, but I will assume that you are already familiar with how to use them and so I will not give step-by-step instructions for using them in this book.

More Information: You can read a comparison of Visual Studio Code and Visual Studio 2019 at the following link: `https://www.itworld.com/article/3403683/visual-studio-code-stepping-on-visual-studios-toes.html`.

Using Visual Studio 2019 for Windows app development

Microsoft Visual Studio 2019 only runs on Windows, version 7 SP1 or later. You must run it on Windows 10 to create **Universal Windows Platform** (**UWP**) apps. It is the only Microsoft developer tool that can create Windows apps, so we will use it in *Chapter 20*, *Building Windows Desktop Apps*.

Using Visual Studio for Mac for mobile development

To create apps for the Apple operating systems like iOS to run on devices like iPhone and iPad, you must have Xcode, but that tool only runs on macOS. Although you can use Visual Studio 2019 on Windows with its Xamarin extensions to write a cross-platform mobile app, you still need macOS and Xcode to compile it.

So, we will use Visual Studio 2019 for Mac on macOS in *Chapter 21*, *Building Cross-Platform Mobile Apps Using Xamarin.Forms*.

Recommended tools for chapters

To help you to set up the best environment to use in this book, the following table summarizes which tools and operating systems I recommend be used for each of the chapters in this book:

Chapters	Tool	Operating systems
Chapters 1 to 19	Visual Studio Code	Windows, macOS, Linux
Chapter 20	Visual Studio 2019	Windows 10
Chapter 21	Visual Studio 2019 for Mac	macOS

To write this book, I used my MacBook Pro and the following listed software:

- Visual Studio Code on macOS as my primary code editor.
- Visual Studio Code on Windows 10 in a virtual machine to test OS-specific behavior like working with the filesystem.
- Visual Studio 2019 on Windows 10 in a virtual machine to build Windows apps.
- Visual Studio 2019 for Mac on macOS to build mobile apps.

More Information: Google and Amazon are supporters of Visual Studio Code, as you can read at the following link: `https://www.cnbc.com/2018/12/20/microsoft-cmo-capossela-says-google-employees-use-visual-studio-code.html`.

Deploying cross-platform

Your choice of code editor and operating system for development does not limit where your code gets deployed.

.NET Core 3.0 supports the following platforms for deployment:

- **Windows**: Windows 7 SP1, or later. Windows 10 version 1607, or later. Windows Server 2012 R2 SP1, or later. Nano Server version 1803, or later.
- **Mac**: macOS High Sierra (version 10.13), or later.
- **Linux**: RHEL 6, or later. RHEL, CentOS, Oracle Linux version 7, or later. Ubuntu 16.04, or later. Fedora 29, or later. Debian 9, or later. openSUSE 15, or later.

More Information: You can read the official list of supported operating systems at the following link: `https://github.com/dotnet/core/blob/master/release-notes/3.0/3.0-supported-os.md`.

Understanding Microsoft Visual Studio Code versions

Microsoft releases a new feature version of Visual Studio Code (almost) every month and bug fix versions more frequently. For example:

- Version 1.38, August 2019 feature release.
- Version 1.38.1, August 2019 bug fix release.

More Information: You can read about the latest versions at the following link: `https://code.visualstudio.com/updates`.

The version used in this book is 1.38.1 released on 11 September 2019, but the version of Microsoft Visual Studio Code is less important than the version of the **C# for Visual Studio Code** extension that you will install later.

While the C# extension is not required, it provides IntelliSense as you type, code navigation, and debugging features, so it's something that's very handy to install. To support C# 8.0, you should install C# extension version 1.21.3 or later.

In this book, I will show keyboard shortcuts and screenshots of Visual Studio Code using the macOS version. Visual Studio Code on Windows and variants of Linux are practically identical, although keyboard shortcuts are likely different.

Some common keyboard shortcuts that we will use are shown in the following table:

Action	macOS	Windows
Show Command Palette	*Cmd + Shift + P,* *F1*	*Ctrl + Shift + P,* *F1*
Go To Definition	*F12*	*F12*
Go Back	*Ctrl + -*	*Alt + ←*
Go Forward	*Ctrl + Shift + -*	*Alt + →*
Show Terminal	*Ctrl +* ` (backtick)	*Ctrl + '* (quote)
New Terminal	*Ctrl + Shift +* ` (backtick)	*Ctrl + Shift + '* (quote)
Toggle Line Comment	*Ctrl + /*	*Ctrl + /*
Toggle Block Comment	*Shift + Option + A*	*Shift + Alt + A*

I recommend that you download a PDF of keyboard shortcuts for your operating system from the following list:

- Windows: https://code.visualstudio.com/shortcuts/keyboard-shortcuts-windows.pdf

- macOS: https://code.visualstudio.com/shortcuts/keyboard-shortcuts-macos.pdf

- Linux: https://code.visualstudio.com/shortcuts/keyboard-shortcuts-linux.pdf

 More Information: You can learn about the default key bindings for Visual Studio Code and how to customize them at the following link: https://code.visualstudio.com/docs/getstarted/keybindings.

Visual Studio Code has rapidly improved over the past couple of years and has pleasantly surprised Microsoft with its popularity. If you are brave and like to live on the bleeding edge, then there is an Insiders edition, which is a daily build of the next version.

Downloading and installing Visual Studio Code

Now you are ready to download and install Visual Studio Code, its C# extension, and the .NET Core 3.0 SDK.

1. Download and install either the Stable build or the Insiders edition of Visual Studio Code from the following link: `https://code.visualstudio.com/`.

2. Download and install the .NET Core SDK from the following link: `https://www.microsoft.com/net/download`.

3. To install the C# extension, you must first launch the Visual Studio Code application.

4. In Visual Studio Code, click the **Extensions** icon or navigate to **View | Extensions**.

5. C# is one of the most popular extensions available, so you should see it at the top of the list, or you can enter C# in the search box, as shown in the following screenshot:

6. Click **Install** and wait for supporting packages to download and install.

 More Information: You can read more about Visual Studio Code support for C# at the following link: `https://code.visualstudio.com/docs/languages/csharp`.

Installing other extensions

In later chapters of this book, you will use more extensions. If you want to install them now, all the extensions that we will use are shown in the following table:

Extension	Description
C# for Visual Studio Code (powered by OmniSharp) `ms-vscode.csharp`	C# editing support, including syntax highlighting, IntelliSense, Go to Definition, Find All References, debugging support for .NET Core (CoreCLR), and support for `project.json` and `csproj` projects on Windows, macOS, and Linux.
C# XML Documentation Comments `k--kato.docomment`	Generate XML documentation comments for Visual Studio Code.
C# Extensions `jchannon.csharpextensions`	Add C# class, add C# interface, add fields and properties from constructors, add constructor from properties.
REST Client `humao.rest-client`	Send an HTTP request and view the response directly in Visual Studio Code.
ILSpy .NET Decompiler `icsharpcode.ilspy-vscode`	Decompile MSIL assemblies – support for .NET Framework, .NET Core, and .NET Standard.
SharpPad `jmazouri.sharppad`	Easily inspect the results of your code. It works similarly to standalone tools like LinqPad and RoslynPad.

Understanding .NET

.NET Framework, .NET Core, Xamarin, and .NET Standard are related and overlapping platforms for developers used to build applications and services. In this section, we're going to introduce you to each of these .NET concepts.

Understanding the .NET Framework

.NET Framework is a development platform that includes a **Common Language Runtime (CLR)**, which manages the execution of code, and a **Base Class Library (BCL)**, which provides a rich library of classes to build applications from. Microsoft originally designed the .NET Framework to have the possibility of being cross-platform, but Microsoft put their implementation effort into making it work best with Windows.

Since .NET Framework 4.5.2 it has been an official component of the Windows operating system. .NET Framework is installed on over one billion computers so it must change as little as possible. Even bug fixes can cause problems, so it is updated infrequently.

All of the apps on a computer written for the .NET Framework share the same version of the CLR and libraries stored in the **Global Assembly Cache (GAC)**, which can lead to issues if some of them need a specific version for compatibility.

Good Practice: Practically speaking, .NET Framework is Windows-only and a legacy platform. Do not create new apps using it.

Understanding the Mono and Xamarin projects

Third parties developed a .NET Framework implementation named the **Mono** project. Mono is cross-platform, but it fell well behind the official implementation of .NET Framework.

More Information: You can read more about the project at the following link: `http://www.mono-project.com/`.

Mono has found a niche as the foundation of the **Xamarin** mobile platform as well as cross-platform game development platforms like **Unity**.

More Information: You can read more about Unity at the following link: `https://docs.unity3d.com/`.

Microsoft purchased Xamarin in 2016 and now gives away what used to be an expensive Xamarin extension for free with Visual Studio 2019. Microsoft renamed the **Xamarin Studio** development tool, which could only create mobile apps, to **Visual Studio for Mac** and gave it the ability to create other types of apps. With Visual Studio 2019 for Mac, Microsoft has replaced parts of the Xamarin Studio editor with parts from Visual Studio for Windows to provide closer parity of experience and performance.

Understanding .NET Core

Today, we live in a truly cross-platform world where modern mobile and cloud development have made Windows, as an operating system, much less important. Because of that, Microsoft has been working on an effort to decouple .NET from its close ties with Windows. While rewriting .NET Framework to be truly cross-platform, they've taken the opportunity to refactor and remove major parts that are no longer considered core.

This new product was branded **.NET Core** and includes a cross-platform implementation of the CLR known as **CoreCLR** and a streamlined library of classes known as **CoreFX**.

Scott Hunter, Microsoft Partner Director Program Manager for .NET, has said that "Forty percent of our .NET Core customers are brand-new developers to the platform, which is what we want with .NET Core. We want to bring new people in."

.NET Core is fast moving and because it can be deployed side by side with an app, it can change frequently knowing those changes will not affect other .NET Core apps on the same machine. Improvements that Microsoft can make to .NET Core cannot be added to .NET Framework.

More Information: You can read more about Microsoft's positioning of .NET Core and .NET Framework at the following link: `https://devblogs.microsoft.com/dotnet/update-on-net-core-3-0-and-net-framework-4-8/`.

Understanding future versions of .NET

At the Microsoft Build developer conference in May 2019, the .NET team announced that after .NET Core 3.0 is released in September 2019, .NET Core will be renamed .NET and the major version number will skip the number four to avoid confusion with .NET Framework 4.x. So, the next version of .NET Core will be .NET 5.0 and it is scheduled for release in November 2020. After that, Microsoft plans on annual major version releases every November, rather like Apple does major version number releases of iOS every second week in September.

More Information: You can read more about Microsoft's plans for .NET 5.0 at the following link: `https://devblogs.microsoft.com/dotnet/introducing-net-5/`

The following table shows when the key versions of .NET Core were released, when future releases are planned, and which version is used by the various editions of this book:

Version	Released	Edition	Published
.NET Core RC1	November 2015	First	March 2016
.NET Core 1.0	June 2016		
.NET Core 1.1	November 2016		

.NET Core 1.0.4 and .NET Core 1.1.1	March 2017	Second	March 2017
.NET Core 2.0	August 2017		
.NET Core for UWP in Windows 10 Fall Creators Update	October 2017	Third	November 2017
.NET Core 2.1	May 2018		
.NET Core 2.2	December 2018		
.NET Core 3.0 (Current)	September 2019	Fourth	October 2019
.NET Core 3.1 (LTS)	November 2019		
.NET 5.0	November 2020		
.NET 6.0	November 2021		

I cannot promise 5th and 6th editions of this book to match future releases of .NET, but that would be a safe bet.

Understanding .NET Core support

.NET Core versions are either **Long-Term Support (LTS)** or Current, as described in the following list:

- **LTS** releases are stable and require fewer updates over their lifetime. These are a good choice for applications that you do not intend to update frequently. LTS releases will be supported for 3 years after general availability. .NET Core 3.1 will be an LTS release.

.NET Core 1.0 and 1.1 reached end of life and went out of support on 27 June 2019, 3 years after the initial .NET Core 1.0 release.

- **Current** releases include features that may change based on feedback. These are a good choice for applications that you are actively developing because they provide access to the latest improvements. After a 3-month maintenance period, the previous minor version will no longer be supported. For example, after 1.2 releases systems running version 1.1 will have 3 months to update to 1.2 to remain eligible for support. .NET Core 3.0 is a Current release so if .NET Core 3.1 releases in November 2019 as planned, then you will need to upgrade to it by February 2020.

Both receive critical fixes throughout their lifetime for security and reliability. You must stay up to date with the latest patches to get support. For example, if a system is running 1.0 and 1.0.1 has been released, 1.0.1 will need to be installed.

What is different about .NET Core?

.NET Core is smaller than the current version of .NET Framework due to the fact that legacy technologies have been removed. For example, **Windows Forms** and **Windows Presentation Foundation (WPF)** can be used to build graphical user interface (GUI) applications, but they are tightly bound to the Windows ecosystem, so they have been removed from .NET Core on macOS and Linux.

One of the new features of .NET Core 3.0 is support for running old Windows Forms and WPF applications using the **Windows Desktop Pack** that is included with the Windows version of .NET Core 3.0 which is why it is bigger than the SDKs for macOS and Linux. You can make some small changes to your legacy Windows app if necessary, and then rebuild it for .NET Core to take advantage of new features and performance improvements. You'll learn about support for building these types of Windows apps in *Chapter 20, Building Windows Desktop Apps*.

The latest technology used to build Windows apps is the **Universal Windows Platform (UWP)**, which is built on a custom version of .NET Core. UWP is not part of .NET Core because it is not cross-platform.

ASP.NET Web Forms and **Windows Communication Foundation (WCF)** are old web application and service technologies that fewer developers are choosing to use for new development projects today, so they have also been removed from .NET Core. Instead, developers prefer to use ASP.NET MVC and ASP.NET Web API. These two technologies have been refactored and combined into a new product that runs on .NET Core, named **ASP.NET Core**. You'll learn about the technologies in *Chapter 15, Building Websites Using ASP.NET Core Razor Pages*, *Chapter 16, Building Websites Using the Model-View-Controller Pattern*, and *Chapter 18, Building and Consuming Web Services*.

More Information: Some .NET Framework developers are upset that ASP.NET Web Forms, WCF, and Windows Workflow (WF) are missing from .NET Core and would like Microsoft to change their minds. There are open source projects to enable WCF and WF to migrate to .NET Core. You can read more at the following link: `https://devblogs.microsoft.com/dotnet/supporting-the-community-with-wf-and-wcf-oss-projects/`.

Entity Framework (EF) 6 is an object-relational mapping technology that is designed to work with data that is stored in relational databases such as Oracle and Microsoft SQL Server. It has gained baggage over the years, so the cross-platform API has been slimmed down, will be given support for non-relational databases like Microsoft Azure Cosmos DB, and named **Entity Framework Core**. You will learn about it in *Chapter 11, Working with Databases Using Entity Framework Core*.

If you have existing apps that use the old EF then version 6.3 is supported on .NET Core 3.0.

In addition to removing large pieces from .NET Framework in order to make .NET Core, Microsoft has componentized the .NET Core into NuGet packages, those being small chunks of functionality that can be deployed independently.

Microsoft's primary goal is not to make .NET Core smaller than .NET Framework. The goal is to componentize .NET Core to support modern technologies and to have fewer dependencies, so that deployment requires only those packages that your application needs.

Understanding .NET Standard

The situation with .NET in 2019 is that there are three forked .NET platforms controlled by Microsoft, as shown in the following list:

- .NET Core: for cross-platform and new apps.
- .NET Framework: for legacy apps.
- Xamarin: for mobile apps.

Each has strengths and weaknesses because they are all designed for different scenarios. This has led to the problem that a developer must learn three platforms, each with annoying quirks and limitations. Because of that, Microsoft defined **.NET Standard**: a specification for a set of APIs that all .NET platforms can implement to indicate what level of compatibility they have. For example, basic support is indicated by a platform being compliant with .NET Standard 1.4.

With .NET Standard 2.0 and later, Microsoft made all three platforms converge on a modern minimum standard, which makes it much easier for developers to share code between any flavor of .NET.

For .NET Core 2.0 and later, this added a number of the missing APIs that developers need to port old code written for .NET Framework to the cross-platform .NET Core. However, some APIs are implemented, but throw an exception to indicate to a developer that they should not actually be used! This is usually due to differences in the operating system on which you run .NET Core. You'll learn how to handle these exceptions in *Chapter 2*, *Speaking C#*.

It is important to understand that .NET Standard is just a standard. You are not able to install .NET Standard in the same way that you cannot install HTML5. To use HTML5, you must install a web browser that implements the HTML5 standard.

To use the .NET Standard, you must install a .NET platform that implements the .NET Standard specification. .NET Standard 2.0 is implemented by the latest versions of .NET Framework, .NET Core, and Xamarin.

The latest .NET Standard, 2.1, is only implemented by .NET Core 3.0, Mono, and Xamarin. Some features of C# 8.0 require .NET Standard 2.1. .NET Standard 2.1 is not implemented by .NET Framework 4.8 so we should treat .NET Framework as legacy.

 More Information: .NET Standard versions and which .NET platforms support them are listed at the following link: `https://github.com/dotnet/standard/blob/master/docs/versions.md`.

.NET platforms and tools used by the book editions

For the first edition of this book, which was written in March 2016, I focused on .NET Core functionality but used .NET Framework when important or useful features had not yet been implemented in .NET Core, because that was before the final release of .NET Core 1.0. Visual Studio 2015 was used for most examples, with Visual Studio Code shown only briefly.

The second edition was (almost) completely purged of all .NET Framework code examples so that readers were able to focus on .NET Core examples that truly run cross-platform. The third edition completed the switch. It was rewritten so that all of the code was pure .NET Core. But giving step-by-step instructions for multiple tools added unnecessary complexity.

In this fourth edition, we'll continue the trend by only showing coding examples using Visual Studio Code for all but the last two chapters of this book. In *Chapter 20, Building Windows Desktop Apps*, you'll need to use Visual Studio 2019 running on Windows 10, and in *Chapter 21, Building Cross-Platform Mobile Apps Using Xamarin. Forms*, you'll need to use Visual Studio 2019 for Mac.

Understanding intermediate language

The C# compiler (named **Roslyn**) used by the `dotnet` CLI tool converts your C# source code into **intermediate language** (**IL**) code and stores the IL in an assembly (a DLL or EXE file). IL code statements are like assembly language instructions, which are executed by .NET Core's virtual machine, known as CoreCLR.

At runtime, CoreCLR loads the IL code from the assembly, the just-in-time (JIT) compiler compiles it into native CPU instructions, and then it is executed by the CPU on your machine. The benefit of this three-step compilation process is that Microsoft is able to create CLRs for Linux and macOS, as well as for Windows. The same IL code runs everywhere because of the second compilation process, which generates code for the native operating system and CPU instruction set.

Regardless of which language the source code is written in, for example, C#, Visual Basic or F#, all .NET applications use IL code for their instructions stored in an assembly. Microsoft and others provide disassembler tools that can open an assembly and reveal this IL code like the ILSpy .NET Decompiler extension.

Understanding .NET Native

Another .NET initiative is called .NET Native. This compiles C# code to native CPU instructions **ahead of time (AoT)**, rather than using the CLR to compile IL code JIT to native code later. .NET Native improves execution speed and reduces the memory footprint for applications because the native code is generated at build time and then deployed instead of the IL code.

 More Information: You can read more about .NET Native at the following link: `https://github.com/dotnet/corert/blob/master/Documentation/intro-to-corert.md`.

Comparing .NET technologies

We can summarize and compare .NET technologies in 2019, as shown in the following table:

Technology	Description	Host OSes
.NET Core	Modern feature set, full C# 8.0 support, port existing and create new Windows and Web apps and services.	Windows, macOS, Linux
.NET Framework	Legacy feature set, limited C# 8.0 support, maintain existing applications.	Windows only
Xamarin	Mobile and desktop apps.	Android, iOS, macOS

By the end of 2020, Microsoft promises that there will be a single .NET platform instead of three. .NET 5.0 is planned to have a single BCL and two runtimes: one optimized for server or desktop scenarios like websites and Windows desktop apps based on the .NET Core runtime, and one optimized for mobile apps based on the Xamarin runtime.

Building console apps using Visual Studio Code

The goal of this section is to showcase how to build a console app using Visual Studio Code. Both instructions and screenshots in this section are for macOS, but the same actions will work with Visual Studio Code on Windows and Linux variants.

The main differences will be native command-line actions such as deleting a file: both the command and the path are likely to be different on Windows or macOS and Linux. Luckily, the `dotnet` command-line tool will be identical on all platforms.

Writing code using Visual Studio Code

Let's get started writing code!

1. Start Visual Studio Code.
2. On macOS, navigate to **File** | **Open...**, or press *Cmd + O*. On Windows, navigate to **File** | **Open Folder...**, or press *Ctrl + K Ctrl + O*. On both OSes, you can click the **Open Folder** button in the **EXPLORER** pane or click the **Open Folder...** link on the **Welcome** page, as shown in the following screenshot:

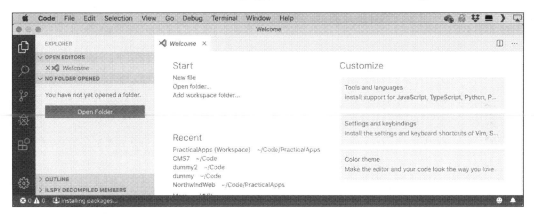

3. In the dialog box, navigate to your user folder on macOS (mine is named `markjprice`), your `Documents` folder on Windows, or any directory or drive in which you want to save your projects.
4. Click the **New Folder** button and name the folder `Code`.
5. In the `Code` folder, create a new folder named `Chapter01`.
6. In the `Chapter01` folder, create a new folder named `HelloCS`.
7. Select the `HelloCS` folder and on macOS click **Open** or on Windows click **Select Folder**.

8. Navigate to **View | Terminal**, or on macOS press *Ctrl + `* (backtick) and on Windows press *Ctrl + '* (single quote). Confusingly on Windows the key combination *Ctrl + `* (backtick) splits the current window!

9. In **TERMINAL**, enter the following command:

```
dotnet new console
```

10. You will see that the `dotnet` command-line tool creates a new **Console Application** project for you in the current folder, and the **EXPLORER** window shows the two files created, `HelloCS.proj` and `Program.cs`, as shown in the following screenshot:

11. In **EXPLORER**, click on the file named `Program.cs` to open it in the editor window. The first time that you do this, Visual Studio Code may have to download and install C# dependencies like OmniSharp, the Razor Language Server, and the .NET Core debugger, if it did not do this when you installed the C# extension.

12. If you see a warning saying that required assets are missing, click **Yes**, as shown in the following screenshot:

13. After a few seconds, a folder named .vscode will appear in the **EXPLORER** pane. These are used during debugging, as you will learn in *Chapter 4, Writing, Debugging, and Testing Functions*.

14. In Program.cs, modify line 9 so that the text that is being written to the console says, **Hello, C#!**

15. Navigate to **File | Auto Save**. This toggle will save the annoyance of remembering to save before rebuilding your application each time.

Compiling and running code using dotnet CLI

The next task is to compile and run the code.

1. Navigate to **View | Terminal** and enter the following command:

    ```
    dotnet run
    ```

2. The output in the **TERMINAL** window will show the result of running your application, as shown in the following screenshot:

Downloading solution code from a GitHub repository

Git is a commonly used source code management system. GitHub is a company, website, and desktop application that makes it easier to manage Git. Microsoft recently purchased GitHub, so it will continue to get closer integration with Microsoft tools.

I used GitHub to store solutions to all the practical exercises that are featured at the end of each chapter. You will find the repository for this chapter at the following link: https://github.com/markjprice/cs8dotnetcore3.

Using Git with Visual Studio Code

Visual Studio Code has support for Git, but it will use your OS's Git installation, so you must install Git 2.0 or later first before you get these features. You can install Git from the following link: `https://git-scm.com/download`.

If you like to use a GUI, you can download GitHub Desktop from the following link:

`https://desktop.github.com`

Cloning the book solution code repository

Let's clone the book solution code repository.

1. Create a folder named `Repos` in your user or `Documents` folder, or wherever you want to store your Git repositories.
2. In Visual Studio Code, open the `Repos` folder.
3. Navigate to **View | Terminal**, and enter the following command:
   ```
   git clone https://github.com/markjprice/cs8dotnetcore3.git
   ```
4. Cloning all of the solutions for all of the chapters will take a minute or so, as shown in the following screenshot:

More Information: For more information about source code version control with Visual Studio Code, visit the following link: `https://code.visualstudio.com/Docs/editor/versioncontrol`

Looking for help

This section is all about how to find quality information about programming on the web.

Reading Microsoft documentation

The definitive resource for getting help with Microsoft developer tools and platforms used to be **Microsoft Developer Network (MSDN)**. Now, it is **Microsoft Docs**, and you can find it at the following link: https://docs.microsoft.com/.

Getting help for the dotnet tool

At the command line, you can ask the dotnet tool for help about its commands.

1. To open the official documentation in a browser window for the dotnet new command, enter the following at the command line or in Visual Studio Code Terminal:

    ```
    dotnet help new
    ```

2. To get help output at the command line, use the -h or --help flag, as shown in the following command:

    ```
    dotnet new console -h
    ```

3. You will see the following partial output:

    ```
    Console Application (C#)
    Author: Microsoft
    Description: A project for creating a command-line application
    that can run on .NET Core on Windows, Linux and macOS
    Options:
      --langVersion  Sets langVersion in the created project file
                     text - Optional
      --no-restore   If specified, skips the automatic restore of the
    project on create.
                     bool - Optional
                     Default: false / (*) true
    * Indicates the value used if the switch is provided without
    a value.
    ```

Getting definitions of types and their members

One of the most useful keyboard shortcuts in Visual Studio Code is *F12* to **Go To Definition**. This will show what the public definition of the type or member looks like by reading the metadata in the compiled assembly. Some tools like ILSpy .NET Decompiler will even reverse-engineer from the metadata and IL code back into C# for you.

1. In Visual Studio Code, open the `HelloCS` folder.

2. In `Program.cs`, inside the `Main` method, enter the following statement to declare an integer variable named `z`:

   ```
   int z;
   ```

3. Click inside `int` and then press *F12*, or right-click and choose **Go To Definition**. In the new code window that appears, you can see how the `int` data type is defined, as shown in the following screenshot:

You can see that `int`:

- ° Is defined using the `struct` keyword.
- ° Is in the `System.Runtime` assembly.
- ° Is in the `System` namespace.
- ° Is named `Int32`.
- ° Is therefore an alias for the `System.Int32` type.
- ° Implements interfaces such as `IComparable`.
- ° Has constant values for its maximum and minimum values.
- ° Has methods like `Parse`.

Good Practice: When you try to use **Go To Definition** you will sometimes see an error saying, **No definition found**. This is because the C# extension does not know about the current project. Navigate to **View | Command Palette**, enter and select **OmniSharp: Select Project**, and then select the correct project that you want to work with.

Right now, the **Go To Definition** feature is not that useful to you because you do not yet know what these terms mean.

By the end of the first part of this book, which teaches you about C#, you will know enough for this feature to become very handy.

4. In the code editor window, scroll down to find the `Parse` method with a single `string` parameter starting on line 86, as shown in the following screenshot:

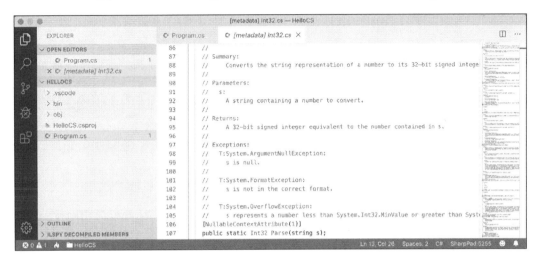

In the comment, you will see that Microsoft has documented what exceptions might occur if you call this method, including `ArgumentNullException`, `FormatException`, and `OverflowException`. Now, we know that we need to wrap a call to this method in a `try` statement and which exceptions to catch.

Hopefully, you are getting impatient to learn what all this means!

Be patient for a little longer. You are almost at the end of this chapter, and in the next chapter you will dive into the details of the C# language. But first, let's see where else you can look for help.

Looking for answers on Stack Overflow

Stack Overflow is the most popular third-party website for getting answers to difficult programming questions. It's so popular that search engines such as **DuckDuckGo** have a special way to write a query to search the site.

1. Start your favorite web browser.

2. Navigate to `DuckDuckGo.com`, enter the following query, and note the search results, which are also shown in the following screenshot:

```
!so securestring
```

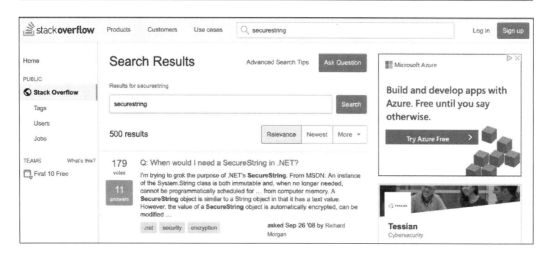

Searching for answers using Google

You can search **Google** with advanced search options to increase the likelihood of finding what you need.

1. Navigate to Google.

2. Search for information about `garbage collection` using a simple Google query, and note that you will probably see a Wikipedia definition of garbage collection in computer science, and then a list of garbage collection services in your local area, as shown in the following screenshot:

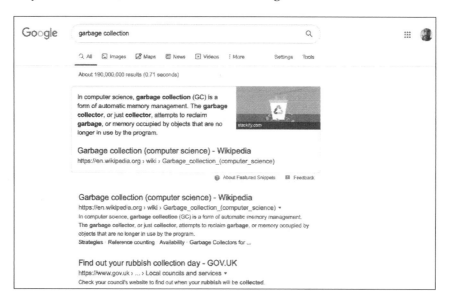

3. Improve the search by restricting it to a useful site such as Stack Overflow, and by removing languages that we might not care about such as C++, Rust, and Python, or by adding C# and .NET explicitly, as shown in the following search query:

```
garbage collection site:stackoverflow.com +C# -Java
```

Subscribing to the official .NET blog

To keep up to date with .NET, an excellent blog to subscribe to is the official **.NET Blog** written by the .NET engineering teams, and you can find it at the following link: `https://blogs.msdn.microsoft.com/dotnet/`

Practicing and exploring

Let's now test your knowledge and understanding by trying to answer some questions, getting some hands-on practice, and exploring with deeper research into the topics covered throughout this chapter.

Exercise 1.1 – Test your knowledge

Try to answer the following questions, remembering that although most answers can be found in this chapter, some online research or code writing will be needed to answer others:

1. Why can a programmer use different languages, for example, C# and F#, to write applications that run on .NET Core?

2. What do you type at the prompt to create a console app?

3. What do you type at the prompt to build and execute C# source code?

4. What is the Visual Studio Code keyboard shortcut to view Terminal?

5. Is Visual Studio 2019 better than Visual Studio Code?

6. Is .NET Core better than .NET Framework?

7. What is .NET Standard and why is it important?

8. What is the name of the entry point method of a .NET console application and how should it be declared?

9. Where would you look for help about a C# keyword?

10. Where would you look for solutions to common programming problems?

Exercise 1.2 – Practice C# anywhere

You don't need Visual Studio Code, or even Visual Studio 2019 or Visual Studio 2019 for Mac to write C#. You can go to .NET Fiddle - `https://dotnetfiddle.net/` - and start coding online.

Microsoft is also working on an online version of Visual Studio Code that can run in any browser but currently it is only available in private preview. Eventually, it will be accessible to everyone at the following link: `https://online.visualstudio.com/`

Exercise 1.3 – Explore topics

You can use the following links to read more details about the topics we've covered in this chapter:

- **Welcome to .NET Core**: `http://dotnet.github.io`
- **.NET Core Command-Line Interface (CLI) tool**: `https://aka.ms/dotnet-cli-docs`
- **.NET Core runtime, CoreCLR**: `https://github.com/dotnet/coreclr/`
- **.NET Core Roadmap**: `https://github.com/dotnet/core/blob/master/roadmap.md`
- **.NET Standard FAQ**: `https://github.com/dotnet/standard/blob/master/docs/faq.md`
- **Stack Overflow**: `http://stackoverflow.com/`
- **Google Advanced Search**: `http://www.google.com/advanced_search`
- **Microsoft Virtual Academy**: `https://mva.microsoft.com/`
- **Microsoft Channel 9: Developer Videos**: `https://channel9.msdn.com/`

Summary

In this chapter, we set up your development environment, discussed the differences between .NET Framework, .NET Core, Xamarin, and .NET Standard, we used Visual Studio Code and .NET Core SDK to create a simple console application, we learned how to download the solution code for this book from a GitHub repository, and most importantly, how to find help.

In the next chapter, you will learn to speak C#.

Chapter 02
Speaking C#

This chapter is all about the basics of the C# programming language. Over the course of this chapter, you'll learn how to write statements using the grammar of C#, as well as being introduced to some of the common vocabulary that you will use every day. In addition to this, by the end of the chapter you'll feel confident in knowing how to temporarily store and work with information in your computer's memory.

This chapter covers the following topics:

- Introducing C#
- Understanding the basics of C#
- Working with variables
- Working with null values
- Further exploring console applications

Introducing C#

This part of the book is about the C# language—the grammar and vocabulary that you will use every day to write the source code for your applications.

Programming languages have many similarities to human languages, except that in programming languages, you can make up your own words, just like Dr. Seuss!

In a book written by Dr. Seuss in 1950, *If I Ran the Zoo*, he states this:

> *"And then, just to show them, I'll sail to Ka-Troo And Bring Back an It-Kutch, a Preep, and a Proo, A Nerkle, a Nerd, and a Seersucker, too!"*

Understanding language versions and features

This part of the book covers the C# programming language and is written primarily for beginners, so it covers the fundamental topics that all developers need to know, from declaring variables to storing data to how to define your own custom data types.

Advanced and obscure topics like `ref` local variable reassignment and reference semantics with value types are not covered.

This book covers features of the C# language from version 1.0 up to the latest version, 8.0. If you already have some familiarity with older versions of C# and are excited to find out about the new features in the most recent versions of C#, I have made it easier for you to jump around by listing language versions and their important new features below, along with the chapter number and topic title where you can learn about them.

C# 1.0

C# 1.0 was released in 2002 and included all the important features of a statically typed object-oriented modern language, as you will see throughout all the chapters in Part 1.

C# 2.0

C# 2.0 was released in 2005 and focused on enabling strong data typing using generics, to improve code performance and reduce type errors, including the topics listed in the following table:

Feature	Chapter	Topic
Nullable value types	2	Making a value type nullable
Generics	6	Making types more reusable with generics

C# 3.0

C# 3.0 was released in 2007 and focused on enabling declarative coding with **Language INtegrated Queries (LINQ)** and related features like anonymous types and lambda expressions, including the topics listed in the following table:

Feature	Chapter	Topic
Implicitly typed local variables	2	Inferring the type of a local variable
LINQ	12	All topics in *Chapter 12, Querying and Manipulating Data Using LINQ*

C# 4.0

C# 4.0 was released in 2010 and focused on improving interoperability with dynamic languages like F# and Python, including the topics listed in the following table:

Feature	Chapter	Topic
Dynamic types	2	The dynamic type
Named/optional arguments	5	Optional parameters and named arguments

C# 5.0

C# 5.0 was released in 2012 and focused on simplifying asynchronous operation support by automatically implementing complex state machines while writing what looks like synchronous statements, including the topics listed in the following table:

Feature	Chapter	Topic
Simplified asynchronous tasks	13	Understanding async and await

C# 6.0

C# 6.0 was released in 2015 and focused on minor refinements to the language, including the topics listed in the following table:

Feature	Chapter	Topic
static imports	2	Simplifying the usage of the console
Interpolated strings	2	Displaying output to the user
Expression bodied members	5	Defining read-only properties

C# 7.0

C# 7.0 was released in March 2017 and focused on adding functional language features like tuples and pattern matching, as well as minor refinements to the language, including the topics listed in the following table:

Feature	Chapter	Topic
Binary literals and digit separators	2	Storing whole numbers
Pattern matching	3	Pattern matching with the if statement
out variables	5	Controlling how parameters are passed
Tuples	5	Combining multiple values with tuples
Local functions	6	Defining local functions

C# 7.1

C# 7.1 was released in August 2017 and focused on minor refinements to the language, including the topics listed in the following table:

Feature	Chapter	Topic
Default literal expressions	5	Setting fields with default literal
Inferred tuple element names	5	Inferring tuple names
`async Main`	13	Improving responsiveness for console apps

C# 7.2

C# 7.2 was released in November 2017 and focused on minor refinements to the language, including the topics listed in the following table:

Feature	Chapter	Topic
Leading underscores in numeric literals	2	Storing whole numbers
Non-trailing named arguments	5	Optional parameters and named arguments
`private protected` access modifier	5	Understanding access modifiers
You can test `==` and `!=` with tuple types	5	Comparing tuples

C# 7.3

C# 7.3 was released in May 2018 and focused on performance-oriented safe code that improve `ref` variables, pointers, and stackalloc. These are advanced and rarely needed for most developers so they are not covered in this book.

 More Information: If you're interested, you can read the details at the following link: `https://docs.microsoft.com/en-us/dotnet/csharp/whats-new/csharp-7-3`

C# 8.0

C# 8.0 was released in September 2019 and focused on a major change to the language related to null handling, including the topics listed in the following table:

Feature	Chapter	Topic
Nullable reference types	2	Making a reference type nullable
Switch expressions	3	Simplifying switch statements with switch expressions

Default interface methods	6	Understanding default interface methods

More Information: You can learn more about the current status of the C# language at this link: `https://github.com/dotnet/roslyn/blob/master/docs/Language%20Feature%20Status.md`.

Discovering your C# compiler versions

With the C# 7.x generation, Microsoft decided to increase the cadence of language releases, releasing minor version numbers, also known as point releases, for the first time since C# 1.1.

.NET language compilers for C#, Visual Basic, and F#, also known as Roslyn, are distributed as part of .NET Core SDK. To use a specific version of C#, you must have at least that version of .NET Core SDK installed, as shown in the following table:

.NET Core SDK	Roslyn	C#
1.0.4	2.0 - 2.2	7.0
1.1.4	2.3 - 2.4	7.1
2.1.2	2.6 - 2.7	7.2
2.1.200	2.8 - 2.10	7.3
3.0	3.0 - 3.3	8.0

More Information: You can see a list of versions at the following link: `https://github.com/dotnet/roslyn/wiki/NuGet-packages`

Let's see what C# language compiler versions you have available.

1. Start Visual Studio Code.

2. Navigate to **View | Terminal**.

3. To determine which version of the .NET Core SDK you have available, enter the following command:

```
dotnet --version
```

4. Note the version at the time of writing is .NET Core 3.0, as shown in the following output:

```
3.0.100
```

5. To determine which versions of the C# compiler you have available, enter the following command:

```
csc -langversion:?
```

6. Note all the versions available at the time of writing, as shown in the following output:

```
Supported language versions:
default
1
2
3
4
5
6
7.0
7.1
7.2
7.3
8.0 (default)
latestmajor
preview
latest
```

Enabling a specific language version compiler

Developer tools like Visual Studio Code and the dotnet command-line interface assume that you want to use the latest major version of a C# language compiler by default. So before C# 8.0 was released, C# 7.0 was the latest major version and was used by default. To use the improvements in a C# point release like 7.1, 7.2, or 7.3, you had to add a configuration element to the project file, as shown in the following markup:

```
<LangVersion>7.3</LangVersion>
```

If Microsoft releases a C# 8.1 compiler and you want to use its new language features then you will have to add a configuration element to your project file, as shown in the following markup:

```
<LangVersion>8.1</LangVersion>
```

Potential values for the <LangVersion> are shown in the following table:

LangVersion	Description
7, 7.1, 7.2, 7.3, 8	Entering a specific version number will use that compiler if it has been installed.
latestmajor	Uses the highest major number, for example, 7.0 in August 2019, 8.0 in October 2019.
latest	Uses the highest major and highest minor number, for example, 7.2 in 2017, 7.3 in 2018, 8 in 2019, perhaps 8.1 in 2020.
preview	Uses the highest available preview version, for example, 8.0 in January 2019 with .NET Core 3.0 Preview 1 installed.

After creating a new project with the `dotnet` command-line tool, you can edit the `csproj` file and add the `<LangVersion>` element, as shown highlighted in the following markup:

```
<Project Sdk="Microsoft.NET.Sdk">

  <PropertyGroup>
    <OutputType>Exe</OutputType>
    <TargetFramework>netcoreapp3.0</TargetFramework>
    <LangVersion>preview</LangVersion>
  </PropertyGroup>

</Project>
```

Your projects must target either `netcoreapp3.0` or `netstandard2.1` to use the full features of C# 8.0.

More Information: The version of C# used by your project is determined by the target framework, as described at the following link: `https://devblogs.microsoft.com/dotnet/an-update-to-c-versions-and-c-tooling/`.

Understanding C# basics

To learn C#, you will need to create some simple applications. To avoid overloading you with too much information too soon, the chapters in the first part of this book will use the simplest type of application: a console application.

Let's start by looking at the basics of the grammar and vocabulary of C#. Throughout this chapter, you will create multiple console applications, with each one showing a feature of the C# language.

1. If you've completed *Chapter 1, Hello, C#! Welcome, .NET!*, then you will already have a `Code` folder in your user folder. If not, then you'll need to create it.

2. Create a subfolder named `Chapter02`, with a sub-subfolder named `Basics`.

3. Start Visual Studio Code and open the `Chapter02/Basics` folder.

4. In Visual Studio Code, navigate to **View** | **Terminal**, and enter the following command:

    ```
    dotnet new console
    ```

5. In **EXPLORER**, click the `Program.cs` file, and then click on **Yes** to add the missing required assets.

Understanding C# grammar

The grammar of C# includes statements and blocks. To document your code, you can use comments.

 Good Practice: Comments should never be the only way that you document your code. Choosing sensible names for variables and functions, writing unit tests, and creating literal documents are other ways to document your code.

Statements

In English, we indicate the end of a sentence with a full stop. A sentence can be composed of multiple words and phrases, with the order of words being part of the grammar. For example, in English, we say: "the black cat."

The adjective, *black*, comes before the noun, *cat*. Whereas French grammar has a different order; the adjective comes after the noun, "le chat noir." What's important to take away from this is that the order matters.

C# indicates the end of a **statement** with a semicolon. A statement can be composed of multiple **variables** and **expressions**. For example, in the following statement, `totalPrice` is a variable and `subtotal + salesTax` is an expression:

```
var totalPrice = subtotal + salesTax;
```

The expression is made up of an operand named `subtotal`, an operator +, and another operand named `salesTax`. The order of operands and operators matters.

Comments

When writing your code, you're able to add comments to explain your code using a double slash, //. By inserting // the compiler will ignore everything after the // until the end of the line, as shown in the following code:

```
// sales tax must be added to the subtotal
var totalPrice = subtotal + salesTax;
```

Visual Studio Code will add or remove the comment double slashes at the start of the currently selected line(s) if you press *Ctrl + K + C* to add them or *Ctrl + K + U* to remove them. In macOS, press *Cmd* instead of *Ctrl*.

To write a multiline comment, use /* at the beginning and */ at the end of the comment, as shown in the following code:

```
/*
This is a multi-line
comment.
*/
```

Blocks

In English, we indicate a paragraph by starting a new line. C# indicates a **block** of code with the use of curly brackets, { }. Blocks start with a declaration to indicate what it is being defined. For example, a block can define a **namespace**, **class**, **method**, or a **statement**, something we will learn more about later.

In your current project, note that the grammar of C# is written for you by the dotnet CLI tool. I've added some comments to the statements written by the project template, as shown in the following code:

```
using System; // a semicolon indicates the end of a statement

namespace Basics
{
  class Program
  {
    static void Main(string[] args)
    { // the start of a block
      Console.WriteLine("Hello World!"); // a statement
    } // the end of a block
  }
}
```

Understanding C# vocabulary

The C# vocabulary is made up of **keywords**, **symbol characters**, and **types**.

Some of the predefined, reserved keywords that you will see in this book include using, namespace, class, static, int, string, double, bool, if, switch, break, while, do, for, and foreach.

Some of the symbol characters that you will see include ", ', +, -, *, /, %, @, and $.

By default, Visual Studio Code shows C# keywords in blue in order to make them easier to differentiate from other code. Visual Studio Code allows you to customize the color scheme.

1. In Visual Studio Code, navigate to **Code | Preferences | Color Theme** (it is on the **File** menu on Windows), or press *Ctrl* or *Cmd* + *K*, *Ctrl* or *Cmd* + *T*.

2. Select a color theme. For reference, I'll use the **Light+ (default light)** color theme so that the screenshots look good in a printed book.

There are other contextual keywords that only have a special meaning in a specific context. However, that still means that there are only about 100 actual C# keywords in the language.

The English language has more than 250,000 distinct words, so how does C# get away with only having about one hundred keywords? Moreover, why is C# so difficult to learn if it has only 0.0416% of the amount of words compared to the English language?

One of the key differences between a human language and a programming language is that developers need to be able to define the new "words" with new meanings. Apart from the 104 keywords in the C# language, this book will teach you about some of the hundreds of thousands of "words" that other developers have defined, but you will also learn how to define your own "words."

More Information: Programmers all over the world must learn English because most programming languages use English words such as namespace and class. There are programming languages that use other human languages, such as Arabic, but they are rare. If you are interested in learning, this YouTube video shows a demonstration of an Arabic programming language: `https://youtu.be/dk08cdwf6v8`

Help for writing correct code

Plain text editors such as Notepad don't help you write correct English. Likewise, Notepad won't help you write correct C# either.

Microsoft Word can help you write English by highlighting spelling mistakes with red squiggles, with Word saying that "icecream" should be ice-cream or ice cream, and grammatical errors with blue squiggles, like a sentence should have an uppercase first letter.

Similarly, Visual Studio Code's C# extension helps you write C# code by highlighting spelling mistakes, like the method name should be `WriteLine` with an uppercase `L`, and grammatical errors, like statements that must end with a semicolon.

The C# extension constantly watches what you type and gives you feedback by highlighting problems with colored squiggly lines, similar to that of Microsoft Word.

Let's see it in action.

1. In `Program.cs`, change the `L` in the `WriteLine` method to lowercase.

2. Delete the semicolon at the end of the statement.

3. Navigate to **View | Problems**, or press *Ctrl* or *Cmd + Shift + M*, and note that a red squiggle appears under the code mistakes and details are shown in the **PROBLEMS** window, as you can see in the following screenshot:

4. Fix the two coding mistakes.

Verbs are methods

In English, verbs are doing or action words, like run and jump. In C#, doing or action words are called **methods**. There are hundreds of thousands of methods available to C#. In English, verbs change how they are written based on when in time the action happens. For example, Amir *was jumping* in the past, Beth *jumps* in the present, they *jumped* in the past, and Charlie *will jump* in the future.

In C#, methods such as `WriteLine` change how they are called or executed based on the specifics of the action. This is called **overloading**, which is something we will cover in more detail during *Chapter 5, Building Your Own Types with Object-Oriented Programming*. But for now, consider the following example:

```
// outputs a carriage-return
Console.WriteLine();
```

```
// outputs the greeting and a carriage-return
Console.WriteLine("Hello Ahmed");

// outputs a formatted number and date and a carriage-return
Console.WriteLine(
  "Temperature on {0:D} is {1}°C.", DateTime.Today, 23.4);
```

A different analogy is that some words are spelled the same, but have different meanings depending on the context.

Nouns are types, fields, and variables

In English, nouns are names that refer to things. For example, Fido is the name of a dog. The word "dog" tells us the type of thing that Fido is, and so in order for Fido to fetch a ball, we would use his name.

In C#, their equivalents are **types**, **fields**, and **variables**. For example, Animal and Car are **types**; that is, they are nouns for categorizing things. Head and Engine are fields, that is, nouns that belong to Animal and Car. Whilst Fido and Bob are variables, that is, nouns for referring to a specific thing.

There are tens of thousands of types available to C#, though have you noticed how I didn't say, "There are tens of thousands of types in C#?" The difference is subtle but important. The language of C# only has a few keywords for types, such as string and int, and strictly speaking, C# doesn't define any types. Keywords such as string that look like types are **aliases**, which represent types provided by the platform on which C# runs.

It's important to know that C# cannot exist alone; after all, it's a language that runs on variants of .NET. In theory, someone could write a compiler for C# that uses a different platform, with different underlying types. In practice, the platform for C# is .NET, which provides tens of thousands of types to C#, including System.Int32, which is the C# keyword alias int maps to, as well as many more complex types, such as System.Xml.Linq.XDocument.

It's worth taking note that the term **type** is often confused with **class**. Have you ever played the parlor game *Twenty Questions*, also known as *Animal, Vegetable, or Mineral*? In the game, everything can be categorized as an animal, vegetable, or mineral. In C#, every **type** can be categorized as a class, struct, enum, interface, or delegate. The C# keyword string is a class, but int is a struct. So, it is best to use the term **type** to refer to both.

Revealing the extent of the C# vocabulary

We know that there are more than one hundred keywords in C#, but how many types are there? Let's now write some code in order to find out how many types (and their methods) are available to C# in our simple console application.

Don't worry about how this code works for now; it uses a technique called reflection.

1. We'll start by adding the following statements at the top of the `Program.cs` file, as shown in the following code:

```
using System.Linq;
using System.Reflection;
```

2. Inside the `Main` method, delete the statement that writes `Hello World!` and replace it with the following code:

```
// loop through the assemblies that this app references
foreach (var r in Assembly.GetEntryAssembly()
  .GetReferencedAssemblies())
{
  // load the assembly so we can read its details
  var a = Assembly.Load(new AssemblyName(r.FullName));

  // declare a variable to count the number of methods
  int methodCount = 0;

  // loop through all the types in the assembly
  foreach (var t in a.DefinedTypes)
  {
    // add up the counts of methods
    methodCount += t.GetMethods().Count();
  }
  // output the count of types and their methods
  Console.WriteLine(
  "{0:N0} types with {1:N0} methods in {2} assembly.",
  arg0: a.DefinedTypes.Count(),
  arg1: methodCount,
  arg2: r.Name);
}
```

3. Navigate to **View | Terminal**.

4. In **TERMINAL**, enter the following command:

```
dotnet run
```

5. After running that command, you will see the following output, which shows the actual number of types and methods that are available to you in the simplest application when running on macOS. The numbers of types and methods displayed may be different depending on the operating system that you are using, as shown in the following output:

```
30 types with 325 methods in System.Runtime assembly.

99 types with 1,068 methods in System.Linq assembly.

56 types with 691 methods in System.Console assembly.
```

6. Add statements to the top of the Main method to declare some variables, as shown highlighted in the following code:

```
static void Main(string[] args)
{
  // declare some unused variables using types
  // in additional assemblies
  System.Data.DataSet ds;
  System.Net.Http.HttpClient client;
```

By declaring variables that use types in other assemblies, those assemblies are loaded with our application, which allows our code to see all the types and methods in them. The compiler will warn you that you have unused variables but that won't stop your code from running.

7. Run the console application again and view the results, which should look similar to the following output:

```
30 types with 325 methods in System.Runtime assembly.
371 types with 6,735 methods in System.Data.Common assembly.
406 types with 4,228 methods in System.Net.Http assembly.
99 types with 1,068 methods in System.Linq assembly.
56 types with 691 methods in System.Console assembly.
```

Now, you have a better sense of why learning C# is a challenge, because there are so many types and methods to learn. Methods are only one category of a member that a type can have, and other programmers are constantly defining new members!

Working with variables

All applications process data. Data comes in, data is processed, and then data goes out. Data usually comes into our program from files, databases, or user input, and it can be put temporarily into variables that will be stored in the memory of the running program. When the program ends, the data in memory is lost. Data is usually output to files and databases, or to the screen or a printer. When using variables, you should think about, firstly, how much space it takes in the memory, and, secondly, how fast it can be processed.

We control this by picking an appropriate type. You can think of simple common types such as int and double as being different-sized storage boxes, where a smaller box would take less memory but may not be as fast at being processed; for example, adding 16-bit numbers might not be processed as fast as adding 64-bit numbers on a 64-bit operating system. Some of these boxes may be stacked close by, and some may be thrown into a big heap further away.

Naming things and assigning values

There are naming conventions for things, and it is good practice to follow them, as shown in the following table:

Naming convention	Examples	Use for
Camel case	`cost`, `orderDetail`, `dateOfBirth`	Local variables, private fields.
Title case	`String`, `Int32`, `Cost`, `DateOfBirth`, `Run`	Types, non-private fields, and other members like methods.

 Good Practice: Following a consistent set of naming conventions will enable your code to be easily understood by other developers (and yourself in the future!).

 You can find more information about Naming Guidelines at `https://docs.microsoft.com/en-us/dotnet/standard/design-guidelines/naming-guidelines`

The following code block shows an example of declaring a named local variable and assigning a value to it with the = symbol. You should note that you can output the name of a variable using a keyword introduced in C# 6.0, `nameof`:

```
// let the heightInMetres variable become equal to the value 1.88
double heightInMetres = 1.88;
Console.WriteLine($"The variable {nameof(heightInMetres)} has the value {heightInMetres}.");
```

The message in double quotes in the preceding code wraps onto a second line because the width of a printed page is too narrow. When entering a statement like this in your code editor, type it all in a single line.

Literal values

When you assign to a variable, you often, but not always, assign a **literal** value. But what is a literal value? A literal is a notation that represents a fixed value. Data types have different notations for their literal values, and over the next few sections, you will see examples of using literal notation to assign values to variables.

Storing text

For text, a single letter, such as an A, is stored as a char type and is assigned using single quotes around the literal value, or assigning the return value of a function call, as shown in the following code:

```
char letter = 'A'; // assigning literal characters
char digit = '1';
char symbol = '$';
char userChoice = GetKeystroke(); // assigning from a function
```

For text, multiple letters, such as Bob, are stored as a string type and are assigned using double quotes around the literal value, or assigning the return value of a function call, as shown in the following code:

```
string firstName = "Bob"; // assigning literal strings
string lastName = "Smith";
string phoneNumber = "(215) 555-4256";

// assigning a string returned from a function call
string address = GetAddressFromDatabase(id: 563);
```

Understanding verbatim strings

When storing text in a string variable, you can include escape sequences, which represent special characters like tabs and new lines using a backslash, as shown in the following code:

```
string fullNameWithTabSeparator = "Bob\tSmith";
```

More Information: You can read more about escape sequences at the following link: https://devblogs.microsoft.com/csharpfaq/what-character-escape-sequences-are-available/.

But what if you are storing the path to a file, and one of the folder names starts with a T, as shown in the following code:

```
string filePath = "C:\televisions\sony\bravia.txt";
```

The compiler will convert the \t into a tab character and you will get errors!

You must prefix with the @ symbol to use a **verbatim** literal string, as shown in the following code:

```
string filePath = @"C:\televisions\sony\bravia.txt";
```

More Information: You can read more about verbatim strings at the following link: https://docs.microsoft.com/en-us/dotnet/csharp/language-reference/tokens/verbatim.

To summarize:

- **Literal string**: Characters enclosed in double-quote characters. They can use escape characters like \t for tab.

- **Verbatim string**: A literal string prefixed with @ to disable escape characters so that a backslash is a backslash.

- **Interpolated string**: A literal string prefixed with $ to enable embedded formatted variables. You will learn more about this later in this chapter.

Storing numbers

Numbers are data that we want to perform an arithmetic calculation on, for example, multiplying. A telephone number is not a number. To decide whether a variable should be stored as a number or not, ask yourself whether you need to perform arithmetic operations on the number or whether the number includes non-digit characters such as parentheses or hyphens to format the number as (414) 555-1234. In this case, the number is a sequence of characters, so it should be stored as a string.

Numbers can be **natural numbers**, such as 42, used for counting (also called **whole numbers**); they can also be negative numbers, such as -42 (called **integers**); or, they can be **real numbers**, such as 3.9 (with a fractional part), which are called **single** or **double-precision floating point numbers** in computing.

Let's explore numbers.

1. Create a new folder inside the Chapter02 folder named Numbers.

2. In Visual Studio Code, open the Numbers folder.

3. In **TERMINAL**, create a new console application using the dotnet new console command.

4. Inside the Main method, type statements to declare some number variables using various data types, as shown in the following code:

```
// unsigned integer means positive whole number
// including 0
uint naturalNumber = 23;

// integer means negative or positive whole number
// including 0
```

```
int integerNumber = -23;

// float means single-precision floating point
// F suffix makes it a float literal
float realNumber = 2.3F;

// double means double-precision floating point
double anotherRealNumber = 2.3; // double literal
```

Storing whole numbers

You might know that computers store everything as bits. The value of a bit is either 0 or 1. This is called a **binary number system**. Humans use a **decimal number system**.

The decimal number system, also known as Base 10, has 10 as its **base,** meaning there are ten digits, from 0 to 9. Although it is the number base most commonly used by human civilizations, other number-base systems are popular in science, engineering, and computing. The binary number system also known as Base 2 has two as its base, meaning there are two digits, 0 and 1.

The following table shows how computers store the decimal number 10. Take note of the bits with the value 1 in the 8 and the 2 columns; 8 + 2 = 10:

128	64	32	16	8	4	2	1
0	0	0	0	1	0	1	0

So, 10 in decimal is 00001010 in binary.

Two of the improvements seen in C# 7.0 and later are the use of the underscore character, _, as a digit separator and support for binary literals. You can insert underscores anywhere into the digits of a number literal, including decimal, binary, or hexadecimal notation, to improve legibility. For example, you could write the value for one million in decimal notation, that is, Base 10, as 1_000_000

To use binary notation, that is, Base 2, using only 1s and 0s, start the number literal with 0b. To use hexadecimal notation, that is, Base 16, using 0 to 9 and A to F, start the number literal with 0x.

1. At the bottom of the Main method, type statements to declare some number variables using underscore separators, as shown in the following code:

   ```
   // three variables that store the number 2 million
   int decimalNotation = 2_000_000;
   int binaryNotation = 0b_0001_1110_1000_0100_1000_0000;
   int hexadecimalNotation = 0x_001E_8480;
   ```

```
// check the three variables have the same value
// both statements output true
Console.WriteLine($"{decimalNotation == binaryNotation}");
Console.WriteLine(
  $"{decimalNotation == hexadecimalNotation}");
```

2. Run the console app and note the result is that all three numbers are the same, as shown in the following output:

```
True

True
```

Computers can always exactly represent integers using the int type or one of its sibling types such as long and short.

Storing real numbers

Computers cannot always exactly represent floating point numbers. The float and double types store real numbers using single and double precision floating points.

Most programming languages implement the IEEE Standard for Floating-Point Arithmetic. IEEE 754 is a technical standard for floating-point arithmetic established in 1985 by the Institute of Electrical and Electronics Engineers (IEEE).

 More Information: If you want to dive deep into understanding floating point numbers then you can read an excellent primer at the following link: https://ciechanow.ski/exposing-floating-point/.

The following table shows how a computer represents the number 12.75 in binary notation. Note the bits with the value 1 in the 8, 4, ½, and ¼ columns.

$8 + 4 + ½ + ¼ = 12¾ = 12.75.$

128	64	32	16	8	4	2	1	.	½	¼	1/8	1/16
0	0	0	0	1	1	0	0	.	1	1	0	0

So, 12.75 in decimal is 00001100.1100 in binary. As you can see, the number 12.75 can be exactly represented using bits. However, some numbers can't, something that we'll be exploring shortly.

Writing code to explore number sizes

C# has an **operator** named `sizeof()` that returns the number of bytes that a type uses in memory. Some types have members named `MinValue` and `MaxValue`, which return the minimum and maximum values that can be stored in a variable of that type. We are now going to use these features to create a console application to explore number types.

1. Inside the `Main` method, type statements to show the size of three number data types, as shown in the following code:

```
Console.WriteLine($"int uses {sizeof(int)} bytes and can store
numbers in the range {int.MinValue:N0} to {int.MaxValue:N0}.");
Console.WriteLine($"double uses {sizeof(double)} bytes and can
store numbers in the range {double.MinValue:N0} to {double.
MaxValue:N0}.");
Console.WriteLine($"decimal uses {sizeof(decimal)} bytes and can
store numbers in the range {decimal.MinValue:N0} to {decimal.
MaxValue:N0}.");
```

The width of printed pages in this book make the `string` values (in double-quotes) to wrap over multiple lines. You must type them on a single line, or you will get compile errors.

2. Run the console application by entering `dotnet run`, and view the output, as shown in the following screenshot:

An `int` variable uses four bytes of memory and can store positive or negative numbers up to about 2 billion. A `double` variable uses eight bytes of memory and can store much bigger values! A `decimal` variable uses 16 bytes of memory and can store big numbers, but not as big as a `double` type.

But you may be asking yourself, why might a `double` variable be able to store bigger numbers than a `decimal` variable, yet it's only using half the space in memory? Well, let's now find out!

Comparing double and decimal types

You will now write some code to compare double and decimal values. Although it isn't hard to follow, don't worry about understanding the syntax right now.

1. Under the previous statements, enter statements to declare two `double` variables, add them together and compare them to the expected result, and write the result to the console, as shown in the following code:

```
Console.WriteLine("Using doubles:");

double a = 0.1;
double b = 0.2;

if (a + b == 0.3)
{
  Console.WriteLine($"{a} + {b} equals 0.3");
}
else
{
  Console.WriteLine($"{a} + {b} does NOT equal 0.3");
}
```

2. Run the console application and view the result, as shown in the following output:

```
Using doubles:

0.1 + 0.2 does NOT equal 0.3
```

The `double` type is not guaranteed to be accurate because some numbers literally cannot be represented as floating-point values.

 More Information: Read more about why 0.1 does not exist in floating-point numbers: https://www.exploringbinary. com/why-0-point-1-does-not-exist-in-floating- point/.

As a rule of thumb, you should only use `double` when accuracy, especially when comparing the equality of two numbers, is not important. An example of this may be when you're measuring a person's height.

The problem with the preceding code is illustrated by how the computer stores the number `0.1`, or multiples of `0.1`. To represent `0.1` in binary, the computer stores 1 in the 1/16 column, 1 in the 1/32 column, 1 in the 1/256 column, 1 in the 1/512 column, and so on.

The number `0.1` in decimal is `0.00011001100110011...` repeating forever:

4	2	1	.	½	¼	1/8	1/16	1/32	1/64	1/128	1/256	1/512	1/1024	1/2048
0	0	0	.	0	0	0	1	1	0	0	1	1	0	0

Good Practice: Never compare `double` values using `==`. During the First Gulf War, an American Patriot missile battery used `double` values in its calculations. The inaccuracy caused it to fail to track and intercept an incoming Iraqi Scud missile, and 28 soldiers were killed; you can read about this at `https://www.ima.umn.edu/~arnold/disasters/patriot.html`.

3. Copy and paste the statements that you wrote before (that used the `double` variables).

4. Modify the statements to use `decimal` and rename the variables to `c` and `d`, as shown in the following code:

```
Console.WriteLine("Using decimals:");

decimal c = 0.1M; // M suffix means a decimal literal value
decimal d = 0.2M;

if (c + d == 0.3M)
{
  Console.WriteLine($"{c} + {d} equals 0.3");
}
else
{
  Console.WriteLine($"{c} + {d} does NOT equal 0.3");
}
```

5. Run the console application and view the result, as shown in the following output:

```
Using decimals:
0.1 + 0.2 equals 0.3
```

The `decimal` type is accurate because it stores the number as a large integer and shifts the decimal point. For example, 0.1 is stored as 1, with a note to shift the decimal point one place to the left. 12.75 is stored as 1275, with a note to shift the decimal point two places to the left.

Good Practice: Use `int` for whole numbers and `double` for real numbers that will not be compared to other values. Use `decimal` for money, CAD drawings, general engineering, and wherever accuracy of a real number is important.

The double type has some useful special values; double.NaN means not-a-number, double.Epsilon is the smallest positive number that can be stored in a double, and double.Infinity means an infinitely large value.

Storing Booleans

Booleans can only contain one of the two literal values: true or false, as shown in the following code:

```
bool happy = true;
bool sad = false;
```

They are most commonly used to branch and loop. You don't need to fully understand them yet, as they are covered more in *Chapter 3, Controlling Flow and Converting Types*.

Using Visual Studio Code workspaces

Before we create any more projects, let's talk about workspaces.

Although we could continue to create and open separate folders for each project, it can be useful to have multiple folders open at the same time. Visual Studio has a feature called workspaces that enables this.

Let's create a workspace for the two projects we have created so far in this chapter.

1. In Visual Studio Code, navigate to **File | Save Workspace As...**.

2. Enter Chapter02 for the workspace name, change to the Chapter02 folder, and click **Save**, as shown in the following screenshot:

3. Navigate to **File | Add Folder to Workspace...**

4. Select the Basics folder, click **Add**, and note that both Basics and Numbers are now part of the Chapter02 workspace.

Good Practice: When using workspaces, be careful when entering commands in Terminal. Be sure that you are in the correct folder before entering potentially destructive commands! You will see how in the next task.

Storing any type of object

There is a special type named `object` which can store any type of data, but its flexibility comes at the cost of messier code and possibly poor performance. Because of those two reasons, you should avoid it whenever possible.

1. Create a new folder named `Variables` and add it to the `Chapter02` workspace.

2. Navigate to **Terminal | New Terminal**.

3. Select the **Variables** project, as shown in the following screenshot:

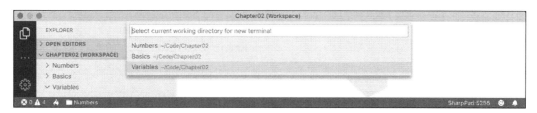

4. Enter the command to create a new console application: `dotnet new console`.

5. Navigate to **View | Command Palette**.

6. Enter and select **OmniSharp: Select Project**.

7. Select the **Variables** project, and if prompted, click **Yes** to add required assets to debug.

8. In **EXPLORER**, in the **Variables** project, open `Program.cs`.

9. In the `Main` method, add statements to declare and use some variables using the `object` type, as shown in the following code:

```
object height = 1.88; // storing a double in an object
object name = "Amir"; // storing a string in an object

Console.WriteLine($"{name} is {height} metres tall.");

int length1 = name.Length; // gives compile error!
int length2 = ((string)name).Length; // tell compiler it is a
string
```

```
Console.WriteLine($"{name} has {length2} characters.");
```

10. In Terminal, execute the code by entering `dotnet run`, and note that the fourth statement cannot compile because the data type of the `name` variable is not known by the compiler.

11. Add comment double slashes to the beginning of the statement that cannot compile to "comment it out."

12. In Terminal, execute the code by entering `dotnet run`, and note that the compiler can access the length of a `string` if the programmer explicitly tells the compiler that the `object` variable contains a `string`, as shown in the following output:

```
Amir is 1.88 metres tall.
Amir has 4 characters.
```

The `object` type has been available since the first version of C#, but C# 2.0 and later have a better alternative called **generics**, which we will cover in *Chapter 6, Implementing Interfaces and Inheriting Classes*, which will provide us with the flexibility we want, but without the performance overhead.

Storing dynamic types

There is another special type named `dynamic` that can also store any type of data, but even more than `object`, its flexibility comes at the cost of performance. The `dynamic` keyword was introduced in C# 4.0. However, unlike an `object`, the value stored in the variable can have its members invoked without an explicit cast.

1. In the `Main` method, add statements to declare a `dynamic` variable and assign a `string` value, as shown in the following code:

```
// storing a string in a dynamic object
dynamic anotherName = "Ahmed";
```

2. Add a statement to get the length of the `string` value, as shown in the following code:

```
// this compiles but would throw an exception at run-time
// if you later store a data type that does not have a
// property named Length
int length = anotherName.Length;
```

One limitation of `dynamic` is that Visual Studio Code cannot show IntelliSense to help you write the code. This is because the compiler cannot check what the type is during build time. Instead, CLR checks for the member at runtime and throws an exception if it is missing.

Exceptions are a way to indicate that something has gone wrong. You will learn more about them and how to handle them in *Chapter 3, Controlling Flow and Converting Types*.

Declaring local variables

Local variables are declared inside methods, and they only exist during the execution of that method, and once the method returns, the memory allocated to any local variables is released.

Strictly speaking, value types are released while reference types must wait for a garbage collection. You will learn about the difference between value types and reference types in *Chapter 6, Implementing Interfaces and Inheriting Classes*.

Specifying and inferring the type of a local variable

Let's explore local variables declared with specific types and using type inference.

1. Inside the `Main` method, enter statements to declare and assign values to some local variables using specific types, as shown in the following code:

```
int population = 66_000_000; // 66 million in UK
double weight = 1.88; // in kilograms
decimal price = 4.99M; // in pounds sterling
string fruit = "Apples"; // strings use double-quotes
char letter = 'Z'; // chars use single-quotes
bool happy = true; // Booleans have value of true or false
```

Visual Studio Code will show green squiggles under each of the variable names to warn you that the variable is assigned, but its value is never used.

You can use the `var` keyword to declare local variables. The compiler will infer the type from the value that you assign after the assignment operator, `=`.

A literal number without a decimal point is inferred as an `int` variable, that is, unless you add the `L` suffix, in which case, it infers a `long` variable.

A literal number with a decimal point is inferred as `double` unless you add the `M` suffix, in which case, it infers a `decimal` variable, or the `F` suffix, in which case, it infers a `float` variable. Double quotes indicate a `string` variable, single quotes indicate a `char` variable, and the `true` and `false` values infer a `bool` type.

2. Modify the previous statements to use `var`, as shown in the following code:

```
var population = 66_000_000; // 66 million in UK
var weight = 1.88; // in kilograms
```

```
var price = 4.99M; // in pounds sterling
var fruit = "Apples"; // strings use double-quotes
var letter = 'Z'; // chars use single-quotes
var happy = true; // Booleans have value of true or false
```

 Good Practice: Although using var is convenient, some developers avoid using it, to make it easier for a code reader to understand the types in use. Personally, I use it only when the type is obvious. For example, in the following code statements, the first statement is just as clear as the second in stating what the type of the xml variable is, but it is shorter. However, the third statement isn't clear, so the fourth is better. If in doubt, spell it out!

```
// good use of var because it avoids the repeated type
// as shown in the more verbose second statement
var xml1 = new XmlDocument();
XmlDocument xml2 = new XmlDocument();

// bad use of var because we cannot tell the type, so we
// should use a specific type declaration as shown in
// the second statement
var file1 = File.CreateText(@"C:\something.txt");
StreamWriter file2 = File.CreateText(@"C:\something.txt");
```

Getting default values for types

Most of the primitive types except string are **value types**, which means that they must have a value. You can determine the default value of a type using the default() operator.

The string type is a **reference type**. This means that string variables contain the memory address of a value, not the value itself. A reference type variable can have a null value, which is a literal that indicates that the variable does not reference anything (yet). null is the default for all reference types.

You'll learn more about value types and reference types in *Chapter 6, Implementing Interfaces and Inheriting Classes.*

Let's explore default values.

1. In the Main method, add statements to show the default values of an int, bool, DateTime, and string, as shown in the following code:
    ```
    Console.WriteLine($"default(int) = {default(int)}");
    Console.WriteLine($"default(bool) = {default(bool)}");
    ```

```
Console.WriteLine(
  $"default(DateTime) = {default(DateTime)}");
Console.WriteLine(
  $"default(string) = {default(string)}");
```

2. Run the console app and view the result, as shown in the following output:

```
default(int) = 0

default(bool) = False

default(DateTime) = 01/01/0001 00:00:00

default(string) =
```

Storing multiple values

When you need to store multiple values of the same type, you can declare an **array**. For example, you may do this when you need to store four names in a `string` array.

The following code will allocate memory for an array for storing four `string` values. It will then store `string` values at index positions 0 to 3 (arrays count from zero, so the last item is one less than the length of the array). Finally, it will loop through each item in the array using a `for` statement, something that we will cover in more detail in *Chapter 3, Controlling Flow and Converting Types*.

1. In the `Chapter02` folder, create a new folder named `Arrays`.
2. Add the `Arrays` folder to the `Chapter02` workspace.
3. Create a new Terminal window for the `Arrays` project.
4. Create a new console application project in the `Arrays` folder.
5. Select `Arrays` as the current project for OmniSharp.
6. In the `Arrays` project, in `Program.cs`, in the `Main` method, add statements to declare and use an array of string values, as shown in the following code:

    ```
    string[] names; // can reference any array of strings

    // allocating memory for four strings in an array
    names = new string[4];

    // storing items at index positions
    names[0] = "Kate";
    names[1] = "Jack";
    names[2] = "Rebecca";
    names[3] = "Tom";

    // looping through the names
    ```

```
for (int i = 0; i < names.Length; i++)
{
  // output the item at index position i
  Console.WriteLine(names[i]);
}
```

7. Run the console app and note the result, as shown in the following output:

```
Kate
Jack
Rebecca
Tom
```

Arrays are always of a fixed size at the time of memory allocation, so you need to decide how many items you want to store before instantiating them.

Arrays are useful for temporarily storing multiple items, but **collections** are a more flexible option when adding and removing items dynamically. You don't need to worry about collections right now, as we will cover them in *Chapter 8, Working with Common .NET Types*.

Working with null values

You have now seen how to store primitive values like numbers in variables. But what if a variable does not yet have a value? How can we indicate that? C# has the concept of a null value, which can be used to indicate that a variable has not been set.

Making a value type nullable

By default, value types like int and DateTime must always have a value, hence their name. Sometimes, for example, when reading values stored in a database that allows empty, missing, or null values, it is convenient to allow a value type to be null, we call this a **nullable value type**.

You can enable this by adding a question mark as a suffix to the type when declaring a variable. Let's see an example.

1. In the Chapter02 folder, create a new folder named NullHandling.
2. Add the NullHandling folder to the Chapter02 workspace.
3. Create a new Terminal window for the NullHandling project.
4. Create a new console application project in the NullHandling folder.
5. Select NullHandling as the current project for OmniSharp.

6. In the `NullHandling` project, in `Program.cs`, in the `Main` method, add statements to declare and assign values, including `null`, to `int` variables, as shown in the following code:

```
int thisCannotBeNull = 4;
thisCannotBeNull = null; // compile error!

int? thisCouldBeNull = null;
Console.WriteLine(thisCouldBeNull);
Console.WriteLine(thisCouldBeNull.GetValueOrDefault());

thisCouldBeNull = 7;
Console.WriteLine(thisCouldBeNull);
Console.WriteLine(thisCouldBeNull.GetValueOrDefault());
```

7. Comment out the statement that gives a compile error.

8. Run the application and view the result, as shown in the following output:

```
0
7
7
```

The first line is blank because it is outputting the `null` value!

Understanding nullable reference types

The use of the `null` value is so common, in so many languages, that many experienced programmers never question the need for its existence. But there are many scenarios where we could write better, simpler code, if a variable is not allowed to have a `null` value.

More Information: You can find out more through the following link, where the inventor of `null`, Sir Charles Antony Richard Hoare, admits his mistake in a recorded hour-long talk: `https://www.infoq.com/presentations/Null-References-The-Billion-Dollar-Mistake-Tony-Hoare`.

The most significant change to the language in C# 8.0 is the introduction of nullable and non-nullable reference types. "But wait!", you are probably thinking, "Reference types are already nullable!"

And you would be right, but in C# 8.0, reference types can be configured to no longer allow the `null` value by setting a file- or project-level option to enable this useful new feature. Since this is a big change for C#, Microsoft decided to make the feature opt-in.

It will take multiple years for this new C# language feature to make an impact since there are thousands of existing library packages and apps that will expect the old behavior. Even Microsoft has not had time to fully implement this new feature in all the core .NET packages. During the transition, you can choose between several approaches for your own projects:

- **Default**: No changes needed. Non-nullable references types not supported.
- **Opt-in project, opt-out files**: Enable the feature at the project level and for any files that need to remain compatible with old behavior, opt out. This is the approach Microsoft is using internally while it updates its own packages to use this new feature.
- **Opt-in files**: Only enable the feature for individual files.

Enabling nullable and non-nullable reference types

To enable the feature at the project level, add the following to your project file:

```
<PropertyGroup>
  <Nullable>enable</Nullable>
</PropertyGroup>
```

To disable the feature at the file level, add the following to the top of a code file:

```
#nullable disable
```

To enable the feature at the file level, add the following to the top of a code file:

```
#nullable enable
```

Declaring non-nullable variables and parameters

If you enable nullable reference types and you want a reference type to be assigned the `null` value, then you will have to use the same syntax as making a value type nullable, that is, adding a ? symbol after the type declaration.

So, how do nullable reference types work? Let's look at an example. When storing information about an address, you might want to force a value for the street, city, and region, but building can be left blank, that is, null.

1. In `NullHandling.csproj`, add an element to enable nullable reference types, as shown highlighted in the following markup:

```
<Project Sdk="Microsoft.NET.Sdk">
```

```xml
<PropertyGroup>
  <OutputType>Exe</OutputType>
  <TargetFramework>netcoreapp3.0</TargetFramework>
  <Nullable>enable</Nullable>
</PropertyGroup>

</Project>
```

2. In `Program.cs`, at the top of the file add a statement to enable nullable reference types, as shown in the following code:

```
#nullable enable
```

3. In `Program.cs`, in the `NullHandling` namespace, above the `Program` class, add statements to declare an `Address` class with four fields, as shown in the following code:

```csharp
class Address
{
  public string? Building;
  public string Street;
  public string City;
  public string Region;
}
```

4. After a few seconds, note that the C# extension warns of problems with the non-nullable fields like `Street`, as shown in the following screenshot:

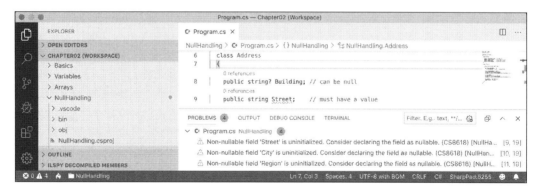

5. Assign the empty string value to each of the three fields that are non-nullable, as shown in the following code:

```csharp
public string Street = string.Empty;
public string City = string.Empty;
public string Region = string.Empty;
```

6. In `Main`, add statements to instantiate an `Address` and set its properties, as shown in the following code:

```
var address = new Address();
address.Building = null;
address.Street = null;
address.City = "London";
address.Region = null;
```

7. Note the warnings, as shown in the following screenshot:

So, this is why the new language feature is named nullable reference types. Starting with C# 8.0, unadorned reference types can become non-nullable, and the same syntax is used to make a reference type nullable, as is used for value types.

More Information: You can watch a video to learn how to get rid of null reference exceptions forever at the following link:
`https://channel9.msdn.com/Shows/On-NET/This-is-how-you-get-rid-of-null-reference-exceptions-forever.`

Checking for null

Checking whether a nullable reference type or nullable value type variable currently contains `null` is important because if you do not, a `NullReferenceException` can be thrown, which results in an error. You should check for a `null` value before using a nullable variable, as shown in the following code:

```
// check that the variable is not null before using it
if (thisCouldBeNull != null)
{
  // access a member of thisCouldBeNull
  int length = thisCouldBeNull.Length; // could throw exception
  ...
}
```

If you are trying to use a member of a variable that might be `null`, use the null-conditional operator `?.`, as shown in the following code:

```
string authorName = null;

// the following throws a NullReferenceException
int x = authorName.Length;

// instead of throwing an exception, null is assigned to y
int? y = authorName?.Length;
```

 More Information: You can read more about the null-conditional operator at the following link: https://docs. microsoft.com/en-us/dotnet/csharp/language-reference/operators/null-conditional-operators

Sometimes you want to either assign a variable to a result or use an alternative value, such as 3, if the variable is `null`. You do this using the null-coalescing operator, `??`, as shown in the following code:

```
// result will be 3 if authorName?.Length is null
var result = authorName?.Length ?? 3;
Console.WriteLine(result);
```

 More Information: You can read about the null-coalescing operator at the following link: https://docs.microsoft. com/en-us/dotnet/csharp/language-reference/operators/null-coalescing-operator

Exploring console applications further

We have already created and used basic console applications, but we're now at a stage where we should delve into them more deeply.

Console applications are text-based and are run at the command line. They typically perform simple tasks that need to be scripted, such as compiling a file or encrypting a section of a configuration file.

Equally they can also have arguments passed to them to control their behavior. An example of this would be to create a new console app using the F# language with a specified name instead of using the name of the current folder, as shown in the following command line:

```
dotnet new console -lang "F#" -name "ExploringConsole"
```

Displaying output to the user

The two most common tasks that a console application performs are writing and reading data. We have already been using the WriteLine method to output, but if we didn't want a carriage return at the end of the lines, we could have used the Write method.

Formatting using numbered positional arguments

One way for generating formatted strings is to use numbered positional arguments.

This feature is supported by methods like Write and WriteLine, and for methods that do not support the feature, the string parameter can be formatted using the Format method of string.

1. Add a new console application project named Formatting to the Chapter02 folder and workspace.

2. In the Main method, add statements to declare some number variables and write them to the console, as shown in the following code:

```
int numberOfApples = 12;
decimal pricePerApple = 0.35M;

Console.WriteLine(
    format: "{0} apples costs {1:C}",
    arg0: numberOfApples,
    arg1: pricePerApple * numberOfApples);

string formatted = string.Format(
    format: "{0} apples costs {1:C}",
    arg0: numberOfApples,
    arg1: pricePerApple * numberOfApples);

//WriteToFile(formatted); // writes the string into a file
```

The WriteToFile method is a nonexistent method used to illustrate the idea.

Formatting using interpolated strings

C# 6.0 and later has a handy feature named **interpolated strings**. A string prefixed with $ can use curly braces around the name of a variable or expression to output the current value of that variable or expression at that position in the string.

1. In the Main method, enter a statement at the bottom of the Main method, as shown in the following code:

```
Console.WriteLine($"{numberOfApples} apples costs {pricePerApple *
numberOfApples:C}");
```

2. Run the console app, and view the result, as shown in the following output:

```
12 apples costs £4.20
```

For short formatted strings, an interpolated string can be easier for people to read. But for code examples in a book, where lines need to wrap over multiple lines, this can be tricky. For many of the code examples in this book I will use numbered positional arguments.

Understanding format strings

A variable or expression can be formatted using a format string after a comma or colon.

An N0 format string means a number with thousand separators and no decimal places, while a C format string means currency. The currency format will be determined by the current thread. For instance, if you run this code on a PC in the UK, you'll get pounds sterling with commas as the thousand separators, but if you run this code on a PC in Germany, you would get Euros with dots as the thousand separators.

The full syntax of a format item is:

```
{ index [, alignment ] [ : formatString ] }
```

Each format item can have an alignment, which is useful when outputting tables of values, some of which might need to the left- or right-aligned within a width of characters. Alignment values are integers. Positive integers are right-aligned and negative integers are left-aligned.

For example, to output a table of fruit and how many of each there are, we might want to left-align the names within a column of 8 characters and right-align the counts formatted as numbers with zero decimal places within a column of six characters.

1. In the Main method, enter statements at the bottom of the Main method:

```
string applesText = "Apples";
int applesCount = 1234;
string bananasText = "Bananas";
int bananasCount = 56789;

Console.WriteLine(
    format: "{0,-8} {1,6:N0}",
    arg0: "Name",
    arg1: "Count");

Console.WriteLine(
```

```
        format: "{0,-8} {1,6:N0}",
        arg0: applesText,
        arg1: applesCount);

Console.WriteLine(
        format: "{0,-8} {1,6:N0}",
        arg0: bananasText,
        arg1: bananasCount);
```

2. Run the console app and note the effect of the alignment and number format, as shown in the following output:

```
Name      Count
Apples    1,234
Bananas   56,789
```

 More Information: You can read more details about formatting types in .NET at the following link: https://docs. microsoft.com/en-us/dotnet/standard/base-types/ formatting-types.

Getting text input from the user

We can get text input from the user using the ReadLine method. This method waits for the user to type some text, then as soon as the user presses *Enter*, whatever the user has typed is returned as a string value.

1. In the Main method, type statements to ask the user for their name and age and then output what they entered, as shown in the following code:

```
Console.Write("Type your first name and press ENTER: ");
string firstName = Console.ReadLine();

Console.Write("Type your age and press ENTER: ");
string age = Console.ReadLine();

Console.WriteLine(
    $"Hello {firstName}, you look good for {age}.");
```

2. Run the console application.

3. Enter name and age, as shown in the following output:

```
Type your name and press ENTER: Gary
Type your age and press ENTER: 34
Hello Gary, you look good for 34.
```

Importing a namespace

You might have noticed that unlike our very first application in *Chapter 1, Hello, C#! Welcome, .NET!*, we have not been typing `System` before `Console`. This is because `System` is a namespace, which is like an address for a type. To refer to someone exactly, you might use `Oxford.HighStreet.BobSmith`, which tells us to look for a person named *Bob Smith on the High Street in the city of Oxford*.

The `System.Console.WriteLine` line tells the compiler to look for a method named `WriteLine` in a type named `Console` in a namespace named `System`. To simplify our code, the `dotnet new console` command added a statement at the top of the code file to tell the compiler to always look in the `System` namespace for types that haven't been prefixed with their namespace, as shown in the following code:

```
using System;
```

We call this *importing the namespace*. The effect of importing a namespace is that all available types in that namespace will be available to your program without needing to enter the namespace prefix and will be seen in IntelliSense while you write code.

Simplifying the usage of the console

In C# 6.0 and later, the `using` statement can be used to further simplify our code. Then, we won't need to enter the `Console` type throughout our code. We can use Visual Studio Code's Replace feature to remove times we have previously wrote `Console`.

1. Add a statement to statically import the `System.Console` class to the top of the `Program.cs` file, as shown in the following code:

    ```
    using static System.Console;
    ```

2. Select the first `Console.` in your code, ensuring that you select the dot after the word `Console` too.

3. Navigate to **Edit | Replace** and note that an overlay dialog appears ready for you to enter what you would like to replace `Console.` with, as shown in the following screenshot:

4. Click on the **Replace All** button (the second of the two buttons to the right of the `replace` box) or press *Alt + A* or *Alt + Cmd + Enter* to replace all, and then close the replace box by clicking on the cross in its top-right corner.

Getting key input from the user

We can get key input from the user using the `ReadKey` method. This method waits for the user to type some text, then as soon as the user presses *Enter*, whatever the user has typed is returned as a `string` value.

1. In the `Main` method, type statements to ask the user to press any key combination and then output information about it, as shown in the following code:

```
Write("Press any key combination: ");
ConsoleKeyInfo key = ReadKey();
WriteLine();
WriteLine("Key: {0}, Char: {1}, Modifiers: {2}",
arg0: key.Key,
arg1: key.KeyChar,
arg2: key.Modifiers);
```

2. Run the console application, press the *K* key, and note the result, as shown in the following output:

```
Press any key combination: k
Key: K, Char: k, Modifiers: 0
```

3. Run the console application, hold down *Shift* and press the *K* key, and note the result, as shown in the following output:

```
Press any key combination: K
Key: K, Char: K, Modifiers: Shift
```

4. Run the console application, press the *F12* key, and note the result, as shown in the following output:

```
Press any key combination:
Key: F12, Char: , Modifiers: 0
```

When running a console application in Terminal within Visual Studio Code, some keyboard combinations will be captured by the code editor or operating system before they can be processed by your app.

Getting arguments

You might have been wondering what the `string[] args` arguments are in the `Main` method. They're an array used to pass arguments into a console application; let's take a look to see how it works.

Command-line arguments are separated by spaces. Other characters like hyphens and colons are treated as part of an argument value. To include spaces in an argument value, enclose the argument value in single or double quotes.

Imagine that we want to be able to enter the names of some colors for the foreground and background, and the dimensions of the Terminal window at the command line. We would be able to read the colors and numbers by reading them from the `args` array, which is always passed into the `Main` method of a console application.

1. Create a new folder for a console application project named `Arguments` and add it to the `Chapter02` workspace.

2. Add a statement to statically import the `System.Console` type and a statement to output the number of arguments passed to the application, as shown highlighted in the following code:

```
using System;
using static System.Console;

namespace Arguments
{
  class Program
  {
    static void Main(string[] args)
    {
      WriteLine($"There are {args.Length} arguments.");
    }
  }
}
```

 Good Practice: Remember to statically import the `System.Console` type in all future projects to simplify your code, as these instructions will not be repeated every time.

3. Run the console application and view the result, as shown in the following output:

```
There are 0 arguments.
```

4. In **TERMINAL**, enter some arguments after the `dotnet run` command, as shown in the following command line:

```
dotnet run firstarg second-arg third:arg "fourth arg"
```

5. Note the result indicates four arguments, as shown in the following output:

```
There are 4 arguments.
```

6. To enumerate or iterate (that is, loop through) the values of those four arguments, add the following statements after outputting the length of the array:

```
foreach (string arg in args)
{
  WriteLine(arg);
}
```

7. In **TERMINAL**, repeat the same arguments after the `dotnet run` command, as shown in the following command line:

```
dotnet run firstarg second-arg third:arg "fourth arg"
```

8. Note the result shows the details of the four arguments, as shown in the following output:

```
There are 4 arguments.
firstarg
second-arg
third:arg
fourth arg
```

Setting options with arguments

We will now use these arguments to allow the user to pick a color for the background, foreground, width, and height of the output window.

The `System` namespace is already imported so that the compiler knows about the `ConsoleColor` and `Enum` types. If you cannot see either of these types in the IntelliSense list, it is because you are missing the `using System;` statement at the top of the file.

1. Add statements to warn the user if they do not enter four arguments and then parse those arguments and use them to set the color and dimensions of the console window, as shown in the following code:

```
if (args.Length < 4)
{
  WriteLine("You must specify two colors and dimensions,
e.g.");
  WriteLine("dotnet run red yellow 80 40");
  return; // stop running
}

ForegroundColor = (ConsoleColor)Enum.Parse(
  enumType: typeof(ConsoleColor),
```

```
    value: args[0],
    ignoreCase: true);

BackgroundColor = (ConsoleColor)Enum.Parse(
    enumType: typeof(ConsoleColor),
    value: args[1],
    ignoreCase: true);

WindowWidth = int.Parse(args[2]);
WindowHeight = int.Parse(args[3]);
```

2. Enter the following command in **TERMINAL**:

```
dotnet run red yellow 50 10
```

On Windows, this will work correctly, although TERMINAL in Visual Studio Code does not change its size. If this is run in an external Windows Command Prompt, that window would change size.

On macOS, you'll see an unhandled exception, as shown in the following screenshot:

Although the compiler did not give an error or warning, at runtime some API calls may fail on some platforms. Although a console application running on Windows can change its size, on macOS, it cannot.

Handling platforms that do not support an API

So how do we solve this problem? We can solve this by using an exception handler. You will learn more details about the `try-catch` statement in *Chapter 3, Controlling the Flow and Converting Types*, so for now, just enter the code.

1. Modify the code to wrap the lines that change the height and width in a `try` statement, as shown in the following code:

```
try
{
  WindowWidth = int.Parse(args[2]);
  WindowHeight = int.Parse(args[3]);
}
catch (PlatformNotSupportedException)
{
  WriteLine("The current platform does not support changing the
size of a console window.");
}
```

2. Rerun the console application; note the exception is caught, and a friendly message is shown to the user, as shown in the following screenshot:

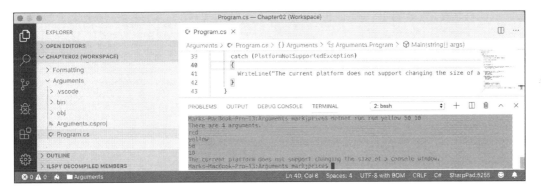

Practicing and exploring

Test your knowledge and understanding by answering some questions, get some hands-on practice, and explore the topics covered in this chapter with deeper research.

Exercise 2.1 – Test your knowledge

To get the best answer to some of these questions you will need to do your own research. I want you to "think outside the book" so I have deliberately not provided all the answers in the book.

I want to encourage you to get in the good habit of looking for help elsewhere, following the principle of "teach a person to fish."

What type would you choose for the following "numbers"?

1. A person's telephone number.

2. A person's height.

3. A person's age.

4. A person's salary.

5. A book's ISBN.

6. A book's price.

7. A book's shipping weight.

8. A country's population.

9. The number of stars in the universe.

10. The number of employees in each of the small or medium businesses in the United Kingdom (up to about 50,000 employees per business).

Exercise 2.2 – Practice number sizes and ranges

Create a console application project named `Exercise02` that outputs the number of bytes in memory that each of the following number types use, and the minimum and maximum values they can have: `sbyte`, `byte`, `short`, `ushort`, `int`, `uint`, `long`, `ulong`, `float`, `double`, and `decimal`.

More Information: You can always read the documentation, available at `https://docs.microsoft.com/en-us/dotnet/standard/base-types/composite-formatting` for Composite Formatting to learn how to align text in a console application.

The result of running your console application should look something like the following screenshot:

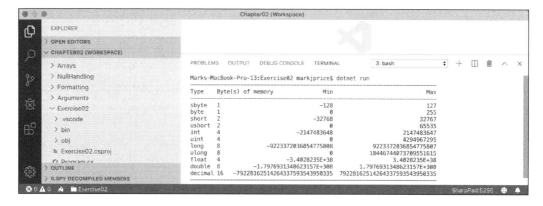

Exercise 2.3 – Explore topics

Use the following links to read more about the topics covered in this chapter:

- **C# Keywords**: https://docs.microsoft.com/en-us/dotnet/csharp/language-reference/keywords/index

- **Main() and command-line arguments (C# Programming Guide)**: https://docs.microsoft.com/en-us/dotnet/csharp/programming-guide/main-and-command-args/

- **Types (C# Programming Guide)**: https://docs.microsoft.com/en-us/dotnet/csharp/programming-guide/types/

- **Statements, Expressions, and Operators (C# Programming Guide)**: https://docs.microsoft.com/en-us/dotnet/csharp/programming-guide/statements-expressions-operators/

- **Strings (C# Programming Guide)**: https://docs.microsoft.com/en-us/dotnet/csharp/programming-guide/strings/

- **Nullable Types (C# Programming Guide)**: https://docs.microsoft.com/en-us/dotnet/csharp/programming-guide/nullable-types/

- **Nullable reference types**: https://docs.microsoft.com/en-us/dotnet/csharp/nullable-references

- **Console Class**: https://docs.microsoft.com/en-us/dotnet/api/system.console?view=netcore-3.0

Summary

In this chapter, you learned how to declare variables with a specified or an inferred type; we discussed some of the built-in types for numbers, text, and Booleans; we covered how to choose between number types; we covered nullability of types; we learned how to control the output formatting in console apps.

In the next chapter, you will learn about operators, branching, looping, and converting between types.

Chapter 03

Controlling Flow and Converting Types

This chapter is all about writing code that performs simple operations on variables, makes decisions, repeats blocks of statements, converts variable or expression values from one type to another, handles exceptions, and checks for overflows in number variables.

This chapter covers the following topics:

- Operating on variables
- Understanding selection statements
- Understanding iteration statements
- Casting and converting between types
- Handling exceptions
- Checking for overflow

Operating on variables

Operators apply simple operations such as addition and multiplication to **operands** such as variables and literal values. They usually return a new value that is the result of the operation that can be assigned to a variable.

Most operators are binary, meaning that they work on two operands, as shown in the following pseudocode:

```
var resultOfOperation = firstOperand operator secondOperand;
```

Some operators are unary, meaning they work on a single operand, and can apply before or after the operand, as shown in the following pseudocode:

```
var resultOfOperation = onlyOperand operator;
var resultOfOperation2 = operator onlyOperand;
```

Examples of unary operators include incrementors and retrieving a type or its size in bytes, as shown in the following code:

```
int x = 5;
int incrementedByOne = x++;
int incrementedByOneAgain = ++x;

Type theTypeOfAnInteger = typeof(int);
int howManyBytesInAnInteger = sizeof(int);
```

A ternary operator works on three operands, as shown in the following pseudocode:

```
var resultOfOperation = firstOperand firstOperator
    secondOperand secondOperator thirdOperand;
```

Unary operators

Two common unary operators are used to increment, `++`, and decrement, `--`, a number.

1. If you have completed the previous chapters, then you will already have a `Code` folder in your user folder. If not, create it.

2. In the `Code` folder, create a folder named `Chapter03`.

3. Start Visual Studio Code and close any open workspace or folder.

4. Save the current workspace in the `Chapter03` folder as `Chapter03.code-workspace`.

5. Create a new folder named `Operators` and add it to the `Chapter03` workspace.

6. Navigate to **Terminal | New Terminal**.

7. In **Terminal**, enter a command to create a new console application in the `Operators` folder.

8. Open `Program.cs`.

9. Statically import `System.Console`.

10. In the `Main` method, declare two integer variables named `a` and `b`, set `a` to three, increment `a` while assigning the result to `b`, and then output their values, as shown in the following code:

```
int a = 3;
int b = a++;
WriteLine($"a is {a}, b is {b}");
```

11. Before running the console application, ask yourself a question: what do you think the value of b will be when output? Once you've thought about that, run the console application, and compare your prediction against the actual result, as shown in the following output:

```
a is 4, b is 3
```

The variable b has the value 3 because the ++ operator executes *after* the assignment; this is known as a **postfix operator**. If you need to increment *before* the assignment, then use the **prefix operator**.

12. Copy and paste the statements, and then modify them to rename the variables and use the prefix operator, as shown in the following code:

```
int c = 3;
int d = ++c; // increment c before assigning it
WriteLine($"c is {c}, d is {d}");
```

13. Rerun the console application and note the result, as shown in the following output:

```
a is 4, b is 3
c is 4, d is 4
```

 Good Practice: Due to the confusion between prefix and postfix for the increment and decrement operators when combined with assignment, the Swift programming language designers decided to drop support for this operator in version 3. My recommendation for usage in C# is to never combine the use of ++ and -- operators with an assignment operator, =. Perform the operations as separate statements.

Binary arithmetic operators

Increment and decrement are unary arithmetic operators. Other arithmetic operators are usually binary and allow you to perform arithmetic operations on two numbers.

1. Add the statements to the bottom of the Main method to declare and assign values to two integer variables named e and f, and then perform the five common binary arithmetic operators to the two numbers, as shown in the following code:

```
int e = 11;
int f = 3;
WriteLine($"e is {e}, f is {f}");
WriteLine($"e + f = {e + f}");
WriteLine($"e - f = {e - f}");
WriteLine($"e * f = {e * f}");
```

```
WriteLine($"e / f = {e / f}");
WriteLine($"e % f = {e % f}");
```

2. Rerun the console application and note the result, as shown in the following output:

```
e is 11, f is 3
e + f = 14
e - f = 8
e * f = 33
e / f = 3
e % f = 2
```

To understand the divide / and modulo % operators when applied to integers, you need to think back to primary school. Imagine you have eleven sweets and three friends. How can you divide the sweets between your friends? You can give three sweets to each of your friends, and there will be two left over. Those two sweets are the **modulus**, also known as the **remainder** after dividing. If you have twelve sweets, then each friend gets four of them, and there are none left over, so the remainder would be 0.

3. Add statements to declare and assign a value to a double variable named g to show the difference between whole number and real number divisions, as shown in the following code:

```
double g = 11.0;
WriteLine($"g is {g:N1}, f is {f}");
WriteLine($"g / f = {g / f}");
```

4. Rerun the console application and note the result, as shown in the following output:

```
g is 11.0, f is 3
g / f = 3.6666666666666665
```

If the first operand is a floating-point number, such as g with the value 11.0, then the divide operator returns a floating-point value, such as 3.6666666666665, rather than a whole number.

Assignment operators

You have already been using the most common assignment operator, =.

To make your code more concise, you can combine the assignment operator with other operators like arithmetic operators, as shown in the following code:

```
int p = 6;
p += 3; // equivalent to p = p + 3;
p -= 3; // equivalent to p = p - 3;
p *= 3; // equivalent to p = p * 3;
p /= 3; // equivalent to p = p / 3;
```

Logical operators

Logical operators operate on Boolean values, so they return either `true` or `false`.

Let's explore binary logical operators that operate on two Boolean values.

1. Create a new folder and console application named `BooleanOperators` and add it to the `Chapter03` workspace. Remember to use the Command Palette to select `BooleanOperators` as the project.

2. In `Program.cs`, in the `Main` method, add statements to declare two Boolean variables with values `true` and `false`, and then output truth tables showing the results of applying AND, OR, and XOR (exclusive OR) logical operators, as shown in the following code:

```
bool a = true;
bool b = false;

WriteLine($"AND   | a     | b    ");
WriteLine($"a     | {a & a,-5} | {a & b,-5} ");
WriteLine($"b     | {b & a,-5} | {b & b,-5} ");
WriteLine();
WriteLine($"OR    | a     | b    ");
WriteLine($"a     | {a | a,-5} | {a | b,-5} ");
WriteLine($"b     | {b | a,-5} | {b | b,-5} ");
WriteLine();
WriteLine($"XOR   | a     | b    ");
WriteLine($"a     | {a ^ a,-5} | {a ^ b,-5} ");
WriteLine($"b     | {b ^ a,-5} | {b ^ b,-5} ");
```

 More Information: Read about truth tables at the following link: https://en.wikipedia.org/wiki/Truth_table

3. Run the console application and note the results, as shown in the following output:

```
AND   | a     | b

a     | True  | False
```

```
b      | False | False

OR     | a     | b
a      | True  | True
b      | True  | False

XOR    | a     | b
a      | False | True
b      | True  | False
```

For the AND & logical operator, both operands must be `true` for the result to be `true`.
For the OR | logical operator, either operand can be `true` for the result to be `true`.
For the XOR ^ logical operator, either operand can be `true` (but not both!) for the
result to be `true`.

Conditional logical operators

Conditional logical operators are similar to logical operators, but you use two
symbols instead of one, for example, && instead of &, or || instead of |.

In *Chapter 4*, *Writing, Debugging, and Testing Functions*, you will learn about functions
in more detail, but I need to introduce functions now to explain conditional logical
operators, also known as short-circuiting Boolean operators.

A function executes statements and then returns a value. That value could be
a Boolean value like `true` that is used in a Boolean operation.

1. After and outside the `Main` method, write statements to declare a function
    that writes a message to the console and returns `true`, as shown highlighted
    in the following code:

    ```csharp
    class Program
    {
      static void Main(string[] args)
      {
        ...
      }

      private static bool DoStuff()
      {
        WriteLine("I am doing some stuff.");
        return true;
      }
    }
    ```

2. Inside and at the bottom of the `Main` method, perform an AND & operation on the `a` and `b` variables and the result of calling the function, as shown in the following code:

```
WriteLine($"a & DoStuff() = {a & DoStuff()}");
WriteLine($"b & DoStuff() = {b & DoStuff()}");
```

3. Run the console app, view the result, and note that the function was called twice, once for `a` and once for `b`, as shown in the following output:

```
I am doing some stuff.

a & DoStuff() = True

I am doing some stuff.

b & DoStuff() = False
```

4. Change the `&` operators into `&&` operators, as shown in the following code:

```
WriteLine($"a && DoStuff() = {a && DoStuff()}");
WriteLine($"b && DoStuff() = {b && DoStuff()}");
```

5. Run the console app, view the result, and note that the function does run when combined with the `a` variable, but it does not run when combined with the `b` variable because the `b` variable is `false` so the result will be `false` anyway so it does not need to execute the function, as shown in the following output:

```
I am doing some stuff.

a && DoStuff() = True

b && DoStuff() = False // DoStuff function was not executed!
```

 Good Practice: Now you can see why the conditional logical operators are described as being short-circuiting. They can make your apps more efficient, but they can also introduce subtle bugs in cases where you assume that the function would always be called. It is safest to avoid them.

Bitwise and binary shift operators

Bitwise operators effect the bits in a number. Binary shift operators can perform some common arithmetic calculations much faster than traditional operators.

Let's explore bitwise and binary shift operators.

1. Create a new folder and console application named `BitwiseAndShiftOperators` and add it to the workspace.

2. Add statements to the `Main` method to declare two integer variables with values 10 and 6, and then output the results of applying AND, OR, and XOR (exclusive OR) bitwise operators, as shown in the following code:

```
int a = 10; // 0000 1010
int b = 6;  // 0000 0110

WriteLine($"a = {a}");
WriteLine($"b = {b}");
WriteLine($"a & b = {a & b}"); // 2-bit column only
WriteLine($"a | b = {a | b}"); // 8, 4, and 2-bit columns
WriteLine($"a ^ b = {a ^ b}"); // 8 and 4-bit columns
```

3. Run the console application and note the results, as shown in the following output:

```
a = 10

b = 6

a & b = 2

a | b = 14

a ^ b = 12
```

4. Add statements to the `Main` method to output the results of applying the left-shift operator to move the bits of the variable a by three columns, multiplying a by 8, and right-shifting the bits of the variable b by one column, as shown in the following code:

```
// 0101 0000 left-shift a by three bit columns
WriteLine($"a << 3 = {a << 3}");

// multiply a by 8
WriteLine($"a * 8 = {a * 8}");

// 0000 0011 right-shift b by one bit column
WriteLine($"b >> 1 = {b >> 1}");
```

5. Run the console application and note the results, as shown in the following output:

```
a << 3 = 80

a * 8 = 80

b >> 1 = 3
```

The 80 result is because the bits in it were shifted three columns to the left, so the 1-bits moved into the 64- and 16-bit columns and 64 + 16 = 80. This is the equivalent of multiplying by 8 but CPUs can perform a bit-shift faster. The 3 result is because the 1-bits in b were shifted one column into the 2- and 1-bit columns.

Miscellaneous operators

`nameof` and `sizeof` are convenient operators when working with types. `nameof` returns the short name (without namespace) of a variable, type, or member as a string value, which is useful when outputting exception messages. `sizeof` returns the size in bytes of simple types, which is useful for determining efficiency of data storage.

There are many other operators; for example, the dot between a variable and its members is called the member access operator and the round brackets at the end of a function or method name is called the invocation operator, as shown in the following code:

```
int age = 47;

// How many operators in the following statement?
string firstDigit = age.ToString()[0];

// There are four operators:
// = is the assignment operator
// . is the member access operator
// () is the invocation operator
// [] is the indexer access operator
```

 More Information: You can read more about some of these miscellaneous operators at the following link: `https://docs.microsoft.com/en-us/dotnet/csharp/language-reference/operators/member-access-operators`.

Understanding selection statements

Every application needs to be able to select from choices and branch along different code paths. The two selection statements in C# are `if` and `switch`. You can use `if` for all your code, but `switch` can simplify your code in some common scenarios such as when there is a single variable that can have multiple values that each require different processing.

Branching with the if statement

The `if` statement determines which branch to follow by evaluating a Boolean expression. If the expression is `true`, then the block executes. The `else` block is optional, and it executes if the `if` expression is `false`. The `if` statement can be nested.

The `if` statement combined with other `if` statements as `else if` branches, as shown in the following code:

```
if (expression1)
{
  // runs if expression1 is true
}
else if (expression2)
{
  // runs if expression1 is false and expression2 if true
}
else if (expression3)
{
  // runs if expression1 and expression2 are false
  // and expression3 is true
}
else
{
  // runs if all expressions are false
}
```

Each `if` statement's Boolean expression is independent of the others and unlike `switch` statements does not need to reference a single value.

Let's create a console application to explore selection statements like `if`.

1. Create a folder and console application named `SelectionStatements` and add it to the workspace.

 Good Practice: Remember to statically import the `System.Console` type to simplify statements in a console app.

2. Add the following statements inside the `Main` method to check whether this console application has any arguments passed to it:

```
if (args.Length == 0)
{
  WriteLine("There are no arguments.");
}
else
{
  WriteLine("There is at least one argument.");
}
```

3. Run the console application by entering the following command into **Terminal**:

```
dotnet run
```

Why you should always use braces with if statements

As there is only a single statement inside each block, the preceding code *could* be written without the curly braces, as shown in the following code:

```
if (args.Length == 0)
  WriteLine("There are no arguments.");
else
  WriteLine("There is at least one argument.");
```

This style of the `if` statement should be avoided because it can introduce serious bugs, for example, the infamous `#gotofail` bug in Apple's iPhone iOS operating system. For 18 months after Apple's iOS 6 was released, in September 2012, it had a bug in its **Secure Sockets Layer (SSL)** encryption code, which meant that any user running Safari, the device's web browser, who tried to connect to secure websites, such as their bank, was not properly secure because an important check was being accidentally skipped.

You can read about this infamous bug at the following link: `https://gotofail.com/`.

Just because you can leave out the curly braces, doesn't mean you should. Your code is not "more efficient" without them; instead, it is less maintainable and potentially more dangerous.

Pattern matching with the if statement

A feature introduced with C# 7.0 and later is **pattern matching**. The `if` statement can use the `is` keyword in combination with declaring a local variable to make your code safer.

1. Add statements to the end of the `Main` method so that if the value stored in the variable named `o` is an `int`, then the value is assigned to the local variable named `i`, which can then be used inside the `if` statement. This is safer than using the variable named `o` because we know for sure that `i` is an `int` variable and not something else, as shown in the following code:

```
// add and remove the "" to change the behavior
object o = "3";
```

```
int j = 4;

if(o is int i)
{
  WriteLine($"{i} x {j} = {i * j}");
}
else
{
  WriteLine("o is not an int so it cannot multiply!");
}
```

2. Run the console application and view the results, as shown in the following output:

    ```
    o is not an int so it cannot multiply!
    ```

3. Delete the double-quote characters around the "3" value so that the value stored in the variable named o is an int type instead of a string type.

4. Rerun the console application to view the results, as shown in the following output:

    ```
    3 x 4 = 12
    ```

Branching with the switch statement

The switch statement is different from the if statement because it compares a single expression against a list of multiple possible case statements. Every case statement is related to the single expression. Every case section must end with:

- The break keyword (like case 1 in the following code),
- Or the goto case keywords (like case 2 in the following code),
- Or they should have no statements (like case 3 in the following code).

Let's write some code to explore the switch statements.

1. Enter some statements for a switch statement after the if statements that you wrote previously. You should note that the first line is a label that can be jumped to, and the second line generates a random number. The switch statement branches based on the value of this random number, as shown in the following code:

    ```
    A_label:
      var number = (new Random()).Next(1, 7);

      WriteLine($"My random number is {number}");
    ```

```
switch (number)
{
  case 1:
    WriteLine("One");
    break; // jumps to end of switch statement
  case 2:
    WriteLine("Two");
    goto case 1;
  case 3:
  case 4:
    WriteLine("Three or four");
    goto case 1;
  case 5:
    // go to sleep for half a second
    System.Threading.Thread.Sleep(500);
    goto A_label;
  default:
    WriteLine("Default");
    break;
} // end of switch statement
```

 Good Practice: You can use the goto keyword to jump to another case or a label. The goto keyword is frowned upon by most programmers but can be a good solution to code logic in some scenarios. However, you should use it sparingly.

2. Run the console application multiple times in order to see what happens in various cases of random numbers, as shown in the following example output:

```
bash-3.2$ dotnet run
My random number is 4
Three or four
One
bash-3.2$ dotnet run
My random number is 2
Two
One
bash-3.2$ dotnet run
My random number is 1
One
```

Pattern matching with the switch statement

Like the `if` statement, the `switch` statement supports pattern matching in C# 7.0 and later. The `case` values no longer need to be literal values. They can be patterns.

Let's see an example of pattern matching with the `switch` statement using a folder path. If you are using macOS, then swap the commented statement that sets the path variable and replace my username with your user folder name.

1. Add the following statement to the top of the file to import types for working with input/output:

    ```
    using System.IO;
    ```

2. Add statements to the end of the `Main` method to declare a `string` path to a file, open it as a stream, and then show a message based on what type and capabilities the stream has, as shown in the following code:

    ```
    // string path = "/Users/markjprice/Code/Chapter03";
    string path = @"C:\Code\Chapter03";

    Stream s = File.Open(
      Path.Combine(path, "file.txt"), FileMode.OpenOrCreate);

    string message = string.Empty;

    switch (s)
    {
      case FileStream writeableFile when s.CanWrite:
        message = "The stream is a file that I can write to.";
        break;
      case FileStream readOnlyFile:
        message = "The stream is a read-only file.";
        break;
      case MemoryStream ms:
        message = "The stream is a memory address.";
        break;
      default: // always evaluated last despite its current position
        message = "The stream is some other type.";
        break;
      case null:
        message = "The stream is null.";
        break;
    }

    WriteLine(message);
    ```

3. Run the console app and note that the variable named s is declared as a `Stream` type so it could be any subtype of stream like a memory stream or file stream. In this code, the stream is created using the `File.Open` method, which returns a file stream and due to the `FileMode`, it will be writeable, so the result will be a message that describes the situation, as shown in the following output:

```
The stream is a file that I can write to.
```

In .NET, there are multiple subtypes of `Stream`, including `FileStream` and `MemoryStream`. In C# 7.0 and later, your code can more concisely branch, based on the subtype of stream, and declare and assign a local variable to safely use it. You will learn more about the `System.IO` namespace and the `Stream` type in *Chapter 9, Working with Files, Streams, and Serialization*.

Additionally, `case` statements can include a `when` keyword to perform more specific pattern matching. In the first `case` statement in the preceding code, s will only be a match if the stream is a `FileStream` and its `CanWrite` property is `true`.

 More Information: You can read more about pattern matching at the following link: https://docs.microsoft.com/en-us/dotnet/csharp/pattern-matching.

Simplifying switch statements with switch expressions

In C# 8.0 or later, you can simplify `switch` statements using **switch expressions**.

Most `switch` statements are very simple, yet they require a lot of typing. Switch expressions are designed to simplify the code you need to type while still expressing the same intent.

Let's implement the previous code that uses a `switch` statement using a `switch` expression so that you can compare the two styles.

1. Add statements to the end of the `Main` method to set the message based on what type and capabilities the stream has using a `switch` expression, as shown in the following code:

```
message = s switch
{
  FileStream writeableFile when s.CanWrite
    => "The stream is a file that I can write to.",
  FileStream readOnlyFile
    => "The stream is a read-only file.",
  MemoryStream ms
    => "The stream is a memory address.",
```

```
null
  => "The stream is null.",

_
  => "The stream is some other type."
};

WriteLine(message);
```

The main differences are the removal of the `case` and `break` keywords. The underscore character is used to represent the default return value.

2. Run the console app, and note the result is the same as before.

 More Information: You can read more about patterns and switch expressions at the following link: `https://devblogs.microsoft.com/dotnet/do-more-with-patterns-in-c-8-0/`.

Understanding iteration statements

Iteration statements repeat a block of statements either while a condition is true or for each item in a collection. The choice of which statement to use is based on a combination of ease of understanding to solve the logic problem and personal preference.

Looping with the while statement

The `while` statement evaluates a Boolean expression and continues to loop while it is `true`. Let's explore iteration statements.

1. Create a new folder and console application project named `IterationStatements` and add it to the workspace.

2. Type the following code inside the `Main` method:

```
int x = 0;

while (x < 10)
{
  WriteLine(x);
  x++;
}
```

3. Run the console application and view the results, which should be the numbers 0 to 9, as shown in the following output:

```
0
```

```
1
2
3
4
5
6
7
8
9
```

Looping with the do statement

The do statement is like while, except the Boolean expression is checked at the bottom of the block instead of the top, which means that the block always executes at least once.

1. Type the following code at the end of the Main method:

```
string password = string.Empty;

do
{
  Write("Enter your password: ");
  password = ReadLine();
}
while (password != "Pa$$w0rd");

WriteLine("Correct!");
```

2. Run the console application, and note that you are prompted to enter your password repeatedly until you enter it correctly, as shown in the following output:

```
Enter your password: password
Enter your password: 12345678
Enter your password: ninja
Enter your password: correct horse battery staple
Enter your password: Pa$$w0rd
Correct!
```

3. As an optional challenge, add statements so that the user can only make ten attempts before an error message is displayed.

Looping with the for statement

The for statement is like while, except that it is more succinct. It combines:

- An **initializer expression**, which executes once at the start of the loop.
- A **conditional expression**, which that executes on every iteration at the start of the loop to check whether the looping should continue.
- An **iterator expression**, which that executes on every loop at the bottom of the statement.

The for statement is commonly used with an integer counter. Let's explore some code.

1. Enter a for statement to output the numbers 1 to 10, as shown in the following code:

```
for (int y = 1; y <= 10; y++)
{
  WriteLine(y);
}
```

2. Run the console application to view the result, which should be the numbers 1 to 10.

Looping with the foreach statement

The foreach statement is a bit different from the previous three iteration statements.

It is used to perform a block of statements on each item in a sequence, for example, an array or collection. Each item is usually read-only, and if the sequence structure is modified during iteration, for example, by adding or removing an item, then an exception will be thrown.

1. Type statements to create an array of string variables and then output the length of each one, as shown in the following code:

```
string[] names = { "Adam", "Barry", "Charlie" };

foreach (string name in names)
{
  WriteLine($"{name} has {name.Length} characters.");
}
```

2. Run the console application and view the results, as shown in the following output:

```
Adam has 4 characters.
```

```
Barry has 5 characters.
Charlie has 7 characters.
```

Understanding how foreach works internally

Technically, the foreach statement will work on any type that follows these rules:

1. The type must have a method named GetEnumerator that returns an object.
2. The returned object must have a property named Current and a method named MoveNext.
3. The MoveNext method must return true if there are more items to enumerate through or false if there are no more items.

There are interfaces named IEnumerable and IEnumerable<T> that formally define these rules but technically the compiler does not require the type to implement these interfaces.

The compiler turns the foreach statement in the preceding example into something similar to the following pseudocode:

```
IEnumerator e = names.GetEnumerator();

while (e.MoveNext())
{
  string name = (string)e.Current; // Current is read-only!
  WriteLine($"{name} has {name.Length} characters.");
}
```

Due to the use of an iterator, the variable declared in a foreach statement cannot be used to modify the value of the current item.

Casting and converting between types

You will often need to convert values of variables between different types. For example, data input is often entered as text at the console, so it is initially stored in a variable of the string type, but it then needs to be converted into a date/time, or number, or some other data type, depending on how it should be stored and processed.

Sometimes you will need to convert between number types, like between an integer and a floating-point, before performing calculations.

Converting is also known as **casting**, and it has two varieties: **implicit** and **explicit**. Implicit casting happens automatically, and it is safe, meaning that you will not lose any information.

Explicit casting must be performed manually because it may lose information, for example, the precision of a number. By explicitly casting, you are telling the C# compiler that you understand and accept the risk.

Casting numbers implicitly and explicitly

Implicitly casting an `int` variable into a `double` variable is safe because no information can be lost.

1. Create a new folder and console application project named `CastingConverting` and add it to the workspace.

2. In the `Main` method, enter statements to declare and assign an `int` variable and a `double` variable, and then implicitly cast the integer's value when assigning it to the `double` variable, as shown in the following code:

    ```
    int a = 10;
    double b = a; // an int can be safely cast into a double
    WriteLine(b);
    ```

3. In the `Main` method, enter the following statements:

    ```
    double c = 9.8;
    int d = c; // compiler gives an error for this line
    WriteLine(d);
    ```

4. View the **PROBLEMS** window by navigating to **View | Problems**, and note the error message, as shown in the following screenshot:

If you need to create the required assets to show **PROBLEMS**, then try closing and reopening the workspace, select the correct project for OmniSharp, and then click **Yes** when prompted to create missing assets for example, the `.vscode` folder. The status bar should show the currently active project, like **CastingConverting** in the preceding screenshot.

You cannot implicitly cast a `double` variable into an `int` variable because it is potentially unsafe and could lose data.

5. View the **TERMINAL** window, and enter the `dotnet run` command, and note the error message, as shown in the following output:

```
Program.cs(19,15): error CS0266: Cannot implicitly convert type
'double' to 'int'. An explicit conversion exists (are you missing
a cast?) [/Users/markjprice/Code/Chapter03/CastingConverting/
CastingConverting.csproj]

The build failed. Please fix the build errors and run again.
```

You must explicitly cast a `double` variable into an `int` variable using a pair of round brackets around the type you want to cast the `double` type into. The pair of round brackets is the **cast operator**. Even then, you must beware that the part after the decimal point will be trimmed off without warning because you have chosen to perform an explicit cast and therefore understand the consequences.

6. Modify the assignment statement for the d variable, as shown in the following code:

```
int d = (int)c;
WriteLine(d); // d is 9 losing the .8 part
```

7. Run the console application to view the results, as shown in the following output:

```
10

9
```

We must perform a similar operation when converting values between larger integers and smaller integers. Again, beware that you might lose information because any value too big will have its bits copied and then interpreted in ways that you might not expect!

8. Enter statements to declare and assign a `long` 64-bit variable to an `int` 32-bit variable, both using a small value that will work and a too-large value that will not, as shown in the following code:

```
long e = 10;
int f = (int)e;
WriteLine($"e is {e:N0} and f is {f:N0}");

e = long.MaxValue;
f = (int)e;
WriteLine($"e is {e:N0} and f is {f:N0}");
```

9. Run the console application to view the results, as shown in the following output:

```
e is 10 and f is 10
e is 9,223,372,036,854,775,807 and f is -1
```

10. Modify the value of e to 5 billion, as shown in the following code:

```
e = 5_000_000_000;
```

11. Run the console application to view the results, as shown in the following output:

```
e is 5,000,000,000 and f is 705,032,704
```

Converting with the System.Convert type

An alternative to using the cast operator is to use the System.Convert type. The System.Convert type can convert to and from all the C# number types as well as Booleans, strings, and date and time values.

1. At the top of the Program.cs file, statically import the System.Convert class, as shown in the following code:

```
using static System.Convert;
```

2. Add statements to the bottom of the Main method to declare and assign a value to a double variable, convert it to an integer, and then write both values to the console, as shown in the following code:

```
double g = 9.8;
int h = ToInt32(g);
WriteLine($"g is {g} and h is {h}");
```

3. Run the console application and view the result, as shown in the following output:

```
g is 9.8 and h is 10
```

One difference between casting and converting is that converting rounds the double value 9.8 up to 10 instead of trimming the part after the decimal point.

Rounding numbers

You have now seen that the cast operator trims the decimal part of a real number and that the System.Convert methods round up or down. However, what is the rule for rounding?

Understanding the default rounding rules

In British primary schools for children aged 5 to 11, pupils are taught to round *up* if the decimal part is .5 or higher and round *down* if the decimal part is less.

Let's explore if C# follows the same primary school rule.

1. At the bottom of the `Main` method, add statements to declare and assign an array of `double` values, convert each of them to an integer, and then write the result to the console, as shown in the following code:

```
double[] doubles = new[]
  { 9.49, 9.5, 9.51, 10.49, 10.5, 10.51 };

foreach (double n in doubles)
{
  WriteLine($"ToInt({n}) is {ToInt32(n)}");
}
```

2. Run the console application and view the result, as shown in the following output:

```
ToInt(9.49) is 9
ToInt(9.5) is 10
ToInt(9.51) is 10
ToInt(10.49) is 10
ToInt(10.5) is 10
ToInt(10.51) is 11
```

We have shown that the rule for rounding in C# is subtly different from the primary school rule:

- It always rounds *down* if the decimal part is less than the midpoint .5.
- It always rounds *up* if the decimal part is more than the midpoint .5.
- It will round *up* if the decimal part is the midpoint .5 and the non-decimal part is odd, but it will round *down* if the non-decimal part is even.

This rule is known as **Banker's Rounding**, and it is preferred because it reduces bias by alternating when it rounds up or down. Sadly, other languages such as JavaScript use the primary school rule.

Taking control of rounding rules

You can take control of the rounding rules by using the `Round` method of the `Math` class.

1. At the bottom of the `Main` method, add statements to round each of the `double` values using the "away from zero" rounding rule also known as rounding "up", and then write the result to the console, as shown in the following code:

```
foreach (double n in doubles)
{
  WriteLine(format:
    "Math.Round({0}, 0, MidpointRounding.AwayFromZero) is {1}",
    arg0: n,
    arg1: Math.Round(value: n,
     digits: 0,
     mode: MidpointRounding.AwayFromZero));
}
```

2. Run the console application and view the result, as shown in the following output:

```
Math.Round(9.49, 0, MidpointRounding.AwayFromZero) is 9

Math.Round(9.5, 0, MidpointRounding.AwayFromZero) is 10

Math.Round(9.51, 0, MidpointRounding.AwayFromZero) is 10

Math.Round(10.49, 0, MidpointRounding.AwayFromZero) is 10

Math.Round(10.5, 0, MidpointRounding.AwayFromZero) is 11

Math.Round(10.51, 0, MidpointRounding.AwayFromZero) is 11
```

More Information: `MidpointRounding.AwayFromZero` is the primary school rule. You can read more about taking control of rounding at the following link: `https://docs.microsoft.com/en-us/dotnet/api/system.math.round?view=netcore-3.0`.

Good Practice: For every programming language that you use, check its rounding rules. They may not work the way you expect!

Converting from any type to a string

The most common conversion is from any type into a `string` variable for outputting as human-readable text, so all types have a method named `ToString` that they inherit from the `System.Object` class.

The `ToString` method converts the current value of any variable into a textual representation. Some types can't be sensibly represented as text, so they return their namespace and type name.

1. At the bottom of the `Main` method, type statements to declare some variables, convert them to their `string` representation, and write them to the console, as shown on the following code:

```
int number = 12;
WriteLine(number.ToString());

bool boolean = true;
WriteLine(boolean.ToString());

DateTime now = DateTime.Now;
WriteLine(now.ToString());

object me = new object();
WriteLine(me.ToString());
```

2. Run the console application and view the result, as shown in the following output:

```
12
True
27/01/2019 13:48:54
System.Object
```

Converting from a binary object to a string

When you have a binary object like an image or video that you want to either store or transmit, you sometimes do not want to send the raw bits, because you do not know how those bits could be misinterpreted, for example, by the network protocol transmitting them or another operating system that is reading the store binary object.

The safest thing to do is to convert the binary object into a `string` of safe characters. Programmers call this **Base64** encoding.

The `Convert` type has a pair of methods, `ToBase64String` and `FromBase64String`, that perform this conversion for you.

1. Add statements to the end of the `Main` method to create an array of bytes randomly populated with byte values, write each byte nicely formatted to the console, and then write the same bytes converted to Base64 to the console, as shown in the following code:

```
// allocate array of 128 bytes
byte[] binaryObject = new byte[128];
```

```
// populate array with random bytes
(new Random()).NextBytes(binaryObject);

WriteLine("Binary Object as bytes:");

for(int index = 0; index < binaryObject.Length; index++)
{
  Write($"{binaryObject[index]:X} ");
}
WriteLine();

// convert to Base64 string and output as text
string encoded = Convert.ToBase64String(binaryObject);
WriteLine($"Binary Object as Base64: {encoded}");
```

By default, an `int` value would output assuming decimal notation, that is, base10. You can use format codes such as `:X` to format the value using hexadecimal notation.

2. Run the console application and view the result:

```
Binary Object as bytes:

B3 4D 55 DE 2D E BB CF BE 4D E6 53 C3 C2 9B 67 3 45 F9 E5 20 61 7E
4F 7A 81 EC 49 F0 49 1D 8E D4 F7 DB 54 AF A0 81 5 B8 BE CE F8 36
90 7A D4 36 42 4 75 81 1B AB 51 CE 5 63 AC 22 72 DE 74 2F 57 7F CB
E7 47 B7 62 C3 F4 2D 61 93 85 18 EA 6 17 12 AE 44 A8 D B8 4C 89 85
A9 3C D5 E2 46 E0 59 C9 DF 10 AF ED EF 8AA1 B1 8D EE 4A BE 48 EC
79 A5 A 5F 2F 30 87 4A C7 7F 5D C1 D 26 EE
```

```
Binary Object as Base64: s01V3i0Ou8++TeZTw8KbZwNF +eUgYX5PeoHsS
fBJHY7U99tUr6CBBbi+zvg2kHrUNkIEdYEbq1HOBWOsInLedC9Xf8vnR7diw/QtY
ZOFGOoGFxKuRKgNuEyJhak81eJG4FnJ3xCv7e+KobGN7kq+SO x5pQpfLzCHSsd/
XcENJu4=
```

Parsing from strings to numbers or dates and times

The second most common conversion is from strings to numbers or date and time values.

The opposite of `ToString` is `Parse`. Only a few types have a `Parse` method, including all the number types and `DateTime`.

1. Add statements to the `Main` method to parse an integer and a date and time value from strings and then write the result to the console, as shown in the following code:

```
int age = int.Parse("27");
DateTime birthday = DateTime.Parse("4 July 1980");

WriteLine($"I was born {age} years ago.");
WriteLine($"My birthday is {birthday}.");
WriteLine($"My birthday is {birthday:D}.");
```

2. Run the console application and view the result, as shown in the following output:

```
I was born 27 years ago.
My birthday is 04/07/1980 00:00:00.
My birthday is 04 July 1980.
```

By default, a date and time value outputs with the short date and time format. You can use format codes such as D to output only the date part using long date format.

 More Information: There are many other format codes for common scenarios that you can read about at the following link: https://docs.microsoft.com/en-us/dotnet/standard/base-types/standard-date-and-time-format-strings.

One problem with the Parse method is that it gives errors if the string cannot be converted.

3. Add a statement to the bottom of the Main method to attempt to parse a string containing letters into an integer variable, as shown in the following code:

```
int count = int.Parse("abc");
```

4. Run the console application and view the result, as shown in the following output:

```
Unhandled Exception: System.FormatException: Input string was not
in a correct format.
```

As well as the preceding exception message, you will see a stack trace. I have not included stack traces in this book because they take up too much space.

Avoiding exceptions using the TryParse method

To avoid errors, you can use the TryParse method instead. TryParse attempts to convert the input string and returns true if it can convert it and false if it cannot.

The out keyword is required to allow the TryParse method to set the count variable when the conversion works.

1. Replace the int count declaration with statements to use the TryParse method and ask the user to input a count for a number of eggs, as shown in the following code:

```
Write("How many eggs are there? ");
int count;
string input = Console.ReadLine();
if (int.TryParse(input, out count))
{
  WriteLine($"There are {count} eggs.");
}
else
{
  WriteLine("I could not parse the input.");
}
```

2. Run the console application.

3. Enter 12 and view the result, as shown in the following output:

```
How many eggs are there? 12

There are 12 eggs.
```

4. Run the console application again.

5. Enter twelve and view the result, as shown in the following output:

```
How many eggs are there? twelve
I could not parse the input.
```

You can also use methods of the System.Convert type to convert string values into other types; however, like the Parse method, it gives an error if it cannot convert.

Handling exceptions when converting types

You've seen several scenarios when errors have occurred when converting types. When this happens, we say *a runtime exception has been thrown*.

As you have seen, the default behavior of a console application is to write a message about the exception including a stack trace in the output and then stop running the application.

 Good Practice: Avoid writing code that will throw an exception whenever possible, perhaps by performing if statement checks, but sometimes you can't. In those scenarios, you could *catch the exception* and handle it in a better way than the default behavior.

Wrapping error-prone code in a try block

When you know that a statement can cause an error, you should wrap that statement in a `try` block. For example, parsing from text to a number can cause an error. Any statements in the `catch` block will be executed only if an exception is thrown by a statement in the `try` block. We don't have to do anything inside the `catch` block.

1. Create a folder and console application named `HandlingExceptions` and add it to the workspace.

2. In the `Main` method, add statements to prompt the user to enter their age and then write their age to the console, as shown in the following code:

```
WriteLine("Before parsing");

Write("What is your age? ");
string input = Console.ReadLine();

try
{
  int age = int.Parse(input);
  WriteLine($"You are {age} years old.");
}
catch
{

}

WriteLine("After parsing");
```

   This code includes two messages to indicate *before* parsing and *after* parsing to make clearer the flow through the code. These will be especially useful as the example code grows more complex.

3. Run the console application.

4. Enter a valid age, for example, `47`, and view the result, as shown in the following output:

```
Before parsing
What is your age? 47
You are 47 years old.
After parsing
```

5. Run the console application again.

6. Enter an invalid age, for example, `kermit`, and view the result, as shown in the following output:

```
Before parsing
```

```
What is your age? Kermit

After parsing
```

When the code executed, the error exception was caught and the default message and stack trace were not output, and the console application continued running. This is better than the default behavior, but it might be useful to see the type of error that occurred.

Catching all exceptions

To get information about any type of exception that might occur, you can declare a variable of type `System.Exception` to the `catch` block.

1. Add an exception variable declaration to the `catch` block and use it to write information about the exception to the console, as shown in the following code:

```
catch(Exception ex)
{
  WriteLine($"{ex.GetType()} says {ex.Message}");
}
```

2. Run the console application.

3. Enter an invalid age, for example, `kermit`, and view the result, as shown in the following output:

```
Before parsing

What is your age? kermit

System.FormatException says Input string was not in a correct
format.

After parsing
```

Catching specific exceptions

Now that we know which specific type of exception occurred, we can improve our code by catching just that type of exception and customizing the message that we display to the user.

1. Leave the existing `catch` block, and above it, add a new `catch` block for the format exception type, as shown in the following highlighted code:

```
catch (FormatException)
{
  WriteLine("The age you entered is not a valid number format.");
}
catch (Exception ex)
{
```

```
    WriteLine($"{ex.GetType()} says {ex.Message}");
}
```

2. Run the console application.

3. Enter an invalid age, for example, `kermit`, and view the result, as shown in the following output:

```
Before parsing
What is your age? kermit
The age you entered is not a valid number format.
After parsing
```

The reason we want to leave the more general `catch` below is because there might be other types of exceptions that can occur.

4. Run the console application.

5. Enter a number that is too big for an integer, for example, `9876543210`, and view the result, as shown in the following output:

```
Before parsing
What is your age? 9876543210
System.OverflowException says Value was either too large or too
small for an Int32.
After parsing
```

Let's add another `catch` block for this type of exception.

6. Leave the existing `catch` blocks, and add a new `catch` block for the overflow exception type, as shown in the following highlighted code:

```
catch (OverflowException)
{
  WriteLine("Your age is a valid number format but it is either
too big or small.");
}
catch (FormatException)
{
  WriteLine("The age you entered is not a valid number format.");
}
```

7. Run the console application.

8. Enter a number that is too big, and view the result, as shown in the following output:

```
Before parsing
```

```
What is your age? 9876543210
Your age is a valid number format but it is either too big or
small.
After parsing
```

The order in which you catch exceptions is important. The correct order is related to the inheritance hierarchy of the exception types. You will learn about inheritance in *Chapter 5, Building Your Own Types with Object-Oriented Programming*. However, don't worry too much about this—the compiler will give you build errors if you get exceptions in the wrong order anyway.

Checking for overflow

Earlier, we saw that when casting between number types, it was possible to lose information, for example, when casting from a `long` variable to an `int` variable. If the value stored in a type is too big, it will overflow.

Throwing overflow exceptions with the checked statement

The `checked` statement tells .NET to throw an exception when an overflow happens instead of allowing it to happen silently.

We will set the initial value of an `int` variable to its maximum value minus one. Then, we will increment it several times, outputting its value each time. Once it gets above its maximum value, it overflows to its minimum value and continues incrementing from there.

1. Create a folder and console application named `CheckingForOverflow` and add it to the workspace.
2. In the `Main` method, type statements to declare and assign an integer to one less than its maximum possible value, and then increment it and write its value to the console three times, as shown in the following code:

```
int x = int.MaxValue - 1;
WriteLine($"Initial value: {x}");
x++;
WriteLine($"After incrementing: {x}");
x++;
WriteLine($"After incrementing: {x}");
x++;
WriteLine($"After incrementing: {x}");
```

3. Run the console application and view the result, as shown in the following output:

```
Initial value: 2147483646
After incrementing: 2147483647
After incrementing: -2147483648
After incrementing: -2147483647
```

4. Now, let's get the compiler to warn us about the overflow by wrapping the statements using a `checked` statement block, as shown highlighted in the following code:

```
checked
{
    int x = int.MaxValue - 1;
    WriteLine($"Initial value: {x}");
    x++;
    WriteLine($"After incrementing: {x}");
    x++;
    WriteLine($"After incrementing: {x}");
    x++;
    WriteLine($"After incrementing: {x}");
}
```

5. Run the console application and view the result, as shown in the following output:

```
Initial value: 2147483646
After incrementing: 2147483647
Unhandled Exception: System.OverflowException: Arithmetic
operation resulted in an overflow.
```

6. Just like any other exception, we should wrap these statements in a `try` statement block and display a nicer error message for the user, as shown in the following code:

```
try
{
    // previous code goes here
}
catch (OverflowException)
{
    WriteLine("The code overflowed but I caught the exception.");
}
```

7. Run the console application and view the result, as shown in the following output:

```
Initial value: 2147483646
After incrementing: 2147483647
The code overflowed but I caught the exception.
```

Disabling compiler overflow checks with the unchecked statement

A related keyword is `unchecked`. This keyword switches off overflow checks performed by the compiler within a block of code.

1. Type the following statement at the end of the previous statements. The compiler will not compile this statement because it knows it would overflow:

    ```
    int y = int.MaxValue + 1;
    ```

2. View the **PROBLEMS** window by navigating to **View | Problems**, and note a **compile-time** check is shown as an error message, as shown in the following screenshot:

3. To disable compile-time checks, wrap the statement in an `unchecked` block, write the value of y to the console, decrement it, and repeat, as shown in the following code:

    ```
    unchecked
    {
      int y = int.MaxValue + 1;

      WriteLine($"Initial value: {y}");
      y--;
      WriteLine($"After decrementing: {y}");
      y--;
      WriteLine($"After decrementing: {y}");
    }
    ```

4. Run the console application and view the results, as shown in the following output:

    ```
    Initial value: -2147483648
    ```

```
After decrementing: 2147483647
After decrementing: 2147483646
```

Of course, it would be rare that you would want to explicitly switch off a check like this because it allows an overflow to occur. But, perhaps, you can think of a scenario where you might want that behavior.

Practicing and exploring

Test your knowledge and understanding by answering some questions, get some hands-on practice, and explore with deeper research into this chapter's topics.

Exercise 3.1 – Test your knowledge

Answer the following questions:

1. What happens when you divide an `int` variable by 0?
2. What happens when you divide a `double` variable by 0?
3. What happens when you overflow an `int` variable, that is, set it to a value beyond its range?
4. What is the difference between x = y++; and x = ++y;?
5. What is the difference between `break`, `continue`, and `return` when used inside a loop statement?
6. What are the three parts of a `for` statement and which of them are required?
7. What is the difference between the = and == operators?
8. Does the following statement compile? for (; true;) ;
9. What does the underscore _ represent in a switch expression?
10. What interface must an object implement to be enumerated over by using the foreach statement?

Exercise 3.2 – Explore loops and overflow

What will happen if this code executes?

```
int max = 500;
for (byte i = 0; i < max; i++)
{
  WriteLine(i);
}
```

Create a console application in Chapter03 named Exercise02 and enter the preceding code. Run the console application and view the output. What happens?

What code could you add (don't change any of the preceding code) to warn us about the problem?

Exercise 3.3 – Practice loops and operators

FizzBuzz is a group word game for children to teach them about division. Players take turns to count incrementally, replacing any number divisible by three with the word *fizz*, any number divisible by five with the word *buzz*, and any number divisible by both with *fizzbuzz*.

Some interviewers give applicants simple FizzBuzz-style problems to solve during interviews. Most good programmers should be able to write out on paper or whiteboard a program to output a simulated FizzBuzz game in under a couple of minutes.

Want to know something worrisome? Many computer science graduates can't. You can even find senior programmers who take more than 10-15 minutes to write a solution.

> *"199 out of 200 applicants for every programming job can't write code at all. I repeat: they can't write any code whatsoever."*
>
> *– Reginald Braithwaite*

This quote is taken from the following website: http://blog.codinghorror.com/why-cant-programmers-program/.

 More Information: Refer to the following link for more information: http://imranontech.com/2007/01/24/using-fizzbuzz-to-find-developers-who-grok-coding/.

Create a console application in Chapter03 named Exercise03 that outputs a simulated FizzBuzz game counting up to 100. The output should look something like the following screenshot:

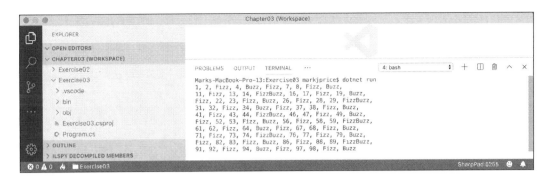

Exercise 3.4 – Practice exception handling

Create a console application in `Chapter03` named `Exercise04` that asks the user for two numbers in the range 0-255 and then divides the first number by the second:

```
Enter a number between 0 and 255: 100

Enter another number between 0 and 255: 8

100 divided by 8 is 12
```

Write exception handlers to catch any thrown errors, as shown in the following output:

```
Enter a number between 0 and 255: apples

Enter another number between 0 and 255: bananas

FormatException: Input string was not in a correct format.
```

Exercise 3.5 – Test your knowledge of operators

What are the values of x and y after the following statements execute?

1. ```
   x = 3;
   y = 2 + ++x;
   ```

2. ```
   x = 3 << 2;
   y = 10 >> 1;
   ```

3. ```
   x = 10 & 8;
   y = 10 | 7;
   ```
   ```

Exercise 3.6 – Explore topics

Use the following links to read in more detail about the topics covered in this chapter:

- **C# Operators**: https://docs.microsoft.com/en-us/dotnet/csharp/programming-guide/statements-expressions-operators/operators

- **Bitwise and shift operators**: https://docs.microsoft.com/en-us/dotnet/csharp/language-reference/operators/bitwise-and-shift-operators#left-shift-operator-

- **Selection Statements (C# Reference)**: https://docs.microsoft.com/en-us/dotnet/articles/csharp/language-reference/keywords/selection-statements

- **Iteration Statements (C# Reference)**: https://docs.microsoft.com/en-us/dotnet/articles/csharp/language-reference/keywords/iteration-statements

- **Jump Statements (C# Reference)**: https://docs.microsoft.com/en-us/dotnet/articles/csharp/language-reference/keywords/jump-statements

- **Casting and Type Conversions (C# Programming Guide)**: https://docs.microsoft.com/en-us/dotnet/articles/csharp/programming-guide/types/casting-and-type-conversions

- **Exception Handling Statements (C# Reference)**: https://docs.microsoft.com/en-us/dotnet/articles/csharp/language-reference/keywords/exception-handling-statements

Summary

In this chapter, you experimented with some operators, learned how to branch and loop, how to convert between types, and how to catch exceptions.

You are now ready to learn how to reuse blocks of code by defining functions, how to pass values into them and get values back, and how to track down bugs in your code and squash them!

Chapter 04

Writing, Debugging, and Testing Functions

This chapter is about writing functions to reuse code, debugging logic errors during development, logging exceptions during runtime, and unit testing your code to remove bugs and ensure stability and reliability.

This chapter covers the following topics:

- Writing functions
- Debugging during development
- Logging during runtime
- Unit testing

Writing functions

A fundamental principle of programming is **Don't Repeat Yourself (DRY)**.

While programming, if you find yourself writing the same statements over and over again, then turn those statements into a function. Functions are like tiny programs that complete one small task. For example, you might write a function to calculate sales tax and then reuse that function in many places in a financial application.

Like programs, functions usually have inputs and outputs. They are sometimes described as black boxes, where you feed some raw materials in one end and a manufactured item emerges at the other. Once created, you don't need to think about how they work.

Let's say that you want to help your child learn their times tables, so you want to make it easy to generate a times table for a number, such as the 12 times table:

```
1 x 12 = 12
2 x 12 = 24
...
12 x 12 = 144
```

You previously learned about the `for` statement earlier in this book, so you know that `for` can be used to generate repeated lines of output when there is a regular pattern, like the 12 times table, as shown in the following code:

```
for (int row = 1; row <= 12; row++)
{
   Console.WriteLine($"{row} x 12 = {row * 12}");
}
```

However, instead of outputting the 12 times table, we want to make this more flexible, so it could output the times table for any number. We can do this by creating a function.

Writing a times table function

Let's explore functions by creating a function to draw a times table.

1. In your `Code` folder, create a folder named `Chapter04`.

2. Start Visual Studio Code. Close any open folder or workspace and save the current workspace in the `Chapter04` folder as `Chapter04.code-workspace`.

3. In the `Chapter04` folder, create a folder named `WritingFunctions`, add it to the `Chapter04` workspace, and create a new console application project in `WritingFunctions`.

4. Modify `Program.cs`, as shown in the following code:

```
using static System.Console;

namespace WritingFunctions
{
  class Program
  {
    static void TimesTable(byte number)
    {
      WriteLine($"This is the {number} times table:");
      for (int row = 1; row <= 12; row++)
      {
        WriteLine(
          $"{row} x {number} = {row * number}");
      }
      WriteLine();
    }

    static void RunTimesTable()
    {
```

```
      bool isNumber;
      do
      {
        Write("Enter a number between 0 and 255: ");

        isNumber = byte.TryParse(
          ReadLine(), out byte number);

        if (isNumber)
        {
          TimesTable(number);
        }
        else
        {
          WriteLine("You did not enter a valid number!");
        }
      }
      while (isNumber);
    }

    static void Main(string[] args)
    {
      RunTimesTable();
    }
  }
}
```

In the preceding code, note the following:

- ○ We have statically imported the `Console` type so that we can simplify calls to its methods such as `WriteLine`.
- ○ We have written a function named `TimesTable` that must have a `byte` value passed to it named `number`.
- ○ `TimesTable` does not return a value to the caller, so it is declared with the `void` keyword before its name.
- ○ `TimesTable` uses a `for` statement to output the times table for the number passed to it.
- ○ We have written a function named `RunTimesTable` that prompts the user to enter a number, and then calls `TimesTable`, passing it the entered number. It loops while the user enters valid numbers.
- ○ We call `RunTimesTable` in the `Main` method.

5. Run the console application.

6. Enter a number, for example, 6, and then view the result, as shown in the following output:

```
Enter a number between 0 and 255: 6
This is the 6 times table:
1 x 6 = 6
2 x 6 = 12
3 x 6 = 18
4 x 6 = 24
5 x 6 = 30
6 x 6 = 36
7 x 6 = 42
8 x 6 = 48
9 x 6 = 54
10 x 6 = 60
11 x 6 = 66
12 x 6 = 72
```

Writing a function that returns a value

The previous function performed actions (looping and writing to the console), but it did not return a value. Let's say that you need to calculate sales or **valued-added tax** (**VAT**). In Europe, VAT rates can range from 8% in Switzerland to 27% in Hungary. In the United States, state sales taxes can range from 0% in Oregon to 8.25% in California.

1. Add a function to the Program class named CalculateTax, with a second function to run it, as shown in the code below. Before you run the code, note the following:

    ◦   The CalculateTax function has two inputs: A parameter named amount that will be the amount of money spent, and a parameter named twoLetterRegionCode that will be the region the amount is spent in.

    ◦   The CalculateTax function will perform a calculation using a switch statement, and then return the sales tax or VAT owed on the amount as a decimal value; so, before the name of the function, we have declared the data type of the return value.

    ◦   The RunCalculateTax function prompts the user to enter an amount and a region code, and then calls CalculateTax and outputs the result.

```csharp
static decimal CalculateTax(
  decimal amount, string twoLetterRegionCode)
{
  decimal rate = 0.0M;
  switch (twoLetterRegionCode)
  {
    case "CH": // Switzerland
      rate = 0.08M;
      break;
    case "DK": // Denmark
    case "NO": // Norway
      rate = 0.25M;
      break;
    case "GB": // United Kingdom
    case "FR": // France
      rate = 0.2M;
      break;
    case "HU": // Hungary
      rate = 0.27M;
      break;
    case "OR": // Oregon
    case "AK": // Alaska
    case "MT": // Montana
      rate = 0.0M; break;
    case "ND": // North Dakota
    case "WI": // Wisconsin
    case "ME": // Maryland
    case "VA": // Virginia
      rate = 0.05M;
      break;
    case "CA": // California
      rate = 0.0825M;
      break;
    default: // most US states
      rate = 0.06M;
      break;
  }
  return amount * rate;
}

static void RunCalculateTax()
{
  Write("Enter an amount: ");
  string amountInText = ReadLine();
```

```
        Write("Enter a two-letter region code: ");
        string region = ReadLine();

        if (decimal.TryParse(amountInText, out decimal amount))
        {
          decimal taxToPay = CalculateTax(amount, region);
          WriteLine($"You must pay {taxToPay} in sales tax.");
        }
        else
        {
          WriteLine("You did not enter a valid amount!");
        }
      }
```

2. In the `Main` method, comment the `RunTimesTable` method call, and call the `RunSalesTax` method, as shown in the following code:

```
// RunTimesTable();
RunCalculateTax();
```

3. Run the console application.

4. Enter an amount like `149` and a valid region code like `FR` to view the result, as shown in the following output:

```
Enter an amount: 149

Enter a two-letter region code: FR

You must pay 29.8 in sales tax.
```

 Challenge: Can you think of any problems with the `CalculateTax` function as written? What would happen if the user enters a code like `fr` or `UK`? How could you rewrite the function to improve it? Would using a **switch expression** instead of a **switch statement** be clearer?

Writing mathematical functions

Although you might never create an application that needs to have mathematical functionality, everyone studies mathematics at school, so using mathematics is a common way to learn about functions.

Converting numbers from ordinal to cardinal

Numbers that are used to count are called **cardinal** numbers, for example, 1, 2, and 3. Whereas numbers that are used to order are **ordinal** numbers, for example, 1st, 2nd, and 3rd.

1. Write a function named `CardinalToOrdinal` that converts a cardinal `int` value into an ordinal `string` value; for example, it converts 1 into 1st, 2 into 2nd, and so on, as shown in the following code:

```
static string CardinalToOrdinal(int number)
{
  switch (number)
  {
    case 11:
    case 12:
    case 13:
      return $"{number}th";
    default:
      string numberAsText = number.ToString();
      char lastDigit = numberAsText[numberAsText.Length - 1];
      string suffix = string.Empty;
      switch (lastDigit)
      {
        case '1':
          suffix = "st";
          break;
        case '2':
          suffix = "nd";
          break;
        case '3':
          suffix = "rd";
          break;
        default:
          suffix = "th";
          break;
      }
      return $"{number}{suffix}";
  }
}

static void RunCardinalToOrdinal()
{
  for (int number = 1; number <= 40; number++)
  {
    Write($"{CardinalToOrdinal(number)} ");
  }
  WriteLine();
}
```

From the preceding code, note the following:

- The `CardinalToOrdinal` function has one input: a parameter of the `int` type named `number`, and one output: a return value of the `string` type.

- A `switch` statement is used to handle the special cases of `11`, `12`, and `13`.

- A nested `switch` statement then handles all other cases: if the last digit is `1`, then use `st` as the suffix, if the last digit is `2`, then use `nd` as the suffix, if the last digit is `3`, then use `rd` as the suffix, and if the last digit is anything else, then use `th` as the suffix.

- The `RunCardinalToOrdinal` function uses a `for` statement to loop from 1 to 40, calling the `CardinalToOrdinal` function for each number and writing the returned string to the console, separated by a space character.

2. In the `Main` method, comment the `RunSalesTax` method call, and call the `RunCardinalToOrdinal` method, as shown in the following code:

```
// RunTimesTable();
// RunSalesTax();
RunCardinalToOrdinal();
```

3. Run the console application and view the results, as shown in the following output:

```
1st 2nd 3rd 4th 5th 6th 7th 8th 9th 10th 11th 12th 13th 14th 15th
16th 17th 18th 19th 20th 21st 22nd 23rd 24th 25th 26th 27th 28th
29th 30th 31st 32nd 33rd 34th 35th 36th 37th 38th 39th 40th
```

Calculating factorials with recursion

The factorial of 5 is 120, because factorials are calculated by multiplying the starting number by one less than itself, and then by one less again, and so on, until the number is reduced to 1. An example can be seen in: 5 x 4 x 3 x 2 x 1 = 120.

We will write a function named `Factorial`; this will calculate the factorial for an `int` passed to it as a parameter. We will use a clever technique called **recursion**, which means a function that calls itself within its implementation, either directly or indirectly.

More Information: Recursion is clever, but it can lead to problems, such as a stack overflow due to too many function calls because memory is used to store data on every function call and it eventually uses too much.

Iteration is a more practical, if less succinct, solution in languages like C#. You can read more about this at the following link:
`https://en.wikipedia.org/wiki/Recursion_(computer_science)#Recursion_versus_iteration`

1. Add a function named `Factorial`, and a function to call it, as shown in the following code:

```csharp
static int Factorial(int number)
{
  if (number < 1)
  {
    return 0;
  }
  else if (number == 1)
  {
    return 1;
  }
  else
  {
    return number * Factorial(number - 1);
  }
}

static void RunFactorial()
{
  bool isNumber;
  do
  {
    Write("Enter a number: ");

    isNumber = int.TryParse(
      ReadLine(), out int number);

    if (isNumber)
    {
      WriteLine(
        $"{number:N0}! = {Factorial(number):N0}");
    }
    else
    {
      WriteLine("You did not enter a valid number!");
    }
  }
  while (isNumber);
}
```

As before, there's several noteworthy elements of the above code, including the following:

- ° If the input number is zero or negative, Factorial returns 0.

- ° If the input number is 1, Factorial returns 1, and therefore stops calling itself. If the input number is larger than one, Factorial multiplies the number by the result of calling itself and passing one less than the number. This makes the function recursive.

- ° RunFactorial prompts the user to enter a number, calls the Factorial function, and then outputs the result, formatted using the code N0, which means number format and use thousands separators with zero decimal places, and repeats in a loop as long as another number is entered.

- ° In the Main method, comment the RunCardinalToOrdinal method call, and call the RunFactorial method.

2. Run the console application.

3. Enter the numbers 3, 5, 31, and 32, and view the results, as shown in the following output:

```
Enter a number: 3
3! = 6
Enter a number: 5
5! = 120
Enter a number: 31
31! = 738,197,504
Enter a number: 32
32! = -2,147,483,648
```

Factorials are written like this: 5!, where the exclamation mark is read as *bang*, so 5! = 120, that is, *five bang equals one hundred and twenty*. Bang is a good name for factorials because they increase in size very rapidly, just like an explosion. As you can see in the previous output, factorials of 32 and higher will overflow the int type because they are so big.

Documenting functions with XML comments

By default, when calling a function like CardinalToOrdinal, Visual Studio Code will show a tooltip with basic information, as shown in the following screenshot:

Let's improve the tooltip by adding extra information.

1. If you haven't already installed the **C# XML Documentation Comments** extension, do so now. Instructions for installing extensions for Visual Studio Code were covered in *Chapter 1, Hello, C#! Welcome, .NET!*.

2. On the line above the `CardinalToOrdinal` function, type three forward slashes, and note the extension expands this into an XML comment and recognizes that it has a single parameter named `number`.

3. Enter suitable information for the XML documentation comment, as shown in the following code and screenshot:

```
/// <summary>
/// Pass a 32-bit integer and it will be converted into its
ordinal equivalent.
/// </summary>
/// <param name="number">Number is a cardinal value e.g. 1, 2, 3,
and so on.</param>
/// <returns>Number as an ordinal value e.g. 1st, 2nd, 3rd, and so
on.</returns>
```

4. Now, when calling the function, you will see more details, as shown in the following screenshot:

Good Practice: Add XML documentation comments to all your functions.

Debugging during development

In this section, you will learn how to debug problems at development time.

Creating code with a deliberate bug

Let's explore debugging by creating a console app with a deliberate bug that we will then use the tools to track down and fix.

1. In Chapter04, create a folder named Debugging, add it to the workspace, and create a console application in the folder.

2. Navigate to **View | Command Palette**, enter and select **OmniSharp: Select Project**, and then select the **Debugging** project.

3. In the Debugging folder, open and modify Program.cs to define a function with a deliberate bug and call it in the Main method, as shown in the following code:

```
using static System.Console;

namespace Debugging
{
  class Program
  {
    static double Add(double a, double b)
    {
      return a * b; // deliberate bug!
    }

    static void Main(string[] args)
    {
```

```
double a = 4.5; // or use var
double b = 2.5;
double answer = Add(a, b);
WriteLine($"{a} + {b} = {answer}");
ReadLine(); // wait for user to press ENTER
        }
    }
}
```

4. Run the console application and view the result, as shown in the following output:

```
4.5 + 2.5 = 11.25
```

5. Press *ENTER* to end the console application.

But wait, there's a bug! `4.5` added to `2.5` should be `7`, not `11.25`!

We will use the debugging tools to hunt for and squash the bug.

Setting a breakpoint

Breakpoints allow us to mark a line of code that we want to pause at to inspect the program state and find bugs.

1. Click the open curly brace at the beginning of the `Main` method.

2. Navigate to **Debug | Toggle Breakpoint** or press *F9*. A red circle will then appear in the margin bar on the left-hand side to indicate that a breakpoint has been set, as shown in the following screenshot:

Breakpoints can be toggled with *F9*. You can also left-click in the margin to toggle the breakpoint on and off, or right-click to see more options, such as remove, disable, or edit an existing breakpoint, or adding a breakpoint, conditional breakpoint, or logpoint when a breakpoint does not yet exist.

3. In Visual Studio Code, go to **View | Debug**, or press *Ctrl* or *Cmd + Shift + D*.

4. At the top of the **DEBUG** window, click on the dropdown to the right of the **Start Debugging** button (green triangular "play" button), and select **.NET Core Launch (console) (Debugging)**, as shown in the following screenshot:

5. At the top of the **DEBUG** window, click the **Start Debugging** button (green triangular "play" button), or press *F5*. Visual Studio Code starts the console application executing and then pauses when it hits the breakpoint. This is known as **break mode**. The line that will be executed next is highlighted in yellow, and a yellow block points at the line from the gray margin bar, as shown in the following screenshot:

Navigating with the debugging toolbar

Visual Studio Code shows a floating toolbar with six buttons to make it easy to access debugging features, as described in the following list:

- **Continue**/*F5* (blue bar and triangle): This button will continue running the program from the current position until it ends or hits another breakpoint.

- **Step Over**/*F10*, **Step Into**/*F11*, and **Step Out**/*Shift + F11* (blue arrows over blue dots): These buttons step through the code statements in various ways, as you will see in a moment.

- **Restart**/*Ctrl* or *Cmd + Shift + F5* (green circular arrow): This button will stop and then immediately restart the program.

- **Stop Debugging**/*Shift + F5* (red square): This button will stop the program.

Debugging windows

DEBUG view on the left-hand side allows you to monitor useful information, such as variables, while you step through your code. It has four sections:

- **VARIABLES**, including **Locals**, which shows the name, value, and type for any local variables automatically. Keep an eye on this window while you step through your code.

- **WATCH**, which shows the value of variables and expressions that you manually enter.

- **CALL STACK**, which shows the stack of function calls.

- **BREAKPOINTS**, which shows all your breakpoints and allows finer control over them.

- **DEBUG CONSOLE** enables live interaction with your code. For example, you can ask a question such as, "What is 1+2?" by typing `1+2` and pressing *Enter*. You can also interrogate the program state, for example, by entering the name of a variable.

Stepping through code

Let's explore some ways to step through the code.

1. Navigate to **Debug | Step Into** or click on the **Step Into** button in the toolbar or press *F11*. The yellow highlight steps forward one line.

2. Navigate to **Debug | Step Over** or click on the **Step Over** button in the toolbar or press *F10*. The yellow highlight steps forward one line. At the moment, you can see that there is no difference between using **Step Into** or **Step Over**.

3. Press *F10* again so that the yellow highlight is on the line that calls the `Add` method, as shown in the following screenshot:

The difference between **Step Into** and **Step Over** can be seen when you are about to execute a method call:

- If you were to click on **Step Into**, the debugger steps *into* the method so that you can step through every line in that method.

- If you were to click on **Step Over**, the whole method is executed in one go; it does *not* skip over the method without executing it.

4. Click on **Step Into** to step inside the method.

5. Select the expression a * b, right-click the expression, and select **Debug: Add to Watch...**

The expression is added to the **WATCH** window, showing that this operator is multiplying a by b to give the result 11.25. We can see that this is the bug, as shown in the following screenshot:

If you hover your mouse pointer over the a or b parameters in the code editing window, then a tooltip appears showing the current value.

6. Fix the bug by changing * to + in both the watch expression and in the function.

7. Stop, recompile, and restart by clicking the green circular arrow **Restart** button or press *Ctrl* or *Cmd* + *Shift* + *F5*.

8. Step into the function, though take a minute to note how it now calculates correctly, click the **Continue** button or press *F5*, and note that when writing to the console during debugging, the output appears in the **DEBUG CONSOLE** window instead of the **TERMINAL** window, as shown in the following screenshot:

Customizing breakpoints

It is easy to make more complex breakpoints.

1. If you are still debugging, click the **Stop** button, or navigate to **Debug | Stop Debugging**, or press *Shift* + *F5*.

2. In the **BREAKPOINTS** window, click the last button in its mini toolbar to **Remove All Breakpoints**, or navigate to **Debug | Remove All Breakpoints**.

3. Click on the WriteLine statement.

4. Set a breakpoint by pressing *F9* or navigating to **Debug | Toggle Breakpoint**.

5. Right-click the breakpoint and choose **Edit Breakpoint.....**

6. Enter an expression, like the `answer` variable must be greater than `9`, and note the expression must evaluate to `true` for the breakpoint to activate, as shown in the following screenshot:

7. Start debugging and note the breakpoint is not hit.

8. Stop debugging.

9. Edit the breakpoint and change its expression to less than `9`.

10. Start debugging and note the breakpoint is hit.

11. Stop debugging.

12. Edit the breakpoint and select **Hit Count**, then enter a number like `3`, meaning that you would have to hit the breakpoint three times before it activates.

13. Hover your mouse over the breakpoint's red circle to see a summary, as shown in the following screenshot:

You have now fixed a bug using some debugging tools and seen some advanced possibilities for setting breakpoints.

Dumping variables using SharpPad

For experienced .NET developers, one of their favorite tools is LINQPad. With complex nested objects it is convenient to be able to quickly output their values into a tool window.

More Information: Despite its name, LINQPad is not just for LINQ, but any C# expression, statement block, or program. If you work on Windows, I recommend it, and you can learn more about it at the following link: `https://www.linqpad.net`.

For a similar tool that works cross-platform, we will use the **SharpPad** extension for Visual Studio Code.

1. In Visual Studio Code, navigate to **View | Extensions**.

2. Search for `SharpPad` and click **Install**.

3. In `Chapter04`, create a folder named `Dumping`, add it to the workspace, and create a console application project in the folder.

4. In **Terminal**, enter the following command to add the `SharpPad` package to the `Dumping` project:

```
dotnet add package SharpPad
```

5. Open `Dumping.csproj` and note the package reference, as shown highlighted in the following markup:

```xml
<Project Sdk="Microsoft.NET.Sdk">

  <PropertyGroup>
    <OutputType>Exe</OutputType>
    <TargetFramework>netcoreapp3.0</TargetFramework>
  </PropertyGroup>

  <ItemGroup>
    <PackageReference Include="SharpPad" Version="1.0.4" />
  </ItemGroup>

</Project>
```

6. Modify `Program.cs` to import the `SharpPad` and `System.Threading.Tasks` namespaces, change the return type of the `Main` method to `async Task`, define a complex object variable, and then dump it to the SharpPad window, as shown in the following code:

```csharp
using System;
using SharpPad;
using System.Threading.Tasks;
using static System.Console;

namespace Dumping
{
```

```
class Program
{
  static async Task Main(string[] args)
  {
    var complexObject = new
    {
      FirstName = "Petr",
      BirthDate = new DateTime(
        year: 1972, month: 12, day: 25),
      Friends = new[] { "Amir", "Geoff", "Sal" }
    };

    WriteLine(
      $"Dumping {nameof(complexObject)} to SharpPad.");

    await complexObject.Dump();
  }
}
```

You will learn more about asynchronous tasks in *Chapter 13, Improving Performance and Scalability Using Multitasking*. For now, I have just shown you enough to be able to await the call to the asynchronous Dump method.

7. Run the application and view the result, as shown in the following screenshot:

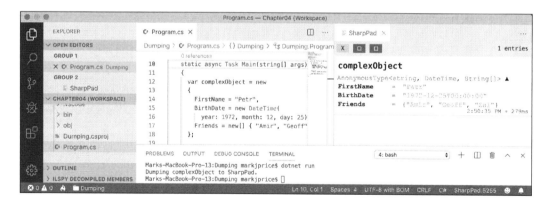

Logging during development and runtime

Once you believe that all the bugs have been removed from your code, you would then compile a release version and deploy the application, so that people can use it. But no code is ever bug free, and during runtime unexpected errors can occur.

End users are notoriously bad about remembering, admitting to, and then accurately describing what they were doing when an error occurred, so you should not rely on them accurately providing useful information to reproduce the problem in order to understand what causes the problem and then fix it.

Good Practice: Add code throughout your application to log what is happening, and especially when exceptions occur, so that you can review the logs and use them to trace the issue and fix the problem.

There are two types that can be used to add simple logging to your code: `Debug` and `Trace`.

Before we delve into them in more detail, let's look at a quick overview of each one:

- `Debug` is used to add logging that gets written during development.
- `Trace` is used to add logging that gets written during both development and runtime.

Instrumenting with Debug and Trace

You have seen the use of the `Console` type and its `WriteLine` method to provide output to the console or **TERMINAL** or **DEBUG CONSOLE** windows in Visual Studio Code.

We also have a pair of types named `Debug` and `Trace` that have more flexibility in where they write out to.

More Information: You can read more about the `Debug` class at the following link: `https://docs.microsoft.com/en-us/dotnet/api/system.diagnostics.debug?view=netcore-3.0`

The `Debug` and `Trace` classes can write to any **trace listener**. A trace listener is a type that can be configured to write output anywhere you like when the `Trace.WriteLine` method is called. There are several trace listeners provided by .NET Core, and you can even make your own by inheriting from the `TraceListener` type.

More Information: You can see the list of trace listeners that derive from `TraceListener` at the following link: `https://docs.microsoft.com/en-us/dotnet/api/system.diagnostics.tracelistener?view=netcore-3.0`

Writing to the default trace listener

One trace listener, the `DefaultTraceListener` class, is configured automatically and writes to Visual Studio Code's **DEBUG CONSOLE** window. You can configure others manually using code.

1. In `Chapter04`, create a folder named `Instrumenting`, add it to the workspace, and create a console application project in the folder.

2. Modify `Program.cs`, as shown in the following code:

```csharp
using System.Diagnostics;

namespace Instrumenting
{
  class Program
  {
    static void Main(string[] args)
    {
      Debug.WriteLine("Debug says, I am watching!");
      Trace.WriteLine("Trace says, I am watching!");
    }
  }
}
```

3. Navigate to the **DEBUG** view.

4. Start debugging by launching the `Instrumenting` console application, and note the **DEBUG CONSOLE** shows the two messages in black, mixed with other debugging information like loaded assembly DLLs in orange, as shown in the following screenshot:

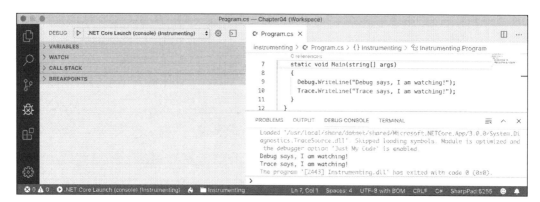

Configuring trace listeners

Now, we will configure another trace listener that will write to a text file.

1. Modify the code to add a statement to import the `System.IO` namespace, create a new text file for logging to, and enable automatic flushing of the buffer, as shown highlighted in the following code:

```
using System.Diagnostics;
using System.IO;

namespace Instrumenting
{
  class Program
  {
    static void Main(string[] args)
    {
      // write to a text file in the project folder
      Trace.Listeners.Add(new TextWriterTraceListener(
        File.CreateText("log.txt")));

      // text writer is buffered, so this option calls
      // Flush() on all listeners after writing
      Trace.AutoFlush = true;

      Debug.WriteLine("Debug says, I am watching!");
      Trace.WriteLine("Trace says, I am watching!");
    }
  }
}
```

Any type that represents a file usually implements a buffer to improve performance. Instead of writing immediately to the file, data is written to an in-memory buffer and only once the buffer is full will it be written in one chunk to the file. This behavior can be confusing while debugging because we do not immediately see the results! Enabling `AutoFlush` means it calls the `Flush` method automatically after every write.

2. Run the console application by entering the following command in the Terminal window for the `Instrumenting` project:

```
dotnet run --configuration Release
```

3. Nothing will appear to have happened.

4. In **EXPLORER**, open the file named `log.txt` and note that it contains the message, "Trace says, I am watching!".

5. Run the console application by entering the following command in the Terminal window for the `Instrumenting` project:

```
dotnet run --configuration Debug
```

6. In **EXPLORER**, open the file named `log.txt` and note that it contains both the message, "Debug says, I am watching!" and "Trace says, I am watching!"

 Good Practice: When running with the Debug configuration, both `Debug` and `Trace` are active and will show their output in **DEBUG CONSOLE**. When running with the Release configuration, only the `Trace` output is shown. You can therefore use `Debug.WriteLine` calls liberally throughout your code, knowing they will be stripped out automatically when you build the release version of your application.

Switching trace levels

The `Trace.WriteLine` calls are left in your code even after release. So, it would be great to have fine control over when they are output. This is something we can do with a **trace switch**.

The value of a trace switch can be set using a number or a word. For example, the number 3 can be replaced with the word **Info**, as shown in the following table:

Number	Word	Description
0	Off	This will output nothing
1	Error	This will output only errors
2	Warning	This will output errors and warnings
3	Info	This will output errors, warnings, and information
4	Verbose	This will output all levels

Let's explore using trace switches. We will need to add some packages to enable loading configuration settings from a JSON `appsettings` file. You will learn more about this in *Chapter 7, Understanding and Packaging .NET Types*.

1. Navigate to the **TERMINAL** window.

2. Enter the following command:

   ```
   dotnet add package Microsoft.Extensions.Configuration
   ```

3. Enter the following command:

   ```
   dotnet add package Microsoft.Extensions.Configuration.Binder
   ```

4. Enter the following command:

   ```
   dotnet add package Microsoft.Extensions.Configuration.Json
   ```

5. Enter the following command:

```
dotnet add package Microsoft.Extensions.Configuration.
FileExtensions
```

6. Open `Instrumenting.csproj` and note the extra `<ItemGroup>` section with the extra packages, as shown highlighted in the following markup:

```xml
<Project Sdk="Microsoft.NET.Sdk">

  <PropertyGroup>
    <OutputType>Exe</OutputType>
    <TargetFramework>netcoreapp3.0</TargetFramework>
  </PropertyGroup>

  <ItemGroup>
    <PackageReference
      Include="Microsoft.Extensions.Configuration"
      Version="3.0.0" />
    <PackageReference
      Include="Microsoft.Extensions.Configuration.Binder"
      Version="3.0.0" />
    <PackageReference
      Include="Microsoft.Extensions.Configuration.FileExtensions"
      Version="3.0.0" />
    <PackageReference
      Include="Microsoft.Extensions.Configuration.Json"
      Version="3.0.0" />
  </ItemGroup>

</Project>
```

7. Add a file named `appsettings.json` to the `Instrumenting` folder.

8. Modify `appsettings.json`, as shown in the following code:

```json
{
  "PacktSwitch": {
    "Level": "Info"
  }
}
```

9. In `Program.cs`, import the `Microsoft.Extensions.Configuration` namespace.

10. Add some statements to the end of the `Main` method to create a configuration builder that looks in the current folder for a file named `appsettings.json`, build the configuration, create a trace switch, set its level by binding to the configuration, and then output the four trace switch levels, as shown in the following code:

```
var builder = new ConfigurationBuilder()
```

```
    .SetBasePath(Directory.GetCurrentDirectory())
    .AddJsonFile("appsettings.json",
      optional: true, reloadOnChange: true);


IConfigurationRoot configuration = builder.Build();


var ts = new TraceSwitch(
    displayName: "PacktSwitch",
    description: "This switch is set via a JSON config.");


configuration.GetSection("PacktSwitch").Bind(ts);


Trace.WriteLineIf(ts.TraceError, "Trace error");
Trace.WriteLineIf(ts.TraceWarning, "Trace warning");
Trace.WriteLineIf(ts.TraceInfo, "Trace information");
Trace.WriteLineIf(ts.TraceVerbose, "Trace verbose");
```

11. Set a breakpoint on the `Bind` statement.

12. Start debugging the `Instrumenting` console application.

13. In the **VARIABLES** window, expand the `ts` variable watch, and note that its `Level` is `Off` and its `TraceError`, `TraceWarning`, and so on are all `false`.

14. Step into the call to the `Bind` method by clicking the **Step Into** button or pressing *F11* and note the `ts` variable watch updates to `Info` level.

15. Step into the four calls to `Trace.WriteLineIf` and note that all levels up to `Info` are written to the **DEBUG CONSOLE** but not `Verbose`, as shown in the following screenshot:

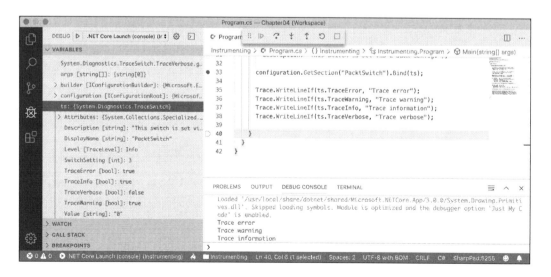

16. Stop debugging.

17. Modify `appsettings.json` to set a level of 2, which means warning, as shown in the following JSON file:

```json
{
  "PacktSwitch": {
    "Level": "2"
  }
}
```

18. Save the changes.

19. Run the console application by entering the following command in the Terminal window for the `Instrumenting` project:

```
dotnet run --configuration Release
```

20. Open the file named `log.txt` and note that this time, only trace error and warning levels are the output of the four potential trace levels, as shown in the following text file:

```
Trace says, I am watching!

Trace error

Trace warning
```

If no argument is passed, the default trace switch level is `Off` (0), so none of the switch levels are output.

Unit testing functions

Fixing bugs in code is expensive. The earlier that a bug is discovered in the development process, the less expensive it will be to fix.

Unit testing is a good way to find bugs early in the development process. Some developers even follow the principle that programmers should create unit tests before they write code, and this is called **Test-Driven Development (TDD)**.

 More Information: You can learn more about TDD at the following link: https://en.wikipedia.org/wiki/Test-driven_development

Microsoft has a proprietary unit testing framework known as **MS Test**; however, we will use the third-party framework **xUnit.net**.

Creating a class library that needs testing

First, we will create a function that needs testing.

1. Inside the `Chapter04` folder, create two subfolders named `CalculatorLib` and `CalculatorLibUnitTests`, and add them each to the workspace.

2. Navigate to **Terminal | New Terminal** and select `CalculatorLib`.

3. Enter the following command in **TERMINAL**:

```
dotnet new classlib
```

4. Rename the file named `Class1.cs` to `Calculator.cs`.

5. Modify the file to define a `Calculator` class (with a deliberate bug!), as shown in the following code:

```
namespace Packt
{
  public class Calculator
  {
    public double Add(double a, double b)
    {
      return a * b;
    }
  }
}
```

6. Enter the following command in **TERMINAL**:

```
dotnet build
```

7. Navigate to **Terminal | New Terminal** and select `CalculatorLibUnitTests`.

8. Enter the following command in **TERMINAL**:

```
dotnet new xunit
```

9. Click on the file named `CalculatorLibUnitTests.csproj`, and modify the configuration to add an item group with a project reference to the `CalculatorLib` project, as shown highlighted in the following markup:

```
<Project Sdk="Microsoft.NET.Sdk">

  <PropertyGroup>
    <TargetFramework>netcoreapp3.0</TargetFramework>
    <IsPackable>false</IsPackable>
  </PropertyGroup>

  <ItemGroup>
```

```
<PackageReference Include="Microsoft.NET.Test.Sdk"
                  Version="16.2.0" />
<PackageReference Include="xunit"
                  Version="2.4.0" />
<PackageReference Include="xunit.runner.visualstudio"
                  Version="2.4.0" />
<PackageReference Include="coverlet.collector"
                  Version="1.0.1" />
</ItemGroup>

<ItemGroup>
  <ProjectReference
    Include="..\CalculatorLib\CalculatorLib.csproj" />
</ItemGroup>

</Project>
```

More Information: You can view Microsoft's NuGet feed for the latest `Microsoft.NET.Test.Sdk` and other packages at the following link: `https://www.nuget.org/packages/Microsoft.NET.Test.Sdk`

10. Rename the file `UnitTest1.cs` to `CalculatorUnitTests.cs`.
11. Enter the following command in **TERMINAL**:
    ```
    dotnet build
    ```

Writing unit tests

A well-written unit test will have three parts:

- **Arrange**: This part will declare and instantiate variables for input and output.
- **Act**: This part will execute the unit that you are testing. In our case, that means calling the method that we want to test.
- **Assert**: This part will make one or more assertions about the output. An assertion is a belief that if not true indicates a failed test. For example, when adding 2 and 2 we would expect the result would be 4.

Now, we will write the unit tests for the `Calculator` class.

1. Open `CalculatorUnitTests.cs`, rename the class to
   `CalculatorUnitTests`, import the `Packt` namespace, and modify
   it to have two test methods for adding 2 and 2, and adding 2 and 3,
   as shown in the following code:

```csharp
using Packt;
using System;
using Xunit;

namespace CalculatorLibUnitTests
{
  public class CalculatorUnitTests
  {
    [Fact]
    public void TestAdding2And2()
    {
      // arrange
      double a = 2;
      double b = 2;
      double expected = 4;
      var calc = new Calculator();

      // act
      double actual = calc.Add(a, b);

      // assert
      Assert.Equal(expected, actual);
    }

    [Fact]
    public void TestAdding2And3()
    {
      // arrange
      double a = 2;
      double b = 3;
      double expected = 5;
      var calc = new Calculator();

      // act
      double actual = calc.Add(a, b);

      // assert
      Assert.Equal(expected, actual);
    }
  }
}
```

Running unit tests

Now we are ready to run the unit tests and see the results.

1. In the `CalculatorLibUnitTest` **TERMINAL** window, enter the following command:

   ```
   dotnet test
   ```

2. Note that the results indicate that two tests ran, one test passed, and one test failed, as shown in the following screenshot:

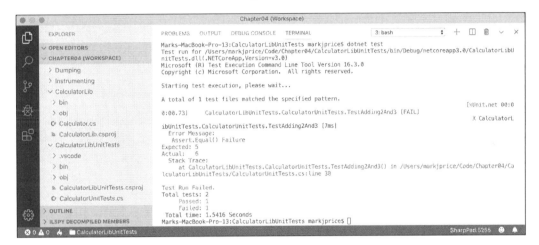

3. Fix the bug in the `Add` method.
4. Run the unit tests again to see that the bug has now been fixed.
5. Close the workspace.

Practicing and exploring

Test your knowledge and understanding by answering some questions, get some hands-on practice, and explore with deeper research into the topics covered in this chapter.

Exercise 4.1 – Test your knowledge

Answer the following questions. If you get stuck, try Googling the answers if necessary:

1. What does the C# keyword `void` mean?
2. How many parameters can a method have?

3. In Visual Studio Code, what is the difference between pressing *F5*, *Ctrl* or *Cmd* + *F5*, *Shift* + *F5*, and *Ctrl* or *Cmd* + *Shift* + *F5*?

4. Where does the `Trace.WriteLine` method write its output to?

5. What are the five trace levels?

6. What is the difference between `Debug` and `Trace`?

7. When writing a unit test, what are the three A's?

8. When writing a unit test using `xUnit`, what attribute must you decorate the test methods with?

9. What `dotnet` command executes `xUnit` tests?

10. What is TDD?

Exercise 4.2 – Practice writing functions with debugging and unit testing

Prime factors are the combination of the smallest prime numbers that, when multiplied together, will produce the original number. Consider the following example:

- Prime factors of 4 are: 2 x 2

- Prime factors of 7 are: 7

- Prime factors of 30 are: 5 x 3 x 2

- Prime factors of 40 are: 5 x 2 x 2 x 2

- Prime factors of 50 are: 5 x 5 x 2

Create a workspace; a class library with a method named `PrimeFactors` that, when passed an `int` variable as a parameter, returns a string showing its prime factors; a unit tests project; and a console application to use it. To keep it simple, you can assume that the largest number entered will be 1000.

Use the debugging tools and write unit tests to ensure that your function works correctly with multiple inputs and returns the correct output.

Exercise 4.3 – Explore topics

Use the following links to read more about the topics covered in this chapter:

- **Debugging in Visual Studio Code**: https://code.visualstudio.com/docs/editor/debugging

- **Instructions for setting up the .NET Core debugger**: https://github.com/OmniSharp/omnisharp-vscode/blob/master/debugger.md

- **System.Diagnostics Namespace**: https://docs.microsoft.com/en-us/dotnet/core/api/system.diagnostics

- **Unit testing in .NET Core and .NET Standard**: https://docs.microsoft.com/en-us/dotnet/core/testing/

- **xUnit.net**: http://xunit.github.io/

Summary

In this chapter, you learned how to write reusable functions and then use the Visual Studio Code debugging and diagnostic features to fix any bugs in them, and then unit tested your code.

In the next chapter, you will learn how to build your own types using object-oriented programming techniques.

Chapter 05

Building Your Own Types with Object-Oriented Programming

This chapter is about making your own types using **object-oriented programming (OOP)**. You will learn about all the different categories of members that a type can have, including fields to store data and methods to perform actions. You will use OOP concepts such as aggregation and encapsulation. You will also learn about language features such as tuple syntax support, `out` variables, inferred tuple names, and default literals.

This chapter will cover the following topics:

- Talking about OOP
- Building class libraries
- Storing data with fields
- Writing and calling methods
- Controlling access with properties and indexers

Talking about object-oriented programming

An object in the real world is a thing, such as a car or a person, whereas an object in programming often represents something in the real world, such as a product or bank account, but this can also be something more abstract.

In C#, we use the `class` (mostly) or `struct` (sometimes) C# keywords to define a type of object. You will learn about the difference between classes and structs in *Chapter 6, Implementing Interfaces and Inheriting Classes*. You can think of a type as being a blueprint or template for an object.

The concepts of object-oriented programming are briefly described here:

- **Encapsulation** is the combination of the data and actions that are related to an object. For example, a `BankAccount` type might have data, such as `Balance` and `AccountName`, as well as actions, such as `Deposit` and `Withdraw`. When encapsulating, you often want to control what can access those actions and the data, for example, restricting how the internal state of an object can be accessed or modified from the outside.

- **Composition** is about what an object is made of. For example, a car is composed of different parts, such as four wheels, several seats, and an engine.

- **Aggregation** is about what can be combined with an object. For example, a person is not part of a car object, but they could sit in the driver's seat and then becomes the car's driver. Two separate objects that are aggregated together to form a new component.

- **Inheritance** is about reusing code by having a subclass derive from a **base** or **super** class. All functionality in the base class is inherited by and becomes available in the derived class. For example, the base or super `Exception` class has some members that have the same implementation across all exceptions, and the sub or derived `SqlException` class inherits those members and has extra members only relevant to when an SQL database exception occurs like a property for the database connection.

- **Abstraction** is about capturing the core idea of an object and ignoring the details or specifics. C# has an `abstract` keyword which formalizes the concept. If a class is not explicitly `abstract` then it can be described as being concrete. Base or super classes are often abstract, for example, the super class `Stream` is `abstract` and its sub classes like `FileStream` and `MemoryStream` are concrete. Abstraction is a tricky balance. If you make a class more abstract, more classes would be able to inherit from it, but at the same time there will be less functionality to share.

- **Polymorphism** is about allowing a derived class to override an inherited action to provide custom behavior.

Building class libraries

Class library assemblies group types together into easily deployable units (DLL files). Apart from when you learned about unit testing, you have only created console applications to contain your code. To make the code that you write reusable across multiple projects, you should put it in class library assemblies, just like Microsoft does.

Good Practice: Put types that you might reuse in a .NET Standard 2.0 class library to enable them to be reused in .NET Core, .NET Framework, and Xamarin projects.

Creating a class library

The first task is to create a reusable .NET Standard class library.

1. In your existing `Code` folder, create a folder named `Chapter05`, with a subfolder named `PacktLibrary`.

2. In Visual Studio Code, navigate to **File | Save Workspace As...**, enter the name `Chapter05`, select the `Chapter05` folder, and click **Save**.

3. Navigate to **File | Add Folder to Workspace...**, select the **PacktLibrary** folder, and click **Add**.

4. In **TERMINAL**, enter the following command: `dotnet new classlib`.

Defining a class

The next task is to define a class that will represent a person.

1. In **EXPLORER**, rename the file named `Class1.cs` to `Person.cs`.

2. Click `Person.cs` to open it and change the class name to `Person`.

3. Change the namespace to `Packt.Shared`.

Good Practice: We're doing this because it is important to put your classes in a logically named namespace. A better namespace name would be domain-specific, for example, `System.Numerics` for types related to advanced numbers, but in this case the types we will create are `Person`, `BankAccount`, and `WondersOfTheWorld` and they do not have a normal domain.

Your class file should now look like the following code:

```
using System;

namespace Packt.Shared
{
  public class Person
  {
  }
}
```

Note that the C# keyword `public` is applied before `class`. This keyword is called an **access modifier**, and it allows for all the other code to access this class.

If you do not explicitly apply the `public` keyword, then it would only be accessible within the assembly that defined it. This is because the implicit access modifier for a class is `internal`. We need this class to be accessible outside the assembly, so we must make sure it is `public`.

Understanding members

This type does not yet have any members encapsulated within it. We will create some over the following pages. Members can be fields, methods, or specialized versions of both. You'll find a description of them below:

- **Fields** are used to store data. There are also three specialized categories of field, as shown in the following bullets:
    - ° **Constant**: The data never changes. The compiler literally copies the data into any code that reads it.
    - ° **Read-only**: The data cannot change after the class is instantiated, but the data can be calculated or loaded from an external source at the time of instantiation.
    - ° **Event**: The data references one or more methods that you want to execute when something happens, such as clicking on a button, or responding to a request from other code. Events will be covered in *Chapter 6*, *Implementing Interfaces and Inheriting Classes*.

- **Methods** are used to execute statements. You saw some examples when you learned about functions in *Chapter 4*, *Writing, Debugging, and Testing Functions*. There are also four specialized categories of method:
    - ° **Constructor**: The statements execute when you use the `new` keyword to allocate memory and instantiate a class.
    - ° **Property**: The statements execute when you get or set data. The data is commonly stored in a field, but could be stored externally, or calculated at runtime. Properties are the preferred way to encapsulate fields unless the memory address of the field needs to be exposed.
    - ° **Indexer**: The statements execute when you get or set data using array syntax `[]`.
    - ° **Operator**: The statements execute when you use an operator like `+` and `/` on operands of your type.

Instantiating a class

In this section, we will make an **instance** of the Person class, which is described as **instantiating** a class.

Referencing an assembly

Before we can instantiate a class, we need to reference the assembly that contains it.

1. Create a subfolder under Chapter05 named PeopleApp.
2. In Visual Studio Code, navigate to **File | Add Folder to Workspace...**, select the PeopleApp folder, and click **Add**.
3. Navigate to **Terminal | New Terminal** and select **PeopleApp**.
4. In **TERMINAL**, enter the following command: dotnet new console.
5. In **EXPLORER**, click on the file named PeopleApp.csproj.
6. Add a project reference to PacktLibrary, as shown highlighted in the following markup:

```
<Project Sdk="Microsoft.NET.Sdk>

  <PropertyGroup>
    <OutputType>Exe</OutputType>
    <TargetFramework>netcoreapp3.0</TargetFramework>
  </PropertyGroup>

  <ItemGroup>
    <ProjectReference Include="../PacktLibrary/PacktLibrary.
csproj" />
  </ItemGroup>

</Project>
```

7. In **TERMINAL**, enter a command to compile the PeopleApp project and its dependency PacktLibrary project, as shown in the following command: dotnet build.

Importing a namespace to use a type

Now, we are ready to write statements to work with the Person class.

1. In Visual Studio Code, in the PeopleApp folder, open Program.cs.

2. At the top of the `Program.cs` file, enter statements to import the namespace for our `People` class and statically import the `Console` class, as shown in the following code:

```
using Packt.Shared;
using static System.Console;
```

3. In the `Main` method, enter statements to:

   ° Create an instance of the `Person` type.

   ° Output the instance using a textual description of itself.

   The `new` keyword allocates memory for the object and initializes any internal data. We could use `Person` in place of the `var` keyword, but the use of `var` involves less typing and is still just as clear, as shown in the following code:

```
var bob = new Person();
WriteLine(bob.ToString());
```

   You might be wondering, "Why does the `bob` variable have a method named `ToString`? The `Person` class is empty!" Don't worry, we're about to find out!

4. Run the application, by entering `dotnet run` in **TERMINAL**, and then view the result, as shown in the following output:

```
Packt.Shared.Person
```

Managing multiple files

If you have multiple files that you want to work with at the same time, then you can put them side-by-side as you edit them.

1. In **EXPLORER**, expand the two projects.

2. Open both `Person.cs` and `Program.cs`.

3. Click, hold, and drag the edit window tab for one of your open files to arrange them so that you can see both `Person.cs` and `Program.cs` at the same time.

You can click on the **Split Editor Right** button or press *Cmd + * so that you have two files open side by side vertically.

Understanding objects

Although our `Person` class did not explicitly choose to inherit from a type, all types ultimately inherit directly or indirectly from a special type named `System.Object`.

The implementation of the `ToString` method in the `System.Object` type simply outputs the full namespace and type name.

Back in the original `Person` class, we could have explicitly told the compiler that `Person` inherits from the `System.Object` type, as shown in the following code:

```
public class Person : System.Object
```

When class B **inherits** from class A, we say that A is the **base** or **super** class and B is the **derived** or **subclass**. In this case, `System.Object` is the base or super class and `Person` is the derived or subclass.

You can also use the C# alias keyword `object`:

```
public class Person : object
```

Inheriting from System.Object

Let's make our class explicitly inherit from `object` and then review what members all objects have.

1. Modify your `Person` class to explicitly inherit from `object`.
2. Click inside the `object` keyword and press *F12*, or right-click on the `object` keyword and choose **Go to Definition**.

You will see the Microsoft-defined `System.Object` type and its members. This is something you don't need to understand the details of yet, but notice that it has a method named `ToString`, as shown in the following screenshot:

Good Practice: Assume other programmers know that if inheritance is not specified, the class will inherit from System.Object.

Storing data within fields

In this section, we will be defining a selection of fields in the class in order to store information about a person.

Defining fields

Let's say that we have decided that a person is composed of a name and a date of birth. We will encapsulate these two values inside a person, and the values will be visible outside it.

1. Inside the Person class, write statements to declare two public fields for storing a person's name and date of birth, as shown in the following code:

```
public class Person : object
{
  // fields
  public string Name;
  public DateTime DateOfBirth;
}
```

You can use any type for a field, including arrays and collections such as lists and dictionaries. These would be used if you needed to store multiple values in one named field. In this example, a person only has one name and one date of birth.

Understanding access modifiers

Part of encapsulation is choosing how visible the members are.

Note that, like we did with the class, we explicitly applied the public keyword to these fields. If we hadn't, then they would be implicitly private to the class, which means they are accessible only inside the class.

There are four access modifier keywords, and two combinations of access modifier keywords that you can apply to a class member, such as a field or method, as shown in the following table:

Access Modifier	Description
private	Member is accessible inside the type only. This is the default.
internal	Member is accessible inside the type and any type in the same assembly.
protected	Member is accessible inside the type and any type that inherits from the type.
public	Member is accessible everywhere.
internal protected	Member is accessible inside the type, any type in the same assembly, and any type that inherits from the type. Equivalent to a fictional access modifier named internal_or_protected.
private protected	Member is accessible inside the type, or any type that inherits from the type and is in the same assembly. Equivalent to a fictional access modifier named internal_and_protected. This combination is only available with C# 7.2 or later.

Good Practice: Explicitly apply one of the access modifiers to all type members, even if you want to use the implicit access modifier for members, which is private. Additionally, fields should usually be private or protected, and you should then create public properties to get or set the field values. This is because it controls access.

Setting and outputting field values

Now we will use those fields in the console app.

1. At the top of Program.cs, make sure the System namespace is imported.

2. Inside the Main method, change the statements to set the person's name and date of birth, and then output those fields nicely formatted, as shown in the following code:

```
var bob = new Person();
bob.Name = "Bob Smith";
bob.DateOfBirth = new DateTime(1965, 12, 22);

WriteLine(
  format: "{0} was born on {1:dddd, d MMMM yyyy}",
  arg0: bob.Name,
  arg1: bob.DateOfBirth);
```

We could have used string interpolation too, but for long strings it will wrap over multiple lines, which can be harder to read in a printed book. In the code examples in this book, remember that {0} is a placeholder for arg0, and so on.

3. Run the application and view the result, as shown in the following output:

```
Bob Smith was born on Wednesday, 22 December 1965
```

The format code for arg1 is made of several parts. dddd means the name of the day of the week. d means the number of the day of the month. MMMM means the name of the month. Lower case 'm's are used for minutes in time values. yyyy means the full number of the year. yy would mean the two-digit year.

You can also initialize fields using a shorthand object initializer syntax using curly braces. Let's see how.

4. Add the following code underneath the existing code to create another new person. Notice the different format code for the date of birth when writing to the console:

```
var alice = new Person
{
  Name = "Alice Jones",
  DateOfBirth = new DateTime(1998, 3, 7)
};

WriteLine(
  format: "{0} was born on {1:dd MMM yy}",
  arg0: alice.Name,
  arg1: alice.DateOfBirth);
```

5. Run the application and view the result, as shown in the following output:

```
Bob Smith was born on Wednesday, 22 December 1965
Alice Jones was born on 07 Mar 98
```

Storing a value using an enum type

Sometimes, a value needs to be one of a limited set of options. For example, there are seven ancient wonders of the world, and a person may have one favorite. In other times, a value needs to be a combination of a limited set of options. For example, a person may have a bucket list of ancient world wonders they want to visit.

We are able to store this data by defining an enum type.

An enum type is a very efficient way of storing one or more choices because, internally, it uses integer values in combination with a lookup table of string descriptions.

1. Add a new class to the class library by selecting PacktLibrary, clicking on the **New File** button in the mini toolbar, and entering the name WondersOfTheAncientWorld.cs.

2. Modify the WondersOfTheAncientWorld.cs file, as shown in the following code:

```
namespace Packt.Shared
{
  public enum WondersOfTheAncientWorld
  {
    GreatPyramidOfGiza,
    HangingGardensOfBabylon,
    StatueOfZeusAtOlympia,
    TempleOfArtemisAtEphesus,
    MausoleumAtHalicarnassus,
    ColossusOfRhodes,
    LighthouseOfAlexandria
  }
}
```

3. In the Person class, add the following statement to your list of fields:

```
public WondersOfTheAncientWorld FavoriteAncientWonder;
```

4. In the Main method of Program.cs, add the following statements:

```
bob.FavoriteAncientWonder =
  WondersOfTheAncientWorld.StatueOfZeusAtOlympia;

WriteLine(format:
  "{0}'s favorite wonder is {1}. It's integer is {2}.",
  arg0: bob.Name,
  arg1: bob.FavoriteAncientWonder,
  arg2: (int)bob.FavoriteAncientWonder);
```

5. Run the application and view the result, as shown in the following output:

```
Bob Smith's favorite wonder is StatueOfZeusAtOlympia. Its
integer is 2.
```

The enum value is internally stored as an int for efficiency. The int values are automatically assigned starting at 0, so the third world wonder in our enum has a value of 2. You can assign int values that are not listed in the enum. They will output as the int value instead of a name since a match will not be found.

Storing multiple values using an enum type

For the bucket list, we could create a collection of instances of the enum, and collections will be explained later in this chapter, but there is a better way. We can combine multiple choices into a single value using **flags**.

1. Modify the enum by decorating it with the [System.Flags] attribute.

2. Explicitly set byte value for each wonder that represent different bit columns, as shown in the following code:

```
namespace Packt.Shared
{
  [System.Flags]
  public enum WondersOfTheAncientWorld : byte
  {
    None                     = 0b_0000_0000, // i.e. 0
    GreatPyramidOfGiza       = 0b_0000_0001, // i.e. 1
    HangingGardensOfBabylon  = 0b_0000_0010, // i.e. 2
    StatueOfZeusAtOlympia    = 0b_0000_0100, // i.e. 4
    TempleOfArtemisAtEphesus = 0b_0000_1000, // i.e. 8
    MausoleumAtHalicarnassus = 0b_0001_0000, // i.e. 16
    ColossusOfRhodes         = 0b_0010_0000, // i.e. 32
    LighthouseOfAlexandria   = 0b_0100_0000  // i.e. 64
  }
}
```

We are assigning explicit values for each choice that would not overlap when looking at the bits stored in memory. We should also decorate the enum type with the System.Flags attribute so that when the value is returned it can automatically match with multiple values as a comma-separated string instead of returning an int value. Normally, an enum type uses an int variable internally, but since we don't need values that big, we can reduce memory requirements by 75%, that is, 1 byte per value instead of 4 bytes, by telling it to use a byte variable.

If we want to indicate that our bucket list includes the *Hanging Gardens* and *Mausoleum at Halicarnassus* ancient world wonders, then we would want the 16 and 2 bits set to 1. In other words, we would store the value 18:

64	32	16	8	4	2	1	0
0	0	1	0	0	1	0	0

In the Person class, add the following statement to your list of fields:

```
public WondersOfTheAncientWorld BucketList;
```

3. In the `Main` method of `PeopleApp`, add the following statements to set the bucket list using the `|` operator (logical OR) to combine the `enum` values. We could also set the value using the number `18` cast into the `enum` type, as shown in the comment, but we shouldn't because that would make the code harder to understand:

```
bob.BucketList =
    WondersOfTheAncientWorld.HangingGardensOfBabylon
    | WondersOfTheAncientWorld.MausoleumAtHalicarnassus;

// bob.BucketList = (WondersOfTheAncientWorld)18;

WriteLine($"{bob.Name}'s bucket list is {bob.BucketList}");
```

4. Run the application and view the result, as shown in the following output:

```
Bob Smith's bucket list is HangingGardensOfBabylon,
MausoleumAtHalicarnassus
```

 Good Practice: Use the `enum` values to store combinations of discreet options. Derive an `enum` type from `byte` if there are up to eight options, from `short` if there are up to 16 options, from `int` if there are up to 32 options, and from `long` if there are up to 64 options.

Storing multiple values using collections

Let's now add a field to store a person's children. This is an example of aggregation because children are instances of a class that is related to the current person but are not part of the person itself. We will use a generic `List<T>` collection type.

1. Import the `System.Collections.Generic` namespace at the top of the `Person.cs` class file, as shown in the following code:

```
using System.Collections.Generic;
```

You will learn more about collections in *Chapter 8, Working with Common .NET Types*. For now, just follow along.

2. Declare a new field in the `Person` class, as shown in the following code:

```
public List<Person> Children = new List<Person>();
```

`List<Person>` is read aloud as "list of `Person`," for example, "the type of the property named `Children` is a list of `Person` instances." We must ensure the collection is initialized to a new instance of a list of `Person` before we can add items to it otherwise the field will be `null` and it will throw runtime exceptions.

The angle brackets in the `List<T>` type is a feature of C# called **generics** that was introduced in 2005 with C# 2.0. It's just a fancy term for making a collection **strongly typed**, that is, the compiler knows more specifically what type of object can be stored in the collection. Generics improve the performance and correctness of your code.

Strongly typed is different from **statically typed**. The old `System.Collection` types are statically typed to contain weakly typed `System.Object` items. The newer `System.Collection.Generic` types are statically typed to contain strongly typed `<T>` instances. Ironically, the term *generics* means we can use a more specific static type!

1. In the `Main` method, add statements to add two children for Bob and then show how many children he has and what their names are, as shown in the following code:

    ```
    bob.Children.Add(new Person { Name = "Alfred" });
    bob.Children.Add(new Person { Name = "Zoe" });

    WriteLine(
      $"{bob.Name} has {bob.Children.Count} children:");

    for (int child = 0; child < bob.Children.Count; child++)
    {
      WriteLine($"  {bob.Children[child].Name}");
    }
    ```

    We could also use a `foreach` statement. As an extra challenge, change the `for` statement to output the same information using `foreach`.

2. Run the application and view the result, as shown in the following output:

    ```
    Bob Smith has 2 children:
      Alfred
      Zoe
    ```

Making a field static

The fields that we have created so far have all been **instance** members, meaning that a different value of each field exists for each instance of the class that is created. The `bob` variable has a different `Name` value to `alice`.

Sometimes, you want to define a field that only has one value that is shared across all instances. These are called **static** members because fields are not the only members that can be `static`.

Let's see what can be achieved using `static` fields.

1. In the `PacktLibrary` project, add a new class file named `BankAccount.cs`.

2. Modify the class to give it three fields, two instance fields and one static field, as shown in the following code:

```
namespace Packt.Shared
{
  public class BankAccount
  {
    public string AccountName;          // instance member
    public decimal Balance;             // instance member
    public static decimal InterestRate; // shared member
  }
}
```

Each instance of `BankAccount` will have its own `AccountName` and `Balance` values, but all instances will share a single `InterestRate` value.

3. In `Program.cs` and its `Main` method, add statements to set the shared interest rate and then create two instances of the `BankAccount` type, as shown in the following code:

```
BankAccount.InterestRate = 0.012M; // store a shared value

var jonesAccount = new BankAccount();
jonesAccount.AccountName = "Mrs. Jones";
jonesAccount.Balance = 2400;

WriteLine(format: "{0} earned {1:C} interest.",
  arg0: jonesAccount.AccountName,
  arg1: jonesAccount.Balance * BankAccount.InterestRate);

var gerrierAccount = new BankAccount();
gerrierAccount.AccountName = "Ms. Gerrier";
gerrierAccount.Balance = 98;

WriteLine(format: "{0} earned {1:C} interest.",
  arg0: gerrierAccount.AccountName,
  arg1: gerrierAccount.Balance * BankAccount.InterestRate);
```

`:C` is a format code that tells .NET to use the currency format for the numbers. In *Chapter 8, Working with Common .NET Types*, you will learn how to control the culture that determines the currency symbol. For now, it will use the default for your operating system installation. I live in London, UK, hence my output shows British Pounds (£).

4. Run the application and view the additional output:

```
Mrs. Jones earned £28.80 interest.
Ms. Gerrier earned £1.18 interest.
```

Making a field constant

If the value of a field will never *ever* change, you can use the const keyword and assign a literal value at compile time.

1. In the Person class, add the following code:

```
// constants
public const string Species = "Homo Sapien";
```

2. In the Main method, add a statement to write Bob's name and species to the console, as shown in the following code:

```
WriteLine($"{bob.Name} is a {Person.Species}");
```

To get the value of a constant field, you must write the name of the class, not the name of an instance of the class.

3. Run the application and view the result, as shown in the following output:

```
Bob Smith is a Homo Sapien
```

Examples of the const fields in Microsoft types include System.Int32.MaxValue and System.Math.PI because neither value will ever change, as you can see in the following screenshot:

Good Practice: Constants should be avoided for two important reasons: the value must be known at compile time, and it must be expressible as a literal string, Boolean, or number value. Every reference to the const field is replaced with the literal value at compile time, which will, therefore, not be reflected if the value changes in a future version and you do not recompile any assemblies that reference it to get the new value.

Making a field read-only

A better choice for fields that should not change is to mark them as read-only.

1. Inside the `Person` class, add a statement to declare an instance read-only field to store a person's home planet, as shown in the following code:

```
// read-only fields
public readonly string HomePlanet = "Earth";
```

You can also declare `static readonly` fields whose value would be shared across all instances of the type.

2. Inside the `Main` method, add a statement to write Bob's name and home planet to the console, as shown in the following code:

```
WriteLine($"{bob.Name} was born on {bob.HomePlanet}");
```

3. Run the application and view the result, as shown in the following output:

```
Bob Smith was born on Earth
```

Good Practice: Use read-only fields over the const fields for two important reasons: the value can be calculated or loaded at runtime and can be expressed using any executable statement. So, a read-only field can be set using a constructor or a field assignment. Every reference to the field is a live reference, so any future changes will be correctly reflected by calling code.

Initializing fields with constructors

Fields often need to be initialized at runtime. You do this in a constructor that will be called when you make an instance of the class using the `new` keyword. Constructors execute before any fields are set by the code that is using the type.

1. Inside the `Person` class, add the following highlighted code after the existing read-only `HomePlanet` field:

```
// read-only fields
```

```
public readonly string HomePlanet = "Earth";
public readonly DateTime Instantiated;

// constructors
public Person()
{
  // set default values for fields
  // including read-only fields
  Name = "Unknown";
  Instantiated = DateTime.Now;
}
```

2. Inside the `Main` method, add statements to instantiate a new person and then output its initial field values, as shown in the following code:

```
var blankPerson = new Person();

WriteLine(format:
  "{0} of {1} was created at {2:hh:mm:ss} on a {2:dddd}.",
  arg0: blankPerson.Name,
  arg1: blankPerson.HomePlanet,
  arg2: blankPerson.Instantiated);
```

3. Run the application and view the result, as shown in the following output:

```
Unknown of Earth was created at 11:58:12 on a Sunday
```

You can have multiple constructors in a type. This is especially useful to encourage developers to set initial values for fields.

4. In the `Person` class, add statements to define a second constructor that allows a developer to set initial values for the person's name and home planet, as shown in the following code:

```
public Person(string initialName, string homePlanet)
{
  Name = initialName;
  HomePlanet = homePlanet;
  Instantiated = DateTime.Now;
}
```

5. Inside the `Main` method, add the following code:

```
var gunny = new Person("Gunny", "Mars");

WriteLine(format:
  "{0} of {1} was created at {2:hh:mm:ss} on a {2:dddd}.",
  arg0: gunny.Name,
```

```
arg1: gunny.HomePlanet,
arg2: gunny.Instantiated);
```

6. Run the application and view the result:

```
Gunny of Mars was created at 11:59:25 on a Sunday
```

Setting fields with default literals

A language feature introduced in C# 7.1 was **default literals**. Back in *Chapter 2, Speaking C#*, you learned about the `default(type)` keyword.

As a reminder, if you had some fields in a class that you wanted to initialize to their default type values in a constructor, you have been able to use `default(type)` since C# 2.0.

1. In the `PacktLibrary` folder, add a new file named `ThingOfDefaults.cs`.

2. In the `ThingOfDefaults.cs` file, add statements to declare a class with four fields of various types and set them to their default values in a constructor, as shown in the following code:

```
using System;
using System.Collections.Generic;

namespace Packt.Shared
{
  public class ThingOfDefaults
  {
    public int Population;
    public DateTime When;
    public string Name;
    public List<Person> People;

    public ThingOfDefaults()
    {
      Population = default(int); // C# 2.0 and later
      When = default(DateTime);
      Name = default(string);
      People = default(List<Person>);
    }
  }
}
```

You might think that the compiler ought to be able to work out what type we mean without being explicitly told, and you'd be right, but for the first 15 years of the C# compiler's life, it didn't. Finally, with the C# 7.1 and later compilers it does.

3. Simplify the statements setting the defaults, as shown highlighted in the following code:

```
using System;
using System.Collections.Generic;

namespace Packt.Shared
{
  public class ThingOfDefaults
  {
    public int Population;
    public DateTime When;
    public string Name;
    public List<Person> People;

    public ThingOfDefaults()
    {
      Population = default; // C# 7.1 and later
      When = default;
      Name = default;
      People = default;
    }
  }
}
```

Constructors are a special category of method. Let's look at methods in more detail.

Writing and calling methods

Methods are members of a type that execute a block of statements.

Returning values from methods

Methods can return a single value or return nothing.

- A method that performs some actions but does not return a value indicates this with the void type before the name of the method.

- A method that performs some actions and returns a value indicates this with the type of the return value before the name of the method.

For example, you will create two methods:

- WriteToConsole: This will perform an action (writing some text to the console), but it will return nothing from the method, indicated by the void keyword.

- `GetOrigin`: This will return a string value, indicated by the `string` keyword.

Let's write the code.

1. Inside the `Person` class, statically import `System.Console`.

2. Add statements to define the two methods, as shown in the following code:

```
// methods
public void WriteToConsole()
{
  WriteLine($"{Name} was born on a {DateOfBirth:dddd}.");
}

public string GetOrigin()
{
  return $"{Name} was born on {HomePlanet}.";
}
```

3. Inside the `Main` method, add statements to call the two methods, as shown in the following code:

```
bob.WriteToConsole();
WriteLine(bob.GetOrigin());
```

4. Run the application and view the result, as shown in the following output:

```
Bob Smith was born on a Wednesday.
Bob Smith was born on Earth.
```

Combining multiple returned values using tuples

Each method can only return a single value that has a single type. That type could be a simple type, such as `string` in the previous example, a complex type, such as `Person`, or a collection type, such as `List<Person>`.

Imagine that we want to define a method named `GetTheData` that returns both a `string` value and an `int` value. We could define a new class named `TextAndNumber` with a `string` field and an `int` field, and return an instance of that complex type, as shown in the following code:

```
public class TextAndNumber
{
  public string Text;
  public int Number;
```

```
    }

    public class Processor
    {
      public TextAndNumber GetTheData()
      {
        return new TextAndNumber
        {
          Text = "What's the meaning of life?",
          Number = 42
        };
      }
    }
}
```

But defining a class just to combine two values together is unnecessary, because in modern versions of C# we can use tuples. I pronounce them as tuh-ples but I have heard other developers pronounce them as too-ples. To-may-toe, to-mah-toe, po-tay-toe, po-tah-toe, I guess.

Tuples have been a part of some languages such as F# since their first version, but .NET only added support for them in .NET 4.0 with the `System.Tuple` type.

It was only in C# 7.0 that C# added language syntax support for tuples and at the same time, .NET added a new `System.ValueTuple` type that is more efficient in some common scenarios than the old .NET 4.0 `System.Tuple` type, and the C# tuple uses the more efficient one.

`System.ValueTuple` is not part of .NET Standard 1.6, and therefore not available by default in .NET Core 1.0 or 1.1 projects. `System.ValueTuple` is built in with .NET Standard 2.0, and therefore, .NET Core 2.0 and later.

Let's explore tuples.

1. In the `Person` class, add statements to define a method that returns a `string` and `int` tuple, as shown in the following code:

    ```
    public (string, int) GetFruit()
    {
      return ("Apples", 5);
    }
    ```

2. In the `Main` method, add statements to call the `GetFruit` method and then output the tuple's fields, as shown in the following code:

    ```
    (string, int) fruit = bob.GetFruit();
    WriteLine($"{fruit.Item1}, {fruit.Item2} there are.");
    ```

3. Run the application and view the result, as shown in the following output:

```
Apples, 5 there are.
```

Naming the fields of a tuple

To access the fields of a tuple, the default names are `Item1`, `Item2`, and so on.

You can explicitly specify the field names.

1. In the `Person` class, add statements to define a method that returns a tuple with named fields, as shown in the following code:

```
public (string Name, int Number) GetNamedFruit()
{
    return (Name: "Apples", Number: 5);
}
```

2. In the `Main` method, add statements to call the method and output the tuple's named fields, as shown in the following code:

```
var fruitNamed = bob.GetNamedFruit();
WriteLine($"There are {fruitNamed.Number} {fruitNamed.Name}.");
```

3. Run the application and view the result, as shown in the following output:

```
There are 5 Apples.
```

Inferring tuple names

If you are constructing a tuple from another object, you can use a feature introduced in C# 7.1 called **tuple name inference**.

1. In the `Main` method, create two tuples, made of a `string` and `int` value each, as shown in the following code:

```
var thing1 = ("Neville", 4);
WriteLine($"{thing1.Item1} has {thing1.Item2} children.");

var thing2 = (bob.Name, bob.Children.Count);
WriteLine($"{thing2.Name} has {thing2.Count} children.");
```

In C# 7.0, both things would use the `Item1` and `Item2` naming schemes. In C# 7.1 and later, the second thing can infer the names `Name` and `Count`.

Deconstructing tuples

You can also deconstruct tuples into separate variables. The deconstructing declaration has the same syntax as named field tuples, but without a variable name for the tuple, as shown in the following code:

```
// store return value in a tuple variable with two fields
(string name, int age) tupleWithNamedFields = GetPerson();
// tupleWithNamedFields.name
// tupleWithNamedFields.age

// deconstruct return value into two separate variables
(string name, int age) = GetPerson();
// name
// age
```

This has the effect of splitting the tuple into its parts and assigning those parts to new variables.

1. In the `Main` method, add the following code:

   ```
   (string fruitName, int fruitNumber) = bob.GetFruit();
   WriteLine($"Deconstructed: {fruitName}, {fruitNumber}");
   ```

2. Run the application and view the result, as shown in the following output:

   ```
   Deconstructed: Apples, 5
   ```

 More Information: Deconstruction is not just for tuples. Any type can be deconstructed if it has a **Deconstruct** method. You can read about this at the following link: https://docs.microsoft.com/en-us/dotnet/csharp/ tuples#deconstruction

Defining and passing parameters to methods

Methods can have parameters passed to them to change their behavior. Parameters are defined a bit like variable declarations, but inside the parentheses of the method.

1. In the `Person` class, add statements to define two methods, the first without parameters and the second with one parameter, as shown in the following code:

   ```
   public string SayHello()
   {
     return $"{Name} says 'Hello!'";
   }
   ```

```
public string SayHelloTo(string name)
{
  return $"{Name} says 'Hello {name}!'";
}
```

2. In the `Main` method, add statements to call the two methods and write the return value to the console, as shown in the following code:

```
WriteLine(bob.SayHello());
WriteLine(bob.SayHelloTo("Emily"));
```

3. Run the application and view the result:

```
Bob Smith says 'Hello!'
Bob Smith says 'Hello Emily!'
```

When typing a statement that calls a method, IntelliSense shows a tooltip with the name and type of any parameters, and the return type of the method, as shown in the following screenshot:

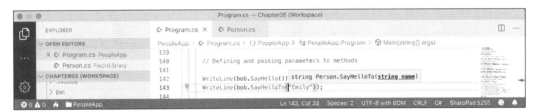

Overloading methods

Instead of having two different method names, we could give both methods the same name. This is allowed because the methods each have a different signature.

A **method signature** is a list of parameter types that can be passed when calling the method (as well as the type of the return value).

1. In the `Person` class, change the name of the `SayHelloTo` method to `SayHello`.

2. In `Main`, change the method call to use the `SayHello` method, and note that the quick info for the method tells you that it has one additional overload, 1/2, as well as 2/2, as shown in the following screenshot:

Good Practice: Use overloaded methods to simplify your class by making it appear to have fewer methods.

Passing optional parameters and naming arguments

Another way to simplify methods is to make parameters optional. You make a parameter optional by assigning a default value inside the method parameter list. Optional parameters must always come last in the list of parameters.

More Information: There is one exception to optional parameters always coming last. C# has a `params` keyword that allows you to pass a comma-separated list of parameters of any length as an array. You can read about `params` at the following link: https://docs.microsoft.com/en-us/dotnet/csharp/language-reference/keywords/params

We will now create a method with three optional parameters.

1. In the `Person` class, add statements to define the method, as shown in the following code:

```
public string OptionalParameters(
  string command = "Run!",
  double number = 0.0,
  bool active = true)
{
  return string.Format(
    format: "command is {0}, number is {1}, active is {2}",
    arg0: command, arg1: number, arg2: active);
}
```

2. In the `Main` method, add a statement to call the method and write its return value to the console, as shown in the following code:

```
WriteLine(bob.OptionalParameters());
```

3. Watch IntelliSense appear as you type the code. You will see a tooltip, showing the three optional parameters with their default values, as shown in the following screenshot:

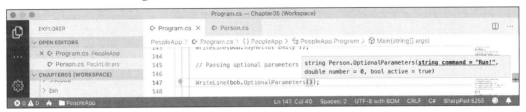

4. Run the application and view the result, as shown in the following output:

```
command is Run!, number is 0, active is True
```

5. In the `Main` method, add a statement to pass a `string` value for the `command` parameter and a `double` value for the `number` parameter, as shown in the following code:

```
WriteLine(bob.OptionalParameters("Jump!", 98.5));
```

6. Run the application and see the result, as shown in the following output:

```
command is Jump!, number is 98.5, active is True
```

The default values for `command` and `number` have been replaced, but the default for `active` is still `true`.

Optional parameters are often combined with naming parameters when you call the method, because naming a parameter allows the values to be passed in a different order than how they were declared.

7. In the `Main` method, add a statement to pass a `string` value for the `command` parameter and a `double` value for the `number` parameter but using named parameters, so that the order they are passed through can be swapped around, as shown in the following code:

```
WriteLine(bob.OptionalParameters(
    number: 52.7, command: "Hide!"));
```

8. Run the application and view the result, as shown in the following output:

```
command is Hide!, number is 52.7, active is True
```

You can even use named parameters to skip over optional parameters.

9. In the `Main` method, add a statement to pass a `string` value for the `command` parameter using positional order, skip the `number` parameter, and use the named `active` parameter, as shown in the following code:

```
WriteLine(bob.OptionalParameters("Poke!", active: false));
```

10. Run the application and view the result, as shown in the following output:

```
command is Poke!, number is 0, active is False
```

Controlling how parameters are passed

When a parameter is passed into a method, it can be passed in one of three ways:

- By **value** (this is the default): Think of these as being *in-only*.
- By **reference** as a `ref` parameter: Think of these as being *in-and-out*.
- As an `out` parameter: Think of these as being *out-only*.

Let's see some examples of passing parameters in and out.

1. In the `Person` class, add statements to define a method with three parameters, one `in` parameter, one `ref` parameter, and one `out` parameter, as shown in the following method:

```
public void PassingParameters(int x, ref int y, out int z)
{
  // out parameters cannot have a default
  // AND must be initialized inside the method
  z = 99;

  // increment each parameter
  x++;
  y++;
  z++;
}
```

2. In the `Main` method, add statements to declare some `int` variables and pass them into the method, as shown in the following code:

```
int a = 10;
int b = 20;
int c = 30;

WriteLine($"Before: a = {a}, b = {b}, c = {c}");

bob.PassingParameters(a, ref b, out c);

WriteLine($"After: a = {a}, b = {b}, c = {c}");
```

3. Run the application and view the result, as shown in the following output:

```
Before: a = 10, b = 20, c = 30
After: a = 10, b = 21, c = 100
```

When passing a variable as a parameter by default, its current *value* gets passed, *not* the variable itself. Therefore, x is a copy of the a variable. The a variable retains its original value of 10. When passing a variable as a ref parameter, a *reference* to the variable gets passed into the method.

Therefore, y is a reference to b. The b variable gets incremented when the y parameter gets incremented. When passing a variable as an out parameter, a *reference* to the variable gets passed into the method.

Therefore, z is a reference to c. The c variable gets replaced by whatever code executes inside the method. We could simplify the code in the Main method by not assigning the value 30 to the c variable, since it will always be replaced anyway.

In C# 7.0 and later, we can simplify code that uses the out variables.

4. In the Main method, add statements to declare some more variables including an out parameter named f declared inline, as shown in the following code:

```
int d = 10;
int e = 20;

WriteLine(
    $"Before: d = {d}, e = {e}, f doesn't exist yet!");

// simplified C# 7.0 syntax for the out parameter
bob.PassingParameters(d, ref e, out int f);

WriteLine($"After: d = {d}, e = {e}, f = {f}");
```

In C# 7.0 and later, the ref keyword is not just for passing parameters into a method: it can also be applied to the return value. This allows an external variable to reference an internal variable and modify its value after the method call. This might be useful in advanced scenarios, for example, passing around placeholders into big data structures, but it's beyond the scope of this book.

Splitting classes using partial

When working on large projects with multiple team members, it is useful to be able to split the definition of a complex class across multiple files. You do this using the partial keyword.

Imagine we want to add statements to the Person class that are automatically generated by a tool like an object-relational mapper that reads schema information from a database. If the class is defined as partial, then we can split the class into an auto-generated code file and a manually edited code file.

1. In the `Person` class, add the `partial` keyword, as shown highlighted in the following code:

```
namespace Packt.Shared
{
  public partial class Person
  {
```

2. In **EXPLORER**, click on the **New File** button in the `PacktLibrary` folder, and enter a name of `PersonAutoGen.cs`.

3. Add statements to the new file, as shown in the following code:

```
namespace Packt.Shared
{
  public partial class Person
  {
  }
}
```

The rest of the code we write for this chapter will be written in the `PersonAutoGen.cs` file.

Controlling access with properties and indexers

Earlier, you created a method named `GetOrigin` that returned a `string` containing the name and origin of the person. Languages such as Java do this a lot. C# has a better way: **properties**.

A property is simply a method (or a pair of methods) that acts and looks like a field when you want to get or set a value, thereby simplifying the syntax.

Defining readonly properties

A `readonly` property only has a `get` implementation.

1. In the `PersonAutoGen.cs` file, in the `Person` class, add statements to define three properties:
    *   The first property will perform the same role as the `GetOrigin` method using the property syntax that works with all versions of C# (although, it uses the C# 6 and later string interpolation syntax).
    *   The second property will return a greeting message using the C# 6 and, later, the lambda expression (`=>`) syntax.
    *   The third property will calculate the person's age.

Here's the code:

```
// a property defined using C# 1 - 5 syntax
public string Origin
{
  get
  {
    return $"{Name} was born on {HomePlanet}";
  }
}

// two properties defined using C# 6+ lambda expression
syntax
public string Greeting => $"{Name} says 'Hello!'";

public int Age => System.DateTime.Today.Year -
DateOfBirth.Year;
```

More Information: Obviously, this isn't the best way to calculate age, but we aren't learning how to calculate ages from dates of birth. If you need to do that properly, you can read a discussion at the following link: https://stackoverflow.com/questions/9/how-do-i-calculate-someones-age-in-c.

2. In the `Main` method, add statements to get the properties, as shown in the following code:

```
var sam = new Person
{
  Name = "Sam",
  DateOfBirth = new DateTime(1972, 1, 27)
};

WriteLine(sam.Origin);
WriteLine(sam.Greeting);
WriteLine(sam.Age);
```

3. Run the application and view the result, as shown in the following output:

```
Sam was born on Earth
Sam says 'Hello!'
47
```

The output shows 47 because I ran the console application on 25th September 2019 when Sam was 47 years old.

Defining settable properties

To create a settable property, you must use the older syntax and provide a pair of methods — not just a get part, but also a set part.

1. In the PersonAutoGen.cs file, add statements to define a string property that has both a get and set method (also known as *getter* and *setter*), as shown in the following code:

    ```
    public string FavoriteIceCream { get; set; } // auto-syntax
    ```

    Although you have not manually created a field to store the person's favorite ice cream, it is there, automatically created by the compiler for you.

    Sometimes, you need more control over what happens when a property is set. In this scenario, you must use a more detailed syntax and manually create a private field to store the value for the property.

2. In the PersonAutoGen.cs file, add statements to define a string field and string property that has both a get and set, as shown in the following code:

    ```
    private string favoritePrimaryColor;

    public string FavoritePrimaryColor
    {
      get
      {
        return favoritePrimaryColor;
      }
      set
      {
        switch (value.ToLower())
        {
          case "red":
          case "green":
          case "blue":
            favoritePrimaryColor = value;
            break;
          default:
            throw new System.ArgumentException(
              $"{value} is not a primary color. " +
              "Choose from: red, green, blue.");
    ```

```
        }
    }
}
```

3. In the `Main` method, add statements to set Sam's favorite ice cream and color, and then write them to the console, as shown in the following code:

    ```
    sam.FavoriteIceCream = "Chocolate Fudge";

    WriteLine($"Sam's favorite ice-cream flavor is {sam.
    FavoriteIceCream}.");

    sam.FavoritePrimaryColor = "Red";

    WriteLine($"Sam's favorite primary color is {sam.
    FavoritePrimaryColor}.");
    ```

4. Run the application and view the result, as shown in the following output:

    ```
    Sam's favorite ice-cream flavor is Chocolate Fudge.
    Sam's favorite primary color is Red.
    ```

If you try to set the color to any value other than red, green, or blue, then the code will throw an exception. The calling code could then use a `try` statement to display the error message.

Good Practice: Use properties instead of fields when you want to validate what value can be stored, when you want to data bind in XAML which we will cover in *Chapter 20, Building Windows Desktop Apps*, and when you want to read and write to fields without using methods.

More Information: You can read more about encapsulation of fields using properties at the following link: `https://stackoverflow.com/questions/1568091/why-use-getters-and-setters-accessors`

Defining indexers

Indexers allow the calling code to use the array syntax to access a property. For example, the `string` type defines an **indexer** so that the calling code can access individual characters in the `string` individually.

We will define an indexer to simplify access to the children of a person.

1. In the `PersonAutoGen.cs` file, add statements to define an indexer to get and set a child using the index of the child, as shown in the following code:

```
// indexers
public Person this[int index]
{
  get
  {
    return Children[index];
  }
  set
  {
    Children[index] = value;
  }
}
```

You can overload indexers so that different types can be used for their parameters. For example, as well as passing an `int` value, you could also pass a `string` value.

2. In the `Main` method, add the following code. After adding to the children, we will access the first and second child using the longer `Children` field and the shorter indexer syntax:

```
sam.Children.Add(new Person { Name = "Charlie" });
sam.Children.Add(new Person { Name = "Ella" });

WriteLine($"Sam's first child is {sam.Children[0].Name}");
WriteLine($"Sam's second child is {sam.Children[1].Name}");
WriteLine($"Sam's first child is {sam[0].Name}");
WriteLine($"Sam's second child is {sam[1].Name}");
```

3. Run the application and view the result, as shown in the following output:

```
Sam's first child is Charlie
Sam's second child is Ella
Sam's first child is Charlie
Sam's second child is Ella
```

 Good Practice: Only use indexers if it makes sense to use the square bracket, also known as array syntax. As you can see from the preceding example, indexers rarely add much value.

Practicing and exploring

Test your knowledge and understanding by answering some questions, get some hands-on practice, and explore this chapter's topics with deeper research.

Exercise 5.1 – Test your knowledge

Answer the following questions:

1. What are the six access modifiers and what do they do?

2. What is the difference between the `static`, `const`, and `readonly` keywords?

3. What does a constructor do?

4. Why should you apply the `[Flags]` attribute to an `enum` type when you want to store combined values?

5. Why is the `partial` keyword useful?

6. What is a tuple?

7. What does the C# `ref` keyword do?

8. What does overloading mean?

9. What is the difference between a field and a property?

10. How do you make a method parameter optional?

Exercise 5.2 – Explore topics

Use the following links to read more about this chapter's topics:

- **Fields (C# programming guide)**: https://docs.microsoft.com/en-us/dotnet/articles/csharp/programming-guide/classes-and-structs/fields

- **Access modifiers (C# programming guide)**: https://docs.microsoft.com/en-us/dotnet/articles/csharp/language-reference/keywords/access-modifiers

- **Constructors (C# programming guide)**: https://docs.microsoft.com/en-us/dotnet/articles/csharp/programming-guide/classes-and-structs/constructors

- **Methods (C# programming guide)**: https://docs.microsoft.com/en-us/dotnet/articles/csharp/methods

- **Properties (C# programming guide)**: https://docs.microsoft.com/en-us/dotnet/articles/csharp/properties

Summary

In this chapter, you learned about making your own types using OOP. You learned about some of the different categories of members that a type can have, including fields to store data and methods to perform actions, and you used OOP concepts, such as aggregation and encapsulation.

In the next chapter, you will take these concepts further by defining delegates and events, implementing interfaces, and inheriting from existing classes.

Chapter 06

Implementing Interfaces and Inheriting Classes

This chapter is about deriving new types from existing ones using **object-oriented programming (OOP)**. You will learn about defining operators and local functions for performing simple actions, delegates and events for exchanging messages between types, implementing interfaces for common functionality, generics, the difference between reference and value types, inheriting from a base class to create a derived class to reuse functionality, overriding a type member, using polymorphism, creating extension methods, and casting between classes in an inheritance hierarchy.

This chapter covers the following topics:

- Setting up a class library and console application
- Simplifying methods
- Raising and handling events
- Implementing interfaces
- Making types more reusable with generics
- Managing memory with reference and value types
- Inheriting from classes
- Casting within inheritance hierarchies
- Inheriting and extending .NET types

Setting up a class library and console application

We will start by defining a workspace with two projects like the one created in *Chapter 5, Building Your Own Types with Object-Oriented Programming*. If you completed all the exercises in that chapter, then you can open the Chapter05 workspace and continue working with its projects.

Otherwise, follow the instructions given in this section:

1. In your existing `Code` folder, create a folder named `Chapter06` with two subfolders named `PacktLibrary` and `PeopleApp`, as shown in the following hierarchy:

   - `Chapter06`
     - ° `PacktLibrary`
     - ° `PeopleApp`

2. Start Visual Studio Code.

3. Navigate to **File | Save As Workspace…**, enter the name `Chapter06`, and click **Save**.

4. Navigate to **File | Add Folder to Workspace…**, select the `PacktLibrary` folder, and click **Add**.

5. Navigate to **File | Add Folder to Workspace…**, select the `PeopleApp` folder, and click **Add**.

6. Navigate to **Terminal | New Terminal** and select `PacktLibrary`.

7. In **TERMINAL**, enter the following command:

   ```
   dotnet new classlib
   ```

8. Navigate to **Terminal | New Terminal** and select **PeopleApp**.

9. In **TERMINAL**, enter the following command:

   ```
   dotnet new console
   ```

10. In the **EXPLORER** pane, in the `PacktLibrary` project, rename the file named `Class1.cs` to `Person.cs`.

11. Modify the file contents, as shown in the following code:

    ```
    using System;

    namespace Packt.Shared
    {
        public class Person
        {
        }
    }
    ```

12. In the **EXPLORER** pane, expand the folder named `PeopleApp` and click on the file named `PeopleApp.csproj`.

13. Add a project reference to `PacktLibrary`, as shown in the following markup:

    ```
    <Project Sdk="Microsoft.NET.Sdk">
    ```

```
<PropertyGroup>
  <OutputType>Exe</OutputType>
  <TargetFramework>netcoreapp3.0</TargetFramework>
</PropertyGroup>

<ItemGroup>
  <ProjectReference
    Include="..\PacktLibrary\PacktLibrary.csproj" />
</ItemGroup>

</Project>
```

14. In the **TERMINAL** window for the `PeopleApp` folder, enter the `dotnet build` command, and note the output indicating that both projects have been built successfully.

15. Add statements to the `Person` class to define three fields and a method, as shown in the following code:

```
using System;
using System.Collections.Generic;
using static System.Console;

namespace Packt.Shared
{
    public class Person
    {
        // fields
        public string Name;
        public DateTime DateOfBirth;
        public List<Person> Children = new List<Person>();

        // methods
        public void WriteToConsole()
        {
            WriteLine($"{Name} was born on a {DateOfBirth:dddd}.");
        }
    }
}
```

Simplifying methods

We might want two instances of `Person` to be able to procreate. We can implement this by writing methods. Instance methods are actions that an object does to itself; static methods are actions the type does.

Which you choose depends on what makes most sense for the action.

Good Practice: Having both the static and instance methods to perform similar actions often makes sense. For example, `string` has both a `Compare` static method and a `CompareTo` instance method. This puts the choice of how to use the functionality in the hands of the programmers using your type, giving them more flexibility.

Implementing functionality using methods

Let's start by implementing some functionality by using methods.

1. Add one instance method and one static method to the `Person` class that will allow two `Person` objects to procreate, as shown in the following code:

```
// static method to "multiply"
public static Person Procreate(Person p1, Person p2)
{
    var baby = new Person
    {
        Name = $"Baby of {p1.Name} and {p2.Name}"
    };

    p1.Children.Add(baby);
    p2.Children.Add(baby);

    return baby;
}

// instance method to "multiply"
public Person ProcreateWith(Person partner)
{
    return Procreate(this, partner);
}
```

Note the following:

○ In the `static` method named `Procreate`, the `Person` objects to procreate are passed as parameters named `p1` and `p2`.

○ A new `Person` class named `baby` is created with a name made of a combination of the two people who have procreated.

○ The `baby` object is added to the `Children` collection of both parents and then returned. Classes are reference types, meaning a reference to the `baby` object stored in memory is added, not a clone of the baby.

○ In the instance method named `ProcreateWith`, the `Person` object to procreate with is passed as a parameter named `partner`, and it, along with `this`, is passed to the static `Procreate` method to reuse the method implementation. `this` is a keyword that references the current instance of the class.

Good Practice: A method that creates a new object, or modifies an existing object, should return a reference to that object so that the caller can see the results.

2. In the `PeopleApp` project, at the top of the `Program.cs` file, import the namespace for our class and statically import the `Console` type, as shown highlighted in the following code:

```
using System;
using Packt.Shared;
using static System.Console;
```

3. In the `Main` method, create three people and have them procreate with each other, noting that to add a double-quote character into a `string`, you must prefix it with a backslash character, like this: `\"`, as shown in the following code:

```
var harry = new Person { Name = "Harry" };
var mary = new Person { Name = "Mary" };
var jill = new Person { Name = "Jill" };

// call instance method
var baby1 = mary.ProcreateWith(harry);

// call static method
var baby2 = Person.Procreate(harry, jill);

WriteLine($"{harry.Name} has {harry.Children.Count} children.");
WriteLine($"{mary.Name} has {mary.Children.Count} children.");
WriteLine($"{jill.Name} has {jill.Children.Count} children.");

WriteLine(
  format: "{0}'s first child is named \"{1}\".",
  arg0: harry.Name,
  arg1: harry.Children[0].Name);
```

4. Run the application and view the result, as shown in the following output:

```
Harry has 2 children.
```

```
Mary has 1 children.
Jill has 1 children.
Harry's first child is named "Baby of Mary and Harry".
```

Implementing functionality using operators

The System.String class has a static method named Concat that concatenates two string values and returns the result, as shown in the following code:

```
string s1 = "Hello ";
string s2 = "World!";
string s3 = string.Concat(s1, s2);
WriteLine(s3); // => Hello World!
```

Calling a method like Concat works, but it might be more natural for a programmer to use the + symbol to *add* two string values together, as shown in the following code:

```
string s1 = "Hello ";
string s2 = "World!";
string s3 = s1 + s2;
WriteLine(s3); // => Hello World!
```

A well-known biblical phrase is *Go forth and multiply*, meaning to procreate. Let's write code so that the * (multiply) symbol will allow two Person objects to procreate.

We do this by defining a static operator for a symbol like *. The syntax is rather like a method, because in effect, an operator is a method, but uses a symbol instead of a method name, which makes the syntax more concise.

 More Information: The * symbol is just one of many that you can implement as an operator. The complete list of symbols is listed at this link: https://docs.microsoft.com/en-us/dotnet/csharp/programming-guide/statements-expressions-operators/overloadable-operators

1. In the PacktLibrary project, in the Person class, create a static operator for the * symbol, as shown in the following code:

```
// operator to "multiply"
public static Person operator *(Person p1, Person p2)
{
    return Person.Procreate(p1, p2);
}
```

Good Practice: Unlike methods, operators do not appear in IntelliSense lists for a type. For every operator you define, make a method as well, because it may not be obvious to a programmer that the operator is available. The implementation of the operator can then call the method, reusing the code you have written. A second reason for providing a method is that operators are not supported by every language compiler.

2. In the `Main` method, after calling the static `Procreate` method, use the `*` operator to make another baby, as shown in the following highlighted code:

```
// call static method
var baby2 = Person.Procreate(harry, jill);

// call an operator
var baby3 = harry * mary;
```

3. Run the application and view the result, as shown in the following output:

```
Harry has 3 children.
Mary has 2 children.
Jill has 1 children.
Harry's first child is named "Baby of Mary and Harry".
```

Implementing functionality using local functions

A language feature introduced in C# 7.0 is the ability to define a **local function**.

Local functions are the method equivalent of local variables. In other words, they are methods that are only accessible from within the containing method in which they have been defined. In other languages, they are sometimes called **nested** or **inner functions**.

Local functions can be defined anywhere inside a method: the top, the bottom, or even somewhere in the middle!

We will use a local function to implement a factorial calculation.

1. In the `Person` class, add statements to define a `Factorial` function that uses a local function inside itself to calculate the result, as shown in the following code:

```
// method with a local function
public static int Factorial(int number)
```

```
    {
        if (number < 0)
        {
            throw new ArgumentException(
                $"{nameof(number)} cannot be less than zero.");
        }
        return localFactorial(number);

        int localFactorial(int localNumber) // local function
        {
            if (localNumber < 1) return 1;
            return localNumber * localFactorial(localNumber - 1);
        }
    }
}
```

2. In `Program.cs`, in the `Main` method, add a statement to call the `Factorial` function and write the return value to the console, as shown in the following code:

```
WriteLine($"5! is {Person.Factorial(5)}");
```

3. Run the application and view the result, as shown in the following output:

```
5! is 120
```

Raising and handling events

Methods are often described as *actions that an object can perform, either on itself or to related objects*. For example, `List` can add an item to itself or clear itself, and `File` can create or delete a file in the filesystem.

Events are often described as *actions that happen to an object*. For example, in a user interface, `Button` has a `Click` event, click being something that happens to a button. Another way of thinking of events is that they provide a way of exchanging messages between two objects.

Events are built on delegates, so let's start by having a look at how delegates work.

Calling methods using delegates

You have already seen the most common way to call or execute a method: use the . operator to access the method using its name. For example, `Console.WriteLine` tells the `Console` type to access its `WriteLine` method.

The other way to call or execute a method is to use a **delegate**. If you have used languages that support **function pointers**, then think of a delegate as being a **type-safe method pointer**. In other words, a delegate contains the memory address of a method that matches the same signature as the delegate so that it can be called safely with the correct parameter types.

For example, imagine there is a method in the `Person` class that must have a `string` type passed as its only parameter, and it returns an `int` type, as shown in the following code:

```
public int MethodIWantToCall(string input)
{
  return input.Length; // it doesn't matter what this does
}
```

I can call this method on an instance of `Person` named `p1` like this:

```
int answer = p1.MethodIWantToCall("Frog");
```

Alternatively, I can define a delegate with a matching signature to call the method indirectly. Note that the names of the parameters do not have to match. Only the types of parameters and return values must match, as shown in the following code:

```
delegate int DelegateWithMatchingSignature(string s);
```

Now, I can create an instance of the delegate, point it at the method, and finally, call the delegate (which calls the method!), as shown in the following code:

```
// create a delegate instance that points to the method
var d = new DelegateWithMatchingSignature(p1.MethodIWantToCall);

// call the delegate, which calls the method
int answer2 = d("Frog");
```

You are probably thinking, "What's the point of that?" Well, it provides flexibility.

For example, we could use delegates to create a queue of methods that need to be called in order. Queuing actions that need to be performed is common in services to provide improved scalability.

Another example is to allow multiple actions to perform in parallel. Delegates have built-in support for asynchronous operations that run on a different thread, and that can provide improved responsiveness. You will learn how to do this in *Chapter 13, Improving Performance and Scalability Using Multitasking*.

The most important example is that delegates allow us to implement **events** for sending messages between different objects that do not need to know about each other.

Delegates and events are two of the most confusing features of C# and can take a few attempts to understand, so don't worry if you feel lost!

Defining and handling delegates

Microsoft has two predefined delegates for use as events. Their signatures are simple, yet flexible, as shown in the following code:

```
public delegate void EventHandler(
  object sender, EventArgs e);

public delegate void EventHandler<TEventArgs>(
  object sender, TEventArgs e);
```

 Good Practice: When you want to define an event in your own types, you should use one of these two predefined delegates.

1. Add statements to the `Person` class and note the following points, as shown in the following code:

    ◦ It defines an `EventHandler` delegate field named `Shout`.

    ◦ It defines an `int` field to store `AngerLevel`.

    ◦ It defines a method named `Poke`.

    ◦ Each time a person is poked, their `AngerLevel` increments. Once their `AngerLevel` reaches three, they raise the `Shout` event, but only if there is at least one event delegate pointing at a method defined somewhere else in the code; that is, it is not `null`.

```
// event delegate field
public EventHandler Shout;

// data field
public int AngerLevel;

// method
public void Poke()
{
   AngerLevel++;
   if (AngerLevel >= 3)
```

```
    {
        // if something is listening...
        if (Shout != null)
        {
            // ...then call the delegate
            Shout(this, EventArgs.Empty);
        }
    }
}
```

Checking whether an object is `null` before calling one of its methods is very common. C# 6.0 and later allows `null` checks to be simplified inline, as shown in the following code:

```
Shout?.Invoke(this, EventArgs.Empty);
```

2. In `Program`, add a method with a matching signature that gets a reference to the `Person` object from the `sender` parameter and outputs some information about them, as shown in the following code:

```
private static void Harry_Shout(object sender, EventArgs e)
{
    Person p = (Person)sender;
    WriteLine($"{p.Name} is this angry: {p.AngerLevel}.");
}
```

Microsoft's convention for method names that handle events is `ObjectName_EventName`.

3. In the `Main` method, add a statement to assign the method to the delegate field, as shown in the following code:

```
harry.Shout = Harry_Shout;
```

4. Add statements to call the `Poke` method four times, after assigning the method to the `Shout` event, as shown highlighted in the following code:

```
harry.Shout = Harry_Shout;

harry.Poke();
harry.Poke();
harry.Poke();
harry.Poke();
```

Delegates are multicast, meaning that you can assign multiple delegates to a single delegate field. Instead of the = assignment, we could have used the += operator so we could add more methods to the same delegate field. When the delegate is called, all the assigned methods are called, although you have no control over the order that they are called.

5. Run the application and view the result, as shown in the following output, and note that Harry says nothing the first two times he is poked, and only gets angry enough to shout once he's been poked at least three times:

```
Harry is this angry: 3.
Harry is this angry: 4.
```

Defining and handling events

You've now seen how delegates implement the most important functionality of events: the ability to define a signature for a method that can be implemented by a completely different piece of code, and then call that method and any others that are hooked up to the delegate field.

But what about events? There is less to them than you might think.

When assigning a method to a delegate field, you should not use the simple assignment operator as we did in the preceding example, and as shown in the following code:

```
harry.Shout = Harry_Shout;
```

If the `Shout` delegate field was already referencing one or more methods, by assigning a method, it would replace all the others. With delegates that are used for events, we usually want to make sure that a programmer only ever uses either the `+=` operator or the `-=` operator to assign and remove methods:

1. To enforce this, add the `event` keyword to the delegate field declaration, as shown in the following code:

   ```
   public event EventHandler Shout;
   ```

2. In **TERMINAL**, enter the command: `dotnet build`, and note the compiler error message, as shown in the following output:

   ```
   Program.cs(41,13): error CS0079: The event 'Person.Shout' can
   only appear on the left hand side of += or -=
   ```

   This is (almost) all that the `event` keyword does! If you will never have more than one method assigned to a delegate field, then you do not need "events".

3. Modify the method assignment to use `+=`, as shown in the following code:

   ```
   harry.Shout += Harry_Shout;
   ```

4. Run the application and note that it has the same behavior as before.

More Information: You can define your own custom `EventArgs`-derived types so that you can pass additional information into an event handler method. You can read more at the following link: `https://docs.microsoft.com/en-us/dotnet/standard/events/how-to-raise-and-consume-events`

Implementing interfaces

Interfaces are a way of connecting different types together to make new things. Think of them like the studs on top of LEGO™ bricks, which allow them to "stick" together, or electrical standards for plugs and sockets.

If a type implements an interface, then it is making a promise to the rest of .NET that it supports a certain feature.

Common interfaces

Here are some common interfaces that your types might need to implement:

Interface	Method(s)	Description
`IComparable`	`CompareTo(other)`	This defines a comparison method that a type implements to order or sort its instances.
`IComparer`	`Compare( first, second)`	This defines a comparison method that a secondary type implements to order or sort instances of a primary type.
`IDisposable`	`Dispose()`	This defines a disposal method to release unmanaged resources more efficiently than waiting for a finalizer.
`IFormattable`	`ToString( format, culture)`	This defines a culture-aware method to format the value of an object into a string representation.
`IFormatter`	`Serialize( stream, object)` and `Deserialize(stream)`	This defines methods to convert an object to and from a stream of bytes for storage or transfer.
`IFormat Provider`	`GetFormat(type)`	This defines a method to format inputs based on a language and region.

Comparing objects when sorting

One of the most common interfaces that you will want to implement is `IComparable`. It allows arrays and collections of any type that implements it to be sorted.

1. In the `Main` method, add statements that create an array of `Person` instances and writes the items to the console, and then attempts to sort the array and writes the items to the console again, as shown in the following code:

```
Person[] people =
{
    new Person { Name = "Simon" },
    new Person { Name = "Jenny" },
    new Person { Name = "Adam" },
    new Person { Name = "Richard" }
};

WriteLine("Initial list of people:");
foreach (var person in people)
{
    WriteLine($"{person.Name}");
}

WriteLine("Use Person's IComparable implementation to
sort:");
Array.Sort(people);
foreach (var person in people)
{
    WriteLine($"{person.Name}");
}
```

2. Run the application, and you will see the following runtime error:

```
Unhandled Exception: System.InvalidOperationException: Failed
to compare two elements in the array. --->
System.ArgumentException: At least one object must implement
IComparable.
```

As the error explains, to fix the problem, our type must implement `IComparable`.

3. In the `PacktLibrary` project, in the `Person` class, after the class name, add a colon and enter `IComparable<Person>`, as shown in the following code:

```
public class Person : IComparable<Person>
```

Visual Studio Code will draw a red squiggle under the new code to warn you that you have not yet implemented the method you have promised to. It can write the skeleton implementation for you if you click on the light bulb and choose the **Implement interface** option.

Interfaces can be implemented implicitly and explicitly. Implicit implementations are simpler. Explicit implementations are only necessary if a type must have multiple methods with the same name and signature. For example, both `IGamePlayer` and `IKeyHolder` might have a method called `Lose` with the same parameters. In a type that must implement both interfaces, only one implementation of `Lose` can be the implicit method. If both interfaces can share the same implementation, that works, but if not then the other `Lose` method will have to be implemented differently and called explicitly.

 More Information: You can read more about explicit interface implementations at the following link: `https://docs.microsoft.com/en-us/dotnet/csharp/programming-guide/interfaces/explicit-interface-implementation`

4. Scroll down to find the method that was written for you and delete the statement that throws the `NotImplementedException` error.

5. Add a statement to call the `CompareTo` method of the `Name` field, which uses the string type's implementation of `CompareTo`, as shown highlighted in the following code:

```
public int CompareTo(Person other)
{
    return Name.CompareTo(other.Name);
}
```

We have chosen to compare two `Person` instances by comparing their `Name` fields. `Person` instances will, therefore, be sorted alphabetically by their name.

For simplicity I have not added `null` checks throughout these examples.

6. Run the application, and note that this time it works as expected, as shown in the following output:

```
Initial list of people:
Simon
Jenny
Adam
Richard
Use Person's IComparable implementation to sort:
Adam
Jenny
Richard
Simon
```

Good Practice: If anyone will want to sort an array or collection of instances of your type, then implement the IComparable interface.

Comparing objects using a separate class

Sometimes, you won't have access to the source code for a type, and it might not implement the IComparable interface. Luckily, there is another way to sort instances of a type. You can create a separate type that implements a slightly different interface, named IComparer.

1. In the PacktLibrary project, add a new class named PersonComparer that implements the IComparer interface that will compare two people, that is, two Person instances by comparing the length of their Name field, or if the names are the same length, then by comparing the names alphabetically, as shown in the following code:

```
using System.Collections.Generic;

namespace Packt.Shared
{
    public class PersonComparer : IComparer<Person>
    {
        public int Compare(Person x, Person y)
        {
            // Compare the Name lengths...
            int result = x.Name.Length
              .CompareTo(y.Name.Length);

            /// ...if they are equal...
            if (result == 0)
            {
                // ...then compare by the Names...
                return x.Name.CompareTo(y.Name);
            }
            else
            {
                // ...otherwise compare by the lengths.
                return result;
            }
        }
    }
}
```

2. In `PeopleApp`, in the `Program` class, in the `Main` method, add statements to sort the array using this alternative implementation, as shown in the following code:

```
WriteLine("Use PersonComparer's IComparer implementation to
sort:");
Array.Sort(people, new PersonComparer());
foreach (var person in people)
{
    WriteLine($"{person.Name}");
}
```

3. Run the application and view the result, as shown in the following output:

```
Initial list of people:
Simon
Jenny
Adam
Richard
Use Person's IComparable implementation to sort:
Adam
Jenny
Richard
Simon
Use PersonComparer's IComparer implementation to sort:
Adam
Jenny
Simon
Richard
```

This time, when we sort the `people` array, we explicitly ask the sorting algorithm to use the `PersonComparer` type instead, so that the people are sorted with the shortest names first, and when the lengths of two or more names are equal, to sort them alphabetically.

Defining interfaces with default implementations

A language feature introduced in C# 8.0 is **default implementations** for an interface.

1. In the `PacktLibrary` project, add a new file named `IPlayable.cs`. If you have installed **C# Extensions**, then you can right-click the `PacktLibrary` folder and choose **Add C# Interface**.

2. Modify the statements to define a public `IPlayable` interface with two methods to `Play` and `Pause`, as shown in the following code:

```
using static System.Console;

namespace Packt.Shared
{
  public interface IPlayable
  {
    void Play();

    void Pause();
  }
}
```

3. In the `PacktLibrary` project, add a new file named `DvdPlayer.cs`. If you have installed **C# Extensions**, then you can right-click the `PacktLibrary` folder and choose **Add C# Class**.

4. Modify the statements in the file to implement the `IPlayable` interface, as shown in the following code:

```
using static System.Console;

namespace Packt.Shared
{
  public class DvdPlayer : IPlayable
  {
    public void Pause()
    {
      WriteLine("DVD player is pausing.");
    }

    public void Play()
    {
      WriteLine("DVD player is playing.");
    }
  }
}
```

This is useful, but what if we decide to add a third method, `Stop`? Before C# 8.0 this would be impossible once at least one type implements the original interface. One of the main points of an interface is that it is a fixed contract.

C# 8.0 allows an interface to add new members after release as long as they have a default implementation. C# purists do not like the idea, but for practical reasons it is useful, and other languages such as Java and Swift enable similar techniques.

More Information: You can read about the design decisions around default interface implementations at the following link: https://docs.microsoft.com/en-us/dotnet/csharp/ language-reference/proposals/csharp-8.0/default- interface-methods

Support for default interface implementations requires some fundamental changes to the underlying platform, so they are only supported with C# 8.0 if the target framework is either .NET Core 3.0 or .NET Standard 2.1. they are therefore not supported by .NET Framework.

5. Modify the IPlayable interface to add a Stop method with a default implementation, as shown highlighted in the following code:

```
using static System.Console;

namespace Packt.Shared
{
  public interface IPlayable
  {
    void Play();

    void Pause();

    void Stop()
    {
      WriteLine("Default implementation of Stop.");
    }
  }
}
```

6. In **Terminal**, compile the PeopleApp project by entering the following command: dotnet build, and note the compiler errors, as shown in the following output:

```
IPlayable.cs(12,10): error CS8370: Feature 'default interface
implementation' is not available in C# 7.3. Please use
language version 8.0 or greater.
[/Users/markjprice/Code/Chapter06/PacktLibrary/PacktLibrary.cs
proj]

IPlayable.cs(12,10): error CS8701: Target runtime doesn't
support default interface implementation.
[/Users/markjprice/Code/Chapter06/PacktLibrary/PacktLibrary.cs
proj]
```

7. Open `PacktLibrary.csproj` and modify the target framework to use .NET Standard 2.1, as shown in the following markup:

```
<Project Sdk="Microsoft.NET.Sdk">

  <PropertyGroup>
    <TargetFramework>netstandard2.1</TargetFramework>
  </PropertyGroup>

</Project>
```

8. In **Terminal**, compile the `PeopleApp` project by entering the following command: `dotnet build`, and note the projects compile successfully.

 More Information: You can read a tutorial about updating interfaces with default interface members at the following link: `https://docs.microsoft.com/en-us/dotnet/csharp/tutorials/default-interface-members-versions`

Making types safely reusable with generics

In 2005, with C# 2.0 and .NET Framework 2.0, Microsoft introduced a feature named **generics**, which enables your types to be more safely reusable and more efficient. It does this by allowing a programmer to pass types as parameters, similar to how you can pass objects as parameters.

First, let's look at an example of a non-generic type, so that you can understand the problem that generics is designed to solve.

1. In the `PacktLibrary` project, add a new class named `Thing`, as shown in the following code, and note the following:
   - `Thing` has an `object` field named `Data`.
   - `Thing` has a method named `Process` that accepts an `object` input parameter and returns a `string` value.

```
using System;

namespace Packt.Shared
{
  public class Thing
  {
    public object Data = default(object);
```

```
      public string Process(object input)
      {
        if (Data == input)
        {
          return "Data and input are the same.";
        }
        else
        {
          return "Data and input are NOT the same.";
        }
      }
    }
  }
}
```

2. In the `PeopleApp` project, add some statements to the end of `Main`, as shown in the following code:

```
var t1 = new Thing();
t1.Data = 42;
WriteLine($"Thing with an integer: {t1.Process(42)}");

var t2 = new Thing();
t2.Data = "apple";
WriteLine($"Thing with a string: {t2.Process("apple")}");
```

3. Run the application and view the result, as shown in the following output:

```
Thing with an integer: Data and input are NOT the same.
Thing with a string: Data and input are the same.
```

`Thing` is currently flexible, because any type can be set for the `Data` field and `input` parameter. But there is no type checking, so inside the `Process` method we cannot safely do much and the results are sometimes wrong; for example, when passing `int` values into an `object` parameter!

Working with generic types

We can solve this problem using generics:

1. In the `PacktLibrary` project, add a new class named `GenericThing`, as shown in the following code:

```
using System;

namespace Packt.Shared
```

```
{
  public class GenericThing<T> where T : IComparable
  {
    public T Data = default(T);

    public string Process(T input)
    {
      if (Data.CompareTo(input) == 0)
      {
        return "Data and input are the same.";
      }
      else
      {
        return "Data and input are NOT the same.";
      }
    }
  }
}
```

Note the following:

- ° GenericThing has a generic type parameter named T, which can be any type that implements IComparable, so it must have a method named CompareTo that returns 0 if two objects are equal. By convention, name the type parameter T if there is only one type parameter.

- ° GenericThing has a T field named Data.

- ° GenericThing has a method named Process that accepts a T input parameter, and returns a string value.

2. In the PeopleApp project, add some statements to the end of Main, as shown in the following code:

```
var gt1 = new GenericThing<int>();
gt1.Data = 42;
WriteLine($"GenericThing with an integer:
{gt1.Process(42)}");

var gt2 = new GenericThing<string>();
gt2.Data = "apple";
WriteLine($"GenericThing with a string:
{gt2.Process("apple")}");
```

Note the following:

- ◦ When instantiating an instance of a generic type, the developer must pass a type parameter. In this example, we pass int as the type parameter for gt1 and string as the type parameter for gt2, so wherever T appears in the GenericThing class, it is replaced with int and string.

- ◦ When setting the Data field and passing the input parameter, the compiler enforces the use of an int value, such as 42, for the gt1 variable, and a string value, such as "apples", for the gt2 variable.

3. Run the application, view the result, and note the logic of the Process method correctly works for GenericThing for both int and string values, as shown in the following output:

```
Thing with an integer: Data and input are NOT the same.
Thing with a string: Data and input are the same.
GenericThing with an integer: Data and input are the same.
GenericThing with a string: Data and input are the same.
```

Working with generic methods

Generics can be used for methods as well as types, even inside a non-generic type:

1. In PacktLibrary, add a new class named Squarer, with a generic method named Square, as shown in the following code:

```
using System;
using System.Threading;

namespace Packt.Shared
{
  public static class Squarer
  {
    public static double Square<T>(T input)
      where T : IConvertible
    {
      // convert using the current culture
      double d = input.ToDouble(
        Thread.CurrentThread.CurrentCulture);

      return d * d;
    }
  }
}
```

Note the following:

- ° The `Squarer` class is non-generic.

- ° The `Square` method is generic, and its type parameter `T` must implement `IConvertible`, so the compiler will make sure that it has a `ToDouble` method.

- ° `T` is used as the type for the `input` parameter.

- ° `ToDouble` requires a parameter that implements `IFormatProvider` to understand the format of numbers for a language and region. We can pass the `CurrentCulture` property of the current thread to specify the language and region used by your computer. You will learn about cultures in *Chapter 8, Working with Common .NET Types*.

- ° The return value is the `input` parameter multiplied by itself, that is, squared.

2. In `PeopleApp`, in the `Program` class, at the bottom of the `Main` method, add the following code. Note that when calling a generic method, you can specify the type parameter to make it clearer, as shown in the first example, although the compiler can work it out on its own, as shown in the second example:

```
string number1 = "4";
WriteLine("{0} squared is {1}",
  arg0: number1,
  arg1: Squarer.Square<string>(number1));

byte number2 = 3;
WriteLine("{0} squared is {1}",
  arg0: number2,
  arg1: Squarer.Square(number2));
```

3. Run the application and view the result, as shown in the following output:

```
4 squared is 16
3 squared is 9
```

Managing memory with reference and value types

There are two categories of memory: **stack** memory and **heap** memory. With modern operating systems, the stack and heap can be anywhere in physical or virtual memory.

Stack memory is faster to work with (because it is managed directly by the CPU and because it uses a first-in, first-out mechanism, it is more likely to have the data in its L1 or L2 cache) but limited in size, while heap memory is slower but much more plentiful. For example, on my macOS, in Terminal, I can enter the command: `ulimit -a` to discover that stack size is limited to 8,192 KB and other memory is "unlimited." This is why it is so easy to get a "stack overflow."

There are two C# keywords that you can use to create object types: `class` and `struct`. Both can have the same members, such as fields and methods. The difference between the two is how memory is allocated.

When you define a type using `class`, you are defining a **reference type**. This means that the memory for the object itself is allocated on the heap, and only the memory address of the object (and a little overhead) is stored on the stack.

 More Information: If you are interested in the technical details of the internal memory layout of types in .NET, you can read the article at the following link: `https://adamsitnik.com/Value-Types-vs-Reference-Types/`

When you define a type using `struct`, you are defining a **value type**. This means that the memory for the object itself is allocated on the stack.

If a `struct` uses field types that are not of the `struct` type, then those fields will be stored on the heap, meaning the data for that object is stored in both the stack and the heap!

These are the most common `struct` types:

- **Numbers**: `byte`, `sbyte`, `short`, `ushort`, `int`, `uint`, `long`, `ulong`, `float`, `double`, and `decimal`
- **Miscellaneous**: `char` and `bool`
- **System.Drawing**: `Color`, `Point`, and `Rectangle`

Almost all the other types are `class` types, including `string`.

Apart from the difference in where in memory the data for a type is stored, the other major difference is that you cannot inherit from a `struct`.

Working with struct types

Let's explore working with value types:

1. Add a file named `DisplacementVector.cs` to the `PacktLibrary` project.

2. Modify the file, as shown in the following code, and note the following:

  ○ The type is declared using `struct` instead of `class`.

  ○ It has two `int` fields, named `X` and `Y`.

  ○ It has a constructor for setting initial values for `X` and `Y`.

  ○ It has an operator for adding two instances together that returns a new instance of the type with `X` added to `X`, and `Y` added to `Y`.

```
namespace Packt.Shared
{
  public struct DisplacementVector
  {
    public int X;
    public int Y;

    public DisplacementVector(int initialX, int initialY)
    {
      X = initialX;
      Y = initialY;
    }

    public static DisplacementVector operator +(
      DisplacementVector vector1,
      DisplacementVector vector2)
    {
      return new DisplacementVector(
        vector1.X + vector2.X,
        vector1.Y + vector2.Y);
    }
  }
}
```

3. In the `PeopleApp` project, in the `Program` class, in the `Main` method, add statements to create two new instances of `DisplacementVector`, add them together, and output the result, as shown in the following code:

```
var dv1 = new DisplacementVector(3, 5);
var dv2 = new DisplacementVector(-2, 7);
var dv3 = dv1 + dv2;
WriteLine($"({dv1.X}, {dv1.Y}) + ({dv2.X}, {dv2.Y}) =
({dv3.X}, {dv3.Y})");
```

4. Run the application and view the result, as shown in the following output:

```
(3, 5) + (-2, 7) = (1, 12)
```

Good Practice: If the total bytes used by all the fields in your type is 16 bytes or less, your type only uses `struct` types for its fields, and you will never want to derive from your type, then Microsoft recommends that you use `struct`. If your type uses more than 16 bytes of stack memory, if it uses class types for its fields, or if you might want to inherit from it, then use `class`.

Releasing unmanaged resources

In the previous chapter, we saw that constructors can be used to initialize fields and that a type may have multiple constructors. Imagine that a constructor allocates an unmanaged resource; that is, anything that is not controlled by .NET, such as a file or mutex under the control of the operating system. The unmanaged resource must be manually released because .NET cannot do it for us.

For this topic, I will show some code examples, but you do not need to create them in your current project.

Each type can have a single **finalizer** that will be called by the .NET runtime when the resources need to be released. A finalizer has the same name as a constructor; that is, the type name, but it is prefixed with a tilde, ~, as shown in the following code:

```
public class Animal
{
    public Animal()
    {
        // allocate any unmanaged resources
    }

    ~Animal() // Finalizer aka destructor
    {
        // deallocate any unmanaged resources
    }
}
```

Do not confuse a finalizer (also known as a **destructor**) with a **deconstruct** method. A destructor releases resources; that is, it destroys an object. A deconstruct method returns an object split up into its constituent parts and uses the C# deconstruction syntax, for example, when working with tuples.

The preceding code example is the minimum you should do when working with unmanaged resources. But the problem with only providing a finalizer is that the .NET garbage collector requires two garbage collections to completely release the allocated resources for this type.

Though optional, it is recommended to also provide a method to allow a developer who uses your type to explicitly release resources so that the garbage collector can release an unmanaged resource, such as a file, immediately and deterministically, and then release the managed memory part of the object in a single collection.

There is a standard mechanism to do this by implementing the IDisposable interface, as shown in the following example:

```
public class Animal : IDisposable
{
  public Animal()
  {
    // allocate unmanaged resource
  }

  ~Animal() // Finalizer
  {
    if (disposed) return;
    Dispose(false);
  }

  bool disposed = false; // have resources been released?

  public void Dispose()
  {
    Dispose(true);
    GC.SuppressFinalize(this);
  }

  protected virtual void Dispose(bool disposing)
  {
    if (disposed) return;

    // deallocate the *unmanaged* resource
    // ...

    if (disposing)
    {
      // deallocate any other *managed* resources
      // ...
    }

    disposed = true;
  }
}
```

There are two `Dispose` methods, `public` and `private`:

- The `public Dispose` method will be called by a developer using your type. When called, both unmanaged and managed resources need to be deallocated.

- The `private Dispose` method with a `bool` parameter is used internally to implement the deallocation of resources. It needs to check the `disposing` parameter and `disposed` flag because if the finalizer has already run, then only unmanaged resources need to be deallocated.

The call to `GC.SuppressFinalize(this)` is what notifies the garbage collector that it no longer needs to run the finalizer, and removes the need for a second collection.

Ensuring that Dispose is called

When someone uses a type that implements `IDisposable`, they can ensure that the public `Dispose` method is called with the `using` statement, as shown in the following code:

```
using (Animal a = new Animal())
{
  // code that uses the Animal instance
}
```

The compiler converts your code into something like the following, which guarantees that even if an exception occurs, the `Dispose` method will still be called:

```
Animal a = new Animal();
try
{
  // code that uses the Animal instance
}
finally
{
  if (a != null) a.Dispose();
}
```

You will see practical examples of releasing unmanaged resources with `IDisposable`, the `using` statements, and the `try...finally` blocks in *Chapter 9, Working with Files, Streams, and Serialization.*

Inheriting from classes

The `Person` type we created earlier implicitly derived (inherited) from `System.Object`. Now, we will create a class that inherits from `Person`:

1. Add a new class named `Employee` to the `PacktLibrary` project.

2. Modify its statements, as shown in the following code:

```
using System;

namespace Packt.Shared
{
  public class Employee : Person
  {
  }
}
```

3. Add statements to the `Main` method to create an instance of the `Employee` class, as shown in the following code:

```
Employee john = new Employee
{
  Name = "John Jones",
  DateOfBirth = new DateTime(1990, 7, 28)
};
john.WriteToConsole();
```

4. Run the console application and view the result, as shown in the following output:

```
John Jones was born on a Saturday
```

Note that the `Employee` class has inherited all the members of `Person`.

Extending classes

Now, we will add some employee-specific members to extend the class.

1. In the `Employee` class, add the following code to define two properties:

```
public string EmployeeCode { get; set; }
public DateTime HireDate { get; set; }
```

2. Back in the `Main` method, add statements to set John's employee code and hire date, as shown in the following code:

```
john.EmployeeCode = "JJ001";
john.HireDate = new DateTime(2014, 11, 23);
WriteLine($"{john.Name} was hired on
{john.HireDate:dd/MM/yy}");
```

3. Run the console application and view the result, as shown in the following output:

```
John Jones was hired on 23/11/14
```

Hiding members

So far, the `WriteToConsole` method is being inherited from `Person`, and it only outputs the employee's name and date of birth. We might want to change what this method does for an employee:

1. In the `Employee` class, add the following highlighted code to redefine the `WriteToConsole` method:

```
using System;
using static System.Console;

namespace Packt.Shared
{
  public class Employee : Person
  {
    public string EmployeeCode { get; set; }

    public DateTime HireDate { get; set; }

    public void WriteToConsole()
    {
      WriteLine(format:
        "{0} was born on {1:dd/MM/yy} and hired on {2:dd/MM/yy}",
        arg0: Name,
        arg1: DateOfBirth,
        arg2: HireDate));
    }
  }
}
```

2. Run the application and view the result, as shown in the following output:

```
John Jones was born on 28/07/90 and hired on 01/01/01
John Jones was hired on 23/11/14
```

The Visual Studio Code C# extension warns you that your method now hides the method by drawing a squiggle under the method name, the **PROBLEMS** window includes more details, and the compiler would output the warning when you build and run the console application, as shown in the following screenshot:

As the warning describes, you can remove this by applying the `new` keyword to the method, to indicate that you are deliberately replacing the old method, as shown highlighted in the following code:

```
public new void WriteToConsole()
```

Overriding members

Rather than hiding a method, it is usually better to **override** it. You can only override if the base class chooses to allow overriding, by applying the `virtual` keyword:

1. In the `Main` method, add a statement to write the value of the `john` variable to the console as a string, as shown in the following code:

```
WriteLine(john.ToString());
```

2. Run the application and note that the `ToString` method is inherited from `System.Object` so the implementation returns the namespace and type name, as shown in the following output:

```
Packt.Shared.Employee
```

3. Override this behavior for the `Person` class by adding a `ToString` method to output the name of the person as well as the type name, as shown in the following code:

```
// overridden methods
public override string ToString()
{
    return $"{Name} is a {base.ToString()}";
}
```

The `base` keyword allows a subclass to access members of its super class; that is, the base class that it inherits or derives from.

4. Run the application and view the result. Now, when the `ToString` method is called, it outputs the person's name, as well as the base class's implementation of `ToString`, as shown in the following output:

```
John Jones is a Packt.Shared.Employee
```

 Good Practice: Many real-world APIs, for example, Microsoft's Entity Framework Core, Castle's DynamicProxy, and Episerver's content models, require the properties that you define in your classes to be marked as `virtual` so that they can be overridden. Unless you have a good reason not to, mark your method and property members as `virtual`.

Preventing inheritance and overriding

You can prevent someone from inheriting from your class by applying the `sealed` keyword to its definition. No one can inherit from Scrooge McDuck, as shown in the following code:

```
public sealed class ScroogeMcDuck
{
}
```

An example of `sealed` in .NET Core is the `string` class. Microsoft has implemented some extreme optimizations inside the `string` class that could be negatively affected by your inheritance; so, Microsoft prevents that.

You can prevent someone from further overriding a `virtual` method in your class by applying the `sealed` keyword to the method. No one can change the way Lady Gaga sings, as shown in the following code:

```
using static System.Console;

namespace Packt.Shared
{
  public class Singer
  {
    // virtual allows this method to be overridden
    public virtual void Sing()
    {
      WriteLine("Singing...");
    }
```

```
    }

    public class LadyGaga : Singer
    {
      // sealed prevents overriding the method in subclasses
      public sealed override void Sing()
      {
        WriteLine("Singing with style...");
      }
    }
  }
```

You can only seal an overridden method.

Understanding polymorphism

You have now seen two ways to change the behavior of an inherited method. We can hide it using the new keyword (known as **non-polymorphic inheritance**), or we can override it (known as **polymorphic inheritance**).

Both ways can access members of the base class by using the base keyword, so what is the difference?

It all depends on the type of the variable holding a reference to the object. For example, a variable of the Person type can hold a reference to a Person class, or any type that derives from Person:

1. In the Employee class, add statements to override the ToString method so it writes the employee's name and code to the console, as shown in the following code:

```
public override string ToString()
{
  return $"{Name}'s code is {EmployeeCode}";
}
```

2. In the Main method, write statements to create a new employee named Alice, store it in a variable of type Person, and call both variables' WriteToConsole and ToString methods, as shown in the following code:

```
Employee aliceInEmployee = new Employee
  { Name = "Alice", EmployeeCode = "AA123" };

Person aliceInPerson = aliceInEmployee;

aliceInEmployee.WriteToConsole();
```

```
aliceInPerson.WriteToConsole();

WriteLine(aliceInEmployee.ToString());

WriteLine(aliceInPerson.ToString());
```

3. Run the application and view the result, as shown in the following output:

```
Alice was born on 01/01/01 and hired on 01/01/01
Alice was born on a Monday
Alice's code is AA123
Alice's code is AA123
```

When a method is hidden with `new`, the compiler is not smart enough to know that the object is an `Employee`, so it calls the `WriteToConsole` method in `Person`.

When a method is overridden with `virtual` and `override`, the compiler is smart enough to know that although the variable is declared as a `Person` class, the object itself is an `Employee` class and, therefore, the `Employee` implementation of `ToString` is called.

The access modifiers and the effect they have is summarized in the following table:

Variable type	Access modifier	Method executed	In class
Person		WriteToConsole	Person
Employee	new	WriteToConsole	Employee
Person	virtual	ToString	Employee
Employee	override	ToString	Employee

In my opinion, polymorphism is literally academic to most programmers. If you get the concept, that's cool; but, if not, I suggest that you don't worry about it. Some people like to make others feel inferior by saying understanding polymorphism is important, but IMHO it's not. You can have a successful career with C# and never need to be able to explain polymorphism, just as a racing car driver doesn't need to be able to explain the engineering behind fuel injection.

Casting within inheritance hierarchies

Casting between types is subtly different from converting between types.

Implicit casting

In the previous example, you saw how an instance of a derived type can be stored in a variable of its base type (or its base's base type, and so on). When we do this, it is called **implicit casting**.

Explicit casting

Going the other way is an explicit cast, and you must use parentheses around the type you want to cast into as a prefix to do it:

1. In the `Main` method, add a statement to assign the `aliceInPerson` variable to a new `Employee` variable, as shown in the following code:

   ```
   Employee explicitAlice = aliceInPerson;
   ```

2. Visual Studio Code displays a red squiggle and a compile error, as shown in the following screenshot:

3. Change the statement to prefix the assigned variable named with a cast to the `Employee` type, as shown in the following code:

   ```
   Employee explicitAlice = (Employee)aliceInPerson;
   ```

Avoiding casting exceptions

The compiler is now happy; *but*, because `aliceInPerson` might be a different derived type, like `Student` instead of `Employee`, we need to be careful. In a real application with more complex code, the current value of this variable could have been set to a `Student` instance and then this statement would throw an `InvalidCastException` error.

We can handle this by writing a `try` statement, but there is a better way. We can check the type of an object using the `is` keyword:

1. Wrap the explicit cast statement in an `if` statement, as shown in the following code:

```
if (aliceInPerson is Employee)
{
  WriteLine($"{nameof(aliceInPerson)} IS an Employee");

  Employee explicitAlice = (Employee)aliceInPerson;
   // safely do something with explicitAlice
}
```

2. Run the application and view the result, as shown in the following output:

```
aliceInPerson IS an Employee
```

   Alternatively, you can use the `as` keyword to cast. Instead of throwing an exception, the `as` keyword returns `null` if the type cannot be cast.

3. Add the following statements to the end of the `Main` method:

```
Employee aliceAsEmployee = aliceInPerson as Employee;

if (aliceAsEmployee != null)
{
  WriteLine($"{nameof(aliceInPerson)} AS an Employee");
   // do something with aliceAsEmployee
}
```

   Since accessing a `null` variable can throw a `NullReferenceException` error, you should always check for `null` before using the result.

4. Run the application and view the result, as shown in the following output:

```
aliceInPerson AS an Employee
```

 Good Practice: Use the `is` and `as` keywords to avoid throwing exceptions when casting between derived types. If you don't do this, you must write `try...catch` statements for `InvalidCastException`.

Inheriting and extending .NET types

.NET has prebuilt class libraries containing hundreds of thousands of types. Rather than creating your own completely new types, you can often get a head start by deriving from one of Microsoft's types to inherit some or all of its behavior and then overriding or extending it.

Inheriting exceptions

As an example of inheritance, we will derive a new type of exception:

1. In the `PacktLibrary` project, add a new class named `PersonException`, with three constructors, as shown in the following code:

```
using System;

namespace Packt.Shared
{
  public class PersonException : Exception
  {
    public PersonException() : base() { }

    public PersonException(string message) : base(message) { }

    public PersonException(
      string message, Exception innerException)
      : base(message, innerException) { }
  }
}
```

   Unlike ordinary methods, constructors are not inherited, so we must explicitly declare and explicitly call the `base` constructor implementations in `System.Exception` to make them available to programmers who might want to use those constructors with our custom exception.

2. In the `Person` class, add statements to define a method that throws an exception if a date/time parameter is earlier than a person's date of birth, as shown in the following code:

```
public void TimeTravel(DateTime when)
{
  if (when <= DateOfBirth)
  {
    throw new PersonException("If you travel back in time to
a date earlier than your own birth, then the universe will
explode!");
  }
  else
  {
    WriteLine($"Welcome to {when:yyyy}!");
  }
}
```

3. In the `Main` method, add statements to test what happens when employee John Jones tries to time travel too far back, as shown in the following code:

```
try
{
  john.TimeTravel(new DateTime(1999, 12, 31));
  john.TimeTravel(new DateTime(1950, 12, 25));
}
catch (PersonException ex)
{
  WriteLine(ex.Message);
}
```

4. Run the application and view the result, as shown in the following output:

```
Welcome to 1999!

If you travel back in time to a date earlier than your own
birth, then the universe will explode!
```

 Good Practice: When defining your own exceptions, give them the same three constructors that explicitly call the built-in ones.

Extending types when you can't inherit

Earlier, we saw how the `sealed` modifier can be used to prevent inheritance.

Microsoft has applied the `sealed` keyword to the `System.String` class so that no one can inherit and potentially break the behavior of strings.

Can we still add new methods to strings? Yes, if we use a language feature named extension methods, which was introduced with C# 3.0.

Using static methods to reuse functionality

Since the first version of C#, we've been able to create `static` methods to reuse functionality, such as the ability to validate that a `string` contains an email address. This implementation will use a regular expression that you will learn more about in *Chapter 8, Working with Common .NET Types*:

1. In the `PacktLibrary` project, add a new class named `StringExtensions`, as shown in the following code, and note the following:

    ° The class imports a namespace for handling regular expressions.

- The `IsValidEmail` static method uses the `Regex` type to check for matches against a simple email pattern that looks for valid characters before and after the @ symbol.

```
using System.Text.RegularExpressions;

namespace Packt.Shared
{
    public static class StringExtensions
    {
        public static bool IsValidEmail(this string input)
        {
            // use simple regular expression to check
            // that the input string is a valid email
            return Regex.IsMatch(input,
@"[a-zA-Z0-9\.-_]+@[a-zA-Z0-9\.-_]+");
        }
    }
}
```

2. Add statements to the bottom of the `Main` method to validate two examples of email addresses, as shown in the following code:

```
string email1 = "pamela@test.com";
string email2 = "ian&test.com";

WriteLine(
  "{0} is a valid e-mail address: {1}",
  arg0: email1,
  arg1: StringExtensions.IsValidEmail(email1));

WriteLine(
  "{0} is a valid e-mail address: {1}",
  arg0: email2,
  arg1: StringExtensions.IsValidEmail(email2));
```

3. Run the application and view the result, as shown in the following output:

```
pamela@test.com is a valid e-mail address: True
ian&test.com is a valid e-mail address: False
```

This works, but extension methods can reduce the amount of code we must type and simplify the usage of this function.

Using extension methods to reuse functionality

It is easy to make `static` methods into extension methods for their usage:

1. In the `StringExtensions` class, add the `static` modifier before the class, and add the `this` modifier before the `string` type, as highlighted in the following code:

    ```
    public static class StringExtensions
    {
        public static bool IsValidEmail(this string input)
        {
    ```

    These two changes tell the compiler that it should treat the method as one that extends the `string` type.

2. Back in the `Program` class, add some new statements to use the extension method for `string` values:

    ```
    WriteLine(
        "{0} is a valid e-mail address: {1}",
        arg0: email1,
        arg1: email1.IsValidEmail());

    WriteLine(
        "{0} is a valid e-mail address: {1}",
        arg0: email2,
        arg1: email2.IsValidEmail());
    ```

    Note the subtle simplification in the syntax. The older, longer syntax still works too.

3. The `IsValidEmail` extension method now appears to be an instance method just like all the actual instance methods of the `string` type, such as `IsNormalized` and `Insert`, as shown in the following screenshot:

Extension methods cannot replace or override existing instance methods, so you cannot, for example, redefine the `Insert` method. The extension method will appear as an overload in IntelliSense, but an instance method will be called in preference to an extension method with the same name and signature.

Although extension methods might not seem to give a big benefit, in *Chapter 12, Querying and Manipulating Data Using LINQ,* you will see some extremely powerful uses of extension methods.

Practicing and exploring

Test your knowledge and understanding by answering some questions. Get some hands-on practice and explore with deeper research into this chapter's topics.

Exercise 6.1 – Test your knowledge

Answer the following questions:

1. What is a delegate?
2. What is an event?
3. How are a base class and a derived class related?
4. What is the difference between `is` and `as operators`?
5. Which keyword is used to prevent a class from being derived from, or a method from being further overridden?
6. Which keyword is used to prevent a class from being instantiated with the `new` keyword?
7. Which keyword is used to allow a member to be overridden?
8. What's the difference between a destructor and a deconstruct method?
9. What are the signatures of the constructors that all exceptions should have?
10. What is an extension method and how do you define one?

Exercise 6.2 – Practice creating an inheritance hierarchy

Explore inheritance hierarchies by following these steps:

1. Add a new console application named `Exercise02` to your workspace.

2. Create a class named `Shape` with properties named `Height`, `Width`, and `Area`.

3. Add three classes that derive from it—`Rectangle`, `Square`, and `Circle`—with any additional members you feel are appropriate and that override and implement the `Area` property correctly.

4. In `Program.cs`, in the `Main` method, add statements to create one instance of each shape, as shown in the following code:

```
var r = new Rectangle(3, 4.5);
WriteLine($"Rectangle H: {r.Height}, W: {r.Width}, Area:
{r.Area}");

var s = new Square(5);
WriteLine($"Square    H: {s.Height}, W: {s.Width}, Area:
{s.Area}");

var c = new Circle(2.5);
WriteLine($"Circle    H: {c.Height}, W: {c.Width}, Area:
{c.Area}");
```

5. Run the console application and ensure that the result looks like the following output:

```
Rectangle H: 3, W: 4.5, Area: 13.5

Square    H: 5, W: 5, Area: 25

Circle    H: 5, W: 5, Area: 19.6349540849362
```

Exercise 6.3 – Explore topics

Use the following links to read more about the topics covered in this chapter:

- **Operator (C# reference)**: https://docs.microsoft.com/en-us/dotnet/articles/csharp/language-reference/keywords/operator

- **Delegates**: https://docs.microsoft.com/en-us/dotnet/articles/csharp/tour-of-csharp/delegates

- **Events (C# programming guide)**: https://docs.microsoft.com/en-us/dotnet/articles/csharp/language-reference/keywords/event

- **Interfaces**: https://docs.microsoft.com/en-us/dotnet/articles/csharp/tour-of-csharp/interfaces

- **Generics (C# Programming Guide)**: https://docs.microsoft.com/en-us/dotnet/csharp/programming-guide/generics

- **Reference Types (C# Reference)**: https://docs.microsoft.com/en-us/dotnet/articles/csharp/language-reference/keywords/reference-types

- **Value Types (C# Reference)**: https://docs.microsoft.com/en-us/dotnet/articles/csharp/language-reference/keywords/value-types

- **Inheritance (C# Programming Guide)**: https://docs.microsoft.com/en-us/dotnet/articles/csharp/programming-guide/classes-and-structs/inheritance

- **Finalizers (C# Programming Guide)**: https://docs.microsoft.com/en-us/dotnet/articles/csharp/programming-guide/classes-and-structs/destructors

Summary

In this chapter, you learned about local functions and operators, delegates and events, implementing interfaces, generics, and deriving types using inheritance and OOP. You also learned about base and derived classes, how to override a type member, use polymorphism, and cast between types.

In the next chapter, you will learn about .NET Core 3.0 and .NET Standard 2.1, and the types that they provide you with to implement common functionality such as file handling, database access, encryption, and multitasking.

Chapter 07

Understanding and Packaging .NET Types

This chapter is about how .NET Core implements the types that are defined in the .NET Standard. Over the course of this chapter, you'll learn how C# keywords are related to .NET types, and about the relationship between namespaces and assemblies. You'll also become familiar with how to package and publish your .NET Core apps and libraries for use cross-platform, how to use existing .NET Framework libraries in .NET Standard libraries, and the possibility of porting .NET Framework code bases to .NET Core.

This chapter covers the following topics:

- Introducing .NET Core 3.0
- Understanding .NET Core components
- Publishing your applications for deployment
- Decompiling assemblies
- Packaging your libraries for NuGet distribution
- Porting from .NET Framework to .NET Core

Introducing .NET Core 3.0

This part of the book is about the functionality in the APIs provided by .NET Core 3.0, and how to reuse functionality across all the different .NET platforms using .NET Standard. .NET Core 2.0 and later's support for a minimum of .NET Standard 2.0 is important because it provides many of the APIs that were missing from the first version of .NET Core. The 15 years' worth of libraries and applications that .NET Framework developers had available to them that are relevant for modern development have now been migrated to .NET Core and can run cross-platform on macOS and Linux variants, as well as on Windows. For example, API support increased by 142% from .NET Core 1.1 to .NET Core 2.0.

.NET Standard 2.1 adds about 3,000 new APIs. Some of those APIs need runtime changes that would break backwards compatibility, so .NET Framework 4.8 only implements .NET Standard 2.0. .NET Core 3.0, Xamarin, Mono, and Unity implement .NET Standard 2.1.

 More Information: The full list of .NET Standard 2.1 APIs and a comparison with .NET Standard 2.0 are documented at the following link: `https://github.com/dotnet/standard/blob/master/docs/versions/netstandard2.1.md`

To summarize the progress that .NET Core has made over the past three years I have compared the major .NET Core versions with the equivalent .NET Framework versions in the following list:

- .NET Core 1.0: much smaller API compared to .NET Framework 4.6.1, which was the current version in March 2016.

- .NET Core 2.0: reached API parity with .NET Framework 4.7.1 for modern APIs because they both implement .NET Standard 2.0.

- .NET Core 3.0: larger API compared to .NET Framework for modern APIs because .NET Framework 4.8 does not implement .NET Standard 2.1.

 More Information: You can search and browse all .NET APIs at the following link: `https://docs.microsoft.com/en-us/dotnet/api/`

.NET Core 1.0

.NET Core 1.0 was released in June 2016 and focused on implementing an API suitable for building modern cross-platform apps, including web and cloud applications and services for Linux using ASP.NET Core.

 More Information: You can read the .NET Core 1.0 announcement at the following link: `https://blogs.msdn.microsoft.com/dotnet/2016/06/27/announcing-net-core-1-0/`

.NET Core 1.1

.NET Core 1.1 was released in November 2016 and focused on fixing bugs, increasing the number of Linux distributions supported, supporting .NET Standard 1.6, and improving performance, especially with ASP.NET Core for web apps and services.

More Information: You can read the .NET Core 1.1 announcement at the following link: `https://blogs.msdn.microsoft.com/dotnet/2016/11/16/announcing-net-core-1-1/`

.NET Core 2.0

.NET Core 2.0 was released in August 2017 and focused on implementing .NET Standard 2.0, the ability to reference .NET Framework libraries, and more performance improvements. .NET Core for UWP apps was released with Windows 10 Fall Creators Update in October 2017.

More Information: You can read the .NET Core 2.0 announcement at the following link: `https://blogs.msdn.microsoft.com/dotnet/2017/08/14/announcing-net-core-2-0/`

The third edition of this book was published in November 2017, so it covered up to .NET Core 2.0 and .NET Core for UWP apps. This fourth edition covers some of the new APIs added in later versions up to .NET Core 3.0.

.NET Core 2.1

.NET Core 2.1 was released in May 2018 and focused on an extendable tooling system, adding new types like `Span<T>`, new APIs for cryptography and compression, a Windows Compatibility Pack with an additional 20,000 APIs to help port old Windows applications, Entity Framework Core value conversions, LINQ `GroupBy` conversions, data seeding, query types, and even more performance improvements, including the topics listed in the following table:

Feature	Chapter	Topic
Spans, indexes, ranges	8	Working with spans, indexes, and ranges
Brotli compression	9	Compressing with the Brotli algorithm
Cryptography	10	What's new in cryptography?
Lazy loading	11	Enabling lazy loading
Data seeding	11	Understanding data seeding

More Information: You can read the .NET Core 2.1 announcement at the following link: `https://blogs.msdn.microsoft.com/dotnet/2018/05/30/announcing-net-core-2-1/`

.NET Core 2.2

.NET Core 2.2 was released in December 2018 and focused on diagnostic improvements for the runtime, optional tiered compilation, and adding new features to ASP.NET Core and Entity Framework Core like spatial data support using types from the **NetTopologySuite (NTS)** library, query tags, and collections of owned entities.

More Information: You can read the .NET Core 2.2 announcement at the following link: `https://blogs.msdn.microsoft.com/dotnet/2018/12/04/announcing-net-core-2-2/`

.NET Core 3.0

.NET Core 3.0 was released in September 2019 and focused on adding support for building Windows desktop applications using Windows Forms (2001), Windows Presentation Foundation (WPF; 2006), and Entity Framework 6.3, side-by-side and app-local deployments, a fast JSON reader, serial port access and other PIN access for **Internet of Things (IoT)** solutions, and tiered compilation on by default, including the topics listed in the following table:

Feature	Chapter	Topic
Embedding .NET Core in app	7	Publishing your applications for deployment
Index and Range	8	Working with spans, indexes, and ranges
System.Text.Json	9	High-performance JSON processing
Async streams	13	Working with async streams

More Information: You can read the .NET Core 3.0 announcement at the following link: `https://devblogs.microsoft.com/dotnet/announcing-net-core-3-0/`

Understanding .NET Core components

.NET Core is made up of several pieces, which are as follows:

- **Language compilers**: These turn your source code written with languages such as C#, F#, and Visual Basic into **intermediate language** (IL) code stored in assemblies. With C# 6.0 and later, Microsoft switched to an open source rewritten compiler known as Roslyn that is also used by Visual Basic. You can read more about Roslyn at the following link: `https://github.com/dotnet/roslyn`

- **Common Language Runtime (CoreCLR)**: This runtime loads assemblies, compiles the IL code stored in them into native code instructions for your computer's CPU, and executes the code within an environment that manages resources such as threads and memory.

- **Base Class Libraries (BCL) of assemblies in NuGet packages (CoreFX)**: These are prebuilt assemblies of types packaged and distributed using NuGet for performing common tasks when building applications.

- You can use them to quickly build anything you want rather like combining LEGO™ pieces. .NET Core 2.0 implemented .NET Standard 2.0, which is a superset of all previous versions of .NET Standard, and lifted .NET Core up to parity with .NET Framework and Xamarin. .NET Core 3.0 implements .NET Standard 2.1, which adds new capabilities and enables performance improvements beyond those available in .NET Framework.

 More Information: You can read the announcement of .NET Standard 2.1 at the following link: `https://blogs.msdn.microsoft.com/dotnet/2018/11/05/announcing-net-standard-2-1/`

Understanding assemblies, packages, and namespaces

An **assembly** is where a type is stored in the filesystem. Assemblies are a mechanism for deploying code. For example, the `System.Data.dll` assembly contains types for managing data. To use types in other assemblies, they must be referenced.

Assemblies are often distributed as **NuGet packages**, which can contain multiple assemblies and other resources. You will also hear about **metapackages** and **platforms**, which are combinations of NuGet packages.

A **namespace** is the address of a type. Namespaces are a mechanism to uniquely identify a type by requiring a full address rather than just a short name. In the real world, *Bob of 34 Sycamore Street* is different from *Bob of 12 Willow Drive*.

In .NET, the `IActionFilter` interface of the `System.Web.Mvc` namespace is different from the `IActionFilter` interface of the `System.Web.Http.Filters` namespace.

Understanding dependent assemblies

If an assembly is compiled as a class library and provides types for other assemblies to use, then it has the file extension `.dll` (dynamic link library), and it cannot be executed standalone.

Likewise, if an assembly is compiled as an application, then it has the file extension `.exe` (executable) and can be executed standalone. Before .NET Core 3.0, console apps were compiled to `.dll` files and had to be executed by the `dotnet run` command or a host executable.

Any assembly can reference one or more class library assemblies as dependencies, but you cannot have circular references. So, assembly *B* cannot reference assembly *A*, if assembly *A* already references assembly *B*. The compiler will warn you if you attempt to add a dependency reference that would cause a circular reference.

Good Practice: Circular references are often a warning sign of poor code design. If you are sure that you need a circular reference, then use an interface to solve it, as explained in the Stack Overflow answer at the following link: `https://stackoverflow.com/questions/6928387/how-to-solve-circular-reference`

Understanding the Microsoft .NET Core App platform

By default, console applications have a dependency reference on the Microsoft .NET Core App platform. This platform contains thousands of types in NuGet packages that almost all applications would need, such as the `int` and `string` types.

When using .NET Core, you reference the dependency assemblies, NuGet packages, and platforms that your application needs in a project file.

Let's explore the relationship between assemblies and namespaces.

1. In Visual Studio Code, create a folder named `Chapter07` with a subfolder named `AssembliesAndNamespaces`, and enter `dotnet new console` to create a console application.

2. Save the current workspace as `Chapter07` in the `Chapter07` folder and add the `AssembliesAndNamespaces` folder to the workspace.

3. Open `AssembliesAndNamespaces.csproj`, and note that it is a typical project file for a .NET Core application, as shown in the following markup:

```
<Project Sdk="Microsoft.NET.Sdk">

  <PropertyGroup>
    <OutputType>Exe</OutputType>
    <TargetFramework>netcoreapp3.0</TargetFramework>
  </PropertyGroup>

</Project>
```

Although it is possible to include the assemblies that your application uses with its deployment package, by default the project will probe for shared assemblies installed in well-known paths.

First, it will look for the specified version of .NET Core in the current user's `.dotnet/store` and `.nuget` folders, and then it looks in a fallback folder that depends on your OS, as shown in the following root paths:

- Windows: `C:\Program Files\dotnet\sdk`
- macOS: `/usr/local/share/dotnet/sdk`

Most common .NET Core types are in the `System.Runtime.dll` assembly. You can see the relationship between some assemblies and the namespaces that they supply types for, and note that there is not always a one-to-one mapping between assemblies and namespaces, as shown in the following table:

Assembly	Example namespaces	Example types
`System.Runtime.dll`	`System, System.Collections, System.Collections.Generic`	`Int32, String, IEnumerable<T>`
`System.Console.dll`	`System`	`Console`
`System.Threading.dll`	`System.Threading`	`Interlocked, Monitor, Mutex`
`System.Xml.XDocument.dll`	`System.Xml.Linq`	`XDocument, XElement, XNode`

Understanding NuGet packages

.NET Core is split into a set of packages, distributed using a Microsoft-supported package management technology named NuGet. Each of these packages represents a single assembly of the same name. For example, the `System.Collections` package contains the `System.Collections.dll` assembly.

The following are the benefits of packages:

- Packages can ship on their own schedule.

- Packages can be tested independently of other packages.

- Packages can support different OSes and CPUs by including multiple versions of the same assembly built for different OSes and CPUs.

- Packages can have dependencies specific to only one library.

- Apps are smaller because unreferenced packages aren't part of the distribution.

The following table lists some of the more important packages and their important types:

Package	Important types
`System.Runtime`	`Object, String, Int32, Array`
`System.Collections`	`List<T>, Dictionary<TKey, TValue>`
`System.Net.Http`	`HttpClient, HttpResponseMessage`
`System.IO.FileSystem`	`File, Directory`
`System.Reflection`	`Assembly, TypeInfo, MethodInfo`

Understanding frameworks

There is a two-way relationship between frameworks and packages. Packages define the APIs, while frameworks group packages. A framework without any packages would not define any APIs.

More Information: If you have a strong understanding of interfaces and types that implement them, you might find the following URL useful for grasping how packages, and their APIs, relate to frameworks such as the various .NET Standard versions: `https://gist.github.com/davidfowl/8939f3055 67e1755412d6dc0b8baf1b7`

.NET packages each support a set of frameworks. For example, the System.IO.FileSystem package version 4.3.0 supports the following frameworks:

- .NET Standard, version 1.3 or later.
- .NET Framework, version 4.6 or later.
- Six Mono and Xamarin platforms (for example, Xamarin.iOS 1.0).

 More Information: You can read the details at the following link: https://www.nuget.org/packages/System.IO.FileSystem/

Importing a namespace to use a type

Let's explore how namespaces are related to assemblies and types.

1. In the AssembliesAndNamespaces project, in the Main method, enter the following code:

```
var doc = new XDocument();
```

The XDocument type is not recognized because we have not told the compiler what the namespace of the type is. Although this project already has a reference to the assembly that contains the type, we also need to either prefix the type name with its namespace or to import the namespace.

2. Click inside the XDocument class name. Visual Studio Code displays a light bulb, showing that it recognizes the type and can automatically fix the problem for you.

3. Click the light bulb, or in Windows, press *Ctrl + .* (dot), or in macOS, press *Cmd + .* (dot).

4. Select using System.Xml.Linq; from the menu.

This will import the namespace by adding a using statement to the top of the file. Once a namespace is imported at the top of a code file, then all the types within the namespace are available for use in that code file by just typing their name without the type name needing to be fully qualified by prefixing with its namespace.

Relating C# keywords to .NET types

One of the common questions I get from new C# programmers is, *What is the difference between* string *with a lowercase and* String *with an uppercase?*

The short answer is easy: none. The long answer is that all C# type keywords are aliases for a .NET type in a class library assembly.

When you use the `string` keyword, the compiler turns it into a `System.String` type. When you use the `int` type, the compiler turns it into a `System.Int32` type.

1. In the `Main` method, declare two variables to hold `string` values, one using lowercase and one using uppercase, as shown in the following code:

   ```
   string s1 = "Hello";
   String s2 = "World";
   ```

   At the moment, they both work equally well, and literally mean the same thing.

2. At the top of the class file, comment out the `using System;` statement by prefixing the statement with `//`, and note the compiler error.

3. Remove the comment slashes to fix the error.

Good Practice: When you have a choice, use the C# keyword instead of the actual type because the keywords do not need the namespace imported.

The following table shows the 16 C# type keywords along with their actual .NET types:

Keyword	.NET type	Keyword	.NET type
string	System.String	char	System.Char
sbyte	System.SByte	byte	System.Byte
short	System.Int16	ushort	System.UInt16
int	System.Int32	uint	System.UInt32
long	System.Int64	ulong	System.UInt64
float	System.Single	double	System.Double
decimal	System.Decimal	bool	System.Boolean
object	System.Object	dynamic	System.Dynamic.DynamicObject

Other .NET programming language compilers can do the same thing. For example, the Visual Basic .NET language has a type named `Integer` that is its alias for `System.Int32`.

4. Right-click inside `XDocument` and choose **Go to Definition** or press *F12*.

5. Navigate to the top of the code file and note the assembly filename is `System.Xml.XDocument.dll` but the class is in the `System.Xml.Linq` namespace, as shown in the following screenshot:

6. Close the **[metadata] XDocument.cs** tab.

7. Right-click inside `string` or `String` and choose **Go to Definition** or press *F12*.

8. Navigate to the top of the code file and note the assembly filename is `System.Runtime.dll` but the class is in the `System` namespace.

Sharing code cross-platform with .NET Standard class libraries

Before .NET Standard, there were **Portable Class Libraries** (PCLs). With PCLs, you could create a library of code and explicitly specify which platforms you want the library to support, such as Xamarin, Silverlight, and Windows 8. Your library could then use the intersection of APIs that are supported by the specified platforms.

Microsoft realized that this is unsustainable, so they created .NET Standard—a single API that all future .NET platforms will support. There are older versions of .NET Standard, but only .NET Standard 2.0 and later is supported by multiple .NET platforms. For the rest of this book I will use the term .NET Standard to mean .NET Standard 2.0 or later.

.NET Standard is similar to HTML5 in that they are both standards that a platform should support. Just as Google's Chrome browser and Microsoft's Edge browser implement the HTML5 standard, so .NET Core, .NET Framework, and Xamarin all implement .NET Standard. If you want to create a library of types that will work across variants of .NET, you can do so most easily with .NET Standard.

Your choice of which .NET Standard version to target comes down to a balance between maximizing platform support or available functionality. A lower version supports more platforms but has a smaller set of APIs. A higher version supports fewer platforms but has a larger set of APIs. Generally, you should choose the lowest version that supports all the APIs that you need.

The versions of .NET Standard and which platforms they support are summarized in the following table:

Platform	1.1	1.2	1.3	1.4	1.5	1.6	2.0	2.1
.NET Core	→	→	→	→	→	1.0, 1.1	2.0	3.0
.NET Framework	4.5	4.5.1	4.6	→	→	→	4.6.1	n/a
Mono	→	→	→	→	→	4.6	5.4	6.2
Xamarin.iOS	→	→	→	→	→	10.0	10.14	12.12
UWP	→	→	→	10	→	→	10.0.16299	n/a

More Information: An online tool for visualizing which platforms support which version of .NET Standard can be found at the following link: `http://immo.landwerth.net/netstandard-versions/`

Good Practice: Since many of the API additions in .NET Standard 2.1 require runtime changes, and .NET Framework is Microsoft's legacy platform that needs to remain as unchanging as possible, .NET Framework 4.8 will remain on .NET Standard 2.0 rather than implement .NET Standard 2.1. If you need to support .NET Framework customers, then you should create class libraries on .NET Standard 2.0 even though it is not the latest and does not support all the new features in C# 8.0 and .NET Core 3.0.

We will create a class library using .NET Standard 2.0 so that it can be used across all important .NET platforms and cross-platform on Windows, macOS, and Linux operating systems while also having access to a wide set of .NET APIs.

1. In the `Code/Chapter07` folder, create a subfolder named `SharedLibrary`.

2. In Visual Studio Code, add the `SharedLibrary` folder to the `Chapter07` workspace.

3. Navigate to **Terminal | New Terminal** and select `SharedLibrary`.

4. In Terminal, enter the following command:

   ```
   dotnet new classlib
   ```

5. Click on `SharedLibrary.csproj` and note that a class library generated by the `dotnet` CLI targets .NET Standard 2.0 by default, as shown in the following markup:

```
<Project Sdk="Microsoft.NET.Sdk">

  <PropertyGroup>
    <TargetFramework>netstandard2.0</TargetFramework>
  </PropertyGroup>

</Project>
```

 Good Practice: If you need to create a type that uses new features in .NET Standard 2.1 then create separate class libraries: one targeting .NET Standard 2.0 and one targeting .NET Standard 2.1. You will see this in action in *Chapter 11, Working with Databases Using Entity Framework Core*.

Publishing your applications for deployment

There are three ways to publish and deploy a .NET Core application. They are:

- Framework-dependent deployment (FDD).
- Framework-dependent executables (FDEs).
- Self-contained.

If you choose to deploy your application and its package dependencies, but not .NET Core itself, then you rely on .NET Core already being on the target computer. This works well for web applications deployed to a server because .NET Core and lots of other web applications are likely already on the server.

Sometimes, you want to be able to give someone a USB stick containing your application and know that it can execute on their computer. You want to perform a self-contained deployment. While the size of the deployment files will be larger, you'll know that it will work.

Creating a console application to publish

Let's explore how to publish a console application.

1. Create a new console application project named `DotNetCoreEverywhere` and add it to the `Chapter07` workspace.

2. In `Program.cs`, add a statement to output a message saying the console app can run everywhere, as shown in the following code:

```
using static System.Console;
```

```
namespace DotNetCoreEverywhere
{
  class Program
  {
    static void Main(string[] args)
    {
      WriteLine("I can run everywhere!");
    }
  }
}
```

3. Open `DotNetCoreEverywhere.csproj` and add the runtime identifiers to target three operating systems inside the `<PropertyGroup>` element, as shown in the following markup:

```
<Project Sdk="Microsoft.NET.Sdk">

  <PropertyGroup>
    <OutputType>Exe</OutputType>
    <TargetFramework>netcoreapp3.0</TargetFramework>
    <RuntimeIdentifiers>
      win10-x64;osx-x64;rhel.7.4-x64
    </RuntimeIdentifiers>
  </PropertyGroup>

</Project>
```

- The `win10-x64` RID value means Windows 10 or Windows Server 2016.

- The `osx-x64` RID value means macOS Sierra 10.12 or later.

- The `rhel.7.4-x64` RID value means **Red Hat Enterprise Linux (RHEL)** 7.4 or later.

> **More Information**: You can find the currently supported **Runtime IDentifier (RID)** values at the following link:
> `https://docs.microsoft.com/en-us/dotnet/articles/core/rid-catalog`

Understanding dotnet commands

When you install .NET Core SDK, it includes the **command-line interface (CLI)** named `dotnet`.

Creating new projects

The `dotnet` CLI has commands that work on the current folder to create a new project using templates.

You can install additional templates from the following link:

`https://dotnetnew.azurewebsites.net/`

More Information: You can define your own project templates, as explained in the official documentation for the `dotnet new` command at the following link: `https://docs.microsoft.com/en-us/dotnet/core/tutorials/create-custom-template`

4. In Visual Studio Code, navigate to **Terminal**.

5. Enter the `dotnet new -l` command to list your currently installed templates, as shown in the following screenshot:

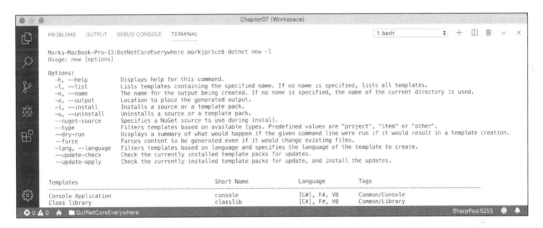

Managing projects

The `dotnet` CLI has the following commands that work on the project in the current folder, to manage the project:

- `dotnet restore`: This downloads dependencies for the project.

- `dotnet build`: This compiles the project.

- `dotnet test`: This runs unit tests on the project.

- `dotnet run`: This runs the project.

- `dotnet pack`: This creates a NuGet package for the project.

- `dotnet publish`: This compiles and then publishes the project, either with dependencies or as a self-contained application.

- `add`: This adds a reference to a package or class library to the project.

- remove: This removes a reference to a package or class library from the project.
- list: This lists the package or class library references for the project.

Publishing a self-contained app

Now we can publish our cross-platform console app.

1. In Visual Studio Code, navigate to **Terminal**, and enter the following command to build the release version of the console application for Windows 10:

```
dotnet publish -c Release -r win10-x64
```

   Microsoft Build Engine will then compile and publish the console application.

2. In **Terminal**, enter the following commands to build release versions for macOS and RHEL:

```
dotnet publish -c Release -r osx-x64
```

```
dotnet publish -c Release -r rhel.7.4-x64
```

3. Open a macOS Finder window or Windows File Explorer, navigate to DotNetCoreEverywhere\bin\Release\netcoreapp3.0, and note the output folders for the three operating systems and the files, including a Linux executable named DotNetCoreEverywhere, as shown in the following screenshot:

If you copy any of those folders to the appropriate operating system, the console application will run; this is because it is a self-contained deployable .NET Core application.

Decompiling assemblies

One of the best ways to learn how to code for .NET is to see how professionals do it.

For learning purposes, you can decompile any .NET assembly with a tool like **ILSpy**.

Good Practice: You could decompile someone else's assemblies for non-learning purposes but remember that you are viewing their intellectual property so please respect that.

1. If you have not already installed the **ILSpy .NET Decompiler** extension for Visual Studio Code, then search for it and install it now.

2. In Visual Studio Code, navigate to **View | Command Palette...** or press *Cmd + Shift + P*.

3. Type `ilspy` and then select **ILSpy: Decompile IL Assembly (pick file)**.

4. Navigate to the `Code/Chapter07/DotNetCodeEverywhere/bin / Release/netcoreapp3.0/win10-x64` folder.

5. Select the **System.IO.FileSystem.dll** assembly and click **Select assembly**.

6. In the **EXPLORER** window, expand **ILSPY DECOMPILED MEMBERS**, select the assembly, and note the two edit windows that open showing assembly attributes using C# code and external DLL and assembly references using IL code, as shown in the following screenshot:

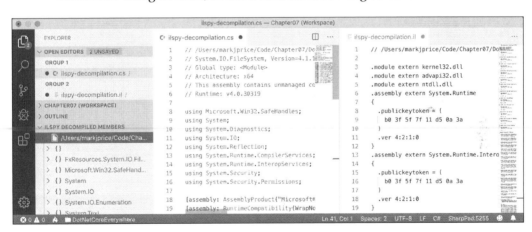

7. In the IL code, note the reference to the `System.Runtime` assembly including version number, as shown in the following code:

```
.assembly extern System.Runtime
{
    .publickeytoken = (
        b0 3f 5f 7f 11 d5 0a 3a
    )
    .ver 4:2:1:0
}
```

`.module extern kernel32.dll` means this assembly makes function calls to Win32 APIs as you would expect from code that interacts with the filesystem.

8. In the **EXPLORER** window, expand the namespaces, expand the **System. IO** namespace, select **Directory**, and note the two edit windows that open showing the decompiled `Directory` class using C# code and IL code, as shown in the following screenshot:

9. Compare the C# source code for the `GetParent` method, shown in the following code:

```csharp
public static DirectoryInfo GetParent(string path)
{
  if (path == null)
  {
    throw new ArgumentNullException("path");
  }
  if (path.Length == 0)
  {
    throw new ArgumentException(SR.Argument_PathEmpty, "path");
  }
  string fullPath = Path.GetFullPath(path);
  string directoryName = Path.GetDirectoryName(fullPath);
  if (directoryName == null)
  {
    return null;
  }
  return new DirectoryInfo(directoryName);
}
```

10. With the equivalent IL source code of the `GetParent` method, as shown in the following code:

```
.method /* 06000067 */ public hidebysig static
  class System.IO.DirectoryInfo GetParent (
    string path
  ) cil managed
{
  // Method begins at RVA 0x62d4
  // Code size 64 (0x40)
  .maxstack 2
  .locals /* 1100000E */ (
    [0] string,
    [1] string
  )

  IL_0000: ldarg.0
  IL_0001: brtrue.s IL_000e

  IL_0003: ldstr "path" /* 700005CB */
  IL_0008: newobj instance void [System.Runtime]System.
ArgumentNullException::.ctor(string) /* 0A000035 */
  IL_000d: throw

  IL_000e: ldarg.0
  IL_000f: callvirt instance int32 [System.Runtime]System.
String::get_Length() /* 0A000022 */
  IL_0014: brtrue.s IL_0026

  IL_0016: call string System.SR::get_Argument_PathEmpty() /*
0600004C */
  IL_001b: ldstr "path" /* 700005CB */
  IL_0020: newobj instance void [System.Runtime]System.
ArgumentException::.ctor(string, string) /* 0A000036 */
  IL_0025: throw

  IL_0026: ldarg.0
  IL_0027: call string [System.Runtime.Extensions]System.
IO.Path::GetFullPath(string) /* 0A000037 */
  IL_002c: stloc.0
  IL_002d: ldloc.0
  IL_002e: call string [System.Runtime.Extensions]System.IO.Path::
GetDirectoryName(string) /* 0A000038 */
  IL_0033: stloc.1
  IL_0034: ldloc.1
  IL_0035: brtrue.s IL_0039

  IL_0037: ldnull
  IL_0038: ret

  IL_0039: ldloc.1
  IL_003a: newobj instance void System.IO.DirectoryInfo::.
ctor(string) /* 06000097 */
  IL_003f: ret
} // end of method Directory::GetParent
```

Good Practice: The IL code edit windows are not especially useful unless you get very advanced with C# and .NET development where knowing how the C# compiler translates your source code into IL code can be important. The much more useful edit windows contain the equivalent C# source code written by Microsoft experts. You can learn a lot of good practices from seeing how professionals implement types.

11. Close the edit windows without saving changes.

12. In the **EXPLORER** window, in **ILSPY DECOMPILED MEMBERS**, right-click the assembly and choose **Unload Assembly**.

Packaging your libraries for NuGet distribution

Before we learn how to create and package our own libraries, we will review how a project can use an existing package.

Referencing a NuGet package

Let's say that you want to add a package created by a third-party developer, for example, Newtonsoft.Json, a popular package for working with the **JavaScript Object Notation (JSON)** serialization format.

1. In Visual Studio Code, open the AssembliesAndNamespaces project.

2. Enter the following command in **Terminal**:

```
dotnet add package newtonsoft.json
```

3. Open AssembliesAndNamespaces.csproj, and you will see the package reference has been added, as shown in the following markup:

```
<Project Sdk="Microsoft.NET.Sdk">

  <PropertyGroup>
    <OutputType>Exe</OutputType>
    <TargetFramework>netcoreapp3.0</TargetFramework>
  </PropertyGroup>

  <ItemGroup>
    <PackageReference Include="newtonsoft.json"
                      Version="12.0.2" />
  </ItemGroup>

</Project>
```

You might have a more recent version of the `newtonsoft.json` package because it has likely been updated since this book was published.

Fixing dependencies

To consistently restore packages and write reliable code, it's important that you **fix dependencies**. Fixing dependencies means you are using the same family of packages released for a specific version of .NET Core, for example, 3.0.

To fix dependencies, every package should have a single version with no additional qualifiers. Additional qualifiers include betas (`beta1`), release candidates (`rc4`), and wildcards (`*`). Wildcards allow future versions to be automatically referenced and used because they always represent the most recent release. But wildcards are therefore dangerous because it could result in the use of future incompatible packages that break your code.

If you use the `dotnet add package` command, then it will always use the latest specific version of a package. But if you copy and paste configuration from a blog article or manually add a reference yourself, you might include wildcard qualifiers.

The following dependencies are NOT fixed and should be avoided:

```
<PackageReference Include="System.Net.Http"
                  Version="4.1.0-*" />
<PackageReference Include="Newtonsoft.Json"
                  Version="12.0.3-beta1" />
```

 Good Practice: Microsoft guarantees that if you fixed your dependencies to what ships with a specific version of .NET Core, for example, 3.0, those packages will all work together. Always fix your dependencies.

Packaging a library for NuGet

Now, let's package the `SharedLibrary` project that you created earlier.

1. In the `SharedLibrary` project, rename `Class1.cs` to `StringExtensions.cs`, and modify its contents, as shown in the following code:

    ```
    using System.Text.RegularExpressions;

    namespace Packt.Shared
    {
      public static class StringExtensions
      {
        public static bool IsValidXmlTag(this string input)
    ```

```
    {
      return Regex.IsMatch(input,
        @"^<([a-z]+)([^<]+)*(?:>(.*)<\/\1>|\s+\/>)$");
    }

    public static bool IsValidPassword(this string input)
    {
      // minimum of eight valid characters
      return Regex.IsMatch(input, "^[a-zA-Z0-9_-]{8,}$");
    }

    public static bool IsValidHex(this string input)
    {
      // three or six valid hex number characters
      return Regex.IsMatch(input,
        "^#?([a-fA-F0-9]{3}|[a-fA-F0-9]{6})$");
    }
  }
}
```

These extension methods use regular expressions to validate the `string` value. You will learn how to write regular expressions in *Chapter 8, Working with Common .NET Types*.

2. Edit `SharedLibrary.csproj`, and modify its contents, as shown in the following markup, and note the following:

   ° `PackageId` must be globally unique, so you must use a different value if you want to publish this NuGet package to the `https://www.nuget.org/` public feed for others to reference and download.

   ° `PackageLicenseExpression` must be a value from the following link: `https://spdx.org/licenses/` or you could specify a custom license.

   ° All the other elements are self-explanatory:

```
<Project Sdk="Microsoft.NET.Sdk">

  <PropertyGroup>
    <TargetFramework>netstandard2.0</TargetFramework>
    <GeneratePackageOnBuild>true</GeneratePackageOnBuild>
    <PackageId>Packt.CS8.SharedLibrary</PackageId>
    <PackageVersion>1.0.0.0</PackageVersion>
    <Authors>Mark J Price</Authors>
    <PackageLicenseExpression>
      MS-PL
    </PackageLicenseExpression>
    <PackageProjectUrl>
      http://github.com/markjprice/cs8dotnetcore3
    </PackageProjectUrl>
```

```
<PackageIcon>packt-cs8-sharedlibrary.png</PackageIcon>
<PackageRequireLicenseAcceptance>true
  </PackageRequireLicenseAcceptance>
<PackageReleaseNotes>
  Example shared library packaged for NuGet.
</PackageReleaseNotes>
<Description>
  Three extension methods to validate a string value.
</Description>
<Copyright>
  Copyright © 2019 Packt Publishing Limited
</Copyright>
<PackageTags>string extension packt cs8</PackageTags>
</PropertyGroup>

<ItemGroup>
  <None Include="packt-cs8-sharedlibrary.png">
    <Pack>True</Pack>
    <PackagePath></PackagePath>
  </None>
</ItemGroup>

</Project>
```

Configuration property values that are `true` or `false` values cannot have any whitespace so the `<PackageRequireLicenseAcceptance>` entry cannot have a carriage-return and indentation as shown in the preceding markup.

3. Download the icon file and save it in the `SharedLibrary` folder from the following link: `https://github.com/markjprice/cs8dotnetcore3/tree/master/Chapter07/SharedLibrary/packt-cs8-sharedlibrary.png`

4. Navigate to **Terminal** | **New Terminal** and select `SharedLibrary`.

5. In **Terminal**, enter commands to build the release assembly and then generate a NuGet package, as shown in the following commands:

```
dotnet build -c Release

dotnet pack -c Release
```

6. Start your favorite browser and navigate to the following link: `https://www.nuget.org/packages/manage/upload`

7. You will need to sign in with a Microsoft account at `https://www.nuget.org/` if you want to upload a NuGet package for other developers to reference as a dependency package.

8. Click on **Browse...** and select the `.nupkg` file that was created by the `pack` command. The folder path should be `Code\Chapter07\SharedLibrary\bin\Release` and the file is named `Packt.CS8.SharedLibrary.1.0.0.nupkg`

9. Verify that the information you entered in the `SharedLibrary.csproj` file has been correctly filled in, and then click on **Submit**.

10. Wait a few seconds, and you will see a success message showing that your package has been uploaded, as shown in the following screenshot:

More Information: If you get an error, then review the project file for mistakes, or read more information about the `PackageReference` format at the link: `https://docs.microsoft.com/en-us/nuget/reference/msbuild-targets`

Testing your package

You will now test your uploaded package by referencing it in the `AssembliesAndNamespaces` project.

1. Open `AssembliesAndNamespaces.csproj`.

2. Modify it to reference your package (or you could use the `dotnet add package` command), as shown highlighted in the following markup:

```
<Project Sdk="Microsoft.NET.Sdk">

  <PropertyGroup>
    <OutputType>Exe</OutputType>
    <TargetFramework>netcoreapp3.0</TargetFramework>
  </PropertyGroup>

  <ItemGroup>
    <PackageReference Include="newtonsoft.json"
                      Version="12.0.2" />
    <PackageReference Include="packt.cs8.sharedlibrary"
                      Version="1.0.0" />
```

```
    </ItemGroup>

</Project>
```

In the preceding markup I used my package reference. You should use your own if you successfully uploaded it.

3. Edit `Program.cs` to import the `Packt.Shared` namespace.

4. In the `Main` method, prompt the user to enter some `string` values, and then validate them using the extension methods in the package, as shown in the following code:

```
Write("Enter a color value in hex: ");
string hex = ReadLine();

WriteLine("Is {0} a valid color value? {1}",
  arg0: hex, arg1: hex.IsValidHex());

Write("Enter a XML tag: ");
string xmlTag = ReadLine();

WriteLine("Is {0} a valid XML tag? {1}",
  arg0: xmlTag, arg1: xmlTag.IsValidXmlTag());

Write("Enter a password: ");
string password = ReadLine();

WriteLine("Is {0} a valid password? {1}",
  arg0: password, arg1: password.IsValidPassword());
```

5. Run the application and view the result, as shown in the following output:

```
Enter a color value in hex: 00ffc8
Is 00ffc8 a valid color value? True
Enter an XML tag: <h1 class="<" />
Is <h1 class="<" /> a valid XML tag? False
Enter a password: secretsauce
Is secretsauce a valid password? True
```

Porting from .NET Framework to .NET Core

If you are an existing .NET Framework developer, then you may have existing applications that you are wondering if you should port to .NET Core. You should consider if porting is the right choice for your code, because sometimes, the best choice is not to port.

Could you port?

.NET Core has great support for the following types of applications on Windows, macOS, and Linux:

- **ASP.NET Core MVC** web applications.
- **ASP.NET Core Web API** web services (REST/HTTP).
- **Console** applications.

.NET Core has great support for the following types of applications on Windows:

- **Windows Forms** applications.
- **Windows Presentation Foundation (WPF)** applications.
- **Universal Windows Platform (UWP)** applications.

> **More Information**: UWP apps can be created using C++, JavaScript, C#, and Visual Basic using a custom version of .NET Core. You can read more about this at the following link: https://docs.microsoft.com/en-us/windows/uwp/get-started/universal-application-platform-guide

.NET Core does not support the following types of legacy Microsoft applications and many others:

- **ASP.NET Web Forms** web applications.
- **Windows Communication Foundation** services.
- **Silverlight** applications.

Silverlight and ASP.NET Web Forms applications will never be able to be ported to .NET Core, but existing Windows Forms and WPF applications could be ported to .NET Core 3.0 on Windows in order to benefit from the new APIs and faster performance. Existing ASP.NET MVC web applications and ASP.NET Web API web services could be ported to .NET Core 3.0 on Windows, Linux, or macOS.

Should you port?

Even if you *could* port, *should* you? What benefits do you gain? Some common benefits include the following:

- **Deployment to Linux or Docker for web applications and web services**: These OSes are lightweight and cost-effective as web application and web service platforms, especially when compared to Windows Server.

- **Removal of dependency on IIS and System.Web.dll**: Even if you continue to deploy to Windows Server, ASP.NET Core can be hosted on lightweight, higher-performance Kestrel (or other) web servers.

- **Command-line tools**: Tools that developers and administrators use to automate their tasks are often built as console applications. The ability to run a single tool cross-platform is very useful.

Differences between .NET Framework and .NET Core

There are three key differences, as shown in the following table:

.NET Core	.NET Framework
Distributed as NuGet packages, so each application can be deployed with its own app-local copy of the version of .NET Core that it needs.	Distributed as a system-wide, shared set of assemblies (literally, in the Global Assembly Cache (GAC)).
Split into small, layered components, so a minimal deployment can be performed.	Single, monolithic deployment.
Removes older technologies, such as ASP.NET Web Forms, and non-cross-platform features, such as AppDomains, .NET Remoting, and binary serialization.	As well as the technologies in .NET Core, it retains some older technologies such as ASP.NET Web Forms.

Understanding the .NET Portability Analyzer

Microsoft has a useful tool that you can run against your existing applications to generate a report for porting. You can watch a demonstration of the tool at the following link:

```
https://channel9.msdn.com/Blogs/Seth-Juarez/A-Brief-Look-at-the-NET-
Portability-Analyzer
```

Using non-.NET Standard libraries

Most existing NuGet packages can be used with .NET Core, even if they are not compiled for .NET Standard. If you find a package that does not officially support .NET Standard, as shown on its nuget.org web page, you do not have to give up. You should try it and see if it works.

 More Information: You can search for useful NuGet packages at the following link: https://www.nuget.org/packages

For example, there is a package of custom collections for handling matrices created by Dialect Software LLC, documented at the following link:

https://www.nuget.org/packages/DialectSoftware.Collections.Matrix/

This package was last updated in 2013, which was long before .NET Core existed, so this package was built for .NET Framework. As long as an assembly package like this only uses APIs available in .NET Standard, it can be used in a .NET Core project.

Let's try using it and see if it works.

1. Open AssembliesAndNamespaces.csproj.

2. Add <PackageReference> for Dialect Software's package, as shown in the following markup:

   ```
   <PackageReference Include="dialectsoftware.collections.matrix"
                     Version="1.0.0" />
   ```

3. In **Terminal**, restore the dependent packages, as shown in the following command:

   ```
   dotnet restore
   ```

4. Open Program.cs and add statements to import the DialectSoftware.Collections and DialectSoftware.Collections.Generics namespaces.

5. Add statements to create instances of Axis and Matrix<T>, populate them with values, and output them, as shown in the following code:

   ```
   var x = new Axis("x", 0, 10, 1);
   var y = new Axis("y", 0, 4, 1);

   var matrix = new Matrix<long>(new[] { x, y });
   for (int i = 0; i < matrix.Axes[0].Points.Length; i++)
   {
     matrix.Axes[0].Points[i].Label = "x" + i.ToString();
   }

   for (int i = 0; i < matrix.Axes[1].Points.Length; i++)
   ```

```
{
  matrix.Axes[1].Points[i].Label = "y" + i.ToString();
}

foreach (long[] c in matrix)
{
  matrix[c] = c[0] + c[1];
}

foreach (long[] c in matrix)
{
  WriteLine("{0},{1} ({2},{3}) = {4}",
    matrix.Axes[0].Points[c[0]].Label,
    matrix.Axes[1].Points[c[1]].Label,
    c[0], c[1], matrix[c]);
}
```

6. Run the console application, view the output, and note the warning message:

```
warning NU1701: Package 'DialectSoftware.Collections.Matrix 1.0.0'
was restored using '.NETFramework,Version=v4.6.1' instead of the
project target framework '.NETCoreApp,Version=v3.0'. This package
may not be fully compatible with your project.
x0,y0 (0,0) = 0
x0,y1 (0,1) = 1
x0,y2 (0,2) = 2
x0,y3 (0,3) = 3
...and so on.
```

Even though this package was created before .NET Core existed, and the compiler and runtime have no way of knowing if it will work and therefore show warnings, because it happens to only call .NET Standard-compatible APIs, it works.

Practicing and exploring

Test your knowledge and understanding by answering some questions, get some hands-on practice, and explore, with deeper research into topics of this chapter.

Exercise 7.1 – Test your knowledge

Answer the following questions:

1. What is the difference between a namespace and an assembly?

2. How do you reference another project in a `.csproj` file?

3. What is the difference between a package and a metapackage? Give an example of each.

4. Which .NET type does the C# `float` alias represent?

5. What is the difference between the packages named `NETStandard.Library` and `Microsoft.NETCore.App`?

6. What is the difference between framework-dependent and self-contained deployments of .NET Core applications?

7. What is a RID?

8. What is the difference between the `dotnet pack` and `dotnet publish` commands?

9. What types of applications written for the .NET Framework can be ported to .NET Core?

10. Can you use packages written for .NET Framework with .NET Core?

Exercise 7.2 – Explore topics

Use the following links to read in more detail the topics covered in this chapter:

- **Porting to .NET Core from .NET Framework**: `https://docs.microsoft.com/en-us/dotnet/articles/core/porting/`

- **Packages, Metapackages, and Frameworks**: `https://docs.microsoft.com/en-us/dotnet/articles/core/packages`

- **.NET Blog**: `https://blogs.msdn.microsoft.com/dotnet/`

- **What .NET Developers ought to know to start in 2017**: `https://www.hanselman.com/blog/WhatNETDevelopersOughtToKnowToStartIn2017.aspx`

- **CoreFX README.md**: `https://github.com/dotnet/corefx/blob/master/Documentation/README.md`

- **.NET Core Application Deployment**: `https://docs.microsoft.com/en-us/dotnet/articles/core/deploying/`

- **Announcing .NET Standard 2.1**: `https://devblogs.microsoft.com/dotnet/announcing-net-standard-2-1/`

Summary

In this chapter, you explored the relationship between assemblies and namespaces, and we also discussed options for porting existing .NET Framework code bases, published your apps and libraries, and deployed your code cross-platform.

In the next chapter, you will learn about some common .NET Standard types that are included with .NET Core.

Chapter 08

Working with Common .NET Types

This chapter is about some common .NET Standard types that are included with .NET Core. This includes types for manipulating numbers, text, collections, network access, reflection, attributes, improving working with spans, indexes, and ranges, and internationalization.

This chapter covers the following topics:

- Working with numbers
- Working with text
- Pattern matching with regular expressions
- Storing multiple objects in collections
- Working with spans, indexes, and ranges
- Working with network resources
- Working with types and attributes
- Internationalizing your code

Working with numbers

One of the most common types of data are numbers. The most common types in .NET Standard for working with numbers are shown in the following table:

Namespace	Example type(s)	Description
System	SByte, Int16, Int32, Int64	Integers; that is, zero and positive and negative whole numbers.
System	Byte, UInt16, UInt32, UInt64	Cardinals; that is, zero and positive whole numbers.

System	Single, Double	Reals; that is, floating point numbers.
System	Decimal	Accurate reals; that is, for use in science, engineering, or financial scenarios.
System .Numerics	BigInteger, Complex, Quaternion	Arbitrarily large integers, complex numbers, and quaternion numbers.

 More Information: You can read more about this subject at the following link: https://docs.microsoft.com/en-us/dotnet/standard/numerics

Working with big integers

The largest whole number that can be stored in .NET Standard types that have a C# alias is about eighteen and a half quintillion, stored in an unsigned long. But what if you need to store numbers larger than that? Let's explore numerics:

1. Create a new console application named WorkingWithNumbers in a folder named Chapter08.

2. Save the workspace as Chapter08 and add WorkingWithNumbers to it.

3. In Program.cs, add a statement to import System.Numerics, as shown in the following code:

   ```
   using System.Numerics;
   ```

4. In Main, add statements to output the largest value of ulong, and a number with 30 digits using BigInteger, as shown in the following code:

   ```
   var largest = ulong.MaxValue;

   WriteLine($"{largest,40:N0}");

   var atomsInTheUniverse =
       BigInteger.Parse("123456789012345678901234567890");

   WriteLine($"{atomsInTheUniverse,40:N0}");
   ```

   The 40 in the format code means right-align 40 characters, so both numbers are lined up to the right-hand edge. The N0 means use thousand separators and zero decimal places.

5. Run the console application and view the result, as shown in the following output:

   ```
                18,446,744,073,709,551,615
   123,456,789,012,345,678,901,234,567,890
   ```

Working with complex numbers

A complex number can be expressed as $a + bi$, where a and b are real numbers, and i is the imaginary unit, where $i^2 = -1$. If the real part is zero, it is a pure imaginary number. If the imaginary part is zero, it is a real number.

Complex numbers have practical applications in many **STEM** (**science, technology, engineering**, and **mathematics**) fields of study. Additionally, they are added by separately adding the real and imaginary parts of the summands; consider this:

```
(a + bi) + (c + di) = (a + c) + (b + d)i
```

Let's explore complex numbers:

1. In `Main`, add statements to add two complex numbers, as shown in the following code:

   ```
   var c1 = new Complex(4, 2);
   var c2 = new Complex(3, 7);
   var c3 = c1 + c2;
   WriteLine($"{c1} added to {c2} is {c3}");
   ```

2. Run the console application and view the result, as shown in the following output:

   ```
   (4, 2) added to (3, 7) is (7, 9)
   ```

Quaternions are a number system that extends complex numbers. They form a four-dimensional associative normed division algebra over the real numbers, and therefore also a domain.

Huh? Yes, I know. I don't understand that either. Don't worry; we're not going to write any code using them! Suffice to say, they are good at describing spatial rotations, so video game engines use them, as do many computer simulations and flight control systems.

Working with text

One of the other most common types of data for variables is text. The most common types in .NET Standard for working with text are shown in the following table:

Namespace	Type	Description
System	Char	Storage for a single text character
System	String	Storage for multiple text characters

System.Text	StringBuilder	Efficiently manipulates strings
System.Text .RegularExpressions	Regex	Efficiently pattern-matches strings

Getting the length of a string

Let's explore some common tasks when working with text, for example, sometimes you need to find out the length of a piece of text stored in a `string` variable:

1. Create a new console application project named `WorkingWithText` in the `Chapter08` folder and add it to the `Chapter08` workspace.

2. Navigate to **View | Command Palette**, enter and select **OmniSharp: Select Project**, and select **WorkingWithText**.

3. In the `WorkingWithText` project, in `Program.cs`, in `Main`, add statements to define a variable to store the name of the city London, and then write its name and length to the console, as shown in the following code:

```
string city = "London";
WriteLine($"{city} is {city.Length} characters long.");
```

4. Run the console application and view the result, as shown in the following output:

```
London is 6 characters long.
```

Getting the characters of a string

The `string` class uses an array of `char` internally to store the text. It also has an indexer, which means that we can use the array syntax to read its characters:

1. Add a statement to write the characters at the first and third position in the string variable, as shown in the following code:

```
WriteLine($"First char is {city[0]} and third is {city[2]}.");
```

2. Run the console application and view the result, as shown in the following output:

```
First char is L and third is n.
```

Array indexes start at zero, so the third character is at index 2.

Splitting a string

Sometimes, you need to split some text wherever there is a character, such as a comma:

1. Add statements to define a single `string` variable containing comma-separated city names, then use the `Split` method and specify that you want to treat commas as the separator, and then enumerate the returned array of `string` values, as shown in the following code:

    ```
    string cities = "Paris,Berlin,Madrid,New York";

    string[] citiesArray = cities.Split(',');

    foreach (string item in citiesArray)
    {
      WriteLine(item);
    }
    ```

2. Run the console application and view the result, as shown in the following output:

    ```
    Paris
    Berlin
    Madrid
    New York
    ```

Later in this chapter you will learn how to handle more complex scenarios, for example, what if a `string` variable contains film titles, as shown in the following example: `""Monsters, Inc.","I, Tonya","Lock, Stock and Two Smoking Barrels""`.

Getting part of a string

Sometimes, you need to get part of some text. The `IndexOf` method has nine overloads that return the index position of a specified `char` or `string`. The `Substring` method has two overloads, as shown in the following list:

*   `Substring(startIndex, length)`: returns a substring starting at `startIndex` and containing the next length characters.

*   `Substring(startIndex)`: returns a substring starting at `startIndex` and containing all characters up to the end of the string.

Let's explore a simple example:

1. Add statements to store a person's full name in a `string` variable with a space character between the first and last name, find the position of the space, and then extract the first name and last name as two parts so that they can be recombined in a different order, as shown in the following code:

```
string fullName = "Alan Jones";

int indexOfTheSpace = fullName.IndexOf(' ');

string firstName = fullName.Substring(
  startIndex: 0, length: indexOfTheSpace);

string lastName = fullName.Substring(
  startIndex: indexOfTheSpace + 1);

WriteLine($"{lastName}, {firstName}");
```

2. Run the console application and view the result, as shown in the following output:

```
Jones, Alan
```

If the format of the initial full name was different, for example, `"LastName, FirstName"`, then the code would need to be different. As an optional exercise, try writing some statements that would change the input `"Jones, Alan"` into `"Alan Jones"`.

Checking a string for content

Sometimes, you need to check whether a piece of text starts or ends with some characters or contains some characters. You can achieve this with methods named `StartsWith`, `EndsWith`, and `Contains`:

1. Add statements to store a string value and then check if it starts with or contains a couple of different string values, as shown in the following code:

```
string company = "Microsoft";
bool startsWithM = company.StartsWith("M");
bool containsN = company.Contains("N");
WriteLine($"Starts with M: {startsWithM}, contains an N:
{containsN}");
```

2. Run the console application and view the result, as shown in the following output:

```
Starts with M: True, contains an N: False
```

Joining, formatting, and other string members

There are many other `string` members, as shown in the following table:

Member	Description
`Trim`, `TrimStart`, and `TrimEnd`	These trim whitespace characters such as space, tab, and carriage-return from the beginning and/or end of the `string` variable.
`ToUpper` and `ToLower`	These convert all the characters in the `string` variable into uppercase or lowercase.
`Insert` and `Remove`	These insert or remove some text in the `string` variable.
`Replace`	This replaces some text with other text.
`string.Concat`	This concatenates two `string` variables. The + operator calls this method when used between `string` variables.
`string.Join`	This concatenates one or more `string` variables with a character in between each one.
`string.IsNullOrEmpty`	This checks whether a `string` variable is `null` or empty (`""`).
`string.IsNullOrWhitespace`	This checks whether a `string` variable is `null` or whitespace; that is, a mix of any number of horizontal and vertical spacing characters, for example, tab, space, carriage return, line feed, and so on.
`string.Empty`	This can be used instead of allocating memory each time you use a literal `string` value using an empty pair of double quotes (`""`).
`string.Format`	An older, alternative method to string interpolation to output formatted `string` variables, which uses positioned instead of named parameters.

Some of the preceding methods are `static` methods. This means that the method can only be called from the type, not from a variable instance. In the preceding table, I indicated the `static` methods by prefixing them with `string.` like `string.Format`.

Let's explore some of these methods:

1. Add statements to take an array of `string` values and combine them back together into a single `string` variable with separators using the `Join` method, as shown in the following code:

```
string recombined = string.Join(" => ", citiesArray);
WriteLine(recombined);
```

2. Run the console application and view the result, as shown in the following output:

```
Paris => Berlin => Madrid => New York
```

3. Add statements to use positioned parameters and interpolated `string` formatting syntax to output the same three variables twice, as shown in the following code:

```
string fruit = "Apples";
decimal price = 0.39M;
DateTime when = DateTime.Today;

WriteLine($"{fruit} cost {price:C} on {when:dddd}s.");

WriteLine(string.Format("{0} cost {1:C} on {2:dddd}s.",
    fruit, price, when));
```

4. Run the console application and view the result, as shown in the following output:

```
Apples cost £0.39 on Thursdays.
Apples cost £0.39 on Thursdays.
```

Building strings efficiently

You can concatenate two strings to make a new `string` variable using the `String.Concat` method or simply using the + operator. But both of these choices are bad practice because .NET must create a completely new `string` variable in memory.

This might not be noticeable if you are only adding two `string` values, but if you concatenate inside a loop with many iterations, it can have a significant negative impact on performance and memory use.

In *Chapter 13, Improving Performance and Scalability Using Multitasking,* you will learn how to concatenate `string` variables efficiently using the `StringBuilder` type.

Pattern matching with regular expressions

Regular expressions are useful for validating input from the user. They are very powerful and can get very complicated. Almost all programming languages have support for regular expressions and use a common set of special characters to define them:

5. Create a new console application project named WorkingWithRegularExpressions, add it to the workspace, and select it as the active project for OmniSharp.

6. At the top of the file, import the following namespace:

```
using System.Text.RegularExpressions;
```

Checking for digits entered as text

1. In the Main method, add statements to prompt the user to enter their age and then check that it is valid using a regular expression that looks for a digit character, as shown in the following code:

```
Write("Enter your age: ");
string input = ReadLine();

var ageChecker = new Regex(@"\d");

if (ageChecker.IsMatch(input))
{
  WriteLine("Thank you!");
}
else
{
  WriteLine($"This is not a valid age: {input}");
}
```

The @ character switches off the ability to use escape characters in the string. Escape characters are prefixed with a backslash. For example, \t means a tab and \n means a new line.

When writing regular expressions, we need to disable this feature. To paraphrase the television show *The West Wing*, "Let backslash be backslash."

Once escape characters are disabled with @, then they can be interpreted by a regular expression. For example, \d means digit. You will learn more regular expressions that are prefixed with a backslash later in this topic.

2. Run the console application, enter a whole number such as 34 for the age, and view the result, as shown in the following output:

```
Enter your age: 34
Thank you!
```

3. Run the console application again, enter carrots, and view the result, as shown in the following output:

```
Enter your age: carrots
This is not a valid age: carrots
```

4. Run the console application again, enter `bob30smith`, and view the result, as shown in the following output:

```
Enter your age: bob30smith
Thank you!
```

The regular expression we used is \d, which means one digit. However, it does not specify what can be entered *before* and *after* that one digit. This regular expression could be described in English as "Enter any characters you want as long as you enter at least one digit character."

5. Change the regular expression to `^\d$`, as shown in the following code:

```
var ageChecker = new Regex(@"^\d$");
```

6. Rerun the application. Now, it rejects anything except a single digit.

We want to allow one or more digits. To do this, we add a + after the \d expression to modify the meaning to *one or more*.

7. Change the regular expression, as shown in the following code:

```
var ageChecker = new Regex(@"^\d+$");
```

8. Run the application and see how the regular expression now only allows zero or positive whole numbers of any length.

Understanding the syntax of a regular expression

Here are some common regular expression **symbols** that you can use in regular expressions:

Symbol	Meaning	Symbol	Meaning
^	Start of input	$	End of input
\d	A single digit	\D	A single NON-digit
\w	Whitespace	\W	NON-whitespace
[A-Za-z0-9]	Range(s) of characters	\^	^ (caret) character
[aeiou]	Set of characters	[^aeiou]	NOT in a set of characters
.	Any single character	\.	. (dot) character

More Information: To specify a Unicode character, use \u followed by four characters specifying the number of the character. For example, \u00c0 is the À character. You can learn more at the following link: https://www.regular-expressions.info/unicode.html

In addition, here are some regular expression **quantifiers** that affect the previous symbols in a regular expression:

Symbol	Meaning	Symbol	Meaning
+	One or more	?	One or none
{3}	Exactly three	{3,5}	Three to five
{3,}	At least three	{,3}	Up to three

Examples of regular expressions

Here are some examples of regular expressions with a description of their meaning:

Expression	Meaning
\d	A single digit somewhere in the input
a	The character a somewhere in the input
Bob	The word Bob somewhere in the input
^Bob	The word Bob at the start of the input
Bob$	The word Bob at the end of the input
^\d{2}$	Exactly two digits
^[0-9]{2}$	Exactly two digits
^[A-Z]{4,}$	At least four uppercase English letters in the ASCII character set only
^[A-Za-z]{4,}$	At least four upper or lowercase English letters in the ASCII character set only
^[A-Z]{2}\d{3}$	Two uppercase English letters in the ASCII character set and three digits only
^[A-Za-z \u00c0-\u017e] +$	At least one uppercase or lowercase English letter in the ASCII character set or European letters in the Unicode character set, as shown in the following list: ÀÁÂÃÄÅÆÇÈÉÊËÌÍÎÏÐÑÒÓÔÕÖ×ØÙÚÛÜÝÞß àáâãäåæçèéêëìíîïðñòóôõö÷øùúûüýþÿıŒœŠšŸŽž

| `^d.g$` | The letter d, then any character, and then the letter g, so it would match both `dig` and `dog` or any single character between the d and g |
| `^d\.g$` | The letter d, then a dot (.), and then the letter g, so it would match `d.g` only |

Good Practice: Use regular expressions to validate input from the user. The same regular expressions can be reused in other languages such as JavaScript.

Splitting a complex comma-separated string

Earlier in this chapter you learned how to split a simple comma-separated `string` variable. But what about the following example of film titles?

```
"Monsters, Inc.","I, Tonya","Lock, Stock and Two Smoking Barrels"
```

The `string` value uses double-quotes around each film title. We can use these to identify whether we need to split on a comma (or not). The `Split` method is not powerful enough so we can use a regular expression instead.

To include double-quotes inside a `string` value, we prefix them with a backslash:

1. Add statements to store a complex comma-separated `string` variable, and then split it in a dumb way using the `Split` method, as shown in the following code:

   ```
   string films = "\"Monsters, Inc.\",\"I, Tonya\",\"Lock, Stock and
   Two Smoking Barrels\"";

   string[] filmsDumb = films.Split(',');

   WriteLine("Dumb attempt at splitting:");
   foreach (string film in filmsDumb)
   {
     WriteLine(film);
   }
   ```

2. Add statements to define a regular expression to split and write the film titles in a smart way, as shown in the following code:

   ```
   var csv = new Regex(
     "(?:^|,)(?=[^\"]|(\")?)\"?((?(1)[^\"]*|[^,\"]*))\"?(?=,|$)");

   MatchCollection filmsSmart = csv.Matches(films);

   WriteLine("Smart attempt at splitting:");
   ```

```
foreach (Match film in filmsSmart)
{
  WriteLine(film.Groups[2].Value);
}
```

3. Run the console application and view the result, as shown in the following output:

```
Dumb attempt at splitting:
"Monsters
 Inc."
"I
 Tonya"
"Lock
 Stock and Two Smoking Barrels"
Smart attempt at splitting:
Monsters, Inc.
I, Tonya
Lock, Stock and Two Smoking Barrels
```

 More Information: Regular expressions are a massive topic. Books more than an inch thick have been written about them. You can read more about them at the following link: `https://www.regular-expressions.info`

Storing multiple objects in collections

Another of the most common types of data is collections. If you need to store multiple values in a variable, then you can use a collection.

A **collection** is a data structure in memory that can manage multiple items in different ways, although all collections have some shared functionality.

The most common types in .NET Standard for working with collections are shown in the following table:

Namespace	Example type(s)	Description
System.Collections	IEnumerable, IEnumerable<T>	Interfaces and base classes used by collections.

System .Collections .Generic	List<T>, Dictionary<T>, Queue<T>, Stack<T>	Introduced in C# 2.0 with .NET Framework 2.0. These collections allow you to specify the type you want to store using a generic type parameter (which is safer, faster, and more efficient).
System .Collections .Concurrent	BlockingCollection, ConcurrentDictionary, ConcurrentQueue	These collections are safe to use in multithreaded scenarios.
System .Collections .Immutable	ImmutableArray, ImmutableDictionary, ImmutableList, ImmutableQueue	Designed for scenarios where the contents of the original collection will never change, although they can create modified collections as a new instance.

More Information: You can read more about collections at the following link: https://docs.microsoft.com/en-us/dotnet/standard/collections

Common features of all collections

All collections implement the ICollection interface; this means that they must have a Count property to tell you how many objects are in them.

For example, if we had a collection named passengers, we could do this:

```
int howMany = passengers.Count;
```

All collections implement the IEnumerable interface, which means that they must have a GetEnumerator method that returns an object that implements IEnumerator; this means that the returned object must have a MoveNext method and a Current property so that they can be iterated using the foreach statement.

For example, to perform an action on each object in the passengers collection, we could do this:

```
foreach (var passenger in passengers)
{
  // do something with each passenger
}
```

To understand collections, it can be useful to see the most common interfaces that collections implement, as shown in the following diagram:

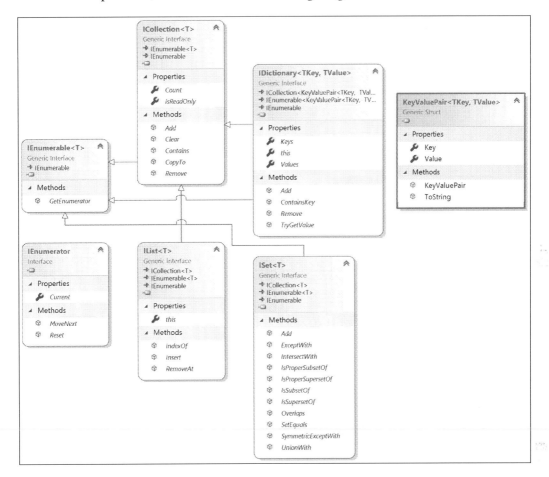

Lists, that is, a type that implements `IList`, are *ordered collections*. As you can see in the preceding diagram, `IList<T>` includes `ICollection<T>` so they must have a `Count` property, and an `Add` method to put an item at the end of the collection, as well as an `Insert` method to put an item in the list at a specified position, and `RemoveAt` to remove an item at a specified position.

Understanding collection choices

There are several different choices of collection that you can use for different purposes: lists, dictionaries, stacks, queues, sets, and many other more specialized collections.

Lists

Lists are a good choice when you want to manually control the order of items in a collection. Each item in a list has a unique index (or position) that is automatically assigned. Items can be any type defined by `T` and items can be duplicated. Indexes are `int` types and start from 0, so the first item in a list is at index 0, as shown in the following table:

Index	Item
0	London
1	Paris
2	London
3	Sydney

If a new item (for example, **Santiago**) is inserted between **London** and **Sydney**, then the index of **Sydney** is automatically incremented. Therefore, you must be aware that an item's index can change after inserting or removing items, as shown in the following table:

Index	Item
0	London
1	Paris
2	London
3	Santiago
4	Sydney

Dictionaries

Dictionaries are a good choice when each **value** (or object) has a unique sub value (or a made-up value) that can be used as a **key** to quickly find the value in the collection later. The key must be unique. For example, if you are storing a list of people, you could choose to use a government-issued identity number as the key.

Think of the key as being like an index entry in a real-world dictionary. It allows you to quickly find the definition of a word because the words (for example, keys) are kept sorted, and if we know we're looking for the definition of *manatee*, we would jump to the middle of the dictionary to start looking, because the letter M is in the middle of the alphabet.

Dictionaries in programming are similarly smart when looking something up. They must implement the interface `IDictionary<TKey, TValue>`.

The key and value can be any types defined by `TKey` and `TValue`. The example `Dictionary<string, Person>` uses a `string` as the key and a `Person` instance as the value. `Dictionary<string, string>` uses `string` values for both, as shown in the following table:

Key	Value
BSA	Bob Smith
MW	Max Williams
BSB	Bob Smith
AM	Amir Mohammed

Stacks

Stacks are a good choice when you want to implement the **last-in, first-out** (LIFO) behavior. With a stack, you can only directly access or remove the one item at the top of the stack, although you can enumerate to read through the whole stack of items. You cannot, for example, directly access the second item in a stack.

For example, word processors use a stack to remember the sequence of actions you have recently performed, and then when you press *Ctrl* + *Z*, it will undo the last action in the stack, and then the next to last action, and so on.

Queues

Queues are a good choice when you want to implement the **first-in, first-out** (FIFO) behavior. With a queue, you can only directly access or remove the one item at the front of the queue, although you can enumerate to read through the whole queue of items. You cannot, for example, directly access the second item in a queue.

For example, background processes use a queue to process work items in the order that they arrive, just like people standing in line at the post office.

Sets

Sets are a good choice when you want to perform set operations between two collections. For example, you may have two collections of city names, and you want to know which names appear in both sets (known as the **intersect** between the sets). Items in a set must be unique.

Working with lists

Let's explore lists.

1. Create a new console application project named `WorkingWithLists`, add it to the workspace, and select it as the active project for OmniSharp.

2. At the top of the file, import the following namespace:

```
using System.Collections.Generic;
```

3. In the `Main` method, type statements that illustrate some of the common ways of working with lists, as shown in the following code:

```
var cities = new List<string>();
cities.Add("London");
cities.Add("Paris");
cities.Add("Milan");

WriteLine("Initial list");
foreach (string city in cities)
{
  WriteLine($"  {city}");
}
WriteLine($"The first city is {cities[0]}.");
WriteLine($"The last city is {cities[cities.Count - 1]}.");

cities.Insert(0, "Sydney");
WriteLine("After inserting Sydney at index 0");
foreach (string city in cities)
{
  WriteLine($"  {city}");
}

cities.RemoveAt(1);
cities.Remove("Milan");
WriteLine("After removing two cities");
foreach (string city in cities)
{
  WriteLine($"  {city}");
}
```

4. Run the console application and view the result, as shown in the following output:

```
Initial list
  London
  Paris
  Milan
The first city is London.
The last city is Milan.
After inserting Sydney at index 0
  Sydney
```

```
        London
        Paris
        Milan
After removing two cities
        Sydney
        Paris
```

Working with dictionaries

Let's explore dictionaries:

1. Create a new console application project named `WorkingWithDictionaries`, add it to the workspace, and select it as the active project for OmniSharp.

2. Import the `System.Collections.Generic` namespace.

3. In the `Main` method, type statements that illustrate some of the common ways of working with dictionaries, as shown in the following code:

```
var keywords = new Dictionary<string, string>();
keywords.Add("int", "32-bit integer data type");
keywords.Add("long", "64-bit integer data type");
keywords.Add("float", "Single precision floating point number");

WriteLine("Keywords and their definitions");
foreach (KeyValuePair<string, string> item in keywords)
{
    WriteLine($"  {item.Key}: {item.Value}");
}
WriteLine($"The definition of long is {keywords["long"]}");
```

4. Run the console application and view the result, as shown in the following output:

```
Keywords and their definitions
  int: 32-bit integer data type
  long: 64-bit integer data type
  float: Single precision floating point number
The definition of long is 64-bit integer data type
```

Sorting collections

A `List<T>` class can be sorted by manually calling its `Sort` method (but remember that the indexes of each item will change). Manually sorting a list of `string` values or other built-in types will work without extra effort on your part, but if you create a collection of your own type, then that type must implement an interface named `IComparable`. You learned how to do this in *Chapter 6, Implementing Interfaces and Inheriting Classes*.

A `Dictionary<T>`, `Stack<T>`, or `Queue<T>` collection cannot be sorted because you wouldn't usually want that functionality; for example, you would never sort a queue of guests checking into a hotel. But sometimes, you might want to sort a dictionary or a set.

Sometimes it would be useful to have an automatically sorted collection that is, one that maintains the items in a sorted order as you add and remove them. There are multiple auto-sorting collections to choose from. The differences between these sorted collections are often subtle but can have an impact on the memory requirements and performance of your application, so it is worth putting effort into picking the most appropriate option for your requirements.

Some common auto-sorting collections are shown in the following table:

Collection	Description
`SortedDictionary<TKey, TValue>`	This represents a collection of key/value pairs that are sorted by key.
`SortedList<TKey, TValue>`	This represents a collection of key/value pairs that are sorted by key, based on the associated `IComparer<TKey>` implementation.
`SortedSet<T>`	This represents a collection of unique objects that are maintained in a sorted order.

Using specialized collections

There are a few other collections for special situations, as shown in the following table:

Collection	Description
`System.Collections.BitArray`	This manages a compact array of bit values, which are represented as Booleans, where `true` indicates that the bit is on (1) and `false` indicates the bit is off (0).
`System.Collections.Generics.LinkedList<T>`	This represents a doubly-linked list where every item has a reference to its previous and next items. They provide better performance compared to `List<T>` for scenarios where you will frequently insert and remove items from the middle of the list because in a `LinkedList<T>` the items do not have to be rearranged in memory.

Using immutable collections

Sometimes you need to make a collection **immutable**, meaning that its members cannot change; that is, you cannot add or remove them.

If you import the System.Collections.Immutable namespace, then any collection that implements IEnumerable<T> is given six extension methods to convert it into an immutable list, dictionary, hash set, and so on:

1. In the WorkingWithLists project, in Program.cs, import the System.Collections.Immutable namespace, and then add the following statements to the end of the Main method, as shown in the following code:

```
var immutableCities = cities.ToImmutableList();
var newList = immutableCities.Add("Rio");
Write("Immutable list of cities:");
foreach (string city in immutableCities)
{
  Write($" {city}");
}
WriteLine();

Write("New list of cities:");
foreach (string city in newList)
{
  Write($" {city}");
}
WriteLine();
```

2. Run the console application, view the result, and note that the immutable list of cities does not get modified when you call the Add method on it; instead, it returns a new list with the newly added city, as shown in the following output:

```
Immutable cities: Sydney Paris
New cities: Sydney Paris Rio
```

Good Practice: To improve performance, many applications store a shared copy of commonly accessed objects in a central cache. To safely allow multiple threads to work with those objects knowing they won't change, you should make them immutable.

Working with spans, indexes, and ranges

One of Microsoft's goals with .NET Core 2.1 was to improve performance and resource usage. A key .NET feature that enables this is the Span<T> type.

More Information: You can read the official documentation for Span<T> at the following link: https://docs.microsoft.com/en-us/dotnet/api/system.span-1?view=netstandard-2.1

Using memory efficiently using spans

When manipulating collections of objects, you will often create new collections from existing ones so that you can pass parts of a collection. This is not efficient because duplicate objects are created in memory.

If you need to work with a subset of a collection, instead of replicating the subset into a new collection, a span is like a window into a subset of the original collection. This is more efficient in terms of memory usage and improves performance.

Before we look at spans in more detail, we need to understand some related new objects: indexes and ranges.

Identifying positions with the Index type

C# 8.0 introduces two new features for identifying an item's index within a collection and a range of items using two indexes. Why did I not introduce these new language features in *Part 1: C# 8.0*?

Some C# language features require features of .NET, not all of which have been available since version 1.0. The **index** and **range** language features require the Index and Range value types that were introduced with .NET Core 3.0.

You learned in the previous topic that objects in a list can be accessed by passing an integer into their indexer, as shown in the following code:

```
int index = 3;
Person p = people[index]; // fourth person in list or array
char letter = name[index]; // fourth letter in name
```

The Index value type is a more formal way of identifying a position, and supports counting from the end, as shown in the following code:

```
// two ways to define the same index, 3 in from the start
var i1 = new Index(value: 3); // counts from the start
Index i2 = 3; // using implicit int conversion operator

// two ways to define the same index, 5 in from the end
var i3 = new Index(value: 5, fromEnd: true);
var i4 = ^5; // using the C# 8.0 caret operator
```

We had to explicitly define the Index type in the second statement because otherwise, the compiler would treat it as an int. In the fourth statement, the caret ^ was enough for the compiler to understand our meaning.

Identifying ranges with the Range type

The `Range` value type uses `Index` values to indicate the start and end of its range, using its constructor, C# syntax, or its static methods, as shown in the following code:

```
Range r1 = new Range(start: new Index(3), end: new Index(7));
Range r2 = new Range(start: 3, end: 7); // using implicit int
conversion
Range r3 = 3..7; // using C# 8.0 syntax
Range r4 = Range.StartAt(3); // from index 3 to last index
Range r5 = 3..; // from index 3 to last index
Range r6 = Range.EndAt(3); // from index 0 to index 3
Range r7 = ..3; // from index 0 to index 3
```

Extension methods have been added to `string` values, `int` arrays, and spans to make ranges easier to work with. These extension methods accept a range as a parameter and return a `Span<T>`. This makes them very memory-efficient.

Using indexes and ranges

Let's explore using indexes and ranges to return spans:

1. Create a new console application named `WorkingWithRanges`, add it to the workspace, and select it as the active project for OmniSharp.

2. In the `Main` method, type statements to compare using the `string` type's `Substring` method with using ranges to extract parts of someone's name, as shown in the following code:

```
string name = "Samantha Jones";

int lengthOfFirst = name.IndexOf(' ');
int lengthOfLast = name.Length - name.IndexOf(' ') - 1;

string firstName = name.Substring(
  startIndex: 0,
  length: lengthOfFirst);

string lastName = name.Substring(
  startIndex: name.Length - lengthOfLast,
  length: lengthOfLast);

WriteLine($"First name: {firstName}, Last name: {lastName}");

ReadOnlySpan<char> nameAsSpan = name.AsSpan();

var firstNameSpan = nameAsSpan[0..lengthOfFirst];

var lastNameSpan = nameAsSpan[^lengthOfLast..^0];

WriteLine("First name: {0}, Last name: {1}",
  arg0: firstNameSpan.ToString(),
  arg1: lastNameSpan.ToString());
```

3. Run the console application and view the result, as shown in the following output:

```
First name: Samantha, Last name: Jones
First name: Samantha, Last name: Jones
```

 More Information: You can read more about how spans work internally at the following link: `https://msdn.microsoft.com/en-us/magazine/mt814808.aspx`

Working with network resources

Sometimes you will need to work with network resources. The most common types in .NET for working with network resources are shown in the following table:

Namespace	Example type(s)	Description
System.Net	Dns, Uri, Cookie, WebClient, IPAddress	These are for working with DNS servers, URIs, IP addresses, and so on.
System.Net	FtpStatusCode, FtpWebRequest, FtpWebResponse	These are for working with FTP servers.
System.Net	HttpStatusCode, HttpWebRequest, HttpWebResponse	These are for working with HTTP servers; that is, websites and services. Types from System.Net.Http are easier to use.
System.Net.Http	HttpClient, HttpMethod, HttpRequestMessage, HttpResponseMessage	These are for working with HTTP servers; that is, websites and services. You will learn how to use these in *Chapter 18, Building and Consuming Web Services*.
System.Net.Mail	Attachment, MailAddress, MailMessage, SmtpClient	These are for working with SMTP servers; that is, sending email messages.
System.Net.NetworkInformation	IPStatus, NetworkChange, Ping, TcpStatistics	These are for working with low-level network protocols.

Working with URIs, DNS, and IP addresses

Let's explore some common types for working with network resources:

1. Create a new console application project named `WorkingWithNetwork Resources`, add it to the workspace, and select it as the active project for OmniSharp.

2. At the top of the file, import the following namespace:

   ```
   using System.Net;
   ```

3. In the `Main` method, type statements to prompt the user to enter a website address, and then use the `Uri` type to break it down into its parts, including scheme (HTTP, FTP, and so on), port number, and host, as shown in the following code:

   ```
   Write("Enter a valid web address: ");
   string url = ReadLine();
   if (string.IsNullOrWhiteSpace(url))
   {
     url = "https://world.episerver.com/cms/?q=pagetype";
   }

   var uri = new Uri(url);

   WriteLine($"URL: {url}");
   WriteLine($"Scheme: {uri.Scheme}");
   WriteLine($"Port: {uri.Port}");
   WriteLine($"Host: {uri.Host}");
   WriteLine($"Path: {uri.AbsolutePath}");
   WriteLine($"Query: {uri.Query}");
   ```

   For convenience, I have also allowed the user to press *ENTER* to use an example URL:

4. Run the console application, enter a valid website address or press *Enter*, and view the result, as shown in the following output:

   ```
   Enter a valid web address:
   URL: https://world.episerver.com/cms/?q=pagetype
   Scheme: https
   Port: 443
   Host: world.episerver.com
   Path: /cms/
   Query: ?q=pagetype
   ```

5. Add statements to the `Main` method to get the IP address for the entered website, as shown in the following code:

```
IPHostEntry entry = Dns.GetHostEntry(uri.Host);
WriteLine($"{entry.HostName} has the following IP addresses:");
foreach (IPAddress address in entry.AddressList)
{
  WriteLine($" {address}");
}
```

6. Run the console application, enter a valid website address or press *Enter*, and view the result, as shown in the following output:

```
world.episerver.com has the following IP addresses:
  217.114.90.249
```

Pinging a server

Now you will add code to ping a web server to check its health:

1. In `Program.cs`, add a statement to import `System.Net.NetworkInformation`, as shown in the following code:

```
using System.Net.NetworkInformation;
```

2. Add statements to `Main` to get the IP addresses for the entered website, as shown in the following code:

```
try
{
  var ping = new Ping();
  WriteLine("Pinging server. Please wait...");
  PingReply reply = ping.Send(uri.Host);

  WriteLine($"{uri.Host} was pinged and replied: {reply.
Status}.");

  if (reply.Status == IPStatus.Success)
  {
    WriteLine("Reply from {0} took {1:N0}ms",
      reply.Address, reply.RoundtripTime);
  }
}
catch (Exception ex)
{
  WriteLine($"{ex.GetType().ToString()} says {ex.Message}");
}
```

3. Run the console application, press *Enter*, view the result, and note that Episerver's developer site does not respond to ping requests (this is often done to avoid DDoS attacks), as shown in the following output on macOS:

```
world.episerver.com was pinged and replied: TimedOut.
```

Note that on Windows, you will see an exception is caught instead.

4. Run the console application again and enter `http://google.com`, as shown in the following output:

```
Enter a valid web address: http://google.com
URL: http://google.com
Scheme: http
Port: 80
Host: google.com
Path: /
Query:
google.com has the following IP addresses:
  216.58.204.46
  2a00:1450:4009:804::200e
google.com was pinged and replied: Success.
Reply from 216.58.204.46 took 19ms
```

Working with types and attributes

Reflection is a programming feature that allows code to understand and manipulate itself. An assembly is made up of up to four parts:

- **Assembly metadata and manifest**: Name, assembly, and file version, referenced assemblies, and so on.

- **Type metadata**: Information about the types, their members, and so on.

- **IL code**: Implementation of methods, properties, constructors, and so on.

- **Embedded Resources (optional)**: Images, strings, JavaScript, and so on.

The metadata comprises items of information about your code. The metadata is applied to your code using attributes.

Attributes can be applied at multiple levels: to assemblies, to types, and to their members, as shown in the following code:

```
// an assembly-level attribute
```

```
[assembly: AssemblyTitle("Working with Reflection")]

// a type-level attribute
[Serializable]
public class Person

  // a member-level attribute
  [Obsolete("Deprecated: use Run instead.")]
  public void Walk()
  {
    // ...
  }
```

Versioning of assemblies

Version numbers in .NET are a combination of three numbers, with two optional additions. If you follow the rules of semantic versioning:

- **Major**: Breaking changes.
- **Minor**: Non-breaking changes, including new features and bug fixes.
- **Patch**: Non-breaking bug fixes.

Good Practice: When updating a NuGet package, you should specify an optional flag to make sure that you only upgrade to the highest minor to avoid breaking changes, or to the highest patch if you are extra cautious and only want to receive bug fixes, as shown in the following commands:
`Update-Package Newtonsoft.Json -ToHighestMinor`
`Update-Package EPiServer.Cms -ToHighestPatch`

Optionally, a version can include these:

- **Prerelease**: Unsupported preview releases.
- **Build number**: Nightly builds.

Good Practice: Follow the rules of semantic versioning, as described at the following link: `http://semver.org`

Reading assembly metadata

Let's explore working with attributes:

1. Create a new console application project named `WorkingWithReflection`, add it to the workspace, and select it as the active project for OmniSharp.

2. At the top of the file, import the following namespace:

```
using System.Reflection;
```

3. In the `Main` method, enter statements to get the console app's assembly, output its name and location, and get all assembly-level attributes and output their types, as shown in the following code:

```
WriteLine("Assembly metadata:");
Assembly = Assembly.GetEntryAssembly();
WriteLine($"  Full name: {assembly.FullName}");
WriteLine($"  Location: {assembly.Location}");

var attributes = assembly.GetCustomAttributes();
WriteLine($"  Attributes:");
foreach (Attribute a in attributes)
{
    WriteLine($"    {a.GetType()}");
}
```

4. Run the console application and view the result, as shown in the following output:

```
Assembly metadata:
  Full name: WorkingWithReflection, Version=1.0.0.0,
Culture=neutral, PublicKeyToken=null
  Location: /Users/markjprice/Code/Chapter08/
WorkingWithReflection/bin/Debug/netcoreapp 3.0/
WorkingWithReflection.dll
  Attributes:
    System.Runtime.CompilerServices.
CompilationRelaxationsAttribute
    System.Runtime.CompilerServices.RuntimeCompatibilityAttribute
    System.Diagnostics.DebuggableAttribute
    System.Runtime.Versioning.TargetFrameworkAttribute
    System.Reflection.AssemblyCompanyAttribute
    System.Reflection.AssemblyConfigurationAttribute
    System.Reflection.AssemblyFileVersionAttribute
    System.Reflection.AssemblyInformationalVersionAttribute
    System.Reflection.AssemblyProductAttribute
    System.Reflection.AssemblyTitleAttribute
```

Now that we know some of the attributes decorating the assembly, we can ask for them specifically.

5. Add statements to the end of the `Main` method to get the `AssemblyInformationalVersionAttribute` and `AssemblyCompany Attribute` classes, as shown in the following code:

```
var version = assembly.GetCustomAttribute
  <AssemblyInformationalVersionAttribute>();

WriteLine($"   Version: {version.InformationalVersion}");

var company = assembly.GetCustomAttribute
  <AssemblyCompanyAttribute>();

WriteLine($"   Company: {company.Company}");
```

6. Run the console application and view the result, as shown in the following output:

```
Version: 1.0.0
Company: WorkingWithReflection
```

Hmm, let's explicitly set this information. The old .NET Framework way to set these values was to add attributes in the C# source code file, as shown in the following code:

```
[assembly: AssemblyCompany("Packt Publishing")]
[assembly: AssemblyInformationalVersion("1.3.0")]
```

The Roslyn compiler used by .NET Core sets these attributes automatically, so we can't use the old way. Instead, they can be set in the project file.

7. Modify `WorkingWithReflection.csproj`, as shown in the following markup:

```
<Project Sdk="Microsoft.NET.Sdk">

  <PropertyGroup>
    <OutputType>Exe</OutputType>
    <TargetFramework>netcoreapp3.0</TargetFramework>
    <Version>1.3.0</Version>
    <Company>Packt Publishing</Company>
  </PropertyGroup>

</Project>
```

8. Run the console application and view the result, as shown in the following output:

```
Version: 1.3.0
Company: Packt Publishing
```

Creating custom attributes

You can define your own attributes by inheriting from the `Attribute` class:

1. Add a class file to your project named `CoderAttribute.cs`.

2. Define an attribute class that can decorate either classes or methods with two properties to store the name of a coder and the date they last modified some code, as shown in the following code:

```
using System;

[AttributeUsage(AttributeTargets.Class | AttributeTargets.Method,
  AllowMultiple = true)]
public class CoderAttribute : Attribute
{
  public string Coder { get; set; }
  public DateTime LastModified { get; set; }

  public CoderAttribute(string coder, string lastModified)
  {
    Coder = coder;
    LastModified = DateTime.Parse(lastModified);
  }
}
```

3. In the `Program` class, add a method named `DoStuff`, and decorate it with the `Coder` attribute with data about two coders, as shown in the following code:

```
[Coder("Mark Price", "22 August 2019")]
[Coder("Johnni Rasmussen", "13 September 2019")]
public static void DoStuff()
{

}
```

4. In `Program.cs`, import `System.Linq`, as shown in the following code:

```
using System.Linq; // to use OrderByDescending
```

   You will learn more about LINQ in *Chapter 12, Querying and Manipulating Data Using LINQ*. We have imported it to use its `OrderByDescending` method.

5. In the `Main` method, add code to get the types, enumerate their members, read any `Coder` attributes on those members, and write the information to the console, as shown in the following code:

```
WriteLine();
WriteLine($"* Types:");
Type[] types = assembly.GetTypes();
```

```
foreach (Type type in types)
{
  WriteLine();
  WriteLine($"Type: {type.FullName}");
  MemberInfo[] members = type.GetMembers();
  foreach (MemberInfo member in members)
  {
    WriteLine("{0}: {1} ({2})",
      arg0: member.MemberType,
      arg1: member.Name,
      arg2: member.DeclaringType.Name);

    var coders = member.GetCustomAttributes<CoderAttribute>()
      .OrderByDescending(c => c.LastModified);

    foreach (CoderAttribute coder in coders)
    {
      WriteLine("-> Modified by {0} on {1}",
        coder.Coder, coder.LastModified.ToShortDateString());
    }
  }
}
```

6. Run the console application and view the result, as shown in the following output:

```
* Types:

Type: CoderAttribute
Method: get_Coder (CoderAttribute)
Method: set_Coder (CoderAttribute)
Method: get_LastModified (CoderAttribute)
Method: set_LastModified (CoderAttribute)
Method: Equals (Attribute)
Method: GetHashCode (Attribute)
Method: get_TypeId (Attribute)
Method: Match (Attribute)
Method: IsDefaultAttribute (Attribute)
Method: ToString (Object)
Method: GetType (Object)
Constructor: .ctor (CoderAttribute)
Property: Coder (CoderAttribute)
Property: LastModified (CoderAttribute)
```

```
Property: TypeId (Attribute)

Type: WorkingWithReflection.Program
Method: DoStuff (Program)
-> Modified by Johnni Rasmussen on 13/09/2019
-> Modified by Mark Price on 22/08/2019
Method: ToString (Object)
Method: Equals (Object)
Method: GetHashCode (Object)
Method: GetType (Object)
Constructor: .ctor (Program)

Type: WorkingWithReflection.Program+<>c
Method: ToString (Object)
Method: Equals (Object)
Method: GetHashCode (Object)
Method: GetType (Object)
Constructor: .ctor (<>c)
Field: <>9 (<>c)
Field: <>9__0_0 (<>c)
```

More Information: What is the `WorkingWithReflection.Program+<>c` type? It is a compiler-generated display class. `<>` indicates compiler-generated and `c` indicates a display class. You can read more at the following link: `http://stackoverflow.com/a/2509524/55847`

As an optional challenge, add statements to your console application to filter compiler-generated types by skipping types decorated with `CompilerGeneratedAttribute`.

Doing more with reflection

This is just a taster of what can be achieved with reflection. We only used reflection to read metadata from our code. Reflection can also do the following:

- **Dynamically load assemblies that are not currently referenced**: `https://docs.microsoft.com/en-us/dotnet/standard/assembly/unloadability-howto`

- **Dynamically execute code**: `https://docs.microsoft.com/en-us/dotnet/api/system.reflection.methodbase.invoke?view=netcore-3.0`

- **Dynamically generate new code and assemblies**: `https://docs.microsoft.com/en-us/dotnet/api/system.reflection.emit.assemblybuilder?view=netcore-3.0`

Internationalizing your code

Internationalization is the process of enabling your code to run correctly all over the world. It has two parts: **globalization** and **localization**.

Globalization is about writing your code to accommodate multiple languages and region combinations. The combination of a language and a region is known as a culture. It is important for your code to know both the language and region because the date and currency formats are different in Quebec and Paris, despite them both using the French language.

There are **International Organization for Standardization (ISO)** codes for all culture combinations. For example, in the code `da-DK`, `da` indicates the Danish language and `DK` indicates the Denmark region, and in the code `fr-CA`, `fr` indicates the French language and `CA` indicates the Canadian region.

ISO is not an acronym. ISO is a reference to the Greek word *isos* (which means equal).

Localization is about customizing the user interface to support a language, for example, changing the label of a button to be **Close** (`en`) or **Fermer** (`fr`). Since localization is more about the language, it doesn't always need to know about the region, although ironically enough, standardization (`en-US`) and standardisation (`en-GB`) suggest otherwise.

Internationalization is a huge topic on which several thousand-page books have been written. In this section, you will get a brief introduction to the basics using the `CultureInfo` type in the `System.Globalization` namespace:

1. Create a new console application project named `Internationalization`, add it to the workspace, and select it as the active project for OmniSharp.

2. At the top of the file, import the following namespace:

   ```
   using System.Globalization;
   ```

3. In the `Main` method, enter statements to get the current globalization and localization cultures and write some information about them to the console, and then prompt the user to enter a new culture code and show how that affects the formatting of common values such as dates and currency, as shown in the following code:

```
CultureInfo globalization = CultureInfo.CurrentCulture;
CultureInfo localization = CultureInfo.CurrentUICulture;

WriteLine("The current globalization culture is {0}: {1}",
  globalization.Name, globalization.DisplayName);
WriteLine("The current localization culture is {0}: {1}",
  localization.Name, localization.DisplayName);
WriteLine();

WriteLine("en-US: English (United States)");
WriteLine("da-DK: Danish (Denmark)");
WriteLine("fr-CA: French (Canada)");
Write("Enter an ISO culture code: ");
string newCulture = ReadLine();
if (!string.IsNullOrEmpty(newCulture))
{
  var ci = new CultureInfo(newCulture);
  CultureInfo.CurrentCulture = ci;
  CultureInfo.CurrentUICulture = ci;
}
WriteLine();

Write("Enter your name: ");
string name = ReadLine();
Write("Enter your date of birth: ");
string dob = ReadLine();
Write("Enter your salary: ");
string salary = ReadLine();

DateTime date = DateTime.Parse(dob);
int minutes = (int)DateTime.Today.Subtract(date).TotalMinutes;
decimal earns = decimal.Parse(salary);

WriteLine(
  "{0} was born on a {1:dddd}, is {2:N0} minutes old, and earns
{3:C}",
  name, date, minutes, earns);
```

When you run an application, it automatically sets its thread to use the culture of the operating system. I am running my code in London, UK, so the thread is set to English (United Kingdom).

The code prompts the user to enter an alternative ISO code. This allows your applications to replace the default culture at runtime.

The application then uses standard format codes to output the day of the week using format code dddd; the number of minutes with thousand separators using format code N0; and the salary with the currency symbol. These adapt automatically, based on the thread's culture.

4. Run the console application and enter `en-GB` for the ISO code and then enter some sample data including a date in a format valid for British English, as shown in the following output:

```
Enter an ISO culture code: en-GB

Enter your name: Alice

Enter your date of birth: 30/3/1967

Enter your salary: 23500

Alice was born on a Thursday, is 25,469,280 minutes old, and earns
£23,500.00
```

Rerun the application and try a different culture, such as Danish in Denmark, as shown in the following output:

```
Enter an ISO culture code: da-DK

Enter your name: Mikkel

Enter your date of birth: 12/3/1980

Enter your salary: 340000

Mikkel was born on a onsdag, is 18.656.640 minutes old, and earns
340.000,00 kr.
```

Good Practice: Consider whether your application needs to be internationalized and plan for that before you start coding! Write down all the pieces of text in the user interface that will need to be localized. Think about all the data that will need to be globalized (date formats, number formats, and sorting text behavior).

Practicing and exploring

Test your knowledge and understanding by answering some questions, get some hands-on practice, and explore with deeper research into the topics in this chapter.

Exercise 8.1 – Test your knowledge

Use the web to answer the following questions:

1. What is the maximum number of characters that can be stored in a `string` variable?

2. When and why should you use a `SecureString` class?

3. When is it appropriate to use a `StringBuilder` type?

4. When should you use a `LinkedList<T>` class?

5. When should you use a `SortedDictionary<T>` class rather than a `SortedList<T>` class?

6. What is the ISO culture code for Welsh?

7. What is the difference between localization, globalization, and internationalization?

8. In a regular expression, what does $ mean?

9. In a regular expression, how could you represent digits?

10. Why should you *not* use the official standard for email addresses to create a regular expression to validate a user's email address?

Exercise 8.2 – Practice regular expressions

Create a console application named `Exercise02` that prompts the user to enter a regular expression, and then prompts the user to enter some input and compare the two for a match until the user presses *Esc*, as shown in the following output:

```
The default regular expression checks for at least one digit.

Enter a regular expression (or press ENTER to use the default): ^[a-z]+$

Enter some input: apples

apples matches ^[a-z]+$? True

Press ESC to end or any key to try again.

Enter a regular expression (or press ENTER to use the default): ^[a-z]+$

Enter some input: abc123xyz

abc123xyz matches ^[a-z]+$? False

Press ESC to end or any key to try again.
```

Exercise 8.3 – Practice writing extension methods

Create a class library named `Exercise03` that defines extension methods that extend number types such as `BigInteger` and `int` with a method named `ToWords` that returns a `string` describing the number; for example, 18,000,000 would be eighteen million, and 18,456,002,032,011,000,007 would be eighteen quintillion, four hundred and fifty six quadrillion, two trillion, thirty two billion, eleven million, and seven.

More Information: You can read more about names for large numbers at the following link: https://en.wikipedia.org/wiki/Names_of_large_numbers

Exercise 8.4 – Explore topics

Use the following links to read in more detail the topics covered in this chapter:

- **.NET Core API Reference**: `https://docs.microsoft.com/en-us/dotnet/api/index?view=netcore-3.0`

- **String Class**: `https://docs.microsoft.com/en-us/dotnet/api/system.string?view=netcore-3.0`

- **Regex Class**: `https://docs.microsoft.com/en-us/dotnet/api/system.text.regularexpressions.regex?view=netcore-3.0`

- **Regular expressions in .NET**: `https://docs.microsoft.com/en-us/dotnet/articles/standard/base-types/regular-expressions`

- **Regular Expression Language - Quick Reference**: `https://docs.microsoft.com/en-us/dotnet/articles/standard/base-types/quick-ref`

- **Collections (C# and Visual Basic)**: `https://docs.microsoft.com/en-us/dotnet/api/system.collections?view=netcore-3.0`

- **Extending Metadata Using Attributes**: `https://docs.microsoft.com/en-us/dotnet/standard/attributes/`

- **Globalizing and localizing .NET applications**: `https://docs.microsoft.com/en-us/dotnet/standard/globalization-localization/`

Summary

In this chapter, you explored some choices for types to store and manipulate numbers and text, including regular expressions, which collections to use for storing multiple items; worked with indexes, ranges, and spans; used some network resources; reflected on code and attributes; and learned how to internationalize your code. In the next chapter, we will manage files and streams, encode and decode text, and perform serialization.

Chapter 09

Working with Files, Streams, and Serialization

This chapter is about reading and writing to files and streams, text encoding, and serialization. We will be covering the following topics:

- Managing the filesystem
- Reading and writing with streams
- Encoding and decoding text
- Serializing object graphs

Managing the filesystem

Your applications will often need to perform input and output with files and directories in different environments. The System and System.IO namespaces contain classes for this purpose.

Handling cross-platform environments and filesystems

Let's explore how to handle cross-platform environments like the differences between Windows and Linux or macOS.

1. Create a new console application named WorkingWithFileSystems in a folder named Chapter09.

2. Save the workspace as Chapter09 and add WorkingWithFileSystems to it.

3. Import the System.IO namespace, and statically import the System.Console, System.IO.Directory, System.Environment, and System.IO.Path types, as shown in the following code:

    ```
    using System.IO; // types for managing the filesystem
    ```

```
using static System.Console;
using static System.IO.Directory;
using static System.IO.Path;
using static System.Environment;
```

Paths are different for Windows, macOS, and Linux, so we will start by exploring how .NET Core handles this.

4. Create a static `OutputFileSystemInfo` method, and write statements to do the following:

    ○ Output the path and directory separation characters

    ○ Output the path of the current directory

    ○ Output some special paths for system files, temporary files, and documents

```
static void OutputFileSystemInfo()
{
  WriteLine("{0,-33} {1}", "Path.PathSeparator", PathSeparator);
  WriteLine("{0,-33} {1}", "Path.DirectorySeparatorChar",
    DirectorySeparatorChar);
  WriteLine("{0,-33} {1}", "Directory.GetCurrentDirectory()",
    GetCurrentDirectory());
  WriteLine("{0,-33} {1}", "Environment.CurrentDirectory",
    CurrentDirectory);
  WriteLine("{0,-33} {1}", "Environment.SystemDirectory",
    SystemDirectory);
  WriteLine("{0,-33} {1}", "Path.GetTempPath()", GetTempPath());

  WriteLine("GetFolderPath(SpecialFolder");
  WriteLine("{0,-33} {1}", "  .System)",
    GetFolderPath(SpecialFolder.System));
  WriteLine("{0,-33} {1}", "  .ApplicationData)",
    GetFolderPath(SpecialFolder.ApplicationData));
  WriteLine("{0,-33} {1}", "  .MyDocuments)",
    GetFolderPath(SpecialFolder.MyDocuments));
  WriteLine("{0,-33} {1}", "  .Personal)",
    GetFolderPath(SpecialFolder.Personal));
}
```

The `Environment` type has many other useful members, including the `GetEnvironmentVariables` method and the `OSVersion` and `ProcessorCount` properties.

5. In the `Main` method, call `OutputFileSystemInfo`, as shown in the following code:

```
static void Main(string[] args)
{
  OutputFileSystemInfo();
}
```

6. Run the console application and view the result, as shown in the following screenshot when run on Windows:

Windows uses a backslash for the directory separator character. macOS and Linux use a forward slash for the directory separator character.

Managing drives

To manage drives, use `DriveInfo`, which has a static method that returns information about all the drives connected to your computer. Each drive has a drive type.

1. Create a `WorkWithDrives` method, and write statements to get all the drives and output their name, type, size, available free space, and format, but only if the drive is ready, as shown in the following code:

```
static void WorkWithDrives()
{
  WriteLine("{0,-30} | {1,-10} | {2,-7} | {3,18} | {4,18}",
    "NAME", "TYPE", "FORMAT", "SIZE (BYTES)", "FREE SPACE");

  foreach (DriveInfo drive in DriveInfo.GetDrives())
  {
    if (drive.IsReady)
    {
      WriteLine(
        "{0,-30} | {1,-10} | {2,-7} | {3,18:N0} | {4,18:N0}",
        drive.Name, drive.DriveType, drive.DriveFormat,
        drive.TotalSize, drive.AvailableFreeSpace);
    }
    else
    {
      WriteLine("{0,-30} | {1,-10}", drive.Name, drive.DriveType);
    }
  }
```

```
    }
}
```

Good Practice: Check that a drive is ready before reading properties such as `TotalSize` or you will see an exception thrown with removable drives.

2. In `Main`, comment out the previous method call, and add a call to `WorkWithDrives`, as shown in the following code:

```
static void Main(string[] args)
{
  // OutputFileSystemInfo();
  WorkWithDrives();
}
```

3. Run the console application and view the result, as shown in the following screenshot:

Managing directories

To manage directories, use the `Directory`, `Path`, and `Environment` static classes.

These types include many properties and methods for working with the filesystem, as shown in the following diagram:

When constructing custom paths, you must be careful to write your code so that it makes no assumptions about the platform, for example, what to use for the directory separator character.

1. Create a `WorkWithDirectories` method, and write statements to do the following:
   - Define a custom path under the user's home directory by creating an array of strings for the directory names, and then properly combining them with the `Path` type's static `Combine` method.

- ○ Check for the existence of the custom directory path using the static Exists method of the Directory class.
- ○ Create and then delete the directory, including files and subdirectories within it, using the static CreateDirectory and Delete methods of the Directory class.

```
static void WorkWithDirectories()
{
  // define a directory path for a new folder
  // starting in the user's folder
  var newFolder = Combine(
    GetFolderPath(SpecialFolder.Personal),
    "Code", "Chapter09", "NewFolder");

  WriteLine($"Working with: {newFolder}");

  // check if it exists
  WriteLine($"Does it exist? {Exists(newFolder)}");

  // create directory
  WriteLine("Creating it...");
  CreateDirectory(newFolder);
  WriteLine($"Does it exist? {Exists(newFolder)}");

  Write("Confirm the directory exists, and then press ENTER: ");
  ReadLine();

  // delete directory
  WriteLine("Deleting it...");
  Delete(newFolder, recursive: true);
  WriteLine($"Does it exist? {Exists(newFolder)}");
}
```

2. In the Main method, comment out the previous method call, and add a call to WorkWithDirectories, as shown in the following code:

```
static void Main(string[] args)
{
  // OutputFileSystemInfo();
  // WorkWithDrives();
  WorkWithDirectories();
}
```

3. Run the console application and view the result, and use your favorite file management tool to confirm that the directory has been created before pressing *Enter* to delete it, as shown in the following output:

```
Working with: /Users/markjprice/Code/Chapter09/NewFolder

Does it exist? False
```

```
Creating it...
Does it exist? True
Confirm the directory exists, and then press ENTER:
Deleting it...
Does it exist? False
```

Managing files

When working with files, you could statically import the `File` type, just as we did for the `Directory` type, but, for the next example, we will not, because it has some of the same methods as the `Directory` type and they would conflict. The `File` type has a short enough name not to matter in this case.

1. Create a `WorkWithFiles` method, and write statements to do the following:

    ○   Check for the existence of a file.

    ○   Create a text file.

    ○   Write a line of text to the file.

    ○   Close the file to release system resources and file locks (this would normally be done inside a `try-finally` statement block to ensure that the file is closed even if an exception occurs when writing to it).

    ○   Copy the file to a backup.

    ○   Delete the original file.

    ○   Read the backup file's contents and then close it.

```
static void WorkWithFiles()
{
  // define a directory path to output files
  // starting in the user's folder
  var dir = Combine(
    GetFolderPath(SpecialFolder.Personal),
    "Code", "Chapter09", "OutputFiles");

  CreateDirectory(dir);

  // define file paths
  string textFile = Combine(dir, "Dummy.txt");
  string backupFile = Combine(dir, "Dummy.bak");

  WriteLine($"Working with: {textFile}");
```

```
        // check if a file exists
        WriteLine($"Does it exist? {File.Exists(textFile)}");

        // create a new text file and write a line to it
        StreamWriter textWriter = File.CreateText(textFile);
        textWriter.WriteLine("Hello, C#!");
        textWriter.Close(); // close file and release resources

        WriteLine($"Does it exist? {File.Exists(textFile)}");

        // copy the file, and overwrite if it already exists
        File.Copy(sourceFileName: textFile,
          destFileName: backupFile, overwrite: true);

        WriteLine(
          $"Does {backupFile} exist? {File.Exists(backupFile)}");

        Write("Confirm the files exist, and then press ENTER: ");
        ReadLine();

        // delete file
        File.Delete(textFile);

        WriteLine($"Does it exist? {File.Exists(textFile)}");

        // read from the text file backup
        WriteLine($"Reading contents of {backupFile}:");
        StreamReader textReader = File.OpenText(backupFile);
        WriteLine(textReader.ReadToEnd());
        textReader.Close();
    }
```

2. In `Main`, comment out the previous method call, and add a call to `WorkWithFiles`.

3. Run the application and view the result, as shown in the following output:

```
Working with: /Users/markjprice/Code/Chapter09/OutputFiles/Dummy.
txt

Does it exist? False

Does it exist? True

Does /Users/markjprice/Code/Chapter09/OutputFiles/Dummy.bak exist?
True
```

```
Confirm the files exist, and then press ENTER:

Does it exist? False

Reading contents of /Users/markjprice/Code/Chapter09/OutputFiles/
Dummy.bak:

Hello, C#!
```

Managing paths

Sometimes, you need to work with parts of a path; for example, you might want to extract just the folder name, the filename, or the extension. Sometimes, you need to generate temporary folders and filenames. You can do this with static methods of the `Path` class.

1. Add the following statements to the end of the `WorkWithFiles` method:

```
// Managing paths
WriteLine($"Folder Name: {GetDirectoryName(textFile)}");
WriteLine($"File Name: {GetFileName(textFile)}");
WriteLine("File Name without Extension: {0}",
  GetFileNameWithoutExtension(textFile));
WriteLine($"File Extension: {GetExtension(textFile)}");
WriteLine($"Random File Name: {GetRandomFileName()}");
WriteLine($"Temporary File Name: {GetTempFileName()}");
```

2. Run the application and view the result, as shown in the following output:

```
Folder Name: /Users/markjprice/Code/Chapter09/OutputFiles

File Name: Dummy.txt

File Name without Extension: Dummy

File Extension: .txt

Random File Name: u45w1zki.co3

Temporary File Name:

/var/folders/tz/xx0y_wld5sx0nv0fjtq4tnpc0000gn/T/tmpyqrepP.tmp
```

`GetTempFileName` creates a zero-byte file and returns its name, ready for you to use. `GetRandomFileName` just returns a filename; it doesn't create the file.

Getting file information

To get more information about a file or directory, for example, its size or when it was last accessed, you can create an instance of the `FileInfo` or `DirectoryInfo` class.

`FileInfo` and `DirectoryInfo` both inherit from `FileSystemInfo`, so they both have members such as `LastAccessTime` and `Delete`, as shown in the following diagram:

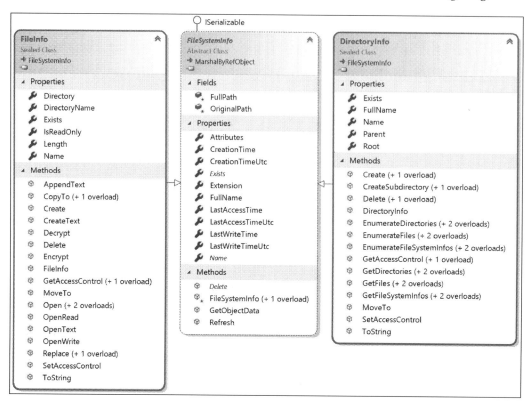

1. Let's write some code that uses a `FileInfo` instance for efficiently performing multiple actions on a file. Add statements to the end of the `WorkWithFiles` method to create an instance of `FileInfo` for the backup file and write information about it to the console, as shown in the following code:

```
var info = new FileInfo(backupFile);
WriteLine($"{backupFile}:");
WriteLine($"Contains {info.Length} bytes");
WriteLine($"Last accessed {info.LastAccessTime}");
WriteLine($"Has readonly set to {info.IsReadOnly}");
```

2. Run the application and view the result, as shown in the following output:

```
/Users/markjprice/Code/Chapter09/OutputFiles/Dummy.bak:

Contains 11 bytes

Last accessed 26/11/2018 09:08:26

Has readonly set to False
```

The number of bytes might be different on your operating system because operating systems can use different line endings.

Controlling how you work with files

When working with files, you often need to control how they are opened. The `File.Open` method has overloads to specify additional options using `enum` values. The `enum` types are as follows:

- `FileMode`: This controls what you want to do with the file, like `CreateNew`, `OpenOrCreate`, or `Truncate`.

- `FileAccess`: This controls what level of access you need, like `ReadWrite`.

- `FileShare`: This controls locks on the file to allow other processes the specified level of access, like `Read`.

You might want to open a file and read from it, and allow other processes to read it too, as shown in the following code:

```
FileStream file = File.Open(pathToFile,
    FileMode.Open, FileAccess.Read, FileShare.Read);
```

There is also an `enum` for attributes of a file as follows:

- `FileAttributes`: This is to check a `FileSystemInfo`-derived types `Attributes` property for values like `Archive` and `Encrypted`.

You could check a file or directory's attributes, as shown in the following code:

```
var info = new FileInfo(backupFile);
WriteLine("Is the backup file compressed? {0}",
    info.Attributes.HasFlag(FileAttributes.Compressed));
```

Reading and writing with streams

A **stream** is a sequence of bytes that can be read from and written to. Although files can be processed rather like arrays, with random access provided by knowing the position of a byte within the file, it can be useful to process files as a stream in which the bytes can be accessed in sequential order.

Streams can also be used to process terminal input and output and networking resources such as sockets and ports that do not provide random access and cannot seek to a position. You can write code to process some arbitrary bytes without knowing or caring where it comes from. Your code simply reads or writes to a stream, and another piece of code handles where the bytes are actually stored.

There is an abstract class named Stream that represents a stream. There are many classes that inherit from this base class, including FileStream, MemoryStream, BufferedStream, GZipStream, and SslStream, so they all work the same way.

All streams implement IDisposable, so they have a Dispose method to release unmanaged resources.

In the following table are some of the common members of the Stream class:

Member	Description
CanRead, CanWrite	This determines whether you can read from and write to the stream.
Length, Position	This determines the total number of bytes and the current position within the stream. These properties may throw an exception for some types of stream.
Dispose()	This closes the stream and releases its resources.
Flush()	If the stream has a buffer, then the bytes in the buffer are written to the stream and the buffer is cleared.
Read(), ReadAsync()	This reads a specified number of bytes from the stream into a byte array and advances the position.
ReadByte()	This reads the next byte from the stream and advances the position.
Seek()	This moves the position to the specified position (if CanSeek is true).
Write(), WriteAsync()	This writes the contents of a byte array into the stream.
WriteByte()	This writes a byte to the stream.

In the following table are some **storage streams** that represent a location where the bytes will be stored:

Namespace	Class	Description
System.IO	FileStream	Bytes stored in the filesystem.
System.IO	MemoryStream	Bytes stored in memory in the current process.
System.Net.Sockets	NetworkStream	Bytes stored at a network location.

In the following table are some **function streams** that cannot exist on their own. They can only be "plugged onto" other streams to add functionality:

Namespace	Class	Description
`System.Security.Cryptography`	`CryptoStream`	This encrypts and decrypts the stream.
`System.IO.Compression`	`GZipStream, DeflateStream`	This compresses and decompresses the stream.
`System.Net.Security`	`AuthenticatedStream`	This sends credentials across the stream.

Although there will be occasions where you need to work with streams at a low level, most often, you can plug helper classes into the chain to make things easier.

All the helper types for streams implement `IDisposable`, so they have a `Dispose` method to release unmanaged resources.

In the following table are some helper classes to handle common scenarios:

Namespace	Class	Description
`System.IO`	`StreamReader`	This reads from the underlying stream as text.
`System.IO`	`StreamWriter`	This writes to the underlying stream as text.
`System.IO`	`BinaryReader`	This reads from streams as .NET types. For example, the `ReadDecimal` method reads the next 16 bytes from the underlying stream as a `decimal` value and the `ReadInt32` method reads the next 4 bytes as an `int` value.
`System.IO`	`BinaryWriter`	This writes to streams as .NET types. For example, the `Write` method with a `decimal` parameter writes 16 bytes to the underlying stream and the `Write` method with an `int` parameter writes 4 bytes.
`System.Xml`	`XmlReader`	This reads from the underlying stream as XML.
`System.Xml`	`XmlWriter`	This writes to the underlying stream as XML.

Writing to text streams

Let's type some code to write text to a stream.

1. Create a new console application project named `WorkingWithStreams`, add it to the `Chapter09` workspace, and select the project as active for OmniSharp.

2. Import the `System.IO` and `System.Xml` namespaces, and statically import the `System.Console`, `System.Environment` and `System.IO.Path` types.

3. Define an array of `string` values, perhaps containing Viper pilot call signs, and create a `WorkWithText` method that enumerates the call signs, writing each one on its own line in a single text file, as shown in the following code:

```
// define an array of Viper pilot call signs
static string[] callsigns = new string[] {
  "Husker", "Starbuck", "Apollo", "Boomer",
  "Bulldog", "Athena", "Helo", "Racetrack" };

static void WorkWithText()
{
  // define a file to write to
  string textFile = Combine(CurrentDirectory, "streams.txt");

  // create a text file and return a helper writer
  StreamWriter text = File.CreateText(textFile);

  // enumerate the strings, writing each one
  // to the stream on a separate line
  foreach (string item in callsigns)
  {
    text.WriteLine(item);
  }
  text.Close(); // release resources

  // output the contents of the file
  WriteLine("{0} contains {1:N0} bytes.",
    arg0: textFile,
    arg1: new FileInfo(textFile).Length);

  WriteLine(File.ReadAllText(textFile));
}
```

4. In `Main`, call the `WorkWithText` method.

5. Run the application and view the result, as shown in the following output:

```
/Users/markjprice/Code/Chapter09/WorkingWithStreams/streams.txt
contains 60 bytes.

Husker

Starbuck

Apollo

Boomer

Bulldog

Athena

Helo

Racetrack
```

6. Open the file that was created and check that it contains the list of call signs.

Writing to XML streams

There are two ways to write an XML element, as follows:

- WriteStartElement and WriteEndElement: use this pair when an element might have child elements.

- , WriteElementString: use this when an element does not have children.

Now, let's try storing the same array of string values in an XML file.

1. Create a WorkWithXml method that enumerates the call signs, writing each one as an element in a single XML file, as shown in the following code:

```
static void WorkWithXml()
{
  // define a file to write to
  string xmlFile = Combine(CurrentDirectory, "streams.xml");

  // create a file stream
  FileStream xmlFileStream = File.Create(xmlFile);

  // wrap the file stream in an XML writer helper
  // and automatically indent nested elements
  XmlWriter xml = XmlWriter.Create(xmlFileStream,
    new XmlWriterSettings { Indent = true });

  // write the XML declaration
  xml.WriteStartDocument();

  // write a root element
  xml.WriteStartElement("callsigns");

  // enumerate the strings writing each one to the stream
  foreach (string item in callsigns)
  {
    xml.WriteElementString("callsign", item);
  }

  // write the close root element
  xml.WriteEndElement();

  // close helper and stream
  xml.Close();
  xmlFileStream.Close();

  // output all the contents of the file
  WriteLine("{0} contains {1:N0} bytes.",
    arg0: xmlFile,
```

```
    arg1: new FileInfo(xmlFile).Length);

  WriteLine(File.ReadAllText(xmlFile));
}
```

2. In `Main`, comment the previous method call, and add a call to the `WorkWithXml` method.

3. Run the application and view the result, as shown in the following the output:

```
/Users/markjprice/Code/Chapter09/WorkingWithStreams/streams.xml
contains 310 bytes.

<?xml version="1.0" encoding="utf-8"?>

<callsigns>

  <callsign>Husker</callsign>

  <callsign>Starbuck</callsign>

  <callsign>Apollo</callsign>

  <callsign>Boomer</callsign>

  <callsign>Bulldog</callsign>

  <callsign>Athena</callsign>

  <callsign>Helo</callsign>

  <callsign>Racetrack</callsign>

</callsigns>
```

Disposing of file resources

When you open a file to read or write to it, you are using resources outside of .NET. These are called unmanaged resources and must be disposed of when you are done working with them. To guarantee that they are disposed of, we can call the `Dispose` method inside of a `finally` block.

Let's improve our previous code that works with XML to properly dispose of its unmanaged resources.

1. Modify the `WorkWithXml` method, as shown highlighted in the following code:

```
static void WorkWithXml()
{
  FileStream xmlFileStream = null;
  XmlWriter xml = null;

  try
  {
```

```
  // define a file to write to
  string xmlFile = Combine(CurrentDirectory, "streams.xml");

  // create a file stream
  xmlFileStream = File.Create(xmlFile);

  // wrap the file stream in an XML writer helper
  // and automatically indent nested elements
  xml = XmlWriter.Create(xmlFileStream,
    new XmlWriterSettings { Indent = true });

  // write the XML declaration
  xml.WriteStartDocument();

  // write a root element
  xml.WriteStartElement("callsigns");

  // enumerate the strings writing each one to the stream
  foreach (string item in callsigns)
  {
    xml.WriteElementString("callsign", item);
  }

  // write the close root element
  xml.WriteEndElement();

  // close helper and stream
  xml.Close();
  xmlFileStream.Close();

  // output all the contents of the file
  WriteLine($"{0} contains {1:N0} bytes.",
    arg0: xmlFile,
    arg1: new FileInfo(xmlFile).Length);

  WriteLine(File.ReadAllText(xmlFile));
}
catch(Exception ex)
{
  // if the path doesn't exist the exception will be caught
  WriteLine($"{ex.GetType()} says {ex.Message}");
}
finally
{
  if (xml != null)
  {
    xml.Dispose();
    WriteLine("The XML writer's unmanaged resources have been
disposed.");
```

```
    }
    if (xmlFileStream != null)
    {
      xmlFileStream.Dispose();
      WriteLine("The file stream's unmanaged resources have been
disposed.");
    }
  }
}
```

You could also go back and modify the other methods you previously created but I will leave that as an optional exercise for you.

2. Run the application and view the result, as shown in the following output:

```
The XML writer's unmanaged resources have been disposed.
The file stream's unmanaged resources have been disposed.
```

Good Practice: Before calling `Dispose`, check that the object is not `null`.

You can simplify the code that needs to check for a `null` object and then call its `Dispose` method by using the `using` statement.

Confusingly, there are two uses for the `using` keyword: importing a namespace and generating a `finally` statement that calls `Dispose` on an object that implements `IDisposable`.

The compiler changes a `using` statement block into a `try-finally` statement without a `catch` statement. You can use nested `try` statements; so, if you do want to catch any exceptions, you can, as shown in the following code example:

```
using (FileStream file2 = File.OpenWrite(
  Path.Combine(path, "file2.txt")))
{
  using (StreamWriter writer2 = new StreamWriter(file2))
  {
    try
    {
      writer2.WriteLine("Welcome, .NET Core!");
    }
    catch(Exception ex)
    {
      WriteLine($"{ex.GetType()} says {ex.Message}");
    }
  } // automatically calls Dispose if the object is not null
} // automatically calls Dispose if the object is not null
```

Compressing streams

XML is relatively verbose, so it takes up more space in bytes than plain text. We can squeeze the XML using a common compression algorithm known as **GZIP**.

1. Import the following namespace:

```
using System.IO.Compression;
```

2. Add a `WorkWithCompression` method, which uses instances of `GZipSteam` to create a compressed file containing the same XML elements as before and then decompresses it while reading it and outputting to the console, as shown in the following code:

```
static void WorkWithCompression()
{
  // compress the XML output
  string gzipFilePath = Combine(
    CurrentDirectory, "streams.gzip");

  FileStream gzipFile = File.Create(gzipFilePath);

  using (GZipStream compressor = new GZipStream(
    gzipFile, CompressionMode.Compress))
  {
    using (XmlWriter xmlGzip = XmlWriter.Create(compressor))
    {
      xmlGzip.WriteStartDocument();
      xmlGzip.WriteStartElement("callsigns");

      foreach (string item in callsigns)
      {
        xmlGzip.WriteElementString("callsign", item);
      }
      // the normal call to WriteEndElement is not necessary
      // because when the XmlWriter disposes, it will
      // automatically end any elements of any depth
    }
  } // also closes the underlying stream

  // output all the contents of the compressed file
  WriteLine("{0} contains {1:N0} bytes.",
    gzipFilePath, new FileInfo(gzipFilePath).Length);

  WriteLine($"The compressed contents:");
  WriteLine(File.ReadAllText(gzipFilePath));

  // read a compressed file
  WriteLine("Reading the compressed XML file:");
  gzipFile = File.Open(gzipFilePath, FileMode.Open);
```

```
    using (GZipStream decompressor = new GZipStream(
      gzipFile, CompressionMode.Decompress))
    {
      using (XmlReader reader = XmlReader.Create(decompressor))
      {
        while (reader.Read()) // read the next XML node
        {
          // check if we are on an element node named callsign
          if ((reader.NodeType == XmlNodeType.Element)
            && (reader.Name == "callsign"))
          {
            reader.Read(); // move to the text inside element
            WriteLine($"{reader.Value}"); // read its value
          }
        }
      }
    }
}
```

3. In `Main`, leave the call to `WorkWithXml`, and add a call to `WorkWithCompression`, as shown in the following code:

```
static void Main(string[] args)
{
  // WorkWithText();
  WorkWithXml();
  WorkWithCompression();
}
```

4. Run the console application and compare the sizes of the XML file and the compressed XML file. It is less than half the size of the same XML without compression, as shown in the following edited output:

```
/Users/markjprice/Code/Chapter09/WorkingWithStreams/streams.xml
contains 310 bytes.
```

```
/Users/markjprice/Code/Chapter09/WorkingWithStreams/streams.gzip
contains 150 bytes.
```

Compressing with the Brotli algorithm

In .NET Core 2.1, Microsoft introduced an implementation of the Brotli compression algorithm. In performance, Brotli is similar to the algorithm used in DEFLATE and GZIP, but the output is about 20% denser.

1. Modify the `WorkWithCompression` method to have an optional parameter to indicate if Brotli should be used and to use Brotli by default, as shown highlighted in the following code:

```csharp
static void WorkWithCompression(bool useBrotli = true)
{
  string fileExt = useBrotli ? "brotli" : "gzip";

  // compress the XML output
  string filePath = Combine(
    CurrentDirectory, $"streams.{fileExt}");

  FileStream file = File.Create(filePath);

  Stream compressor;

  if (useBrotli)
  {
    compressor = new BrotliStream(file, CompressionMode.Compress);
  }
  else
  {
    compressor = new GZipStream(file, CompressionMode.Compress);
  }

  using (compressor)
  {
    using (XmlWriter xml = XmlWriter.Create(compressor))
    {
      xml.WriteStartDocument();
      xml.WriteStartElement("callsigns");
      foreach (string item in callsigns)
      {
        xml.WriteElementString("callsign", item);
      }
    }
  } // also closes the underlying stream

  // output all the contents of the compressed file
  WriteLine("{0} contains {1:N0} bytes.",
    filePath, new FileInfo(filePath).Length);

  WriteLine(File.ReadAllText(filePath));

  // read a compressed file
  WriteLine("Reading the compressed XML file:");
  file = File.Open(filePath, FileMode.Open);

  Stream decompressor;

  if (useBrotli)
  {
    decompressor = new BrotliStream(
```

```
      file, CompressionMode.Decompress);
}
else
{
  decompressor = new GZipStream(
    file, CompressionMode.Decompress);
}

using (decompressor)
{
  using (XmlReader reader = XmlReader.Create(decompressor))
  {
    while (reader.Read())
    {
      // check if we are on an element node named callsign
      if ((reader.NodeType == XmlNodeType.Element)
        && (reader.Name == "callsign"))
      {
        reader.Read(); // move to the text inside element
        WriteLine($"{reader.Value}"); // read its value
      }
    }
  }
}
}
```

2. Modify the `Main` method to call `WorkWithCompression` twice, once with the default using Brotli and once with GZIP, as shown in the following code:

```
WorkWithCompression();
WorkWithCompression(useBrotli: false);
```

3. Run the console application and compare the sizes of the two compressed XML files. Brotli is more than 21% denser, as shown in the following edited output:

```
/Users/markjprice/Code/Chapter09/WorkingWithStreams/streams.brotli
contains 118 bytes.
```

```
/Users/markjprice/Code/Chapter09/WorkingWithStreams/streams.gzip
contains 150 bytes.
```

High-performance streams using pipelines

In .NET Core 2.1, Microsoft introduced **pipelines**. Processing data from a stream correctly requires a lot of complex boilerplate code that is difficult to maintain. Testing on your local laptop often works with small example files, but it fails in the real world due to poor assumptions. Pipelines help with this.

More Information: Although pipelines are powerful for real-world use and eventually you will want to learn about them, a decent example gets complicated so I have no plans to cover them in this book. You can read a detailed description of the problem and how pipelines help at the following link: `https://blogs.msdn.microsoft.com/dotnet/2018/07/09/system-io-pipelines-high-performance-io-in-net/`

Asynchronous streams

With C# 8.0 and .NET Core 3.0, Microsoft introduced asynchronous processing of streams. You will learn about this in *Chapter 13, Improving Performance and Scalability Using Multitasking*.

More Information: You can complete a tutorial about async streams at the following link: `https://docs.microsoft.com/en-us/dotnet/csharp/tutorials/generate-consume-asynchronous-stream`

Encoding and decoding text

Text characters can be represented in different ways. For example, the alphabet can be encoded using Morse code into a series of dots and dashes for transmission over a telegraph line.

In a similar way, text inside a computer is stored as bits (ones and zeros) representing a code point within a code space. Most code points represent a single character, but they can also have other meanings like formatting.

For example, ASCII has a code space with 128 code points. .NET uses a standard called **Unicode** to encode text internally. Unicode has more than one million code points.

Sometimes, you will need to move text outside .NET for use by systems that do not use Unicode or use a variation of Unicode so it is important to learn how to convert between encodings.

The following table lists some alternative text encodings commonly used by computers:

Encoding	Description
ASCII	This encodes a limited range of characters using the lower seven bits of a byte.
UTF-8	This represents each Unicode code point as a sequence of one to four bytes.
UTF-7	This is designed to be more efficient over 7-bit channels than UTF-8 but it has security and robustness issues so UTF-8 is recommended over UTF-7.
UTF-16	This represents each Unicode code point as a sequence of one or two 16-bit integers.
UTF-32	This represents each Unicode code point as a 32-bit integer and is therefore a fixed-length encoding unlike the other Unicode encodings, which are all variable-length encodings.
ANSI/ISO encodings	This provides support for a variety of code pages that are used to support a specific language or group of languages.

In most cases today, UTF-8 is a good default, which is why it is literally the default encoding, that is, `Encoding.Default`.

Encoding strings as byte arrays

Let's explore text encodings.

1. Create a new console application project named `WorkingWithEncodings`, add it to the `Chapter09` workspace, and select the project as active for OmniSharp.

2. Import the `System.Text` namespace and statically import the `Console` class.

3. Add statements to the `Main` method to encode a `string` using an encoding chosen by the user, loop through each byte, and then decode it back into a `string` and output it, as shown in the following code:

```
WriteLine("Encodings");
WriteLine("[1] ASCII");
WriteLine("[2] UTF-7");
WriteLine("[3] UTF-8");
WriteLine("[4] UTF-16 (Unicode)");
WriteLine("[5] UTF-32");
WriteLine("[any other key] Default");

// choose an encoding
```

```
Write("Press a number to choose an encoding: ");
ConsoleKey number = ReadKey(intercept: false).Key;
WriteLine();
WriteLine();

Encoding encoder = number switch
{
  ConsoleKey.D1 => Encoding.ASCII,
  ConsoleKey.D2 => Encoding.UTF7,
  ConsoleKey.D3 => Encoding.UTF8,
  ConsoleKey.D4 => Encoding.Unicode,
  ConsoleKey.D5 => Encoding.UTF32,
              _ => Encoding.Default
};

// define a string to encode
string message = "A pint of milk is £1.99";

// encode the string into a byte array
byte[] encoded = encoder.GetBytes(message);

// check how many bytes the encoding needed
WriteLine("{0} uses {1:N0} bytes.",
  encoder.GetType().Name, encoded.Length);

// enumerate each byte
WriteLine($"BYTE  HEX  CHAR");
foreach (byte b in encoded)
{
  WriteLine($"{b,4} {b.ToString("X"),4} {(char)b,5}");
}

// decode the byte array back into a string and display it
string decoded = encoder.GetString(encoded);
WriteLine(decoded);
```

4. Run the application and press 1 to choose ASCII and note that when
    outputting the bytes, the pound sign (£) cannot be represented in ASCII,
    so it uses a question mark instead, as shown in the following output:

```
ASCIIEncodingSealed uses 23 bytes.

BYTE  HEX  CHAR
  65   41    A
  32   20
 112   70    p
 105   69    i
 110   6E    n
```

116	74	t
32	20	
111	6F	o
102	66	f
32	20	
109	6D	m
105	69	i
108	6C	l
107	6B	k
32	20	
105	69	i
115	73	s
32	20	
63	3F	?
49	31	1
46	2E	.
57	39	9
57	39	9

```
A pint of milk is ?1.99
```

5. Rerun the application and press 3 to choose UTF-8 and note that UTF-8 requires one extra byte (24 bytes instead of 23 bytes) but it can store the £ sign.

6. Rerun the application and press 4 to choose Unicode (UTF-16) and note that UTF-16 requires two bytes for every character, taking 46 total bytes, and it can store the £ sign. This encoding is used internally by .NET to store char and string values.

Encoding and decoding text in files

When using stream helper classes, such as StreamReader and StreamWriter, you can specify the encoding you want to use. As you write to the helper, the text will automatically be encoded, and as you read from the helper, the bytes will be automatically decoded.

To specify an encoding, pass the encoding as a second parameter to the helper type's constructor, as shown in the following code:

```
var reader = new StreamReader(stream, Encoding.UTF7);
var writer = new StreamWriter(stream, Encoding.UTF7);
```

Good Practice: Often, you won't have the choice of which encoding to use, because you will be generating a file for use by another system. However, if you do, pick one that uses the least number of bytes, but can store every character you need.

Serializing object graphs

Serialization is the process of converting a live object into a sequence of bytes using a specified format. **Deserialization** is the reverse process.

There are dozens of formats you can specify, but the two most common ones are **eXtensible Markup Language (XML)** and **JavaScript Object Notation (JSON)**.

Good Practice: JSON is more compact and is best for web and mobile applications. XML is more verbose but is better supported in more legacy systems. Use JSON to minimize the size of serialized object graphs. JSON is also a good choice when sending object graphs to web applications and mobile applications because JSON is the native serialization format for JavaScript and mobile apps often make calls over limited bandwidth, so the number of bytes is important.

.NET Core has multiple classes that will serialize to and from XML and JSON. We will start by looking at `XmlSerializer` and `JsonSerializer`.

Serializing as XML

Let's start by looking at XML, probably the world's most used serialization format (for now).

1. Create a new console application project named `WorkingWithSerialization`, add it to the `Chapter09` workspace, and select the project as active for OmniSharp.

    To show a typical example, we will define a custom class to store information about a person and then create an object graph using a list of `Person` instances with nesting.

2. Add a class named `Person` with a `Salary` property that is `protected`, meaning it is only accessible to itself and derived classes. To populate the salary, the class has a constructor with a single parameter to set the initial salary, as shown in the following code:

    ```
    using System;
    ```

```
using System.Collections.Generic;

namespace Packt.Shared
{
  public class Person
  {
    public Person(decimal initialSalary)
    {
      Salary = initialSalary;
    }

    public string FirstName { get; set; }
    public string LastName { get; set; }
    public DateTime DateOfBirth { get; set; }
    public HashSet<Person> Children { get; set; }
    protected decimal Salary { get; set; }
  }
}
```

3. Back in `Program.cs`, import the following namespaces:

```
using System;                      // DateTime
using System.Collections.Generic;  // List<T>, HashSet<T>
using System.Xml.Serialization;    // XmlSerializer
using System.IO;                   // FileStream
using Packt.Shared;                // Person
using static System.Console;
using static System.Environment;
using static System.IO.Path;
```

4. Add the following statements to the `Main` method:

```
// create an object graph
var people = new List<Person>
{
  new Person(30000M) { FirstName = "Alice",
    LastName = "Smith",
    DateOfBirth = new DateTime(1974, 3, 14) },

  new Person(40000M) { FirstName = "Bob",
    LastName = "Jones",
    DateOfBirth = new DateTime(1969, 11, 23) },

  new Person(20000M) { FirstName = "Charlie",
    LastName = "Cox",
    DateOfBirth = new DateTime(1984, 5, 4),
    Children = new HashSet<Person>
    { new Person(0M) { FirstName = "Sally",
      LastName = "Cox",
      DateOfBirth = new DateTime(2000, 7, 12) } } }
```

```
};

// create object that will format a List of Persons as XML
var xs = new XmlSerializer(typeof(List<Person>));

// create a file to write to
string path = Combine(CurrentDirectory, "people.xml");

using (FileStream stream = File.Create(path))
{
  // serialize the object graph to the stream
  xs.Serialize(stream, people);
}

WriteLine("Written {0:N0} bytes of XML to {1}",
  arg0: new FileInfo(path).Length,
  arg1: path);

WriteLine();

// Display the serialized object graph
WriteLine(File.ReadAllText(path));
```

5. Run the console application, view the result, and note that an exception is thrown, as shown in the following output:

```
Unhandled Exception: System.InvalidOperationException: Packt.
Shared.Person cannot be serialized because it does not have a
parameterless constructor.
```

6. Back in the `Person.cs` file, add the following statement to define a parameter-less constructor, as shown in the following code:

```
public Person() { }
```

The constructor does not need to do anything, but it must exist so that the `XmlSerializer` can call it to instantiate new `Person` instances during the deserialization process.

7. Rerun the console application and view the result, and note that the object graph is serialized as XML and the `Salary` property is not included, as shown in the following output:

```
Written 752 bytes of XML to
```

```
/Users/markjprice/Code/Chapter09/WorkingWithSerialization/people.
xml
```

```
<?xml version="1.0"?>
```

```
<ArrayOfPerson xmlns:xsi="http://www.w3.org/2001/XMLSchema-
instance" xmlns:xsd="http://www.w3.org/2001/XMLSchema">
```

```
<Person>
  <FirstName>Alice</FirstName>
  <LastName>Smith</LastName>
  <DateOfBirth>1974-03-14T00:00:00</DateOfBirth>
</Person>
<Person>
  <FirstName>Bob</FirstName>
  <LastName>Jones</LastName>
  <DateOfBirth>1969-11-23T00:00:00</DateOfBirth>
</Person>
<Person>
  <FirstName>Charlie</FirstName>
  <LastName>Cox</LastName>
  <DateOfBirth>1984-05-04T00:00:00</DateOfBirth>
  <Children>
    <Person>
      <FirstName>Sally</FirstName>
      <LastName>Cox</LastName>
      <DateOfBirth>2000-07-12T00:00:00</DateOfBirth>
    </Person>
  </Children>
</Person>
</ArrayOfPerson>
```

Generating compact XML

We could make the XML more compact using attributes instead of elements for some fields.

1. In the `Person.cs` file, import the `System.Xml.Serialization` namespace.

2. Decorate all the properties, except `Children`, with the `[XmlAttribute]` attribute, and set a short name for each property, as shown in the following code:

```
[XmlAttribute("fname")]
public string FirstName { get; set; }

[XmlAttribute("lname")]
public string LastName { get; set; }
```

```
[XmlAttribute("dob")]
public DateTime DateOfBirth { get; set; }
```

3. Rerun the application and note that the size of the file has been reduced from 752 to 462 bytes, a space saving of more than a third, as shown in the following output:

```
Written 462 bytes of XML to /Users/markjprice/Code/Chapter09/
WorkingWithSerialization/people.xml


<?xml version="1.0"?>
<ArrayOfPerson xmlns:xsi="http://www.w3.org/2001/XMLSchema-
instance" xmlns:xsd="http://www.w3.org/2001/XMLSchema">
    <Person fname="Alice" lname="Smith" dob="1974-03-14T00:00:00" />
    <Person fname="Bob" lname="Jones" dob="1969-11-23T00:00:00" />
    <Person fname="Charlie" lname="Cox" dob="1984-05-04T00:00:00">
      <Children>
        <Person fname="Sally" lname="Cox" dob="2000-07-12T00:00:00"
/>
      </Children>
    </Person>
</ArrayOfPerson>
```

Deserializing XML files

Now let's try deserializing the XML file back into live objects in memory.

1. Add statements to the end of the Main method to open the XML file and then deserialize it, as shown in the following code:

```
using (FileStream xmlLoad = File.Open(path, FileMode.Open))
{
  // deserialize and cast the object graph into a List of Person
  var loadedPeople = (List<Person>)xs.Deserialize(xmlLoad);

  foreach (var item in loadedPeople)
  {
    WriteLine("{0} has {1} children.",
      item.LastName, item.Children.Count);
  }
}
```

2. Rerun the application and note that the people are loaded successfully from the XML file, as shown in the following output:

```
Smith has 0 children.
Jones has 0 children.
Cox has 1 children.
```

There are many other attributes that can be used to control the XML generated.

Good Practice: When using `XmlSerializer`, remember that only the public fields and properties are included, and the type must have a parameter-less constructor. You can customize the output with attributes.

Serializing with JSON

One of the most popular .NET libraries for working with the JSON serialization format is `Newtonsoft.Json`, known as **Json.NET**. It is mature and powerful.

Let's see it in action.

1. Edit the `WorkingWithSerialization.csproj` file to add a package reference for the latest version of `Newtonsoft.Json`, as shown highlighted in the following markup:

```xml
<Project Sdk="Microsoft.NET.Sdk">

  <PropertyGroup>
    <OutputType>Exe</OutputType>
    <TargetFramework>netcoreapp3.0</TargetFramework>
  </PropertyGroup>

  <ItemGroup>
    <PackageReference Include="Newtonsoft.Json"
                      Version="12.0.2" />
  </ItemGroup>

</Project>
```

Good Practice: Search for NuGet packages on Microsoft's NuGet feed to discover the latest supported version, as shown at the following link: `https://www.nuget.org/packages/Newtonsoft.Json/`

2. Add statements to the end of the `Main` method to create a text file and then serialize the people into the file as JSON, as shown in the following code:

```csharp
// create a file to write to
string jsonPath = Combine(CurrentDirectory, "people.json");

using (StreamWriter jsonStream = File.CreateText(jsonPath))
{
  // create an object that will format as JSON
```

```
    var jss = new Newtonsoft.Json.JsonSerializer();

    // serialize the object graph into a string
    jss.Serialize(jsonStream, people);
}

WriteLine();
WriteLine("Written {0:N0} bytes of JSON to: {1}",
  arg0: new FileInfo(jsonPath).Length,
  arg1: jsonPath);

// Display the serialized object graph
WriteLine(File.ReadAllText(jsonPath));
```

3. Rerun the application and note that JSON requires less than half the number of bytes compared to XML with elements. It's even smaller than the XML file, which uses attributes, as shown in the following output:

```
Written 366 bytes of JSON to: /Users/markjprice/Code/Chapter09/
WorkingWithSerialization/people.json
```

```
[{"FirstName":"Alice","LastName":"Smith","DateOfBirth":"1974-
03-14T00:00:00","Children":null},{"FirstName":"Bob","LastN
ame":"Jones","DateOfBirth":"1969-11-23T00:00:00","Children
":null},{"FirstName":"Charlie","LastName":"Cox","DateOfBir
th":"1984-05-04T00:00:00","Children":[{"FirstName":"Sally","LastN-
ame":"Cox","DateOfBirth":"2000-07-12T00:00:00","Children":null}]}]
```

High-performance JSON processing

.NET Core 3.0 introduces a new namespace for working with JSON:
`System.Text.Json`, which is optimized for performance by leveraging APIs like `Span<T>`.

Also, Json.NET is implemented by reading UTF-16. It would be more performant to read and write JSON documents using UTF-8 because most network protocols including HTTP use UTF-8 and you can avoid transcoding UTF-8 to and from Json.NET's Unicode `string` values. With the new API, Microsoft achieved between 1.3x and 5x improvement, depending on the scenario.

 More Information: You can read more about the new `System.Text.Json` APIs at the following link: `https://devblogs.microsoft.com/dotnet/try-the-new-system-text-json-apis/`

The original author of Json.NET, James Newton-King, joined Microsoft and has been working with them to develop their new JSON types. As he says in a comment discussing the new JSON APIs, "Json.NET isn't going away," as shown in the following screenshot:

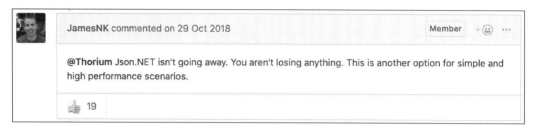

JamesNK commented on 29 Oct 2018   Member

@**Thorium** Json.NET isn't going away. You aren't losing anything. This is another option for simple and high performance scenarios.

👍 19

> **More Information**: You can read more about the issues solved by the new JSON APIs, including JamesNK's comments, at the following link: `https://github.com/dotnet/corefx/issues/33115`

Let's explore the new JSON APIs.

1. Import the `System.Threading.Tasks` namespace.

2. Modify the `Main` method to enable awaiting on tasks by changing `void` to `async Task`, as shown highlighted in the following code:

```
static async Task Main(string[] args)
```

3. Import the new JSON class for performing serialization using an alias to avoid conflicting names with the Json.NET one we used before, as shown in the following code:

```
using NuJson = System.Text.Json.JsonSerializer;
```

4. Add statements to open the JSON file, deserialize it, and output the names and counts of the children of the people, as shown in the following code:

```
using (FileStream jsonLoad = File.Open(
  jsonPath, FileMode.Open))
{
  // deserialize object graph into a List of Person
  var loadedPeople = (List<Person>)
    await NuJson.DeserializeAsync(
      utf8Json: jsonLoad,
      returnType: typeof(List<Person>));

  foreach (var item in loadedPeople)
  {
```

```
WriteLine("{0} has {1} children.",
    item.LastName, item.Children?.Count);
  }
}
```

5. Run the console application and view the result, as shown in the following output:

```
Smith has   children.
Jones has   children.
Cox has 1 children.
```

 Good Practice: Choose Json.NET for developer productivity and a large feature set or System.Text.Json for performance.

Practicing and exploring

Test your knowledge and understanding by answering some questions, get some hands-on practice, and explore this chapter's topics with more in-depth research.

Exercise 9.1 – Test your knowledge

Answer the following questions:

1. What is the difference between using the File class and the FileInfo class?
2. What is the difference between the ReadByte method and the Read method of a stream?
3. When would you use the StringReader, TextReader, and StreamReader classes?
4. What does the DeflateStream type do?
5. How many bytes per character does the UTF-8 encoding use?
6. What is an object graph?
7. What is the best serialization format to choose for minimizing space requirements?
8. What is the best serialization format to choose for cross-platform compatibility?
9. Why is it bad to use a string value like \Code\Chapter01 to represent a path and what should you do instead?
10. Where can you find information about NuGet packages and their dependencies?

Exercise 9.2 – Practice serializing as XML

Create a console application named `Exercise02` that creates a list of shapes, uses serialization to save it to the filesystem using XML, and then deserializes it back:

```
// create a list of Shapes to serialize
var listOfShapes = new List<Shape>
{
  new Circle { Colour = "Red", Radius = 2.5 },
  new Rectangle { Colour = "Blue", Height = 20.0, Width = 10.0 },
  new Circle { Colour = "Green", Radius = 8.0 },
  new Circle { Colour = "Purple", Radius = 12.3 },
  new Rectangle { Colour = "Blue", Height = 45.0, Width = 18.0 }
};
```

Shapes should have a read-only property named `Area` so that when you deserialize, you can output a list of shapes, including their areas, as shown here:

```
List<Shape> loadedShapesXml =
  serializerXml.Deserialize(fileXml) as List<Shape>;
foreach (Shape item in loadedShapesXml)
{
  WriteLine("{0} is {1} and has an area of {2:N2}",
    item.GetType().Name, item.Colour, item.Area);
}
```

This is what your output should look like when you run the application:

```
Loading shapes from XML:
Circle is Red and has an area of 19.63
Rectangle is Blue and has an area of 200.00
Circle is Green and has an area of 201.06
Circle is Purple and has an area of 475.29
Rectangle is Blue and has an area of 810.00
```

Exercise 9.3 – Explore topics

Use the following links to read more on this chapter's topics:

- **File System and the Registry (C# Programming Guide)**: https://docs.microsoft.com/en-us/dotnet/csharp/programming-guide/file-system/

- **Character encoding in .NET**: https://docs.microsoft.com/en-us/dotnet/articles/standard/base-types/character-encoding

- **Serialization (C#)**: https://docs.microsoft.com/en-us/dotnet/articles/csharp/programming-guide/concepts/serialization/

- **Serializing to Files, TextWriters, and XmlWriters**: https://docs.
microsoft.com/en-us/dotnet/articles/csharp/programming-guide/
concepts/linq/serializing-to-files-textwriters-and-xmlwriters

- **Newtonsoft Json.NET**: http://www.newtonsoft.com/json

Summary

In this chapter, you learned how to read from and write to text files and XML files, how to compress and decompress files, how to encode and decode text, and how to serialize an object into JSON and XML (and deserialize it back again).

In the next chapter, you will learn how to protect data and files using hashing, signing encryption, authentication, and authorization.

Chapter 10

Protecting Your Data
and Applications

This chapter is about protecting your data from being viewed by malicious users using encryption, and from being manipulated or corrupted using hashing and signing.

In .NET Core 2.1, Microsoft introduced new Span<T>-based cryptography APIs for hashing, random number generation, asymmetric signature generation and processing, and RSA encryption. This chapter covers the following topics:

- Understanding the vocabulary of protection
- Encrypting and decrypting data
- Hashing data
- Signing data
- Generating random numbers
- What's new in cryptography?
- Authenticating and authorizing users

Understanding the vocabulary of protection

There are many techniques to protect your data; below we'll briefly introduce six of the most popular ones and you will see more detailed explanations and practical implementations throughout this chapter:

- **Encryption and decryption**: These are a two-way process to convert your data from clear-text into crypto-text and back again.
- **Hashes**: This is a one-way process to generate a hash value to securely store passwords, or can be used to detect malicious changes or corruption of your data.

- **Signatures**: This technique is used to ensure that data has come from someone you trust by validating a signature that has been applied to some data against someone's public key.

- **Authentication**: This technique is used to identify someone by checking their credentials.

- **Authorization**: This technique is used to ensure that someone has permission to perform an action or work with some data by checking the roles or groups they belong to.

Good Practice: If security is important to you (and it should be!), then hire an experienced security expert for guidance rather than relying on advice found online. It is very easy to make small mistakes and leave your applications and data vulnerable without realizing until it is too late!

Keys and key sizes

Protection algorithms often use a **key**. Keys are represented by byte arrays of varying size.

Good Practice: Choose a bigger key size for stronger protection.

Keys can be symmetric (also known as shared or secret because the same key is used to encrypt and decrypt) or asymmetric (a public-private key pair where the public key is used to encrypt and only the private key can be used to decrypt).

Good Practice: Symmetric key encryption algorithms are fast and can encrypt large amounts of data using a stream. Asymmetric key encryption algorithms are slow and can only encrypt small byte arrays.

In the real world, get the best of both worlds by using a symmetric key to encrypt your data, and an asymmetric key to share the symmetric key. This is how **Secure Sockets Layer** (**SSL**) encryption on the internet works.

Keys come in various byte array sizes.

IVs and block sizes

When encrypting large amounts of data, there are likely to be repeating sequences. For example, in an English document, in the sequence of characters, `the` would appear frequently, and each time it might get encrypted as `hQ2`. A good cracker would use this knowledge to make it easier to crack the encryption, as shown in the following output:

```
When the wind blew hard the umbrella broke.

5:s4&hQ2aj#D f9d1d£8fh"&hQ2s0)an DF8SFd#][1
```

We can avoid repeating sequences by dividing data into **blocks**. After encrypting a block, a byte array value is generated from that block, and this value is fed into the next block to adjust the algorithm so that `the` isn't encrypted in the same way. To encrypt the first block, we need a byte array to feed in. This is called the **initialization vector (IV)**.

Good Practice: Choose a small block size for stronger encryption.

Salts

A **salt** is a random byte array that is used as an additional input to a one-way hash function. If you do not use a salt when generating hashes, then when many of your users register with `123456` as their password (about 8% of users still did this in 2016!), they will all have the same hashed value, and their accounts will be vulnerable to a dictionary attack.

More Information: Dictionary Attacks 101: `https://blog.codinghorror.com/dictionary-attacks-101/`

When a user registers, the salt should be randomly generated and concatenated with their chosen password before being hashed. The output (but not the original password) is stored with the salt in the database.

Then, when the user next logs in and enters their password, you look up their salt, concatenate it with the entered password, regenerate a hash, and then compare its value with the hash stored in the database. If they are the same, you know they entered the correct password.

Generating keys and IVs

Keys and IVs are byte arrays. Both of the two parties that want to exchange encrypted data need the key and IV values, but byte arrays can be difficult to exchange reliably.

You can reliably generate a key or IV using a **password-based key derivation function (PBKDF2)**. A good one is the `Rfc2898DeriveBytes` class, which takes a password, a salt, and an iteration count, and then generates keys and IVs by making calls to its `GetBytes` method.

 Good Practice: The salt size should be 8 bytes or larger, and the iteration count should be greater than zero. The minimum recommended number of iterations is 1,000.

Encrypting and decrypting data

In .NET Core, there are multiple encryption algorithms you can choose from.

Some algorithms are implemented by the operating system and their names are suffixed with `CryptoServiceProvider`. Some algorithms are implemented in .NET Core and their names are suffixed with `Managed`.

Some algorithms use symmetric keys, and some use asymmetric keys. The main asymmetric encryption algorithm is RSA.

Symmetric encryption algorithms use `CryptoStream` to encrypt or decrypt large amounts of bytes efficiently. Asymmetric algorithms can only handle small amounts of bytes, stored in a byte array instead of a stream.

The most common symmetric encryption algorithms derive from the `abstract` class named `SymmetricAlgorithm` and are shown in the following list:

- AES
- DESCryptoServiceProvider
- TripleDESCryptoServiceProvider
- RC2CryptoServiceProvider
- RijndaelManaged

If you need to write code to decrypt some data sent by an external system, then you will have to use whatever algorithm the external system used to encrypt the data. Or if you need to send encrypted data to a system that can only decrypt using a specific algorithm then again you will not have a choice of algorithm.

If your code will both encrypt and decrypt then you can choose the algorithm that best suits your requirements for strength, performance, and so on.

Good Practice: Choose the **Advanced Encryption Standard (AES)**, which is based on the Rijndael algorithm for symmetric encryption. Choose RSA for asymmetric encryption. Do not confuse RSA with DSA. **Digital Signature Algorithm (DSA)** cannot encrypt data. It can only generate hashes and signatures.

Encrypting symmetrically with AES

To make it easier to reuse your protection code in the future, we will create a `static` class named `Protector` in its own class library.

1. In the `Code` folder, create a folder named `Chapter10`, with two subfolders named `CryptographyLib` and `EncryptionApp`.

2. In Visual Studio Code, save a workspace as `Chapter10` in the `Chapter10` folder.

3. Add the folder named `CryptographyLib` to the workspace.

4. Navigate to **Terminal | New Terminal**.

5. In **Terminal**, enter the following command:

    ```
    dotnet new classlib
    ```

6. Add the folder named `EncryptionApp` to the workspace.

7. Navigate to **Terminal | New Terminal** and select `EncryptionApp`.

8. In **Terminal**, enter the following command:

    ```
    dotnet new console
    ```

9. In **EXPLORER**, expand `CryptographyLib` and rename the `Class1.cs` file to `Protector.cs`.

10. In the `EncryptionApp` project folder, open the file named `EncryptionApp.csproj`, and add a package reference to the `CryptographyLib` library, as shown highlighted in the following markup:

    ```
    <Project Sdk="Microsoft.NET.Sdk">

      <PropertyGroup>
        <OutputType>Exe</OutputType>
        <TargetFramework>netcoreapp3.0</TargetFramework>
      </PropertyGroup>

      <ItemGroup>
    ```

```
  <ProjectReference
    Include="..\CryptographyLib\CryptographyLib.csproj" />
  </ItemGroup>

</Project>
```

11. In **Terminal**, enter the following command:

```
dotnet build
```

12. Open the `Protector.cs` file and change its contents to define a static class named `Protector` with fields for storing a salt byte array and a number of iterations, and methods to `Encrypt` and `Decrypt`, as shown in the following code:

```
using System;
using System.Collections.Generic;
using System.IO;
using System.Security.Cryptography;
using System.Security.Principal;
using System.Text;
using System.Xml.Linq;
using static System.Convert;

namespace Packt.Shared
{
  public static class Protector
  {
    // salt size must be at least 8 bytes, we will use 16 bytes
    private static readonly byte[] salt =
      Encoding.Unicode.GetBytes("7BANANAS");

    // iterations must be at least 1000, we will use 2000
    private static readonly int iterations = 2000;

    public static string Encrypt(
      string plainText, string password)
    {
      byte[] encryptedBytes;
      byte[] plainBytes = Encoding.Unicode
        .GetBytes(plainText);
      var aes = Aes.Create();
      var pbkdf2 = new Rfc2898DeriveBytes(
        password, salt, iterations);
      aes.Key = pbkdf2.GetBytes(32); // set a 256-bit key
```

```csharp
    aes.IV = pbkdf2.GetBytes(16); // set a 128-bit IV

    using (var ms = new MemoryStream())
    {
      using (var cs = new CryptoStream(
        ms, aes.CreateEncryptor(),
        CryptoStreamMode.Write))
      {
        cs.Write(plainBytes, 0, plainBytes.Length);
      }
      encryptedBytes = ms.ToArray();
    }

    return Convert.ToBase64String(encryptedBytes);
  }

  public static string Decrypt(
    string cryptoText, string password)
  {
    byte[] plainBytes;
    byte[] cryptoBytes = Convert
      .FromBase64String(cryptoText);
    var aes = Aes.Create();
    var pbkdf2 = new Rfc2898DeriveBytes(
      password, salt, iterations);
    aes.Key = pbkdf2.GetBytes(32);
    aes.IV = pbkdf2.GetBytes(16);

    using (var ms = new MemoryStream())
    {
      using (var cs = new CryptoStream(
        ms, aes.CreateDecryptor(),
        CryptoStreamMode.Write))
      {
        cs.Write(cryptoBytes, 0, cryptoBytes.Length);
      }
      plainBytes = ms.ToArray();
    }

    return Encoding.Unicode.GetString(plainBytes);
  }
 }
}
```

Note the following points about the preceding code:

- ○ We used double the recommended salt size and iteration count.
- ○ Although the salt and iteration count can be hardcoded, the password *must* be passed at runtime when calling the Encrypt and Decrypt methods.
- ○ We use a temporary MemoryStream type to store the results of encrypting and decrypting, and then call ToArray to turn the stream into a byte array.
- ○ We convert the encrypted byte arrays to and from a Base64 encoding to make them easier to read.

 Good Practice: Never hardcode a password in your source code because, even after compilation, the password can be read in the assembly by using disassembler tools.

13. In the EncryptionApp project, open the Program.cs file and then import the namespace for the Protector class and statically import the Console class, as shown in the following code:

```
using Packt.Shared;
using static System.Console;
```

14. In Main, add statements to prompt the user for a message and a password, and then encrypt and decrypt, as shown in the following code:

```
Write("Enter a message that you want to encrypt: ");
string message = ReadLine();
Write("Enter a password: ");
string password = ReadLine();

string cryptoText = Protector.Encrypt(message, password);

WriteLine($"Encrypted text: {cryptoText}");
Write("Enter the password: ");
string password2 = ReadLine();

try
{
  string clearText = Protector.Decrypt(cryptoText, password2);
  WriteLine($"Decrypted text: {clearText}");
}
catch (CryptographicException ex)
{
```

```
WriteLine("{0}\nMore details: {1}",
  arg0: "You entered the wrong password!",
  arg1: ex.Message);
}
catch (Exception ex)
{
  WriteLine("Non-cryptographic exception: {0}, {1}",
    arg0: ex.GetType().Name,
    arg1: ex.Message);
}
```

15. Run the console application, try entering a message and password, and view the result, as shown in the following output:

```
Enter a message that you want to encrypt: Hello Bob
Enter a password: secret
Encrypted text: pV5qPDf1CCZmGzUMH2gapFSkn5731g7tMj5ajice3cQ=
Enter the password: secret
Decrypted text: Hello Bob
```

16. Rerun the application and try entering a message and password, but this time enter the password incorrectly after encrypting and view the output:

```
Enter a message that you want to encrypt: Hello Bob
Enter a password: secret
Encrypted text: pV5qPDf1CCZmGzUMH2gapFSkn5731g7tMj5ajice3cQ=
Enter the password: 123456
You entered the wrong password!
More details: Padding is invalid and cannot be removed.
```

Hashing data

In .NET Core, there are multiple hash algorithms you can choose from. Some do not use any key, some use symmetric keys, and some use asymmetric keys.

There are two important factors to consider when choosing a hash algorithm:

- **Collision resistance**: How rare is it to find two inputs that share the same hash?
- **Preimage resistance**: For a hash, how difficult would it be to find another input that shares the same hash?

Some common non-keyed hashing algorithms are shown in the following table:

Algorithm	Hash size	Description
MD5	16 bytes	This is commonly used because it is fast, but it is not collision-resistant
SHA1	20 bytes	The use of SHA1 on the internet has been deprecated since 2011
SHA256 SHA384 SHA512	32 bytes 48 bytes 64 bytes	These are the **Secure Hashing Algorithm 2nd generation** (**SHA2**) algorithms with different hash sizes

Good Practice: Avoid MD5 and SHA1 because they have known weaknesses. Choose a larger hash size to reduce the possibility of repeated hashes. The first publicly known MD5 collision happened in 2010. The first publicly known SHA1 collision happened in 2017. You can read more at the following link: https://arstechnica.co.uk/information-technology/2017/02/at-deaths-door-for-years-widely-used-sha1-function-is-now-dead/

Hashing with the commonly used SHA256

We will now add a class to represent a user stored in memory, a file, or a database. We will use a dictionary to store multiple users in memory.

1. In the `CryptographyLib` class library project, add a new class file named `User.cs`, as shown in the following code:

```
namespace Packt.Shared
{
  public class User
  {
    public string Name { get; set; }
    public string Salt { get; set; }
    public string SaltedHashedPassword { get; set; }
  }
}
```

2. Add statements to the `Protector` class to declare a dictionary to store users and define two methods, one to register a new user and one to validate their password when they subsequently log in, as shown in the following code:

```
private static Dictionary<string, User> Users =
  new Dictionary<string, User>();
```

```
public static User Register(
  string username, string password)
{
  // generate a random salt
  var rng = RandomNumberGenerator.Create();
  var saltBytes = new byte[16];
  rng.GetBytes(saltBytes);
  var saltText = Convert.ToBase64String(saltBytes);

  // generate the salted and hashed password
  var saltedhashedPassword = SaltAndHashPassword(
    password, saltText);

  var user = new User
  {
    Name = username, Salt = saltText,
    SaltedHashedPassword = saltedhashedPassword
  };
  Users.Add(user.Name, user);

  return user;
}

public static bool CheckPassword(
  string username, string password)
{
  if (!Users.ContainsKey(username))
  {
    return false;
  }
  var user = Users[username];

  // re-generate the salted and hashed password
  var saltedhashedPassword = SaltAndHashPassword(
    password, user.Salt);

  return (saltedhashedPassword == user.SaltedHashedPassword);
}

private static string SaltAndHashPassword(
  string password, string salt)
{
```

```
    var sha = SHA256.Create();
    var saltedPassword = password + salt;
    return Convert.ToBase64String(
      sha.ComputeHash(Encoding.Unicode.GetBytes(
      saltedPassword)));
  }
```

3. Create a new console application project named `HashingApp`, add it to the workspace, and select the project as active for OmniSharp.

4. Add a reference to the `CryptographyLib` assembly as you did before and import the `Packt.Shared` namespace.

5. In the `Main` method, add statements to register a user and prompt to register a second user, and then prompt to log in as one of those users and validate the password, as shown in the following code:

```
WriteLine("Registering Alice with Pa$$w0rd.");
var alice = Protector.Register("Alice", "Pa$$w0rd");
WriteLine($"Name: {alice.Name}");
WriteLine($"Salt: {alice.Salt}");
WriteLine("Password (salted and hashed): {0}",
  arg0: alice.SaltedHashedPassword);
WriteLine();

Write("Enter a new user to register: ");
string username = ReadLine();
Write($"Enter a password for {username}: ");
string password = ReadLine();
var user = Protector.Register(username, password);
WriteLine($"Name: {user.Name}");
WriteLine($"Salt: {user.Salt}");
WriteLine("Password (salted and hashed): {0}",
  arg0: user.SaltedHashedPassword);
WriteLine();

bool correctPassword = false;
while (!correctPassword)
{
  Write("Enter a username to log in: ");
  string loginUsername = ReadLine();
  Write("Enter a password to log in: ");
  string loginPassword = ReadLine();

  correctPassword = Protector.CheckPassword(
    loginUsername, loginPassword);

  if (correctPassword)
  {
```

```
      WriteLine($"Correct! {loginUsername} has been logged in.");
    }
    else
    {
      WriteLine("Invalid username or password. Try again.");
    }
  }
```

When using multiple projects, remember to use a Terminal window for the correct console application before entering the `dotnet build` and `dotnet run` commands.

6. Run the console application, register a new user with the same password as Alice, and view the result, as shown in the following output:

```
Registering Alice with Pa$$w0rd.

Name: Alice

Salt: I1I1dzIjkd7EYDf/6jaf4w==

Password (salted and hashed): pIoadjE4W/XaRFkqS3br3UuAuPv/3LVQ8kzj
6mvcz+s=


Enter a new user to register: Bob

Enter a password for Bob: Pa$$w0rd

Name: Bob

Salt: 1X7ym/UjxTiuEWBC/vIHpw==

Password (salted and hashed):
DoBFtDhKeN0aaaLVdErtrZ3mpZSvpWDQ9TXDosTq0sQ=


Enter a username to log in: Alice

Enter a password to log in: secret

Invalid username or password. Try again.

Enter a username to log in: Bob

Enter a password to log in: secret

Invalid username or password. Try again.

Enter a username to log in: Bob

Enter a password to log in: Pa$$w0rd

Correct! Bob has been logged in.
```

Even if two users register with the same password, they have randomly generated salts so that their salted and hashed passwords are different.

Signing data

To prove that some data has come from someone we trust, it can be signed. Actually, you do not sign the data itself; instead, you sign a hash of the data.

We will be using the SHA256 algorithm for generating the hash, combined with the RSA algorithm for signing the hash.

We could use DSA for both hashing and signing. DSA is faster than RSA for generating a signature, but it is slower than RSA for validating a signature. Since a signature is generated once but validated many times, it is best to have faster validation than a generation.

More Information: The RSA algorithm is based on the factorization of large integers, compared to the DSA algorithm, which is based on the discrete logarithm calculation. You can read more at the following link: http://mathworld.wolfram. com/RSAEncryption.html

Signing with SHA256 and RSA

Let's explore signing data and checking the signature with a public key.

1. In the `CryptographyLib` class library project, add statements to the `Protector` class to declare a field for the public key, two extension methods to convert an RSA instance to and from XML, and two methods to generate and validate a signature, as shown in the following code:

```
public static string PublicKey;

public static string ToXmlStringExt(
  this RSA rsa, bool includePrivateParameters)
{
  var p = rsa.ExportParameters(includePrivateParameters);
  XElement xml;
  if (includePrivateParameters)
  {
    xml = new XElement("RSAKeyValue",
      new XElement("Modulus", ToBase64String(p.Modulus)),
      new XElement("Exponent", ToBase64String(p.Exponent)),
      new XElement("P", ToBase64String(p.P)),
      new XElement("Q", ToBase64String(p.Q)),
      new XElement("DP", ToBase64String(p.DP)),
      new XElement("DQ", ToBase64String(p.DQ)),
      new XElement("InverseQ", ToBase64String(p.InverseQ))
```

```
    );
  }
  else
  {
    xml = new XElement("RSAKeyValue",
      new XElement("Modulus", ToBase64String(p.Modulus)),
      new XElement("Exponent",
        ToBase64String(p.Exponent)));
  }
  return xml?.ToString();
}

public static void FromXmlStringExt(
  this RSA rsa, string parametersAsXml)
{
  var xml = XDocument.Parse(parametersAsXml);
    var root = xml.Element("RSAKeyValue");
    var p = new RSAParameters
  {
    Modulus = FromBase64String(
      root.Element("Modulus").Value),
    Exponent = FromBase64String(
      root.Element("Exponent").Value)
  };

  if (root.Element("P") != null)
  {
    p.P = FromBase64String(root.Element("P").Value);
    p.Q = FromBase64String(root.Element("Q").Value);
    p.DP = FromBase64String(root.Element("DP").Value);
    p.DQ = FromBase64String(root.Element("DQ").Value);
    p.InverseQ = FromBase64String(
      root.Element("InverseQ").Value);
  }
  rsa.ImportParameters(p);
}

public static string GenerateSignature(string data)
{
  byte[] dataBytes = Encoding.Unicode.GetBytes(data);
  var sha = SHA256.Create();
  var hashedData = sha.ComputeHash(dataBytes);
```

```
    var rsa = RSA.Create();
    PublicKey = rsa.ToXmlStringExt(false); // exclude private key

    return ToBase64String(rsa.SignHash(hashedData,
      HashAlgorithmName.SHA256, RSASignaturePadding.Pkcs1));
}

public static bool ValidateSignature(
  string data, string signature)
{
  byte[] dataBytes = Encoding.Unicode.GetBytes(data);
  var sha = SHA256.Create();
  var hashedData = sha.ComputeHash(dataBytes);
  byte[] signatureBytes = FromBase64String(signature);
  var rsa = RSA.Create();
  rsa.FromXmlStringExt(PublicKey);

  return rsa.VerifyHash(hashedData, signatureBytes,
    HashAlgorithmName.SHA256, RSASignaturePadding.Pkcs1);
}
```

Note the following from the preceding code:

- The RSA type has two methods named ToXmlString and FromXmlString. These serialize and deserialize the RSAParameters structure, which contains the public and private keys. However, the implementation of these methods on macOS throws a PlatformNotSupportedException exception. I have had to re-implement them myself as extension methods named ToXmlStringExt and FromXmlStringExt using LINQ to XML types such as XDocument, which you will learn about in *Chapter 12, Querying and Manipulating Data Using LINQ*.

- Only the public part of the public-private key pair needs to be made available to the code that is checking the signature so that we can pass the false value when we call the ToXmlStringExt method. The private part is required to sign data and must be kept secret because anyone with the private part can sign data as if they are you!

- The hash algorithm used to generate the hash from the data by calling the SignHash method must match the hash algorithm set when calling the VerifyHash method. In the preceding code, we used SHA256.

Now we can test signing some data and checking its signature.

2. Create a new console application project named `SigningApp`, add it to the workspace, and select the project as active for OmniSharp.

3. Add a reference to the `CryptographyLib` assembly, in `Program.cs` import the appropriate namespaces, and then in `Main`, add statements to prompt the user to enter some text, sign it, check its signature, then modify the text, check the signature again to deliberately cause a mismatch, as shown in the following code:

```
Write("Enter some text to sign: ");
string data = ReadLine();
var signature = Protector.GenerateSignature(data);
WriteLine($"Signature: {signature}");
WriteLine("Public key used to check signature:");
WriteLine(Protector.PublicKey);

if (Protector.ValidateSignature(data, signature))
{
  WriteLine("Correct! Signature is valid.");
}
else
{
  WriteLine("Invalid signature.");
}

// simulate a fake signature by replacing the
// first character with an X
var fakeSignature = signature.Replace(signature[0], 'X');

if (Protector.ValidateSignature(data, fakeSignature))
{
  WriteLine("Correct! Signature is valid.");
}
else
{
  WriteLine($"Invalid signature: {fakeSignature}");
}
```

4. Run the console application and enter some text, as shown in the following output (edited for length):

```
Enter some text to sign: The cat sat on the mat.
Signature: BXSTdM...4Wrg==
Public key used to check signature:
<RSAKeyValue>
```

```
<Modulus>nHtwl3...mw3w==</Modulus>

<Exponent>AQAB</Exponent>

</RSAKeyValue>

Correct! Signature is valid.

Invalid signature: XXSTdM...4Wrg==
```

Generating random numbers

Sometimes you need to generate random numbers, perhaps in a game that simulates rolls of a die, or for use with cryptography in encryption or signing. There are a couple of classes that can generate random numbers in .NET Core.

Generating random numbers for games

In scenarios that don't need truly random numbers like games, you can create an instance of the Random class, as shown in the following code example:

```
var r = new Random();
```

Random has a constructor with a parameter for specifying a seed value used to initialize its pseudo-random number generator, as shown in the following code:

```
var r = new Random(Seed: 12345);
```

 Good Practice: Shared seed values act as a secret key, so if you use the same random number generation algorithm with the same seed value in two applications, then they can generate the same "random" sequences of numbers. Sometimes this is necessary, for example, when synchronizing a GPS receiver with a satellite. But usually, you want to keep your seed secret.

As you learned in *Chapter 2, Speaking C#*, parameter names should use camel case. The developer who defined the constructor for the Random class broke this convention! The parameter name should be seed, not Seed.

Once you have a Random object, you can call its methods to generate random numbers, as shown in the following code examples:

```
int dieRoll = r.Next(minValue: 1, maxValue: 7); // returns 1 to 6
double randomReal = r.NextDouble(); // returns 0.0 to 1.0
var arrayOfBytes = new byte[256];
r.NextBytes(arrayOfBytes); // 256 random bytes in an array
```

The `Next` method takes two parameters: `minValue` and `maxValue`. Now, `maxValue` is not the maximum value that the method returns! It is an *exclusive* upper bound, meaning it is one more than the maximum value.

Generating random numbers for cryptography

`Random` generates pseudo-random numbers. This is not good enough for cryptography! If the random numbers are not truly random then they are repeatable, and if they are repeatable, then a cracker can break your protection.

For truly random numbers, you must use a `RandomNumberGenerator` derived type, such as `RNGCryptoServiceProvider`.

We will now create a method to generate a truly random byte array that can be used in algorithms like encryption for key and IV values.

1. In the `CryptographyLib` class library project, add statements to the `Protector` class to define a method to get a random key or IV for use in encryption, as shown in the following code:

    ```
    public static byte[] GetRandomKeyOrIV(int size)
    {
      var r = RandomNumberGenerator.Create();
      var data = new byte[size];
      r.GetNonZeroBytes(data);
      // data is an array now filled with
      // cryptographically strong random bytes
      return data;
    }
    ```

    Now we can test the random bytes generated for a truly random encryption key or IV.

2. Create a new console application project named `RandomizingApp`, add it to the workspace, and select the project as active for OmniSharp.

3. Add a reference to the `CryptographyLib` assembly, import the appropriate namespaces, and in `Main`, add statements to prompt the user to enter a size of byte array and then generate random byte values and write them to the console, as shown in the following code:

    ```
    Write("How big do you want the key (in bytes): ");
    string size = ReadLine();

    byte[] key = Protector.GetRandomKeyOrIV(int.Parse(size));
    ```

```
WriteLine($"Key as byte array:");
for (int b = 0; b < key.Length; b++)
{
  Write($"{key[b]:x2} ");
  if (((b + 1) % 16) == 0) WriteLine();
}
WriteLine();
```

4. Run the console application, enter a typical size for the key, such as 256, and view the randomly generated key, as shown in the following output:

```
How big do you want the key (in bytes): 256
Key as byte array:
f1 57 3f 44 80 e7 93 dc 8e 55 04 6c 76 6f 51 b9
e8 84 59 e5 8d eb 08 d5 e6 59 65 20 b1 56 fa 68
...
```

What's new in cryptography

An automatic benefit of using .NET Core 3.0 is that algorithms for hashing, HMAC, random number generation, asymmetric signature generation and processing, and RSA encryption have been rewritten to use Span<T> so they achieve better performance. For example, Rfc2898DeriveBytes is about 15% faster.

Some enhancements have been made to the cryptography APIs that are useful in advanced scenarios, including:

*   Signing and verifying of CMS/PKCS #7 messages.

*   Enable X509Certificate.GetCertHash and X509Certificate. GetCertHashString to get certificate thumbprint values using algorithms other than SHA-1.

*   The CryptographicOperations class with useful methods like ZeroMemory to securely clear memory.

*   RandomNumberGenerator has a Fill method that will fill a span with random values and doesn't require you to manage an IDisposable resource.

- APIs to read, validate, and create RFC 3161 `TimestampToken` values.
- Elliptic-Curve Diffie-Hellman support using the `ECDiffieHellman` classes.
- Support for RSA-OAEP-SHA2 and RSA-PSS on Linux platforms.

Authenticating and authorizing users

Authentication is the process of verifying the identity of a user by validating their credentials against some authority. Credentials include a username and password combination, or a fingerprint or face scan.

Once authenticated, the authority can make claims about the user, for example, what their email address is, and what groups or roles they belong to.

Authorization is the process of verifying membership of groups or roles before allowing access to resources such as application functions and data. Although authorization can be based on individual identity, it is good security practice to authorize based on group or role membership (that can be indicated via claims) even when there is only one user in the role or group. This is because that allows the user's membership to change in future without reassigning the user's individual access rights.

For example, instead of assigning access rights to launch a nuclear strike to Donald Trump (a user), you would assign access rights to launch a nuclear strike to the President of the United States (a role) and then add Donald Trump as a member of that role.

There are multiple authentication and authorization mechanisms to choose from. They all implement a pair of interfaces in the `System.Security.Principal` namespace: `IIdentity` and `IPrincipal`.

`IIdentity` represents a user, so it has a `Name` property and an `IsAuthenticated` property to indicate if they are anonymous or if they have been successfully authenticated from their credentials.

The most common class that implements this interface is `GenericIdentity`, which inherits from `ClaimsIdentity`, as shown in the following diagram:

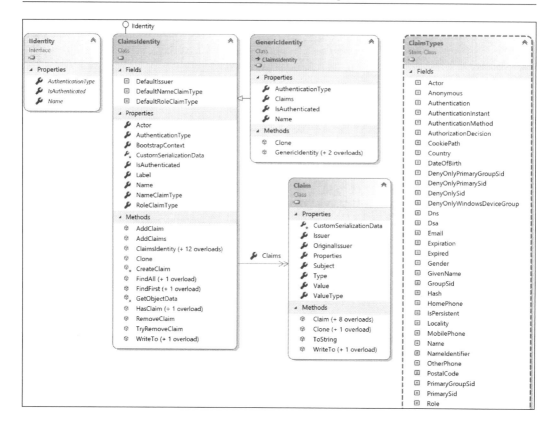

Each ClaimsIdentity class has a Claims property that is shown in the preceding diagram as a double-arrowhead between the ClaimsIdentity and Claim classes.

The Claim objects have a Type property that indicates if the claim is for their name, their membership of a role or group, their date of birth, and so on.

IPrincipal is used to associate an identity with the roles and groups that they are members of, so it can be used for authorization purposes. The current thread executing your code has a CurrentPrincipal property that can be set to any object that implements IPrincipal, and it will be checked when permission is needed to perform a secure action.

The most common class that implements this interface is GenericPrincipal, which inherits from ClaimsPrincipal, as shown in the following diagram:

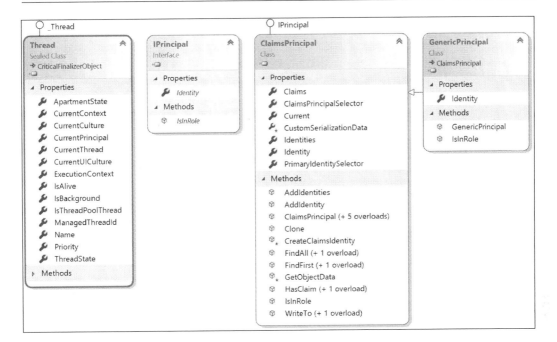

Implementing authentication and authorization

Let's explore authentication and authorization.

1. In the `CryptographyLib` class library project, add a property to the `User` class to store an array of roles, as shown in the following code:

    ```
    public string[] Roles { get; set; }
    ```

2. Modify the `Register` method in the `Protector` class to allow an array of roles to be passed as an optional parameter, as shown highlighted in the following code:

    ```
    public static User Register(
      string username, string password,
      string[] roles = null)
    ```

3. Modify the `Register` method in the `Protector` class to set the array of roles in the `User` object, as shown in the following code:

    ```
    var user = new User
    {
      Name = username, Salt = saltText,
      SaltedHashedPassword = saltedhashedPassword,
    ```

```
    Roles = roles
};
```

4. In the `CryptographyLib` class library project, add statements to the `Protector` class to define a `LogIn` method to log in a user, and use generic identity and principal to assign them to the current thread, as shown in the following code:

```
public static void LogIn(string username, string password)
{
  if (CheckPassword(username, password))
  {
    var identity = new GenericIdentity(
      username, "PacktAuth");
    var principal = new GenericPrincipal(
      identity, Users[username].Roles);
    System.Threading.Thread.CurrentPrincipal = principal;
  }
}
```

5. Create a new console application project named `SecureApp`, add it to the workspace, and select the project as active for OmniSharp.

6. Add a reference to the `CryptographyLib` assembly, and then in `Program.cs`, import the following namespaces:

```
using static System.Console;
using Packt.Shared;
using System.Threading;
using System.Security;
using System.Security.Permissions;
using System.Security.Principal;
using System.Security.Claims;
```

7. In the `Main` method, write statements to register three users named Alice, Bob, and Eve, in various roles, prompt the user to log in, and then output information about them, as shown in the following code:

```
Protector.Register("Alice", "Pa$$w0rd",
  new[] { "Admins" });
Protector.Register("Bob", "Pa$$w0rd",
  new[] { "Sales", "TeamLeads" });
Protector.Register("Eve", "Pa$$w0rd");

Write($"Enter your user name: ");
string username = ReadLine();
Write($"Enter your password: ");
```

```
string password = ReadLine();

Protector.LogIn(username, password);
if (Thread.CurrentPrincipal == null)
{
  WriteLine("Log in failed.");
  return;
}

var p = Thread.CurrentPrincipal;

WriteLine(
  $"IsAuthenticated: {p.Identity.IsAuthenticated}");
WriteLine(
  $"AuthenticationType: {p.Identity.AuthenticationType}");
WriteLine($"Name: {p.Identity.Name}");
WriteLine($"IsInRole(\"Admins\"): {p.IsInRole("Admins")}");
WriteLine($"IsInRole(\"Sales\"): {p.IsInRole("Sales")}");

if (p is ClaimsPrincipal)
{
  WriteLine(
    $"{p.Identity.Name} has the following claims:");

  foreach (Claim claim in (p as ClaimsPrincipal).Claims)
  {
    WriteLine($"{claim.Type}: {claim.Value}");
  }
}
```

8. Run the console application, log in as `Alice` with `Pa$$word`, and view the results, as shown in the following output:

```
Enter your user name: Alice
Enter your password: Pa$$w0rd
IsAuthenticated: True
AuthenticationType: PacktAuth
Name: Alice
IsInRole("Admins"): True
IsInRole("Sales"): False
Alice has the following claims: http://schemas.xmlsoap.org/
ws/2005/05/identity/claims/name: Alice http://schemas.microsoft.
com/ws/2008/06/identity/claims/role: Admins
```

9. Run the console application, log in as `Alice` with `secret`, and view the results, as shown in the following output:

```
Enter your user name: Alice

Enter your password: secret

Log in failed.
```

10. Run the console application, log in as `Bob` with `Pa$$word`, and view the results, as shown in the following output:

```
Enter your user name: Bob

Enter your password: Pa$$w0rd

IsAuthenticated: True

AuthenticationType: PacktAuth

Name: Bob

IsInRole("Admins"): False

IsInRole("Sales"): True

Bob has the following claims:

http://schemas.xmlsoap.org/ws/2005/05/identity/claims/name: Bob

http://schemas.microsoft.com/ws/2008/06/identity/claims/role:
Sales http://schemas.microsoft.com/ws/2008/06/identity/claims/
role: TeamLeads
```

Protecting application functionality

Now let's explore how we can use authorization to prevent some users from accessing some features of an application.

1. Add a method to the `Program` class, secured by checking for permission inside the method, and throw appropriate exceptions if the user is anonymous or not a member of the `Admins` role, as shown in the following code:

```
static void SecureFeature()
{
  if (Thread.CurrentPrincipal == null)
  {
    throw new SecurityException(
      "A user must be logged in to access this feature.");
  }

  if (!Thread.CurrentPrincipal.IsInRole("Admins"))
  {
```

```
      throw new SecurityException(
        "User must be a member of Admins to access this feature.");
    }

    WriteLine("You have access to this secure feature.");
  }
```

2. Add statements to the end of the Main method to call the SecureFeature method in a try statement, as shown in the following code:

```
try
{
  SecureFeature();
}
catch (System.Exception ex)
{
  WriteLine($"{ex.GetType()}: {ex.Message}");
}
```

3. Run the console application, log in as Alice with Pa$$word, and view the results:

```
You have access to this secure feature.
```

4. Run the console application, log in as Bob with Pa$$word, and view the results:

```
System.Security.SecurityException: User must be a member of Admins
to access this feature.
```

Practicing and exploring

Test your knowledge and understanding by answering some questions, get some hands-on practice, and explore the topics covered in this chapter with deeper research.

Exercise 10.1 – Test your knowledge

Answer the following questions:

1. Of the encryption algorithms provided by .NET, which is the best choice for symmetric encryption?

2. Of the encryption algorithms provided by .NET, which is the best choice for asymmetric encryption?

3. What is a rainbow attack?

4. For encryption algorithms, is it better to have a larger or smaller block size?

5. What is a hash?

6. What is a signature?

7. What is the difference between symmetric and asymmetric encryption?

8. What does RSA stand for?

9. Why should passwords be salted before being stored?

10. SHA1 is a hashing algorithm designed by the United States National Security Agency. Why should you never use it?

Exercise 10.2 – Practice protecting data with encryption and hashing

Create a console application named `Exercise02` that protects an XML file, such as the following example:

```xml
<?xml version="1.0" encoding="utf-8" ?>
<customers>
  <customer>
    <name>Bob Smith</name>
    <creditcard>1234-5678-9012-3456</creditcard>
    <password>Pa$$w0rd</password>
  </customer>
  ...
</customers>
```

The customer's credit card number and password are currently stored in clear text. The credit card must be encrypted so that it can be decrypted and used later, and the password must be salted and hashed.

Exercise 10.3 – Practice protecting data with decryption

Create a console application named `Exercise03` that opens the XML file that you protected in the preceding code and decrypts the credit card number.

Exercise 10.4 – Explore topics

Use the following links to read more about the topics covered in this chapter:

- **Key Security Concepts**: https://docs.microsoft.com/en-us/dotnet/standard/security/key-security-concepts

- **Encrypting Data**: https://docs.microsoft.com/en-us/dotnet/standard/security/encrypting-data

- **Cryptographic Signatures**: https://docs.microsoft.com/en-us/dotnet/standard/security/cryptographic-signatures

- **Principal and Identity Objects**: https://docs.microsoft.com/en-us/dotnet/standard/security/principal-and-identity-objects

Summary

In this chapter, you learned how to encrypt and decrypt using symmetric encryption, how to generate a salted hash, how to sign data and check the signature on the data, how to generate truly random numbers, and how to use authentication and authorization to protect features of your applications.

In the next chapter, you will learn how to work with databases using Entity Framework Core.

Chapter 11

Working with Databases Using Entity Framework Core

This chapter is about reading and writing to data stores, such as Microsoft SQL Server, SQLite, and Azure Cosmos DB, by using the object-to-data store mapping technology named **Entity Framework Core (EF Core)**.

This chapter will cover the following topics:

- Understanding modern databases
- Setting up EF Core
- Defining EF Core models
- Querying EF Core models
- Loading patterns with EF Core
- Manipulating data with EF Core

Understanding modern databases

Two of the most common places to store data are in a **Relational Database Management System (RDBMS)** such as Microsoft SQL Server, PostgreSQL, MySQL, and SQLite, or in a **NoSQL** data store such as Microsoft Azure Cosmos DB, Redis, MongoDB, and Apache Cassandra.

This chapter will focus on RDBMSes such as SQL Server and SQLite. If you wish to learn more about NoSQL databases, such as Cosmos DB and MongoDB, and how to use them with EF Core, then I recommend the following links, which will go over them in detail:

- **Welcome to Azure Cosmos DB**: https://docs.microsoft.com/en-us/azure/cosmos-db/introduction

- **Use NoSQL databases as a persistence infrastructure**: `https://docs.microsoft.com/en-us/dotnet/standard/microservices-architecture/microservice-ddd-cqrs-patterns/nosql-database-persistence-infrastructure`

- **Document Database Providers for Entity Framework Core**: `https://github.com/BlueshiftSoftware/EntityFrameworkCore`

Understanding Entity Framework

Entity Framework (EF) was first released as part of the .NET Framework 3.5 with Service Pack 1 back in late 2008. Since then, Entity Framework has evolved, as Microsoft has observed how programmers use an **object-relational mapping (ORM)** tool in the real world.

ORMs use a mapping definition to associate columns in tables to properties in classes. Then, a programmer can interact with objects of different types in a way that they are familiar with, instead of having to deal with knowing how to store the values in a relational table or other structure provided by a NoSQL data store.

The version of EF included with the last version of .NET Framework is **Entity Framework 6 (EF6)**. It is mature, stable, and supports an old EDMX (XML file) way of defining the model as well as complex inheritance models, and a few other advanced features.

EF 6.3 is supported on .NET Core 3.0 cross-platform in order to enable existing projects like web applications and services to be ported. However, EF6 should be considered a legacy technology, has some limitations when running cross-platform, and no new features will be added to it.

 More Information: You can read more about Entity Framework 6.3 and its .NET Core 3.0 support at the following link: `https://devblogs.microsoft.com/dotnet/announcing-ef-core-3-0-and-ef-6-3-general-availability/`

The truly cross-platform version, EF Core, is different. Although EF Core has a similar name, you should be aware of how it varies from EF6. For example, as well as traditional RDBMSes, EF Core also supports modern cloud-based, nonrelational, schema-less data stores, such as Microsoft Azure Cosmos DB and MongoDB, sometimes with third-party providers.

 More Information: You can read a preview article about the EF Core Cosmos DB provider at the following link: `https://msdn.microsoft.com/en-us/magazine/mt833286.aspx`

Using a sample relational database

To learn how to manage an RDBMS using .NET Core, it would be useful to have a sample one so that you can practice on one that has a medium complexity and a decent amount of sample records. Microsoft offers several sample databases, most of which are too complex for our needs, so instead, we will use a database that was first created in the early 1990s known as **Northwind**.

Let's take a minute to look at a diagram of the Northwind database. You can use the diagram below to refer to as we write code and queries throughout this book:

You will write code to work with the Categories and Products tables later in this chapter and other tables in later chapters. But before we do, note that:

- Each category has a unique identifier, name, description, and picture.
- Each product has a unique identifier, name, unit price, units in stock, and other fields.
- Each product is associated with a category by storing the category's unique identifier.
- The relationship between Categories and Products is one-to-many, meaning each category can have zero or more products.

SQLite is a small, cross-platform, self-contained RDBMS that is available in the public domain. It's the most common RDBMS for mobile platforms such as iOS (iPhone and iPad) and Android.

Setting up SQLite for macOS

SQLite is included in macOS in the `/usr/bin/` directory as a command-line application named `sqlite3`.

Setting up SQLite for Windows

SQLite can be downloaded and installed for other OSes. On Windows, we also need to add the folder for SQLite to the system path so it will be found when we enter commands in Command Prompt.

1. Start your favorite browser and navigate to the following link: `https://www.sqlite.org/download.html`
2. Scroll down the page to the **Precompiled Binaries for Windows** section.
3. Click `sqlite-tools-win32-x86-3290000.zip`.
4. Extract the ZIP file into a folder named `C:\Sqlite\`
5. Navigate to Windows Settings.
6. Search for `environment` and choose **Edit the system environment variables**.
7. Click the **Environment Variables** button.
8. In **System variables**, select **Path** in the list, and then click **Edit...**
9. Click **New**, enter `C:\Sqlite`, and press *Enter*.
10. Click **OK**.
11. Click **OK**.
12. Click **OK**.
13. Close **Windows Settings**.

Creating the Northwind sample database for SQLite

Now we can create the `Northwind` sample database using an SQL script.

1. Create a folder named `Chapter11` with a subfolder named `WorkingWithEFCore`.

2. Download the script to create the `Northwind` database for SQLite from the following link: `https://github.com/markjprice/cs8dotnetcore3/blob/master/sql-scripts/Northwind.sql`

3. Copy `Northwind.sql` into the `WorkingWithEFCore` folder.

4. In Visual Studio Code, open the `WorkingWithEFCore` folder, navigate to **Terminal**, and pipe the script to SQLite to create the `Northwind.db` database, as shown in the following command:

```
sqlite3 Northwind.db < Northwind.sql
```

Be patient because this command might take a while to create all the database structure.

 More Information: You can read about the SQL statements supported by SQLite at the following link: `https://sqlite.org/lang.html`

Managing the Northwind sample database with SQLiteStudio

You can use a cross-platform graphical database manager named **SQLiteStudio** to easily manage SQLite databases.

1. Navigate to the following link: `http://sqlitestudio.pl` and download and install the application.

2. Launch **SQLiteStudio**.

3. On the **Database** menu, choose **Add a database**, or press *Cmd + O* on macOS or *Ctrl + O* on Windows.

4. In the **Database** dialog, click on the folder button to browse for an existing database file on the local computer, and select the `Northwind.db` file in the `WorkingWithEFCore` folder, and then click **OK**.

5. Right-click on the `Northwind` database and choose **Connect to the database**. You will see the tables that were created by the script.

6. Right-click on the `Products` table and choose **Edit the table**.

In the table editor window, you will see the structure of the `Products` table, including column names, data types, keys, and constraints, as shown in the following screenshot:

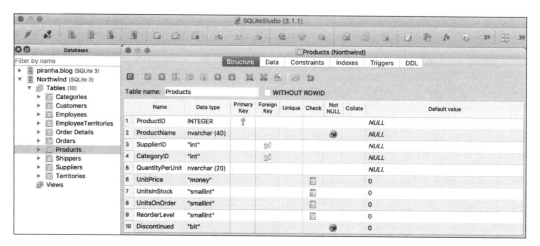

7. In the table editor window, click the **Data** tab. You will see 77 products, as shown in the following screenshot:

Setting up EF Core

Before we dive into the practicalities of managing data using EF Core, let's briefly talk about choosing between **EF Core data providers**.

Choosing an EF Core data provider

To manage data in a specific database, we need classes that know how to efficiently *talk* to that database. EF Core data providers are sets of classes that are optimized for a specific data store. There is even a provider for storing the data in the memory of the current process, which is useful for high-performance unit testing since it avoids hitting an external system.

They are distributed as NuGet packages, as shown in the following table:

To manage this data store	Install this NuGet package
Microsoft SQL Server 2008 or later	`Microsoft.EntityFrameworkCore.SqlServer`
SQLite 3.7 or later	`Microsoft.EntityFrameworkCore.SQLite`
MySQL	`MySQL.Data.EntityFrameworkCore`
In-memory	`Microsoft.EntityFrameworkCore.InMemory`

More Information: Devart is a third party that offers EF Core providers for a wide range of data stores. Find out more at the following link: `https://www.devart.com/dotconnect/entityframework.html`

Connecting to the database

To connect to SQLite, we just need to know the database filename. We specify this information in a connection string.

1. In Visual Studio Code, make sure that you have opened the `WorkingWithEFCore` folder, and then in **Terminal**, enter the `dotnet new console` command.

2. Edit `WorkingWithEFCore.csproj` to add a package reference to the EF Core data provider for SQLite, as shown highlighted in the following markup:

```xml
<Project Sdk="Microsoft.NET.Sdk">

  <PropertyGroup>
    <OutputType>Exe</OutputType>
    <TargetFramework>netcoreapp3.0</TargetFramework>
  </PropertyGroup>

  <ItemGroup>
    <PackageReference
      Include="Microsoft.EntityFrameworkCore.Sqlite"
      Version="3.0.0" />
  </ItemGroup>

</Project>
```

3. In **Terminal**, build the project to restore packages, as shown in the following command:

```
dotnet build
```

More Information: You can check the most recent version at the following link: `https://www.nuget.org/packages/Microsoft.EntityFrameworkCore.Sqlite/`

Defining EF Core models

EF Core uses a combination of **conventions**, **annotation attributes**, and **Fluent API** statements to build an entity model at runtime so that any actions performed on the classes can later be automatically translated into actions performed on the actual database. An entity class represents the structure of a table and an instance of the class represents a row in that table.

First we will review the three ways to define a model, with code examples, and then we will create some classes that implement those techniques.

EF Core conventions

The code we will write will use the following conventions:

- The name of a table is assumed to match the name of a `DbSet<T>` property in the `DbContext` class, for example, `Products`.

- The names of the columns are assumed to match the names of properties in the class, for example, `ProductID`.

- The `string` .NET type is assumed to be a `nvarchar` type in the database.

- The `int` .NET type is assumed to be an `int` type in the database.

- A property that is named `ID`, or if the class is named `Product`, then the property can be named `ProductID`. That property is then assumed to be a primary key. If this property is an integer type or the `Guid` type, then it is also assumed to be `IDENTITY` (a column type that automatically assigns a value when inserting).

More Information: There are many other conventions, and you can even define your own, but that is beyond the scope of this book. You can read about them at the following link:

`https://docs.microsoft.com/en-us/ef/core/modeling/`

EF Core annotation attributes

Conventions often aren't enough to completely map the classes to the database objects. A simple way of adding more smarts to your model is to apply annotation attributes.

For example, in the database, the maximum length of a product name is 40, and the value cannot be null. In a Product class, we could apply attributes to specify this, as shown in the following code:

```
[Required]
[StringLength(40)]
public string ProductName { get; set; }
```

When there isn't an obvious map between .NET types and database types, an attribute can be used.

For example, in the database, the column type of UnitPrice for the Products table is money. .NET Core does not have a money type, so it should use decimal instead, as shown in the following code:

```
[Column(TypeName = "money")]
public decimal? UnitPrice { get; set; }
```

In the Category table, the Description column can be longer than the 8,000 characters that can be stored in a nvarchar variable, so it needs to map to ntext instead, as shown in the following code:

```
[Column(TypeName = "ntext")]
public string Description { get; set; }
```

EF Core Fluent API

The last way that the model can be defined is by using the **Fluent API**. This API can be used instead of attributes, as well as being used in addition to them. For example, let's look at the following two attributes in a Product class, as shown in the following code:

```
[Required]
[StringLength(40)]
public string ProductName { get; set; }
```

The attributes could be removed from the class to keep it simpler, and replaced with an equivalent Fluent API statement in the OnModelCreating method of a database context class, as shown in the following code:

```
modelBuilder.Entity<Product>()
```

```
    .Property(product => product.ProductName)
    .IsRequired()
    .HasMaxLength(40);
```

Understanding data seeding

You can use the Fluent API to provide initial data to populate a database. EF Core automatically works out what insert, update, or delete operations must be executed. If we wanted to make sure that a new database has at least one row in the `Product` table then we would call the `HasData` method, as shown in the following code:

```
modelBuilder.Entity<Product>()
  .HasData(new Product
  {
    ProductID = 1,
    ProductName = "Chai",
    UnitPrice = 8.99M
  });
```

Our model will map to an existing database that is already populated with data so we will not need to use this technique in our code.

 More Information: You can read more about data seeding at the following link: https://docs.microsoft.com/en-us/ef/core/modeling/data-seeding

Building an EF Core model

Now that you've learned about model conventions, let's build a model to represent two tables and the `Northwind` database. To make the classes more reusable, we will define them in the `Packt.Shared` namespace. These three classes will refer to each other, so to avoid compiler errors we will create the three classes without any members first.

1. Add three class files to the `WorkingWithEFCore` project named `Northwind.cs`, `Category.cs`, and `Product.cs`.

2. In the file named `Northwind.cs`, define a class named `Northwind`, as shown in the following code:

```
namespace Packt.Shared
{
    public class Northwind
    {
    }
}
```

3. In the file named `Category.cs`, define a class named `Category`, as shown in the following code:

```
namespace Packt.Shared
{
    public class Category
    {
    }
}
```

4. In the file named `Product.cs`, define a class named `Product`, as shown in the following code:

```
namespace Packt.Shared
{
    public class Product
    {
    }
}
```

Defining the Category and Product entity classes

`Category` will be used to represent a row in the `Categories` table, which has four columns, as shown in the following screenshot:

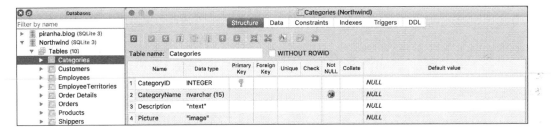

We will use conventions to define three of the four properties (we will not map the `Picture` column), the primary key, and the one-to-many relationship to the `Products` table. To map the `Description` column to the correct database type, we will need to decorate the `string` property with the `Column` attribute.

Later on in this chapter, we will use the Fluent API to define that `CategoryName` cannot be `null` and is limited to a maximum of 15 characters.

1. Modify `Category.cs`, as shown in the following code:

```
using System.Collections.Generic;
using System.ComponentModel.DataAnnotations.Schema;
```

```
namespace Packt.Shared
{
  public class Category
  {
    // these properties map to columns in the database
    public int CategoryID { get; set; }

    public string CategoryName { get; set; }

    [Column(TypeName = "ntext")]
    public string Description { get; set; }

    // defines a navigation property for related rows
    public virtual ICollection<Product> Products { get; set; }

    public Category()
    {
      // to enable developers to add products to a Category we must
      // initialize the navigation property to an empty list
      this.Products = new List<Product>();
    }
  }
}
```

Product will be used to represent a row in the Products table, which has ten columns. You do not need to include all columns from a table as properties of a class. We will only map six properties: ProductID, ProductName, UnitPrice, UnitsInStock, Discontinued, and CategoryID.

Columns that are not mapped to properties cannot be read or set using the class instances. If you use the class to create a new object, then the new row in the table will have NULL or some other default value for the unmapped column values in that row. In this scenario, the rows already have data values and I have decided that I do not need to read those values in the console application.

We can rename a column by defining a property with a different name, like Cost, and then decorating the property with the [Column] attribute and specifying its column name, like UnitPrice.

The final property, CategoryID, is associated with a Category property that will be used to map each product to its parent category.

2. Modify Product.cs, as shown in the following code:

```
using System.ComponentModel.DataAnnotations;
```

```
using System.ComponentModel.DataAnnotations.Schema;

namespace Packt.Shared
{
  public class Product
  {
    public int ProductID { get; set; }

    [Required]
    [StringLength(40)]
    public string ProductName { get; set; }

    [Column("UnitPrice", TypeName = "money")]
    public decimal? Cost { get; set; }

    [Column("UnitsInStock")]
    public short? Stock { get; set; }

    public bool Discontinued { get; set; }

    // these two define the foreign key relationship
    // to the Categories table
    public int CategoryID { get; set; }

    public virtual Category Category { get; set; }
  }
}
```

The two properties that relate the two entities, Category.Products and Product. Category, are both marked as virtual. This allows EF Core to inherit and override the properties to provide extra features, such as lazy loading. Lazy loading is not available in .NET Core 2.0 or earlier.

Defining the Northwind database context class

The Northwind class will be used to represent the database. To use EF Core, the class must inherit from DbContext. This class understands how to communicate with databases and dynamically generate SQL statements to query and manipulate data.

Inside your DbContext-derived class, you must define at least one property of the DbSet<T> type. These properties represent the tables. To tell EF Core what columns each table has, the DbSet properties use generics to specify a class that represents a row in the table, with properties that represent its columns.

Your `DbContext`-derived class should have an overridden method named `OnConfiguring`, which will set the database connection string.

Likewise, your `DbContext`-derived class can optionally have an overridden method named `OnModelCreating`. This is where you can write Fluent API statements as an alternative to decorating your entity classes with attributes.

1. Modify `Northwind.cs`, as shown in the following code:

```
using Microsoft.EntityFrameworkCore;

namespace Packt.Shared
{
  // this manages the connection to the database
  public class Northwind : DbContext
  {
    // these properties map to tables in the database
    public DbSet<Category> Categories { get; set; }
    public DbSet<Product> Products { get; set; }

    protected override void OnConfiguring(
      DbContextOptionsBuilder optionsBuilder)
    {
      string path = System.IO.Path.Combine(
        System.Environment.CurrentDirectory, "Northwind.db");

      optionsBuilder.UseSqlite($"Filename={path}");
    }

    protected override void OnModelCreating(
      ModelBuilder modelBuilder)
    {
      // example of using Fluent API instead of attributes
      // to limit the length of a category name to 15
      modelBuilder.Entity<Category>()
        .Property(category => category.CategoryName)
        .IsRequired() // NOT NULL
        .HasMaxLength(15);
    }
  }
}
```

Querying EF Core models

Now that we have a model that maps to the `Northwind` database and two of its tables, we can write some simple LINQ queries to fetch data. You will learn much more about writing LINQ queries in *Chapter 12, Querying and Manipulating Data Using LINQ*. For now, just write the code and view the results.

1. Open `Program.cs` and import the following namespaces:

```
using static System.Console;
using Packt.Shared;
using Microsoft.EntityFrameworkCore;
using System.Linq;
```

2. In `Program`, define a `QueryingCategories` method, and add statements to do these tasks, as shown in the following code:

   ◦ Create an instance of the `Northwind` class that will manage the database.

   ◦ Create a query for all categories that include their related products.

   ◦ Enumerate through the categories, outputting the name and number of products for each one.

```
static void QueryingCategories()
{
  using (var db = new Northwind())
  {
    WriteLine("Categories and how many products they have:");

    // a query to get all categories and their related products
    IQueryable<Category> cats = db.Categories
      .Include(c => c.Products);

    foreach (Category c in cats)
    {
      WriteLine($"{c.CategoryName} has {c.Products.Count}
products.");
    }
  }
}
```

3. In `Main`, call the `QueryingCategories` method, as shown in the following code:

```
static void Main(string[] args)
{
  QueryingCategories();
}
```

4. Run the application and view the result, as shown in the following output:

```
Categories and how many products they have:
Beverages has 12 products.
Condiments has 12 products.
```

```
Confections has 13 products.
Dairy Products has 10 products.
Grains/Cereals has 7 products.
Meat/Poultry has 6 products.
Produce has 5 products.
Seafood has 12 products.
```

Filtering and sorting products

Let's explore a more complex query that filters and sorts data.

1. In Program, define a QueryingProducts method, and add statements to do the following, as shown in the following code:

   ° Create an instance of the Northwind class that will manage the database.

   ° Prompt the user for a price for products.

   ° Create a query for products that cost more than the price using LINQ.

   ° Loop through the results, outputting the ID, name, cost (formatted with US dollars), and the number of units in stock.

```
static void QueryingProducts()
{
  using (var db = new Northwind())
  {
    WriteLine("Products that cost more than a price, highest at
top.");
    string input;
    decimal price;
    do
    {
      Write("Enter a product price: ");
      input = ReadLine();
    } while(!decimal.TryParse(input, out price));

    IOrderedEnumerable<Product> prods = db.Products
      .AsEnumerable()
      .Where(product => product.Cost > price)
      .OrderByDescending(product => product.Cost);

    foreach (Product item in prods)
    {
```

```
    WriteLine(
      "{0}: {1} costs {2:$#,##0.00} and has {3} in stock.",
      item.ProductID, item.ProductName, item.Cost, item.Stock);
    }
  }
}
```

2. In `Main`, comment the previous method, and call the method, as shown in the following code:

```
static void Main(string[] args)
{
  // QueryingCategories();
  QueryingProducts();
}
```

3. Run the application, enter `50` when prompted to enter a product price, and view the result, as shown in the following output:

```
Products that cost more than a price, highest at top.
Enter a product price: 50
38: Côte de Blaye costs $263.50 and has 17 in stock.
29: Thüringer Rostbratwurst costs $123.79 and has 0 in stock.
9: Mishi Kobe Niku costs $97.00 and has 29 in stock.
20: Sir Rodney's Marmalade costs $81.00 and has 40 in stock.
18: Carnarvon Tigers costs $62.50 and has 42 in stock.
59: Raclette Courdavault costs $55.00 and has 79 in stock.
51: Manjimup Dried Apples costs $53.00 and has 20 in stock.
```

There is a limitation with the console provided by Microsoft on versions of Windows before the Windows 10 Fall Creators Update. By default, the console cannot display Unicode characters. You can temporarily change the code page (also known as the character set) in a console to Unicode UTF-8 by entering the following command at the prompt before running the app:

```
chcp 65001
```

Logging EF Core

To monitor the interaction between EF Core and the database, we can enable logging. This requires the following two tasks:

*   The registering of a **logging provider**
*   The implementation of a **logger**

1. Add a file to your project named `ConsoleLogger.cs`.

2. Modify the file to define two classes, one to implement `ILoggerProvider` and one to implement `ILogger`, as shown in the following code, and note the following:

   - `ConsoleLoggerProvider` returns an instance of `ConsoleLogger`. It does not need any unmanaged resources, so the `Dispose` method does not do anything, but it must exist.

   - `ConsoleLogger` is disabled for log levels `None`, `Trace`, and `Information`. It is enabled for all other log levels.

   - `ConsoleLogger` implements its `Log` method by writing to `Console`.

```csharp
using Microsoft.Extensions.Logging;
using System;
using static System.Console;

namespace Packt.Shared
{
  public class ConsoleLoggerProvider : ILoggerProvider
  {
    public ILogger CreateLogger(string categoryName)
    {
      return new ConsoleLogger();
    }

    // if your logger uses unmanaged resources,
    // you can release the memory here
    public void Dispose() { }
  }

  public class ConsoleLogger : ILogger
  {
    // if your logger uses unmanaged resources, you can
    // return the class that implements IDisposable here
    public IDisposable BeginScope<TState>(TState state)
    {
      return null;
    }

    public bool IsEnabled(LogLevel logLevel)
    {
      // to avoid overlogging, you can filter
      // on the log level
      switch(logLevel)
      {
```

```
      case LogLevel.Trace:
      case LogLevel.Information:
      case LogLevel.None:
        return false;
      case LogLevel.Debug:
      case LogLevel.Warning:
      case LogLevel.Error:
      case LogLevel.Critical:
      default:
        return true;
    };
  }

  public void Log<TState>(LogLevel logLevel,
    EventId eventId, TState state, Exception exception,
    Func<TState, Exception, string> formatter)
  {
    // log the level and event identifier
    Write($"Level: {logLevel}, Event ID: {eventId.Id}");

    // only output the state or exception if it exists
    if (state != null)
    {
      Write($", State: {state}");
    }
    if (exception != null)
    {
      Write($", Exception: {exception.Message}");
    }
    WriteLine();
  }
 }
}
```

3. At the top of the `Program.cs` file, add statements to import the namespaces needed for logging, as shown in the following code:

```
using Microsoft.EntityFrameworkCore.Infrastructure;
using Microsoft.Extensions.DependencyInjection;
using Microsoft.Extensions.Logging;
```

4. To both the `QueryingCategories` and `QueryingProducts` methods, add statements immediately inside the using block for the `Northwind` database context to get the logging factory and register your custom console logger, as shown highlighted in the following code:

```
using (var db = new Northwind())
```

```
{
    var loggerFactory = db.GetService<ILoggerFactory>();
    loggerFactory.AddProvider(new ConsoleLoggerProvider());
```

5. Run the console application and view the logs, which are partially shown in the following output:

```
Level: Debug, Event ID: 20000, State: Opening connection to
database 'main' on server '/Users/markjprice/Code/Chapter11/
WorkingWithEFCore/Northwind.db'.

Level: Debug, Event ID: 20001, State: Opened connection to
database 'main' on server '/Users/markjprice/Code/Chapter11/
WorkingWithEFCore/Northwind.db'.

Level: Debug, Event ID: 20100, State: Executing DbCommand
[Parameters=[], CommandType='Text', CommandTimeout='30']

PRAGMA foreign_keys=ON;

Level: Debug, Event ID: 20100, State: Executing DbCommand
[Parameters=[], CommandType='Text', CommandTimeout='30']

SELECT "product"."ProductID", "product"."CategoryID",
"product"."UnitPrice", "product"."Discontinued",
"product"."ProductName", "product"."UnitsInStock"

FROM "Products" AS "product"

ORDER BY "product"."UnitPrice" DESC
```

The event ID values and what they mean will be specific to the .NET data provider. If we want to know how the LINQ query has been translated into SQL statements and is executing, then the Event ID to output has an Id value of 20100.

6. Modify the Log method in ConsoleLogger to only output events with Id of 20100, as highlighted in the following code:

```
public void Log<TState>(LogLevel logLevel, EventId eventId, TState
state,
    Exception exception, Func<TState, Exception, string> formatter)
{
    if (eventId.Id == 20100)
    {
        // log the level and event identifier
        Write("Level: {0}, Event ID: {1}, Event: {2}"
            logLevel, eventId.Id, eventId.Name);

        // only output the state or exception if it exists
        if (state != null)
        {
            Write($", State: {state}");
```

```
      }
      if (exception != null)
      {
        Write($", Exception: {exception.Message}");
      }
      WriteLine();
    }
  }
}
```

7. In `Main`, uncomment the `QueryingCategories` method and comment the `QueryingProducts` method so that we can monitor the SQL statements that are generated when joining two tables.

8. Run the console application, and note the following SQL statements that were logged, as shown in the following output:

```
Categories and how many products they have:
Level: Debug, Event ID: 20100, State: Executing DbCommand
[Parameters=[], CommandType='Text', CommandTimeout='30']
PRAGMA foreign_keys=ON;
Level: Debug, Event ID: 20100, State: Executing DbCommand
[Parameters=[], CommandType='Text', CommandTimeout='30']
SELECT "c"."CategoryID", "c"."CategoryName", "c"."Description"
FROM "Categories" AS "c"
ORDER BY "c"."CategoryID"
Level: Debug, Event ID: 20100, State: Executing DbCommand
[Parameters=[], CommandType='Text', CommandTimeout='30']
SELECT "c.Products"."ProductID", "c.Products"."CategoryID",
"c.Products"."UnitPrice", "c.Products"."Discontinued",
"c.Products"."ProductName", "c.Products"."UnitsInStock"
FROM "Products" AS "c.Products"
INNER JOIN (
    SELECT "c0"."CategoryID"
    FROM "Categories" AS "c0"
) AS "t" ON "c.Products"."CategoryID" = "t"."CategoryID"
ORDER BY "t"."CategoryID"
Beverages has 12 products.
Condiments has 12 products.
Confections has 13 products.
Dairy Products has 10 products.
Grains/Cereals has 7 products.
Meat/Poultry has 6 products.
Produce has 5 products.
Seafood has 12 products.
```

Logging with query tags

When logging LINQ queries it can be tricky to correlate log messages in complex scenarios. EF Core 2.2 introduced the query tags feature to help by allowing you to add SQL comments to the log.

You can annotate a LINQ query using the `TagWith` method, as shown in the following code:

```
IQueryable<Product> prods = db.Products
  .TagWith("Products filtered by price and sorted.")
  .Where(product => product.Cost > price)
  .OrderByDescending(product => product.Cost);
```

This will add an SQL comment to the log, as shown in the following output:

```
-- Products filtered by price and sorted.
```

> **More Information**: You can read more about query tags at the following link: https://docs.microsoft.com/en-us/ef/core/querying/tags

Pattern matching with Like

EF Core supports common SQL statements including `Like` for pattern matching.

1. In `Program`, add a method named `QueryingWithLike`, as shown in the following code, and note:

    ○ We have enabled logging.

    ○ We prompt the user to enter part of a product name and then use the `EF.Functions.Like` method to search anywhere in the `ProductName` property.

    ○ For each matching product, we output its name, stock, and if it is discontinued.

```
static void QueryingWithLike()
{
  using (var db = new Northwind())
  {
    var loggerFactory = db.GetService<ILoggerFactory>();
    loggerFactory.AddProvider(new ConsoleLoggerProvider());
```

```
Write("Enter part of a product name: ");
string input = ReadLine();

IQueryable<Product> prods = db.Products
  .Where(p => EF.Functions.Like(p.ProductName, $"%{input}%"));

foreach (Product item in prods)
{
  WriteLine("{0} has {1} units in stock. Discontinued? {2}",
    item.ProductName, item.Stock, item.Discontinued);
}
}
}
```

2. In `Main`, comment the existing methods, and call `QueryingWithLike`, as shown in the following code:

```
static void Main(string[] args)
{
  // QueryingCategories();
  // QueryingProducts();
  QueryingWithLike();
}
```

3. Run the console application, enter a partial product name such as `che`, and view the result, as shown in the following output:

```
Enter part of a product name: che

Level: Debug, Event ID: 20100, State: Executing DbCommand
[Parameters=[], CommandType='Text', CommandTimeout='30']

PRAGMA foreign_keys=ON;

Level: Debug, Event ID: 20100, State: Executing DbCommand
[Parameters=[@__Format_1='?' (Size = 5)], CommandType='Text',
CommandTimeout='30']

SELECT "p"."ProductID", "p"."CategoryID", "p"."UnitPrice",
"p"."Discontinued", "p"."ProductName", "p"."UnitsInStock"

FROM "Products" AS "p"

WHERE "p"."ProductName" LIKE @__Format_1

Chef Anton's Cajun Seasoning has 53 units in stock. Discontinued?
False

Chef Anton's Gumbo Mix has 0 units in stock. Discontinued? True

Queso Manchego La Pastora has 86 units in stock. Discontinued?
False

Gumbär Gummibärchen has 15 units in stock. Discontinued? False
```

Defining global filters

The Northwind products can be discontinued, so it might be useful to ensure that discontinued products are never returned in results, even if the programmer forgets to use Where to filter them out.

1. Modify the OnModelCreating method in the Northwind class to add a global filter to remove discontinued products, as shown highlighted in the following code:

```
protected override void OnModelCreating(ModelBuilder modelBuilder)
{
  // example of using Fluent API instead of attributes
  // to limit the length of a category name to under 15
  modelBuilder.Entity<Category>()
    .Property(category => category.CategoryName)
    .IsRequired() // NOT NULL
    .HasMaxLength(15);

  // global filter to remove discontinued products
  modelBuilder.Entity<Product>()
    .HasQueryFilter(p => !p.Discontinued);
}
```

2. Run the console application, enter the partial product name che, view the result, and note that **Chef Anton's Gumbo Mix** is now missing, because the SQL statement generated includes a filter for the Discontinued column, as shown in the following output:

```
SELECT "p"."ProductID", "p"."CategoryID", "p"."UnitPrice",
"p"."Discontinued", "p"."ProductName", "p"."UnitsInStock"

FROM "Products" AS "p"

WHERE ("p"."Discontinued" = 0) AND "p"."ProductName" LIKE @__
Format_1

Chef Anton's Cajun Seasoning has 53 units in stock. Discontinued?
False

Queso Manchego La Pastora has 86 units in stock. Discontinued?
False

Gumbär Gummibärchen has 15 units in stock. Discontinued? False
```

Loading patterns with EF Core

There are three **loading patterns** that are commonly used with EF: **lazy loading**, **eager loading**, and **explicit loading**. In this section, we're going to introduce each of them.

Eager loading entities

In the `QueryingCategories` method, the code currently uses the `Categories` property to loop through each category, outputting the category name and the number of products in that category. This works because when we wrote the query, we used the `Include` method to use eager loading (also known as **early loading**) for the related products.

1. Modify the query to comment out the `Include` method call, as shown in the following code:

```
IQueryable<Category> cats =
    db.Categories; //.Include(c => c.Products);
```

2. In `Main`, comment all methods except `QueryingCategories`, as shown in the following code:

```
static void Main(string[] args)
{
  QueryingCategories();
  // QueryingProducts();
  // QueryingWithLike();
}
```

3. Run the console application and view the result, as shown in the following partial output:

```
Beverages has 0 products.
Condiments has 0 products.
Confections has 0 products.
Dairy Products has 0 products.
Grains/Cereals has 0 products.
Meat/Poultry has 0 products.
Produce has 0 products.
Seafood has 0 products.
```

Each item in `foreach` is an instance of the `Category` class, which has a property named `Products`, that is, the list of products in that category. Since the original query is only selected from the `Categories` table, this property is empty for each category.

Lazy loading was introduced in EF Core 2.1, and it can automatically load missing related data.

Enabling lazy loading

To enable lazy loading, developers must:

- Reference a NuGet package for proxies.
- Configure lazy loading to using a proxy.

1. Open `WorkingWithEFCore.csproj` and add a package reference, as shown in the following markup:

```
<PackageReference
  Include="Microsoft.EntityFrameworkCore.Proxies"
  Version="3.0.0" />
```

2. In **Terminal**, build the project to restore packages, as shown in the following command:

```
dotnet build
```

3. Open `Northwind.cs`, import the `Microsoft.EntityFrameworkCore.Proxies` namespace, and call an extension method to use lazy loading proxies before using SQLite, as shown highlighted in the following code:

```
optionsBuilder.UseLazyLoadingProxies()
  .UseSqlite($"Filename={path}");
```

Now, every time the loop enumerates and an attempt is made to read the `Products` property, the lazy loading proxy will check if they are loaded. If not, it will load them for us "lazily" by executing a `SELECT` statement to load just that set of products for the current category, and then the correct count would be returned to the output.

4. Run the console app and you will see that the problem with lazy loading is that multiple round trips to the database server are required to eventually fetch all the data, as shown in the following partial output:

```
Categories and how many products they have:
Level: Debug, Event ID: 20100, State: Executing DbCommand
[Parameters=[], CommandType='Text', CommandTimeout='30']
PRAGMA foreign_keys=ON;
Level: Debug, Event ID: 20100, State: Executing DbCommand
[Parameters=[], CommandType='Text', CommandTimeout='30']
SELECT "c"."CategoryID", "c"."CategoryName", "c"."Description"
FROM "Categories" AS "c"
Level: Debug, Event ID: 20100, State: Executing DbCommand
[Parameters=[@__p_0='?'], CommandType='Text', CommandTimeout='30']
SELECT "p"."ProductID", "p"."CategoryID", "p"."UnitPrice",
```

```
"p"."Discontinued", "p"."ProductName", "p"."UnitsInStock"
FROM "Products" AS "p"
WHERE ("p"."Discontinued" = 0) AND ("p"."CategoryID" = @__p_0)
Beverages has 11 products.
Level: Debug, Event ID: 20100, State: Executing DbCommand
[Parameters=[@__p_0='?'], CommandType='Text', CommandTimeout='30']
SELECT "p"."ProductID", "p"."CategoryID", "p"."UnitPrice",
"p"."Discontinued", "p"."ProductName", "p"."UnitsInStock"
FROM "Products" AS "p"
WHERE ("p"."Discontinued" = 0) AND ("p"."CategoryID" = @__p_0)
Condiments has 11 products.
```

Explicit loading entities

Another type of loading is explicit loading. It works in a similar way to lazy loading, with the difference being that you are in control of exactly what related data is loaded and when.

1. In the `QueryingCategories` method, modify the statements to disable lazy loading and then prompt the user if they want to enable eager loading and explicit loading, as shown in the following code:

```
IQueryable<Category> cats;
// = db.Categories;
// .Include(c => c.Products);

db.ChangeTracker.LazyLoadingEnabled = false;

Write("Enable eager loading? (Y/N): ");
bool eagerloading = (ReadKey().Key == ConsoleKey.Y);
bool explicitloading = false;
WriteLine();

if (eagerloading)
{
  cats = db.Categories.Include(c => c.Products);
}
else
{
  cats = db.Categories;
  Write("Enable explicit loading? (Y/N): ");
  explicitloading = (ReadKey().Key == ConsoleKey.Y);
  WriteLine();
}
```

2. Inside the `foreach` loop, before the `WriteLine` method call, add statements to check if explicit loading is enabled, and if so, prompt the user if they want to explicitly load each individual category, as shown in the following code:

```
if (explicitloading)
{
  Write($"Explicitly load products for {c.CategoryName}? (Y/N): ");
  ConsoleKeyInfo key = ReadKey();
  WriteLine();
  if (key.Key == ConsoleKey.Y)
  {
    var products = db.Entry(c).Collection(c2 => c2.Products);
    if (!products.IsLoaded) products.Load();
  }
}
WriteLine($"{c.CategoryName} has {c.Products.Count} products.");
```

3. Run the console application; press *N* to disable eager loading, and press *Y* to enable explicit loading. For each category, press *Y* or *N* to load its products as you wish. I chose to load products for only two of the eight categories, `Beverages` and `Seafood`, as shown in the following output:

```
Categories and how many products they have:
Enable eager loading? (Y/N): n
Enable explicit loading? (Y/N): y
Level: Debug, Event ID: 20100, State: Executing DbCommand
[Parameters=[], CommandType='Text', CommandTimeout='30']
PRAGMA foreign_keys=ON;
Level: Debug, Event ID: 20100, State: Executing DbCommand
[Parameters=[], CommandType='Text', CommandTimeout='30']
SELECT "c"."CategoryID", "c"."CategoryName", "c"."Description"
FROM "Categories" AS "c"
Explicitly load products for Beverages? (Y/N): y
Level: Debug, Event ID: 20100, State: Executing DbCommand
[Parameters=[@__p_0='?'], CommandType='Text', CommandTimeout='30']
SELECT "p"."ProductID", "p"."CategoryID", "p"."UnitPrice",
"p"."Discontinued", "p"."ProductName", "p"."UnitsInStock"
FROM "Products" AS "p"
WHERE ("p"."Discontinued" = 0) AND ("p"."CategoryID" = @__p_0)
Beverages has 11 products.
Explicitly load products for Condiments? (Y/N): n
Condiments has 0 products.
Explicitly load products for Confections? (Y/N): n
```

```
Confections has 0 products.
Explicitly load products for Dairy Products? (Y/N): n
Dairy Products has 0 products.
Explicitly load products for Grains/Cereals? (Y/N): n
Grains/Cereals has 0 products.
Explicitly load products for Meat/Poultry? (Y/N): n
Meat/Poultry has 0 products.
Explicitly load products for Produce? (Y/N): n
Produce has 0 products.
Explicitly load products for Seafood? (Y/N): y
Level: Debug, Event ID: 20100, State: Executing DbCommand
[Parameters=[@__p_0='?'], CommandType='Text', CommandTimeout='30']
SELECT "p"."ProductID", "p"."CategoryID", "p"."UnitPrice",
"p"."Discontinued", "p"."ProductName", "p"."UnitsInStock"
FROM "Products" AS "p"
WHERE ("p"."Discontinued" = 0) AND ("p"."CategoryID" = @__p_0)
Seafood has 12 products.
```

Good Practice: Carefully consider which loading pattern is best for your code. Lazy loading could literally make you a lazy database developer! Read more about loading patterns at the following link: https://docs.microsoft.com/en-us/ef/core/querying/related-data

Manipulating data with EF Core

Inserting, updating, and deleting entities using EF Core is an easy task to accomplish. DbContext maintains change tracking automatically, so the local entities can have multiple changes tracked, including adding new entities, modifying existing entities, and removing entities. When you are ready to send those changes to the underlying database, call the SaveChanges method. The number of entities successfully changed will be returned.

Inserting entities

Let's start by looking at how to add a new row to a table.

1. In Program, create a new method named AddProduct, as shown in the following code:

    ```
    static bool AddProduct(int categoryID, string productName,
    decimal? price)
    ```

```
    {
      using (var db = new Northwind())
      {
        var newProduct = new Product
        {
          CategoryID = categoryID,
          ProductName = productName,
          Cost = price
        };

        // mark product as added in change tracking
        db.Products.Add(newProduct);

        // save tracked change to database
        int affected = db.SaveChanges();
        return (affected == 1);
      }
    }
```

2. In `Program`, create a new method named `ListProducts` that outputs the ID, name, cost, stock, and discontinued properties of each product sorted with the costliest first, as shown in the following code:

```
static void ListProducts()
{
  using (var db = new Northwind())
  {
    WriteLine("{0,-3} {1,-35} {2,8} {3,5} {4}",
      "ID", "Product Name", "Cost", "Stock", "Disc.");

    foreach (var item in db.Products.OrderByDescending(p =>
p.Cost))
    {
      WriteLine("{0:000} {1,-35} {2,8:$#,##0.00} {3,5} {4}",
        item.ProductID, item.ProductName, item.Cost,
        item.Stock, item.Discontinued);
    }
  }
}
```

Remember that `1,-35` means left-align argument number 1 within a 35 character-wide column and `3,5` means right-align argument number 3 within a 5 character-wide column.

3. In `Main`, comment previous method calls, and then call `AddProduct` and `ListProducts`, as shown in the following code:

```
static void Main(string[] args)
{
  // QueryingCategories();
  // QueryingProducts();
  // QueryingWithLike();

  if (AddProduct(6, "Bob's Burgers", 500M))
  {
    WriteLine("Add product successful.");
  }

  ListProducts();
}
```

4. Run the application, view the result, and note the new product has been added, as shown in the following partial output:

```
Add product successful.
ID   Product Name                    Cost Stock Disc.
078 Bob's Burgers                 $500.00       False
038 Côte de Blaye                 $263.50    17 False
020 Sir Rodney's Marmalade         $81.00    40 False
```

Updating entities

Now, let's modify an existing row in a table.

1. In `Program`, add a method to increase the price of the first product with a name that begins with `Bob` by $20, as shown in the following code:

```
static bool IncreaseProductPrice(string name, decimal amount)
{
  using (var db = new Northwind())
  {
    // get first product whose name starts with name
    Product updateProduct = db.Products.First(
      p => p.ProductName.StartsWith(name));

    updateProduct.Cost += amount;

    int affected = db.SaveChanges();
    return (affected == 1);
  }
}
```

2. In `Main`, comment the whole `if` statement block that calls `AddProduct`, and add a call to `IncreaseProductPrice` before the call to list products, as shown highlighted in the following code:

```
if (IncreaseProductPrice("Bob", 20M))
{
  WriteLine("Update product price successful.");
}

ListProducts();
```

3. Run the console application, view the result, and note that the existing entity for Bob's Burgers has increased in price by $20, as shown in the following output:

```
Update product price successful.
ID   Product Name                         Cost Stock Disc.
078 Bob's Burgers                      $520.00       False
038 Côte de Blaye                      $263.50    17 False
```

Deleting entities

Now let's see how to delete a row from a table.

1. In `Program`, import `System.Collections.Generic`, and then add a method to delete all products with a name that begins with `Bob`, as shown in the following code:

```
static int DeleteProducts(string name)
{
  using (var db = new Northwind())
  {
    IEnumerable<Product> products = db.Products.Where(
      p => p.ProductName.StartsWith(name));

    db.Products.RemoveRange(products);

    int affected = db.SaveChanges();
    return affected;
  }
}
```

You can remove individual entities with the `Remove` method. `RemoveRange` is more efficient when you want to delete multiple entities.

2. In `Main`, comment the whole `if` statement block that calls `IncreaseProductPrice`, and add a call to `DeleteProducts`, as shown highlighted in the following code:

```
int deleted = DeleteProducts("Bob");
WriteLine($"{deleted} product(s) were deleted.");

ListProducts();
```

3. Run the console application and view the result, as shown in the following output:

```
1 product(s) were deleted.
ID   Product Name                        Cost Stock Disc.
038 Côte de Blaye                     $263.50    17 False
020 Sir Rodney's Marmalade            $81.00     40 False
```

If multiple product names started with Bob, then they are all deleted. As an optional challenge, uncomment the statements to add three new products that start with Bob and then delete them.

Pooling database contexts

The DbContext class is disposable and is designed following the single-unit-of-work principle. In the previous code examples, we created all the DbContext-derived Northwind instances in a using block.

A feature of ASP.NET Core that is related to EF Core is that it makes your code more efficient by pooling database contexts when building web applications and web services.

This allows you to create and dispose of as many DbContext-derived objects as you want, knowing your code is still very efficient.

 More Information: You can read more about pooling database contexts at the following link: https://docs.microsoft.com/en-us/ef/core/what-is-new/ef-core-2.0#dbcontext-pooling

Transactions

Every time you call the SaveChanges method, an **implicit transaction** is started so that if something goes wrong, it would automatically roll back all the changes. If the multiple changes within the transaction succeed, then the transaction and all changes are committed.

Transactions maintain the integrity of your database by applying locks to prevent reads and writes while a sequence of changes is occurring.

Transactions are **ACID**, which is an acronym explained in the following list:

- **A** is for atomic. Either all the operations in the transaction commit, or none of them do.

- **C** is for consistent. The state of the database before and after a transaction is consistent. This is dependent on your code logic; for example, when transferring money between bank accounts it is up to your business logic to ensure that if you debit $100 in one account, you credit $100 in the other account.

- **I** is for isolated. During a transaction, changes are hidden from other processes. There are multiple isolation levels that you can pick from (refer to the following table). The stronger the level, the better the integrity of the data. However, more locks must be applied, which will negatively affect other processes. Snapshot is a special case because it creates multiple copies of rows to avoid locks, but this will increase the size of your database while transactions occur.

- **D** is for durable. If a failure occurs during a transaction, it can be recovered. This is often implemented as a two-phase commit and transaction logs. The opposite of durable is volatile.

Isolation level	Lock(s)	Integrity problems allowed
ReadUncommitted	None	Dirty reads, nonrepeatable reads, and phantom data
ReadCommitted	When editing, it applies read lock(s) to block other users from reading the record(s) until the transaction ends	Nonrepeatable reads and phantom data
RepeatableRead	When reading, it applies edit lock(s) to block other users from editing the record(s) until the transaction ends	Phantom data
Serializable	Applies key-range locks to prevent any action that would affect the results, including inserts and deletes	None
Snapshot	None	None

Defining an explicit transaction

You can control explicit transactions using the `Database` property of the database context.

1. Import the following namespace in `Program.cs` to use the `IDbContextTransaction` interface:

```
using Microsoft.EntityFrameworkCore.Storage;
```

2. In the `DeleteProducts` method, after the instantiation of the db variable, add the following highlighted statements to start an explicit transaction and output its isolation level. At the bottom of the method, commit the transaction, and close the brace, as shown in the following code:

```
static int DeleteProducts(string name)
{
  using (var db = new Northwind())
  {
    using (IDbContextTransaction t = db.Database.
BeginTransaction())
    {
      WriteLine("Transaction isolation level: {0}",
        t.GetDbTransaction().IsolationLevel);

      var products = db.Products.Where(
        p => p.ProductName.StartsWith(name));

      db.Products.RemoveRange(products);

      int affected = db.SaveChanges();
      t.Commit();
      return affected;
    }
  }
}
```

3. Run the console application and view the result, as shown in the following output:

```
Transaction isolation level: Serializable
```

Practicing and exploring

Test your knowledge and understanding by answering some questions, get some hands-on practice, and explore this chapter's topics with deeper research.

Exercise 11.1 – Test your knowledge

Answer the following questions:

1. What type would you use for the property that represents a table, for example, the `Products` property of a database context?

2. What type would you use for the property that represents a one-to-many relationship, for example, the `Products` property of a `Category` entity?

3. What is the EF Core convention for primary keys?

4. When would you use an `annotation` attribute in an `entity` class?

5. Why might you choose the Fluent API in preference to annotation attributes?

6. What does a transaction isolation level of Serializable mean?

7. What does the `DbContext.SaveChanges()` method return?

8. What is the difference between eager loading and explicit loading?

9. How should you define an EF Core entity class to match the following table?

```
CREATE TABLE Employees(
  EmpID INT IDENTITY,
  FirstName NVARCHAR(40) NOT NULL,
  Salary MONEY
)
```

10. What benefit do you get from declaring entity navigation properties as `virtual`?

Exercise 11.2 – Practice exporting data using different serialization formats

Create a console application named `Exercise02` that queries the `Northwind` database for all the categories and products, and then serializes the data using at least three formats of serialization available to .NET Core.

Which format of serialization uses the least number of bytes?

Exercise 11.3 – Explore the EF Core documentation

Use the following link to read more about the topics covered in this chapter:

`https://docs.microsoft.com/en-us/ef/core/index`

Summary

In this chapter, you learned how to connect to a database, how to execute a simple LINQ query and process the results, how to add, modify, and delete data, and how to build entity data models for an existing database, such as `Northwind`. In the next chapter, you will learn how to write more advanced LINQ queries to select, filter, sort, join, and group.

Chapter 12

Querying and Manipulating Data Using LINQ

This chapter is about **Language INtegrated Query (LINQ)**, a set of language extensions that add the ability to work with sequences of items and then filter, sort, and project them into different outputs.

This chapter will cover the following topics:

- Writing LINQ queries
- Working with sets using LINQ
- Using LINQ with EF Core
- Sweetening LINQ syntax with syntactic sugar
- Using multiple threads with parallel LINQ
- Creating your own LINQ extension methods
- Working with LINQ to XML

Writing LINQ queries

Although we wrote a few LINQ queries in *Chapter 11, Working with Databases Using Entity Framework Core*, they weren't the focus, and so I didn't properly explain how LINQ works, but let's now take time to properly understand them.

LINQ has several parts; some are required, and some are optional:

- **Extension methods (required)**: These include examples such as `Where`, `OrderBy`, and `Select`. These are what provide the functionality of LINQ.

- **LINQ providers (required)**: These include LINQ to Objects, LINQ to Entities, LINQ to XML, LINQ to OData, and LINQ to Amazon. These are what convert standard LINQ operations into specific commands for different types of data.

- **Lambda expressions (optional)**: These can be used instead of named methods to simplify LINQ extension method calls.

- **LINQ query comprehension syntax (optional)**: These include `from`, `in`, `where`, `orderby`, `descending`, and `select`. These are C# keywords that are aliases for some of the LINQ extension methods, and their use can simplify the queries you write, especially if you already have experience with other query languages, such as **Structured Query Language (SQL)**.

When programmers are first introduced to LINQ, they often believe that LINQ query comprehension syntax is LINQ, but ironically, that is one of the parts of LINQ that is optional!

Extending sequences with the Enumerable class

The LINQ extension methods, such as `Where` and `Select`, are appended by the `Enumerable` static class to any type, known as a **sequence**, that implements `IEnumerable<T>`.

For example, an array of any type implements the `IEnumerable<T>` class, where `T` is the type of item in the array, so all arrays support LINQ to query and manipulate them.

All generic collections, such as `List<T>`, `Dictionary<TKey, TValue>`, `Stack<T>`, and `Queue<T>`, implement `IEnumerable<T>`, so they can be queried and manipulated with LINQ.

`Enumerable` defines more than 45 extension methods, as summarized in the following table:

Method(s)	Description
`First, FirstOrDefault, Last, LastOrDefault`	Gets the first or last item in the sequence or returns the default value for the type, for example, `0` for an `int`, `null` for a reference type, if there is no first or last item.
`Where`	Returns a sequence of items that match a specified filter.
`Single, SingleOrDefault`	Returns an item that matches a specific filter or throws an exception, or returns the default value for the type, if there is not exactly one match.

ElementAt, ElementAtOrDefault	Returns an item at a specified index position or throws an exception, or returns the default value for the type, if there is not an item at that position.
Select, SelectMany	Projects items into a different shape, that is, type, and flattens a nested hierarchy of items.
OrderBy, OrderByDescending, ThenBy, ThenByDescending	Sorts items by a specified property.
Reverse	Reverses the order of items.
GroupBy, GroupJoin, Join	Group and join sequences.
Skip, SkipWhile	Skip a number of items or skip while an expression is true.
Take, TakeWhile	Take a number of items or take while an expression is true.
Aggregate, Average, Count, LongCount, Max, Min, Sum	Calculates aggregate values.
All, Any, Contains	Returns true if all or any of the items match the filter, or if the sequence contains a specified item.
Cast	Converts items into a specified type.
OfType	Removes items that do not match a specified type.
Except, Intersect, Union	Performs operations that return sets. Sets cannot have duplicate items. Although the inputs of these methods can be any sequence so can have duplicates, the result is always a set.
Append, Concat, Prepend	Performs sequence combining operations.
Zip	Performs a match operation based on the position of items.
Distinct	Removes duplicate items from the sequence.
ToArray, ToList, ToDictionary, ToLookup	Convert the sequence into an array or collection.

Filtering entities with Where

The most common reason for using LINQ is to filter items in a sequence using the Where extension method. Let's explore filtering by defining a sequence of names and then applying LINQ operations on it.

1. In the Code folder, create a folder named Chapter12, with a subfolder named LinqWithObjects.

2. In Visual Studio Code, save a workspace as Chapter12.code-workspace in the Chapter12 folder.

3. Add the folder named `LinqWithObjects` to the workspace.

4. Navigate to **Terminal | New Terminal**.

5. In **Terminal**, enter the following command:

```
dotnet new console
```

6. In `Program.cs`, add a `LinqWithArrayOfStrings` method, which defines an array of `string` values and then attempts to call the `Where` extension method on it, as shown in the following code:

```
static void LinqWithArrayOfStrings()
{
  var names = new string[] { "Michael", "Pam", "Jim", "Dwight",
    "Angela", "Kevin", "Toby", "Creed" };

  var query = names.
}
```

7. As you type the `Where` method, note that it is missing from the IntelliSense list of members of a `string` array, as shown in the following screenshot:

This is because `Where` is an **extension method**. It does not exist on the array type. To make the `Where` extension method available, we must import the `System.Linq` namespace.

8. Add the following statement to the top of the `Program.cs` file:

```
using System.Linq;
```

9. Retype the `Where` method and note that the IntelliSense list shows many more methods, including the extension methods added by the `Enumerable` class, as shown in the following screenshot:

10. As you type the parentheses for the `Where` method, IntelliSense tells us that to call `Where`, we must pass in an instance of a `Func<string, bool>` delegate, as shown in the following screenshot:

11. Enter an expression to create a new instance of a `Func<string, bool>` delegate, and for now note that we have not yet supplied a method name because we will define it in the next step, as shown in the following code:

```
var query = names.Where(new Func<string, bool>())
```

The `Func<string, bool>` delegate tells us that for each `string` variable passed to the method, the method must return a `bool` value. If the method returns `true`, it indicates that we should include the `string` in the results, and if the method returns `false`, it indicates that we should exclude it.

Targeting a named method

Let's define a method that only includes names that are longer than four characters.

1. Add a method to `Program`, as shown in the following code:

```
static bool NameLongerThanFour(string name)
{
  return name.Length > 4;
}
```

2. Back in the `LinqWithArrayOfStrings` method, pass the method's name into the `Func<string, bool>` delegate, and then loop through the query items, as shown in the following code:

```
var query = names.Where(
  new Func<string, bool>(NameLongerThanFour));

foreach (string item in query)
{
  WriteLine(item);
}
```

3. In `Main`, call the `LinqWithArrayOfStrings` method, run the console application, and view the results, noting that only names longer than four letters are listed, as shown in the following output:

```
Michael
Dwight
Angela
Kevin
Creed
```

Simplifying the code by removing the explicit delegate instantiation

We can simplify the code by deleting the explicit instantiation of the `Func<string, bool>` delegate because the C# compiler can instantiate the delegate for us.

1. To help you learn by seeing progressively improved code, copy and paste the query.

2. Comment out the first example, as shown in the following code:

```
// var query = names.Where(
//   new Func<string, bool>(NameLongerThanFour));
```

3. Modify the copy to remove the explicit instantiation of the delegate, as shown in the following code:

```
var query = names.Where(NameLongerThanFour);
```

4. Rerun the application and note that it has the same behavior.

Targeting a lambda expression

We can simplify our code even further using a **lambda expression** in place of a named method.

Although it can look complicated at first, a lambda expression is simply a **nameless function**. It uses the `=>` (read as "goes to") symbol to indicate the return value.

1. Copy and paste the query, comment the second example, and modify the query, as shown in the following code:

```
var query = names.Where(name => name.Length > 4);
```

Note that the syntax for a lambda expression includes all the important parts of the `NameLongerThanFour` method, but nothing more. A lambda expression only needs to define the following:

   ○ The names of input parameters.

   ○ A return value expression

The type of the `name` input parameter is inferred from the fact that the sequence contains `string` values, and the return type must be a `bool` value for `Where` to work, so the expression after the `=>` symbol must return a `bool` value.

The compiler does most of the work for us, so our code can be as concise as possible.

2. Rerun the application and note that it has the same behavior.

Sorting entities

Other commonly used extension methods are `OrderBy` and `ThenBy`, used for sorting a sequence.

Extension methods can be chained if the previous method returns another sequence, that is, a type that implements the `IEnumerable<T>` interface.

Sorting by a single property using OrderBy

Let's continue working with the current project to explore sorting.

1. Append a call to `OrderBy` to the end of the existing query, as shown in the following code:

```
var query = names
  .Where(name => name.Length > 4)
  .OrderBy(name => name.Length);
```

 Good Practice: Format the LINQ statement so that each extension method call happens on its own line to make them easier to read.

2. Rerun the application and note that the names are now sorted by shortest first, as shown in the following output:

```
Kevin
Creed
Dwight
Angela
Michael
```

To put the longest name first, you would use `OrderByDescending`.

Sorting by a subsequent property using ThenBy

We might want to sort by more than one property, for example, to sort names of the same length in alphabetical order.

1. Add a call to the `ThenBy` method at the end of the existing query, as shown highlighted in the following code:

```
var query = names
    .Where(name => name.Length > 4)
    .OrderBy(name => name.Length)
    .ThenBy(name => name);
```

2. Rerun the application and note the slight difference in the following sort order. Within a group of names of the same length, the names are sorted alphabetically by the full value of the `string`, so `Creed` comes before `Kevin`, and `Angela` comes before `Dwight`, as shown in the following output:

```
Creed
Kevin
Angela
Dwight
Michael
```

Filtering by type

`Where` is great for filtering by values, such as text and numbers. But what if the sequence contains multiple types, and you want to filter by a specific type and respect any inheritance hierarchy?

Imagine that you have a sequence of exceptions. Exceptions have a complex hierarchy, as shown in the following diagram:

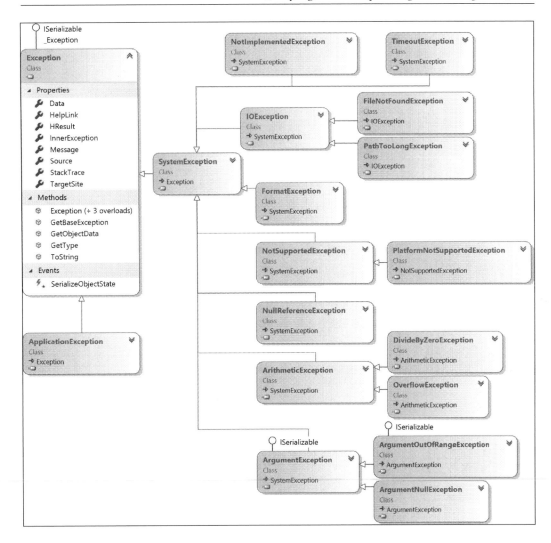

Let's explore filtering by type.

1. In `Program`, add a `LinqWithArrayOfExceptions` method, which defines an array of `Exception`-derived objects, as shown in the following code:

```
static void LinqWithArrayOfExceptions()
{
  var errors = new Exception[]
  {
    new ArgumentException(),
    new SystemException(),
    new IndexOutOfRangeException(),
    new InvalidOperationException(),
```

```
      new NullReferenceException(),
      new InvalidCastException(),
      new OverflowException(),
      new DivideByZeroException(),
      new ApplicationException()
   };
}
```

2. Write statements using the `OfType<T>` extension method to filter exceptions that are not arithmetic exceptions and write them to the console, as shown in the following code:

```
var numberErrors = errors.OfType<ArithmeticException>();

foreach (var error in numberErrors)
{
  WriteLine(error);
}
```

3. In the `Main` method, comment out the call to the `LinqWithArrayOfStrings` method and add a call to the `LinqWithArrayOfExceptions` method.

4. Run the console application and note that the results only include exceptions of the `ArithmeticException` type, or the `ArithmeticException`-derived types, as shown in the following output:

```
System.OverflowException: Arithmetic operation resulted in an
overflow.
System.DivideByZeroException: Attempted to divide by zero.
```

Working with sets and bags using LINQ

Sets are one of the most fundamental concepts in mathematics. A **set** is a collection of one or more unique objects. A **multiset** or **bag** is a collection of one or more objects that can have duplicates. You might remember being taught about Venn diagrams in school. Common set operations include the **intersect** or **union** between sets.

Let's create a console application that will define three arrays of `string` values for cohorts of apprentices and then perform some common set and multiset operations on them.

1. Create a new console application project named `LinqWithSets`, add it to the workspace for this chapter, and select the project as active for OmniSharp.

2. Import the following additional namespaces:

```
using System.Collections.Generic; // for IEnumerable<T>
using System.Linq; // for LINQ extension methods
```

3. In `Program`, before the `Main` method, add the following method that outputs any sequence of `string` variables as a comma-separated single `string` to the console output, along with an optional description:

```
static void Output(IEnumerable<string> cohort,
  string description = "")
{
  if (!string.IsNullOrEmpty(description))
  {
    WriteLine(description);
  }
  Write("  ");
  WriteLine(string.Join(", ", cohort.ToArray()));
}
```

4. In `Main`, add statements to define three arrays of names, output them, and then perform various set operations on them, as shown in the following code:

```
var cohort1 = new string[]
  { "Rachel", "Gareth", "Jonathan", "George" };
var cohort2 = new string[]
  { "Jack", "Stephen", "Daniel", "Jack", "Jared" };
var cohort3 = new string[]
  { "Declan", "Jack", "Jack", "Jasmine", "Conor" };

Output(cohort1, "Cohort 1");
Output(cohort2, "Cohort 2");
Output(cohort3, "Cohort 3");
WriteLine();
Output(cohort2.Distinct(), "cohort2.Distinct():");
WriteLine();
Output(cohort2.Union(cohort3), "cohort2.Union(cohort3):");
WriteLine();
Output(cohort2.Concat(cohort3), "cohort2.Concat(cohort3):");
WriteLine();
Output(cohort2.Intersect(cohort3), "cohort2.Intersect(cohort3):");
WriteLine();
Output(cohort2.Except(cohort3), "cohort2.Except(cohort3):");
WriteLine();
Output(cohort1.Zip(cohort2, (c1, c2) => $"{c1} matched with {c2}"),
  "cohort1.Zip(cohort2):");
```

5. Run the console application and view the results, as shown in the following output:

```
Cohort 1
  Rachel, Gareth, Jonathan, George
Cohort 2
  Jack, Stephen, Daniel, Jack, Jared
```

```
Cohort 3
  Declan, Jack, Jack, Jasmine, Conor

cohort2.Distinct():
  Jack, Stephen, Daniel, Jared

cohort2.Union(cohort3):
  Jack, Stephen, Daniel, Jared, Declan, Jasmine, Conor

cohort2.Concat(cohort3):
  Jack, Stephen, Daniel, Jack, Jared, Declan, Jack, Jack, Jasmine,
Conor

cohort2.Intersect(cohort3):
  Jack

cohort2.Except(cohort3):
  Stephen, Daniel, Jared

cohort1.Zip(cohort2):
  Rachel matched with Jack, Gareth matched with Stephen, Jonathan
matched with Daniel, George matched with Jack
```

With `Zip`, if there are unequal numbers of items in the two sequences, then some items will not have a matching partner. Those without a partner will not be included in the result.

Using LINQ with EF Core

To learn about **projection**, it is best to have some more complex sequences to work with, so in the next project, we will use the `Northwind` sample database.

1. Create a new console application project named `LinqWithEFCore`, add it to the workspace for this chapter, and select the project as active for OmniSharp.

2. Modify the `LinqWithEFCore.csproj` file, as shown highlighted in the following markup:

```
<Project Sdk="Microsoft.NET.Sdk">

  <PropertyGroup>
    <OutputType>Exe</OutputType>
```

```
    <TargetFramework>netcoreapp3.0</TargetFramework>
  </PropertyGroup>

  <ItemGroup>
    <PackageReference
      Include="Microsoft.EntityFrameworkCore.Sqlite"
      Version="3.0.0" />
  </ItemGroup>

</Project>
```

3. In **Terminal**, download the referenced package and compile the current project, as shown in the following command:

   ```
   dotnet build
   ```

4. Copy the `Northwind.sql` file into the `LinqWithEFCore` folder, and then use **Terminal** to create the Northwind database by executing the following command:

   ```
   sqlite3 Northwind.db < Northwind.sql
   ```

Detailed instructions of how to create the Northwind database were in *Chapter 11, Working with Databases Using Entity Framework Core*.

Building an EF Core model

Let's define an Entity Framework Core model to represent the database and tables that we will work with. Your `DbContext`-derived class must have an overridden method named `OnConfiguring`. This will set the database connection string.

1. Add three class files to the project named `Northwind.cs`, `Category.cs`, and `Product.cs`.

2. Modify the class file named `Northwind.cs`, as shown in the following code:

   ```
   using Microsoft.EntityFrameworkCore;

   namespace Packt.Shared
   {
     // this manages the connection to the database
     public class Northwind : DbContext
     {
       // these properties map to tables in the database
       public DbSet<Category> Categories { get; set; }
       public DbSet<Product> Products { get; set; }
   ```

```
    protected override void OnConfiguring(
      DbContextOptionsBuilder optionsBuilder)
    {
      string path = System.IO.Path.Combine(
        System.Environment.CurrentDirectory, "Northwind.db");

      optionsBuilder.UseSqlite($"Filename={path}");
    }
  }
}
```

3. Modify the class file named `Category.cs`, as shown in the following code:

```
using System.ComponentModel.DataAnnotations;

namespace Packt.Shared
{
  public class Category
  {
    public int CategoryID { get; set; }

    [Required]
    [StringLength(15)]
    public string CategoryName { get; set; }

    public string Description { get; set; }
  }
}
```

4. Modify the class file named `Product.cs`, as shown in the following code:

```
using System.ComponentModel.DataAnnotations;

namespace Packt.Shared
{
  public class Product
  {
    public int ProductID { get; set; }

    [Required]
    [StringLength(40)]
    public string ProductName { get; set; }

    public int? SupplierID { get; set; }

    public int? CategoryID { get; set; }

    [StringLength(20)]
    public string QuantityPerUnit { get; set; }
```

```
        public decimal? UnitPrice { get; set; }

        public short? UnitsInStock { get; set; }

        public short? UnitsOnOrder { get; set; }

        public short? ReorderLevel { get; set; }

        public bool Discontinued { get; set; }
    }
}
```

We have not defined relationships between the two entity classes. This is deliberate. Later, you will use LINQ to join the two entity sets.

Filtering and sorting sequences

Now let's write statements to filter and sort sequences of rows from the tables.

1. Open the `Program.cs` file and import the following type and namespaces:

```
using static System.Console;
using Packt.Shared;
using Microsoft.EntityFrameworkCore;
using System.Linq;
```

2. Create a method to filter and sort products, as shown in the following code:

```
static void FilterAndSort()
{
  using (var db = new Northwind())
  {
    var query = db.Products
      .Where(product => product.UnitPrice < 10M)
      // IQueryable<Product>
      .OrderByDescending(product => product.UnitPrice);

    WriteLine("Products that cost less than $10:");
    foreach (var item in query)
    {
      WriteLine("{0}: {1} costs {2:$#,##0.00}",
        item.ProductID, item.ProductName, item.UnitPrice);
    }
    WriteLine();
  }
}
```

`DbSet<T>` implements `IQueryable<T>`, which implements `IEnumerable<T>`, so LINQ can be used to query and manipulate collections of entities in models built for EF Core.

You might have also noticed that the sequences implement `IQueryable<T>` (or `IOrderedQueryable<T>` after a call to an ordering LINQ method) instead of `IEnumerable<T>` or `IOrderedEnumerable<T>`.

This is an indication that we are using a LINQ provider that builds the query in memory using expression trees. They represent code in a tree-like data structure and enable the creation of dynamic queries, which is useful for building LINQ queries for external data providers like SQLite.

More Information: You can read more about expression trees at the following link: https://docs.microsoft.com/en-us/dotnet/csharp/programming-guide/concepts/expression-trees/

The LINQ query will be converted into another query language, such as SQL. Enumerating the query with `foreach` or calling a method such as `ToArray` will force execution of the query.

1. In `Main`, call the `FilterAndSort` method.

2. Run the console application and view the result, as shown in the following output:

```
Products that cost less than $10:
41: Jack's New England Clam Chowder costs $9.65
45: Rogede sild costs $9.50
47: Zaanse koeken costs $9.50
19: Teatime Chocolate Biscuits costs $9.20
23: Tunnbröd costs $9.00
75: Rhönbräu Klosterbier costs $7.75
54: Tourtière costs $7.45
52: Filo Mix costs $7.00
13: Konbu costs $6.00
24: Guaraná Fantástica costs $4.50
33: Geitost costs $2.50
```

Although this query outputs the information we want, it does so inefficiently because it gets all columns from the `Products` table instead of just the three columns we need, which is the equivalent of the following SQL statement:

```
SELECT * FROM Products;
```

In *Chapter 11, Working with Databases Using Entity Framework Core*, you learned how to log the SQL commands executed against SQLite to see this for yourself.

Projecting sequences into new types

Before we look at projection, we need to review object initialization syntax. If you have a class defined, then you can instantiate an object using new, the class name, and curly braces to set initial values for fields and properties, as shown in the following code:

```
var alice = new Person
{
  Name = "Alice Jones",
  DateOfBirth = new DateTime(1998, 3, 7)
};
```

C# 3.0 and later allows instances of **anonymous types** to be instantiated, as shown in the following code:

```
var anonymouslyTypedObject = new
{
  Name = "Alice Jones",
  DateOfBirth = new DateTime(1998, 3, 7)
};
```

Although we did not specify a type name, the compiler could infer an anonymous type from the setting of two properties named Name and DateOfBirth. This capability is especially useful when writing LINQ queries to project an existing type into a new type without having to explicitly define the new type. Since the type is anonymous, this can only work with var-declared local variables.

Let's add a call to the Select method to make the SQL command executed against the database table more efficient by projecting instances of the Product class into instances of a new anonymous type with only three properties.

1. In Main, modify the LINQ query to use the Select method to return only the three properties (that is, table columns) that we need, as shown highlighted in the following code:

    ```
    var query = db.Products
      .Where(product => product.UnitPrice < 10M) //
    IQueryable<Product>
      .OrderByDescending(product => product.UnitPrice)
      // IOrderedQueryable<Product>
      .Select(product => new // anonymous type
        {
    ```

```
      product.ProductID,
      product.ProductName,
      product.UnitPrice
  });
```

2. Run the console application and confirm that the output is the same as before.

Joining and grouping sequences

There are two extension methods for joining and grouping:

*   `Join`: This method has four parameters: the sequence that you want to join with, the property or properties on the *left* sequence to match on, the property or properties on the *right* sequence to match on, and a projection.

*   `GroupJoin`: This method has the same parameters, but it combines the matches into a group object with a `Key` property for the matching value and an `IEnumerable<T>` type for the multiple matches.

Let's explore these methods when working with two tables: categories and products.

1. Create a method to select categories and products, join them and output them, as shown in the following code:

```
static void JoinCategoriesAndProducts()
{
  using (var db = new Northwind())
  {
    // join every product to its category to return 77 matches
    var queryJoin = db.Categories.Join(
      inner: db.Products,
      outerKeySelector: category => category.CategoryID,
      innerKeySelector: product => product.CategoryID,
      resultSelector: (c, p) =>
        new { c.CategoryName, p.ProductName, p.ProductID });

    foreach (var item in queryJoin)
    {
      WriteLine("{0}: {1} is in {2}.",
        arg0: item.ProductID,
        arg1: item.ProductName,
        arg2: item.CategoryName);
    }
  }
}
```

In a join there are two sequences, `outer` and `inner`. In the previous example, `categories` is the outer sequence and `products` is the inner sequence.

2. In `Main`, comment out the call to `FilterAndJoin` and call `JoinCategoriesAndProducts`.

3. Run the console application and view the results. Note that there is a single line output for each of the 77 products, and the results show all products in the `Beverages` category first, then the `Condiments` category, and so on, as shown in the following output:

```
1: Chai is in Beverages.
2: Chang is in Beverages.
24: Guaraná Fantástica is in Beverages.
34: Sasquatch Ale is in Beverages.
35: Steeleye Stout is in Beverages.
38: Côte de Blaye is in Beverages.
39: Chartreuse verte is in Beverages.
43: Ipoh Coffee is in Beverages.
67: Laughing Lumberjack Lager is in Beverages.
70: Outback Lager is in Beverages.
75: Rhönbräu Klosterbier is in Beverages.
76: Lakkalikööri is in Beverages.
3: Aniseed Syrup is in Condiments.
4: Chef Anton's Cajun Seasoning is in Condiments.
```

4. At the end of the existing query, call the `OrderBy` method to sort by `ProductID`, as shown in the following code:

```
.OrderBy(cp => cp.ProductID);
```

5. Rerun the application and view the results, as shown in the following output (edited to only include the first 10 items):

```
1: Chai is in Beverages.
2: Chang is in Beverages.
3: Aniseed Syrup is in Condiments.
4: Chef Anton's Cajun Seasoning is in Condiments.
5: Chef Anton's Gumbo Mix is in Condiments.
6: Grandma's Boysenberry Spread is in Condiments.
7: Uncle Bob's Organic Dried Pears is in Produce.
8: Northwoods Cranberry Sauce is in Condiments.
9: Mishi Kobe Niku is in Meat/Poultry.
10: Ikura is in Seafood.
```

6. Create a method to group and join, show the group name, and then show all the items within each group, as shown in the following code:

```
static void GroupJoinCategoriesAndProducts()
{
  using (var db = new Northwind())
  {
    // group all products by their category to return 8 matches
    var queryGroup = db.Categories.AsEnumerable().GroupJoin(
      inner: db.Products,
      outerKeySelector: category => category.CategoryID,
      innerKeySelector: product => product.CategoryID,
      resultSelector: (c, matchingProducts) => new {
        c.CategoryName,
        Products = matchingProducts.OrderBy(p => p.ProductName)
      });

    foreach (var item in queryGroup)
    {
      WriteLine("{0} has {1} products.",
        arg0: item.CategoryName,
        arg1: item.Products.Count());

      foreach (var product in item.Products)
      {
        WriteLine($"  {product.ProductName}");
      }
    }
  }
}
```

If we had not called the AsEnumerable method, then a runtime exception is thrown, as shown in the following output:

```
Unhandled exception. System.NotImplementedException: The method or
operation is not implemented.
    at Microsoft.EntityFrameworkCore.Relational.Query.Pipeline.
RelationalQueryableMethodTranslatingExpressionVisitor.Translat
eGroupJoin(ShapedQueryExpression outer, ShapedQueryExpression
inner, LambdaExpression outerKeySelector, LambdaExpression
innerKeySelector, LambdaExpression resultSelector)
```

This is because not all LINQ extension methods can be converted from expression trees into other query syntax like SQL. In these cases, we can convert from IQueryable<T> to IEnumerable<T> by calling the AsEnumerable method, which forces query processing to use LINQ to EF Core only to bring the data into the application and then use LINQ to Objects to execute more complex processing in-memory. But, often, this is less efficient.

7. In `Main`, comment the previous method call and call `GroupJoinCategoriesAndProducts`.

8. Rerun the console application, view the results, and note that the products inside each category have been sorted by their name, as defined in the query and shown in the following partial output:

```
Beverages has 12 products.
  Chai
  Chang
  Chartreuse verte
  Côte de Blaye
  Guaraná Fantástica
  Ipoh Coffee
  Lakkalikööri
  Laughing Lumberjack Lager
  Outback Lager
  Rhönbräu Klosterbier
  Sasquatch Ale
  Steeleye Stout
Condiments has 12 products.
  Aniseed Syrup
  Chef Anton's Cajun Seasoning
  Chef Anton's Gumbo Mix
```

Aggregating sequences

There are LINQ extension methods to perform aggregation functions, such as `Average` and `Sum`. Let's write some code to see some of these methods in action aggregating information from the `Products` table.

1. Create a method to show the use of the aggregation extension methods, as shown in the following code:

```
static void AggregateProducts()
{
  using (var db = new Northwind())
  {
    WriteLine("{0,-25} {1,10}",
      arg0: "Product count:",
      arg1: db.Products.Count());

    WriteLine("{0,-25} {1,10:$#,##0.00}",
      arg0: "Highest product price:",
      arg1: db.Products.Max(p => p.UnitPrice));

    WriteLine("{0,-25} {1,10:N0}",
```

```
            arg0: "Sum of units in stock:",
            arg1: db.Products.Sum(p => p.UnitsInStock));

        WriteLine("{0,-25} {1,10:N0}",
            arg0: "Sum of units on order:",
            arg1: db.Products.Sum(p => p.UnitsOnOrder));

        WriteLine("{0,-25} {1,10:$#,##0.00}",
            arg0: "Average unit price:",
            arg1: db.Products.Average(p => p.UnitPrice));

        WriteLine("{0,-25} {1,10:$#,##0.00}",
            arg0: "Value of units in stock:",
                arg1: db.Products.AsEnumerable()
                   .Sum(p => p.UnitPrice * p.UnitsInStock));
    }
}
```

2. In `Main`, comment the previous method and call `AggregateProducts`.

3. Run the console application and view the result, as shown in the following output:

```
Product count:                  77
Highest product price:      $263.50
Sum of units in stock:        3,119
Sum of units on order:          780
Average unit price:          $28.87
Value of units in stock:  $74,050.85
```

In Entity Framework Core 3.0 and later, LINQ operations that cannot be translated to SQL are no longer automatically evaluated on the client side, so you must explicitly call `AsEnumerable` to force further processing of the query on the client.

More Information: You can learn more about this breaking change at the following link: `https://docs.microsoft.com/en-us/ef/core/what-is-new/ef-core-3.0/breaking-changes-linq-queries-are-no-longer-evaluated-on-the-client`

Sweetening LINQ syntax with syntactic sugar

C# 3.0 introduced some new language keywords in 2008 in order to make it easier for programmers with experience with SQL to write LINQ queries. This *syntactic sugar* is sometimes called the **LINQ query comprehension syntax**.

More Information: The LINQ query comprehension syntax is limited in functionality. It only provides C# keywords for the most commonly used LINQ features. You must use extension methods to access all the features of LINQ. You can read more about why it is called comprehension syntax at the following link: `https://stackoverflow.com/questions/6229187/linq-why-is-it-called-comprehension-syntax`

Consider the following array of `string` values:

```
var names = new string[] { "Michael", "Pam", "Jim", "Dwight",
"Angela", "Kevin", "Toby", "Creed" };
```

To filter and sort the names, you could use **extension methods** and **lambda expressions**, as shown in the following code:

```
var query = names
  .Where(name => name.Length > 4)
  .OrderBy(name => name.Length)
  .ThenBy(name => name);
```

Or you could achieve the same results by using **query comprehension syntax**, as shown in the following code:

```
var query = from name in names
  where name.Length > 4
  orderby name.Length, name
  select name;
```

The compiler changes the query comprehension syntax to the equivalent extension methods and lambda expressions for you.

The `select` keyword is always required for LINQ query comprehension syntax. The `Select` extension method is optional when using extension methods and lambda expressions because the whole item is implicitly selected.

Not all extension methods have a C# keyword equivalent, for example, the `Skip` and `Take` extension methods, which are commonly used to implement paging for lots of data.

A query that skips and takes cannot be written using only the query comprehension syntax so we could write the query using all extension methods, as shown in the following code:

```
var query = names
  .Where(name => name.Length > 4)
  .Skip(80)
  .Take(10);
```

Or, you can wrap query comprehension syntax in parentheses and then switch to using extension methods, as shown in the following code:

```
var query = (from name in names
             where name.Length > 4
             select name)
  .Skip(80)
  .Take(10);
```

Good Practice: Learn both extension methods with lambda expressions and the query comprehension syntax ways of writing LINQ queries, because you are likely to have to maintain code that uses both.

Using multiple threads with parallel LINQ

By default, only one thread is used to execute a LINQ query. **Parallel LINQ (PLINQ)** is an easy way to enable multiple threads to execute a LINQ query.

Good Practice: Do not assume that using parallel threads will improve the performance of your applications. Always measure real-world timings and resource usage.

Creating an app that benefits from multiple threads

To see it in action, we will start with some code that only uses a single thread to square 200 million integers. We will use the `StopWatch` type to measure the change in performance.

We will use operating system tools to monitor CPU and CPU core usage. If you do not have multiple CPUs or at least multiple cores, then this exercise won't show much!

1. Create a new console application project named `LinqInParallel`, add it to the workspace for this chapter, and select the project as active for OmniSharp.

2. Import the `System.Diagnostics` namespace so that we can use the `StopWatch` type; `System.Collections.Generic` so that we can use the `IEnumerable<T>` type, `System.Linq` so that we can use LINQ; and statically import the `System.Console` type.

3. Add statements to Main to create a stopwatch to record timings, wait for a key press before starting the timer, create 200 million integers, square each of them, stop the timer, and display the elapsed milliseconds, as shown in the following code:

```
var watch = Stopwatch.StartNew();
Write("Press ENTER to start: ");
ReadLine();
watch.Start();

IEnumerable<int> numbers = Enumerable.Range(1, 200_000_000);

var squares = numbers.Select(number => number * number).ToArray();

watch.Stop();
WriteLine("{0:#,##0} elapsed milliseconds.",
  watch.ElapsedMilliseconds);
```

4. Run the console application, but *do not* press *Enter* to start yet.

Using Windows 10

1. If you are using Windows 10, then right-click on the Windows **Start** button or press *Ctrl + Alt + Delete*, and then click on **Task Manager**.

2. At the bottom of the **Task Manager** window, click on the **More details** button. At the top of the **Task Manager** window, click on the **Performance** tab.

3. Right-click on the **CPU Utilization** graph, choose **Change graph to**, and then select **Logical processors**.

Using macOS

1. If you are using macOS, then launch **Activity Monitor**.

2. Navigate to **View | Update Frequency | Very often (1 sec)**.

3. To see the CPU graphs, navigate to **Window | CPU History**.

For all operating systems

1. Rearrange **Task Manager** or **CPU History** or your Linux tool and Visual Studio Code so that they are side by side.

2. Wait for the CPUs to settle and then press *Enter* to start the stopwatch and run the query.

The result should be an amount of elapsed milliseconds, as shown in the following output and screenshot:

```
Press ENTER to start.
173,689 elapsed milliseconds.
```

The **Task Manager** or **CPU History** windows should show that one or two CPUs were used the most. Others may execute background tasks at the same time, such as the garbage collector, so the other CPUs or cores won't be completely flat, but the work is certainly not being evenly spread among all the possible CPUs or cores.

3. In `Main`, modify the query to make a call to the `AsParallel` extension method, as shown in the following code:

```
var squares = numbers.AsParallel()
    .Select(number => number * number).ToArray();
```

4. Run the application again.

5. Wait for the **Task Manager** or **CPU History** windows to settle and then press *Enter* to start the stopwatch and run the query. This time, the application should complete in less time (although it might not be as less as you might hope for—managing those multiple threads takes extra effort!):

```
Press ENTER to start.
145,904 elapsed milliseconds.
```

6. The **Task Manager** or **CPU History** windows should show that all CPUs were used equally to execute the LINQ query, as shown in the following screenshot:

You will learn more about managing multiple threads in *Chapter 13, Improving Performance and Scalability Using Multitasking*.

Creating your own LINQ extension methods

In *Chapter 6, Implementing Interfaces and Inheriting Classes*, you learned how to create your own extension methods. To create LINQ extension methods, all you must do is extend the IEnumerable<T> type.

 Good Practice: Put your own extension methods in a separate class library so that they can be easily deployed as their own assembly or NuGet package.

We will look at the Average extension method as an example. Any school child will tell you that *average* can mean one of three things:

- **Mean**: Sum the numbers and divide by the count.

- **Mode**: The most common number.
- **Median**: The number in the middle of the numbers when ordered.

Microsoft's implementation of the `Average` extension method calculates the mean. We might want to define our own extension methods for `Mode` and `Median`.

1. In the `LinqWithEFCore` project, add a new class file named `MyLinqExtensions.cs`.

2. Modify the class, as shown in the following code:

```
using System.Collections.Generic;

namespace System.Linq
{
  public static class MyLinqExtensions
  {
    // this is a chainable LINQ extension method
    public static IEnumerable<T> ProcessSequence<T>(
      this IEnumerable<T> sequence)
    {
      // you could do some processing here
      return sequence;
    }

    // these are scalar LINQ extension methods
    public static int? Median(this IEnumerable<int?> sequence)
    {
      var ordered = sequence.OrderBy(item => item);
      int middlePosition = ordered.Count() / 2;
      return ordered.ElementAt(middlePosition);
    }

    public static int? Median<T>(
      this IEnumerable<T> sequence, Func<T, int?> selector)
    {
      return sequence.Select(selector).Median();
    }

    public static decimal? Median(
      this IEnumerable<decimal?> sequence)
    {
      var ordered = sequence.OrderBy(item => item);
      int middlePosition = ordered.Count() / 2;
      return ordered.ElementAt(middlePosition);
    }

    public static decimal? Median<T>(
```

```
      this IEnumerable<T> sequence, Func<T, decimal?> selector)
  {
    return sequence.Select(selector).Median();
  }

  public static int? Mode(this IEnumerable<int?> sequence)
  {
    var grouped = sequence.GroupBy(item => item);
    var orderedGroups = grouped.OrderBy(group => group.Count());
    return orderedGroups.FirstOrDefault().Key;
  }

  public static int? Mode<T>(
    this IEnumerable<T> sequence, Func<T, int?> selector)
  {
    return sequence.Select(selector).Mode();
  }

  public static decimal? Mode(
    this IEnumerable<decimal?> sequence)
  {
    var grouped = sequence.GroupBy(item => item);
    var orderedGroups = grouped.OrderBy(group => group.Count());
    return orderedGroups.FirstOrDefault().Key;
  }

  public static decimal? Mode<T>(
    this IEnumerable<T> sequence, Func<T, decimal?> selector)
  {
    return sequence.Select(selector).Mode();
  }
 }
}
```

If this class was in a separate class library, to use your LINQ extension
methods, you simply need to reference the class library assembly because the
System.Linq namespace is often already imported.

3. In Program.cs, in the FilterAndSort method, modify the LINQ query for
   Products to call your custom chainable extension method, as shown in the
   following code:

```
var query = db.Products
  .ProcessSequence()
  .Where(product => product.UnitPrice < 10M)
  .OrderByDescending(product => product.UnitPrice)
  .Select(product => new
  {
    product.ProductID,
```

```
        product.ProductName,
        product.UnitPrice
    });
```

4. In the `Main` method, uncomment the `FilterAndSort` method and comment out any calls to other methods.

5. Run the console application and note that you see the same output as before because your method doesn't modify the sequence. But you now know how to extend LINQ with your own functionality.

6. Create a method to output the mean, median, and mode, for `UnitsInStock` and `UnitPrice` for products, using your custom extension methods and the built-in `Average` extension method, as shown in the following code:

```
static void CustomExtensionMethods()
{
  using (var db = new Northwind())
  {
    WriteLine("Mean units in stock: {0:N0}",
      db.Products.Average(p => p.UnitsInStock));

    WriteLine("Mean unit price: {0:$#,##0.00}",
      db.Products.Average(p => p.UnitPrice));

    WriteLine("Median units in stock: {0:N0}",
      db.Products.Median(p => p.UnitsInStock));

    WriteLine("Median unit price: {0:$#,##0.00}",
      db.Products.Median(p => p.UnitPrice));

    WriteLine("Mode units in stock: {0:N0}",
      db.Products.Mode(p => p.UnitsInStock));

    WriteLine("Mode unit price: {0:$#,##0.00}",
      db.Products.Mode(p => p.UnitPrice));
  }
}
```

7. In `Main`, comment any previous method calls and call `CustomExtensionMethods`.

8. Run the console application and view the result, as shown in the following output:

```
Mean units in stock: 41
Mean unit price: $28.87
Median units in stock: 26
Median unit price: $19.50
Mode units in stock: 13
Mode unit price: $22.00
```

Working with LINQ to XML

LINQ to XML is a LINQ provider that allows you to query and manipulate XML.

Generating XML using LINQ to XML

Let's create a method to convert the Products table into XML.

1. In Program.cs, import the System.Xml.Linq namespace.

2. Create a method to output the products in XML format, as shown in the following code:

```
static void OutputProductsAsXml()
{
  using (var db = new Northwind())
  {
    var productsForXml = db.Products.ToArray();

    var xml = new XElement("products",
      from p in productsForXml
      select new XElement("product",
        new XAttribute("id", p.ProductID),
        new XAttribute("price", p.UnitPrice),
        new XElement("name", p.ProductName)));

    WriteLine(xml.ToString());
  }
}
```

3. In Main, comment the previous method call and call OutputProductsAsXml.

4. Run the console application, view the result, and note that the structure of the XML generated matches the elements and attributes that the LINQ to XML statement declaratively described in the preceding code, as shown in the following partial output:

```
<products>
  <product id="1" price="18">
    <name>Chai</name>
  </product>
  <product id="2" price="19">
    <name>Chang</name>
  </product>
  . . .
```

Reading XML using LINQ to XML

You might want to use LINQ to XML to easily query or process XML files.

1. In the `LinqWithEFCore` project, add a file named `settings.xml`.

2. Modify its contents, as shown in the following markup:

```xml
<?xml version="1.0" encoding="utf-8" ?>
<appSettings>
  <add key="color" value="red" />
  <add key="size" value="large" />
  <add key="price" value="23.99" />
</appSettings>
```

3. Create a method to complete these tasks:

   ○ Load the XML file.

   ○ Use LINQ to XML to search for an element named `appSettings` and its descendants named `add`.

   ○ Project the XML into an array of an anonymous type with a `Key` and `Value` property.

   ○ Enumerate through the array to show the results:

```csharp
static void ProcessSettings()
{
  XDocument doc = XDocument.Load("settings.xml");

  var appSettings = doc.Descendants("appSettings")
    .Descendants("add")
    .Select(node => new
    {
      Key = node.Attribute("key").Value,
      Value = node.Attribute("value").Value
    }).ToArray();

  foreach (var item in appSettings)
  {
    WriteLine($"{item.Key}: {item.Value}");
  }
}
```

4. In `Main`, comment the previous method call and call `ProcessSettings`.

5. Run the console application and view the result, as shown in the following output:

```
color: red
size: large
price: 23.99
```

Practicing and exploring

Test your knowledge and understanding by answering some questions, get some hands-on practice, and explore with deeper research into the topics covered in this chapter.

Exercise 12.1 – Test your knowledge

Answer the following questions:

1. What are the two required parts of LINQ?
2. Which LINQ extension method would you use to return a subset of properties from a type?
3. Which LINQ extension method would you use to filter a sequence?
4. List five LINQ extension methods that perform aggregation.
5. What is the difference between the `Select` and `SelectMany` extension methods?
6. What is the difference between `IEnumerable<T>` and `IQueryable<T>`? and how do you switch between them
7. What does the last type parameter in the generic `Func` delegates represent?
8. What is the benefit of a LINQ extension method that ends with `OrDefault`?
9. Why is query comprehension syntax optional?
10. How can you create your own LINQ extension methods?

Exercise 12.2 – Practice querying with LINQ

Create a console application, named `Exercise02`, that prompts the user for a city and then lists the company names for Northwind customers in that city, as shown in the following output:

```
Enter the name of a city: London
There are 6 customers in London:
Around the Horn
B's Beverages
Consolidated Holdings
Eastern Connection
North/South
Seven Seas Imports
```

Then, enhance the application by displaying a list of all unique cities that customers already reside in as a prompt to the user before they enter their preferred city, as shown in the following output:

```
Aachen, Albuquerque, Anchorage, Århus, Barcelona, Barquisimeto,
Bergamo, Berlin, Bern, Boise, Bräcke, Brandenburg, Bruxelles,
Buenos Aires, Butte, Campinas, Caracas, Charleroi, Cork, Cowes,
Cunewalde, Elgin, Eugene, Frankfurt a.M., Genève, Graz, Helsinki,
I. de Margarita, Kirkland, Kobenhavn, Köln, Lander, Leipzig,
Lille, Lisboa, London, Luleå, Lyon, Madrid, Mannheim, Marseille,
México D.F., Montréal, München, Münster, Nantes, Oulu, Paris,
Portland, Reggio Emilia, Reims, Resende, Rio de Janeiro, Salzburg,
San Cristóbal, San Francisco, Sao Paulo, Seattle, Sevilla,
Stavern, Strasbourg, Stuttgart, Torino, Toulouse, Tsawassen,
Vancouver, Versailles, Walla Walla, Warszawa
```

Exercise 12.3 – Explore topics

Use the following links to read more details about the topics covered in this chapter:

- **LINQ in C#**: https://docs.microsoft.com/en-us/dotnet/csharp/linq/linq-in-csharp
- **101 LINQ Samples**: https://code.msdn.microsoft.com/101-LINQ-Samples-3fb9811b
- **Parallel LINQ (PLINQ)**: https://docs.microsoft.com/en-us/dotnet/standard/parallel-programming/parallel-linq-plinq
- **LINQ to XML Overview (C#)**: https://docs.microsoft.com/en-gb/dotnet/csharp/programming-guide/concepts/linq/linq-to-xml-overview
- **LINQPad 6 for .NET Core 3.0**: https://www.linqpad.net/LINQPad6.aspx

Summary

In this chapter, you learned how to write LINQ queries to select, project, filter, sort, join, and group data in many different formats, including XML, which are tasks you will perform every day.

In the next chapter, you will use the `Task` type to improve the performance of your applications.

Chapter 13
Improving Performance and Scalability Using Multitasking

This chapter is about allowing multiple actions to occur at the same time to improve performance, scalability, and user productivity for the applications that you build.

In this chapter, we will cover the following topics:

- Understanding processes, threads, and tasks
- Monitoring performance and resource usage
- Running tasks asynchronously
- Synchronizing access to shared resources
- Understanding `async` and `await`

Understanding processes, threads, and tasks

A **process**, with one example being each of the console applications we have created, has resources, like memory and threads allocated to it. A **thread** executes your code, statement by statement. By default, each process only has one thread, and this can cause problems when we need to do more than one **task** at the same time. Threads are also responsible for keeping track of things like the currently authenticated user and any internationalization rules that should be followed for the current language and region.

Windows and most other modern operating systems use **preemptive multitasking**, which simulates the parallel execution of tasks. It divides the processor time among the threads, allocating a **time slice** to each thread one after another. The current thread is suspended when its time slice finishes. The processor then allows another thread to run for a time slice.

When Windows switches from one thread to another, it saves the context of the thread and reloads the previously saved context of the next thread in the thread queue. This takes both time and resources to complete.

Threads have a `Priority` property and a `ThreadState` property. In addition, there is a `ThreadPool` class, which is for managing a pool of background worker threads, as shown in the following diagram:

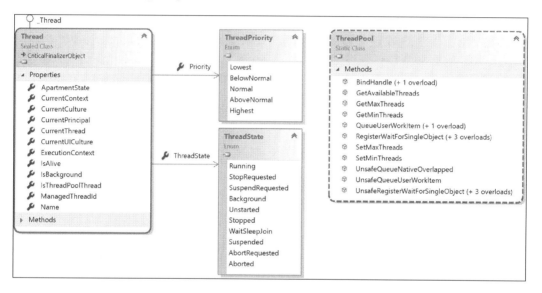

As a developer, if you have a small number of complex pieces of work and you want complete control over them, then you can create and manage individual `Thread` instances. If you have one main thread and multiple small pieces of work that can be executed in the background, then you can add delegate instances that point to those pieces of work implemented as methods to a queue, and they will be automatically allocated to threads in the thread pool.

More Information: You can read more about the thread pool at the following link: https://docs.microsoft.com/en-us/dotnet/standard/threading/the-managed-thread-pool

Threads may have to compete for and also wait for access to shared resources, such as variables, files, and database objects.

Depending on the task, doubling the number of threads (workers) to perform a task does not halve the number of seconds that it will take to complete that task. In fact, it can *increase* the duration of the task, as pointed out in the following tweet:

Carl T. Bergstrom @CT_Bergstrom · Dec 17
My son clearly has a better grasp on the real world than his teacher does.

8. If 6 workers can make a car in 90 hours, how long would it take 12 workers to make the same car?

(A) 12 hours
(B) 25 hours
(C) 30 hours
(D) 45 hours
(E) 180 hours

↩ 253   ↻ 10K   ♥ 16K   •••

Good Practice: Never assume that more threads will improve performance! Run performance tests on a baseline code implementation without multiple threads, and then again on a code implementation with multiple threads. You should also perform performance tests in a staging environment that is as close as possible to the production environment.

Monitoring performance and resource usage

Before we can improve the performance of any code, we need to be able to monitor its speed and efficiency in order to record a baseline that we can then measure improvements from.

Evaluating the efficiency of types

What is the best type to use for a scenario? To answer this question, we need to carefully consider what we mean by *best*, and through this, we should consider the following factors:

- **Functionality**: This can be decided by checking whether the type provides the features you need.

- **Memory size**: This can be decided by the number of bytes of memory the type takes up.

- **Performance**: This can be decided by how fast the type is.
- **Future needs**: This depends on the changes in requirements and maintainability.

There will be scenarios, such as when storing numbers, where multiple types have the same functionality, so we will need to consider the memory and performance to make a choice.

If we need to store millions of numbers, then the best type to use would be the one that requires the least bytes of memory. But if we only need to store a few numbers, yet we need to perform lots of calculations on them, then the best type to use would be the one that runs fastest on a specific CPU.

You have seen the use of the `sizeof()` function, which shows the number of bytes a single instance of a type uses in memory. When we are storing a large number of values in more complex data structures, such as arrays and lists, then we need a better way of measuring memory usage.

You can read lots of advice online and in books, but the only way to know for sure what the best type would be for your code is to compare the types yourself.

In the next section, you will learn how to write the code to monitor the actual memory requirements and the performance when using different types.

Today a `short` variable might be the best choice, but it might be an even better choice to use an `int` variable, even though it takes twice as much space in the memory. This is because we might need a wider range of values to be stored in the future.

There is another metric we should consider: maintenance. This is a measure of how much effort another programmer would have to put in to understand and modify your code. If you use a nonobvious type choice without explaining that choice with a helpful comment, then it might confuse the programmer who comes along later and needs to fix a bug or add a feature.

Monitoring performance and memory use

The `System.Diagnostics` namespace has lots of useful types for monitoring your code. The first one we will look at is the `Stopwatch` type.

1. In the `Code` folder, create a folder named `Chapter13` with two subfolders named `MonitoringLib` and `MonitoringApp`.
2. In Visual Studio Code, save a workspace as `Chapter13.code-workspace`.

3. Add the folder named `MonitoringLib` to the workspace, open a new **Terminal** window for it, and create a new class library project, as shown in the following command:

```
dotnet new classlib
```

4. Add the folder named `MonitoringApp` to the workspace, open a new **Terminal** window for it, and create a new console app project, as shown in the following command:

```
dotnet new console
```

5. In the `MonitoringLib` project, rename the `Class1.cs` file to `Recorder.cs`.

6. In the `MonitoringApp` project, open `MonitoringApp.csproj` and add a project reference to the `MonitoringLib` class library, as shown highlighted in the following markup:

```
<Project Sdk="Microsoft.NET.Sdk">

  <PropertyGroup>
    <OutputType>Exe</OutputType>
    <TargetFramework>netcoreapp3.0</TargetFramework>
  </PropertyGroup>

  <ItemGroup>
    <ProjectReference
      Include="..\MonitoringLib\MonitoringLib.csproj" />
  </ItemGroup>

</Project>
```

7. In **Terminal**, compile the projects, as shown in the following command:

```
dotnet build
```

Implementing the Recorder class

The `Stopwatch` type has some useful members, as shown in the following table:

Member	Description
`Restart` method	This resets the elapsed time to zero and then starts the timer.
`Stop` method	This stops the timer.
`Elapsed` property	This is the elapsed time stored as a `TimeSpan` format (for example, hours:minutes:seconds)

ElapsedMilliseconds property	This is the elapsed time in milliseconds stored as a long.

The `Process` type has some useful members, as shown in the following table:

Member	Description
VirtualMemorySize64	This displays the amount of virtual memory, in bytes, allocated for the process.
WorkingSet64	This displays the amount of physical memory, in bytes, allocated for the process.

To implement our `Recorder` class, we will use the `Stopwatch` and `Process` classes.

1. Open `Recorder.cs`, and change its contents to use a `Stopwatch` instance to record timings and the current `Process` instance to record memory usage, as shown in the following code:

```
using System;
using System.Diagnostics;
using static System.Console;
using static System.Diagnostics.Process;

namespace Packt.Shared
{
  public static class Recorder
  {
    static Stopwatch timer = new Stopwatch();
    static long bytesPhysicalBefore = 0;
    static long bytesVirtualBefore = 0;

    public static void Start()
    {
      // force two garbage collections to release memory that is
      // no longer referenced but has not been released yet
      GC.Collect();
      GC.WaitForPendingFinalizers();
      GC.Collect();

      // store the current physical and virtual memory use
      bytesPhysicalBefore = GetCurrentProcess().WorkingSet64;
      bytesVirtualBefore = GetCurrentProcess().
VirtualMemorySize64;
      timer.Restart();
    }

    public static void Stop()
    {
```

```
      timer.Stop();
      long bytesPhysicalAfter = GetCurrentProcess().WorkingSet64;
      long bytesVirtualAfter =
        GetCurrentProcess().VirtualMemorySize64;

      WriteLine("{0:N0} physical bytes used.",
        bytesPhysicalAfter - bytesPhysicalBefore);

      WriteLine("{0:N0} virtual bytes used.",
        bytesVirtualAfter - bytesVirtualBefore);

      WriteLine("{0} time span ellapsed.", timer.Elapsed);

      WriteLine("{0:N0} total milliseconds ellapsed.",
        timer.ElapsedMilliseconds);
    }
  }
}
```

The `Start` method of the `Recorder` class uses the garbage collector (the `GC` class) type to ensure that any currently allocated but not referenced memory is collected before recording the amount of used memory. This is an advanced technique that you should almost never use in application code.

2. In the `Program` class, in `Main`, write statements to start and stop the `Recorder` while generating an array of 10,000 integers, as shown in the following code:

```
using System.Linq;
using Packt.Shared;
using static System.Console;

namespace MonitoringApp
{
  class Program
  {
    static void Main(string[] args)
    {
      WriteLine("Processing. Please wait...");
      Recorder.Start();

      // simulate a process that requires some memory resources...
      int[] largeArrayOfInts =
        Enumerable.Range(1, 10_000).ToArray();

      // ...and takes some time to complete
      System.Threading.Thread.Sleep(
        new Random().Next(5, 10) * 1000);

      Recorder.Stop();
```

```
        }
      }
    }
```

3. Run the console application and view the result, as shown in the following output:

```
Processing. Please wait...
655,360 physical bytes used.
536,576 virtual bytes used.
00:00:09.0038702 time span ellapsed.
9,003 total milliseconds ellapsed.
```

Measuring the efficiency of processing strings

Now that you've seen how the Stopwatch and Process types can be used to monitor your code, we will use them to evaluate the best way to process string variables.

1. Comment out the previous statements in the Main method by wrapping them in /* */.

2. Add statements to the Main method to create an array of 50,000 int variables and then concatenate them with commas as separators using a string and StringBuilder class, as shown in the following code:

```
int[] numbers = Enumerable.Range(1, 50_000).ToArray();

Recorder.Start();
WriteLine("Using string with +");
string s = "";
for (int i = 0; i < numbers.Length; i++)
{
  s += numbers[i] + ", ";
}
Recorder.Stop();

Recorder.Start();
WriteLine("Using StringBuilder");
var builder = new System.Text.StringBuilder();
for (int i = 0; i < numbers.Length; i++)
{
  builder.Append(numbers[i]); builder.Append(", ");
}
Recorder.Stop();
```

3. Run the console application and view the result, as shown in the following output:

```
Using string with +
11,231,232 physical bytes used.
29,843,456 virtual bytes used.
00:00:02.6908216 time span ellapsed.
2,690 total milliseconds ellapsed.
Using StringBuilder
4,096 physical bytes used.
0 virtual bytes used.
00:00:00.0023091 time span ellapsed.
2 total milliseconds ellapsed.
```

We can summarize the results as follows:

- The `string` class with the + operator used about 11 MB of physical memory, 29 MB of virtual memory, and took 2.7 seconds.
- The `StringBuilder` class used 4 KB of physical memory, 0 virtual memory, and took a little more than 2 milliseconds.

In this scenario, `StringBuilder` is more than 1,000 times faster and about 10,000 times more memory efficient when concatenating text!

Good Practice: Avoid using the `String.Concat` method or the + operator inside loops. Use `StringBuilder` instead.

Now that you've learned how to measure the performance and resource efficiency of your code, let's learn about processes, threads, and tasks.

Running tasks asynchronously

To understand how multiple tasks can be run simultaneously (at the same time), we will create a console application that needs to execute three methods.

There will be three methods that need to be executed: the first takes 3 seconds, the second takes 2 seconds, and the third takes 1 second. To simulate that work, we can use the `Thread` class to tell the current thread to go to sleep for a specified number of milliseconds.

Running multiple actions synchronously

Before we make the tasks run simultaneously, we will run them synchronously, that is, one after the other.

1. Create a new console application named `WorkingWithTasks`, add its folder to your `Chapter13` workspace, and select the project as active for OmniSharp.

2. In `Program.cs`, import namespace to work with threading and tasks, as shown in the following code:

```
using System;
using System.Threading;
using System.Threading.Tasks;
using System.Diagnostics;
using static System.Console;
```

3. In the `Program` class, add the three methods, as shown in the following code:

```
static void MethodA()
{
  WriteLine("Starting Method A...");
  Thread.Sleep(3000); // simulate three seconds of work
  WriteLine("Finished Method A.");
}

static void MethodB()
{
  WriteLine("Starting Method B...");
  Thread.Sleep(2000); // simulate two seconds of work
  WriteLine("Finished Method B.");
}

static void MethodC()
{
  WriteLine("Starting Method C...");
  Thread.Sleep(1000); // simulate one second of work
  WriteLine("Finished Method C.");
}
```

4. In `Main`, add statements to define a stopwatch and output the milliseconds elapsed, as shown in the following code:

```
static void Main(string[] args)
{
  var timer = Stopwatch.StartNew();

  WriteLine("Running methods synchronously on one thread.");

  MethodA();
  MethodB();
  MethodC();

  WriteLine($"{timer.ElapsedMilliseconds:#,##0}ms elapsed.");
}
```

5. Run the console application, view the result, and note that when there is only one thread doing the work the total time required is just over 6 seconds, as shown in the following output:

```
Running methods synchronously on one thread.
Starting Method A...
Finished Method A.
Starting Method B...
Finished Method B.
Starting Method C...
Finished Method C.
6,015ms elapsed.
```

Running multiple actions asynchronously using tasks

The Thread class has been available since the first version of .NET and can be used to create new threads and manage them, but it can be tricky to work with directly.

.NET Framework 4.0 introduced the Task class in 2010, which is a wrapper around a thread that enables easier creating and management. Managing multiple threads wrapped in tasks will allow our code to execute at the same time, aka asynchronously.

Each `Task` has a `Status` property, and a `CreationOptions` property has a `ContinueWith` method that can be customized with the `TaskContinuationOptions` enum, and can be managed with the `TaskFactory` class, as shown in the following diagram:

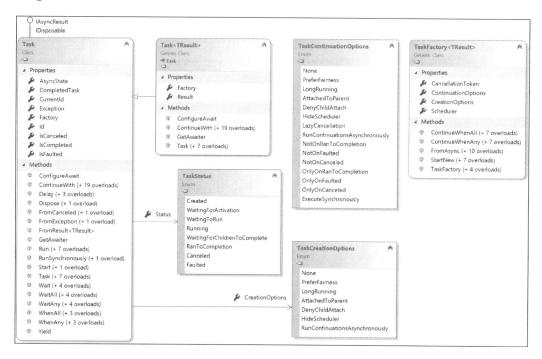

We will look at three ways to start the methods using `Task` instances. Each has a slightly different syntax, but they all define a `Task` and start it.

1. Comment out the calls to the three methods and the associated console message.

2. Add statements to create and start three tasks, one for each method, as shown highlighted in the following code:

```
static void Main(string[] args)
{
  var timer = Stopwatch.StartNew();

  // WriteLine("Running methods synchronously on one thread.");

  // MethodA();
  // MethodB();
  // MethodC();

  WriteLine("Running methods asynchronously on multiple
```

```
threads.");

    Task taskA = new Task(MethodA);
    taskA.Start();
    Task taskB = Task.Factory.StartNew(MethodB);
    Task taskC = Task.Run(new Action(MethodC));

    WriteLine($"{timer.ElapsedMilliseconds:#,##0}ms elapsed.");
}
```

3. Run the console application, view the result, and note that the elapsed milliseconds appear almost immediately. This is because each of the three methods is now being executed by three *new* threads and the original thread can, therefore, write the elapsed time before they finish, as shown in the following output:

```
Running methods asynchronously on multiple threads.
Starting Method A...
Starting Method B...
Starting Method C...
3ms elapsed.
```

It is even possible that the console app will end before one or more of the tasks have a chance to start and write to the console!

 More Information: You can read more about the pros and cons of different ways to start tasks at the following link: https://devblogs.microsoft.com/pfxteam/task-factory-startnew-vs-new-task-start/

Waiting for tasks

Sometimes, you need to wait for a task to complete before continuing. To do this, you can use the `Wait` method on a `Task` instance, or the `WaitAll` or `WaitAny` static methods on an array of tasks, as described in the following table:

Method	Description
`t.Wait()`	This waits for the task instance named `t` to complete execution.
`Task.WaitAny(Task[])`	This waits for any of the tasks in the array to complete execution.
`Task.WaitAll(Task[])`	This waits for all the tasks in the array to complete execution.

Let's see how we can use these wait methods to fix the problem with our console app.

1. Add statements to the `Main` method (after creating the three tasks and before outputting the elapsed time) to combine references to the three tasks into an array and pass them to the `WaitAll` method, as shown in the following code:

```
Task[] tasks = { taskA, taskB, taskC };
Task.WaitAll(tasks);
```

Now, the original thread will pause on that statement, waiting for all three tasks to finish before outputting the elapsed time.

2. Run the console application and view the result, as shown in the following output:

```
Running methods asynchronously on multiple threads.
Starting Method C...
Starting Method A...
Starting Method B...
Finished Method C.
Finished Method B.
Finished Method A.
3,006ms elapsed.
```

The three new threads execute their code simultaneously, and they start in any order. `MethodC` should finish first because it takes only 1 second, then `MethodB`, which takes 2 seconds, and finally `MethodA`, because it takes 3 seconds.

However, the actual CPU used has a big effect on the results. It is the CPU that allocates time slices to each process to allow them to execute their threads. You have no control over when the methods run.

Continuing with another task

If all three tasks can be performed at the same time, then waiting for all tasks to finish will be all we need to do. However, often a task is dependent on the output from another task. To handle this scenario, we need to define **continuation tasks**.

We will create some methods to simulate a call to a web service that returns a monetary amount that then needs to be used to retrieve how many products cost more than that amount in a database. The result returned from the first method needs to be fed into the input of the second method. We will use the `Random` class to wait for a random interval of between 2 and 4 seconds for each method call to simulate the work.

1. Add two methods to the `Program` class that simulate calling a web service and a database stored procedure, as shown in the following code:

```
static decimal CallWebService()
{
  WriteLine("Starting call to web service...");
  Thread.Sleep((new Random()).Next(2000, 4000));
  WriteLine("Finished call to web service.");
  return 89.99M;
}

static string CallStoredProcedure(decimal amount)
{
  WriteLine("Starting call to stored procedure...");
  Thread.Sleep((new Random()).Next(2000, 4000));
  WriteLine("Finished call to stored procedure.");
  return $"12 products cost more than {amount:C}.";
}
```

2. In the `Main` method, comment out the previous three tasks by wrapping them in multiline comment characters, `/* */`. Leave the statement that outputs the elapsed milliseconds.

3. Add statements before the existing statement to output the total time elapsed and then call `ReadLine` to wait for the user to press *Enter*, as shown in the following code:

```
WriteLine("Passing the result of one task as an input into
another.");

var taskCallWebServiceAndThenStoredProcedure =
  Task.Factory.StartNew(CallWebService)
    .ContinueWith(previousTask =>
      CallStoredProcedure(previousTask.Result));

WriteLine($"Result: {taskCallWebServiceAndThenStoredProcedure.
Result}");
```

4. Run the console application and view the result, as shown in the following output:

```
Passing the result of one task as an input into another.
Starting call to web service...
Finished call to web service.
Starting call to stored procedure...
Finished call to stored procedure.
Result: 12 products cost more than £89.99.
5,971ms elapsed.
```

Nested and child tasks

As well as defining dependencies between tasks, you can define nested and child tasks. A **nested task** is a task that is created inside another task. A **child task** is a nested task that must finish before its parent task is allowed to finish.

Let's explore how these types of task work.

1. Create a new console application named `NestedAndChildTasks`, add it to the `Chapter13` workspace, and select the project as active for OmniSharp.

2. In `Program.cs`, import namespaces to work with threads and tasks, as shown in the following code:

```
using System;
using System.Threading;
using System.Threading.Tasks;
using System.Diagnostics;
using static System.Console;
```

3. Add two methods, one of which starts a task to run the other, as shown in the following code:

```
static void OuterMethod()
{
  WriteLine("Outer method starting...");
  var inner = Task.Factory.StartNew(InnerMethod);
  WriteLine("Outer method finished.");
}

static void InnerMethod()
{
  WriteLine("Inner method starting...");
  Thread.Sleep(2000);
  WriteLine("Inner method finished.");
}
```

4. In `Main`, add statements to start a task to run the outer method and wait for it to finish before stopping, as shown in the following code:

```
var outer = Task.Factory.StartNew(OuterMethod);
outer.Wait();
WriteLine("Console app is stopping.");
```

5. Run the console application and view the result, as shown in the following output:

```
Outer method starting...
Outer method finished.
Console app is stopping.
Inner method starting...
```

Note that, although we wait for the outer task to finish, its inner task does not have to finish as well. In fact, the outer task might finish, and the console app could end, before the inner task even starts! To link these nested tasks, we must use a special option.

6. Modify the existing code that defines the inner task to add a `TaskCreationOption` value of `AttachedToParent`, as shown highlighted in the following code:

```
var inner = Task.Factory.StartNew(InnerMethod,
    TaskCreationOptions.AttachedToParent);
```

7. Run the console application, view the result, and note that the inner task must finish before the outer task can, as shown in the following output:

```
Outer method starting...
Outer method finished.
Inner method starting...
Inner method finished.
Console app is stopping.
```

The `OuterMethod` can finish before the `InnerMethod`, as shown by its writing to the console, but its task must wait, as shown by the console not stopping until both the outer and inner tasks finish.

Synchronizing access to shared resources

When you have multiple threads executing at the same time, there is a possibility that two or more of the threads may access the same variable or another resource at the same time, and as a result, may cause a problem. For this reason, you should carefully consider how to make your code *thread safe*.

The simplest mechanism for implementing thread safety is to use an object variable as a *flag* or *traffic light* to indicate when a shared resource has an exclusive lock applied.

In William Golding's *Lord of the Flies*, Piggy and Ralph spot a conch shell and use it to call a meeting. The boys impose a "rule of the conch" on themselves, deciding that no one can speak unless they're holding the conch.

I like to name the object variable I use for implementing thread-safe code the "conch." When a thread has the conch, no other thread can access the shared resource(s) represented by that conch.

We will explore a couple of types that can be used to synchronize access to resources:

- `Monitor`: A flag to prevent multiple threads accessing a resource simultaneously within the same process.

- `Interlocked`: An object for manipulating simple numeric types at the CPU level.

Accessing a resource from multiple threads

1. Create a console application named `SynchronizingResourceAccess`, add it to the `Chapter13` workspace, and select the project as active for OmniSharp.

2. Import namespaces for working with threads and tasks, as shown in the following code:

```
using System;
using System.Threading;
using System.Threading.Tasks;
using System.Diagnostics;
using static System.Console;
```

3. In `Program`, add statements to do the following:
   - Declare and instantiate an object to generate random wait times.
   - Declare a `string` variable to store a message (this is the shared resource).
   - Declare two methods that add a letter, A or B, to the shared `string` five times in a loop, and wait for a random interval of up to 2 seconds for each iteration:

```
static Random r = new Random();
static string Message; // a shared resource

static void MethodA()
{
  for (int i = 0; i < 5; i++)
  {
    Thread.Sleep(r.Next(2000));
    Message += "A";
    Write(".");
  }
}

static void MethodB()
{
  for (int i = 0; i < 5; i++)
  {
    Thread.Sleep(r.Next(2000));
    Message += "B";
```

```
        Write(".");
      }
   }
}
```

4. In `Main`, execute both methods on separate threads using a pair of tasks and wait for them to complete before outputting the elapsed milliseconds, as shown in the following code:

```
WriteLine("Please wait for the tasks to complete.");
Stopwatch watch = Stopwatch.StartNew();

Task a = Task.Factory.StartNew(MethodA);
Task b = Task.Factory.StartNew(MethodB);

Task.WaitAll(new Task[] { a, b });

WriteLine();
WriteLine($"Results: {Message}.");
WriteLine($"{watch.ElapsedMilliseconds:#,##0} elapsed
milliseconds.");
```

5. Run the console application and view the result, as shown in the following output:

```
Please wait for the tasks to complete.
..........
Results: BABABAABBA.
5,753 elapsed milliseconds.
```

This shows that both threads were modifying the message concurrently. In an actual application, this could be a problem. But we can prevent concurrent access by applying a mutually exclusive lock to the resource, which we will do in the following section.

Applying a mutually exclusive lock to a resource

Now, let's use a conch to ensure that only one thread has access to the share resource at a time.

1. In `Program`, declare and instantiate an object variable to act as a *conch*, as shown in the following code:

```
static object conch = new object();
```

2. In both `MethodA` and `MethodB`, add a `lock` statement around the `for` statement, as shown highlighted in the following code:

```
lock (conch)
```

```
{
  for (int i = 0; i < 5; i++)
  {
    Thread.Sleep(r.Next(2000));
    Message += "A";
    Write(".");
  }
}
```

3. Run the console application and view the result, as shown in the following output:

```
Please wait for the tasks to complete.
. . . . . . . . . .
Results: BBBBBAAAAA.
10,345 elapsed milliseconds.
```

Although the time elapsed was longer, only one method at a time could access the shared resource. Either `MethodA` or `MethodB` can start first. Once a method has finished its work on the shared resource, then the conch gets released, and the other method has the chance to do its work.

Understanding the lock statement and avoiding deadlocks

You might wonder how the `lock` statement works when it *locks* an object variable, as shown in the following code:

```
lock (conch)
{
  // work with shared resource
}
```

The C# compiler changes the `lock` statement into a `try-finally` statement that uses the `Monitor` class to enter and exit the `conch` object variable, as shown in the following code:

```
try
{
  Monitor.Enter(conch);
  // work with shared resource
}
finally
{
  Monitor.Exit(conch);
}
```

Knowing how the `lock` statement works internally is important because using the `lock` statement can cause a deadlock.

Deadlocks occur when there are two or more shared resources (and therefore conches), and the following sequence of events happens:

- Thread X locks conch A.
- Thread Y locks conch B.
- Thread X attempts to lock conch B but is blocked because thread Y already has it.
- Thread Y attempts to lock conch A but is blocked because thread X already has it.

A proven way to prevent deadlocks is to specify a timeout when attempting to get a lock. To do this, you must manually use the `Monitor` class instead of using the `lock` statement.

1. Modify your code to replace the `lock` statements with code that tries to enter the `conch` with a timeout, as shown in the following code:

```
try
{
  Monitor.TryEnter(conch, TimeSpan.FromSeconds(15));

  for (int i = 0; i < 5; i++)
  {
    Thread.Sleep(r.Next(2000));
    Message += "A";
    Write(".");
  }
}
finally
{
  Monitor.Exit(conch);
}
```

2. Run the console application and view the result, which should return the same results as before (although either A or B could grab the conch first) but is better code because it will avoid potential deadlocks.

Good Practice: Only use the `lock` keyword if you can write your code such that it avoids potential deadlocks. If you cannot avoid potential deadlocks, then always use the `Monitor.TryEnter` method instead of `lock`, in combination with a `try-finally` statement, so that you can supply a timeout and one of the threads will back out of a deadlock if it occurs.

Making CPU operations atomic

Atomic is from the Greek word **atomos**, which means *undividable*. Is the C# increment operator atomic, as shown in the following code?

```
int x = 3;
x++; // is this an atomic CPU operation?
```

It is not atomic! Incrementing an integer requires the following three CPU operations:

1. Load a value from an instance variable into a register.

2. Increment the value.

3. Store the value in the instance variable.

A thread could be preempted after executing the first two steps. A second thread could then execute all three steps. When the first thread resumes execution, it will overwrite the value in the variable, and the effect of the increment or decrement performed by the second thread will be lost!

There is a type named `Interlocked` that can perform atomic actions on value types, such as integers and floats.

1. Declare another shared resource that will count how many operations have occurred, as shown in the following code:

    ```
    static int Counter; // another shared resource
    ```

2. In both methods, inside the `for` statement and after modifying the `string` value, add a statement to safely increment the counter, as shown in the following code:

    ```
    Interlocked.Increment(ref Counter);
    ```

3. After outputting the elapsed time, write the current value of the counter to the console, as shown in the following code:

    ```
    WriteLine($"{Counter} string modifications.");
    ```

4. Run the console application and view the result, as shown in the following partial output:

    ```
    10 string modifications.
    ```

Observant readers will realize that the existing `conch` object variable protects *all* shared resources accessed within a block of code locked by the conch, and therefore it is actually unnecessary to use `Interlocked` in this specific example. But if we had not already been protecting another shared resource like `Message` then using `Interlocked` would be necessary.

Applying other types of synchronization

`Monitor` and `Interlocked` are mutually exclusive locks that are simple and effective, but sometimes, you need more advanced options to synchronize access to shared resources, as shown in the following table:

Type	Description
`ReaderWriterLock` and `ReaderWriterLockSlim` (recommended)	These allow multiple threads to be in **read mode**, one thread to be in the **write mode** with exclusive ownership of the lock, and one thread that has read access to be in the **upgradeable read mode**, from which the thread can upgrade to the write mode without having to relinquish its read access to the resource.
`Mutex`	Like `Monitor`, this provides exclusive access to a shared resource, except it is used for **inter-process** synchronization.
`Semaphore` and `SemaphoreSlim`	These limit the number of threads that can access a resource or pool of resources concurrently by defining **slots**.
`AutoResetEvent` and `ManualResetEvent`	Event wait handles allow threads to synchronize activities by signaling each other and by waiting for each other's signals.

Understanding async and await

C# 5 introduced two keywords to simplify working with the `Task` type. They are especially useful for the following:

- Implementing multitasking for a **graphical user interface (GUI)**
- Improving the scalability of web applications and web services

In *Chapter 16, Building Websites Using the Model-View-Controller Pattern*, we will explore how the `async` and `await` keywords can improve scalability in websites.

In *Chapter 20, Building Windows Desktop Apps*, we will explore how the `async` and `await` keywords can implement multitasking with a GUI. But for now, let's learn the theory of why these two C# keywords were introduced, and then later you will see them used in practice.

Improving responsiveness for console apps

One of the limitations with console applications is that you can only use the `await` keyword inside methods that are marked as `async...`, and C# 7 and earlier do not allow the `Main` method to be marked as `async`! Luckily, a new feature introduced in C# 7.1 was support for `async` in `Main`.

1. Create a console app named `AsyncConsole`, add it to the `Chapter13` workspace, and select the project as active for OmniSharp.

2. Import namespaces for making HTTP requests and working with tasks, and statically import `Console`, as shown in the following code:

```
using System.Net.Http;
using System.Threading.Tasks;
using static System.Console;
```

3. In the `Main` method, add statements to create an `HttpClient` instance, make a request for Apple's home page, and output how many bytes it has, as shown in the following code:

```
var client = new HttpClient();

HttpResponseMessage response =
    await client.GetAsync("http://www.apple.com/");

WriteLine("Apple's home page has {0:N0} bytes.",
    response.Content.Headers.ContentLength);
```

4. Build the project and note the error message, as shown in the following output:

```
Program.cs(14,9): error CS4033: The 'await' operator can only be
used within an async method. Consider marking this method with the
'async' modifier and changing its return type to 'Task'. [/Users/
markjprice/Code/Chapter13/AsyncConsole/AsyncConsole.csproj]
```

5. Add the `async` keyword to the `Main` method and change its return type to `Task`.

6. Build the project and note that it now builds successfully.

7. Run the console application and view the result, as shown in the following output:

```
Apple's home page has 40,252 bytes.
```

Improving responsiveness for GUI apps

So far in this book, we have only built console applications. Life for a programmer gets more complicated when building web applications, web services, and apps with GUIs such as Windows desktop and mobile apps.

One reason for this is that for a GUI app, there is a special thread: the **user interface (UI)** thread.

There are two rules for working in GUIs:

- Do not perform long-running tasks on the UI thread.
- Do not access UI elements on any thread except the UI thread.

To handle these rules, programmers used to have to write complex code to ensure that long-running tasks were executed by a non-UI thread, but once complete, the results of the task were safely passed to the UI thread to present to the user. It could quickly get messy!

Luckily, with C# 5 and later, you have the use of `async` and `await`. They allow you to continue to write your code as if it is synchronous, which keeps your code clean and easy to understand, but underneath, the C# compiler creates a complex state machine and keeps track of running threads. It's kind of magical!

Improving scalability for web applications and web services

The `async` and `await` keywords can also be applied on the server side when building websites, applications, and services. From the client application's point of view, nothing changes (or they might even notice a small increase in the time for a request to return). So, from a single client's point of view, the use of `async` and `await` to implement multitasking on the server side makes their experience worse!

On the server side, additional, cheaper worker threads are created to wait for long-running tasks to finish so that expensive I/O threads can handle other client requests instead of being blocked. This improves the overall scalability of a web application or service. More clients can be supported simultaneously.

Common types that support multitasking

There are many common types that have asynchronous methods that you can await, as shown in the following table:

Type	Methods
`DbContext<T>`	`AddAsync`, `AddRangeAsync`, `FindAsync`, and `SaveChangesAsync`
`DbSet<T>`	`AddAsync`, `AddRangeAsync`, `ForEachAsync`, `SumAsync`, `ToListAsync`, `ToDictionaryAsync`, `AverageAsync`, and `CountAsync`
`HttpClient`	`GetAsync`, `PostAsync`, `PutAsync`, `DeleteAsync`, and `SendAsync`
`StreamReader`	`ReadAsync`, `ReadLineAsync`, and `ReadToEndAsync`
`StreamWriter`	`WriteAsync`, `WriteLineAsync`, and `FlushAsync`

Good Practice: Any time you see a method that ends in the suffix Async, check to see whether it returns `Task` or `Task<T>`. If it does, then you should use it instead of the synchronous non-Async suffixed method. Remember to call it using `await` and decorate your method with `async`.

Using await in catch blocks

In C# 5, it was only possible to use the `await` keyword in a `try` block, but not in a `catch` block. In C# 6 and later, it is now possible to use `await` in both the `try` and `catch` blocks.

Working with async streams

Before C# 8.0 and .NET Core 3.0, the `await` keyword only worked with tasks that return scalar values. Async stream support in .NET Standard 2.1 allows an `async` method to return a sequence of values.

Let's see a simulated example.

1. Create a console app named `AsyncEnumerable`, add it to the `Chapter13` workspace, and select the project as active for OmniSharp.

2. Import namespaces for working with tasks, and statically import `Console`, as shown in the following code:

```
using System.Collections.Generic;
using System.Threading.Tasks;
using static System.Console;
```

3. Create a method that yield returns a random sequence of three numbers asynchronously, as shown in the following code:

```
static async IAsyncEnumerable<int> GetNumbers()
{
  var r = new Random();

  // simulate work
  System.Threading.Thread.Sleep(r.Next(1000, 2000));
  yield return r.Next(0, 101);

  System.Threading.Thread.Sleep(r.Next(1000, 2000));
  yield return r.Next(0, 101);

  System.Threading.Thread.Sleep(r.Next(1000, 2000));
  yield return r.Next(0, 101);
}
```

4. In the `Main` method, add statements to enumerate the sequence of numbers, as shown in the following code:

```
static async Task Main(string[] args)
{
  await foreach (int number in GetNumbers())
  {
    WriteLine($"Number: {number}");
  }
}
```

5. Run the console application and view the result, as shown in the following output:

```
Number: 509
Number: 813
Number: 307
```

Practicing and exploring

Test your knowledge and understanding by answering some questions, get some hands-on practice, and explore this chapter's topics with deeper research.

Exercise 13.1 – Test your knowledge

Answer the following questions:

1. What information can you find out about a process?

2. How accurate is the `Stopwatch` class?

3. By convention, what suffix should be applied to a method that returns `Task` or `Task<T>`?

4. To use the `await` keyword inside a method, what keyword must be applied to the method declaration?

5. How do you create a child task?

6. Why should you avoid the `lock` keyword?

7. When should you use the `Interlocked` class?

8. When should you use the `Mutex` class instead of the `Monitor` class?

9. What is the benefit of using `async` and `await` in a website or web service?

10. Can you cancel a task? How?

Exercise 13.2 – Explore topics

Use the following links to read more about this chapter's topics:

- **Threads and threading**: `https://docs.microsoft.com/en-us/dotnet/standard/threading/threads-and-threading`

- **Async in depth**: `https://docs.microsoft.com/en-us/dotnet/standard/async-in-depth`

- **await (C# Reference)**: `https://docs.microsoft.com/en-us/dotnet/csharp/language-reference/keywords/await`

- **Parallel Programming in .NET**: `https://docs.microsoft.com/en-us/dotnet/standard/parallel-programming/`

- **Overview of synchronization primitives**: `https://docs.microsoft.com/en-us/dotnet/standard/threading/overview-of-synchronization-primitives`

Summary

In this chapter, you have learned not only how to define and start a task, but also how to wait for one or more tasks to finish, and how to control task completion order. You've also learned how to synchronize access to shared resources, and the theory behind `async` and `await`.

In the remaining chapters, you will learn how to create applications for the **App Models** supported by .NET Core, such as websites, web applications, and web services. As a bonus, you will also learn how you can build Windows desktop apps using .NET Core 3.0 and cross-platform mobile apps using Xamarin.Forms.

Chapter 14

Practical Applications of C# and .NET

The third part of this book is about practical applications of C# and .NET. You will learn how to build complete cross-platform applications such as websites, web services, Windows desktop and mobile apps, and how to add intelligence to them with machine learning. Microsoft calls platforms for building applications **App Models**.

In this chapter, we will cover the following topics:

- Understanding app models for C# and .NET
- New features in ASP.NET Core
- Understanding SignalR
- Understanding Blazor
- Understanding the bonus chapters
- Building an entity data model for Northwind

Understanding app models for C# and .NET

Since this book is about C# 8.0 and .NET Core 3.0, we will learn about app models that use them to build the practical applications that we will encounter in the remaining chapters of this book.

More Information: Microsoft has extensive guidance for implementing App Models such as ASP.NET Web Applications, Xamarin Mobile Apps, and UWP Apps in its .NET Application Architecture Guidance documentation, which you can read at the following link: https://www.microsoft.com/net/learn/architecture

Building websites using ASP.NET Core

Websites are made up of multiple web pages loaded statically from the filesystem or generated dynamically by a server-side technology such as ASP.NET Core. A web browser makes GET requests using URLs that identify each page and can manipulate data stored on the server using the POST, PUT, and DELETE requests.

With many websites, the web browser is treated as a presentation layer, with almost all of the processing performed on the server side. A small amount of JavaScript might be used on the client side to implement some presentation features, such as carousels.

ASP.NET Core 3.0 provides three technologies for building websites:

- **ASP.NET Core Razor Pages** and **Razor class libraries** are ways to dynamically generate HTML for simple websites. You will learn about them in detail in *Chapter 15, Building Websites Using ASP.NET Core Razor Pages*.

- **ASP.NET Core MVC** is an implementation of the Model-View-Controller design pattern that is popular for developing complex websites. You will learn about it in detail in *Chapter 16, Building Websites Using the Model-View-Controller Pattern*.

- **Blazor** lets you build server-side or client-side components and user interfaces using C# instead of JavaScript. Blazor is still very new, and is not included in this edition of the book.

Building websites using a web content management system

Most websites have a lot of content, and if developers had to be involved every time some content needed to be changed, that would not scale well. A web **Content Management System (CMS)** enables developers to define content structure and templates to provide consistency and good design, while making it easy for a non-technical content owner to manage the actual content. They can create new pages or blocks of content, and update existing content, knowing it will look great for the visitors with minimal effort.

There are a multitude of CMSs available for all web platforms, like WordPress for PHP or Django for Python. Enterprise-level CMSs for .NET Framework include Episerver and Sitecore, but neither are yet available for .NET Core. CMSs that support .NET Core include Piranha CMS, Squidex, and Orchard Core.

The key benefit of using a CMS is that it provides a friendly content management user interface. Content owners log in to the website and manage the content themselves. The content is then rendered and returned to visitors using ASP.NET MVC controllers and views.

In summary, C# and .NET can be used on both the server-side and the client-side to build websites, as shown in the following diagram:

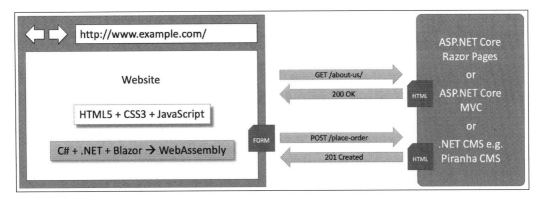

Understanding web applications

Web applications, also known as **Single-Page Applications** (SPAs), are made up of a single web page built with a frontend technology such as Angular, React, Vue, or a proprietary JavaScript library that can make requests to a backend web service for getting more data when needed and posting updated data, using common serialization formats, such as XML and JSON. The canonical examples are Google web apps like Gmail, Maps, and Docs.

With a web application, the client-side uses JavaScript libraries to implement sophisticated user interactions, but most of the important processing and data access still happens on the server-side, because the web browser has limited access to local system resources.

.NET Core has project templates for JavaScript-based SPAs, but we will not spend any time learning how to build JavaScript-based SPAs in this book, even though these are commonly used with ASP.NET Core as the backend.

More Information: To learn more about building frontends to .NET Core using JavaScript SPAs, Packt has two books of interest, which you can read about at the following links:

ASP.NET Core 2 and Vue.js: `https://www.packtpub.com/application-development/hands-aspnet-core-2-and-vuejs`

ASP.NET Core 2 and Angular 5: `https://www.packtpub.com/application-development/aspnet-core-2-and-angular-5`

Building and consuming web services

Although we will not learn about JavaScript-based SPAs, we will learn how to build a web service using **ASP.NET Core Web API**, call that web service from the server-side code in our ASP.NET Core websites, and then later, we will call that web service from Windows desktop and cross-platform mobile apps.

Building intelligent apps

In a traditional app, the algorithms it uses to process its data are designed and implemented by a human. Humans are good at many things, but writing complex algorithms is not one of them, especially algorithms for spotting useful patterns in vast quantities of data.

Machine learning algorithms that work with custom models like those provided by Microsoft's **ML.NET** for .NET Core can add intelligence to your apps. We will use ML.NET algorithms with custom models to process the tracked behavior of visitors to a website and then make recommendations for other pages that they might be interested in. It will work rather like how Netflix recommends films and TV shows you might like based on your previous behavior and the behavior of people who have expressed similar interests to you.

New features for ASP.NET Core

Over the past few years, Microsoft has rapidly expanded the capabilities of ASP.NET Core. You should note which .NET platforms are supported, as shown in the following list:

- ASP.NET 1.0 to 2.2 runs on either .NET Core or .NET Framework.
- ASP.NET Core 3.0 only runs on .NET Core 3.0.

ASP.NET Core 1.0

ASP.NET Core 1.0 was released in June 2016 and focused on implementing an API suitable for building modern cross-platform web and services for Windows, macOS, and Linux.

More Information: You can read the ASP.NET Core 1.0 announcement at the following link: `https://blogs.msdn.microsoft.com/webdev/2016/06/27/announcing-asp-net-core-1-0/`

ASP.NET Core 1.1

ASP.NET Core 1.1 was released in November 2016 and focused on bug fixes and general improvements to features and performance.

 More Information: You can read the ASP.NET Core 1.1 announcement at the following link: `https://blogs.msdn. microsoft.com/webdev/2016/11/16/announcing-asp- net-core-1-1/`

ASP.NET Core 2.0

ASP.NET Core 2.0 was released in August 2017 and focused on adding new features such as Razor Pages, bundling assemblies into a `Microsoft.AspNetCore.All` metapackage, targeting .NET Standard 2.0, providing a new authentication model, and performance improvements. The biggest new feature is covered in *Chapter 15, Building Websites Using ASP.NET Core Razor Pages*.

 More Information: You can read the ASP.NET Core 2.0 announcement at the following link: `https://blogs.msdn. microsoft.com/webdev/2017/08/14/announcing-asp- net-core-2-0/`

ASP.NET Core 2.1

ASP.NET Core 2.1 was released in May 2018 and focused on adding new features such as SignalR for real-time communication, Razor class libraries, ASP.NET Core Identity, and better support for HTTPS and the European Union's **General Data Protection Regulation (GDPR)**, including the topics listed in the following table:

Feature	Chapter	Topic
SignalR	14	Understanding SignalR
Razor class libraries	15	Using Razor class libraries
GDPR support	16	Creating and exploring an ASP.NET Core MVC website
Identity UI library and scaffolding	16	Exploring an ASP.NET Core MVC website
Integration tests	16	Testing an ASP.NET Core MVC website
`[ApiController]`, `ActionResult<T>`	18	Creating an ASP.NET Core Web API project

Problem details	18	Implementing a Web API controller
IHttpClientFactory	18	Configuring HTTP clients using HttpClientFactory

More Information: You can read the ASP.NET Core 2.1 announcement at the following link: `https://blogs.msdn.microsoft.com/webdev/2018/05/30/asp-net-core-2-1-0-now-available/`

ASP.NET Core 2.2

ASP.NET Core 2.2 was released in December 2018 and focused on improving the building of RESTful HTTP APIs, updating the project templates to Bootstrap 4 and Angular 6, an optimized configuration for hosting in Azure, and performance improvements, including the topics listed in the following table:

Feature	Chapter	Topic
HTTP/2 in Kestrel	15	Classic ASP.NET versus modern ASP.NET Core
In-process hosting model	15	Creating an ASP.NET Core project
Health Check API	18	Implementing Health Check API
Open API Analyzers	18	Implementing Open API analyzers and conventions
Endpoint Routing	18	Understanding endpoint routing

More Information: You can read the ASP.NET Core 2.2 announcement at the following link: `https://blogs.msdn.microsoft.com/webdev/2018/12/04/asp-net-core-2-2-available-today/`

ASP.NET Core 3.0

ASP.NET Core 3.0 was released in September 2019 and focused on fully leveraging .NET Core 3.0, which means it can no longer support .NET Framework, and added useful refinements, including the topics listed in the following table:

Feature	Chapter	Topic
Blazor; server- and client-side	14	Understanding Blazor
Static assets in Razor class libraries	15	Using Razor class libraries
New options for MVC service registration	16	Understanding ASP.NET Core MVC startup

More Information: You can read the ASP.NET Core 3.0 announcement at the following link: `https://blogs.msdn.microsoft.com/webdev/2018/10/29/a-first-look-at-changes-coming-in-asp-net-core-3-0/`

Understanding SignalR

In the early days of the Web in the 1990s, browsers had to make a full-page HTTP GET request to the web server to get fresh information to show to the visitor.

In late 1999, Microsoft released Internet Explorer 5.0 with a component named **XMLHttpRequest** that could make asynchronous HTTP calls in the background. This alongside **dynamic HTML (DHTML)** allowed parts of the web page to be updated with fresh data smoothly.

The benefits of this technique were obvious and soon all browsers added the same component. Google took maximum advantage of this capability to build clever web applications such as Google Maps and Gmail. A few years later, the technique became popularly known as **Asynchronous JavaScript and XML (AJAX)**.

AJAX still uses HTTP to communicate, however, and that has limitations. First, HTTP is a request-response communication protocol, meaning that the server cannot push data to the client. It must wait for the client to make a request. Second, HTTP request and response messages have headers with lots of potentially unnecessary overhead. Third, HTTP typically requires a new underlying TCP connection to be created on each request.

WebSocket is full-duplex, meaning that either client or server can initiate communicating new data. WebSocket uses the same TCP connection for the lifecycle of the connection. It is also more efficient in the message sizes that it sends because they are minimally framed with 2 bytes.

WebSocket works over HTTP ports 80 and 443 so it is compatible with the HTTP protocol and the WebSocket handshake uses the HTTP Upgrade header to switch from the HTTP protocol to the WebSocket protocol.

More Information: You can read more about WebSocket at the following link: `https://en.wikipedia.org/wiki/WebSocket`

Modern web apps are expected to deliver up-to-date information. Live chat is the canonical example, but there are lots of potential applications, from stock prices to games.

Whenever you need the server to push updates to the web page, you need a web-compatible real-time communication technology. WebSocket could be used but it is not supported by all clients.

ASP.NET Core SignalR is an open-source library that simplifies adding real-time web functionality to apps by being an abstraction over multiple underlying communication technologies, which allows you to add real-time communication capabilities using C# code.

The developer does not need to understand or implement the underlying technology used, and SignalR will automatically switch between underlying technologies depending on what the visitor's web browser supports. For example, SignalR will use WebSocket when it's available, and gracefully falls back on other technologies such as AJAX long polling when it isn't, while your application code stays the same.

SignalR is an API for server-to-client **remote procedure calls** (**RPC**). The RPCs call JavaScript functions on clients from server-side .NET Core code. SignalR has hubs to define the pipeline and handles the message dispatching automatically using two built-in hub protocols: JSON and a binary one based on MessagePack.

 More Information: You can read more about MessagePack at the following link: `https://msgpack.org`

On the server-side, SignalR runs everywhere that ASP.NET Core runs: Windows, macOS, or Linux servers. SignalR supports the following client platforms:

- JavaScript clients for current browsers including Chrome, Firefox, Safari, Edge, and Internet Explorer 11.
- .NET clients including Xamarin for Android and iOS mobile apps.
- Java 8 and later.

 More Information: You can read more about SignalR at the following link: `https://docs.microsoft.com/en-us/aspnet/core/signalr/introduction?view=aspnetcore-3.0`

Understanding Blazor

Blazor lets you build shared components and interactive web user interfaces using C# instead of JavaScript. In April 2019, Microsoft announced that Blazor "is no longer experimental and we are committing to ship it as a supported web UI framework including support for running client-side in the browser on WebAssembly."

JavaScript and friends

Traditionally, any code that needs to execute in a web browser is written using the JavaScript programming language or a higher-level technology that transpiles (transforms or compiles) into JavaScript. This is because all browsers have supported JavaScript for about two decades, so it has become the lowest-common denominator for implementing business logic on the client-side.

JavaScript does have some issues, however. First, although it has superficial similarities to C-style languages like C# and Java, it is actually very different once you dig beneath the surface. Second, it is a dynamically-typed pseudo-functional language that uses prototypes instead of class inheritance for object reuse. It might look Human, but you will get a surprise when it's revealed to actually be a Skrull.

Wouldn't it be great if we could use the same language and libraries in a web browser as we do on the server-side?

Silverlight – C# and .NET using a plugin

Microsoft made a previous attempt at achieving this goal with a technology named **Silverlight**. When Silverlight 2.0 was released in 2008, a C# and .NET developer could use their skills to build libraries and visual components that were executed in the web browser by the Silverlight plugin.

By 2011 and Silverlight 5.0, Apple's success with the iPhone and Steve Job's hatred of browser plugins like Flash eventually led to Microsoft abandoning Silverlight since, like Flash, Silverlight is banned from iPhones and iPads.

WebAssembly – a target for Blazor

A recent development in browsers has given Microsoft the opportunity to make another attempt. In 2017, the WebAssembly Consensus was completed and all major browsers now support it: Chromium (Chrome, Edge, Opera, Brave), Firefox, and WebKit (Safari). It is not supported by Microsoft's Internet Explorer because it is a legacy web browser.

WebAssembly (Wasm) is a binary instruction format for a virtual machine that provides a way to run code written in multiple languages on the web at near native speed. Wasm is designed as a portable target for the compilation of high-level languages like C#.

 More Information: You can learn more about WebAssembly at the following link: https://webassembly.org

Blazor on the server-side or client-side

Blazor is a single programming or *app* model with two *hosting* models:

- Server-side Blazor runs on the server-side using SignalR to communicate with the client-side and it shipped as part of .NET Core 3.0.
- Client-side Blazor runs on the client-side using WebAssembly and it will ship as part of a future .NET Core release.

This means that a web developer can write Blazor components once, and then run them either on the server-side or client-side.

 More Information: You can read the official documentation for Blazor at the following link: `https://dotnet.microsoft.com/apps/aspnet/web-apps/client`

Since the most interesting hosting option for Blazor might not ship until .NET 5.0 in 2020, I decided to wait until the publication of the next edition to write a whole new chapter about the Blazor technology.

 More Information: You can find lots of Blazor resources at the community-driven Awesome Blazor site at the following link: `https://github.com/AdrienTorris/awesome-blazor`

Understanding the bonus chapters

The bonus chapters in this book are the last two chapters:

- *Chapter 20, Building Windows Desktop Apps*
- *Chapter 21, Building Cross-Platform Mobile Apps Using Xamarin.Forms*

Since this book is about modern cross-platform development using C# 8.0 and .NET Core 3.0, technically, it should not include coverage of Windows desktop apps because they are Windows-only. Nor should it include coverage of cross-platform mobile apps because they use Xamarin instead of .NET Core.

In Chapters 1 to 19 we are using cross-platform Visual Studio Code to build all the apps. Windows desktop apps are built using Visual Studio 2019 on Windows 10. Cross-platform mobile apps are built using Visual Studio 2019 for Mac and require macOS to compile.

But Windows and mobile are important platforms for current and future client app development using C# and .NET, so I did not want to take away the opportunity to introduce you to them.

Building Windows desktop apps

With the first version of C# and .NET Framework released in 2002, Microsoft provided a technology for building Windows desktop applications named **Windows Forms**. (The equivalent at the time for web development was named **Web Forms**, hence the complementary names).

In 2007, Microsoft released a more powerful technology for building Windows desktop applications, named **Windows Presentation Foundation (WPF)**. WPF can use **eXtensible Application Markup Language (XAML)** to specify its user interface, which is easy for both humans and code to understand. Visual Studio 2019 is built with WPF.

There are many enterprise applications built using Windows Forms and WPF that need to be maintained or enhanced with new features, but until now they were stuck on .NET Framework, which is now a legacy platform. With .NET Core 3.0 and Windows Desktop Pack, these apps can now use the full modern capabilities of .NET Core (and in future .NET 5.0).

In 2015 Microsoft released Windows 10, and with it a new technology named **Universal Windows Platform (UWP)**. UWP can use a custom fork of .NET Core that is not cross-platform but provides full access to the underlying Windows APIs.

UWP apps can only execute on the Windows 10 platform, not earlier versions of Windows. UWP apps can also run on Xbox and Windows Mixed Reality headsets with motion controllers.

With Windows apps, the client side can provide extremely sophisticated user interactions, and has full access to all local system resources; so the app only needs the server side if the app needs to implement cross-device functionality, for example, creating a document on a tablet device, and continuing to work on the document on a desktop device, or having gameplay progress shared across devices.

Building cross-platform mobile apps

There are two major mobile platforms: Apple's iOS and Google's Android, each with their own different programming languages and platform APIs.

Cross-platform mobile apps can be built once for the Xamarin platform using C#, and then can run on both Apple and Android mobile platforms. Xamarin.Forms makes it even easier to develop mobile apps by sharing user interface components as well as business logic.

Mobile apps have similar benefits as Windows apps, except they are cross-platform, not just cross-device. Much of the XAML for defining the user interface can be shared with WPF and UWP apps.

The apps can exist on their own, but they usually call web services to provide an experience that spans across all of your computing devices, from servers and laptops to phones and gaming systems.

Once .NET 5.0 is released in late 2020, you will be able to create cross-platform mobile apps that target the same .NET 5.0 APIs as used by console apps, websites, web services, and Windows desktop apps, and it will be executed by the Xamarin runtime on mobile devices.

Building an entity data model for Northwind

Practical applications usually need to work with data in a relational database or another data store. In this chapter, we will define an entity data model for the Northwind database stored in SQLite. It will be used in most of the apps that we create in subsequent chapters.

Although macOS includes an installation of SQLite by default, if you are using Windows or a variety of Linux then you might need to download, install, and configure SQLite for your operating system. Instructions to do so can be found in *Chapter 11*, *Working with Databases Using Entity Framework Core*.

Good Practice: You should create a separate class library project for your entity data models that does not have a dependency on anything except .NET Standard 2.0. This allows easier sharing between backend servers and frontend clients without the client needing to reference Entity Framework Core 3.0, that is dependent on .NET Standard 2.1.

Creating a class library for Northwind entity models

You will now define entity data models in a .NET Standard 2.0 class library so that they can be reused in other types of projects including client-side app models such as Windows desktop and mobile apps:

1. In your existing Code folder, create a folder named PracticalApps.

2. In Visual Studio, open the `PracticalApps` folder.

3. Create the `Northwind.db` file by copying the `Northwind.sql` file into the `PracticalApps` folder, and then enter the following command in **Terminal**:

   ```
   sqlite3 Northwind.db < Northwind.sql
   ```

4. In the `PracticalApps` folder, create a folder named `NorthwindEntitiesLib`.

5. In Visual Studio Code, navigate to **File | Save Workspace As...**, enter the name `PracticalApps`, change to the `PracticalApps` folder, and click **Save**.

6. Add the `NorthwindEntitiesLib` folder to the workspace.

7. Navigate to **Terminal | New Terminal** and select **NorthwindEntitiesLib**.

8. In **Terminal**, enter the following command: `dotnet new classlib`

9. Delete the `Class1.cs` file.

10. Add the following class files to the `NorthwindEntitiesLib` project: `Category.cs`, `Customer.cs`, `Employee.cs`, `Order.cs`, `OrderDetail.cs`, `Product.cs`, `Shipper.cs`, and `Supplier.cs`. To save time, you could get these files from the GitHub repository for this book.

11. `Category.cs` should have three scalar properties for a category, and a property for related products, as shown in the following code:

    ```
    using System.Collections.Generic;

    namespace Packt.Shared
    {
      public class Category
      {
        public int CategoryID { get; set; }
        public string CategoryName { get; set; }
        public string Description { get; set; }

        // related entities
        public ICollection<Product> Products { get; set; }
      }
    }
    ```

12. `Customer.cs` should have 11 scalar properties for a customer, and a property for related orders, as shown in the following code:

    ```
    using System.Collections.Generic;

    namespace Packt.Shared
    {
      public class Customer
      {
        public string CustomerID { get; set; }
    ```

```
        public string CompanyName { get; set; }
        public string ContactName { get; set; }
        public string ContactTitle { get; set; }
        public string Address { get; set; }
        public string City { get; set; }
        public string Region { get; set; }
        public string PostalCode { get; set; }
        public string Country { get; set; }
        public string Phone { get; set; }
        public string Fax { get; set; }

        // related entities
        public ICollection<Order> Orders { get; set; }
    }
}
```

13. `Employee.cs` should have 15 scalar properties for an employee, and a property for related orders, as shown in the following code:

```
using System;
using System.Collections.Generic;

namespace Packt.Shared
{
  public class Employee
  {
    public int EmployeeID { get; set; }
    public string LastName { get; set; }
    public string FirstName { get; set; }
    public string Title { get; set; }
    public string TitleOfCourtesy { get; set; }
    public DateTime? BirthDate { get; set; }
    public DateTime? HireDate { get; set; }
    public string Address { get; set; }
    public string City { get; set; }
    public string Region { get; set; }
    public string PostalCode { get; set; }
    public string Country { get; set; }
    public string HomePhone { get; set; }
    public string Extension { get; set; }
    public string Notes { get; set; }

    // related entities
    public ICollection<Order> Orders { get; set; }
  }
}
```

14. `Order.cs` should have eight scalar properties for an order, and four properties for related order details, the customer who made the order, the employee who took the order, and the company that shipped the order, as shown in the following code:

```
using System;
using System.Collections.Generic;

namespace Packt.Shared
{
  public class Order
  {
    public int OrderID { get; set; }
    public string CustomerID { get; set; }
    public int EmployeeID { get; set; }
    public DateTime? OrderDate { get; set; }
    public DateTime? RequiredDate { get; set; }
    public DateTime? ShippedDate { get; set; }
    public int ShipVia { get; set; }
    public decimal? Freight { get; set; } = 0;

    // related entities
    public Customer Customer { get; set; }
    public Employee Employee { get; set; }
    public Shipper Shipper { get; set; }
    public ICollection<OrderDetail> OrderDetails { get; set; }
  }
}
```

15. `OrderDetail.cs` should have five scalar properties for an order detail, and two properties for the related order and product, as shown in the following code:

```
namespace Packt.Shared
{
  public class OrderDetail
  {
    public int OrderID { get; set; }
    public int ProductID { get; set; }
    public decimal UnitPrice { get; set; } = 0;
    public short Quantity { get; set; } = 1;
    public double Discount { get; set; } = 0;

    // related entities
    public Order Order { get; set; }
    public Product Product { get; set; }
  }
}
```

16. `Product.cs` should have 10 scalar properties for a product, and two properties for the related category and supplier, as shown in the following code:

```
namespace Packt.Shared
{
  public class Product
  {
    public int ProductID { get; set; }
    public string ProductName { get; set; }
    public int? SupplierID { get; set; }
```

```
        public int? CategoryID { get; set; }
        public string QuantityPerUnit { get; set; }
        public decimal? UnitPrice { get; set; } = 0;
        public short? UnitsInStock { get; set; } = 0;
        public short? UnitsOnOrder { get; set; } = 0;
        public short? ReorderLevel { get; set; } = 0;
        public bool Discontinued { get; set; } = false;

        // related entities
        public Category Category { get; set; }
        public Supplier Supplier { get; set; }
    }
}
```

17. `Shipper.cs` should have three scalar properties for a shipper, and a property for the related orders, as shown in the following code:

```
using System.Collections.Generic;

namespace Packt.Shared
{
  public class Shipper
  {
    public int ShipperID { get; set; }
    public string ShipperName { get; set; }
    public string Phone { get; set; }

    // related entities
    public ICollection<Order> Orders { get; set; }
  }
}
```

18. `Supplier.cs` should have 12 scalar properties for a supplier, and a property for the related products, as shown in the following code:

```
using System.Collections.Generic;

namespace Packt.Shared
{
  public class Supplier
  {
    public int SupplierID { get; set; }
    public string CompanyName { get; set; }
    public string ContactName { get; set; }
    public string ContactTitle { get; set; }
    public string Address { get; set; }
    public string City { get; set; }
    public string Region { get; set; }
    public string PostalCode { get; set; }
    public string Country { get; set; }
    public string Phone { get; set; }
    public string Fax { get; set; }
    public string HomePage { get; set; }
```

```
        // related entities
        public ICollection<Product> Products { get; set; }
    }
}
```

Creating a class library for a Northwind database context

You will now define a database context class library dependent on EF Core, which therefore needs to target .NET Standard 2.1:

1. In the `PracticalApps` folder, create a folder named `NorthwindContextLib`.

2. Add the `NorthwindContextLib` folder to the workspace.

3. Navigate to **View | Command Palette**, enter and select **OmniSharp: Select Project**, and select the `NorthwindContextLib` project.

4. Navigate to **Terminal | New Terminal** and select `NorthwindContextLib`.

5. In **Terminal**, enter the following command: `dotnet new classlib`

6. Modify `NorthwindContextLib.csproj` to target .NET Standard 2.1, and add a reference to the `NorthwindEntitiesLib` project and the Entity Framework Core package for SQLite, as shown in the following markup:

    ```
    <Project Sdk="Microsoft.NET.Sdk">

      <PropertyGroup>
        <TargetFramework>netstandard2.1</TargetFramework>
      </PropertyGroup>

      <ItemGroup>
        <ProjectReference Include=
          "..\NorthwindEntitiesLib\NorthwindEntitiesLib.csproj" />
        <PackageReference
          Include="Microsoft.EntityFrameworkCore.SQLite"
          Version="3.0.0" />
      </ItemGroup>

    </Project>
    ```

7. In **Terminal**, restore packages and compile the class libraries to check for errors by entering the following command: `dotnet build`

8. In the `NorthwindContextLib` project, rename the `Class1.cs` class file as `Northwind.cs`.

9. Add statements to define properties to represent all the Northwind tables, and define validation rules and relationships between entities, as shown in the following code:
    ```
    using Microsoft.EntityFrameworkCore;
    ```

```csharp
namespace Packt.Shared
{
  public class Northwind : DbContext
  {
    public DbSet<Category> Categories { get; set; }
    public DbSet<Customer> Customers { get; set; }
    public DbSet<Employee> Employees { get; set; }
    public DbSet<Order> Orders { get; set; }
    public DbSet<OrderDetail> OrderDetails { get; set; }
    public DbSet<Product> Products { get; set; }
    public DbSet<Shipper> Shippers { get; set; }
    public DbSet<Supplier> Suppliers { get; set; }

    public Northwind(DbContextOptions<Northwind> options)
      : base(options) { }

    protected override void OnModelCreating(
      ModelBuilder modelBuilder)
    {
      base.OnModelCreating(modelBuilder);

      modelBuilder.Entity<Category>()
        .Property(c => c.CategoryName)
        .IsRequired()
        .HasMaxLength(15);

      // define a one-to-many relationship
      modelBuilder.Entity<Category>()
        .HasMany(c => c.Products)
        .WithOne(p => p.Category);

      modelBuilder.Entity<Customer>()
        .Property(c => c.CustomerID)
        .IsRequired()
        .HasMaxLength(5);

      modelBuilder.Entity<Customer>()
        .Property(c => c.CompanyName)
        .IsRequired()
        .HasMaxLength(40);

      modelBuilder.Entity<Customer>()
        .Property(c => c.ContactName)
        .HasMaxLength(30);

      modelBuilder.Entity<Customer>()
        .Property(c => c.Country)
        .HasMaxLength(15);

      // define a one-to-many relationship
      modelBuilder.Entity<Customer>()
        .HasMany(c => c.Orders)
        .WithOne(o => o.Customer);
```

```csharp
modelBuilder.Entity<Employee>()
  .Property(c => c.LastName)
  .IsRequired()
  .HasMaxLength(20);

modelBuilder.Entity<Employee>()
  .Property(c => c.FirstName)
  .IsRequired()
  .HasMaxLength(10);

modelBuilder.Entity<Employee>()
  .Property(c => c.Country)
  .HasMaxLength(15);

// define a one-to-many relationship
modelBuilder.Entity<Employee>()
  .HasMany(e => e.Orders)
  .WithOne(o => o.Employee);

modelBuilder.Entity<Product>()
  .Property(c => c.ProductName)
  .IsRequired()
  .HasMaxLength(40);

modelBuilder.Entity<Product>()
  .HasOne(p => p.Category)
  .WithMany(c => c.Products);

modelBuilder.Entity<Product>()
  .HasOne(p => p.Supplier)
  .WithMany(s => s.Products);

// define a one-to-many relationship
// with a property key that does not
// follow naming conventions
modelBuilder.Entity<Order>()
  .HasOne(o => o.Shipper)
  .WithMany(s => s.Orders)
  .HasForeignKey(o => o.ShipVia);

// the table name has a space in it
modelBuilder.Entity<OrderDetail>()
  .ToTable("Order Details");

// define multi-column primary key
// for Order Details table
modelBuilder.Entity<OrderDetail>()
  .HasKey(od => new { od.OrderID, od.ProductID });

modelBuilder.Entity<Supplier>()
  .Property(c => c.CompanyName)
  .IsRequired()
  .HasMaxLength(40);
```

```
        modelBuilder.Entity<Supplier>()
          .HasMany(s => s.Products)
          .WithOne(p => p.Supplier);
      }
    }
}
```

10. In **Terminal**, compile the class libraries to check for errors by entering the following command: `dotnet build`

We will set the database connection string in any projects such as websites that need to work with the Northwind database, so that it does not need to be done in the `Northwind` class, but the class derived from `DbContext` must have a constructor with a `DbContextOptions` parameter for this to work.

Summary

In this chapter, you have been introduced to some of the app models that you can use to build practical applications using C# and .NET Core, and you have created two class libraries to define an entity data model for working with the Northwind database.

In the following chapters, you will learn the details about how to build the following:

- Simple websites with static HTML pages and dynamic Razor Pages.

- Complex websites with the **Model-View-Controller** (**MVC**) design pattern.

- Complex websites with content that can be managed by end users with a **Content Management System** (**CMS**).

- Web services that can be called by any platform that can make an HTTP request and clients of those services.

- Intelligent apps with machine learning.

- Windows desktop apps with Windows Forms, WPF, and UWP.

- Cross-platform mobile apps with Xamarin.Forms.

Chapter 15

Building Websites Using ASP.NET Core Razor Pages

This chapter is about building websites with a modern HTTP architecture on the server side using Microsoft ASP.NET Core. You will learn about building simple websites using the ASP.NET Core Razor Pages feature introduced with .NET Core 2.0 and the Razor class library feature introduced with .NET Core 2.1.

This chapter will cover the following topics:

- Understanding web development
- Understanding ASP.NET Core
- Exploring Razor Pages
- Using Entity Framework Core with ASP.NET Core
- Using Razor class libraries

Understanding web development

Developing for the web is developing with **Hypertext Transfer Protocol (HTTP)**.

Understanding HTTP

To communicate with a web server, the client, also known as the **user agent**, makes calls over the network using HTTP. As such, HTTP is the technical underpinning of the *web*. So, when we talk about web applications or web services, we mean that they use HTTP to communicate between a client (often a web browser) and a server.

A client makes an HTTP request for a resource, such as a page, uniquely identified by a **Uniform Resource Locator (URL)**, and the server sends back an HTTP response, as shown in the following diagram:

You can use Google Chrome and other browsers to record requests and responses.

Good Practice: **Google Chrome** is available on more operating systems than any other browser, and it has powerful, built-in developer tools, so it is a good first choice of browser for testing your websites. Always test your web application with Chrome and at least two other browsers, for example, Firefox and Safari for macOS and iPhone. Microsoft Edge will switch from using Microsoft's own rendering engine to using Chromium in 2019 so it is less important to test with it. If Microsoft's Internet Explorer is used at all, it tends to mostly be inside organizations for intranets.

Let's explore how to use Google Chrome to make HTTP requests.

1. Start **Google Chrome**.

2. To show developer tools in Chrome, do the following:
    ° On macOS, press *Alt + Cmd + I*
    ° On Windows, press *F12* or *Ctrl + Shift + I*

3. Click on the **Network** tab, and Chrome should immediately start recording the network traffic between your browser and any web servers, as shown in the following screenshot:

4. In Chrome's address box, enter the following URL: `https://dotnet.microsoft.com/learn/web`

5. In the **Developer tools** window, in the list of recorded requests, scroll to the top and click on the first entry, as shown in the following screenshot:

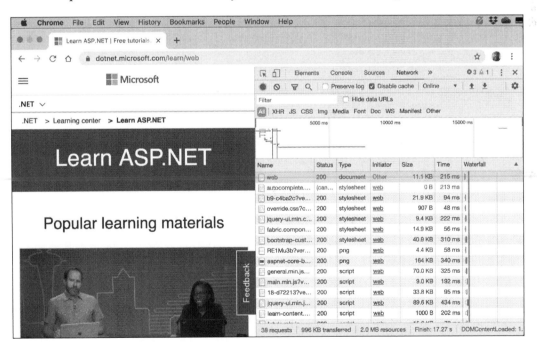

6. On the right-hand side, click on the **Headers** tab, and you will see details about the request and the response, as shown in the following screenshot:

Note the following aspects:

- ○ **Request Method** is GET. Other methods that HTTP defines include POST, PUT, DELETE, HEAD, and PATCH.

- ○ **Status Code** is 200 OK. This means that the server found the resource that the browser requested and has returned it in the body of the response. Other status codes that you might see in response to a GET request include 301 Moved Permanently, 400 Bad Request, 401 Unauthorized, and 404 Not Found.

- ○ **Request Headers** sent by the browser to the web server include:

- **accept**, which lists what formats the browser accepts. In this case, the browser is saying it understands HTML, XHTML, XML, and some image formats, but it will accept all other files */*. Default weightings, also known as quality values, are 1.0. XML is specified with a quality value of 0.9 so it is preferred less than HTML or XHTML. All other file types are given a quality value of 0.8 so are least preferred.
- **accept-encoding**, which lists what compression algorithms the browser understands. In this case, GZIP, DEFLATE, and Brotli.
- **accept-language**, which lists the human languages it would prefer the content to use. In this case, US English which has a default quality value of 1.0, and then any dialect of English that has an explicitly specified quality value of 0.9.
  - A Google Analytics cookie, named _ga, is being sent to the server so that the website can track me, along with lots of other cookies.
  - The server has sent back the HTML web page response compressed using the GZIP algorithm because it knows that the client can decompress that format.

7. Close Chrome.

Client-side web development

When building websites, a developer needs to know more than just C# and .NET Core. On the client (that is, in the web browser), you will use a combination of the following technologies:

- **HTML5**: This is used for the content and structure of a web page.
- **CSS3**: This is used for the styles applied to elements on the web page.
- **JavaScript**: This is used to code any business logic needed on the web page, for example, validating form input or making calls to a web service to fetch more data needed by the web page.

Although HTML5, CSS3, and JavaScript are the fundamental components of frontend web development, there are many additional technologies that can make frontend web development more productive, including Bootstrap and CSS preprocessors like SASS and LESS for styling, Microsoft's TypeScript language for writing more robust code, and JavaScript libraries like jQuery, Angular, React, and Vue. All these higher-level technologies ultimately translate or compile to the underlying three core technologies, so they work across all modern browsers.

As part of the build and deploy process, you will likely use technologies like Node.js; **Node Package Manager** (**NPM**) and Bower, which are both client-side package managers; and Webpack, which is a popular module bundler, a tool for compiling, transforming, and bundling website source files.

 More Information: This book is about C# and .NET Core, so we will cover some of the basics of frontend web development, but for more detail, try *HTML5 and CSS3: Building Responsive Websites* at: `https://www.packtpub.com/web-development/html5-and-css3-building-responsive-websites`.

Understanding ASP.NET Core

Microsoft ASP.NET Core is part of a history of Microsoft technologies used to build websites and web services that have evolved over the years:

- **Active Server Pages** (**ASP**) was released in 1996 and was Microsoft's first attempt at a platform for dynamic server-side execution of website code. ASP files contain a mix of HTML and code that executes on the server written in the VBScript language.

- **ASP.NET Web Forms** was released in 2002 with the .NET Framework, and is designed to enable non-web developers, such as those familiar with Visual Basic, to quickly create websites by dragging and dropping visual components and writing event-driven code in Visual Basic or C#. Web Forms can only be hosted on Windows, but it is still used today in products such as Microsoft SharePoint. It should be avoided for new web projects in favor of ASP.NET Core.

- **Windows Communication Foundation** (**WCF**) was released in 2006 and enables developers to build SOAP and REST services. SOAP is powerful but complex, so it should be avoided unless you need advanced features, such as distributed transactions and complex messaging topologies.

- **ASP.NET MVC** was released in 2009 and is designed to cleanly separate the concerns of web developers between the *models*, which temporarily store the data; the *views* that present the data using various formats in the UI; and the *controllers*, which fetch the model and pass it to a view. This separation enables improved reuse and unit testing.

- **ASP.NET Web API** was released in 2012 and enables developers to create HTTP services, also known as REST services that are simpler and more scalable than SOAP services.

- **ASP.NET SignalR** was released in 2013 and enables real-time communication in websites by abstracting underlying technologies and techniques, such as WebSockets and Long Polling. This enables website features like live chat or updates to time-sensitive data like stock prices across a wide variety of web browsers even when they do not support an underlying technology like Web Sockets.

- **ASP.NET Core** was released in 2016 and combines MVC, Web API, and SignalR, running on .NET Core. Therefore, it can execute cross-platform. ASP.NET Core has many project templates to get you started with its supported technologies.

> **Good Practice**: Choose ASP.NET Core to develop websites and web services because it includes web-related technologies that are modern and cross-platform.

ASP.NET Core 2.0 to 2.2 can run on .NET Framework 4.6.1 or later (Windows only) as well as .NET Core 2.0 or later (cross-platform). ASP.NET Core 3.0 only supports .NET Core 3.0.

Classic ASP.NET versus modern ASP.NET Core

Until now, ASP.NET has been built on top of a large assembly in the .NET Framework named `System.Web.dll` and it is tightly coupled to Microsoft's Windows-only web server named **Internet Information Services (IIS)**. Over the years, this assembly has accumulated a lot of features, many of which are not suitable for modern cross-platform development.

ASP.NET Core is a major redesign of ASP.NET. It removes the dependency on the `System.Web.dll` assembly and IIS and is composed of modular lightweight packages, just like the rest of .NET Core.

You can develop and run ASP.NET Core applications cross-platform on Windows, macOS, and Linux. Microsoft has even created a cross-platform, super-performant web server named **Kestrel**, and the entire stack is open source.

> **More Information**: You can read more about Kestrel, including its HTTP/2 support, at the following link: `https://docs.microsoft.com/en-us/aspnet/core/fundamentals/servers/kestrel`.

ASP.NET Core 2.2 or later projects default to the new in-process hosting model. This gives a 400% performance improvement when hosting in Microsoft IIS, but Microsoft still recommends using Kestrel for even better performance.

I recommend that you work through the chapters in the rest of the book sequentially because later chapters will reference projects in earlier chapters, and you will build up sufficient knowledge and skill to tackle the trickier problems in later chapters.

Creating an ASP.NET Core project

We will create an ASP.NET Core project that will show a list of suppliers from the Northwind database.

The dotnet tool has many project templates that do a lot of work for you, but it can be difficult to discern which work best in a given situation, so we will start with the simplest web template and slowly add features step by step so that you can understand all the pieces.

1. In your existing PracticalApps folder, create a subfolder named NorthwindWeb, and add it to the PracticalApps workspace.

2. Navigate to **Terminal** | **New Terminal** and select NorthwindWeb.

3. In **Terminal**, enter the following command to create an **ASP.NET Core Empty** website: dotnet new web

4. In **Terminal**, enter the following command to restore packages and compile the website: dotnet build

5. Edit NorthwindWeb.csproj, and note the SDK is Microsoft.NET.Sdk.Web, as shown in the following markup:

```
<Project Sdk="Microsoft.NET.Sdk.Web">

  <PropertyGroup>
    <TargetFramework>netcoreapp3.0</TargetFramework>
  </PropertyGroup>

</Project>
```

In ASP.NET Core 1.0, you would need to include lots of references. With ASP.NET Core 2.0, you would need a package reference named Microsoft.AspNetCore.All. With ASP.NET Core 3.0, simply using this Web SDK is enough.

6. Open Program.cs, and note the following:
   ° A website is like a console application, with a Main method as its entry point.

- ○ A website has a `CreateHostBuilder` method that specifies a `Startup` class that is used to configure the website, which is then built and run, as shown in the following code:

```
public class Program
{
  public static void Main(string[] args)
  {
    CreateHostBuilder(args).Build().Run();
  }

  public static IHostBuilder CreateHostBuilder(
    string[] args) =>
    Host.CreateDefaultBuilder(args)
      .ConfigureWebHostDefaults(webBuilder =>
      {
        webBuilder.UseStartup<Startup>();
      });
}
```

7. Open `Startup.cs`, and note its two methods:

- ○ The `ConfigureServices` method is currently empty. We will use it later to add services like MVC.

- ○ The `Configure` method currently does three things: first, it configures that when developing, any unhandled exceptions will be shown in the browser window for the developer to see its details; second, it uses routing; and third, it uses endpoints to wait for requests, and then for each HTTP GET request it asynchronously responds by returning the plain text "Hello World!", as shown in the following code:

```
public class Startup
{
  // This method gets called by the runtime.
  // Use this method to add services to the container.
  public void ConfigureServices(
    IServiceCollection services)
  {
  }

  // This method gets called by the runtime.
  // Use this method to configure the HTTP request pipeline.
  public void Configure(
    IApplicationBuilder app, IWebHostEnvironment env)
  {
    if (env.IsDevelopment())
    {
```

```
        app.UseDeveloperExceptionPage();
    }

    app.UseRouting();

    app.UseEndpoints(endpoints =>
    {
        endpoints.MapGet("/", async context =>
        {
            await context.Response.WriteAsync("Hello World!");
        });
    });
  }
}
```

8. Close the `Startup.cs` class file.

Testing and securing the website

We will now test the functionality of the ASP.NET Core Empty website project. We will also enable encryption of all traffic between the browser and web server for privacy by switching from HTTP to HTTPS. HTTPS is the secure encrypted version of HTTP.

1. In **Terminal**, enter the `dotnet run` command, and note the web server has started listening on ports 5000 and 5001, as shown in the following output:

```
info: Microsoft.Hosting.Lifetime[0]
        Now listening on: https://localhost:5001
info: Microsoft.Hosting.Lifetime[0]
        Now listening on: http://localhost:5000
info: Microsoft.Hosting.Lifetime[0]
        Application started. Press Ctrl+C to shut down.
info: Microsoft.Hosting.Lifetime[0]
        Hosting environment: Development
info: Microsoft.Hosting.Lifetime[0]
        Content root path: /Users/markjprice/Code/PracticalApps/
NorthwindWeb
```

2. Start Chrome.

3. Enter the address `http://localhost:5000/`, and note the response is `Hello World!` in plain text, from the cross-platform Kestrel web server, as shown in the following screenshot:

4. Enter the address `https://localhost:5001/`, and note the response is a privacy error, as shown in the following screenshot:

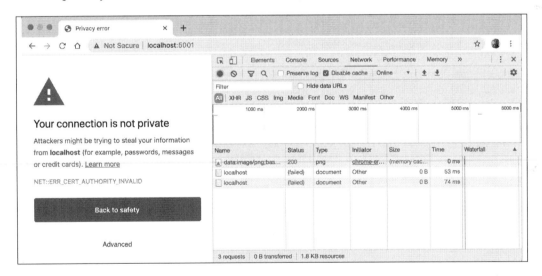

This is because we have not configured a certificate that the browser can trust to encrypt and decrypt HTTP traffic (so if you do not see this error, it is because you have already configured a certificate). In a production environment you would want to pay a company like Verisign for one because they provide liability protection and technical support.

More Information: If you do not mind reapplying for a new certificate every 90 days then you can get a free certificate from the following link: `https://letsencrypt.org`.

During development, you can tell your OS to trust a temporary development certificate provided by ASP.NET Core.

5. In Visual Studio Code, press *Ctrl + C* to stop the web server.

6. In **Terminal**, enter the `dotnet dev-certs https --trust` command, and note the message, **Trusting the HTTPS development certificate was requested**. You might be prompted to enter your password and a valid HTTPS certificate may already be present.

7. If Chrome is still running, close and restart it to ensure it has read the new certificate.

8. In `Startup.cs`, in the `Configure` method, add an `else` statement to enable HSTS when not in development, as shown highlighted in the following code:

```
if (env.IsDevelopment())
{
  app.UseDeveloperExceptionPage();
}
else
{
  app.UseHsts();
}
```

HTTP Strict Transport Security (HSTS) is an opt-in security enhancement. If a website specifies it and a browser supports it, then it forces all communication over HTTPS and prevents the visitor from using untrusted or invalid certificates.

9. Add a statement after the call to `app.UseRouting` to redirect HTTP requests to HTTPS, as shown in the following code:

```
app.UseHttpsRedirection();
```

10. In **Terminal**, enter the `dotnet run` command to start the web server.

11. In Chrome, request the address `http://localhost:5000/`, and note how the server responds with a **307 Temporary Redirect** to port 5001, and that the certificate is now valid and trusted, as shown in the following screenshot:

12. Close Chrome.

13. In Visual Studio Code, press *Ctrl + C* to stop the web server.

Remember to stop the Kestrel web server whenever you have finished testing a website.

Enabling static and default files

A website that only ever returns a single plain text message isn't very useful!

At a minimum, it ought to return static HTML pages, CSS that the web pages will use for styling, and any other static resources such as images and videos.

You will now create a folder for your static website resources and a basic index page that uses Bootstrap for styling.

 More Information: Web technologies like Bootstrap commonly use a **Content Delivery Network (CDN)** to efficiently deliver their source files globally. You can read more about CDNs at the following link: https://en.wikipedia.org/wiki/Content_delivery_network.

1. In the NorthwindWeb folder, create a folder named wwwroot.

2. Add a new file to the wwwroot folder named index.html.

3. Modify its content to link to CDN-hosted Bootstrap for styling, and use modern good practices such as setting the viewport, as shown in the following markup:

```
<!DOCTYPE html>
<html lang="en">
<head>
  <!-- Required meta tags -->
  <meta charset="utf-8" />
  <meta name="viewport" content=
    "width=device-width, initial-scale=1, shrink-to-fit=no" />

  <!-- Bootstrap CSS -->
  <link rel="stylesheet" href="https://stackpath.bootstrapcdn.
com/bootstrap/4.3.1/css/bootstrap.min.css" integrity="sha384-gg
OyR0iXCbMQv3Xipma34MD+dH/1fQ784/j6cY/iJTQUOhcWr7x9JvoRxT2MZw1T"
crossorigin="anonymous">

  <title>Welcome ASP.NET Core!</title>
</head>
<body>
  <div class="container">
    <div class="jumbotron">
      <h1 class="display-3">Welcome to Northwind!</h1>
      <p class="lead">We supply products to our customers.</p>
      <hr />
      <p>Our customers include restaurants, hotels, and cruise
lines.</p>
      <p>
        <a class="btn btn-primary"
           href="https://www.asp.net/">Learn more</a>
      </p>
    </div>
  </div>
</body>
</html>
```

More Information: To get the latest <link> element for Bootstrap, copy and paste it from the **Getting Started - Introduction** page at the following link: https://getbootstrap.com/.

If you were to start the website now, and enter http://localhost:5000/index.html in the address box, the website would return a 404 Not Found error saying no web page was found. To enable the website to return static files such as index.html, we must explicitly configure that feature.

Even if we enable static files, if you were to start the website and enter `http://localhost:5000/` in the address box, the website would return a `404 Not Found` error because the web server doesn't know what to return by default if no named file is requested.

You will now enable static files and explicitly configure default files.

1. In `Startup.cs`, in the `Configure` method, comment the statement that maps a GET request to returning the `Hello World!` plain text response, and add statements to enable static files and default files, as shown highlighted in the following code:

```
public void Configure(
   IApplicationBuilder app, IHostingEnvironment env)
{
  if (env.IsDevelopment())
  {
    app.UseDeveloperExceptionPage();
  }
  else
  {
    app.UseHsts();
  }

  app.UseRouting();

  app.UseHttpsRedirection();

  app.UseDefaultFiles(); // index.html, default.html, and so on
  app.UseStaticFiles();

  app.UseEndpoints(endpoints =>
  {
  // endpoints.MapGet("/", async context =>
  //      {
  //        await context.Response.WriteAsync("Hello World!");
  //      });
  });
}
```

The call to `UseDefaultFiles` must be before the call to `UseStaticFiles`, or it won't work!

2. Start the website by entering `dotnet run` in **Terminal**.

3. In Chrome, enter `http://localhost:5000/`, and note that you are redirected to the HTTPS address on port 5001, and the `index.html` file is now returned because it is one of the possible default files for this website.

If all web pages are static, that is, they only get changed manually by a web editor, then our website programming work is complete. But almost all websites need dynamic content, which means a web page that is generated at runtime by executing code.

The easiest way to do that is to use a feature of ASP.NET Core named **Razor Pages**.

Exploring Razor Pages

Razor Pages allow a developer to easily mix HTML markup with C# code statements. That is why they use the .cshtml file extension.

By default, ASP.NET Core looks for Razor Pages in a folder named Pages.

Enabling Razor Pages

You will now change the static HTML page into a dynamic Razor Page, and then add and enable the Razor Pages service.

1. In the NorthwindWeb project, create a folder named Pages.

2. Move the index.html file into the Pages folder.

3. Rename the file extension from .html to .cshtml.

4. In Startup.cs, in the ConfigureServices method, add statements to add Razor Pages and its related services like model binding, authorization, antiforgery, views, and tag helpers, as shown highlighted in the following code:

```
public void ConfigureServices(IServiceCollection services)
{
    services.AddRazorPages();
}
```

5. In Startup.cs, in the Configure method, in the configuration to use endpoints, add a statement to use MapRazorPages, as shown highlighted in the following code:

```
app.UseEndpoints(endpoints =>
{
// endpoints.MapGet("/", async context =>
//     {
//     await context.Response.WriteAsync("Hello World!");
//     });
    endpoints.MapRazorPages();
});
```

Defining a Razor Page

In the HTML markup of a web page, Razor syntax is indicated by the @ symbol.

Razor Pages can be described as follows:

- They require the @page directive at the top of the file.
- They can have an @functions section that defines any of the following:
  - Properties for storing data values, like in a class definition. An instance of that class is automatically instantiated named Model that can have its properties set in special methods and you can get the property values in the markup.
  - Methods named OnGet, OnPost, OnDelete, and so on, that execute when HTTP requests are made such as GET, POST, and DELETE.

Let's now convert the static HTML page into a Razor page.

1. In Visual Studio Code, open index.cshtml.

2. Add the @page statement to the top of the file.

3. After the @page statement, add an @functions statement block.

4. Define a property to store the name of the current day as a string value.

5. Define a method to set DayName that executes when an HTTP GET request is made for the page, as shown in the following code:

```
@page
@functions
{
  public string DayName { get; set; }

  public void OnGet()
  {
    Model.DayName = DateTime.Now.ToString("dddd");
  }
}
```

6. Output the day name inside one of the paragraphs, as shown highlighted in the following markup:

```
<p>It's @Model.DayName! Our customers include restaurants, hotels,
and cruise lines.</p>
```

7. Start the website, visit it with Chrome, and note the current day name is output on the page, as shown in the following screenshot:

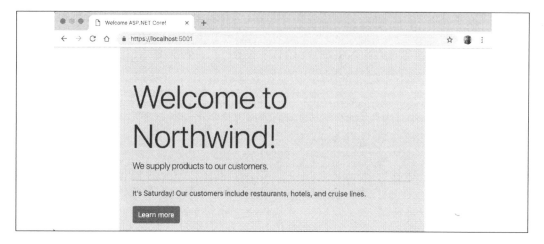

Using shared layouts with Razor Pages

Most websites have more than one page. If every page had to contain all of the boilerplate markup that is currently in `index.cshtml`, that would become a pain to manage. So, ASP.NET Core has **layouts**.

To use layouts, we must create a Razor file to define the default layout for all Razor Pages (and all MVC views) and store it in a `Shared` folder so that it can be easily found by convention. The name of this file can be anything, but `_Layout.cshtml` is good practice. We must also create a specially named file to set the default layout for all Razor Pages (and all MVC views). This file must be named `_ViewStart.cshtml`.

1. In the `Pages` folder, create a file named `_ViewStart.cshtml`.

2. Modify its content, as shown in the following markup:

```
@{
    Layout = "_Layout";
}
```

3. In the `Pages` folder, create a folder named `Shared`.

4. In the `Shared` folder, create a file named `_Layout.cshtml`.

5. Modify the content of `_Layout.cshtml` (it is similar to `index.cshtml` so you can copy and paste from there), as shown in the following markup:

```
<!DOCTYPE html>
<html lang="en">
<head>
```

```html
<!-- Required meta tags -->
<meta charset="utf-8" />
<meta name="viewport" content=
"width=device-width, initial-scale=1, shrink-to-fit=no" />

<!-- Bootstrap CSS -->
<link rel="stylesheet" href="https://stackpath.bootstrapcdn.
com/bootstrap/4.3.1/css/bootstrap.min.css" integrity="sha384-gg
OyR0iXCbMQv3Xipma34MD+dH/1fQ784/j6cY/iJTQUOhcWr7x9JvoRxT2MZw1T"
crossorigin="anonymous">

<title>@ViewData["Title"]</title>
</head>
<body>
  <div class="container">
    @RenderBody()
    <hr />
    <footer>
      <p>Copyright &copy; 2019 - @ViewData["Title"]</p>
    </footer>
  </div>
  <!-- JavaScript to enable features like carousel -->
  <!-- jQuery first, then Popper.js, then Bootstrap JS -->
  <script src="https://code.jquery.com/jquery-3.3.1.slim.min.js"
integrity="sha384-q8i/X+965Dz00rT7abK41JStQIAqVgRVzpbzo5smXKp4YfRv
H+8abtTE1Pi6jizo" crossorigin="anonymous"></script>
  <script src="https://cdnjs.cloudflare.com/ajax/libs/
popper.js/1.14.7/umd/popper.min.js" integrity="sha384-UO2eT0
CpHqdSJQ6hJty5KVphtPhzWj9WO1clHTMGa3JDZwrnQq4sF86dIHNDz0W1"
crossorigin="anonymous"></script>
  <script src="https://stackpath.bootstrapcdn.com/bootstrap/4.3.1/
js/bootstrap.min.js" integrity="sha384-JjSmVgyd0p3pXB1rRibZUAYoII
y6OrQ6VrjIEaFf/nJGzIxFDsf4x0xIM+B07jRM" crossorigin="anonymous"></
script>

  @RenderSection("Scripts", required: false)
</body>
</html>
```

While reviewing the preceding markup, note the following:

- ○ `<title>` is set dynamically using server-side code from a dictionary named `ViewData`. This is a simple way to pass data between different parts of an ASP.NET Core website. In this case, the data will be set in a Razor Page class file and then output in the shared layout.

- ○ `@RenderBody()` marks the insertion point for the page being requested.

- ° A horizontal rule and footer will appear at the bottom of each page.
- ° At the bottom of the layout are some scripts to implement some cool features of Bootstrap that we will use later like a carousel of images.
- ° After the `<script>` elements for Bootstrap, we have defined a section named `Scripts` so that a Razor Page can optionally inject additional scripts that it needs.

6. Modify `index.cshtml` to remove all HTML markup except `<div class="jumbotron">` and its contents, and leave the C# code in the `@ functions` block that you added earlier.

7. Add a statement to the `OnGet` method to store a page title in the `ViewData` dictionary, and modify the button to navigate to a suppliers page (which we will create in the next section), as shown highlighted in the following markup:

```
@page
@functions
{
  public string DayName { get; set; }

  public void OnGet()
  {
    ViewData["Title"] = "Northwind Website";
    Model.DayName = DateTime.Now.ToString("dddd");
  }
}
<div class="jumbotron">
  <h1 class="display-3">Welcome to Northwind!</h1>
  <p class="lead">We supply products to our customers.</p>
  <hr />
  <p>It's @Model.DayName! Our customers include restaurants,
hotels, and cruise lines.</p>
  <p>
    <a class="btn btn-primary" href="suppliers">Learn more about
our suppliers</a>
  </p>
</div>
```

8. Start the website, visit it with Chrome, and note that it has similar behavior as before, although clicking the button for suppliers will give a `404 Not Found` error because we have not created that page yet.

Using code-behind files with Razor Pages

Sometimes, it is better to separate the HTML markup from the data and executable code, so Razor Pages allows **code-behind** class files.

You will now create a page that shows a list of suppliers. In this example, we are focusing on learning about code-behind files. In the next topic, we will load the list of suppliers from a database, but for now, we will simulate that with a hard-coded array of `string` values.

1. In the `Pages` folder, add two new files named `suppliers.cshtml` and `suppliers.cshtml.cs`.

2. Add statements to `suppliers.cshtml.cs`, as shown in the following code:

```
using Microsoft.AspNetCore.Mvc.RazorPages;
using System.Collections.Generic;

namespace NorthwindWeb.Pages
{
  public class SuppliersModel : PageModel
  {
    public IEnumerable<string> Suppliers { get; set; }

    public void OnGet()
    {
      ViewData["Title"] = "Northwind Web Site - Suppliers";

      Suppliers = new[] {
        "Alpha Co", "Beta Limited", "Gamma Corp"
      };
    }
  }
}
```

While reviewing the preceding markup, note the following:

- ° `SuppliersModel` inherits from `PageModel`, so it has members such as the `ViewData` dictionary for sharing data. You can click on `PageModel` and press *F12* to see that it has lots more useful features, like the entire `HttpContext` of the current request.

- ° `SuppliersModel` defines a property for storing a collection of `string` values named `Suppliers`.

- ° When a HTTP GET request is made for this Razor Page, the `Suppliers` property is populated with some example supplier names.

3. Modify the contents of `suppliers.cshtml`, as shown in the following markup:

```
@page
@model NorthwindWeb.Pages.SuppliersModel
<div class="row">
```

```
<h1 class="display-2">Suppliers</h1>
<table class="table">
  <thead class="thead-inverse">
    <tr><th>Company Name</th></tr>
  </thead>
  <tbody>
  @foreach(string name in Model.Suppliers)
  {
    <tr><td>@name</td></tr>
  }
  </tbody>
</table>
</div>
```

While reviewing the preceding markup, note the following:

- The model type for this Razor Page is set to `SuppliersModel`.
- The page outputs an HTML table with Bootstrap styles.
- The data rows in the table are generated by looping through the `Suppliers` property of `Model`.

4. Start the website, visit it using Chrome, click on the button to learn more about suppliers, and note the table of suppliers, as shown in the following screenshot:

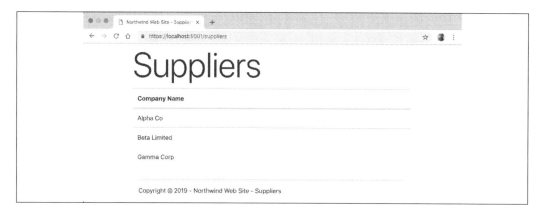

Using Entity Framework Core with ASP.NET Core

Entity Framework Core is a natural way to get real data into a website. In *Chapter 14, Practical Applications of C# and .NET*, you created two class libraries: one for the entity models and one for the Northwind database context.

Configure Entity Framework Core as a service

Functionality like Entity Framework Core database contexts that are needed by ASP.NET Core must be registered as a service during website startup.

1. In the `NorthwindWeb` project, modify `NorthwindWeb.csproj` to add a reference to the `NorthwindContextLib` project, as shown highlighted in the following markup:

```
<Project Sdk="Microsoft.NET.Sdk.Web">

  <PropertyGroup>
    <TargetFramework>netcoreapp3.0</TargetFramework>
  </PropertyGroup>

  <ItemGroup>
    <ProjectReference Include=
      "..\NorthwindContextLib\NorthwindContextLib.csproj" />
  </ItemGroup>

</Project>
```

2. Navigate to **Terminal | New Terminal** and select `NorthwindWeb`.

3. In **Terminal**, restore packages and compile the project by entering the following command: `dotnet build`

4. Open `Startup.cs` and import the `System.IO`, `Microsoft.EntityFrameworkCore` and `Packt.Shared` namespaces, as shown in the following code:

```
using System.IO;
using Microsoft.EntityFrameworkCore;
using Packt.Shared;
```

5. Add a statement to the `ConfigureServices` method to register the `Northwind` database context class to use SQLite as its database provider and specify its database connection string, as shown in the following code:

```
string databasePath = Path.Combine("..", "Northwind.db");

services.AddDbContext<Northwind>(options =>
  options.UseSqlite($"Data Source={databasePath}"));
```

6. In the `NorthwindWeb` project, in the `Pages` folder, open `suppliers.cshtml.cs`, and import the `Packt.Shared` and `System.Linq` namespaces, as shown in the following code:

```
using System.Linq;
using Packt.Shared;
```

7. In the `SuppliersModel` class, add a private field and a constructor to get the `Northwind` database context, as shown in the following code:

```
private Northwind db;

public SuppliersModel(Northwind injectedContext)
{
  db = injectedContext;
}
```

8. In the `OnGet` method, modify the statements to get the names of suppliers by selecting the company names from the `Suppliers` property of the database context, as shown highlighted in the following code:

```
public void OnGet()
{
  ViewData["Title"] = "Northwind Web Site - Suppliers";

  Suppliers = db.Suppliers.Select(s => s.CompanyName);
}
```

9. In **Terminal**, enter the command `dotnet run` to start the website, in Chrome, enter `http://localhost:5000/`, click the button to go to the `Suppliers` page, and note that the supplier table now loads from the database, as shown in the following screenshot:

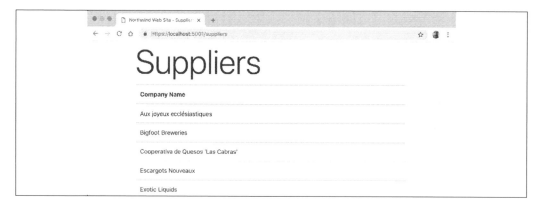

Manipulating data using Razor pages

You will now add functionality to insert a new supplier.

Enabling a model to insert entities

First, you will modify the supplier model so that it responds to HTTP POST requests when a visitor submits a form to insert a new supplier.

1. In the `NorthwindWeb` project, in the `Pages` folder, open `suppliers.cshtml.cs` and import the following namespace:

```
using Microsoft.AspNetCore.Mvc;
```

2. In the `SuppliersModel` class, add a property to store a supplier, and a method named `OnPost` that adds the supplier if its model is valid, as shown in the following code:

```
[BindProperty]
public Supplier Supplier { get; set; }

public IActionResult OnPost()
{
  if (ModelState.IsValid)
  {
    db.Suppliers.Add(Supplier);
    db.SaveChanges();
    return RedirectToPage("/suppliers");
  }
  return Page();
}
```

While reviewing the preceding code, note the following:

- We added a property named `Supplier` that is decorated with the `[BindProperty]` attribute so that we can easily connect HTML elements on the web page to properties in the `Supplier` class.

- We added a method that responds to HTTP POST requests. It checks that all property values conform to validation rules and then adds the supplier to the existing table and saves changed to the database context. This will generate an SQL statement to perform the insert into the database. Then it redirects to the **Suppliers** page so that the visitor sees the newly added supplier.

Defining a form to insert new suppliers

Second, you will modify the Razor page to define a form that a visitor can fill in and submit to insert a new supplier.

1. Open `suppliers.cshtml`, and add tag helpers after the `@model` declaration so that we can use tag helpers like `asp-for` on this Razor page, as shown in the following markup:

```
@addTagHelper *, Microsoft.AspNetCore.Mvc.TagHelpers
```

2. At the bottom of the file, add a form to insert a new supplier, and use the `asp-for` tag helper to connect the `CompanyName` property of the `Supplier` class to the input box, as shown in the following markup:

```
<div class="row">
  <p>Enter a name for a new supplier:</p>
  <form method="POST">
    <div><input asp-for="Supplier.CompanyName" /></div>
    <input type="submit" />
  </form>
</div>
```

While reviewing the preceding markup, note the following:

   ○ The `<form>` element with a `POST` method is normal HTML so an `<input type="submit" />` element inside it will make an HTTP POST request back to the current page with values of any other elements inside that form.

   ○ An `<input>` element with a tag helper named `asp-for` enables data binding to the model behind the Razor page.

3. Start the website, click **Learn more about our suppliers**, scroll down the table of suppliers to the bottom of the form to add a new supplier, enter `Bob's Burgers`, and click on **Submit**, as shown in the following screenshot:

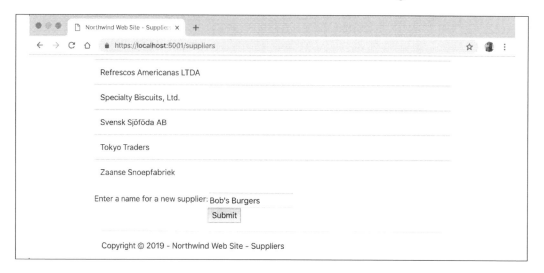

4. Note that you are redirected back to the *Suppliers* list with the new supplier added.

5. Close the browser.

Using Razor class libraries

Everything related to a Razor page can be compiled into a class library for easier reuse. With .NET Core 3.0 and later this can now include static files. A website can either use the Razor page's view as defined in the class library or override it.

1. Create a subfolder in `PracticalApps` named `NorthwindEmployees`.

2. In Visual Studio Code, add the `NorthwindEmployees` folder to the `PracticalApps` workspace.

3. Navigate to **Terminal | New Terminal** and select `NorthwindEmployees`.

4. In **Terminal**, enter the following command to create a **Razor Class Library** project: `dotnet new razorclasslib`

5. Edit `NorthwindEmployees.csproj`, and add a reference to the `NorthwindContextLib` project, as shown in the following markup:

```
<ItemGroup>
  <ProjectReference Include=
    "..\NorthwindContextLib\NorthwindContextLib.csproj" />
</ItemGroup>
```

6. In **Terminal**, enter the following command to restore packages and compile the project: `dotnet build`

7. In **Explorer**, expand the `Areas` folder, and rename the `MyFeature` folder to `PacktFeatures`.

8. In **Explorer**, expand the `PacktFeatures` folder, and in the `Pages` subfolder, add a new file named `_ViewStart.cshtml`.

9. Modify its content, as shown in the following markup:

```
@{
  Layout = "_Layout";
}
```

10. In the `Pages` subfolder, rename `Page1.cshtml` to `employees.cshtml`, and rename `Page1.cshtml.cs` to `employees.cshtml.cs`.

11. Modify `employees.cshtml.cs`, to define a page model with an array of `Employee` entity instances loaded from the `Northwind` database, as shown in the following code:

```
using Microsoft.AspNetCore.Mvc.RazorPages; // PageModel
using Packt.Shared;                        // Employee
using System.Linq;                         // ToArray()
using System.Collections.Generic;          // IEnumerable<T>

namespace PacktFeatures.Pages
```

```
{
  public class EmployeesPageModel : PageModel
  {
    private Northwind db;

    public EmployeesPageModel(Northwind injectedContext)
    {
      db = injectedContext;
    }

    public IEnumerable<Employee> Employees { get; set; }

    public void OnGet()
    {
      Employees = db.Employees.ToArray();
    }
  }
}
```

12. Modify `employees.cshtml`, as shown in the following markup:

```
@page
@using Packt.Shared
@addTagHelper *, Microsoft.AspNetCore.Mvc.TagHelpers
@model PacktFeatures.Pages.EmployeesPageModel
<div class="row">
  <h1 class="display-2">Employees</h2>
</div>
<div class="row">
  @foreach(Employee in Model.Employees)
  {
  <div class="col-sm-3">
    <partial name="_Employee" model="employee" />
  </div>
  }
</div>
```

While reviewing the preceding markup, note the following:

- ° We import the `Packt.Shared` namespace so that we can use classes in it like `Employee`.

- ° We add support for tag helpers so that we can use the `<partial>` element.

- ° We declare the model type for this Razor page to use the class that you just defined.

- ° We enumerate through the `Employees` in the model, outputting each one using a partial view. Partial views are like small pieces of a Razor page and you will create one in the next few steps.

More Information: The `<partial>` tag helper was introduced in ASP.NET Core 2.1. You can read more about it at the following link: `https://docs.microsoft.com/en-us/aspnet/core/ mvc/views/tag-helpers/built-in/partial-tag-helper.`

13. In the `Pages` folder, create a `Shared` folder.

14. In the `Shared` folder, create a file named `_Employee.cshtml`.

15. Modify `_Employee.cshtml`, as shown in the following markup:

```
@model Packt.Shared.Employee
<div class="card border-dark mb-3"
    style="max-width: 18rem;">
  <div class="card-header">@Model.FirstName
    @Model.LastName</div>
  <div class="card-body text-dark">
    <h5 class="card-title">@Model.Country</h5>
    <p class="card-text">@Model.Notes</p>
  </div>
</div>
```

While reviewing the preceding markup, note the following:

- By convention, the names of partial views start with an underscore.

- If you put a partial view in the `Shared` folder then it can be found automatically.

- The model type for this partial view is an `Employee` entity.

- We use Bootstrap card styles to output information about each employee.

Using a Razor class library

You will now reference and use the Razor class library in the website project.

1. Modify the `NorthwindWeb.csproj` file to add a reference to the `NorthwindEmployees` project, as shown highlighted in the following markup:

```
<Project Sdk="Microsoft.NET.Sdk.Web">

  <PropertyGroup>
    <TargetFramework>netcoreapp3.0</TargetFramework>
  </PropertyGroup>

  <ItemGroup>
    <ProjectReference Include=
```

```
         "..\NorthwindContextLib\NorthwindContextLib.csproj" />
    <ProjectReference Include=
         "..\NorthwindEmployees\NorthwindEmployees.csproj" />
    </ItemGroup>

</Project>
```

2. Modify `Pages\index.cshtml` to add a link to the employees page after the link to the suppliers page, as shown in the following markup:

```
<p>
  <a class="btn btn-primary"
     href="packtfeatures/employees">
     Contact our employees
  </a>
</p>
```

3. Start the website, visit the website using Chrome, and click the button to see the cards of employees, as shown in the following screenshot:

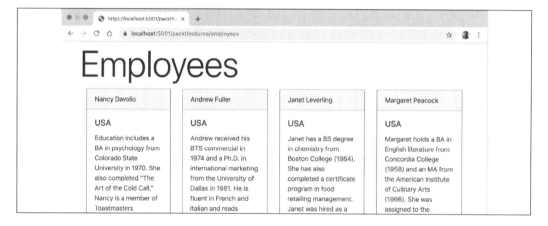

Practicing and exploring

Test your knowledge and understanding by answering some questions, get some hands-on practice, and explore this chapter's topics with deeper research.

Exercise 15.1 – Test your knowledge

Answer the following questions:

1. List six method names that can be specific in an HTTP request.

2. List six status codes and their descriptions that can be returned in an HTTP response.

3. In ASP.NET Core, what is the `Startup` class used for?

4. What does the acronym HSTS stand for and what does it do?

5. How do you enable static HTML pages for a website?

6. How do you mix C# code into the middle of HTML to create a dynamic page?

7. How can you define shared layouts for Razor Pages?

8. How can you separate the markup from the code behind in a Razor Page?

9. How do you configure an Entity Framework Core data context for use with an ASP.NET Core website?

10. How can you reuse Razor Pages with ASP.NET Core 2.2 or later?

Exercise 15.2 – Practice building a data-driven web page

Add a Razor Page to the **NorthwindWeb** website that enables the user to see a list of customers grouped by country. When the user clicks on a customer record, they then see a page showing the full contact details of that customer, and a list of their orders.

Exercise 15.3 – Explore topics

Use the following links to read more details about this chapter's topics:

- **ASP.NET Core fundamentals**: `https://docs.microsoft.com/en-us/aspnet/core/fundamentals/`

- **Static files in ASP.NET Core**: `https://docs.microsoft.com/en-us/aspnet/core/fundamentals/static-files`

- **Introduction to Razor Pages in ASP.NET Core**: `https://docs.microsoft.com/en-us/aspnet/core/razor-pages/`

- **Razor syntax reference for ASP.NET Core**: `https://docs.microsoft.com/en-us/aspnet/core/mvc/views/razor`

- **Layout in ASP.NET Core**: `https://docs.microsoft.com/en-us/aspnet/core/mvc/views/layout`

- **Tag Helpers in ASP.NET Core**: `https://docs.microsoft.com/en-us/aspnet/core/mvc/views/tag-helpers/intro`

- **ASP.NET Core Razor Pages with EF Core**: `https://docs.microsoft.com/en-us/aspnet/core/data/ef-rp/`

- **ASP.NET Core Schedule and Roadmap**: `https://github.com/aspnet/AspNetCore/wiki/Roadmap`

Summary

In this chapter, you learned about the foundations of web development using HTTP, how to build a simple website that returns static files, and you used ASP.NET Core Razor Pages with Entity Framework Core to create web pages that were dynamically generated from information in a database.

In the next chapter, you will learn how to build more complex websites using ASP.NET Core MVC, which separates the technical concerns of building a website into models, views, and controllers to make them easier to manage.

Chapter 16

Building Websites Using the Model-View-Controller Pattern

This chapter is about building websites with a modern HTTP architecture on the server side using Microsoft ASP.NET Core MVC, including the startup configuration, authentication, authorization, routes, models, views, and controllers that make up ASP.NET Core MVC.

This chapter will cover the following topics:

- Setting up an ASP.NET Core MVC website
- Exploring an ASP.NET Core MVC website
- Customizing an ASP.NET Core MVC website
- Using other project templates

Setting up an ASP.NET Core MVC website

ASP.NET Core Razor Pages are great for simple websites. For more complex websites, it would be better to have a more formal structure to manage that complexity.

This is where the **Model-View-Controller (MVC)** design pattern is useful. It uses technologies similar to Razor Pages, but allows a cleaner separation between technical concerns, as shown in the following list:

- **Models**: Classes that represent the data entities and view models used in the website.
- **Views**: Razor files, that is, `.cshtml` files, that render data in view models into HTML web pages. Blazor uses the `.razor` file extension, but do not confuse them with Razor files!

- **Controllers**: Classes that execute code when an HTTP request arrives at the web server. The code usually creates a view model that may contain entity models and passes it to a view to generate an HTTP response to send back to the web browser or other client.

The best way to understand MVC is to see a working example.

Creating and exploring an ASP.NET Core MVC website

You will use the mvc project template to create an ASP.NET Core MVC application with a database for authenticating and authorizing users.

1. In the folder named PracticalApps, create a folder named NorthwindMvc.

2. In Visual Studio Code, open the PracticalApps workspace and then add the NorthwindMvc folder to the workspace.

3. Navigate to **Terminal** | **New Terminal** and select NorthwindMvc.

4. In **Terminal**, create a new MVC website project with authentication stored in a SQLite database, as shown in the following command:

```
dotnet new mvc --auth Individual
```

You can enter the following command to see other options for this template:

```
dotnet new mvc --help
```

5. In **Terminal**, enter the command dotnet run to start the website.

6. Start Chrome and open developer tools.

7. Navigate to http://localhost:5000/ and note the following, as shown in the following screenshot:

   ○ Requests for HTTP are automatically redirected to HTTPS.

   ○ The navigation menu at the top with links to: **Home**, **Privacy**, **Register**, and **Login**. If the viewport width is 575 pixels or less then the navigation collapses into a hamburger menu.

   ○ The temporary message about privacy and cookie use policy that can be hidden by clicking **Accept**.

   ○ The title of the website shown in the header and footer.

8. Click **Register**, enter an email and password, and click the **Register** button. I use Pa$$w0rd in exploring scenarios like this.

   By default, passwords must have at least one non-alphanumeric character, they must have at least one digit ('0'-'9'), and they must have at least one uppercase ('A'-'Z').

   The MVC project template follows best practice for **double-opt-in** (DOI), meaning that after filling in an email and password to register, an email is sent to the email address, and the visitor must click a link in that email to confirm that they want to register.

   We have not yet configured an email provider to send that email, so we must simulate that step.

9. Click the link with the text **Click here to confirm your account** and note that you are redirected to a **Confirm email** web page that you can customize.

10. In the top navigation menu click **Login**, enter your email and password (note that there is an optional check box to remember you, and there are links if the visitor has forgotten their password or they want to register as a new visitor), and then click the **Log in** button.

11. Click your email in the top navigation menu to navigate to an account management page, and note that you can set a phone number, change your email address, change your password, enable two-factor authentication (if you add an authenticator app), and download and delete your personal data, as shown in the following screenshot:

More Information: Some of these built-in features of the basic MVC project template make it easier for your website to be compliant with modern privacy requirements like the European Union's **General Data Protection Regulation (GDPR)** that became active in May 2018. You can read more at the following link: https://docs.microsoft.com/en-us/aspnet/core/security/gdpr

12. Close the browser.

13. In **Terminal**, press *Ctrl + C* to stop the console application and shut down the Kestrel web server that is hosting your ASP.NET Core website.

 More Information: You can read more about ASP.NET Core's support for authenticator apps at the following link: https://docs.microsoft.com/en-us/aspnet/core/security/authentication/identity-enable-qrcodes?view=aspnetcore-3.0

Reviewing the ASP.NET Core MVC website

In Visual Studio Code, look at the **EXPLORER** pane, as shown in the following screenshot:

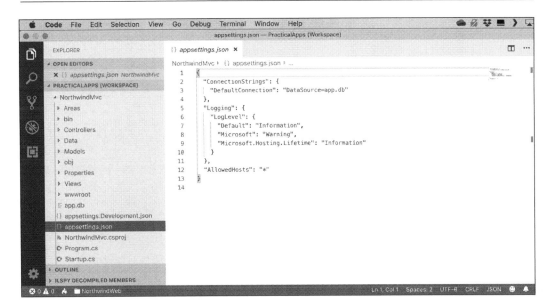

We will look in more detail at some of these parts later, but for now, note the following:

- Areas: This folder contains files needed for features like **ASP.NET Core Identity** for authentication.

- bin, obj: These folders contain the compiled assemblies for the project.

- Controllers: This folder contains C# classes that have methods (known as actions) that fetch a *model* and pass it to a *view*, for example, HomeController.cs.

- Data: This folder contains Entity Framework Core migration classes used by the **ASP.NET Core Identity** system to provide data storage for authentication and authorization, for example, ApplicationDbContext.cs.

- Models: This folder contains C# classes that represent all of the data gathered together by a controller and passed to a view, for example, ErrorViewModel.cs.

- Properties: This folder contains a configuration file for IIS and launching the website during development named launchSettings.json.

- Views: This folder contains the .cshtml Razor files that combine HTML and C# code to dynamically generate HTML responses. The _ViewStart file sets the default layout and the _ViewImports imports common namespaces used in all views like tag helpers.
    - Home: This subfolder contains Razor files for the home and privacy pages.

- ° `Shared`: This subfolder contains Razor files for the shared layout, an error page, and some partial views for logging in, accepting privacy policy, and managing the consent cookie.

- `wwwroot`: This folder contains static content used in the website, such as CSS for styling, images, JavaScript, and a `favicon.ico` file.

- `app.db`: This is the SQLite database that stores registered visitors.

- `appsettings.json` and `appsettings.Development.json`: These files contain settings that your website can load at runtime, for example, the database connection string for the ASP.NET Identity system and logging levels.

- `NorthwindMvc.csproj`: This file contains project settings like use of the Web .NET SDK, an entry to ensure that the `app.db` file is copied to the website's output folder, and a list of NuGet packages that your project requires, including:
  - ° `Microsoft.AspNetCore.Diagnostics.EntityFrameworkCore`
  - ° `Microsoft.AspNetCore.Identity.EntityFrameworkCore`
  - ° `Microsoft.AspNetCore.Identity.UI`
  - ° `Microsoft.EntityFrameworkCore.Sqlite`
  - ° `Microsoft.EntityFrameworkCore.Tools`

- `Program.cs`: This file defines a class that contains the `Main` entry point that builds a pipeline for processing incoming HTTP requests and hosts the website using default options like configuring the Kestrel web server and loading `appsettings`. While building the host it calls the `UseStartup<T>()` method to specify another class that performs additional configuration.

- `Startup.cs`: This file adds and configures services that your website needs, for example, ASP.NET Identity for authentication, SQLite for data storage, and so on, and routes for your application.

 More Information: You can read more about default configuration of web hosts at the following link: `https://docs.microsoft.com/en-us/aspnet/core/fundamentals/host/web-host?view=aspnetcore-3.0`

Reviewing the ASP.NET Core Identity database

If you installed an SQLite tool such as **SQLiteStudio**, then you can open the database and see the tables that the ASP.NET Core Identity system uses to register users and roles, including the `AspNetUsers` table used to store the registered visitor, as shown in the following screenshot:

Good Practice: The ASP.NET Core MVC project template follows good practice by storing a hash of the password instead of the password itself, as you learned how to do in *Chapter 10, Protecting Your Data and Applications*.

Exploring an ASP.NET Core MVC website

Let's walk through the parts that make up a modern ASP.NET Core MVC website.

Understanding ASP.NET Core MVC startup

Appropriately enough, we will start by exploring the MVC website's default startup configuration.

1. Open the `Startup.cs` file.

2. Note that the `ConfigureServices` method adds an application database context using SQLite with its database connection string loaded from the `appsettings.json` file for its data storage, adds ASP.NET Identity for authentication and configures it to use the application database, and adds support for MVC controllers with views as well as Razor Pages, as shown in the following code:

```
public void ConfigureServices(IServiceCollection services)
{
  services.AddDbContext<ApplicationDbContext>(options =>
    options.UseSqlite(
      Configuration
      .GetConnectionString("DefaultConnection")));
```

```
services.AddDefaultIdentity<IdentityUser>(options =>
    options.SignIn.RequireConfirmedAccount = true)
    .AddEntityFrameworkStores<ApplicationDbContext>();

services.AddControllersWithViews();
services.AddRazorPages();
}
```

Although we will not create any Razor Pages in this chapter, we need to leave the method call that adds Razor Page support because our MVC website uses ASP.NET Core Identity for authentication and authorization, and it uses a Razor Class Library for its user interface components, like visitor registration and log in.

More Information: You can learn more about the Identity UI library that is distributed as a Razor class library and can be overridden by a website at the following link: https://docs.microsoft.com/en-us/aspnet/core/security/authentication/scaffold-identity?tabs=netcore-cli

3. The call to AddDbContext is an example of registering a dependency service. ASP.NET Core implements the **dependency injection (DI)** design pattern so that controllers can request needed services through their constructors. Developers register those services in the ConfigureServices method.

More Information: You can read more about dependency injection at the following link: https://docs.microsoft.com/en-us/aspnet/core/fundamentals/dependency-injection?view=aspnetcore-3.0

4. Next, we have the Configure method, which configures a detailed exception and database error page if the website runs in development, or a friendlier error page and HSTS for production. HTTPS redirection, static files, routing, and ASP.NET Identity are enabled, and an MVC default route and Razor Pages are configured, as shown in the following code:

```
public void Configure(IApplicationBuilder app,
    IHostingEnvironment env)
{
    if (env.IsDevelopment())
    {
        app.UseDeveloperExceptionPage();
        app.UseDatabaseErrorPage();
    }
    else
```

```
{
  app.UseExceptionHandler("/Home/Error");
  // The default HSTS value is 30 days.
  app.UseHsts();
}

app.UseHttpsRedirection();
app.UseStaticFiles();

app.UseRouting();

app.UseAuthentication();
app.UseAuthorization();

app.UseEndpoints(endpoints =>
{
  endpoints.MapControllerRoute(
    name: "default",
    pattern: "{controller=Home}/{action=Index}/{id?}");

  endpoints.MapRazorPages();
});
}
```

We learned about most of these methods in *Chapter 15, Building Websites Using ASP.NET Core Razor Pages*. The most important new method in the `Configure` method is `MapControllerRoute`, which maps a default route for use by MVC. This route is very flexible, because it will map to almost any incoming URL, as you will see in the next section.

 More Information: You can read more about configuring middleware at the following link: `https://docs.microsoft.com/en-us/aspnet/core/fundamentals/middleware/index?view=aspnetcore-3.0`

Understanding the default MVC route

The responsibility of a route is to discover the name of a controller class to instantiate and an action method to execute to generate an HTTP response.

A default route is configured for MVC, as shown in the following code:

```
app.UseEndpoints(endpoints =>
{
  endpoints.MapControllerRoute(name: "default",
    pattern: "{controller=Home}/{action=Index}/{id?}");
});
```

The route template has parts in curly brackets { } called **segments**, and they are like named parameters of a method. The value of these segments can be any `string`.

The route template looks at any URL path requested by the browser and matches it to extract the name of a `controller`, the name of an `action`, and an optional `id` value (the `?` symbol makes it optional).

If the user hasn't entered these names, it uses defaults of `Home` for the controller and `Index` for the action (the `=` assignment sets a default for a named segment).

The following table contains example URLs and how the default route would work out the names of a controller and action:

URL	Controller	Action	ID
/	Home	Index	
/Muppet	Muppet	Index	
/Muppet/Kermit	Muppet	Kermit	
/Muppet/Kermit/Green	Muppet	Kermit	Green
/Products	Products	Index	
/Products/Detail	Products	Detail	
/Products/Detail/3	Products	Detail	3

Segments in URLs are not case-sensitive.

Understanding controllers and actions

In ASP.NET Core MVC, the C stands for controller. From the route and an incoming URL, ASP.NET Core MVC knows the name of the controller, so it will then look for a class that is decorated with the `[Controller]` attribute or derives from a class decorated with that attribute, for example, `ControllerBase`, as shown in the following code:

```
namespace Microsoft.AspNetCore.Mvc
{
  //
  // Summary:
  //     A base class for an MVC controller without view support.
  [Controller]
  public abstract class ControllerBase
```

To simplify the requirements, Microsoft supplies a class named `Controller` that your classes can inherit from if they also need view support.

The responsibilities of a controller are as follows:

- Identify the services that the controller needs in order to be in a valid state and to function properly in their class constructor(s).

- Use the `action` name to identify a method to execute.

- Extract parameters from the HTTP request.

- Use the parameters to fetch any additional data needed to construct a view model and pass it to the appropriate view for the client. For example, if the client is a web browser, then a view that renders HTML would be most appropriate. Other clients might prefer alternative renderings like document formats such as a PDF file or an Excel file, or data formats like JSON or XML.

- Return the results from the view to the client as an HTTP response with an appropriate status code.

Let's review the controller used to generate the home, privacy, and error pages.

1. Expand the `Controllers` folder.

2. Open the file named `HomeController.cs`.

3. Note, as shown in the following code, that:

   ○ A private field is declared to store a reference to a logger for the `HomeController` that is set in a constructor.

   ○ All three action methods call a method named `View()` and return the results as an `IActionResult` interface to the client.

   ○ The `Error` action method passes a view model into its view with a request ID used for tracing. The error response will not be cached.

```
public class HomeController : Controller
{
  private readonly ILogger<HomeController> _logger;

  public HomeController(ILogger<HomeController> logger)
  {
    _logger = logger;
  }

  public IActionResult Index()
  {
    return View();
  }

  public IActionResult Privacy()
  {
```

```
      return View();
   }

   [ResponseCache(Duration = 0,
     Location = ResponseCacheLocation.None, NoStore = true)]
   public IActionResult Error()
   {
     return View(new ErrorViewModel { RequestId =
       Activity.Current?.Id ?? HttpContext.TraceIdentifier });
   }
 }
```

If the visitor enters / or /Home, then it is the equivalent of /Home/Index because those were the defaults.

Controllers are where the business logic of your website runs, so it is important to test the correctness of that logic using unit tests as you learned in *Chapter 4, Writing, Debugging, and Testing Functions*.

More Information: You can read more about how to unit test controllers at the following link: https://docs. microsoft.com/en-us/aspnet/core/mvc/controllers/ testing?view=aspnetcore-3.0

Understanding filters

When you need to add some functionality to multiple controllers and actions then you can use or define your own filters that are implemented as an attribute class.

Filters can be applied at the following levels:

- Action-level by decorating the method with the attribute. This will only affect the one method.

- Controller-level by decorating the class with the attribute. This will affect all methods of this controller.

- Global-level by adding an instance of the attribute to the Filters collection of the IServiceCollection in the ConfigureServices method of the Startup class. This will affect all methods of all controllers in the project.

More Information: You can read more about filters at the following link: https://docs.microsoft. com/en-us/aspnet/core/mvc/controllers/ filters?view=aspnetcore-3.0

Using a filter to secure an action method

For example, you might want to ensure that one particular method of a controller can only be called by members of certain security roles. You do this by decorating the method with the [Authorize] attribute, as shown in the following code:

```
[Authorize(Roles = "Sales,Marketing")]
public IActionResult SalesAndMarketingEmployeesOnly()
{
  return View();
}
```

More Information: You can read more about authorization at the following link: https://docs.microsoft.com/en-us/ aspnet/core/security/authorization/introduction?vi ew=aspnetcore-3.0

Using a filter to cache a response

You might want to cache the HTTP response that is generated by an action method by decorating the method with the [ResponseCache] attribute, as shown in the following code:

```
[ResponseCache(Duration = 3600, // in seconds = 1 hour
  Location = ResponseCacheLocation.Any)]
public IActionResult AboutUs()
{
  return View();
}
```

You control where the response is cached and for how long by setting parameters as shown in the following list:

- Duration: In seconds. This sets the max-age HTTP response header.

- Location: One of the ResponseCacheLocation values, Any, Client, or None. This sets the cache-control HTTP response header.

- NoStore: If true, this ignores Duration and Location and sets the cache-control HTTP response header to no-store.

More Information: You can read more about response caching at the following link: https://docs.microsoft. com/en-us/aspnet/core/performance/caching/ response?view=aspnetcore-3.0

Using a filter to define a custom route

You might want to define a simplified route for an action method instead of using the default route.

For example, to show the privacy page currently requires the following URL path which specifies both the controller and action:

`https://localhost:5001/home/privacy`

We could decorate the action method to make the route simpler, as shown in the following code:

```
[Route("private")]
public IActionResult Privacy()
{
  return View();
}
```

Now, we can use the following URL path, which specifies the custom route:

`https://localhost:5001/private`

Understanding entity and view models

In ASP.NET Core MVC, the M stands for model. Models represent the data required to respond to a request. **Entity models** represent entities in a data store like SQLite. Based on the request, one or more entities might need to be retrieved from data storage. All of the data that we want to show in response to a request is the MVC model, sometimes called a **view model**, because it is a *model* that is passed into a *view* for rendering into a response format like HTML or JSON.

For example, the following HTTP GET request might mean that the browser is asking for the product details page for product number 3:

`http://www.example.com/products/details/3`

The controller would need to use the ID value 3 to retrieve the entity for that product and pass it to a view that can then turn the model into HTML for display in the browser.

Imagine that when a user comes to our website, we want to show them a carousel of categories, a list of products, and a count of the number of visitors we have had this month.

We will reference the Entity Framework Core entity data model for the Northwind database that you created in *Chapter 15, Building Websites Using ASP.NET Core Razor Pages.*

1. In the `NorthwindMvc` project, open `NorthwindMvc.csproj`.

2. Add a project reference to `NorthwindContextLib`, as shown in the following markup:

```
<ItemGroup>
  <ProjectReference Include=
    "..\NorthwindContextLib\NorthwindContextLib.csproj" />
</ItemGroup>
```

3. In **Terminal**, enter the following command to rebuild the project:

```
dotnet build
```

4. Modify `Startup.cs`, to import the `System.IO` and `Packt.Shared` namespaces and add a statement to the `ConfigureServices` method to configure the `Northwind` database context, as shown in the following code:

```
string databasePath = Path.Combine("..", "Northwind.db");

services.AddDbContext<Northwind>(options =>
  options.UseSqlite($"Data Source={databasePath}"));
```

5. Add a class file to the `Models` folder and name it `HomeIndexViewModel.cs`.

 Good Practice: Although the `ErrorViewModel` class created by the MVC project template does not follow this convention, I recommend that you use the naming convention `{Controller}{Action}ViewModel` for your view model classes.

6. Modify the class definition to have three properties for a count of the number of visitors, and lists of categories and products, as shown in the following code:

```
using System.Collections.Generic;
using Packt.Shared;

namespace NorthwindMvc.Models
{
  public class HomeIndexViewModel
  {
    public int VisitorCount;
    public IList<Category> Categories { get; set; }
    public IList<Product> Products { get; set; }
  }
}
```

7. Open the `HomeController` class.

8. Import the `Packt.Shared` namespace.

9. Add a field to store a reference to a `Northwind` instance, and initialize it in the constructor, as shown highlighted in the following code:

```
public class HomeController : Controller
{
  private readonly ILogger<HomeController> _logger;

  private Northwind db;

  public HomeController(ILogger<HomeController> logger,
    Northwind injectedContext)
  {
    _logger = logger;
    db = injectedContext;
  }
}
```

ASP.NET Core will use constructor parameter injection to pass an instance of the Northwind database context using the database path you specified in the `Startup` class.

10. Modify the contents of the `Index` action method to create an instance of the view model for this method, simulating a visitor count using the `Random` class to generate a number between 1 and 1001, and using the `Northwind` database to get lists of categories and products, as shown in the following code:

```
var model = new HomeIndexViewModel
{
  VisitorCount = (new Random()).Next(1, 1001),
  Categories = db.Categories.ToList(),
  Products   = db.Products.ToList()
};

return View(model); // pass model to view
```

When the `View()` method is called in a controller's action method, ASP.NET Core MVC looks in the `Views` folder for a subfolder with the same name as the current controller, that is, `Home`. It then looks for a file with the same name as the current action, that is, `Index.cshtml`.

Understanding views

In ASP.NET Core MVC, the V stands for view. The responsibility of a view is to transform a model into HTML or other formats.

There are multiple **view engines** that could be used to do this. The default view engine is called **Razor**, and it uses the @ symbol to indicate server-side code execution.

The Razor Pages feature introduced with ASP.NET Core 2.0 uses the same view engine and so can use the same Razor syntax.

Let's modify the home page view to render the lists of categories and products.

1. Expand the `Views` folder, and then expand the `Home` folder.

2. Open the `Index.cshtml` file and note the block of C# code wrapped in @{ }. This will execute first and can be used to store data that needs to be passed into a shared layout file like the title of the web page, as shown in the following code:

   ```
   @{
       ViewData["Title"] = "Home Page";
   }
   ```

3. Note the static HTML content in the `<div>` element that uses Bootstrap for styling.

   Good Practice: As well as defining your own styles, base your styles on a common library, such as Bootstrap, that implements responsive design.

   Just as with Razor Pages, there is a file named `_ViewStart.cshtml` that gets executed by the `View()` method. It is used to set defaults that apply to all views.

   For example, it sets the `Layout` property of all views to a shared layout file, as shown in the following markup:

   ```
   @{
       Layout = "_Layout";
   }
   ```

4. In the `Shared` folder, open the `_Layout.cshtml` file.

5. Note that the title is being read from the `ViewData` dictionary that was set earlier in the `Index.cshtml` view.

6. Note the rendering of links to support Bootstrap and a site stylesheet, where ~ means the `wwwroot` folder, as shown in the following markup:

   ```
   <link rel="stylesheet"
         href="~/lib/bootstrap/dist/css/bootstrap.css" />
   <link rel="stylesheet" href="~/css/site.css" />
   ```

7. Note the rendering of a navigation bar in the header, as shown in the following markup:

```
<body>
  <header>
    <nav class="navbar ...">
```

8. Note the rendering of a collapsible `<div>` containing a partial view for logging in and hyperlinks to allow users to navigate between pages, as shown in the following markup:

```
<div class=
  "navbar-collapse collapse d-sm-inline-flex flex-sm-row-reverse">
  <partial name="_LoginPartial" />
  <ul class="navbar-nav flex-grow-1">
    <li class="nav-item">
      <a class="nav-link text-dark" asp-area=""
        asp-controller="Home" asp-action="Index">Home</a>
    </li>
    <li class="nav-item">
      <a class="nav-link text-dark"
        asp-area=""
        asp-controller="Home"
        asp-action="Privacy">Privacy</a>
    </li>
  </ul>
</div>
```

The `<a>` elements use tag helper attributes named `asp-controller` and `asp-action` to specify the controller name and action name that will execute when the link is clicked on. If you want to navigate to a feature in a Razor Class Library, then you use `asp-area` to specify the feature name.

9. Note the rendering of the body inside the `<main>` element, as shown in the following markup:

```
<div class="container">
  <main role="main" class="pb-3">
    @RenderBody()
  </main>
</div>
```

The `@RenderBody()` method call injects the contents of a specific Razor view for a page like the `Index.cshtml` file at that point in the shared layout.

More Information: You can read about why it is good to put `<script>` elements at the bottom of the `<body>` at the following link: https://stackoverflow.com/questions/436411/where-should-i-put-script-tags-in-html-markup

10. Note the rendering of `<script>` elements at the bottom of the page so that it doesn't slow down the display of the page and that you can add your own script blocks into an optional defined section named `scripts`, as shown in the following markup:

```
<script src="~/lib/jquery/dist/jquery.js"></script>
<script src="~/lib/bootstrap/dist/js/bootstrap.bundle.js">
</script>
<script src="~/js/site.js" asp-append-version="true"></script>
@RenderSection("scripts", required: false)
```

When `asp-append-version` is specified with a `true` value in any element along with a `src` attribute, the Image Tag Helper is invoked (it does not only affect images!)

It works by automatically appending a query string value named v that is generated from a hash of the referenced source file, as shown in the following example generated output:

```
<script src="~/js/site.js?
v=Kl_dqr9NVtnMdsM2MUg4qthUnWZm5T1fCEimBPWDNgM"></script>
```

If even a single byte within the `site.js` file changes then its hash value will be different, and therefore if a browser or CDN is caching the script file then it will bust the cached copy and replace it with the new version.

More Information: You can read how cache busting using query strings works at the following link: `https://stackoverflow.com/questions/9692665/cache-busting-via-params`

Customizing an ASP.NET Core MVC website

Now that you've reviewed the structure of a basic MVC website, you will customize it. You have already added code to retrieve entities from the Northwind database, so the next task is to output that information in the home page.

More Information: To find suitable images for the eight categories, I searched on a site that has free stock photos for commercial use with no attribution required, at the following link: `https://www.pexels.com`

Defining a custom style

The home page will show a list of the 77 products in the Northwind database. To make efficient use of space we want to show the list in three columns. To do this we need to customize the stylesheet for the website.

1. In the wwwroot\css folder, open the site.css file.
2. At the bottom of the file, add a new style that will apply to an element with the newspaper ID, as shown in the following code:

```
#newspaper
{
  column-count: 3;
}
```

Setting up the category images

The Northwind database includes a table of categories, but they do not have images, and websites look better with some colorful pictures.

1. In the wwwroot folder, create a folder named images.
2. In the images folder, add eight image files named category1.jpeg, category2.jpeg, and so on, up to category8.jpeg.

More Information: You can download images from the GitHub repository for this book at the following link: https://github.com/markjprice/cs8dotnetcore3/tree/master/Assets

Understanding Razor syntax

Before we customize the home page view, let's review an example Razor file that has an initial Razor code block that instantiates an order with price and quantity and then outputs information about the order in the web page, as shown in the following markup:

```
@{
  var order = new Order
  {
    OrderID = 123,
    Product = "Sushi",
    Price = 8.49M,
    Quantity = 3
  };
}
<div>Your order for @order.Quantity of @order.Product has a total cost
of $@order.Price * @order.Quantity</div>
```

The preceding Razor file would result in the following incorrect output:

```
Your order for 3 of Sushi has a total cost of $8.49 * 3
```

Although Razor markup can include the value of any single property using the
`@object.property` syntax, you should wrap expressions in parentheses, as shown
in the following markup:

```
<div>Your order for @order.Quantity of @order.Product has a total cost
of $@(order.Price * @order.Quantity)</div>
```

The preceding Razor expression results in the following correct output:

```
Your order for 3 of Sushi has a total cost of $25.47
```

Defining a typed view

To improve the IntelliSense when writing a view, you can define what type the view
can expect using a `@model` directive at the top.

1. In the `Views\Home` folder, open `Index.cshtml`.

2. At the top of the file, add a statement to set the model type to use the
   `HomeIndexViewModel`, as shown in the following code:

   ```
   @model NorthwindMvc.Models.HomeIndexViewModel
   ```

   Now, whenever we type `Model` in this view, the Visual Studio Code
   C# extension will know the correct type for the model and will provide
   IntelliSense for it.

   While entering code in a view, remember the following:

   - To declare the type for the model, use `@model` (with lowercase m).
   - To interact with the model instance, use `@Model` (with uppercase M).

   Let's continue customizing the view for the home page.

3. In the initial Razor code block, add a statement to declare a `string` variable
   for the current item and replace the existing `<div>` element with the new
   markup to output categories in a carousel and products as an unordered list,
   as shown in the following markup:

   ```
   @model NorthwindMvc.Models.HomeIndexViewModel
   @{
     ViewData["Title"] = "Home Page";
     string currentItem = "";
   }
   <div id="categories" class="carousel slide" data-ride="carousel"
   ```

```
      data-interval="3000" data-keyboard="true">
  <ol class="carousel-indicators">
  @for (int c = 0; c < Model.Categories.Count; c++)
  {
    if (c == 0)
    {
      currentItem = "active";
    }
    else
    {
      currentItem = "";
    }
    <li data-target="#categories" data-slide-to="@c"
      class="@currentItem"></li>
  }
  </ol>
  <div class="carousel-inner">
  @for (int c = 0; c < Model.Categories.Count; c++)
  {
    if (c == 0)
    {
      currentItem = "active";
    }
    else
    {
      currentItem = "";
    }
    <div class="carousel-item @currentItem">
      <img class="d-block w-100" src=
"~/images/category@(Model.Categories[c].CategoryID).jpeg"
        alt="@Model.Categories[c].CategoryName" />
      <div class="carousel-caption d-none d-md-block">
        <h2>@Model.Categories[c].CategoryName</h2>
        <h3>@Model.Categories[c].Description</h3>
        <p>
          <a class="btn btn-primary"
href="/category/@Model.Categories[c].CategoryID">View</a>
        </p>
      </div>
    </div>
  }
  </div>
  <a class="carousel-control-prev" href="#categories"
    role="button" data-slide="prev">
    <span class="carousel-control-prev-icon"
      aria-hidden="true"></span>
    <span class="sr-only">Previous</span>
  </a>
  <a class="carousel-control-next" href="#categories"
    role="button" data-slide="next">
    <span class="carousel-control-next-icon"
      aria-hidden="true"></span>
```

```
      <span class="sr-only">Next</span>
    </a>
</div>
<div class="row">
  <div class="col-md-12">
    <h1>Northwind</h1>
    <p class="lead">
      We have had @Model.VisitorCount visitors this month.
    </p>
    <h2>Products</h2>
      <div id="newspaper">
        <ul>
        @foreach (var item in @Model.Products)
        {
          <li>
            <a asp-controller="Home"
               asp-action="ProductDetail"
               asp-route-id="@item.ProductID">
            @item.ProductName costs
            @item.UnitPrice.Value.ToString("C")
            </a>
          </li>
        }
        </ul>
      </div>
  </div>
</div>
```

While reviewing the preceding Razor markup, note the following:

- It is easy to mix static HTML elements such as `<ul>` and `<li>` with C# code to output the carousel of categories and the list of product names.

- The `<div>` element with the `id` attribute of `newspaper` will use the custom style that we defined earlier, so all of the content in that element will display in three columns.

- The `<img>` element for each category uses parentheses around a Razor expression to ensure that the compiler does not include the `.jpeg` as part of the expression, as shown in the following markup:

  `"~/images/category@(Model.Categories[c].CategoryID).jpeg"`

- The `<a>` elements for the product links use tag helpers to generate URL paths. Clicks on these hyperlinks will be handled by the `Home` controller and its `ProductDetail` action method. This action method does not exist yet, but you will add it later in this chapter. The ID of the product is passed as a route segment named `id`, as shown in the following URL path for Ipoh Coffee:

  `https://localhost:5001/Home/ProductDetail/43`

Testing the customized home page

Let's see the result of our customized home page.

1. Start the website by entering the following command: `dotnet run`

2. Start Chrome and navigate to `http://localhost:5000`

3. Note the home page has a rotating carousel showing categories, a random number of visitors, and a list of products in three columns, as shown in the following screenshot:

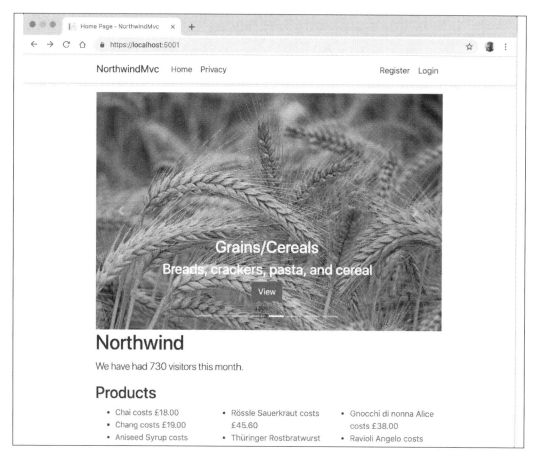

At the moment, clicking on any of the categories or product links gives `404 Not Found` errors, so let's see how we can pass parameters so that we can see the details of a product or category.

4. Close Chrome.

5. Stop the website by pressing *Ctrl + C* in **Terminal**.

Passing parameters using a route value

One way to pass a simple parameter is to use the `id` segment defined in the default route.

1. In the `HomeController` class, add an action method named `ProductDetail`, as shown in the following code:

```
public IActionResult ProductDetail(int? id)
{
  if (!id.HasValue)
  {
    return NotFound("You must pass a product ID in the route, for
example, /Home/ProductDetail/21");
  }

  var model = db.Products
    .SingleOrDefault(p => p.ProductID == id);

  if (model == null)
  {
    return NotFound($"Product with ID of {id} not found.");
  }

  return View(model); // pass model to view and then return result
}
```

Note the following:

  ○ This method uses a feature of ASP.NET Core called **model binding** to automatically match the `id` passed in the route to the parameter named `id` in the method.

  ○ Inside the method, we check to see whether `id` is null, and if so, we call the `NotFound` method to return a `404` status code with a custom message explaining the correct URL path format.

  ○ Otherwise, we can connect to the database and try to retrieve a product using the `id` variable.

  ○ If we find a product, we pass it to a view; otherwise, we call the `NotFound` method to return a `404` status code and a custom message explaining that a product with that ID was not found in the database.

  If the view is named to match the action method and is placed in a folder that matches the controller name then ASP.NET Core MVC's conventions will find it automatically.

2. Inside the `Views/Home` folder, add a new file named `ProductDetail.cshtml`.

3. Modify the contents, as shown in the following markup:

```
@model Packt.Shared.Product
@{
  ViewData["Title"] = "Product Detail - " + Model.ProductName;
}
<h2>Product Detail</h2>
<hr />
<div>
  <dl class="dl-horizontal">
    <dt>Product ID</dt>
    <dd>@Model.ProductID</dd>
    <dt>Product Name</dt>
    <dd>@Model.ProductName</dd>
    <dt>Category ID</dt>
    <dd>@Model.CategoryID</dd>
    <dt>Unit Price</dt>
    <dd>@Model.UnitPrice.Value.ToString("C")</dd>
    <dt>Units In Stock</dt>
    <dd>@Model.UnitsInStock</dd>
  </dl>
</div>
```

4. Start the website by entering the following command: `dotnet run`.

5. Start Chrome and navigate to `http://localhost:5000`.

6. When the home page appears with the list of products, click on one of them, for example, the second product, **Chang**.

7. Note the URL path in the browser's address bar, the page title shown in the browser tab, and the product details page, as shown in the following screenshot:

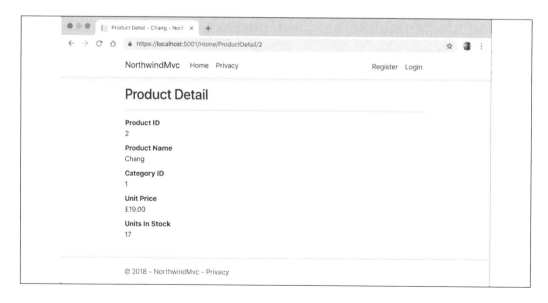

8. Toggle on the developer tools pane.

9. Edit the URL in the address box of Chrome to request a product ID that does not exist, like `99`, and note the `404 Not Found` status code and custom error response, as shown in the following screenshot:

Understanding model binders

Model binders are very powerful, and the default one does a lot for you. After the default route identifies a controller class to instantiate and an action method to call, if that method has parameters then those parameters need to have values set.

Model binders do this by looking for parameter values passed in the HTTP request as any of the following types of parameters:

*   Route parameter, like `id` as we did in the previous section, as shown in the following URL path: `/Home/ProductDetail/2`
*   Query string parameter, as shown in the following URL path: `/Home/ProductDetail?id=2`
*   Form parameter, as shown in the following markup:

```
<form action="post" action="/Home/ProductDetail">
  <input type="text" name="id" />
  <input type="submit" />
</form>
```

Model binders can populate almost any type:

*   Simple types like `int`, `string`, `DateTime`, and `bool`.
*   Complex types defined by `class` or `struct`.
*   Collections types like arrays and lists.

Let's create a somewhat artificial example to illustrate what can be achieved using the default model binder.

1. In the `Models` folder, add a new file named `Thing.cs`.

2. Modify the contents to define a class with two properties for a nullable number named `ID` and a `string` named `color`, as shown in the following code:

```
namespace NorthwindMvc.Models
{
  public class Thing
  {
    public int? ID { get; set; }

    public string Color { get; set; }
  }
}
```

3. Open `HomeController.cs` and add two new action methods, one to show a page with a form and one to display it with a parameter using your new model type, as shown in the following code:

```
public IActionResult ModelBinding()
{
  return View(); // the page with a form to submit
}

public IActionResult ModelBinding(Thing thing)
{
  return View(thing); // show the model bound thing
}
```

4. In the `Views\Home` folder, add a new file named `ModelBinding.cshtml`.

5. Modify its contents, as shown in the following markup:

```
@model NorthwindMvc.Models.Thing
@{
  ViewData["Title"] = "Model Binding Demo";
}
<h1>@ViewData["Title"]</h1>
<div>
  Enter values for your thing in the following form:
</div>
<form method="POST" action="/home/modelbinding?id=3">
  <input name="color" value="Red" />
  <input type="submit" />
</form>
@if (Model != null)
{
```

```
<h2>Submitted Thing</h2>
<hr />
<div>
  <dl class="dl-horizontal">
    <dt>Model.ID</dt>
    <dd>@Model.ID</dd>
    <dt>Model.Color</dt>
    <dd>@Model.Color</dd>
  </dl>
</div>
}
```

6. Start the website, start Chrome, and navigate to: `https://localhost:5001/home/modelbinding`

7. Note the unhandled exception about an ambiguous match, as shown in the following screenshot:

Although the C# compiler can differentiate between the two methods by noting that the signatures are different, from HTTP's point of view, both methods are potential matches. We need an HTTP-specific way to disambiguate the action methods. We could do this by creating different names for the actions, or by specifying that one method should be used for a specific HTTP verb like GET, POST, or DELETE.

8. Stop the website.

9. In `HomeController.cs`, decorate the second `ModelBinding` action method to indicate that it should be used for processing HTTP POST requests, that is, when a form is submitted, as shown highlighted in the following code:

```
[HttpPost]
public IActionResult ModelBinding(Thing thing)
```

10. Start the website, start Chrome, and navigate to `https://localhost:5001/home/modelbinding`.

11. Click the **Submit** button and note the value for `ID` property is set from the query string parameter and the value for the `color` property is set from the form parameter, as shown in the following screenshot:

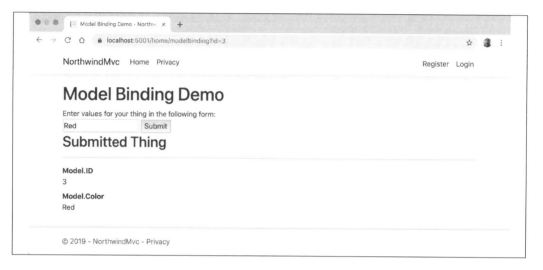

12. Stop the website.

13. Modify the action for the form to pass the value 2 as a route parameter, as shown highlighted in the following markup:

```
<form method="POST" action="/home/modelbinding/2?id=3">
```

14. Start the website, start Chrome, and navigate to `https://localhost:5001/home/modelbinding`

15. Click the **Submit** button and note the value for `ID` property is set from the route parameter and the value for the `color` property is set from the form parameter.

16. Stop the website.

17. Modify the action for the form to pass the value 1 as a form parameter, as shown highlighted in the following markup:

```
<form method="POST" action="/home/modelbinding/2?id=3">
  <input name="id" value="1" />
```

18. Start the website, start Chrome, and navigate to `https://localhost:5001/home/modelbinding`

19. Click the **Submit** button and note the value for `ID` and `color` properties are both set from the form parameters.

If you have multiple parameters with the same name, then form parameters have the highest priority and query string parameters have the lowest priority.

 More Information: For advanced scenarios, you can create your own model binders by implementing the `IModelBinder` interface: `https://docs.microsoft.com/en-us/aspnet/core/mvc/advanced/custom-model-binding?view=aspnetcore-3.0`

Validating the model

The process of model binding can cause errors, for example, data type conversions, or validation errors if the model has been decorated with validation rules. What data has been bound and any binding or validation errors is stored in `ControllerBase.ModelState`.

Let's explore that we can do with model state by applying some validation rules to the bound model and then showing invalid data messages in the view.

1. In the `Models` folder, open `Thing.cs`.

2. Import the `System.ComponentModel.DataAnnotations` namespace.

3. Decorate the `ID` property with a validation attribute to limit the range of allowed numbers to 1 to 10, and one to ensure that the visitor supplies a color, as shown in the following highlighted code:

```
public class Thing
{
  [Range(1, 10)]
  public int? ID { get; set; }

  [Required]
  public string Color { get; set; }
}
```

4. In the `Models` folder, add a new file named `HomeModelBindingViewModel.cs`.

5. Modify its contents to define a class with two properties for the bound model and for any errors, as shown in the following code:

```
using System.Collections.Generic;

namespace NorthwindMvc.Models
{
  public class HomeModelBindingViewModel
  {
    public Thing Thing { get; set; }
```

```
public bool HasErrors { get; set; }

public IEnumerable<string>
  ValidationErrors { get; set; }
  }
}
```

6. In the `Controllers` folder, open `HomeController.cs`.

7. In the second `ModelBinding` method, comment out the previous statement that passed the thing to the view, and instead add statements to create an instance of the view model, validate the model and store an array of error messages, and then pass the view model to the view, as shown in the following code:

```
public IActionResult ModelBinding(Thing thing)
{
  // return View(thing);

  var model = new ModelBindingViewModel
  {
    Thing = thing,
    HasErrors = !ModelState.IsValid,
    ValidationErrors = ModelState.Values
      .SelectMany(state => state.Errors)
      .Select(error => error.ErrorMessage)
  };

  return View(model);
}
```

8. In `Views\Home`, open `ModelBinding.cshtml`.

9. Modify the model type declaration to use the view model class, add a `<div>` to show any model validation errors, and change the output of the thing's properties because the view model has changed, as shown highlighted in the following markup:

```
@model NorthwindMvc.Models.HomeModelBindingViewModel
@{
  ViewData["Title"] = "Model Binding Demo";
}
<h1>@ViewData["Title"]</h1>
<div>
  Enter values for your thing in the following form:
</div>
<form method="POST" action="/home/modelbindingdemo/2?id=3">
  <input name="id" value="1" />
  <input name="color" value="Red" />
  <input type="submit" />
</form>
@if (Model != null)
```

```
{
<h2>Submitted Thing</h2>
<hr />
<div>
  <dl class="dl-horizontal">
    <dt>Model.Thing.ID</dt>
    <dd>@Model.Thing.ID</dd>
    <dt>Model.Thing.Color</dt>
    <dd>@Model.Thing.Color</dd>
  </dl>
</div>
@if (Model.HasErrors)
{
  <div>
  @foreach(string errorMessage in Model.ValidationErrors)
  {
    <div class="alert alert-danger" role="alert">
      @errorMessage</div>
  }
  </div>
}
}
```

10. Start the website, start Chrome, and navigate to:
    `https://localhost:5001/home/modelbinding`

11. Click the **Submit** button and note that `1` and `Red` are valid values.

12. Enter an ID of `99`, clear the color text box, click the **Submit** button, and note the error messages, as shown in the following screenshot:

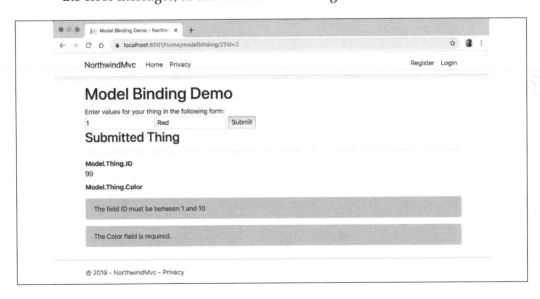

13. Close the browser and stop the website.

More Information: You can read more about model validation at the following link: https://docs. microsoft.com/en-us/aspnet/core/mvc/models/ validation?view=aspnetcore-3.0

Understanding view helper methods

While creating a view for ASP.NET Core MVC, you can use the Html object and its methods to generate markup.

Some useful methods include the following:

- ActionLink: Use this to generate an anchor <a> element that contains a URL path to the specified controller and action.

- AntiForgeryToken: Use this inside a <form> to insert a <hidden> element containing an anti-forgery token that will be validated when the form is submitted.

- Display and DisplayFor: Use this to generate HTML markup for the expression relative to the current model using a display template. There are built-in display templates for .NET types and custom templates can be created in the DisplayTemplates folder. The folder name is case-sensitive on case-sensitive file systems.

- DisplayForModel: Use this to generate HTML markup for an entire model instead of a single expression.

- Editor and EditorFor: Use this to generate HTML markup for the expression relative to the current model using an editor template. There are built-in editor templates for .NET types that use <label> and <input> elements, and custom templates can be created in the EditorTemplates folder. The folder name is case-sensitive on case-sensitive file systems.

- EditorForModel: Use this to generate HTML markup for an entire model instead of a single expression.

- Encode: Use this to safely encode an object or string into HTML. For example, the string value "<script>" would be encoded as "<script>". This is not normally necessary since the Razor @ symbol encodes string values by default.

- Raw: Use this to render a string value *without* encoding as HTML.

- PartialAsync and RenderPartialAsync: Use these to generate HTML markup for a partial view. You can optionally pass a model and view data.

More Information: You can read more about the `HtmlHelper` class at the following link: `https://docs.microsoft.com/en-us/dotnet/api/microsoft.aspnetcore.mvc.viewfeatures.htmlhelper?view=aspnetcore-3.0`

Querying a database and using display templates

Let's create a new action method that can have a query string parameter passed to it and use that to query the Northwind database.

1. In the `HomeController` class, import the `Microsoft.EntityFrameworkCore` namespace. We need this to add the `Include` extension method so that we can include related entities, as you learned in *Chapter 11, Working with Databases Using Entity Framework Core*.

2. Add a new action method, as shown in the following code:

```
public IActionResult ProductsThatCostMoreThan(
  decimal? price)
{
  if (!price.HasValue)
  {
    return NotFound("You must pass a product price in the query
string, for example, /Home/ProductsThatCostMoreThan?price=50");
  }

  IEnumerable<Product> model = db.Products
    .Include(p => p.Category)
    .Include(p => p.Supplier)
    .AsEnumerable() // switch to client-side
    .Where(p => p.UnitPrice > price);

  if (model.Count() == 0)
  {
    return NotFound(
      $"No products cost more than {price:C}.");
  }
  ViewData["MaxPrice"] = price.Value.ToString("C");

  return View(model); // pass model to view
}
```

3. Inside the `Views/Home` folder, add a new file named `ProductsThatCostMoreThan.cshtml`.

4. Modify the contents, as shown in the following code:

```
@model IEnumerable<Packt.Shared.Product>
@{
  ViewData["Title"] =
    "Products That Cost More Than " + ViewData["MaxPrice"];
}
<h2>Products That Cost More Than @ViewData["MaxPrice"]</h2>
<table class="table">
  <tr>
    <th>Category Name</th>
    <th>Supplier's Company Name</th>
    <th>Product Name</th>
    <th>Unit Price</th>
    <th>Units In Stock</th>
  </tr>
  @foreach (var item in Model)
  {
  <tr>
    <td>
      @Html.DisplayFor(modelItem => item.Category.CategoryName)
    </td>
    <td>
      @Html.DisplayFor(modelItem => item.Supplier.CompanyName)
    </td>
    <td>
      @Html.DisplayFor(modelItem => item.ProductName)
    </td>
    <td>
      @Html.DisplayFor(modelItem => item.UnitPrice)
    </td>
    <td>
      @Html.DisplayFor(modelItem => item.UnitsInStock)
    </td>
  </tr>
  }
</table>
```

5. In the `Views/Home` folder, open `Index.cshtml`.

6. Add the following `form` element below the visitor count and above the `Products` heading and its listing of products. This will provide a form for the user to enter a price. The user can then click on a **Submit** button to call the action method that shows only products that cost more than the entered price:

```
<form asp-action="ProductsThatCostMoreThan" method="get">
  <input name="price"
         placeholder="Enter a product price" />
  <input type="submit" />
</form>
```

7. Start the website, use Chrome to navigate to the website, and on the home page, enter a price in the form, for example, 50, and then click on **Submit**. You will see a table of the products that cost more than the price that you entered, as shown in the following screenshot:

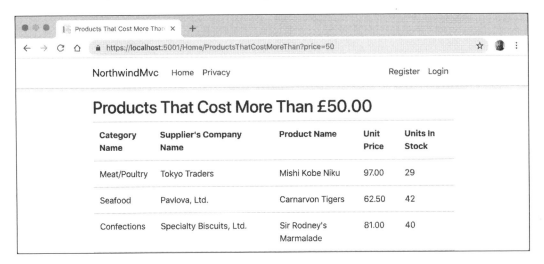

8. Close the browser and stop the website.

Improving scalability using asynchronous tasks

When building a desktop or mobile app, multiple tasks (and their underlying threads) can be used to improve responsiveness, because while one thread is busy with the task, another can handle interactions with the user.

Tasks and their threads can be useful on the server side too, especially with websites that work with files, or request data from a store or a web service that could take a while to respond. But they are detrimental to complex calculations that are CPU-bound so leave these to be processed synchronously as normal.

When an HTTP request arrives at the web server a thread from its pool is allocated to handle the request. But if that thread must wait for a resource, then it is blocked from handling any more incoming requests. If a website receives more simultaneous requests than it has threads in its pool, then some of those requests will respond with a server timeout error `503 Service Unavailable`.

The threads that are locked are not doing useful work. They *could* handle one of those other requests but only if we implement asynchronous code in our websites.

Whenever a thread is waiting for a resource it needs, it can return to the thread pool and handle a different incoming request, improving the scalability of the website, that is, increasing the number of simultaneous requests it can handle.

Why not just have a larger thread pool? In modern operating systems, every thread pool thread has a 1 MB stack. An asynchronous method uses a smaller amount of memory. It also removes the need to create new threads in the pool, which takes time. The rate at which new threads are added to the pool is typically one every two seconds, which is a loooooong time compared to switching between asynchronous threads.

Making controller action methods asynchronous

It is easy to make an existing action method asynchronous.

1. In the `HomeController` class, make sure that the `System.Threading.Tasks` namespace has been imported.

2. Modify the `Index` action method to be asynchronous, to return a `Task<T>`, and to await on the calls to asynchronous methods to get the categories and products, as shown highlighted in the following code:

```
public async Task<IActionResult> Index()
{
  var model = new HomeIndexViewModel
  {
    VisitorCount = (new Random()).Next(1, 1001),
    Categories = await db.Categories.ToListAsync(),
    Products = await db.Products.ToListAsync()
  };

  return View(model); // pass model to view
}
```

3. Modify the `ProductDetail` action method in a similar way, as shown highlighted in the following code:

```
public async Task<IActionResult> ProductDetail(int? id)
{
  if (!id.HasValue)
  {
    return NotFound("You must pass a product ID in the route, for
example, /Home/ProductDetail/21");
  }

  var model = await db.Products
    .SingleOrDefaultAsync(p => p.ProductID == id);

  if (model == null)
  {
    return NotFound($"Product with ID of {id} not found.");
```

```
    }

    return View(model); // pass model to view and then return result
}
```

4. Start the website, use Chrome to navigate to the website, and note that the functionality of the website is the same, but trust that it will now scale better.

5. Close the browser and stop the website.

Using other project templates

When you install the.NET Core SDK, there are many project templates included.

1. In **Terminal**, enter the following command:

```
dotnet new --help
```

2. You will see a list of currently installed templates, as shown in the following screenshot:

```
● ● ●                              ⚙ markjprice — -bash — 153×54
Marks-MacBook-Pro-13:~ markjprice$ dotnet new --help
Usage: new [options]

Options:
  -h, --help            Displays help for this command.
  -l, --list            Lists templates containing the specified name. If no name is specified, lists all templates.
  -n, --name            The name for the output being created. If no name is specified, the name of the current directory is used.
  -o, --output          Location to place the generated output.
  -i, --install         Installs a source or a template pack.
  -u, --uninstall       Uninstalls a source or a template pack.
  --nuget-source        Specifies a NuGet source to use during install.
  --type                Filters templates based on available types. Predefined values are "project", "item" or "other".
  --dry-run             Displays a summary of what would happen if the given command line were run if it would result in a template creation.
  --force               Forces content to be generated even if it would change existing files.
  -lang, --language     Filters templates based on language and specifies the language of the template to create.
  --update-check        Check the currently installed template packs for updates.
  --update-apply        Check the currently installed template packs for update, and install the updates.


Templates                                         Short Name          Language        Tags
----------------------------------------------------------------------------------------------------------------------------------
Console Application                               console             [C#], F#, VB    Common/Console
Class library                                     classlib            [C#], F#, VB    Common/Library
Worker Service                                    worker              [C#]            Common/Worker/Web
Unit Test Project                                 mstest              [C#], F#, VB    Test/MSTest
NUnit 3 Test Project                              nunit               [C#], F#, VB    Test/NUnit
NUnit 3 Test Item                                 nunit-test          [C#], F#, VB    Test/NUnit
xUnit Test Project                                xunit               [C#], F#, VB    Test/xUnit
Razor Component                                   razorcomponent      [C#]            Web/ASP.NET
Razor Page                                        page                [C#]            Web/ASP.NET
MVC ViewImports                                   viewimports         [C#]            Web/ASP.NET
MVC ViewStart                                     viewstart           [C#]            Web/ASP.NET
Blazor (server-side)                              blazorserverside    [C#]            Web/Blazor
ASP.NET Core Empty                                web                 [C#], F#        Web/Empty
ASP.NET Core Web App (Model-View-Controller)      mvc                 [C#], F#        Web/MVC
ASP.NET Core Web App                              webapp              [C#]            Web/MVC/Razor Pages
ASP.NET Core with Angular                         angular             [C#]            Web/MVC/SPA
ASP.NET Core with React.js                        react               [C#]            Web/MVC/SPA
ASP.NET Core with React.js and Redux              reactredux          [C#]            Web/MVC/SPA
Razor Class Library                               razorclasslib       [C#]            Web/Razor/Library/Razor Class Library
ASP.NET Core Web API                              webapi              [C#], F#        Web/WebAPI
ASP.NET Core gRPC Service                         grpc                [C#]            Web/gRPC
dotnet gitignore file                             gitignore                           Config
global.json file                                  globaljson                          Config
NuGet Config                                      nugetconfig                         Config
Dotnet local tool manifest file                   tool-manifest                       Config
Web Config                                        webconfig                           Config
Solution File                                     sln                                 Solution
Protocol Buffer File                              proto                               Web/gRPC

Examples:
    dotnet new mvc --auth Individual
    dotnet new react --auth Individual
    dotnet new --help
```

3. Note the web-related project templates including ones for creating SPAs using React and Angular.

Installing additional template packs

Developers can install lots of additional template packs.

1. Start a browser and navigate to `http://dotnetnew.azurewebsites.net/`.

2. Enter `vue` in the text box, click the **Search templates** button, and note the list of available templates for Vue.js including one published by Microsoft, as shown in the following screenshot:

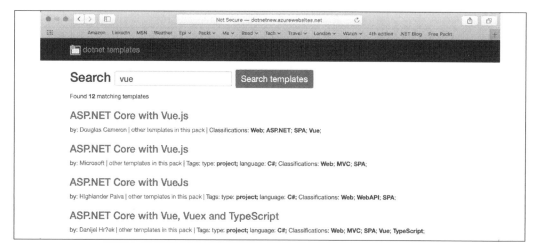

3. Click on **ASP.NET Core with Vue.js**, and note the instructions for installing and using this template, as shown in the following screenshot:

More Information: You can see more templates at the following link: `https://github.com/dotnet/templating/wiki/Available-templates-for-dotnet-new`

Practicing and exploring

Test your knowledge and understanding by answering some questions, get some hands-on practice, and explore this chapter's topics with deeper research.

Exercise 16.1 – Test your knowledge

Answer the following questions:

1. What do the files with the special names `_ViewStart` and `_ViewImports` do when created in the `Views` folder?
2. That are the names of the three segments defined in the default ASP. NET Core MVC route, what do they represent, and which are optional?
3. What does the default model binder do, and what data types can it handle?
4. In a shared layout file like `_Layout.cshtml`, how do you output the content of the current view?
5. In a shared layout file like `_Layout.cshtml`, how do you output a section that the current view can supply content for, and how does the view supply the contents for that section?
6. When calling the `View` method inside a controller's action method, what paths are searched for the view by convention?
7. How can you instruct the visitor's browser to cache the response for 24 hours?
8. Why might you enable Razor Pages even if you are not creating any yourself?
9. How does ASP.NET Core MVC identify classes that can act as controllers?
10. In what ways does ASP.NET Core MVC make it easier to test a website?

Exercise 16.2 – Practice implementing MVC by implementing a category detail page

The `NorthwindMvc` project has a home page that shows categories but when the **View** button is clicked, the website returns a `404 Not Found` error, for example, for the following URL:

```
https://localhost:5001/category/1
```

Extend the `NorthwindMvc` project by adding the ability to show a detail page for a category.

Exercise 16.3 – Practice improving scalability by understanding and implementing async action methods

A few years ago, Stephen Cleary wrote an excellent article for MSDN Magazine explaining the benefits to scalability of implementing async action methods for ASP.NET. The same principles apply to ASP.NET Core, but even more so, because unlike old ASP.NET as described in the article, ASP.NET Core supports asynchronous filters and other components.

Read the article at the following link and change the application that you created in this chapter to use `async` action methods in the controller: `https://msdn.microsoft.com/en-us/magazine/dn802603.aspx`

Exercise 16.4 – Explore topics

Use the following links to read more details about this chapter's topics:

- **Overview of ASP.NET Core MVC**: `https://docs.microsoft.com/en-us/aspnet/core/mvc/overview?view=aspnetcore-3.0`

- **Tutorial: Get started with EF Core in an ASP.NET MVC web app**: `https://docs.microsoft.com/en-us/aspnet/core/data/ef-mvc/intro?view=aspnetcore-3.0`

- **Handle requests with controllers in ASP.NET Core MVC**: `https://docs.microsoft.com/en-us/aspnet/core/mvc/controllers/actions?view=aspnetcore-3.0`

- **Model Binding in ASP.NET Core**: `https://docs.microsoft.com/en-us/aspnet/core/mvc/models/model-binding?view=aspnetcore-3.0`

- **Views in ASP.NET Core MVC**: `https://docs.microsoft.com/en-us/aspnet/core/mvc/views/overview?view=aspnetcore-3.0`

Summary

In this chapter, you learned how to build large, complex websites in a way that is easy to unit test and manage with teams of programmers using ASP.NET Core. You learned about startup configuration, authentication, routes, models, views, and controllers in ASP.NET Core MVC.

In the next chapter, you will learn how to build websites using a cross-platform **Content Management System (CMS)**. This allows developers to put responsibility of the content where it belongs: into the hands of users.

Chapter 17

Building Websites Using a Content Management System

This chapter is about building websites using a modern cross-platform **Content Management System (CMS)**.

There are many choices of CMS for most web development platforms. For cross-platform C# and .NET web developers, the best for learning the important principles is currently Piranha CMS. It was the first CMS to support .NET Core, with Piranha CMS 4.0 released on 1st December 2017.

This chapter will cover the following topics:

- Understanding the benefits of a CMS
- Understanding Piranha CMS
- Defining components, content types, and templates
- Testing the CMS website

Understanding the benefits of a CMS

In previous chapters, you learned how to create static HTML web pages and configure ASP.NET Core to serve them when requested by a visitor's browser.

You also learned how ASP.NET Core Razor Pages can add C# code that executes on the server side to generate HTML dynamically, including from information loaded live from a database. Additionally, you learned how ASP.NET Core MVC provides separation of technical concerns to make building more complex websites more manageable.

On its own, ASP.NET Core does not solve the problem of managing content. In those previous websites, the person creating and managing the content would have to have programming and HTML editing skills, or the ability to edit the data in the Northwind database, to change what visitors see on the website.

This is where a CMS becomes useful. A CMS separates the content (data values) from templates (layout, format, and style). Most CMSs generate web responses like HTML for humans viewing the website with a browser.

Some CMSs generate open data formats like JSON and XML to be processed by a web service or rendered in a browser using client-side technologies like Angular, React, or Vue. This is often called a **headless CMS**.

Developers define the structure of data stored in the CMS using content type classes for different purposes, like a product page, with content templates that render the content data into HTML, JSON, or other formats.

Non-technical content owners can log into the CMS and use a simple user interface to create, edit, delete, and publish content that will fit the structure defined by the content type classes, without needing the involvement of developers or tools like Visual Studio Code.

Understanding basic CMS features

Any decent basic CMS will include the following core features:

- A user interface that allows non-technical content owners to log in and manage their content.
- A content delivery system that converts the content from simple data into one or more formats, like HTML and JSON.

Understanding enterprise CMS features

Any decent commercial enterprise-level CMS would add the following additional features:

- **Search Engine Optimized (SEO)** URLs, page titles and related metadata, sitemaps, and so on.
- Authentication and authorization including management of users, groups, and their access rights to content.
- Media asset management of images, videos, documents, and other files.
- Sharing and reuse of pieces of content, often named *blocks*.
- Forms designer for gathering input from visitors.
- Marketing tools like tracking visitor behavior and A/B testing of content.
- Personalization of content based on rules like geographic location or machine learning processing of tracked visitor behavior.

- Saved drafts of content that are hidden from website visitors until they are published.
- Retaining multiple versions of content and enabling the re-publishing of old versions.
- Translation of content into multiple human languages, like English and German.

Understanding CMS platforms

CMSs exist for most development platforms and languages, as shown in the following table:

Development platform	Content Management Systems
PHP	WordPress, Drupal, Joomla!, Magento
Python	django CMS
Java	Adobe Experience Manager, Hippo CMS
.NET Framework	Episerver CMS, Sitecore, Umbraco, Kentico CMS
.NET Core	Piranha CMS, Orchard Core CMS

More Information: At the time of writing this fourth edition, the latest released version of Orchard Core CMS was `1.0.0-beta3`, so I decided to use Piranha CMS for this edition since it has supported .NET Core since its version 4.0 and it is now up to version 7.0. You can read about Orchard Core CMS at the following link: `https://orchardcore.readthedocs.io/en/dev/`

Understanding Piranha CMS

Piranha CMS is a good choice for learning how to develop for a CMS because it is open source, simple, and flexible.

As described by its lead developer and creator, Håkan Edling, "Piranha CMS is a lightweight, unobtrusive and cross-platform CMS library for .NET Standard 2.0. It can be used to add CMS functionality to an already existing application, build new website from scratch, or even be used as a backend for a mobile application."

Piranha CMS has three design principles:

- An open and extendible platform.
- Easy and intuitive for the content administrators.
- Fast, efficient, and fun for the developers.

Instead of adding more and more complex functions for commercial enterprise customers, Piranha CMS focuses on providing a platform for small to medium sized websites that need non-technical users to edit content on their current websites.

Piranha is not WordPress, meaning it will never have thousands of predefined themes and plugins to install. In the words of Piranha themselves, "The heart and soul of Piranha is about structuring content and editing it in the most intuitive way possible - the rest we leave up to you."

 More Information: You can read the official documentation for Piranha CMS at the following link: `http://piranhacms.org/`

Piranha CMS is built using some open source libraries, including the following:

- **Font Awesome**, the web's most popular icon set and toolkit: `https://fontawesome.com`
- **AutoMapper**, a convention-based object-object mapper: `http://automapper.org`
- **Markdig**, a fast, powerful, CommonMark compliant, extensible Markdown processor for .NET: `https://github.com/lunet-io/markdig`
- **Newtonsoft Json.NET**, a popular high-performance JSON framework for .NET: `https://www.newtonsoft.com/json`

Piranha CMS is released under the MIT license, meaning that it permits reuse within proprietary software provided all copies of the licensed software include a copy of the MIT License terms and the copyright notice.

Creating and exploring a Piranha CMS website

Piranha CMS has three project templates: **Empty**, **Web**, and **Blog**. Web and Blog include models, controllers and views for a blog archive, basic pages and blog posts. Web also has a start page type to use as a landing page. Blog has a more advanced blog archive with paging, category, and tag filtering to use as its default page.

We will need to install these templates before we can create a Piranha CMS website project.

You will use the `piranha.blog` project template to create a Piranha CMS website with an SQLite database for storing content including blog posts and user names and passwords for authentication.

1. In the folder named `PracticalApps`, create a folder named `NorthwindCms`.

2. In Visual Studio Code, open the `PracticalApps` workspace.

3. Add the `NorthwindCms` folder to the workspace.

4. Navigate to **Terminal | New Terminal** and select `NorthwindCms`.

5. In **Terminal**, install Piranha project templates, as shown in the following command:

   ```
   dotnet new -i Piranha.Templates
   ```

6. In **Terminal**, enter a command to list the Piranha CMS templates, as shown in the following command:

   ```
   dotnet new "piranha cms" --list
   ```

7. Note the templates, as shown in the following output:

   ```
   Templates                                 Short Name          Language

   ------------------------------------------------------------------

   ASP.NET Core Empty with Piranha CMS  piranha.empty        [C#]

   ASP.NET Core Blog with Piranha CMS   piranha.blog         [C#]

   ASP.NET Core Web with Piranha CMS    piranha.web          [C#]

   ASP.NET Core Blog with Piranha CMS   piranha.blog.razor   [C#]
   ```

8. In **Terminal**, enter commands to create a Piranha CMS website with extra blog archive support, as shown in the following command:

   ```
   dotnet new piranha.blog
   ```

9. In **EXPLORER**, open the `NorthwindCms.csproj` file, and note that at the time of writing, Piranha CMS is version 7.0 and that it targets ASP.NET Core 2.2, as shown in the following markup:

   ```
   <Project Sdk="Microsoft.NET.Sdk.Web">
     <PropertyGroup>
       <TargetFramework>netcoreapp2.2</TargetFramework>
       <AspNetCoreHostingModel>InProcess</AspNetCoreHostingModel>
     </PropertyGroup>

     <ItemGroup>
       <Folder Include="wwwroot\" />
     </ItemGroup>

     <ItemGroup>
       <PackageReference Include="Microsoft.AspNetCore.App" />
       <PackageReference
         Include="Microsoft.EntityFrameworkCore.Sqlite"
         Version="2.2.4" />
       <PackageReference Include="Piranha" Version="7.0.2" />
   ```

```
<PackageReference Include="Piranha.AspNetCore"
    Version="7.0.0" />
<PackageReference
    Include="Piranha.AspNetCore.Identity.SQLite"
    Version="7.0.0" />
<PackageReference Include="Piranha.AttributeBuilder"
    Version="7.0.0" />
<PackageReference
    Include="Piranha.Data.EF" Version="7.0.1" />
<PackageReference Include="Piranha.ImageSharp"
    Version="7.0.0-rc1" />
<PackageReference Include="Piranha.Local.FileStorage"
    Version="7.0.0" />
<PackageReference
    Include="Piranha.Manager" Version="7.0.4" />
  </ItemGroup>
</Project>
```

I expect Piranha CMS and its project templates to be updated to support
.NET Core 3.0 a few months after its release, so by the time you read this
book the version numbers in your .csproj file are likely to be higher.

10. In **Terminal**, build and start the website, as shown in the following
    command:

```
dotnet run
```

11. Start Chrome and navigate to the following URL: `https://
    localhost:5001/`.

12. Note the default home page for a Piranha CMS website, as shown in the
    following screenshot:

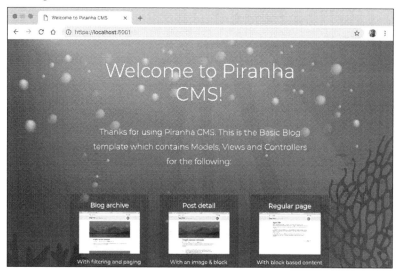

13. At the bottom of the page, click **Seed some data** to create some sample content, and note the following, as shown in the following screenshot:

   ○ The default page for the website is a blog archive that shows the latest posts.

   ○ At the top are links to **Blog**, **About Me**, and developer-oriented social media sites: **Twitter**, **GitHub**, and **LinkedIn**.

   ○ Each blog post has an image, title and publish date, summary text with button to **Read more**, and can be categorized and hash tagged.

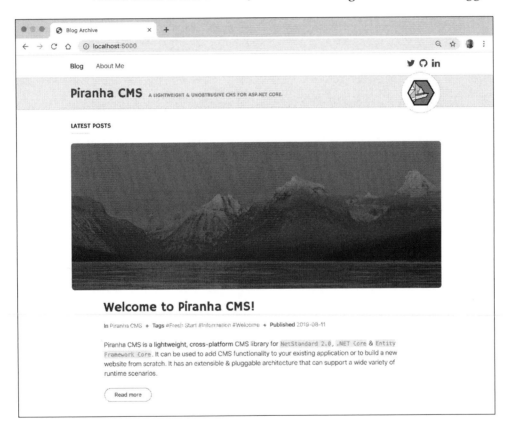

Editing site and page content

Let's log in as if we are the content owner for the website and manage some of the content.

1. In your browsers address box, enter the following URL: `https://localhost:5001/manager`.

2. Enter a username of admin and a password of password, as shown in the following screenshot:

3. In the manager, note the two existing pages named **Blog** (that is an example of the **Blog archive** type) and **About Me** (that is an example of the **Standard page** type), and then click **Default Site**, as shown in the following screenshot:

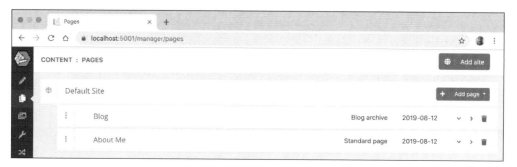

4. In the **Edit site** dialog box, on the **Settings** tab, change the **Title** to Northwind CMS and **Description** to Providing fresh tasty food to restaurants for three generations, as shown in the following screenshot:

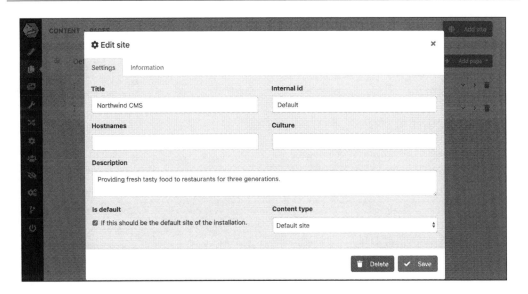

5. In the **Edit site** dialog box, on the **Information** tab, change the **Site Title** to Northwind CMS and **Tag Line** to Providing fresh tasty food to restaurants for three generations. Note that the content owner could also replace the site logo with an alternative image file, and then click **Save**.

6. If you are not already in the **CONTENT : PAGES** section, then in the menu navigation bar on the left, click **Pages**, and then click **About Me** to edit that page.

7. Change the page title to **About Us**, and note that beneath it the content owner can add any number of blocks to the page, as shown in the following screenshot, including:

    ° Horizontal dividers between each block with a circular button to insert a new block.

    ° When a block has the focus it has buttons to collapse, expand, and delete the block, and a menu of additional actions.

    ° A block with one column of rich text, images, and links, easily styled with a toolbar.

    ° A block with plain text styled for a quote.

  ° A block with two columns of rich text, with an extra button to swap the order of the columns.

8. At the top of **CONTENT : PAGES / EDIT**, click the gear icon to show the **Settings** dialog box, where the content owner can set the navigation title, meta keywords, meta description, and the slug used in the URL path, as shown in the following screenshot:

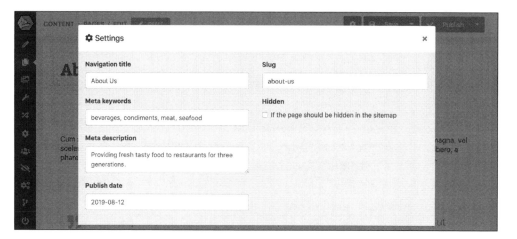

9. Change **Navigation title** to About Us.

10. Change **Meta keywords** to beverages, condiments, meat, seafood.

11. Change **Meta description** to `Providing fresh tasty food to restaurants for three generations`.

12. Change **Slug** to `about-us`. Slug is another name for a segment in a URL path, like the name of a controller or action in MVC.

13. Close the dialog box.

14. At the top of **CONTENT : PAGES / EDIT**, click **Save**, and note that the changes have been saved as a draft, as shown in the following screenshot:

15. Click the **Publish** button to make those changes visible to website visitors.

Creating a new top-level page

Let's create a new page with some blocks for its content.

1. In the menu navigation bar on the left, click **Pages**, click the **+ Add** button, and then click **Standard page**.

2. In the **Your page title** box, enter `Contact Us`.

3. Click the circular **+** button and choose **Columns**, as shown in the following screenshot:

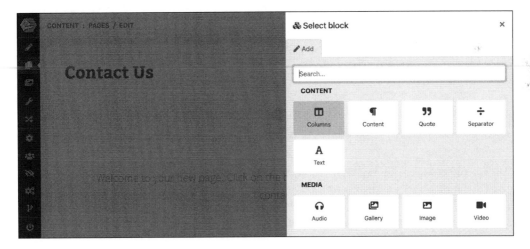

4. At the top of the **COLUMNS** block, click the **+** button, click **Text**, and then enter a fake postal address, like 123 Main Street, New York City, United States.

5. At the top of the **COLUMNS** block, click the **+** button, click **Text**, and then enter a fake email address and phone number, like `admin@northwind.com` and `(123) 555-1234`, as shown in the following screenshot:

6. At the top of **CONTENT : PAGES / EDIT**, click **Publish**.

If you just click the **Save** button, then the new page is saved to the CMS database, but it will not yet be visible to website visitors.

Creating a new child page

To create new pages in Piranha CMS you must consider the page hierarchy.

To create the **Contact Us** page, we clicked the **+ Add page** button at the top of the **Pages** list. But to insert a new page within the existing structure, you must click either the down or right arrow icons.

-   **Down arrow**: Creates a new page *after* the current page, that is, at the same level.
-   **Right arrow**: Creates a new page *under* the current page, that is, a child page.

If you ever create a page in the wrong place, it is easy to drag and drop it into the correct position within the page tree structure. A lot of content owners would probably prefer this technique, that is, always create new pages at the bottom of the list and then drag and drop them to the desired position within the page tree.

Let's try creating a new child page for the **About Us** page.

1. In the menu navigation bar on the left, click **Pages**; in the **About Us** row, click the right arrow icon, and then click **Standard page**.

2. Enter Our Location for the page title and then click **Publish**.

3. In the menu navigation bar on the left, click **Pages**, and note the **Our Location** page is a child of **About Us**, as shown in the following screenshot:

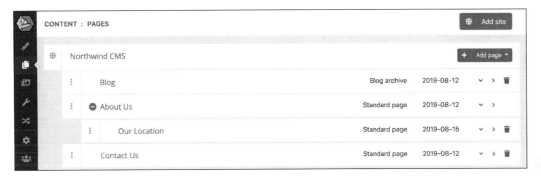

4. Click the **Our Location** page to edit it.

5. Click the gear button to open the **Settings** dialog box, and note the **Slug** has been set automatically based on where the page was initially created, as shown in the following screenshot:

The slug for a page will not automatically change if the page is later dragged and dropped to a different position within the page tree hierarchy. You would have to change the slug manually.

Reviewing the blog archive

1. In the menu navigation bar on the left, click **Pages**, click **Blog**, and note the blog archive type of page has a table of blog post items, each row with the item's title, published date, item type (in this case the one item is a **Blog post**), category (in this case, **Piranha CMS**), and the ability to delete items, as shown in the following screenshot:

2. Click the **+ Add** button and then click **Blog post**.

3. Enter a post title like `Northwind has some cool new fish to sell you!`, enter `Fish` for the category, add some tags like `seafood` and `cool`, and then add at least one block like a quote saying `"This fish is the tastiest ever!"`, as shown in the following screenshot:

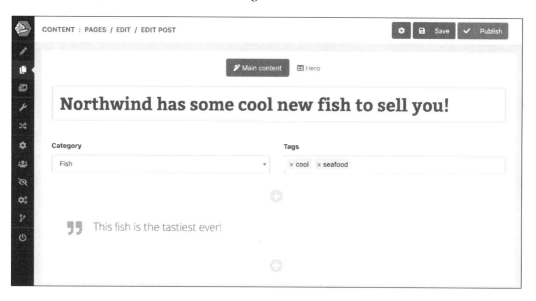

4. Click **Publish**.

5. Click the arrow to the right of the **Save** button and then click **Preview**.

6. In the **Live Preview** browser tab, click **MOBILE** to see how the blog post will look on mobile devices, as shown in the following screenshot:

7. Close the **Live Preview** browser tab.

Exploring authentication and authorization

Let's see what system settings are available to protect content.

1. In the menu navigation bar on the left, click **Users**, and note the **admin** user is a member of the **SysAdmin** role, as shown in the following screenshot:

2. In the menu navigation bar on the left, click **Roles**, click the **SysAdmin** role, and note that you can assign dozens of permissions to a role, as shown in the following screenshot:

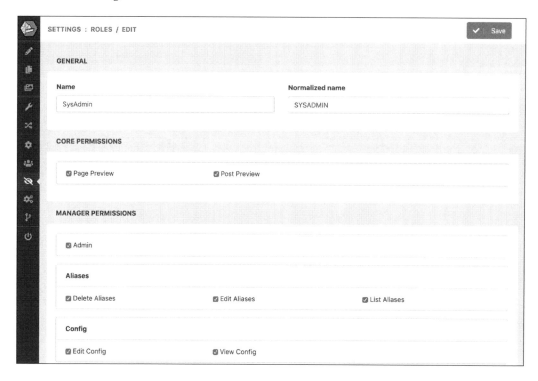

3. In the menu navigation bar on the left, click **Roles**, then then click the **+ Add** button.

4. In the **GENERAL** section, enter the name `Editors`.

5. In the **CORE PERMISSIONS** section, select both permissions.

6. In the **MANAGER PERMISSIONS** section, select the following permissions, as shown in the following screenshot:

    ○   **Media**: Add Media, Add Media Folders, Edit Media, List Media.

    ○   **Pages**: Add Pages, Edit Pages, List Pages, Pages - Save.

    ○   **Posts**: Add Posts, Edit Posts, List Posts, Save Posts.

7. Click **Save**.

8. In the menu navigation bar on the left, click **Users**, then then click the **+ Add** button.

9. Enter a name of Eve, an email address of eve@northwind.com, assign her to the Editors role, set her password to Pa$$w0rd, as shown in the following screenshot:

10. Click **Save**.

> **Good Practice**: You should carefully consider what permissions different roles will need. The **SysAdmin** role should have all permissions. If you were to create an **Editor** role then it might be allowed to add, delete, edit and save pages, posts, and media, but perhaps only a **Publisher** role would be allowed to publish content because only they should control when to allow website visitors to see the content.

Exploring configuration

Let's see how you can control the URL paths, the number of versions of each page and post that are retained in the CMS database, and caching to improve scalability and performance.

1. In the menu navigation bar on the left, click **Config**, and note that by default, five blogs are shown in each archive page, ten revisions are retained for pages and posts, and if the content owner creates a hierarchical tree of pages then the URL path will use hierarchical slugs, as shown in the following example URL path:

    `/about-us/news-and-events/northwind-wins-award`

2. Change the cache time from `0` to `30` minutes for pages and posts, as shown in the following screenshot:

Good Practice: While developing, switch off page caching by setting the minutes to 0 because it is likely to cause you confusion when you make a change to your code, but it is not reflected in the website! After you deploy to production, then log in and set these values to sensible values depending on how frequently content owners update pages and how quickly they expect a website visitor to then see those changes. Caching is a balance.

3. Change the cache expiration for pages and posts back to 0.

4. Click **Save**.

Testing the new content

Let's see if the **Contact Us** and **Our Location** pages are published and therefore visible to website visitors.

1. In the menu navigation bar on the left, click **Logout**.

2. Navigate to the website at `https://localhost:5001/` and note that the **Contact Us** page and the blog post are now shown to visitors, as shown in the following screenshot:

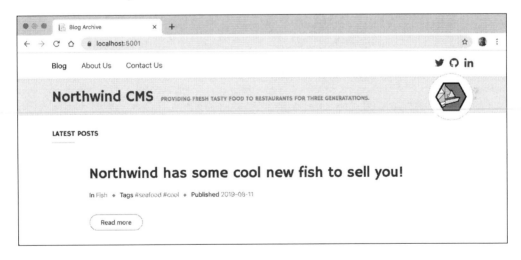

3. Only top-level pages are shown in the navigation menu, so click **About Us** to navigate to that page and then in the browser's address bar, append the rest of the slug and press *Enter*, as shown in the following URL:

   `https://localhost:5001/about-us/our-location`

In a real website, you would want to provide navigation to child pages using something like a Bootstrap `navbar` with dropdown menus.

 More Information: You can read about Bootstrap's `navbar` at the following link: `https://getbootstrap.com/docs/4.0/components/navbar/`

4. Close the browser.
5. Stop the website running by pressing *Ctrl + C* in **Terminal**.

Understanding routing

Piranha CMS uses the normal ASP.NET Core routing system underneath.

In the current website we have four pages that are the responses to HTTP requests for relative paths, also known as slugs, as shown in the following list:

- **Blog**: / or `/blog`
- **About Us**: `/about-us`
- **Our Location**: `/about-us/our-location`
- **Contact Us**: `/contact-us`

When a request arrives for a slug, Piranha CMS looks in the content database for a matching content item. When found, it looks up the type of content, so for `/about-us` it would then know that it is a Standard page.

The Standard page and Archive page do not need custom routes defined in order to work because the following routes are configured by default:

- `/page` for all page types except archive pages.
- `/archive` for archive pages.
- `/post` for post items in an archive.

So, incoming HTTP request URLs are translated into a route that can be processed by ASP.NET Core in the normal way. For example, the following request:

`https://localhost:5001/about-us`

Is translated by Piranha CMS into:

`https://localhost:5001/page?id=154b519d-b5ed-4f75-8aa4-d092559363b0`

This is processed by a normal ASP.NET Core MVC controller. The page `id` is a GUID that can be used to look up the page content data in the Piranha CMS database. Let's see how.

1. In the `Controllers` folder, open `CmsController.cs`.

2. Note that `CmsController` derives from Microsoft's `Controller` class.

3. Scroll down to find the `Page` action method, and note that it uses Microsoft's `[Route]` attribute to indicate that this action method responds to HTTP requests for the relative URL path, `/page`, and will extract the Guid using Microsoft's model binder and use it to look up the page's model from the database using Piranha's API, as shown in the following code:

```
/// <summary>
/// Gets the page with the given id.
/// </summary>
/// <param name="id">The unique page id</param>
/// <param name="draft">If a draft is requested</param>
[Route("page")]
public async Task<IActionResult> Page(
  Guid id, bool draft = false)
{
  var model = await _loader.GetPage<StandardPage>(
    id, HttpContext.User, draft);

  return View(model);
}
```

Note that this controller also has similar action methods with custom simplified routes for archive pages and posts.

So that a request is not processed repeatedly by Piranha, a query string parameter, `piranha_handled=true`, is added to the rewritten URL.

As well as the built-in custom routes, you can define additional ones. For example, if you are building an e-commerce website, then you might want special routes for product catalogs and categories:

- **Product catalog**: `/catalog`
- **Product category**: `/catalog/beverages`

 More Information: You can read about advanced routing for Piranha CMS at the following link: `http://piranhacms.org/docs/architecture/routing/advanced-routing`.

Understanding media

Media files can be uploaded through the manager user interface or programmatically using an API provided by Piranha CMS with streams and byte arrays.

 More Information: You can read more about programmatically uploading media using the Piranha CMS APIs at the following link: http://piranhacms.org/docs/basics/media-files

To make it more likely that uploaded media is compatible with common devices, Piranha CMS limits the types of media that can be uploaded to the following file types by default:

- .jpg, .jpeg, and .png images
- .mp4 videos
- .pdf documents

If you need to upload other types of file, like GIF images, then you can register additional media file types in the Startup class.

1. Open the Startup.cs file.
2. In the Configure method, after Piranha is initialized, register the GIF file extension as a recognized file type, as shown highlighted in the following code:

```
// Initialize Piranha
App.Init(api);

// register GIFs as a media type
App.MediaTypes.Images.Add(".gif", "image/gif");
```

Understanding the application service

ApplicationService simplifies programmatic access to common objects for the current request. It is usually injected into all Razor files using _ViewImports.cshtml with the name WebApp, as shown in the following code:

```
@inject Piranha.AspNetCore.Services.IApplicationService WebApp
```

Common uses of the application service are shown in the following table:

Code	Description
`@WebApp.PageId`	Guid of the requested page.
`@WebApp.Url`	Browser requested original URL before it was rewritten by the middleware.
`@WebApp.Api`	Access to the complete Piranha API.

`@WebApp.Media.ResizeImage(`
`ImageField image,`
`int width, int? height = null)`
	Resizes the given `ImageField` to the specified dimensions and returns the generated URL path to the resized file. `ImageField` is a Piranha type that can reference an uploaded image.

Understanding content types

Piranha allows a developer to define three categories of **content type** as shown in the following list:

- **Sites**: For properties shared across all other content. If you don't need to share properties, then you don't need a site content type. Even if you do need one, each site usually only needs one site content type. The class must be decorated with `[SiteType]`.

- **Pages**: For informational pages like About Us and landing pages like a home or category page that can have other pages as their children. Pages form a hierarchical tree that provides the URL path structure of the site, like `/about-us/locations` and `/about-us/job-vacancies`. Each site usually has multiple page content types, like Standard page, Archive page, Category page, and Product page. The class must be decorated with `[PageType]`.

- **Posts**: for "pages" that do not have children and can only be listed in archive pages. Posts can be filtered and grouped by date, category, and tags. The special archive page type provides the user interaction with the posts. Each site usually has only one or two post content types, like `NewsPost` or `EventPost`. The class must be decorated with `[PostType]`.

Understanding component types

Registered content types are given built-in support for creating, editing, and deleting in the Piranha manager. The structure of a content type is provided by dividing it into three categories of **component type**, as shown in the following list:

- **Fields**: The smallest component of content. They can be as simple as a number, date, or `string` value. Fields are like properties in a C# class. The property must be decorated with `[Field]`.

- **Regions**: Small pieces of content that appear in a fixed location on the page or post rendered to the visitor under the control of the developer. Regions are composed of one or more fields, or a sortable collection of fields.

  Regions are like titled complex properties in a C# class. The property must be decorated with `[Region]`.

- **Blocks**: Small pieces of content that can be added, reordered, and deleted. Blocks provide complete flexibility to the content editor. By default, all pages and posts can contain any number of blocks, although this can be disabled for a specific page or post content type with the `[PageType]` attribute that sets `UseBlocks` to `false`. Standard block types include multi-column rich text, quote, and image. Developers can define custom block types with a custom editing experience in the Piranha manager.

Understanding standard fields

Standard fields each have a built-in editing experience and include the following:

- `CheckBoxField`, `DateField`, `NumberField`, `StringField`, `TextField`: Simple field values.

- `PageField` and `PostField`: Reference a page or post using its GUID.

- `DocumentField`, `ImageField`, `VideoField`, `MediaField`: Reference a document, image, video, or any media file using its `Guid`. By default, `DocumentField` can be `.pdf`, `ImageField` can be `.jpg`, `.jpeg`, or `.png`, `VideoField` can be `.mp4`, and `MediaField` can be any file type.

- `HtmlField`, `MarkdownField`: Formatted text values with a customizable TinyMCE editor with a toolbar and a Markdown editor.

Reviewing some content types

Let's review some of the content types defined by the Piranha Blog project template.

1. Open `Models/BlogSite.cs` and note that a site content class must inherit from `SiteContent<T>`, where `T` is the derived class, and be decorated with the `[SiteType]` attribute. It has a single `Information` property decorated to register the property as a `[Region]` so that it can be easily edited in the Piranha manager, as shown in the following code:

```
using Piranha.AttributeBuilder;
using Piranha.Extend.Fields;
using Piranha.Models;

namespace NorthwindCms.Models
{
  [SiteType(Title = "Default site")]
  public class BlogSite : SiteContent<BlogSite>
  {
    [Region]
    public Regions.SiteInfo Information { get; set; }
  }
}
```

2. Click in `SiteInfo`, press *F12*, and note this region has three properties to share the title, tagline, and logo across the whole website, as shown in the following code:

```
using Piranha.AttributeBuilder;
using Piranha.Extend.Fields;
using Piranha.Models;

namespace NorthwindCms.Models.Regions
{
  public class SiteInfo
  {
    [Field(Title = "Site Title",
      Options = FieldOption.HalfWidth)]
    public StringField SiteTitle { get; set; }

    [Field(Options = FieldOption.HalfWidth)]
    public StringField Tagline { get; set; }

    [Field(Title = "Site Logo")]
    public ImageField SiteLogo { get; set; }
  }
}
```

3. Open `Models/StandardPage.cs`, and note that a page type must inherit from `Page<T>`, where `T` is the derived class, and be decorated with the `[PageType]` attribute, as shown in the following code:

```
using Piranha.AttributeBuilder; // [PageType]
using Piranha.Extend.Fields;
using Piranha.Models; // Page<T>

namespace NorthwindCms.Models
{
  [PageType(Title = "Standard page")]
  public class StandardPage : Page<StandardPage>
  {
  }
}
```

4. Open `Views/Cms/Page.cshtml`, and note this view is strongly typed to be passed an instance of the `StandardPage` class as its `Model` property, stores the `Title` in the `ViewBag` so it can be rendered into a shared layout, and renders the `Title` and `Blocks` in Bootstrap-styled `<div>` elements, as shown in the following code:

```
@model NorthwindCms.Models.StandardPage
@{
  ViewBag.Title = Model.Title;
}

<div class="container">
  <div class="row justify-content-center">
    <div class="col-sm-10">
      <h1>@Model.Title</h1>
    </div>
  </div>
  @Html.DisplayFor(m => m.Blocks)
</div>
```

Blogs on a website require a page type and a post type. The page type acts as a container for listing, filtering, and grouping the blog posts.

5. Open `Models/BlogArchive.cs` and note that a page type for interacting with posts is a page type but it must inherit from `ArchivePage<T>`, where `T` is the derived class, and be decorated with the `[PageType]` attribute, and usually will not need to have a section that the content owner can add blocks to, as shown in the following code:

```
using Piranha.AttributeBuilder;
using Piranha.Models;

namespace NorthwindCms.Models
{
```

```
[PageType(Title = "Blog archive", UseBlocks = false)]
public class BlogArchive  : ArchivePage<BlogArchive>
{
}
}
```

6. Open `Models/BlogPost.cs` and note that a post type must inherit from `Post<T>`, where `T` is the derived class, and be decorated with the `[PostType]` attribute, and that this post has a single property registered as a region, as shown in the following code:

```
using Piranha.AttributeBuilder;
using Piranha.Extend.Fields;
using Piranha.Models;

namespace NorthwindCms.Models
{
   [PostType(Title = "Blog post")]
   public class BlogPost : Post<BlogPost>
   {
      [Region]
      public Regions.Heading Heading { get; set; }
   }
}
```

7. Open `Views/Cms/Archive.cshtml`. Note that it has more than one hundred lines of markup to output lists of posts sorted and filtered by various year, month, category, and tag, and includes page navigation at the bottom.

8. Note the `foreach` statement to output each post in the archive, wrapped in an `<article>` element, as shown in the following markup:

```
@foreach (var post in Model.Archive.Posts)
{
   <article>
     <header>
```

9. Open `Views/Cms/Post.cshtml` and note that `Api` is injected to enable easy access to shared features and properties across the website (or you could use `WebApp.Api` to access the same object), and the `Resize` method of `ImageField` is used to efficiently resize the primary image in the `Heading` of each post, as shown in the following markup:

```
@model NorthwindCms.Models.BlogPost
@inject Piranha.IApi Api
@{
   ViewBag.Title = Model.Title;
}

<div class="container">
  <article>
```

```
<header>
  @if (Model.Heading.PrimaryImage.HasValue)
  {
  <div class="row justify-content-center">
    <div class="col-sm">
      <img src="@Url.Content(Model.Heading
        .PrimaryImage.Resize(Api, 930, 360))">
    </div>
  </div>
  }
  <div class="row justify-content-center">
    <div class="col-sm-10">
      <h1>@Model.Title</h1>
        <p class="post-meta">
          <strong>In</strong>
          <a href="/category/@Model.Category.Slug">
            @Model.Category.Title</a>
          <span class="sep">&#9670;</span>
          <strong>Tags</strong>
          @foreach (var tag in Model.Tags)
          {
          <span class="tag"><a href="/tag/@tag.Slug">
            #@tag.Title</a></span>
          }
          <span class="sep">&#9670;</span>
          <strong>Published</strong>
          @Model.Published.Value.ToString("yyyy-MM-dd")
        </p>
    </div>
  </div>
</header>
@Html.DisplayFor(m => m.Blocks)
</article>
</div>
```

Each post belongs to a single category and can have multiple tags.

Understanding standard blocks

Standard blocks include the following:

- **Columns**: Has an `Items` property with one or more items that are `Block` instances.

- **Image**: Has a `Body` property that is an `ImageField` with a view that outputs it as the `src` for an `<img>` element.

- **Quote**: Has a `Body` property that is a `TextField` with a view that outputs it wrapped in a `<blockquote>` element.

- **Text**: Has a `Body` property that is a `TextField`.

Reviewing component types and standard blocks

Let's review some of the component types defined by the project template.

1. Open `Models/Regions/Heading.cs` and note that a region component type is a C# class that must contain one or more properties that use special `Field` types and the properties must be decorated with the `[Field]` attribute, and this region has a two properties for storing a reference to an image and a rich text property, as shown in the following code:

```
using Piranha.AttributeBuilder;
using Piranha.Extend.Fields;

namespace NorthwindCms.Models.Regions
{
    public class Heading
    {
        [Field(Title = "Primary image")]
        public ImageField PrimaryImage { get; set; }

        [Field]
        public HtmlField Ingress { get; set; }
    }
}
```

2. In the `Regions` folder, add a new temporary class without a namespace named `ExploreBlocks.cs`, and enter statements to define five properties, one for each block type, as shown in the following code:

```
using Piranha.Extend.Blocks;

class ExploreBlocks
{
    HtmlBlock a;
    ColumnBlock b;
    ImageBlock c;
    QuoteBlock d;
    TextBlock e;
}
```

3. Click inside each block type, press *F12*, review its definition, and note that to define a block the class must inherit from `Block` and be decorated with the `[BlockType]` attribute. For example, the `HtmlBlock` class, as shown in the following code:

```
#region Assembly Piranha, Version=7.0.2.0, Culture=neutral,
PublicKeyToken=null
// Piranha.dll
```

```
#endregion

using Piranha.Extend.Fields;

namespace Piranha.Extend.Blocks
{
    [BlockType(Name = "Content", Category = "Content",
      Icon = "fas fa-paragraph", Component = "html-block")]
    public class HtmlBlock : Block
    {
        public HtmlBlock();

        public HtmlField Body { get; set; }

        public override string GetTitle();
    }
}
```

4. Open `Views/Cms/DisplayTemplates/ColumnBlock.cshtml` and note that it renders collection of block items inside `<div>` elements styled with Bootstrap, as shown in the following markup:

```
@model Piranha.Extend.Blocks.ColumnBlock

<div class="row">
    @for (var n = 0; n < Model.Items.Count; n++)
    {
        <div class="col-md">
            @Html.DisplayFor(m => Model.Items[n],
                Model.Items[n].GetType().Name)
        </div>
    }
</div>
```

5. Review the models and views for the other four built-in block types.

6. Comment out the whole class or delete the file from your project. We only created it to review how the built-in block types are implemented.

 More Information: If you are not familiar with the Bootstrap grid system then you can read about it at the following link: https://getbootstrap.com/docs/4.1/layout/grid/

Defining components, content types, and templates

Now that you have seen the functionality of the content and component types provided with the project template, we will review how they were defined in more detail, and then we will define some custom page types to show a catalog of Northwind products.

Reviewing the standard page type

We will review the simplest page type, used for standard pages like About Us.

1. In Visual Studio Code, expand `Models`, open `StandardPage.cs`, and note that standard pages do not currently have any custom properties, as shown in the following code:

```
using Piranha.AttributeBuilder;
using Piranha.Models;

namespace NorthwindCms.Models
{
    [PageType(Title = "Standard page")]
    public class StandardPage  : Page<StandardPage>
    {
    }
}
```

2. Click in `Page<StandardPage>` and press *F12* to view the source.

3. Click in `GenericPage<T>` and press *F12* to view the source.

4. Click in `PageBase<T>` and press *F12* to view the source.

5. Review the `PageBase` class, as shown in the following code, and note that every page has the following properties:

   ○   `SiteId` and `ParentId` that are `Guid` values.

   ○   `ContentType` that is a `string`.

   ○   `Blocks` that is a list of `Block` instances.

```
#region Assembly Piranha, Version=7.0.2.0, Culture=neutral,
PublicKeyToken=null
// Piranha.dll
#endregion

using System;
using System.Collections.Generic;
using System.ComponentModel.DataAnnotations;
```

```
using Piranha.Extend;

namespace Piranha.Models
{
  public abstract class PageBase :
    RoutedContent, IBlockModel, IMeta
  {
    protected PageBase();

    public Guid SiteId { get; set; }
    [StringLength(256)]
    public string ContentType { get; set; }
    public Guid? ParentId { get; set; }
    public int SortOrder { get; set; }
    [StringLength(128)]
    public string NavigationTitle { get; set; }
    public bool IsHidden { get; set; }
    [StringLength(256)]
    public string RedirectUrl { get; set; }
    public RedirectType { get; set; }
    public Guid? OriginalPageId { get; set; }
    public IList<Block> Blocks { get; set; }
  }
}
```

6. Click in `RoutedContent`, press *F12* to view the source, and note that this is the class that defines properties like Slug for the segment name used in URL paths, and metadata like description and keywords for better SEO.

7. Click in `Content` and press *F12* to view the source, as shown in the following code, and note that all content has:

   ○ `Id` as a `Guid`

   ○ `TypeId` as a `string`

   ○ `Title` as a `string`

   ○ `DateTime` values for when it was created and last modified

```
using System;
using System.ComponentModel.DataAnnotations;

namespace Piranha.Models
{
  public abstract class Content
  {
    protected Content();

    public Guid Id { get; set; }
    [StringLength(64)]
    public string TypeId { get; set; }
    [StringLength(128)]
```

```
        public string Title { get; set; }
        public DateTime Created { get; set; }
        public DateTime LastModified { get; set; }
    }
}
```

Reviewing the blog archive page type

We will review the blog archive page type, used to list, sort, and filter blog items.

1. Open `BlogArchive.cs` and note that blog archive pages do not currently have any custom properties and that they do not enable blocks, as shown in the following code:

```
using Piranha.AttributeBuilder;
using Piranha.Models;

namespace NorthwindCms.Models
{
    [PageType(Title = "Blog archive", UseBlocks = false)]
    public class BlogArchive  : ArchivePage<BlogArchive>
    {
    }
}
```

2. Click `ArchivePage<BlogArchive>`, press *F12*, and note that `ArchivePage<T>` inherits from `ArchivePage<T, DynamicPost>`.

3. Click `ArchivePage<T, DynamicPost >`, press *F12*, and note that it has an `Archive` property that is a `PostArchive<TPost>`.

4. Click `PostArchive<TPost>`, press *F12*, and note the `Posts` property and the filtering and grouping properties by `Year`, `Month`, `Category`, and `Tag`, as shown in the following code:

```
using System.Collections.Generic;

namespace Piranha.Models
{
  public class PostArchive<T> where T : PostBase
  {
    public PostArchive();

    public int? Year { get; set; }
    public int? Month { get; set; }
    public int CurrentPage { get; set; }
    public int TotalPages { get; set; }
    public int TotalPosts { get; set; }
    public Taxonomy Category { get; set; }
    public Taxonomy Tag { get; set; }
```

```
        public IList<T> Posts { get; set; }
    }
}
```

Defining custom content and component types

We will define custom pages and regions for storing categories and products imported from the Northwind database. Since Piranha CMS is not yet compatible with .NET Core 3.0, we cannot use the Entity Framework Core database context that we used in previous chapters, although we can reuse the entity models because we put them in a .NET Standard 2.0-compatible class library.

We will create an MVC controller that responds to an HTTP GET request for the /import relative path by querying the Northwind database for categories and their products. Then, using the Piranha CMS API to find a special page that represents the root of the product catalog, and as children of that page, programmatically create instances of a custom CategoryPage type with a custom region to store details like the name, description, and image of each category, and a list of instances of a custom region to store details of each product including name, price, and units in stock, as shown in the following diagram:

Creating custom regions

Let's start by creating custom regions for a category and product so that data can be stored in the Piranha CMS database and edited by a content owner through the manager user interface.

1. In the `Models/Regions` folder, add a new class named `CategoryRegion.cs`, and add statements to define a region for storing information about a category from the Northwind database using suitable field types, as shown in the following code:

```
using Piranha.AttributeBuilder;
using Piranha.Extend.Fields;

namespace NorthwindCms.Models.Regions
{
  public class CategoryRegion
  {
    [Field(Title = "Category ID")]
    public NumberField CategoryID { get; set; }

    [Field(Title = "Category name")]
    public TextField CategoryName { get; set; }

    [Field]
    public HtmlField Description { get; set; }

    [Field(Title = "Category image")]
    public ImageField CategoryImage { get; set; }
  }
}
```

2. In the `Models/Regions` folder, add a new class named `ProductRegion.cs` and add statements to define a region for storing information about a product from the Northwind database using suitable field types, as shown in the following code:

```
using Piranha.AttributeBuilder;
using Piranha.Extend.Fields;
using Piranha.Models;

namespace NorthwindCms.Models.Regions
{
  public class ProductRegion
  {
    [Field(Title = "Product ID")]
    public NumberField ProductID { get; set; }

    [Field(Title = "Product name")]
```

```
        public TextField ProductName { get; set; }

        [Field(Title = "Unit price",
          Options = FieldOption.HalfWidth)]
        public StringField UnitPrice { get; set; }

        [Field(Title = "Units in stock",
          Options = FieldOption.HalfWidth)]
        public NumberField UnitsInStock { get; set; }
    }
}
```

Creating an entity data model

Now we need to reference the entity models in the .NET Standard 2.0 class
library and create a new Northwind database context in the current project that is
compatible with ASP.NET Core 2.2 used by Piranha CMS 7.0.

1. Open the `NorthwindCms.csproj` file and add a project reference to the
   Northwind entity models class library that you created in *Chapter 15, Building
   Websites Using ASP.NET Core Razor Pages*, as shown in the following markup:

```
<ItemGroup>
  <ProjectReference Include=
    "..\NorthwindEntitiesLib\NorthwindEntitiesLib.csproj" />
</ItemGroup>
```

2. In the `Models` folder, add a class named `Northwind.cs`, with statements as
   shown in the following code:

```
using Microsoft.EntityFrameworkCore;

namespace Packt.Shared
{
  public class Northwind : DbContext
  {
    public DbSet<Category> Categories { get; set; }
    public DbSet<Product> Products { get; set; }

    public Northwind(DbContextOptions options)
      : base(options) { }

    protected override void OnModelCreating(
      ModelBuilder modelBuilder)
    {
      base.OnModelCreating(modelBuilder);

      modelBuilder.Entity<Category>()
        .Property(c => c.CategoryName)
        .IsRequired()
```

```
    .HasMaxLength(15);

  // define a one-to-many relationship
  modelBuilder.Entity<Category>()
    .HasMany(c => c.Products)
    .WithOne(p => p.Category);

  modelBuilder.Entity<Product>()
    .Property(c => c.ProductName)
    .IsRequired()
    .HasMaxLength(40);

  modelBuilder.Entity<Product>()
    .HasOne(p => p.Category)
    .WithMany(c => c.Products);
    }
  }
}
```

Creating custom page types

Now we need to define custom page types for the catalog and a product category.

1. In the `Models` folder, add a class named `CatalogPage.cs` that does not allow blocks, has no content regions because it will be populated from the Northwind database, and has a custom route path `/catalog`, as shown in the following code:

```
using Piranha.AttributeBuilder;
using Piranha.Extend.Fields;
using Piranha.Models;
using NorthwindCms.Models.Regions;
using System.Collections.Generic;

namespace NorthwindCms.Models
{
  [PageType(Title = "Catalog page", UseBlocks = false)]
  [PageTypeRoute(Title = "Default", Route = "/catalog")]
  public class CatalogPage : Page<CatalogPage>
  {
  }
}
```

2. In the `Models` folder, add a class named `CategoryPage.cs` that does not allow blocks, has a custom route path `/catalog-category`, and has a property to store details of the category using a region and a property to store a list of products using a region, as shown in the following code:

```
using Piranha.AttributeBuilder;
using Piranha.Extend.Fields;
```

```
using Piranha.Models;
using NorthwindCms.Models.Regions;
using System.Collections.Generic;

namespace NorthwindCms.Models
{
  [PageType(Title = "Category Page", UseBlocks = false)]
  [PageTypeRoute(Title = "Default", Route = "/catalog-category")]
  public class CategoryPage : Page<CategoryPage>
  {
    [Region(Title = "Category detail")]
    [RegionDescription("The details for this category.")]
    public CategoryRegion CategoryDetail { get; set; }

    [Region(Title = "Category products")]
    [RegionDescription("The products for this category.")]
    public IList<ProductRegion> Products { get; set; }
      = new List<ProductRegion>();
  }
}
```

Creating custom view models

Next, we need to define some types for populating the catalog page because it will use the page hierarchy structure to determine product categories to show in the catalog page.

1. In the Models folder, add a class named CategoryItem.cs that has properties to store a summary of a category including links to its image and the full category page, as shown in the following code:

```
namespace NorthwindCms.Models
{
  public class CategoryItem
  {
    public string Title { get; set; }
    public string Description { get; set; }
    public string PageUrl { get; set; }
    public string ImageUrl { get; set; }
  }
}
```

2. In the Models folder, add a class named CatalogViewModel.cs that has a property to reference the catalog page and a property to store a list of category summary items, as shown in the following code:

```
using System.Collections.Generic;

namespace NorthwindCms.Models
```

```
{
  public class CatalogViewModel
  {
    public CatalogPage CatalogPage { get; set; }

    public IEnumerable<CategoryItem> Categories { get; set; }
  }
}
```

Defining custom content templates for content types

Now we must define the controllers and views to render the content types. We will use the sitemap to fetch the children of the catalog page to find out which categories should be shown in the catalog.

1. Open `Controllers/CmsController.cs`, import the `System.Linq` and `NorthwindCMS.Models` namespaces, and add statements to define two new action methods named `Catalog` and `Category` configured for the routes for the catalog and each catalog category, as shown highlighted in the following partial code:

```
using System;
using System.Threading;
using Microsoft.AspNetCore.Mvc;
using Piranha;
using System.Linq;
using NorthwindCms.Models;

namespace NorthwindCms.Controllers
{
  public class CmsController : Controller
  {
    ...

    [Route("catalog")]
    public async Task<IActionResult> Catalog(Guid id)
    {
      var catalog = await _api.Pages.
GetByIdAsync<CatalogPage>(id);

      var model = new CatalogViewModel
      {
        CatalogPage = catalog,
        Categories = (await _api.Sites.GetSitemapAsync())

        // get the catalog page
```

```
            .Where(item => item.Id == catalog.Id)

            // get its children
            .SelectMany(item => item.Items)

            // for each child sitemap item, get the page
            // and return a simplified model for the view
            .Select(item =>
              {
                var page = _api.Pages.GetByIdAsync<CategoryPage>
                  (item.Id).Result;

                var ci = new CategoryItem
                {
                  Title = page.Title,
                  Description = page.CategoryDetail.Description,
                  PageUrl = page.Permalink,
                  ImageUrl = page.CategoryDetail.CategoryImage
                    .Resize(_api, 200)
                };

                return ci;
              })
        };

        return View(model);
    }

    [Route("catalog-category")]
    public async Task<IActionResult> Category(Guid id)
    {
      var model = await _api.Pages
        .GetByIdAsync<Models.CategoryPage>(id);

      return View(model);
    }
  }
}
```

We used `catalog-category` for the name of the route because there is already a route named `category` that is used for grouping blog posts into categories.

2. In `Views/Cms`, add a Razor file named `Catalog.cshtml`, as shown in the following markup:

```
@using Piranha.Models
@using NorthwindCms.Models
@model CatalogViewModel
@{
  ViewBag.Title = Model.CatalogPage.Title;
```

```
}
<div class="container">
  <div class="row justify-content-center">
    <div class="col-sm-10">
      <h1 class="display-3">@Model.CatalogPage.Title</h1>
    </div>
  </div>
  <div class="row">
  @foreach(CategoryItem c in Model.Categories)
  {
    <div class="col-sm-4">
      <a class="card-link" href="@c.PageUrl">
        <div class="card border-dark"
            style="width: 18rem;">
          <img class="card-img-top" src="@c.ImageUrl"
            alt="Image of @c.Title"
            asp-append-version="true" />
          <div class="card-body">
            <h5 class="card-title text-info">@c.Title</h5>
            <p class="card-text text-info">
              @c.Description</p>
          </div>
        </div>
      </a>
    </div>
  }
  </div>
</div>
```

3. In `Views/Cms`, add a Razor file named `Category.cshtml`, as shown in the following markup:

```
@using NorthwindCms.Models.Regions
@model NorthwindCms.Models.CategoryPage
@{
  ViewBag.Title = Model.Title;
}
<div class="container">
  <div class="row justify-content-center">
    <div class="col-sm-10">
      <h1 class="display-4">
        @Model.CategoryDetail.CategoryName
      </h1>
      <p class="lead">@Model.CategoryDetail.Description</p>
    </div>
  </div>
  <div class="row">
  @if (Model.Products.Count == 0)
  {
    <div class="col-sm-10">
      There are no products in this category!
    </div>
```

```
    }
    else
    {
      @foreach(ProductRegion p in Model.Products)
      {
      <div class="col-sm-4">
        <div class="card border-dark" style="width: 18rem;">
          <div class="card-header">
            In Stock: @p.UnitsInStock.Value
          </div>
          <div class="card-body">
            <h5 class="card-title text-info">
              <small class="text-muted">
                @p.ProductID.Value</small>
              @p.ProductName.Value
            </h5>
            <p class="card-text text-info">
              Price: @p.UnitPrice.Value
            </p>
          </div>
        </div>
      </div>
      }
    }
    </div>
</div>
```

Configuring start up and importing from a database

Finally, we must configure the content types and Northwind database connection string.

1. Open `Startup.cs` and import the `System.IO` namespace.

2. At the bottom of the `ConfigureServices` method, add a statement to register the Northwind database context, as shown highlighted in the following partial code:

```
public void ConfigureServices(IServiceCollection services)
{
  ...
  string databasePath = Path.Combine("..", "Northwind.db");

  services.AddDbContext<Packt.Shared.Northwind>(options =>
    options.UseSqlite($"Data Source={databasePath}"));
}
```

3. In the `Configure` method, in the section commented with `// Build content types`, add two calls to the `AddType` method to register the two new page types and add a call to automatically redirect to HTTPS, as shown highlighted in the following code:

```
public void Configure(IApplicationBuilder app,
  IHostingEnvironment env, IApi api)
{
  if (env.IsDevelopment())
  {
    app.UseDeveloperExceptionPage();
  }

  // Initialize Piranha
  App.Init();

  // register GIFs as a media type
  App.MediaTypes.Images.Add(".gif", "image/gif");

  // Configure cache level
  App.CacheLevel = Piranha.Cache.CacheLevel.Basic;

  // Build content types
  var pageTypeBuilder = new Piranha.AttributeBuilder
    .PageTypeBuilder(api)
      .AddType(typeof(Models.BlogArchive))
      .AddType(typeof(Models.StandardPage))
      .AddType(typeof(Models.CatalogPage))
      .AddType(typeof(Models.CategoryPage));

  pageTypeBuilder.Build().DeleteOrphans();

  var postTypeBuilder = new Piranha.AttributeBuilder
    .PostTypeBuilder(api)
      .AddType(typeof(Models.BlogPost));

  postTypeBuilder.Build().DeleteOrphans();

  var siteTypeBuilder = new Piranha.AttributeBuilder
    .SiteTypeBuilder(api)
      .AddType(typeof(Models.BlogSite));

  siteTypeBuilder.Build().DeleteOrphans();

  // Register middleware
  app.UseStaticFiles();
  app.UseAuthentication();
  app.UsePiranha();
```

```
    app.UsePiranhaManager();

    app.UseHttpsRedirection();

    app.UseMvc(routes =>
    {
      routes.MapRoute(name: "areaRoute",
        template: "{area:exists}/{controller}/{action}/{id?}",
      defaults: new { controller = "Home", action = "Index" });

      routes.MapRoute(
        name: "default",
        template: "{controller=home}/{action=index}/{id?}");
    });
}
```

4. In the `Controllers` folder, add a new class named `ImportController.cs` to define a controller to import categories and products from Northwind into instances of the new custom content types, as shown in the following code:

```
using Microsoft.AspNetCore.Mvc;
using Piranha;
using Piranha.Models;
using System;
using System.Linq;
using System.Threading.Tasks;
using Packt.Shared;
using NorthwindCms.Models;
using NorthwindCms.Models.Regions;
using Microsoft.EntityFrameworkCore; // Include() extension method

namespace NorthwindCms.Controllers
{
  public class ImportController : Controller
  {
    private readonly IApi api;

    private readonly Northwind db;

    public ImportController(
      IApi api, Northwind injectedContext)
    {
      this.api = api;
      db = injectedContext;
    }

    [Route("/import")]
    public async Task<IActionResult> Import()
    {
      var site = await api.Sites.GetDefaultAsync();
      var catalog = await api.Pages
```

```
        .GetBySlugAsync<CatalogPage>("catalog");

foreach (var category in
  db.Categories.Include(c => c.Products))
{
  // if the category page already exists,
  // then skip to the next iteration of the loop
  CategoryPage =
    await api.Pages.GetBySlugAsync<CategoryPage>(
    $"catalog/{category.CategoryName.ToLower()}");

  if (categoryPage == null)
  {
    categoryPage = CategoryPage.Create(api);

    categoryPage.Id = Guid.NewGuid();
    categoryPage.SiteId = site.Id;
    categoryPage.ParentId = catalog.Id;

    categoryPage.CategoryDetail.CategoryID =
      category.CategoryID;
    categoryPage.CategoryDetail.CategoryName =
      category.CategoryName;
    categoryPage.CategoryDetail.Description =
      category.Description;

    // find image with correct filename for category id
    var image = (await api.Media.GetAllAsync())
      .First(media => media.Type == MediaType.Image
      && media.Filename ==
      $"category{category.CategoryID}.jpeg");

    categoryPage.CategoryDetail.CategoryImage = image;
  }

  if (categoryPage.Products.Count == 0)
  {
    // convert the products for this category into
    // a list of instances of ProductRegion
    categoryPage.Products = category.Products
      .Select(p => new ProductRegion
      {
        ProductID = p.ProductID,
        ProductName = p.ProductName,
        UnitPrice = p.UnitPrice.HasValue
          ? p.UnitPrice.Value.ToString("c") : "n/a",
        UnitsInStock = p.UnitsInStock ?? 0
      }).ToList();
  }
```

```
                 categoryPage.Title = category.CategoryName;

                 categoryPage.MetaDescription =
                   category.Description;

                 categoryPage.NavigationTitle =
                   category.CategoryName;

                 categoryPage.Published = DateTime.Now;

                 await api.Pages.SaveAsync(categoryPage);
             }

           return Redirect("~/");
         }
       }
     }
```

Testing the Northwind CMS website

We are now ready to run the website.

Uploading images and creating the catalog root

First, we will upload some images to use for the eight categories of products and then we will create a catalog page to act as a root in the page hierarchy that we will later import content from the Northwind database into.

 More Information: You can download images from the GitHub repository for this book at the following link: https://github. com/markjprice/cs8dotnetcore3/tree/master/Assets

1. In **Terminal**, enter the command dotnet run to build and start the website.

2. Start Chrome, navigate to https://localhost:5001/manager/, and log in as admin with password.

3. In the menu navigation bar on the left, click **Media**, and import the eight category images, as shown in the following screenshot:

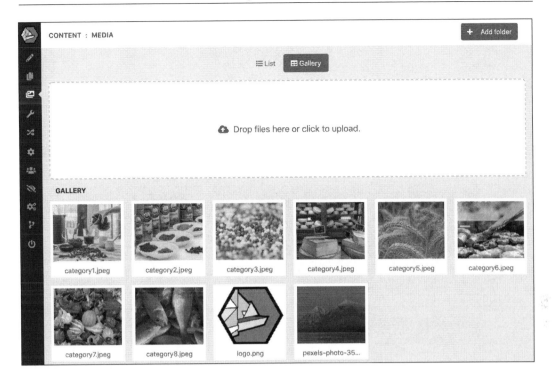

4. In the menu navigation bar on the left, click **Pages**, add a new **Catalog page**, set its title to **Catalog**, and then click **Publish**.

Importing category and product content

In the **CONTENT : PAGES** section, a content owner could manually add a new **Category page** under the **Catalog**, but we will use the import controller to create all the categories and products automatically.

1. In the Chrome address box, change the URL to `https://localhost:5001/`, press *Enter*, click **Catalog**, and note the new page is currently empty.

2. In the Chrome address box, change the URL to `https://localhost:5001/import/`, press *Enter*, and note that after importing the Northwind categories and products you are redirected to the home page.

3. Click **Catalog**, and note the categories have been successfully imported, as shown in the following screenshot:

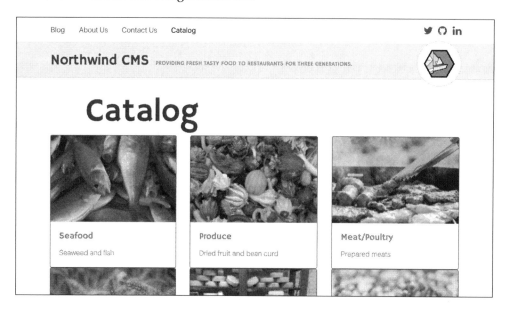

4. Click **Meat/Poultry**. Note that the URL is `https://localhost:5001/catalog/meat/poultry` and that it has some products, as shown in the following screenshot:

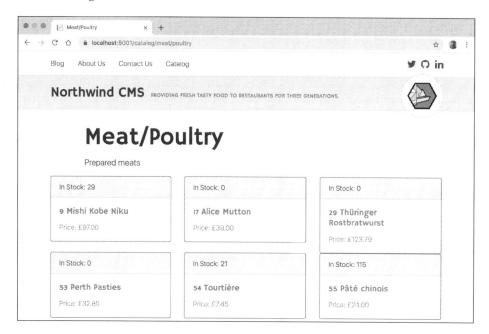

Managing catalog content

Now that we have imported the catalog content, a content owner can use the Piranha manager interface to make changes instead of editing the original data in the Northwind database.

1. In the Chrome address box, change the URL to `https://localhost:5001/manager/` and, if necessary, log in as `admin` with `password`.

2. In **CONTENT : PAGES**, under the **Catalog** page, click the **Meat/Poultry** page, as shown in the following screenshot:

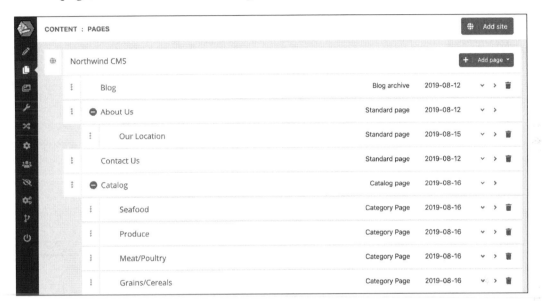

3. In **Meat/Poultry**, note the category details including a link to the uploaded image media, and then click **Category products**, as shown in the following screenshot:

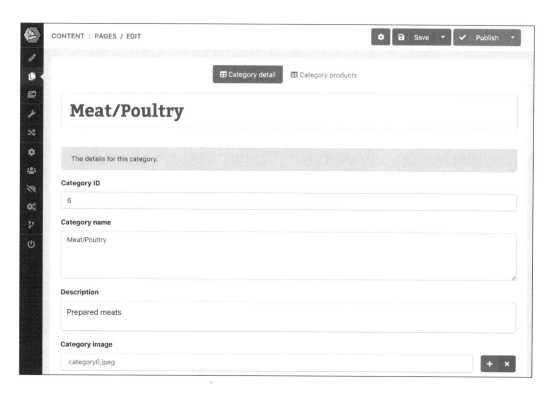

4. In the **Meat/Poultry Category products**, note that although there are six rows representing the six products, the rows do not show the product details.

More Information: You can write manager extensions to improve the view of a product in a row, but at the time of writing there is no documentation at the following link: `http://piranhacms.org/docs/manager-extensions`

5. Click the three dots icons in any row to expand or collapse that row, and note the admin could edit the data, or click the delete icon to completely remove that product, as shown in the following screenshot:

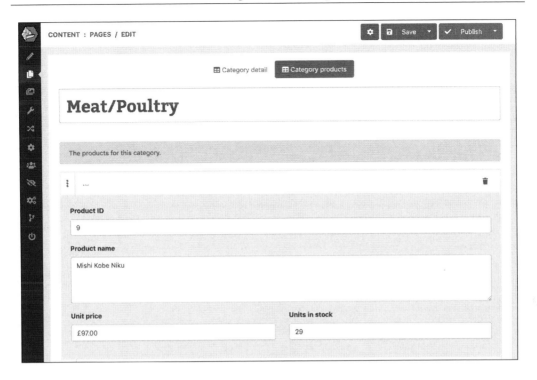

6. Close the browser.

Reviewing how Piranha stores content

Let's see how content is stored in the Piranha CMS database.

1. Start **SQLiteStudio**.
2. Navigate to **Database | Add a database** or press *Cmd + O*.
3. Click the yellow folder to browse for existing database file on the local computer.
4. Navigate to the `Code/PracticalApps/NorthwindCms` folder, select `piranha.blog.db`, and click **Open**.
5. In the **Database** dialog box, click **OK**.
6. Double-click the `piranha.blog` database to connect to it.
7. Expand **Tables**, right-click the `Piranha_Pages` table, and select **Edit the table**.

8. Click the **Data** tab and note the column values stored for each page, including **LastModified**, **MetaDescription**, **NavigationTitle**, and **PageTypeId**, as shown in the following screenshot:

9. Right-click the `Piranha_PageFields` table and select **Edit the table**.

10. Click the **Data** tab, and note the column values stored for each page including **CLRType**, **FieldId**, **RegionId**, and **Value**, as shown in the following screenshot:

11. Right-click the `piranha.blog` database and select **Disconnect from the database**.

12. Close **SQLiteStudio**.

Practicing and exploring

Test your knowledge and understanding by answering some questions, get some hands-on practice, and explore this chapter's topics with deeper research.

Exercise 17.1 – Test your knowledge

Answer the following questions:

1. What are some of the benefits of using a Content Management System to build a website compared to using ASP.NET Core alone?

2. What is the special relative URL path to access the Piranha CMS management user interface and what is the username and password configured by default?

3. What is a slug?

4. What is the difference between saving content and publishing content?

5. What are the three Piranha CMS content types and what are they used for?

6. What are the three Piranha CMS component types and what are they used for?

7. List three properties that a Page type inherits from its base classes and explain what they are used for.

8. How do you define a custom region for a content type?

9. How do you define routes for Piranha CMS?

10. How do you retrieve a page from the Piranha CMS database?

Exercise 17.2 – Practice defining a block type for rendering YouTube videos

Read the following support article and then define a block type with properties to control options like auto play with a display template that uses the correct HTML markup:

`https://support.google.com/youtube/answer/171780`

You should also refer to the official documentation for defining custom blocks. Note that for Piranha CMS 7.0 and later, to define a manager view to enable block editing, you must use Vue.js.

`http://piranhacms.org/docs/extensions/custom-blocks`

Exercise 17.3 – Explore topics

Use the following links to read more details about this chapter's topics:

- **Piranha CMS**: `http://piranhacms.org/`
- **Piranha CMS repository**: `https://github.com/PiranhaCMS/piranha.core`
- **Piranha questions on Stack Overflow**: `https://stackoverflow.com/questions/tagged/piranha-cms`

Summary

In this chapter, you learned how a web content management system can enable developers to rapidly build websites that non-technical users can use to create and manage their own content. As an example, you learned about a simple open source .NET Core-based CMS named Piranha, you reviewed some content types provided by its blog project template, and you defined custom regions and page types for working with content imported from the Northwind sample database.

In the next chapter, you will learn how to build and consume web services.

Chapter 18

Building and Consuming Web Services

This chapter is about learning how to build web services using ASP.NET Core Web API, and then consuming web services using HTTP clients that could be any other type of .NET app, including a website, a Windows desktop app, or a mobile app.

This chapter assumes knowledge and skills that you learned in *Chapter 11, Working with Databases Using Entity Framework Core* and *Chapter 16, Building Websites Using the Model-View-Controller Pattern*.

In this chapter, we will cover the following topics:

- Building web services using ASP.NET Core Web API
- Documenting and testing web services
- Consuming services using HTTP clients
- Implementing advanced features
- Understanding other communication technologies

Building web services using ASP.NET Core Web API

Before we build a modern web service, we need to cover some background to set the context for this chapter.

Understanding web service acronyms

Although HTTP was originally designed to request and respond with HTML and other resources for humans to look at, it is also good for building services.

Roy Fielding stated in his doctoral dissertation, describing the **Representational State Transfer (REST)** architectural style, that the HTTP standard would be great for building services because it defines the following:

- URIs to uniquely identify resources, like `https://localhost:5001/api/products/23`.

- Methods to perform common tasks on those resources, like `GET`, `POST`, `PUT`, and `DELETE`.

- The ability to negotiate the media type of content exchanged in requests and responses, such as XML and JSON. Content negotiation happens when the client specifies a request header like `Accept: application/xml,*/*;q=0.8`. The default response format used by ASP.NET Core Web API is JSON, which means one of the response headers would be `Content-Type: application/json; charset=utf-8`.

More Information: You can read more about media types at the following link: `https://en.wikipedia.org/wiki/Media_type`

Web services are services that use the HTTP communication standard, so they are sometimes called HTTP or RESTful services. HTTP or RESTful services are what this chapter is about.

Web services can also mean **Simple Object Access Protocol (SOAP)** services that implement some of the WS-* standards. Microsoft .NET Framework 3.0 and later includes a technology named **Windows Communication Foundation (WCF)**, which makes it easy for developers to create services including SOAP services that implement WS-* standards, but Microsoft decided it is legacy and has not ported it to modern .NET platforms.

More Information: You can read more about WS-* standards at the following link: `https://en.wikipedia.org/wiki/List_of_web_service_specifications`

Creating an ASP.NET Core Web API project

We will build a web service that provides a way to work with data in the Northwind database using ASP.NET Core so that the data can be used by any client application on any platform that can make HTTP requests and receive HTTP responses:

1. In the folder named `PracticalApps`, create a folder named `NorthwindService`.

2. In Visual Studio Code, open the `PracticalApps` workspace and add the `NorthwindService` folder.

3. Navigate to **Terminal | New Terminal** and select `NorthwindService`.

4. In **Terminal**, use the `webapi` template to create a new ASP.NET Core Web API project, as shown in the following command:

```
dotnet new webapi
```

5. In the `Controllers` folder, open `WeatherForecastController.cs`, as shown in the following code:

```csharp
using System;
using System.Collections.Generic;
using System.Linq;
using System.Threading.Tasks;
using Microsoft.AspNetCore.Mvc;
using Microsoft.Extensions.Logging;

namespace NorthwindService.Controllers
{
  [ApiController]
  [Route("[controller]")]
  public class WeatherForecastController : ControllerBase
  {
    private static readonly string[] Summaries = new[]
    {
      "Freezing", "Bracing", "Chilly", "Cool", "Mild",
      "Warm", "Balmy", "Hot", "Sweltering", "Scorching"
    };

    private readonly ILogger<WeatherForecastController> _logger;

    public WeatherForecastController(
      ILogger<WeatherForecastController> logger)
    {
      _logger = logger;
    }

    [HttpGet]
    public IEnumerable<WeatherForecast> Get()
    {
      var rng = new Random();
      return Enumerable.Range(1, 5).Select(
        index => new WeatherForecast
      {
        Date = DateTime.Now.AddDays(index),
        TemperatureC = rng.Next(-20, 55),
        Summary = Summaries[rng.Next(Summaries.Length)]
      })
      .ToArray();
    }
  }
}
```

While reviewing the preceding code, note the following:

- ° The `Controller` class inherits from `ControllerBase`. This is simpler than the `Controller` class used in MVC because it does not have methods like `View` to generate HTML responses using a Razor file.

- ° The `[Route]` attribute registers the `weatherforecast` relative URL for clients to use to make HTTP requests that will be handled by this controller. For example, an HTTP request for `https://localhost:5001/weatherforecast/` would be handled by this controller. Some developers like to prefix the controller name with `api/` which is a convention to differentiate between MVC and Web API in mixed projects. If you use `[controller]` as shown, it uses the characters before `Controller` in the class name, in this case `WeatherForecast`, or you can simply enter a different name without the brackets, for example `[Route("api/forecast")]`.

- ° The `[ApiController]` attribute was introduced with ASP.NET Core 2.1 and it enables REST-specific behavior for controllers, like automatic HTTP 400 responses for invalid models, as you will see later in this chapter.

- ° The `[HttpGet]` attribute registers the `Get` method in the `Controller` class to respond to HTTP GET requests, and its implementation uses a `Random` object to return an array of `WeatherForecast` values with random temperatures and summaries like `Bracing` or `Balmy` for the next five days of weather.

6. Add a second `Get` method to have an integer parameter named `days`, cut and paste the original `Get` method implementation code statements into the new `Get` method and modify it to create an `IEnumerable` of `int` values up to the number of days requested, and modify the original `Get` method to call the new `Get` method and pass the value `5`, as shown in the following code:

```
// GET /weatherforecast
[HttpGet]
public IEnumerable<WeatherForecast> Get()
{
   return Get(5);
}

// GET /weatherforecast/7
```

```
[HttpGet("{days:int}")]
public IEnumerable<WeatherForecast> Get(int days)
{
  var rng = new Random();
  return Enumerable.Range(1, days)
    .Select(index => new WeatherForecast
  {
    Date = DateTime.Now.AddDays(index),
    TemperatureC = rng.Next(-20, 55),
    Summary = Summaries[rng.Next(Summaries.Length)]
  })
    .ToArray();
}
```

Note the format pattern that constrains the days parameter to int values in the [HttpGet] attribute.

 More Information: You can read more about route constraints at the following link: https://docs.microsoft.com/en-us/aspnet/core/fundamentals/routing?view=aspnetcore-3.0#route-constraint-reference

Reviewing the web service's functionality

Now, we will test the web service's functionality:

1. In **Terminal**, start the website by entering dotnet run.

2. Start Chrome, navigate to https:/localhost:5001/, and note you will get a 404 status code response because we have not enabled static files and there is not an index.html, nor is there an MVC controller with a route configured, either. Remember that this project is not designed for a human to view and interact with.

3. In Chrome, show the **Developer tools**, navigate to https:/localhost:5001/weatherforecast, and note the Web API service should return a JSON document with five random weather forecast objects in an array, as shown in the following screenshot:

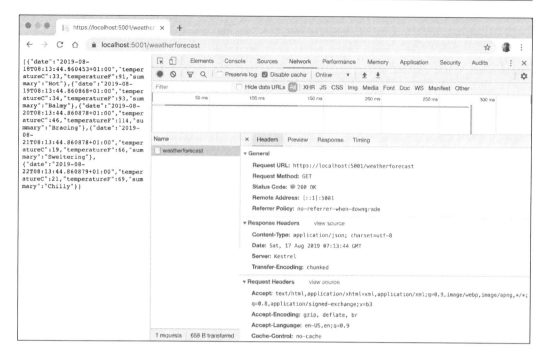

4. Close Developer Tools.

5. Navigate to `https:/localhost:5001/weatherforecast/14`, and note the response when requesting a two-week weather forecast, as shown in the following screenshot:

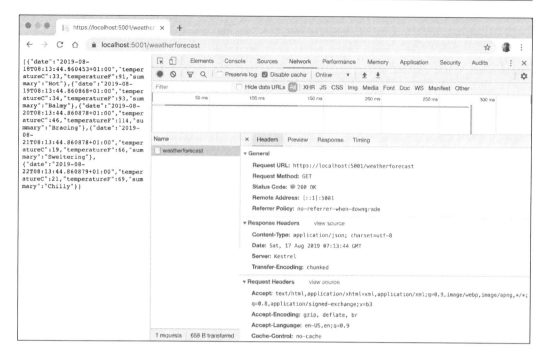

6. Close Chrome.

7. In **Terminal**, press *Ctrl + C* to stop the console application and shut down the Kestrel web server that is hosting your ASP.NET Core Web API service.

Creating a web service for the Northwind database

Unlike MVC controllers, Web API controllers do not call Razor views to return HTML responses for humans to see in browsers. Instead, they use **content negotiation** with the client application that made the HTTP request to return data in formats such as XML, JSON, or X-WWW-FORM-URLENCODED in their HTTP response.

The client application must then deserialize the data from the negotiated format. The most commonly used format for modern web services is **JavaScript Object Notation (JSON)** because it is compact and works natively with JavaScript in a browser when building **Single Page Applications (SPA)** with client-side technologies like Angular, React, and Vue.

We will reference the Entity Framework Core entity data model for the Northwind database that you created in *Chapter 15, Building Websites Using ASP.NET Core Razor Pages*:

1. In the `NorthwindService` project, open `NorthwindService.csproj`.

2. Add a project reference to `NorthwindContextLib`, as shown in the following markup:

    ```
    <ItemGroup>
      <ProjectReference Include=
        "..\NorthwindContextLib\NorthwindContextLib.csproj" />
    </ItemGroup>
    ```

3. In **Terminal**, enter the following command and ensure that the project builds:

    ```
    dotnet build
    ```

4. Open `Startup.cs` and modify it to import the `System.IO`, `Microsoft.EntityFrameworkCore`, and `Packt.Shared` namespaces, and statically import the `System.Console` class.

5. Add statements to the `ConfigureServices` method, before the call to `AddControllers`, to configure the Northwind data context, as shown in the following code:

    ```
    string databasePath = Path.Combine("..", "Northwind.db");

    services.AddDbContext<Northwind>(options =>
      options.UseSqlite($"Data Source={databasePath}"));
    ```

6. Add statements to write the names and supported media types of the default output formatters to the console, and then add XML serializer formatters and set the compatibility to ASP.NET Core 3.0 after the method call to add `controller` support, as shown in the following code:

```
services.AddControllers(options =>
  {
    WriteLine("Default output formatters:");
    foreach(IOutputFormatter formatter in options.
OutputFormatters)
    {
      var mediaFormatter = formatter as OutputFormatter;

      if (mediaFormatter == null)
      {
        WriteLine($"  {formatter.GetType().Name}");
      }
      else // OutputFormatter class has SupportedMediaTypes
      {
        WriteLine("  {0}, Media types: {1}",
          arg0: mediaFormatter.GetType().Name,
          arg1: string.Join(", ",
            mediaFormatter.SupportedMediaTypes));
      }
    }
  })
  .AddXmlDataContractSerializerFormatters()
  .AddXmlSerializerFormatters()
  .SetCompatibilityVersion(CompatibilityVersion.Version_3_0);
```

More Information: You can read more about the benefits of setting version compatibility at the following link: `https://docs.microsoft.com/en-us/aspnet/core/mvc/compatibility-version?view=aspnetcore-3.0`

7. Start the web service and note that there are four default output formatters, including ones that convert `null` values into `204 No Content` and ones to support responses that are plain text and JSON, as shown in the following output:

```
Default output formatters:
  HttpNoContentOutputFormatter
  StringOutputFormatter, Media types: text/plain
  StreamOutputFormatter
  SystemTextJsonOutputFormatter, Media types: application/json,
text/json, application/*+json
```

8. Stop the web service.

Creating data repositories for entities

Defining and implementing a data repository to provide CRUD operations is good practice. The CRUD acronym includes the following operations:

- C for Create
- R for Retrieve (or Read)
- U for Update
- D for Delete

We will create a data repository for the `Customers` table in Northwind. There are only 91 customers in this table, so we will store a copy of the whole table in memory to improve scalability and performance when reading customer records. In a real web service, you should use a distributed cache like **Redis**, an open source data structure store, that can be used as a high-performance, high-availability database, cache, or message broker.

 More Information: You can read more about Redis at the following link: `https://redis.io`

We will follow modern good practice and make the repository API asynchronous. It will be instantiated by a `Controller` class using constructor parameter injection, so a new instance is created to handle every HTTP request:

1. In the `NorthwindService` project, create a `Repositories` folder.

2. Add two class files to the `Repositories` folder named `ICustomerRepository.cs` and `CustomerRepository.cs`.

3. The `ICustomerRepository` interface will define five methods, as shown in the following code:

```
using Packt.Shared;
using System.Collections.Generic;
using System.Threading.Tasks;

namespace NorthwindService.Repositories
{
  public interface ICustomerRepository
  {
    Task<Customer> CreateAsync(Customer c);
    Task<IEnumerable<Customer>> RetrieveAllAsync();
    Task<Customer> RetrieveAsync(string id);
    Task<Customer> UpdateAsync(string id, Customer c);
    Task<bool?> DeleteAsync(string id);
```

```
    }
}
```

4. The `CustomerRepository` class will implement the five methods, as shown in the following code:

```
using Microsoft.EntityFrameworkCore.ChangeTracking;
using Packt.Shared;
using System.Collections.Generic;
using System.Collections.Concurrent;
using System.Linq;
using System.Threading.Tasks;

namespace NorthwindService.Repositories
{
  public class CustomerRepository : ICustomerRepository
  {
    // use a static thread-safe dictionary field to cache the
customers
    private static ConcurrentDictionary
      <string, Customer> customersCache;

    // use an instance data context field because it should not be
    // cached due to their internal caching
    private Northwind db;

    public CustomerRepository(Northwind db)
    {
      this.db = db;

      // pre-load customers from database as a normal
      // Dictionary with CustomerID as the key,
      // then convert to a thread-safe ConcurrentDictionary
      if (customersCache == null)
      {
        customersCache = new ConcurrentDictionary
          <string, Customer>(
          db.Customers.ToDictionary(c => c.CustomerID));
      }
    }

    public async Task<Customer> CreateAsync(Customer c)
    {
      // normalize CustomerID into uppercase
      c.CustomerID = c.CustomerID.ToUpper();

      // add to database using EF Core
      EntityEntry<Customer> added = await db.Customers.
AddAsync(c);
      int affected = await db.SaveChangesAsync();
```

```
      if (affected == 1)
      {
        // if the customer is new, add it to cache, else
        // call UpdateCache method
        return customersCache.AddOrUpdate(c.CustomerID, c,
UpdateCache);
      }
      else
      {
        return null;
      }
    }

    public Task<IEnumerable<Customer>> RetrieveAllAsync()
    {
      // for performance, get from cache
      return Task.Run<IEnumerable<Customer>>(
        () => customersCache.Values);
    }

    public Task<Customer> RetrieveAsync(string id)
    {
      return Task.Run(() =>
      {
        // for performance, get from cache
        id = id.ToUpper();
        Customer c;
        customersCache.TryGetValue(id, out c);
        return c;
      });
    }

    private Customer UpdateCache(string id, Customer c)
    {
      Customer old;
      if (customersCache.TryGetValue(id, out old))
      {
        if (customersCache.TryUpdate(id, c, old))
        {
          return c;
        }
      }
      return null;
    }

    public async Task<Customer> UpdateAsync(string id, Customer c)
    {
      // normalize customer ID
      id = id.ToUpper();
      c.CustomerID = c.CustomerID.ToUpper();
```

```
                // update in database
                db.Customers.Update(c);
                int affected = await db.SaveChangesAsync();

                if (affected == 1)
                {
                  // update in cache
                  return UpdateCache(id, c);
                }
                return null;
            }

            public async Task<bool?> DeleteAsync(string id)
            {
              id = id.ToUpper();

              // remove from database
              Customer c = db.Customers.Find(id);
              db.Customers.Remove(c);
              int affected = await db.SaveChangesAsync();

              if (affected == 1)
              {
                // remove from cache
                return customersCache.TryRemove(id, out c);
              }
              else
              {
                return null;
              }
            }
          }
        }
```

Implementing a Web API controller

There are some useful attributes and methods for implementing a controller that returns data instead of HTML.

With MVC controllers, a route like /home/index/ tells us the Controller class name and the action method name, for example, the HomeController class and the Index action method.

With Web API controllers, a route like /weatherforecast/ only tells uses the Controller class name, for example, WeatherForecastController. To determine the action method name to execute, we must map HTTP methods like GET and POST to methods in the Controller class.

You should decorate `Controller` methods with the following attributes to indicate the HTTP method to respond to:

- `[HttpGet]`, `[HttpHead]`: These action methods respond to HTTP GET or HEAD requests to retrieve a resource and return either the resource and its response headers or just the headers.

- `[HttpPost]`: This action method responds to HTTP POST requests to create a new resource.

- `[HttpPut]`, `[HttpPatch]`: These action methods respond to HTTP PUT or PATCH requests to update an existing resource either by replacing it or updating some of its properties.

- `[HttpDelete]`: This action method responds to HTTP DELETE requests to remove a resource.

- `[HttpOptions]`: This action method responds to HTTP OPTIONS requests.

More Information: You can read more about the HTTP OPTIONS method and other HTTP methods at the following link: https://developer.mozilla.org/en-US/docs/Web/HTTP/Methods/OPTIONS

An action method can return .NET types like a single `string` value, complex objects defined by a `class` or `struct`, or collections of complex objects, and ASP.NET Core Web API will automatically serialize them into the requested data format set in the HTTP request `Accept` header, for example, JSON, if a suitable serializer has been registered.

For more control over the response, there are helper methods that return an `ActionResult` wrapper around the .NET type.

Declare the action method's return type to be `IActionResult` if it could return different return types based on inputs or other variables. Declare the action method's return type to be `ActionResult<T>` if it will only return a single type but with different status codes.

Good Practice: Decorate action methods with the `[ProducesResponseType]` attribute to indicate all the known types and HTTP status codes that the client should expect in a response. This information can then be publicly exposed to document how a client should interact with your web service. Think of it as part of your formal documentation. Later in this chapter you will learn how you can install a code analyzer to give you warnings when you do not decorate your action methods like this.

For example, an action method that gets a product based on an `id` parameter would be decorated with three attributes; one to indicate that it responds to GET requests and has an `id` parameter, and two to indicate what happens when it succeeds and when the client has supplied an invalid product ID, as shown in the following code:

```
[HttpGet("{id}")]
[ProducesResponseType(200, Type = typeof(Product))]
[ProducesResponseType(404)]
public IActionResult Get(string id)
```

The `ControllerBase` class has methods to make it easy to return different responses:

- `Ok`: Return an HTTP 200 status code with a resource converted to the client's preferred format like JSON or XML. Commonly used in response to an HTTP GET request.

- `CreatedAtRoute`: Return an HTTP 201 status code with the path to the new resource. Commonly used in response to a POST request to create a resource that can be performed quickly.

- `Accepted`: Return an HTTP 202 status code to indicate the request is being processed but has not completed. Commonly used in response to a request that triggers a background process that takes a long time to complete.

- `NoContentResult`: Return an HTTP 204 status code. Commonly used in response to a PUT request to update an existing resource and the response does not need to contain the updated resource.

- `BadRequest`: Return an HTTP 400 status code with optional message `string`.

- `NotFound`: Return an HTTP 404 status code with an automatically populated `ProblemDetails` body (requires a compatibility version of 2.2 or later).

Configuring the customers repository and Web API controller

Now you will configure the repository so that it can be called from within a Web API controller.

You will register a scoped dependency service implementation for the repository when the web service starts up and then use constructor parameter injection to get it in a new Web API controller for working with customers.

More Information: You can read more about dependency injection at the following link: https://docs.microsoft.com/en-us/aspnet/core/fundamentals/dependency-injection?view=aspnetcore-3.0

To show an example of differentiating between MVC and Web API controllers using routes, we will use the common /api URL prefix convention for the customers controller:

1. Open Startup.cs and import the NorthwindService.Repositories namespace.

2. Add the following statement to the bottom of the ConfigureServices method, which will register the CustomerRepository for use at runtime, as shown in the following code:

   ```
   services.AddScoped<ICustomerRepository, CustomerRepository>();
   ```

3. In the Controllers folder, add a new class named CustomersController.cs.

4. In the CustomersController class, add statements to define a Web API Controller class to work with customers, as shown in the following code:

   ```
   using Microsoft.AspNetCore.Mvc;
   using Packt.Shared;
   using NorthwindService.Repositories;
   using System.Collections.Generic;
   using System.Linq;
   using System.Threading.Tasks;

   namespace NorthwindService.Controllers
   {
     // base address: api/customers
     [Route("api/[controller]")]
     [ApiController]
     public class CustomersController : ControllerBase
     {
       private ICustomerRepository repo;

       // constructor injects repository registered in Startup
       public CustomersController(ICustomerRepository repo)
       {
         this.repo = repo;
       }

       // GET: api/customers
       // GET: api/customers/?country=[country]
       // this will always return a list of customers even if its
   empty
       [HttpGet]
       [ProducesResponseType(200,
         Type = typeof(IEnumerable<Customer>))]
       public async Task<IEnumerable<Customer>> GetCustomers(
         string country)
   ```

```
    {
      if (string.IsNullOrWhiteSpace(country))
      {
        return await repo.RetrieveAllAsync();
      }
      else
      {
        return (await repo.RetrieveAllAsync())
          .Where(customer => customer.Country == country);
      }
    }

    // GET: api/customers/[id]
    [HttpGet("{id}", Name = nameof(GetCustomer))] // named route
    [ProducesResponseType(200, Type = typeof(Customer))]
    [ProducesResponseType(404)]
    public async Task<IActionResult> GetCustomer(string id)
    {
      Customer c = await repo.RetrieveAsync(id);
      if (c == null)
      {
        return NotFound(); // 404 Resource not found
      }
      return Ok(c); // 200 OK with customer in body
    }

    // POST: api/customers
    // BODY: Customer (JSON, XML)
    [HttpPost]
    [ProducesResponseType(201, Type = typeof(Customer))]
    [ProducesResponseType(400)]
    public async Task<IActionResult> Create([FromBody] Customer c)
    {
      if (c == null)
      {
        return BadRequest(); // 400 Bad request
      }

      if (!ModelState.IsValid)
      {
        return BadRequest(ModelState); // 400 Bad request
      }

      Customer added = await repo.CreateAsync(c);

      return CreatedAtRoute( // 201 Created
        routeName: nameof(GetCustomer),
        routeValues: new { id = added.CustomerID.ToLower() },
        value: added);
    }
```

```
// PUT: api/customers/[id]
// BODY: Customer (JSON, XML)
[HttpPut("{id}")]
[ProducesResponseType(204)]
[ProducesResponseType(400)]
[ProducesResponseType(404)]
public async Task<IActionResult> Update(
  string id, [FromBody] Customer c)
{
  id = id.ToUpper();
  c.CustomerID = c.CustomerID.ToUpper();

  if (c == null || c.CustomerID != id)
  {
    return BadRequest(); // 400 Bad request
  }

  if (!ModelState.IsValid)
  {
    return BadRequest(ModelState); // 400 Bad request
  }

  var existing = await repo.RetrieveAsync(id);

  if (existing == null)
  {
    return NotFound(); // 404 Resource not found
  }

  await repo.UpdateAsync(id, c);

  return new NoContentResult(); // 204 No content
}

// DELETE: api/customers/[id]
[HttpDelete("{id}")]
[ProducesResponseType(204)]
[ProducesResponseType(400)]
[ProducesResponseType(404)]
public async Task<IActionResult> Delete(string id)
{
  var existing = await repo.RetrieveAsync(id);
  if (existing == null)
  {
    return NotFound(); // 404 Resource not found
  }

  bool? deleted = await repo.DeleteAsync(id);
```

```
                  if (deleted.HasValue && deleted.Value) // short circuit AND
                  {
                    return new NoContentResult(); // 204 No content
                  }
                  else
                  {
                    return BadRequest( // 400 Bad request
                      $"Customer {id} was found but failed to delete.");
                  }
                }
              }
            }
```

While reviewing the `Controller` class, note the following:

- The `Controller` class registers a route that starts with `api/` and includes the name of the controller, that is, `api/customers`.

- The constructor uses dependency injection to get the registered repository for working with customers.

- There are five methods to perform CRUD operations on customers — two `GET` methods (all customers or one customer), `POST` (create), `PUT` (update), and `DELETE`.

- `GetCustomers` can have a `string` parameter passed with a country name. If it is missing, all customers are returned. If it is present, it is used to filter customers by country.

- `GetCustomer` has a route explicitly named `GetCustomer` so that it can be used to generate a URL after inserting a new customer.

- `Create` decorates the `customer` parameter with `[FromBody]` to tell the model binder to populate it with values from the body of the HTTP `POST` request.

- `Create` returns a response that uses the `GetCustomer` route so that the client knows how to get the newly created resource in the future. We are matching up to methods to create and then get a customer.

- `Create` and `Update` both check the model state of the customer passed in the body of the HTTP request and return a `400 Bad Request` containing details of the model validation errors if it is not valid.

When an HTTP request is received by the service, then it will create an instance of the `Controller` class, call the appropriate action method, return the response in the format preferred by the client, and release the resources used by the controller, including the repository and its data context.

Specifying problem details

A feature added in ASP.NET Core 2.1 and later is an implementation of a web standard for specifying problem details.

More Information: You can read more about the proposed standard for Problem Details for HTTP APIs at the following link: `https://tools.ietf.org/html/rfc7807`

In controllers attributed with `[ApiController]` in a project with ASP.NET Core 2.2 or later compatibility enabled, action methods that return `IActionResult` that return a client status code, that is, `4xx`, will automatically include a serialized instance of the `ProblemDetails` class in the response body.

More Information: You can read more about implementing problem details at the following link: `https://docs. microsoft.com/en-us/dotnet/api/microsoft. aspnetcore.mvc.problemdetails`

If you want to take control, then you can create a `ProblemDetails` instance yourself and include additional information.

Let's simulate a bad request that needs custom data returned to the client:

1. At the top of the `CustomersController` class, import the `Microsoft.AspNetCore.Http` namespace.

2. At the top of the `Delete` method, add statements to check if the `id` matches the `string` value `"bad"`, and if so, then return a custom problem details object, as shown in the following example code:

```
if (id == "bad")
{
  var problemDetails = new ProblemDetails
  {
    Status = StatusCodes.Status400BadRequest,
    Type = "https://localhost:5001/customers/failed-to-delete",
    Title = $"Customer ID {id} found but failed to delete.",
    Detail = "More details like Company Name, Country and so on.",
    Instance = HttpContext.Request.Path
  };
  return BadRequest(problemDetails); // 400 Bad request
}
```

Documenting and testing web services

You can easily test a web service by making HTTP GET requests, using a browser. To test other HTTP methods, we need a more advanced tool.

Testing GET requests using a browser

You will use Chrome to test the three implementations of a GET request: for all customers, for customers in a specified country, and for a single customer using their unique customer ID:

1. In **Terminal**, start the NorthwindService Web API web service by entering the following command: dotnet run

2. In Chrome, navigate to https://localhost:5001/api/customers and note the JSON document returned, containing all the 91 customers in the Northwind database, as shown in the following screenshot:

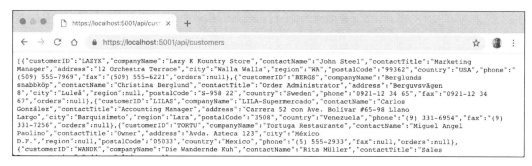

3. Navigate to https://localhost:5001/api/customers/?country=Germany and note the JSON document returned, containing only the customers in Germany, as shown in the following screenshot:

[{"customerID":"WANDK","companyName":"Die Wandernde Kuh","contactName":"Rita Müller","contactTitle":"Sales Representative","address":"Adenauerallee 900","city":"Stuttgart","region":null,"postalCode":"70563","country":"Germany","phone":"0711-020361","fax":"0711-035428","orders":null},{"customerID":"MORGK","companyName":"Morgenstern Gesundkost","contactName":"Alexander Feuer","contactTitle":"Marketing Assistant","address":"Heerstr. 22","city":"Leipzig","region":null,"postalCode":"04179","country":"Germany","phone":"0342-023176","fax":null,"orders":null},{"customerID":"BLAUS","companyName":"Blauer See Delikatessen","contactName":"Hanna Moos","contactTitle":"Sales Representative","address":"Forsterstr. 57","city":"Mannheim","region":null,"postalCode":"68306","country":"Germany","phone":"0621-08460","fax":"0621-08924","orders":null},{"customerID":"KOENE","companyName":"Königlich Essen","contactName":"Philip Cramer","contactTitle":"Sales Associate","address":"Maubelstr. 90","city":"Brandenburg","region":null,"postalCode":"14776","country":"Germany","phone":"0555-

If you get an empty array returned, then make sure you have entered the country name using the correct casing because the database query is case-sensitive.

4. Navigate to `https://localhost:5001/api/customers/alfki` and note the JSON document returned containing only the customer named **Alfreds Futterkiste**, as shown in the following screenshot:

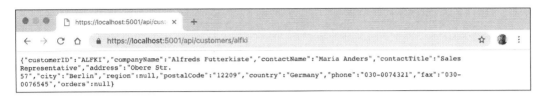

We do not need to worry about casing for the customer `id` value because inside the `Controller` class we normalized the `string` value to uppercase in code.

But how can we test the other HTTP methods such as POST, PUT, and DELETE? And how can we document our web service so it's easy for anyone to understand how to interact with it?

To solve the first problem, we can install a Visual Studio Code extension named **REST Client**. To solve the second, we can enable **Swagger**, the world's most popular technology for documenting and testing HTTP APIs. But first let's see what is possible with the Visual Studio Code extension.

Testing HTTP requests with REST Client extension

REST Client allows you to send an HTTP request and view the response in Visual Studio Code directly:

More Information: You can read more about how you can use REST Client at the following link: `https://github.com/Huachao/vscode-restclient/blob/master/README.md`

1. If you have not already installed REST Client by Huachao Mao (`humao.rest-client`), then install it now.

2. In Visual Studio Code, open the `NorthwindService` project.

3. If the web service is not already running, then start it by entering the following command in **Terminal**: `dotnet run`.

4. In the `NorthwindService` folder, create a `RestClientTests` folder.

5. In the `RestClientTests` folder, create a file named `get-customers.http`, and modify its contents to contain an HTTP GET request to retrieve all customers, as shown in the following code:

```
GET https://localhost:5001/api/customers/ HTTP/1.1
```

6. Navigate to **View | Command Palette**, enter `rest client`, select the command **Rest Client: Send Request**, and press *Enter*, as shown in the following screenshot:

7. Note the **Response** is shown in a new tabbed window pane vertically and that you can rearrange the open tabs to a horizontal layout by dragging and dropping the tab.

8. Enter more HTTP GET requests, each separated by three hash symbols, to test getting customers in various countries and getting a single customer using their ID, as shown in the following code:

```
###
GET https://localhost:5001/api/customers/?country=Germany HTTP/1.1
###
GET https://localhost:5001/api/customers/?country=USA HTTP/1.1
Accept: application/xml
###
GET https://localhost:5001/api/customers/ALFKI HTTP/1.1
```

9. Click inside each statement and press *Ctrl* or *Cmd* + *Alt* + *R* or click the **Send Request** link above each request to send it, as shown in the following screenshot:

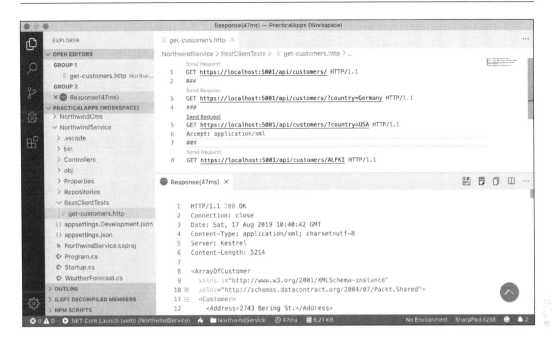

10. Create a file named `create-customer.http` and modify its contents to define a `POST` request to create a new customer, as shown in the following code:

```
POST https://localhost:5001/api/customers/ HTTP/1.1
Content-Type: application/json
Content-Length: 287

{
  "customerID": "ABCXY",
  "companyName": "ABC Corp",
  "contactName": "John Smith",
  "contactTitle": "Sir",
  "address": "Main Street",
  "city": "New York",
  "region": "NY",
  "postalCode": "90210",
  "country": "USA",
  "phone": "(123) 555-1234",
  "fax": null,
  "orders": null
}
```

Note that REST Client will provide IntelliSense while you type common HTTP requests.

Due to different line endings in different operating systems, the value for the Content-Length header will be different on Windows and macOS or Linux. If the value is wrong, then the request will fail.

11. To discover the correct content length, select the body of the request and then look in the status bar for the number of characters, as shown in the following screenshot:

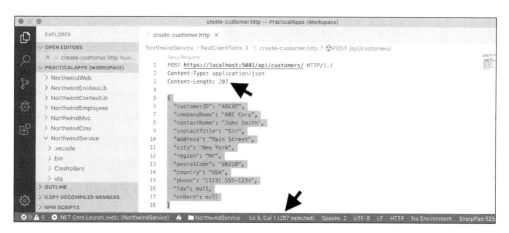

12. Send the request and note the response is 201 Created and includes the newly created customer in the response body, as shown in the following screenshot:

More Information: Learn more details about HTTP POST requests at the following link: https://developer.mozilla.org/en-US/docs/Web/HTTP/Methods/POST

I will leave as an optional challenge to the reader the task of creating REST Client files to test updating a customer (using PUT) and deleting a customer (using DELETE).

Now that we've seen a quick and easy way to test our service, which also happens to be a great way to learn HTTP, what about external developers? We want it to be as easy as possible for them to learn and then call our service. For that purpose, we will use Swagger.

Enabling Swagger

The most important part of Swagger is the **OpenAPI Specification**, which defines a REST-style contract for your API, detailing all of its resources and operations in a human-and machine-readable format for easy development, discovery, and integration.

For us, another useful feature is **Swagger UI**, because it automatically generates documentation for your API with built-in visual testing capabilities.

More Information: You can read more about Swagger at the following link: https://swagger.io

Let's enable Swagger for our web service using the Swashbuckle package:

1. Open NorthwindService.csproj and add a package reference for Swashbuckle.AspNetCore, which at the time of writing was still a release candidate but will likely be fully released as 5.0.0 soon after publishing, as shown highlighted in the following markup:

```
<ItemGroup>
  <ProjectReference Include=
    "..\NorthwindContextLib\NorthwindContextLib.csproj" />
  <PackageReference Include="Swashbuckle.AspNetCore"
                    Version="5.0.0-rc3" />
</ItemGroup>
```

2. In **Terminal**, restore packages and compile your project, as shown in the following command:

```
dotnet build
```

3. Open `Startup.cs` and import Swashbuckle's `Swagger` and `SwaggerUI` namespaces and Microsoft's OpenAPI models namespace, as shown in the following code:

```
using Swashbuckle.AspNetCore.Swagger;
using Swashbuckle.AspNetCore.SwaggerUI;
using Microsoft.OpenApi.Models;
```

4. In the `ConfigureServices` method, add a statement to add Swagger support including documentation for the Northwind service, indicating that this is the first version of your service, as shown in the following code:

```
// Register the Swagger generator and define a Swagger document
// for Northwind service
services.AddSwaggerGen(options =>
{
  options.SwaggerDoc(name: "v1", info: new OpenApiInfo
    { Title = "Northwind Service API", Version = "v1" });
});
```

More Information: You can read about how Swagger can support multiple versions of an API at the following link: https://stackoverflow.com/questions/30789045/ leverage-multipleapiversions-in-swagger-with- attribute-versioning/30789944

5. In the `Configure` method, add statements to use Swagger and Swagger UI, define an endpoint for the OpenAPI specification JSON document, and list the HTTP methods supported by our web service, as shown in the following code:

```
app.UseSwagger();

app.UseSwaggerUI(options =>
{
  options.SwaggerEndpoint("/swagger/v1/swagger.json",
    "Northwind Service API Version 1");

  options.SupportedSubmitMethods(new[] {
    SubmitMethod.Get, SubmitMethod.Post,
    SubmitMethod.Put, SubmitMethod.Delete });
});
```

Testing requests with Swagger UI

You are now ready to test an HTTP request using Swagger:

1. Start the NorthwindService ASP.NET Web API service.

2. In Chrome, navigate to https://localhost:5001/swagger/ and note that both the **Customers** and **WeatherForecast** Web API controllers have been discovered and documented, as well as **Schemas** used by the API.

3. Click **GET /api/Customers/{id}** to expand that endpoint and note the required parameter for the id of a customer, as shown in the following screenshot:

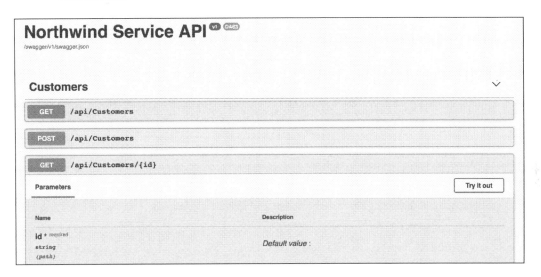

4. Click **Try it out**, enter an ID of ALFKI, and then click the wide blue **Execute** button, as shown in the following screenshot:

5. Scroll down and note the **Request URL**, **Server response** with **Code**, and **Details** including **Response body** and **Response headers**, as shown in the following screenshot:

6. Scroll back up to the top of the page, click `POST /api/Customers` to expand that section and then click **Try it out**.

7. Click inside the **Edit Value** box, and modify the JSON to define a new customer, as shown in the following JSON:

```
{
    "customerID": "SUPER",
    "companyName": "Super Company",
    "contactName": "Rasmus Ibensen",
    "contactTitle": "Sales Leader",
    "address": "Rotterslef 23",
    "city": "Billund",
    "region": null,
    "postalCode": "4371",
    "country": "Denmark",
    "phone": "31 21 43 21",
    "fax": "31 21 43 22",
    "orders": null
}
```

8. Click **Execute**, and note the **Request URL**, **Server response** with **Code**, and **Details** including **Response body** and **Response headers**, as shown in the following screenshot:

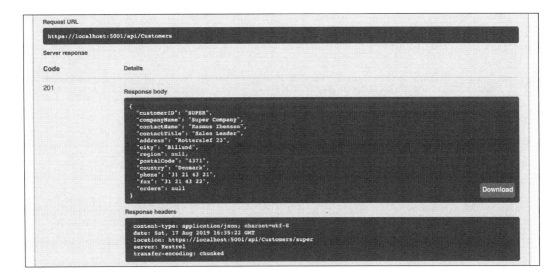

```
Request URL

https://localhost:5001/api/Customers

Server response

Code        Details

201         Response body
            {
              "customerID": "SUPER",
              "companyName": "Super Company",
              "contactName": "Rasmus Ibensen",
              "contactTitle": "Sales Leader",
              "address": "Rotterslef 23",
              "city": "Billund",
              "region": null,
              "postalCode": "4371",
              "country": "Denmark",
              "phone": "31 21 43 21",
              "fax": "31 21 43 22",
              "orders": null
            }

            Response headers
            content-type: application/json; charset=utf-8
            date: Sat, 17 Aug 2019 16:35:22 GMT
            location: https://localhost:5001/api/Customers/super
            server: Kestrel
            transfer-encoding: chunked
```

A response code of `201` means the customer was successfully created.

9. Scroll back up to the top of the page, click `GET /api/Customers`, click **Try it out**, enter `Denmark` for the country parameter, and click **Execute**, to confirm that the new customer was added to the database, as shown in the following screenshot:

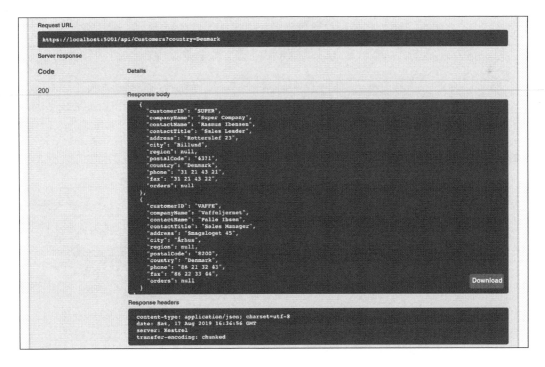

```
Request URL

https://localhost:5001/api/Customers?country=Denmark

Server response

Code        Details

200         Response body
            {
              "customerID": "SUPER",
              "companyName": "Super Company",
              "contactName": "Rasmus Ibensen",
              "contactTitle": "Sales Leader",
              "address": "Rotterslef 23",
              "city": "Billund",
              "region": null,
              "postalCode": "4371",
              "country": "Denmark",
              "phone": "31 21 43 21",
              "fax": "31 21 43 22",
              "orders": null
            },
            {
              "customerID": "VAFFE",
              "companyName": "Vaffeljernet",
              "contactName": "Palle Ibsen",
              "contactTitle": "Sales Manager",
              "address": "Smagsloget 45",
              "city": "Århus",
              "region": null,
              "postalCode": "8200",
              "country": "Denmark",
              "phone": "86 21 32 43",
              "fax": "86 22 33 44",
              "orders": null
            }

            Response headers
            content-type: application/json; charset=utf-8
            date: Sat, 17 Aug 2019 16:36:56 GMT
            server: Kestrel
            transfer-encoding: chunked
```

10. Click `DELETE /api/Customers/{id}`, click **Try it out**, enter `super` for the `id`, click **Execute**, and note that the server response **Code** is `204`, indicating that it was successfully deleted, as shown in the following screenshot:

11. Click **Execute** again, and note that the server response **Code** is `404`, indicating that the customer does not exist anymore, and the response body contains a problem details JSON document, as shown in the following screenshot:

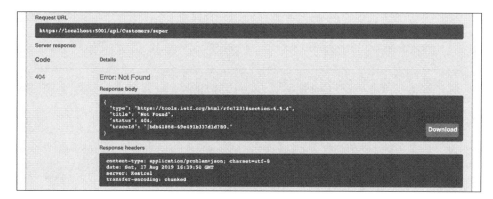

12. Enter `bad`, click **Execute** again, and note that the server response **Code** is `400`, indicating that the customer did exist but failed to delete (in this case, because the web service is simulating this error), and the response body contains a custom problem details JSON document, as shown in the following screenshot:

13. Use the GET methods to confirm that the new customer has been deleted from the database (there were originally only two customers in Denmark).

    I will leave testing updates to an existing customer by using PUT to the reader.

14. Close Chrome.

15. In **Terminal**, press *Ctrl + C* to stop the console application and shut down the Kestrel web server that is hosting your service.

You are now ready to build applications that consume your web service.

Consuming services using HTTP clients

Now that we have built and tested our Northwind service, we will learn how to call it from any .NET Core app using the HttpClient class and its new factory.

Understanding HttpClient

The easiest way to consume a web service is to use the HttpClient class. However, many people use it wrongly because it implements IDisposable and Microsoft's own documentation shows poor usage of it.

Usually when a type implements IDisposable you should create it inside a using statement to ensure that it is disposed as soon as possible. HttpClient is different because it is shared, reentrant, and partially thread safe.

More Information: It is the BaseAddress and DefaultRequestHeaders properties that you should treat with caution with multiple threads. You can read more details and recommendations at the following link: https://medium.com/@nuno.caneco/c-httpclient-should-not-be-disposed-or-should-it-45d2a8f568bc

The problem has to do with how the underlying network sockets have to be managed. The bottom line is that you should use a single instance of it for each HTTP endpoint that you consume during the life of your application.

This will allow each HttpClient instance to have defaults set that are appropriate for the endpoint it works with, while managing the underlying network sockets efficiently.

More Information: You're using `HttpClient` wrong and it is destabilizing your software: `https://aspnetmonsters.com/2016/08/2016-08-27-httpclientwrong/`

Configuring HTTP clients using HttpClientFactory

Microsoft is aware of the issue, and in .NET Core 2.1 they introduced `HttpClientFactory` to encourage best practice; that is the technique we will use.

More Information: You can read more about how to initiate HTTP requests at the following link: `https://docs.microsoft.com/en-us/aspnet/core/fundamentals/http-requests`

In the following example, we will use the Northwind MVC website as a client to the Northwind Web API service. Since both need to be hosted in a web server simultaneously, we first need to configure them to use different port numbers, as shown in the following list:

- Northwind Web API service will continue to listen on port 5001 using HTTPS.

- Northwind MVC will listen on ports 5000 using HTTP and 5002 using HTTPS.

Let's configure those ports.

1. In `NorthwindMvc`, open `Program.cs`, and in the `CreateHostBuilder` method, add an extension method call to `UseUrls` to specify port number `5000` for HTTP and port number `5002` for HTTPS, as shown highlighted in the following code:

```
public static IHostBuilder CreateHostBuilder(string[] args) =>
  Host.CreateDefaultBuilder(args)
    .ConfigureWebHostDefaults(webBuilder =>
    {
      webBuilder.UseStartup<Startup>();
      webBuilder.UseUrls(
        "http://localhost:5000",
        "https://localhost:5002"
      );
    });
```

2. Open `Startup.cs` and import the `System.Net.Http.Headers` namespace.

3. In the `ConfigureServices` method, add a statement to enable `HttpClientFactory` with a named client to make calls to the Northwind Web API service using HTTPS on port `5001` and request JSON as the default response format, as shown in the following code:

```
services.AddHttpClient(name: "NorthwindService",
  configureClient: options =>
  {
    options.BaseAddress = new Uri("https://localhost:5001/");

    options.DefaultRequestHeaders.Accept.Add(
      new MediaTypeWithQualityHeaderValue(
        "application/json", 1.0));
  });
```

4. Open `Controllers/HomeController.cs` and import the `System.Net.Http` and `Newtonsoft.Json` namespaces.

5. Declare a field to store the HTTP client factory, as shown in the following code:

```
private readonly IHttpClientFactory clientFactory;
```

6. Set the field in the constructor, as shown in the following code:

```
public HomeController(
  ILogger<HomeController> logger,
  Northwind injectedContext,
  IHttpClientFactory httpClientFactory)
{
  _logger = logger;
  db = injectedContext;
  clientFactory = httpClientFactory;
}
```

7. Create a new action method for calling the Northwind service, fetching all customers, and passing them to a view, as shown in the following code:

```
public async Task<IActionResult> Customers(string country)
{
  string uri;

  if (string.IsNullOrEmpty(country))
  {
    ViewData["Title"] = "All Customers Worldwide";
    uri = "api/customers/";
  }
  else
  {
    ViewData["Title"] = $"Customers in {country}";
```

```
    uri = $"api/customers/?country={country}";
  }

  var client = clientFactory.CreateClient(
    name: "NorthwindService");

  var request = new HttpRequestMessage(
    method: HttpMethod.Get, requestUri: uri);

  HttpResponseMessage response = await client.SendAsync(request);

  string jsonString = await response.Content.ReadAsStringAsync();

  IEnumerable<Customer> model = JsonConvert
    .DeserializeObject<IEnumerable<Customer>>(jsonString);

  return View(model);
}
```

8. In the `Views/Home` folder, create a Razor file named `Customers.cshtml`.

9. Modify the Razor file to render the customers, as shown in the following markup:

```
@model IEnumerable<Packt.Shared.Customer>
<h2>@ViewData["Title"]</h2>
<table class="table">
  <tr>
    <th>Company Name</th>
    <th>Contact Name</th>
    <th>Address</th>
    <th>Phone</th>
  </tr>
  @foreach (var item in Model)
  {
  <tr>
    <td>
      @Html.DisplayFor(modelItem => item.CompanyName)
    </td>
    <td>
      @Html.DisplayFor(modelItem => item.ContactName)
    </td>
    <td>
      @Html.DisplayFor(modelItem => item.Address)
      @Html.DisplayFor(modelItem => item.City)
      @Html.DisplayFor(modelItem => item.Region)
      @Html.DisplayFor(modelItem => item.Country)
      @Html.DisplayFor(modelItem => item.PostalCode)
    </td>
    <td>
      @Html.DisplayFor(modelItem => item.Phone)
```

```
        </td>
      </tr>
      }
  </table>
```

10. Open `Views/Home/Index.cshtml` and add a form to allow visitors to enter a country and see the customers, as shown in the following markup:

```
<form asp-action="Customers" method="get">
  <input name="country" placeholder="Enter a country" />
  <input type="submit" />
</form>
```

Enabling Cross-Origin Resource Sharing

It would be useful to explicitly specify the port number for the `NorthwindService` so that it does not conflict with the defaults of `5000` for HTTP and `5002` for HTTPS used by websites like `NorthwindMvc`, and to enable **Cross-Origin Resource Sharing (CORS)**.

More Information: Default browser same-origin policy prevents code downloaded from one origin from accessing resources downloaded from a different origin to improve security. CORS can be enabled to allow requests from specified domains. Learn more about CORS and ASP.NET Core at the following link:

https://docs.microsoft.com/en-us/aspnet/core/security/cors

1. In `NorthwindService`, open `Program.cs`, and in the `CreateHostBuilder` method, add an extension method call to `UseUrls` and to specify port number `5001` for HTTPS, as shown highlighted in the following code:

```
public static IHostBuilder CreateHostBuilder(string[] args) =>
  Host.CreateDefaultBuilder(args)
    .ConfigureWebHostDefaults(webBuilder =>
    {
      webBuilder.UseStartup<Startup>();
      webBuilder.UseUrls("https://localhost:5001");
    });
```

2. Open `Startup.cs`, and add a statement to the top of the `ConfigureServices` method, to add support for CORS, as shown highlighted in the following code:

```
public void ConfigureServices(IServiceCollection services)
{
  services.AddCors();
```

3. Add a statement to the `Configure` method, before calling `UseEndpoints`, to use CORS and allow HTTP `GET`, `POST`, `PUT`, and `DELETE` requests from any website like Northwind MVC that has an origin of `https://localhost:5002`, as shown in the following code:

```
// after UseRouting and before UseEndpoints
app.UseCors(configurePolicy: options =>
  {
    options.WithMethods("GET", "POST", "PUT", "DELETE");

    options.WithOrigins(
      "https://localhost:5002" // for MVC client
    );
  });
```

4. Navigate to **Terminal | New Terminal** and select `NorthwindService`.

5. In **Terminal**, start the `NorthwindService` project by entering the command: `dotnet run`.

6. Navigate to **Terminal | New Terminal** and select `NorthwindMvc`.

7. In **Terminal**, start the `NorthwindMvc` project by entering the command: `dotnet run`.

8. Start Chrome, navigate to `http://localhost:5000/`, and note that it redirects to HTTPS on port `5002` and shows the home page of the Northwind MVC website.

9. In the customer form, enter a country like Germany, UK, or USA, click **Submit**, and note the list of customers, as shown in the following screenshot:

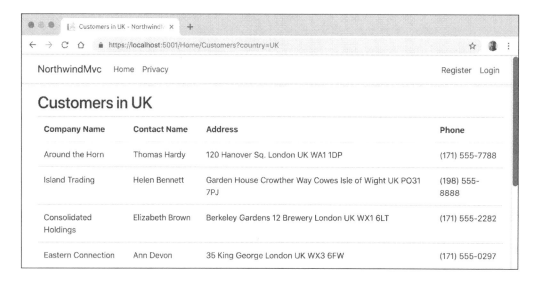

10. Click back in your browser, clear the country text box, click **Submit**, and note the worldwide list of customers.

Implementing advanced features

Since the third edition of this book, published in late 2017, Microsoft has added lots of great features to ASP.NET for building web services.

Implementing Health Check API

There are many paid services that perform site availability tests that are basic pings, some with more advanced analysis of the HTTP response.

ASP.NET Core 2.2 and later makes it easy to implement more detailed website health checks. For example, your website might be live, but is it ready? Can it retrieve data from its database?

1. Open `NorthwindService.csproj`.

2. Add a project reference to enable Entity Framework Core database health checks, as shown in the following markup:

   ```
   <PackageReference Include="Microsoft.Extensions.Diagnostics.
   HealthChecks.EntityFrameworkCore" Version="3.0.0" />
   ```

3. In **Terminal**, restore packages and compile the website project, as shown in the following command:

   ```
   dotnet build
   ```

4. Open `Startup.cs`.

5. In the `ConfigureServices` method, add a statement to add health checks, including to the Northwind database context, as shown in the following code:

   ```
   services.AddHealthChecks()
     .AddDbContextCheck<Northwind>();
   ```

   By default, the database context check calls EF Core's `CanConnectAsync` method. You can customize what operation is run using the `AddDbContextCheck` method.

6. In the `Configure` method, add a statement to use basic health checks, as shown in the following code:

   ```
   app.UseHealthChecks(path: "/howdoyoufeel");
   ```

7. Start the web service, and navigate to `https://localhost:5001/howdoyoufeel`

8. Note the website responds with plain text: `Healthy`

 More Information: You can extend the health check response as much as you want. Read more at the following link: `https://blogs.msdn.microsoft.com/webdev/2018/08/22/asp-net-core-2-2-0-preview1-healthcheck/`

Implementing Open API analyzers and conventions

In this chapter, you learned how to enable Swagger to document a web service by manually decorating a `Controller` class with attributes.

In ASP.NET Core 2.2 or later, there are API analyzers that reflect over `Controller` classes that have been annotated with the `[ApiController]` attribute to document it automatically. The analyzer assumes some API conventions.

To use it, your project must reference the NuGet package, as shown in the following markup:

```
<PackageReference Include="Microsoft.AspNetCore.Mvc.Api.Analyzers"
  Version="3.0.0" PrivateAssets="All" />
```

 More Information: At the time of writing, the package above was version `3.0.0-preview3-19153-02`, but after publishing it should be a full version `3.0.0` release. You can check the latest version to use at the following link: `https://www.nuget.org/packages/Microsoft.AspNetCore.Mvc.Api.Analyzers/`

After installing, controllers that have not been properly decorated should have warnings (green squiggles) and warnings when you compile the source code using the `dotnet build` command. Automatic code fixes can then add the appropriate `[Produces]` and `[ProducesResponseType]` attributes, although this only currently works in Visual Studio 2019. In Visual Studio Code you will see warnings about where the analyzer thinks you should add attributes, but you must add them yourself.

Understanding endpoint routing

In earlier versions of ASP.NET Core, the routing system and the extendable middleware system did not always work easily together, for example, if you wanted to implement a policy like CORS in both middleware and MVC, so Microsoft has invested in improving routing with a new system named **Endpoint Routing**.

Good Practice: Microsoft recommends every ASP.NET Core project migrates to Endpoint Routing if possible.

Endpoint routing is designed to enable better interoperability between frameworks that need routing, like Razor Pages, MVC, or Web API, and middleware that need to understand how routing affects them, like localization, authorization, CORS, and so on.

More Information: You can read more about the design decisions around endpoint routing at the following link: https://devblogs.microsoft.com/aspnet/asp-net-core-2-2-0-preview1-endpoint-routing/

It gets its name because it represents the route table as a compiled tree of endpoints that can be walked efficiently by the routing system. One of the biggest improvements is to performance of routing and action method selection.

It is on by default with ASP.NET Core 2.2 or later if compatibility is set to 2.2 or later. Traditional routes registered using the `MapRoute` method or with attributes are mapped to the new system.

The new routing system includes a link generation service registered as a dependency service that does not need an `HttpContext`.

Configuring endpoint routing

Endpoint routing requires a pair of calls to `app.UseRouting()` and `app.UseEndpoints()`.

- `app.UseRouting()` marks the pipeline position where a routing decision is made.
- `app.UseEndpoints()` marks the pipeline position where the selected endpoint is executed.

Middleware like localization that run in between these can see the selected endpoint and can switch to a different endpoint if necessary.

Endpoint routing uses the same route template syntax that has been used in ASP.NET MVC since 2010 and the [Route] attribute introduced with ASP.NET MVC 5 in 2013. Migration often only requires changes to Startup configuration.

MVC controllers, Razor Pages, and frameworks like SignalR used to be enabled by a call to UseMvc() or similar methods but they are now added inside UseEndpoints() because they are all integrated into the same routing system along with middleware.

Let's define some middleware that can output information about endpoints:

1. Open NorthwindService.csproj.

2. Open Startup.cs and import namespaces for working with endpoint routing, as shown in the following code:

```
using Microsoft.AspNetCore.Http; // GetEndpoint() extension method
using Microsoft.AspNetCore.Routing; // RouteEndpoint
```

3. In the ConfigureServices method, add a statement before UseEndpoints to define a lambda statement to output information about the selected endpoint during every request, as shown in the following code:

```
app.Use(next => (context) =>
  {
    var endpoint = context.GetEndpoint();

    if (endpoint != null)
    {
      WriteLine("*** Name: {0}; Route: {1}; Metadata: {2}",
        arg0: endpoint.DisplayName,
        arg1: (endpoint as RouteEndpoint)?.RoutePattern,
        arg2: string.Join(", ", endpoint.Metadata));
    }

    // pass context to next middleware in pipeline
    return next(context);
  });
```

While reviewing the preceding code, note the following:

- The Use method requires an instance of RequestDelegate or a lambda statement equivalent.

- RequestDelegate has a single HttpContext parameter that wraps all information about the current HTTP request (and its matching response).

- ○ Importing the `Microsoft.AspNetCore.Http` namespace adds the `GetEndpoint` extension method to the `HttpContext` instance.

4. Start the web service.

5. In Chrome, navigate to `https://localhost:5001/weatherforecast`.

6. In **Terminal**, note the result, as shown in the following output:

```
Request starting HTTP/1.1 GET https://localhost:5001/
weatherforecast

*** Name: NorthwindService.Controllers.WeatherForecastController.
Get (NorthwindService); Route: Microsoft.AspNetCore.Routing.
Patterns.RoutePattern; Metadata: Microsoft.AspNetCore.
Mvc.ApiControllerAttribute, Microsoft.AspNetCore.Mvc.
ControllerAttribute, Microsoft.AspNetCore.Mvc.RouteAttribute,
Microsoft.AspNetCore.Mvc.HttpGetAttribute, Microsoft.AspNetCore.
Routing.HttpMethodMetadata, Microsoft.AspNetCore.Mvc.Controllers.
ControllerActionDescriptor, Microsoft.AspNetCore.Routing.
RouteNameMetadata, Microsoft.AspNetCore.Mvc.ModelBinding.
UnsupportedContentTypeFilter, Microsoft.AspNetCore.Mvc.
Infrastructure.ClientErrorResultFilterFactory, Microsoft.
AspNetCore.Mvc.Infrastructure.ModelStateInvalidFilterFactory,
Microsoft.AspNetCore.Mvc.ApiControllerAttribute, Microsoft.
AspNetCore.Mvc.ActionConstraints.HttpMethodActionConstraint
```

7. Close Chrome and stop the web service.

More Information: You can read more about endpoint routing at the following link: `https://docs.microsoft.com/en-us/aspnet/core/fundamentals/routing?view=aspnetcore-3.0`

Endpoint routing replaces the `IRouter`-based routing used in ASP.NET Core 2.1 and earlier.

More Information: If you need to work with ASP.NET Core 2.1 or earlier, then you can read about the old routing system at the following link: `https://docs.microsoft.com/en-us/aspnet/core/fundamentals/routing?view=aspnetcore-2.1`

Understanding other communication technologies

ASP.NET Core Web API is not the only Microsoft technology for implementing services or communicating between components of a distributed application. Although we will not cover these technologies in detail, you should be aware of what they can do and when they should be used.

Understanding Windows Communication Foundation (WCF)

In 2006, Microsoft released .NET Framework 3.0 with some major frameworks, one of which was **Windows Communication Foundation** (**WCF**). It abstracted the business logic implementation of a service from the technology used to communicate with it. It heavily used XML configuration to declaratively define endpoints including their address, binding, and contract (known as the ABCs of endpoints). Once you have understood how to do this, it is a powerful yet flexible technology.

Microsoft has decided not to officially port WCF to .NET Core, but there is a community-owned OSS project named **Core WCF** managed by the .NET Foundation. If you need to migrate an existing service from .NET Framework to .NET Core, or build a client to a WCF service, then you could use Core WCF. Be aware that it can never be a full port since parts of WCF are Windows-specific.

 More Information: You can read more and download the Core WCF repository from the following link: `https://github.com/CoreWCF/CoreWCF`

Technologies like WCF allow for the building of distributed applications. A client application can make **remote procedure calls** (**RPC**) to a server application. Instead of using a port of WCF to do this, we could use an alternative RPC technology.

Understanding gRPC

gRPC is a modern open source high-performance RPC framework that can run in any environment.

Like WCF, gRPC uses a contract-first API development that supports language-agnostic implementations. You write the contracts using `.proto` files with their own language syntax and tools to convert them into various languages like C#. It minimizes network usage by using `Protobuf` binary serialization.

More Information: You can read about gRPC at the following link: `https://grpc.io`

Microsoft officially supports gRPC with ASP.NET Core.

More Information: You can learn how to use gRPC with ASP.NET Core at the following link: `https://docs.microsoft.com/en-us/aspnet/core/grpc/aspnetcore?view=aspnetcore-3.0&tabs=visual-studio-code`

Practicing and exploring

Test your knowledge and understanding by answering some questions, get some hands-on practice, and explore this chapter's topics with deeper research.

Exercise 18.1 – Test your knowledge

Answer the following questions:

1. Which base class should you inherit from to create a controller class for an ASP.NET Core Web API service?

2. If you decorate your `Controller` class with the `[ApiController]` attribute to get default behavior like automatic 400 responses for invalid models, what else must you do?

3. What must you do to specify which controller action method will be executed in response to an HTTP request?

4. What must you do to specify what responses should be expected when calling an action method?

5. List three methods that can be called to return responses with different status codes.

6. List four ways that you can test a web service.

7. Why should you not wrap you use of `HttpClient` in a using statement to dispose of it when you are finished even though it implements the `IDisposable` interface, and what should you use instead?

8. What does the acronym CORS stand for and why is it important to enable it in a web service?

9. How can you enable clients to detect if your web service is healthy with ASP. NET Core 2.2 and later?

10. What benefits does endpoint routing provide?

Exercise 18.2 – Practice creating and deleting customers with HttpClient

Extend the NorthwindMvc website project to have pages where a visitor can fill in a form to create a new customer, or search for a customer and then delete them. The MVC controller should make calls to the Northwind service to create and delete customers.

Exercise 18.3 – Explore topics

Use the following links to read more about this chapter's topics:

- **Create web APIs with ASP.NET Core**: https://docs.microsoft.com/en-us/aspnet/core/web-api/?view=aspnetcore-3.0

- **Swagger Tools**: https://swagger.io/tools/

- **Swashbuckle for ASP.NET Core**: https://github.com/domaindrivendev/Swashbuckle.AspNetCore

- **Health checks in ASP.NET Core**: https://docs.microsoft.com/en-us/aspnet/core/host-and-deploy/health-checks?view=aspnetcore-3.0

- **Use HttpClientFactory to implement resilient HTTP requests**: https://docs.microsoft.com/en-us/dotnet/architecture/microservices/implement-resilient-applications/use-httpclientfactory-to-implement-resilient-http-requests

Summary

In this chapter, you learned how to build an ASP.NET Core Web API service that can be called by any app on any platform that can make an HTTP request and process an HTTP response. You also learned how to test and document web service APIs with Swagger, as well as how to consume services efficiently.

In the next chapter, you will learn how to add intelligence to any type of application using machine learning.

Chapter 19

Building Intelligent Apps Using Machine Learning

This chapter is about embedding intelligence into your apps using machine learning algorithms. Microsoft has created a cross-platform machine learning library named ML.NET designed specifically for C# and .NET developers.

This chapter will cover the following topics:

- Understanding machine learning
- Understanding ML.NET
- Making product recommendations

Understanding machine learning

Marketing folk love to use terms like **artificial intelligence** or **data science** in their promotional materials. **Machine learning** is a subset of data science. It is one practical way to add intelligence to software.

 More Information: You can learn the science behind one of the most popular and successful data science techniques by enrolling in Harvard University's free *Data Science: Machine Learning* 8-week course at the following link: `https://www.edx.org/course/data-science-machine-learning-2`

This book cannot teach machine learning in one chapter. If you need to understand how machine learning algorithms work internally then you would need to understand data science topics including calculus, statistics, probability theory, and linear algebra. Then you would need to learn about machine learning in depth.

More Information: To learn about machine learning in depth, read Python Machine Learning by Sebastian Raschka and Vahid Mirjalili: `https://www.packtpub.com/big-data-and-business-intelligence/python-machine-learning-second-edition`.

My goal with this chapter is to give you the minimum conceptual understanding needed to implement a valuable and practical application of machine learning: making product recommendations in an e-commerce website to increase the value of each order. By seeing all the tasks required, you can then decide for yourself if the effort required to properly learn it all is worth it for you, or if you'd rather put your efforts in to other topics like building websites or mobile apps.

Understanding the machine learning life cycle

The machine learning lifecycle has four steps:

- **Problem analysis**: What is the problem you are trying to solve?

- **Data gathering and processing**: The raw data needed to solve the problem often needs transforming into formats suitable for a machine learning algorithm to process.

- **Modeling** is divided into three sub-steps:
    - **Identifying features**: Features are the values that influence predictions, for example, the distance traveled and time of day that influence the cost of a taxi journey.

    - **Training the model**: Select and apply algorithms and set hyperparameters to generate one or more models. Hyperparameters are set before the learning process begins in contrast to other parameters derived during training.

    - **Evaluating the model**: Choose which model best solves the original problem. Evaluating models is a manual task that can take months.

- **Deploying the model**: Embed the model in an app where it is used to make predictions on real data inputs.

But even then, your work is not done! After deploying the model, you should regularly reassess the model to maintain its efficiency. Over time the predictions it makes could drift and become poorer because data can change over time.

You should not assume a static relationship between inputs and outputs, especially when predicting human behavior, since fashions change. Just because superhero movies are popular in 2019 does not mean they will be popular in 2020. This problem is named **concept drift** or model decay. If you suspect this problem then you should retrain the model, or even switch to a better algorithm or hyperparameter values.

Deciding which algorithm to use and the values for its hyperparameters is tricky because the combination of potential algorithms and hyperparameter values is infinite. This is why machine learning and its wider data science field is a full-time specialized career.

 More Information: You can read more about roles like the types of data scientist who are involved with machine learning at the following link: `https://www.datasciencecentral.com/profiles/blogs/difference-between-machine-learning-data-science-ai-deep-learning`

Understanding datasets for training and testing

You must not use your entire dataset to train your model. You need to split your dataset into a **training dataset** and a **testing dataset**. The training dataset is used to train the model, unsurprisingly. Then, the testing dataset is used to evaluate that the model makes good enough predictions before it is deployed. If you were to use the whole dataset for training, then you would have no data left over to test your model.

The splitting between training and testing can be random for some scenarios, but be careful! You must consider if the dataset could have regular variations. For example, taxi usage varies based on time of day, and even varies based on season and city. For example, New York City will typically be busy for taxis all year, at all hours, but Munich might get extra busy for taxis during Oktoberfest.

When your dataset is affected by seasonality and other factors, you must split the dataset strategically. You also need to ensure that the model is not **overfitted** with the training data. Let's talk about an example of overfitting.

When I was studying Computer Science at the University of Bristol between 1990 and 1993, we were told a story during our Neural Networks class (possibly apocryphal, but it illustrates an important point). The British Army employed data scientists to build a machine learning model to detect Russian tanks camouflaged in the woods of Eastern Europe. The model was fed with thousands of images, yet when it came time to show off its abilities in the real world it failed dismally.

During the project autopsy, the scientists realized that all the images they used to train the model were from Spring when the foliage was lively shades of green, but the live test happened in Autumn when the foliage was reds, yellows, and browns.

The model was *overfitted* to the Spring foliage. If the model was more generalized, then it might have performed better in other seasons. Underfitting is the opposite; it describes a model that is too generalized and doesn't provide satisfactory outputs when applied to specific contexts.

 More Information: You can read more about overfitting and underfitting and how to compensate for it at the following link: https://elitedatascience.com/overfitting-in-machine-learning

Understanding machine learning tasks

There are many tasks or scenarios that machine learning can help developers with:

- **Binary classification** is classifying the items in an input dataset between two groups, predicting which group each item belongs to. For example, deciding if an Amazon book review is *positive* or *negative*, also known as sentiment analysis. Other examples include spam email message and credit card purchase fraud detection.

- **Multi-class classification** is classifying instances into one of three or more classes, predicting which group each one belongs to. For example, deciding if a news article should be categorized as *celebrity gossip*, *sports*, *politics*, or *science and technology*. Binary and multi-class are examples of **supervised** classification because the labels must be predefined.

- **Clustering** is for grouping input data items so that items in the same cluster are more similar to each other than to those in other clusters. It is not the same as classification because it does not give each cluster a label and therefore the labels do not have to be predefined as with classification. Clustering is therefore an example of **unsupervised** classification. After clustering a group can be processed to spot patterns and then assign a label.

- **Ranking** is for ordering input data items based on properties like star reviews, context, likes, and so on.

- **Recommendations** are for suggesting other items like products or content that a user might like based on their past behavior compared to other users.

- **Regression** is for predicting a numeric value from input data. It can be used for forecasting and suggesting how much a product should sell for or how much it will cost to get a taxi from Heathrow airport to a central London hotel, or how many bikes will be needed in a particular area of Amsterdam for a bike sharing scheme.

- **Anomaly detection** is for identifying "black swans" or unusual data that could indicate a problem that needs to be fixed, in fields like medical, financial, and mechanical maintenance.

- **Deep Learning** is for handling large and complex binary input data instead of input data in a more structured format, for example, computer vision tasks like detecting objects and classifying images, or audio tasks like speech recognition and **natural language processing (NLP)**.

Understanding Microsoft Azure Machine Learning

The rest of this chapter will cover using an open source .NET package to implement machine learning, but before we dive into that, let's take a quick diversion to understand an important alternative.

Implementing machine learning well requires people with strong skills in mathematics or related areas. Data scientists are in high demand and the difficulty and cost of hiring them prevents some organizations from adopting machine learning in their own apps. An organization might have access to warehouses of data accumulated over many years, but they struggle to use machine learning to improve the decisions they make.

Microsoft Azure Machine Learning overcomes these obstacles by providing pre-built machine learning models for common tasks like face recognition and language processing. This enables organizations without their own data scientists to get some benefit from their data. As an organization hires their own data scientists, or their developers gain data science skills, they can then develop their own models to work within Azure ML.

But as organizations become more sophisticated and recognize the value of owning their machine learning models and being able to run them anywhere, more and more will need a platform that their existing developers can get started on that has as shallow a learning curve as possible.

Understanding ML.NET

ML.NET is Microsoft's open source and cross-platform machine learning framework for .NET.

C# developers can use their existing skills and familiarity with .NET Standard APIs to integrate custom machine learning inside their apps without knowing details about how to build and maintain machine learning models.

 More Information: You can read the official announcement for ML.NET at the following link: `https://blogs.msdn.microsoft.com/dotnet/2018/05/07/introducing-ml-net-cross-platform-proven-and-open-source-machine-learning-framework/`

Today, ML.NET contains machine learning libraries created by Microsoft Research and used by Microsoft products like PowerPoint for intelligently recommending style templates based on the content of a presentation. Soon, ML.NET will also support other popular libraries like Accord.NET, CNTK, Light GBM, and TensorFlow, but we will not cover those in this book.

 More Information: The **Accord.NET Framework** is a .NET machine learning framework combined with audio and image processing libraries completely written in C#. You can read more at the following link: `http://accord-framework.net`

Understanding Infer.NET

Infer.NET was created by Microsoft Research in Cambridge in 2004. It was made available to academics in 2008. Since then, hundreds of academic papers have been written about Infer.NET.

 More Information: You can read more about Microsoft **Infer.NET** at the following link: `https://www.microsoft.com/en-us/research/blog/the-microsoft-infer-net-machine-learning-framework-goes-open-source/`

Developers can incorporate domain knowledge into a model to create custom algorithms instead of mapping your problem to existing algorithms as you would do with ML.NET.

Infer.NET is used by Microsoft for products including Microsoft Azure, Xbox, and Bing search and translator.

Infer.NET can be used for classification, recommendations, and clustering.

We will not be looking at Infer.NET in this book.

More Information: You can read how to create a game match up list app with Infer.NET and probabilistic programming at the following link: `https://docs.microsoft.com/en-us/dotnet/machine-learning/how-to-guides/matchup-app-infer-net`.

Understanding ML.NET learning pipelines

A typical learning pipeline comprises six steps:

- **Data loading** – ML.NET supports loading data from the following formats: text (CSV, TSV), Parquet, binary, `IEnumerable<T>`, and file sets.

- **Transformations** – ML.NET supports the following transformations: text manipulation, schema (i.e. structure) modification, handling missing values, categorical value encoding, normalization, and feature selection.

- **Algorithms** – ML.NET supports the following algorithms: linear, boosted trees, k-means, **Support Vector Machine** (**SVM**), and averaged perceptron.

- **Model training** – Call the ML.NET `Train` method to create a `PredictionModel` that you can use to make predictions.

- **Model evaluation** – ML.NET supports multiple evaluators to assess the accuracy of your model against various metrics.

- **Model deployment** – ML.NET allows you to export your model as a binary file for deployment with any type of .NET app.

More Information: The traditional "Hello World" app for machine learning is one that can predict the type of iris flower based on four features: petal length, petal width, sepal length, and sepal width. You can follow a 10-minute tutorial for it at the following link: `https://dotnet.microsoft.com/learn/machinelearning-ai/ml-dotnet-get-started-tutorial/intro`

Understanding model training concepts

The .NET type system was not designed for machine learning and data analysis, so it needs some specialized types to make it better suited for these tasks.

ML.NET uses the following .NET types when working with models:

- `IDataView` interface represents a dataset that is:
  - **immutable**, meaning it cannot change,
  - **cursorable**, meaning cursors can iterate over the data,
  - **lazily evaluated**, meaning that work like transformations is only done when a cursor iterates over the data,
  - **heterogenous**, meaning data can have mixed types, and
  - **schematized**, meaning it has a strongly defined structure.

 More Information: You can read more about the design of the `IDataView` interface at the following link: `https://github.com/dotnet/machinelearning/blob/master/docs/code/IDataViewDesignPrinciples.md`

- `DataViewType`: All `IDataView` column types derive from the abstract class `DataViewType`. Vector types require dimensionality information to indicate the length of the vector type.

- The `ITransformer` interface represents a component that accepts input data, changes it in some way, and returns output data. For example, a tokenizer transformer takes a text column containing phrases as input and outputs a vector column with individual words extracted out of the phrases and arranged vertically in a column. Most transformers work on one column at a time. New transformers can be constructed by combining other transformers in a chain.

- The `IDataReader<T>` interface represents a component to create data. It takes an instance of `T` and returns data out of it.

- The `IEstimator<T>` interface represents an object that learns from data. The result of the learning is a transformer. Estimators are eager, meaning every call to their `Fit` method causes learning to occur, which can take a lot of time!

- The `PredictionEngine<TSrc, TDst>` class represents a function that can be seen as a machine that applies a transformer to one row at prediction time. If you have a lot of input data that you want to make predictions for, you would create a data view, call `Transform` on the model to generate prediction rows, and then use a cursor to read the results. In the real world, a common scenario is to have one data row as input that you want to make a prediction for, so to simplify the process you can use a prediction engine.

Understanding missing values and key types

The R language is popular for machine learning and it uses the special value NA to indicate a missing value. ML.NET follows that convention.

Key types are used for data that is represented as number values within a cardinality set, as shown in the following code:

```
[KeyType(10)]
public uint NumberInRange1To10 { get; set; }
```

The representational, also known as underlying, type must be one of the four .NET unsigned integer types: `byte`, `ushort`, `uint`, and `ulong`. The value zero always means NA, indicating its value is missing. The representational value one is always the first valid value of the key type.

The count should be set to one more than the maximum value to account for counting starting at 1, because 0 is reserved for missing values. For example, the cardinality of the 0-9 range should be 10. Any values outside of the specified cardinality will be mapped to the missing value representation: 0.

Understanding features and labels

The inputs of a machine learning model are called **features**. For example, if there was a linear regression where one continuous quantity, like the price of a bottle of wine, is proportional to another, like the rating given by vintners, then price is the only feature.

The values used to train a machine learning model are called **labels**. In the wine example, the rating values in the training dataset are the labels.

In some models, the label value is not important, since the existence of a row represents a match. This is especially common in recommendations.

Making product recommendations

The practical application of machine learning we will implement is making product recommendations on an ecommerce website with the goal being to increase the value of a customer order.

The problem is how to decide what products to recommend to the visitor.

Problem analysis

On 2nd October 2006, Netflix started an open prize challenge for the best algorithm for predicting customer ratings for films based only on previous ratings. The dataset that Netflix provided had 17,000 movies, 500,000 users, and 100 million ratings. For example, user 437822 gives movie 12934 a rating of 4 out of 5.

Singular Value Decomposition (SVD) is a decomposition method for reducing a matrix to make later calculations simpler and Simon Funk shared with the community how he and his team used it to get near the top of the rankings during the competition.

> **More Information**: You can read more about Simon Funk's use of SVD at the following link: `https://sifter.org/~simon/journal/20061027.2.html`

Since Funk's initial work, similar approaches have been proposed for recommender systems. Matrix factorization is a class of collaborative filtering algorithms used in recommender systems that uses SVD.

> **More Information**: You can read more about the use of matrix factorization in recommender systems at the following link: `https://en.wikipedia.org/wiki/Matrix_factorization_(recommender_systems)`

We will use the One-Class Matrix Factorization algorithm because we only have information on purchase order history. The products have not been given ratings or other factors that could be used in other multi-class factorization approaches.

The score produced by matrix factorization tells us the likelihood of being a positive case. The larger the score value, the higher the probability. The score is not a probability so when making predictions we have to predict multiple product co-purchase scores and sort with the highest score at the top.

Matrix factorization uses a supervised collaborative filtering approach, which assumes that if Alice has the same opinion as Bob about a product, Alice is more likely to have Bob's opinion on a different product than that of a random other person. Hence, they are more likely to add that product Bob liked to their shopping cart.

Data gathering and processing

The Northwind sample database has the following tables:

- Products has 77 rows, each with an integer product ID.

- Orders has 830 rows, each order having one or more related detail rows.

- Order Details has 2,155 rows, each with an integer product ID indicating the product that was ordered.

We can use this data to create datasets for training and testing models that can then make predictions of other products a customer might want to add to their cart based on what they have already added to it.

For example, order 10248 was made by customer VINET for three products with IDs of 11, 42, and 72, as shown in the following screenshot:

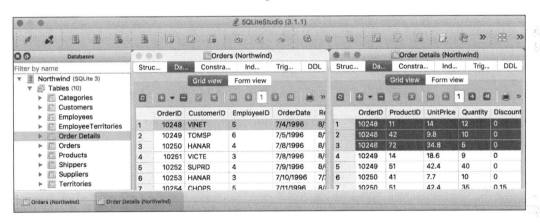

We will write a LINQ query to cross-join this data to generate a simple text file with two columns showing products that are co-bought, as shown in the following output:

```
ProductID    CoboughtProductID
11           42
11           72
42           11
42           72
72           11
72           42
```

Unfortunately, the Northwind database matches almost every product with every other product. To produce more realistic datasets, we will filter by country. We will generate one dataset for Germany, one for the UK, and one for the USA. The USA dataset will be used for testing.

Creating the NorthwindML website project

We will build an ASP.NET Core MVC website that shows a list of all products, grouped by category, and allows a visitor to add products to a shopping cart. Their shopping cart will be stored in a temporary cookie as a dash-separated list of product IDs.

1. In the folder named `PracticalApps`, create a folder named `NorthwindML`.

2. In Visual Studio Code, open the `PracticalApps` workspace and add the `NorthwindML` folder to the workspace.

3. Navigate to **Terminal | New Terminal** and select `NorthwindML`.

4. In **Terminal**, enter the following command to create a new ASP.NET Core MVC project, as shown in the following command:

    ```
    dotnet new mvc
    ```

5. Open the `NorthwindML.csproj` project file, add references to the SQLite, ML.NET, and ML.NET Recommender packages, and to the Northwind context and entity class library projects that you created in *Chapter 14, Practical Applications of C# and .NET*, as shown highlighted in the following markup:

    ```
    <Project Sdk="Microsoft.NET.Sdk.Web">

      <PropertyGroup>
        <TargetFramework>netcoreapp3.0</TargetFramework>
      </PropertyGroup>

      <ItemGroup>
        <PackageReference
          Include="Microsoft.AspNetCore.Mvc.NewtonsoftJson"
          Version="3.0.0" />
        <PackageReference
          Include="Microsoft.EntityFrameworkCore.Sqlite"
          Version="3.0.0" />
        <PackageReference Include="Microsoft.ML" Version="1.3.1" />
        <PackageReference Include="Microsoft.ML.Recommender"
          Version="0.15.1" />
    ```

```
      </ItemGroup>

      <ItemGroup>
        <ProjectReference Include=
        "..\NorthwindContextLib\NorthwindContextLib.csproj" />
        <ProjectReference Include=
          "..\NorthwindEmployees\NorthwindEmployees.csproj" />
      </ItemGroup>

    </Project>
```

6. In **Terminal**, restore packages and compile the project, as shown in the following command:

```
dotnet build
```

7. Open the `Startup.cs` class file and import the `Packt.Shared`, `System.IO`, and `Microsoft.EntityFrameworkCore` namespaces.

8. Add a statement to the `ConfigureServices` method to register the Northwind data context, as shown in the following code:

```
string databasePath = Path.Combine("..", "Northwind.db");

services.AddDbContext<Northwind>(options =>
  options.UseSqlite($"Data Source={databasePath}"));
```

Creating the data and view models

The `NorthwindML` project will simulate an ecommerce website that allows visitors to add products that they want to order to their shopping cart. We will start by defining some models to represent this.

1. In the `Models` folder, create a class file named `CartItem.cs`, and add statements to define a class with properties for the ID and name of a product, as shown in the following code:

```
namespace NorthwindML.Models
{
  public class CartItem
  {
    public int ProductID { get; set; }

    public string ProductName { get; set; }
  }
}
```

2. In the `Models` folder, create a class file named `Cart.cs`, and add statements to define a class with properties for the items in a cart, as shown in the following code:

```
using System.Collections.Generic;

namespace NorthwindML.Models
{
  public class Cart
  {
    public IEnumerable<CartItem> Items { get; set; }
  }
}
```

3. In the `Models` folder, create a class file named `ProductCobought.cs`, and add statements to define a class with properties used to record when a product is purchased with another product, and the cardinality (aka maximum possible value) of the `ProductID` property, as shown in the following code:

```
using Microsoft.ML.Data;

namespace NorthwindML.Models
{
  public class ProductCobought
  {
    [KeyType(77)] // maximum possible value of a ProductID
    public uint ProductID { get; set; }

    [KeyType(77)]
    public uint CoboughtProductID { get; set; }
  }
}
```

4. In the `Models` folder, create a class file named `Recommendation.cs` that will be used as the output of the machine learning algorithm, and add statements to define a class with properties used to show a recommended product ID with its score that will be used as the result of the machine learning algorithm, as shown in the following code:

```
namespace NorthwindML.Models
{
  public class Recommendation
  {
    public uint CoboughtProductID { get; set; }

    public float Score { get; set; }
  }
}
```

5. In the `Models` folder, create a class file named `EnrichedRecommendation.cs`, and add statements to inherit from the `Recommendation` class with an extra property to show the product name for display, as shown in the following code:

```
namespace NorthwindML.Models
{
  public class EnrichedRecommendation : Recommendation
  {
    public string ProductName { get; set; }
  }
}
```

6. In **Terminal**, compile the project, as shown in the following command:

```
dotnet build
```

7. In the `Models` folder, create a class file named `HomeCartViewModel.cs`, and add statements to define a class with properties to store the visitor's shopping cart and a list of recommendations, as shown in the following code:

```
using System.Collections.Generic;

namespace NorthwindML.Models
{
  public class HomeCartViewModel
  {
    public Cart Cart { get; set; }

    public List<EnrichedRecommendation>
      Recommendations { get; set; }
  }
}
```

8. In the `Models` folder, create a class file named `HomeIndexViewModel.cs`, and add statements to define a class with properties to show if the training datasets have been created, as shown in the following code:

```
using System.Collections.Generic;
using Packt.Shared;

namespace NorthwindML.Models
{
  public class HomeIndexViewModel
  {
    public IEnumerable<Category> Categories { get; set; }
    public bool GermanyDatasetExists { get; set; }
    public bool UKDatasetExists { get; set; }
    public bool USADatasetExists { get; set; }
    public long Milliseconds { get; set; }
  }
}
```

Implementing the controller

Now we can modify the existing home controller to perform the operations we need.

1. In the wwwroot folder, create a folder named Data.

2. In the Controllers folder, open HomeController.cs, and import some namespaces, as shown in the following code:

```
using Packt.Shared;
using Microsoft.EntityFrameworkCore;
using Microsoft.AspNetCore.Hosting;
using System.IO;
using Microsoft.ML;
using Microsoft.ML.Data;
using Microsoft.Data;
using Microsoft.ML.Trainers;
```

3. In the HomeController class, declare some fields for the filename and countries that we will generate datasets for, as shown in the following code:

```
private readonly static string datasetName = "dataset.txt";

private readonly static string[] countries =
  new[] { "Germany", "UK", "USA" };
```

4. Declare some fields for the Northwind data context and web host environment dependency services and set them in the constructor, as shown in the following code:

```
// dependency services
private readonly ILogger<HomeController> _logger;
private readonly Northwind db;
private readonly IWebHostEnvironment webHostEnvironment;

public HomeController(ILogger<HomeController> logger,
  Northwind db,
  IWebHostEnvironment webHostEnvironment)
{
  _logger = logger;
  this.db = db;
  this.webHostEnvironment = webHostEnvironment;
}
```

5. Add a private method to return the path to a file stored in the Data folder of the website, as shown in the following code:

```
private string GetDataPath(string file)
{
  return Path.Combine(webHostEnvironment.ContentRootPath,
    "wwwroot", "Data", file);
}
```

6. Add a private method to create an instance of the `HomeIndexViewModel` class loaded with all the products from the Northwind database and indicating if the datasets have been created, as shown in the following code:

```
private HomeIndexViewModel CreateHomeIndexViewModel()
{
  return new HomeIndexViewModel
  {
    Categories = db.Categories
      .Include(category => category.Products),

    GermanyDatasetExists = System.IO.File.Exists(
      GetDataPath("germany-dataset.txt")),

    UKDatasetExists = System.IO.File.Exists(
      GetDataPath("uk-dataset.txt")),

    USADatasetExists = System.IO.File.Exists(
      GetDataPath("usa-dataset.txt"))
  };
}
```

We had to prefix the `File` class with `System.IO` because the `ControllerBase` class has a `File` method that would cause a naming conflict.

7. In the `Index` action method, add statements to create its view model and pass it to its Razor view, as shown highlighted in the following code:

```
public IActionResult Index()
{
  var model = CreateHomeIndexViewModel();
  return View(model);
}
```

8. Add an action method to generate the datasets for each country and then return to the default `Index` view, as shown in the following code:

```
public IActionResult GenerateDatasets()
{
  foreach (string country in countries)
  {
    IEnumerable<Order> ordersInCountry = db.Orders
      // filter by country to create different datasets
      .Where(order => order.Customer.Country == country)
      .Include(order => order.OrderDetails)
      .AsEnumerable(); // switch to client-side

    IEnumerable<ProductCobought> coboughtProducts =
      ordersInCountry.SelectMany(order =>
        from lineItem1 in order.OrderDetails // cross-join
```

```
      from lineItem2 in order.OrderDetails
      select new ProductCobought
      {
        ProductID = (uint)lineItem1.ProductID,
        CoboughtProductID = (uint)lineItem2.ProductID
      })

    // exclude matches between a product and itself
    .Where(p => p.ProductID != p.CoboughtProductID)

    // remove duplicates by grouping by both values
    .GroupBy(p => new { p.ProductID, p.CoboughtProductID })
    .Select(p => p.FirstOrDefault())

    // make it easier for humans to read results by sorting
    .OrderBy(p => p.ProductID)
    .ThenBy(p => p.CoboughtProductID);

  StreamWriter datasetFile = System.IO.File.CreateText(
    path: GetDataPath($"{country.ToLower()}-{datasetName}"));

  // tab-separated header
  datasetFile.WriteLine("ProductID\tCoboughtProductID");

  foreach (var item in coboughtProducts)
  {
    datasetFile.WriteLine("{0}\t{1}",
      item.ProductID, item.CoboughtProductID);
  }

  datasetFile.Close();
  }

  var model = CreateHomeIndexViewModel();
  return View("Index", model);
}
```

Training the recommendation models

In the dataset, we already provide a `KeyType` to set the maximum value for a
product ID and product IDs are already encoded as integers, which is what's needed
for the algorithm we will use, so to train the models all we need to do is call the
`MatrixFactorizationTrainer` with a few extra parameters.

1. In the `HomeController.cs` file, add an action method to train the models, as
    shown in the following code:

```
public IActionResult TrainModels()
{
```

```csharp
var stopWatch = Stopwatch.StartNew();

foreach (string country in countries)
{
  var mlContext = new MLContext();

  IDataView dataView = mlContext.Data.LoadFromTextFile(
    path: GetDataPath($"{country}-{datasetName}"),
    columns: new[]
    {
      new TextLoader.Column(
        name:     "Label",
        dataKind: DataKind.Double,
        index:    0),

      // The key count is the cardinality i.e. maximum
      // valid value. This column is used internally when
      // training the model. When results are shown, the
      // columns are mapped to instances of our model
      // which could have a different cardinality but
      // happen to have the same.
      new TextLoader.Column(
        name:     nameof(ProductCobought.ProductID),
        dataKind: DataKind.UInt32,
        source:   new [] { new TextLoader.Range(0) },
        keyCount: new KeyCount(77)),

      new TextLoader.Column(
        name:     nameof(
          ProductCobought.CoboughtProductID),
        dataKind: DataKind.UInt32,
        source:   new [] { new TextLoader.Range(1) },
        keyCount: new KeyCount(77))
    },
    hasHeader: true,
    separatorChar: '\t');

  var options = new MatrixFactorizationTrainer.Options
  {
    MatrixColumnIndexColumnName =
      nameof(ProductCobought.ProductID),
    MatrixRowIndexColumnName =
      nameof(ProductCobought.CoboughtProductID),
    LabelColumnName = "Label",
    LossFunction = MatrixFactorizationTrainer
      .LossFunctionType.SquareLossOneClass,
    Alpha = 0.01,
    Lambda = 0.025,
```

```
        C = 0.00001
    };

    MatrixFactorizationTrainer mft =
      mlContext.Recommendation()
      .Trainers.MatrixFactorization(options);

    ITransformer trainedModel = mft.Fit(dataView);

    mlContext.Model.Save(trainedModel,
      inputSchema: dataView.Schema,
      filePath: GetDataPath($"{country}-model.zip"));
  }

  stopWatch.Stop();

  var model = CreateHomeIndexViewModel();
  model.Milliseconds = stopWatch.ElapsedMilliseconds;

  return View("Index", model);
}
```

Implementing a shopping cart with recommendations

We will now build a shopping cart feature and allow visitors to add products to their cart. In the cart, they will see recommendations of other products they can quickly add to their cart.

This type of recommendation is known as **co-purchase** or "products frequently bought together," which means it will recommend customers a set of products based upon their and other customers' purchase histories.

In this example, we will always use the Germany model to make predictions. In a real website, you might choose to select the model based on the current location of the visitor so that they get recommendations similar to other visitors from their country.

1. In the `HomeController.cs` file, add an action method to add a product to the shopping cart and then show the cart with the best three recommendations of other products the visitor might like to add, as shown in the following code:

    ```
    // GET /Home/Cart
    // To show the cart and recommendations

    // GET /Home/Cart/5
    // To add a product to the cart

    public IActionResult Cart(int? id)
    ```

```
{
  // the current cart is stored as a cookie
  string cartCookie = Request.Cookies["nw_cart"]
                        ?? string.Empty;

  // if visitor clicked Add to Cart button
  if (id.HasValue)
  {
    if (string.IsNullOrWhiteSpace(cartCookie))
    {
      cartCookie = id.ToString();
    }
    else
    {
      string[] ids = cartCookie.Split('-');

      if (!ids.Contains(id.ToString()))
      {
        cartCookie = string.Join('-',
          cartCookie, id.ToString());
      }
    }

    Response.Cookies.Append("nw_cart", cartCookie);
  }

  var model = new HomeCartViewModel
  {
    Cart = new Cart
    {
      Items = Enumerable.Empty<CartItem>()
    },
    Recommendations = new List<EnrichedRecommendation>()
  };

  if (cartCookie.Length > 0)
  {
    model.Cart.Items = cartCookie.Split('-').Select(item =>
      new CartItem
      {
        ProductID = int.Parse(item),
        ProductName = db.Products.Find(
          int.Parse(item)).ProductName
      });
  }

  if (System.IO.File.Exists(
    GetDataPath("germany-model.zip")))
  {
```

```
var mlContext = new MLContext();

ITransformer modelGermany;

using (var stream = new FileStream(
  path:    GetDataPath("germany-model.zip"),
  mode:    FileMode.Open,
  access:  FileAccess.Read,
  share:   FileShare.Read))
{
  modelGermany = mlContext.Model.Load(stream,
    out DataViewSchema schema);
}

var predictionEngine =
  mlContext.Model.CreatePredictionEngine
  <ProductCobought, Recommendation>(modelGermany);

var products = db.Products.ToArray();

foreach (var item in model.Cart.Items)
{
  var topThree = products
    .Select(product =>
      predictionEngine.Predict(
        new ProductCobought
        {
          ProductID = (uint)item.ProductID,
          CoboughtProductID = (uint)product.ProductID
        })
      ) // returns IEnumerable<Recommendation>
    .OrderByDescending(x => x.Score)
    .Take(3)
    .ToArray();

  model.Recommendations.AddRange(topThree
    .Select(rec => new EnrichedRecommendation
    {
      CoboughtProductID = rec.CoboughtProductID,
      Score = rec.Score,
      ProductName = db.Products.Find(
        (int)rec.CoboughtProductID).ProductName
    }));
}

// show the best three product recommendations
model.Recommendations = model.Recommendations
  .OrderByDescending(rec => rec.Score)
  .Take(3)
  .ToList();
```

```
    }

    return View(model);
}
```

2. In the `Views` folder, in its `Home` subfolder, open `Index.cshtml`, and modify it to output its view model and include links to generate the datasets and train the models, as shown in the following markup:

```
@using Packt.Shared
@model HomeIndexViewModel
@{
    ViewData["Title"] = "Products - Northwind ML";
}
<h1 class="display-3">@ViewData["Title"]</h1>
<p class="lead">
  <div>See product recommendations in your shopping cart.</div>
  <ol>
    <li>First,
      <a asp-controller="Home"
         asp-action="GenerateDatasets">
         generate some datasets</a>.</li>
    <li>Second,
      <a asp-controller="Home" asp-action="TrainModels">
         train the models</a>.</li>
    <li>Third, add some products to your
      <a asp-controller="Home"
         asp-action="Cart">cart</a>.</li>
  </ol>
  <div>
    @if (Model.GermanyDatasetExists || Model.UKDatasetExists)
    {
    <text>Datasets for training:</text>
    }
    @if (Model.GermanyDatasetExists)
    {
    <a href="/Data/germany-dataset.txt">Germany</a>
    }
    @if (Model.UKDatasetExists)
    {
    <a href="/Data/uk-dataset.txt">UK</a>
    }
    @if (Model.USADatasetExists)
    {
    <text>Dataset for testing:</text>
    <a href="/Data/usa-dataset.txt">USA</a>
    }
  </div>
  @if (Model.Milliseconds > 0)
  {
```

```
<div>
  It took @Model.Milliseconds milliseconds to train
  the models.
</div>
}
</p>
<hr />
<h2>Products</h2>
@foreach (Category category in Model.Categories)
{
<h3>@category.CategoryName <small>@category.Description</small></
h3>
<table>
@foreach (Product product in category.Products)
{
  <tr>
    <td>
      <a asp-controller="Home" asp-action="Cart"
        asp-route-id="@product.ProductID"
        class="btn btn-primary">Add to Cart</a>
    </td>
    <td>
      @product.ProductName
    </td>
  </tr>
}
</table>
}
```

3. In the `Views` folder, in its `Home` subfolder, create a new Razor file named `Cart.cshtml`, and modify it to output its view model, as shown in the following markup:

```
@model HomeCartViewModel
@{
  ViewData["Title"] = "Shopping Cart - Northwind ML";
}
<h1>@ViewData["Title"]</h1>
<table class="table table-bordered">
  <tr>
    <th>Product ID</th>
    <th>Product Name</th>
  </tr>
@foreach (CartItem item in Model.Cart.Items)
{
  <tr>
    <td>@item.ProductID</td>
    <td>@item.ProductName</td>
  </tr>
}
```

```
</table>
<h2>Customers who bought items in your cart also bought the
following products</h2>
@if (Model.Recommendations.Count() == 0)
{
  <div>No recommendations.</div>
}
else
{
<table class="table table-bordered">
  <tr>
    <th></th>
    <th>Co-bought Product</th>
    <th>Score</th>
  </tr>
@foreach (EnrichedRecommendation rec
          in Model.Recommendations)
{
  <tr>
    <td>
      <a asp-controller="Home" asp-action="Cart"
        asp-route-id="@rec.CoboughtProductID"
        class="btn btn-primary">Add to Cart</a>
    </td>
    <td>
      @rec.ProductName
    </td>
    <td>
      @rec.Score
    </td>
  </tr>
}
</table>
}
```

Testing the product recommendations website

Now we are ready to test the website product recommendations feature.

1. Start the website using the following command:

   ```
   dotnet run
   ```

2. Start Chrome and navigate to `https://localhost:5001/`

3. On the home page, click **generate some datasets**, and note that links to the three datasets are created, as shown in the following screenshot:

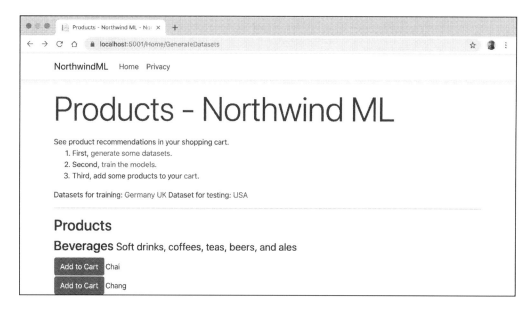

4. Click the **UK** dataset, and note that five products were co-bought with Product ID 1: 5, 11, 23, 68, and 69, as shown in the following screenshot:

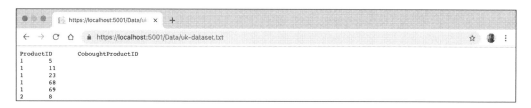

5. Navigate back in your browser.

6. Click **train the models** and note how long it took to train the models, as shown in the following screenshot:

Datasets for training: Germany UK Dataset for testing: USA
It took 324 milliseconds to train the models.

7. In Visual Studio Code, in the `NorthwindML` project, expand the `wwwroot` folder, expand the `Data` folder, and note the models in the filesystem saved as binary ZIP files.

8. In Chrome, on the **Products - Northwind ML** home page, scroll down the list of products, click **Add to Cart** next to any product like **Outback Lager**, and note the **Shopping Cart** page appears with the product as a cart item and recommended products with scores, as shown in the following screenshot:

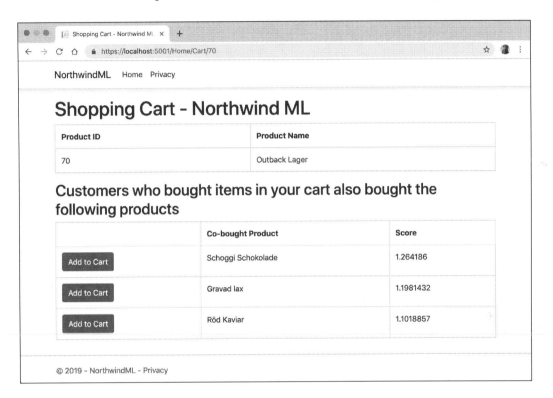

9. Navigate back in your browser, add another product to your cart like **Ipoh Coffee**, and note the changes in the top three product recommendations due to **NuNuCa Nuß-Nougat-Creme** being even more likely to be co-bought than the previous top recommendation, **Schoggi Schokolade**, as shown in the following screenshot:

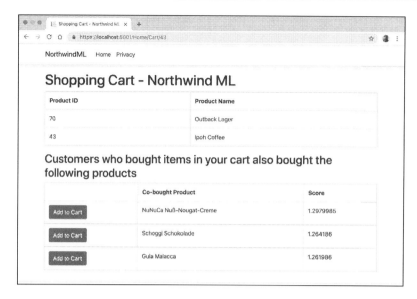

10. Close the browser and stop the website.

Practicing and exploring

Test your knowledge and understanding by answering some questions, get some hands-on practice, and explore this chapter's topics with deeper research.

Exercise 19.1 – Test your knowledge

Answer the following questions:

1. What are the four main steps of the machine learning lifecycle?
2. What are the three sub-steps of the modeling step?
3. Why do models need to be retrained after deployment?
4. Why must you split your dataset into a training dataset and a testing dataset?
5. What are some of the differences between clustering and classification machine learning tasks?
6. What class must you instantiate to perform any machine learning task?
7. What is the difference between a label and a feature?
8. What does `IDataView` represent?
9. What does the `count` parameter in the `[KeyType(count: 10)]` attribute represent?
10. What does the score represent with matrix factorization?

Exercise 19.2 – Practice with samples

Microsoft has many sample projects for learning ML.NET, as shown in the following list:

- **Sentiment Analysis for User Reviews**: `https://github.com/dotnet/machinelearning-samples/tree/master/samples/csharp/getting-started/BinaryClassification_SentimentAnalysis`

- **Customer Segmentation - Clustering sample**: `https://github.com/dotnet/machinelearning-samples/tree/master/samples/csharp/getting-started/Clustering_CustomerSegmentation`

- **Spam Detection for Text Messages**: `https://github.com/dotnet/machinelearning-samples/tree/master/samples/csharp/getting-started/BinaryClassification_SpamDetection`

- **GitHub Issues Labeler**: `https://github.com/dotnet/machinelearning-samples/tree/master/samples/csharp/end-to-end-apps/MulticlassClassification-GitHubLabeler`

- **Movie Recommendation - Matrix Factorization problem sample**: `https://github.com/dotnet/machinelearning-samples/tree/master/samples/csharp/getting-started/MatrixFactorization_MovieRecommendation`

- **Taxi Fare Prediction**: `https://github.com/dotnet/machinelearning-samples/tree/master/samples/csharp/getting-started/Regression_TaxiFarePrediction`

- **Bike Sharing Demand - Regression problem sample**: `https://github.com/dotnet/machinelearning-samples/tree/master/samples/csharp/getting-started/Regression_BikeSharingDemand`

- **eShopDashboardML - Sales forecasting**: `https://github.com/dotnet/machinelearning-samples/tree/master/samples/csharp/end-to-end-apps/Regression-SalesForecast`

Exercise 19.3 – Explore topics

Use the following links to read more details about this chapter's topics:

- **What is ML.NET and how do I understand Machine Learning basics?** `https://docs.microsoft.com/en-us/dotnet/machine-learning/how-does-mldotnet-work`

- **Machine learning glossary of important terms**: `https://docs.microsoft.com/en-us/dotnet/machine-learning/resources/glossary`

- **Channel 9 ML.NET videos**: `https://aka.ms/dotnet3-mlnet`

- **YouTube ML.NET videos**: `https://aka.ms/mlnetyoutube`

- **Machine Learning Explainability vs Interpretability: Two concepts that could help restore trust in AI**: https://www.kdnuggets.com/2018/12/machine-learning-explainability-interpretability-ai.html

- **Machine learning tasks in ML.NET**: https://docs.microsoft.com/en-us/dotnet/machine-learning/resources/tasks

- **Machine learning data transforms - ML.NET**: https://docs.microsoft.com/en-us/dotnet/machine-learning/resources/transforms

- **ML.NET Samples**: https://github.com/dotnet/machinelearning-samples/blob/master/README.md

- **Community Samples**: https://github.com/dotnet/machinelearning-samples/blob/master/docs/COMMUNITY-SAMPLES.md

- **ML.NET API reference**: https://docs.microsoft.com/en-gb/dotnet/api/?view=ml-dotnet

- **ML.NET: The Machine Learning Framework for .NET Developers**: https://msdn.microsoft.com/en-us/magazine/mt848634

- **Building recommendation engine for .NET applications using Azure Machine Learning**: https://devblogs.microsoft.com/dotnet/dot-net-recommendation-system-for-net-applications-using-azure-machine-learning/

Summary

In this chapter, you were introduced to one practical example of how to add intelligence to a website using ML.NET. The current solution would not scale well since it currently loads the entire product list into memory. Building intelligence like this into apps is more than a full-time profession. I hope that this chapter has either sparked an interest in diving deeper into machine learning and data science or has shown you enough that you can make an informed decision to pursue other areas of C# and .NET development.

In the next chapter, you will learn how to build desktop apps for Windows using **Windows Presentation Foundation (WPF)** and **Universal Windows Platform (UWP)**, and how to migrate Windows Forms apps to .NET Core 3.0.

Chapter 20

Building Windows Desktop Apps

This chapter is about building applications for Windows desktop using three technologies: **Windows Forms**, **Windows Presentation Foundation** (**WPF**), and **Universal Windows Platform** (**UWP**). Windows Forms and WPF support using .NET Core 3.0 as their runtime, but current design-time support is limited so I only recommend this if you have existing Windows Forms or WPF apps that must be migrated to .NET Core 3.0. Personally, I would recommend leaving those apps on .NET Framework at least until Visual Studio has much better design-time support for these legacy app models.

Most of this chapter will cover UWP apps that use the modern Windows Runtime and can execute apps built using a custom version of .NET Core 2.0 that compiles to .NET Native. Although most of this chapter does not technically use .NET Core 3.0, in November 2020 Microsoft will release .NET 5.0, which will be the single unified platform for .NET used by all app models, including ASP.NET for web development, Windows Forms, WPF, and UWP for Windows development, and for mobile apps.

 More Information: You can read more about your choices of platform for building Windows desktop apps at the following link: https://docs.microsoft.com/en-us/windows/apps/desktop/choose-your-platform

You will see how **eXtensible Application Markup Language** (**XAML**) makes it easy to define the user interface for a graphical app. You will explore some of the new user interface features of Fluent Design, introduced in the Windows 10 Fall Creators Update in October 2017.

In a single chapter, we will only be able to scratch the surface of what can be achieved using .NET for the Windows desktop. However, I hope to excite you into wanting to learn more about the new ability to migrate legacy Windows applications to the modern .NET Core 3.0 platform, and the cool new UWP technology with its Fluent Design, including template-able controls, data binding, and animation!

Some important points about this chapter

UWP apps are not cross-platform, but they are cross-device, meaning they can run on desktop, laptop, tablet, and mixed reality devices like the HP Windows Mixed Reality Headset. Those devices must run a modern flavor of Windows. You will need Windows 10 May 2019 Update and Visual Studio 2019 version 16.3 or later to use the latest features, like XAML Islands, although older versions of Windows 10 like April 2018 Update should work for creating the example app in this chapter.

In this chapter, we will cover the following topics:

- Understanding legacy Windows application platforms
- Understanding the modern Windows platform
- Creating a modern Windows app
- Using resources and templates
- Using data binding

Understanding legacy Windows application platforms

With the Microsoft Windows 1.0 release in 1985, the only way to create Windows applications was to use the C language and call functions in three core **DLLs** named kernel, user, and GDI. Once Windows became 32-bit with Windows 95, the DLLs were suffixed with 32 and became known as the Win32 API.

In 1991, Microsoft introduced Visual Basic, which provided developers a visual, drag and drop from a toolbox of controls way to build the user interface for Windows applications. It was immensely popular, and the Visual Basic runtime is still part of Windows 10 today.

In 2002, Microsoft introduced .NET Framework, which included Windows Forms for building Windows applications. The code could be written in either Visual Basic or C# languages. Windows Forms had a similar drag and drop visual designer, although it generated C# or Visual Basic code to define the user interface, which can be difficult for humans to understand and edit directly.

In 2006, Microsoft introduced .NET Framework 3.0, which included WPF for building user interfaces using XAML, which is easy for developers to understand and edit directly.

Understanding .NET Core 3.0 support for legacy Windows platforms

The on-disk size of the .NET Core 3.0 SDKs for Linux and macOS are 332 MB and 337 MB respectively. The on-disk size of the .NET Core 3.0 SDK for Windows is 441 MB. This is because it includes the .NET Core Windows Desktop Runtime, which allows the legacy Windows application platforms Windows Forms and WPF to be run on .NET Core 3.0.

Installing Microsoft Visual Studio 2019 for Windows

Since October 2014, Microsoft has made a professional-quality edition of Visual Studio available to everyone for free. It is called Community Edition.

If you have not already installed it, let's do so now.

1. Download Microsoft Visual Studio 2019 version 16.3 or later for Windows from the following link: `https://visualstudio.microsoft.com/downloads/`

2. Start the installer.

3. On the **Workloads** tab, select the following:
    - **.NET desktop development**
    - **Universal Windows Platform development**
    - **.NET Core cross-platform development**

4. Click **Install** and wait for the installer to acquire the selected software and install it.

5. When the installation is complete, click **Launch**.

6. The first time that you run Visual Studio, you will be prompted to sign in. If you have a Microsoft account, you can use that account. If you don't, then register for a new one at the following link: `https://signup.live.com/`

7. The first time that you run Visual Studio, you will be prompted to configure your environment. For **Development Settings**, choose **Visual C#**. For the color theme, I chose **Blue**, but you can choose whatever tickles your fancy.

Working with Windows Forms

We will start by using the `dotnet` command tool to create a new Windows Forms app, then we will use Visual Studio to create a Windows Forms app for .NET Framework to simulate a legacy application, and then we will migrate that application to .NET Core 3.0.

Building a new Windows Forms application

In this task, you will see that it is not a good idea to build new Windows Forms applications for .NET Core 3.0. As a general rule, only migrate existing Windows Forms applications to .NET Core 3.0.

The following instructions start with creating some new folders to store a solution file and a project. You can choose to use another tool to do this instead of the command prompt, but you should at least create the new solution and Windows Forms project by using the `dotnet` command-line tool in the correct folder.

1. From the Windows Start menu, open **Command Prompt**.

2. In Command Prompt, enter commands to perform the following tasks:

    ° Change to the `PracticalApps` folder.

    ° Create a folder named `WindowsDesktopApps` with a new solution file.

    ° Create a subfolder named `BasicWinForms` with a new Windows Forms project.

    ```
    cd C:\Code\PracticalApps\
    mkdir WindowsDesktopApps
    cd WindowsDesktopApps
    dotnet new sln
    mkdir BasicWinForms
    cd BasicWinForms
    dotnet new winforms
    ```

3. Start Visual Studio 2019 and click **Open a project or solution**.

4. Navigate to the `C:\Code\PracticalApps\WindowsDesktopApps` folder, select the `WindowsDesktopApps.sln` solution file, and click **Open**.

5. Navigate to **File | Add | Existing Project...**, select the project named `BasicWinForms.csproj`, and then click **Open**.

6. Navigate to **Project | BasicWinForms Properties...** or right-click the project in **Solution Explorer** and choose **Properties**, and then note that the **Target framework** is **.NET Core 3.0** and the **Output type** is a **Windows Application.**, as shown in the following screenshot:

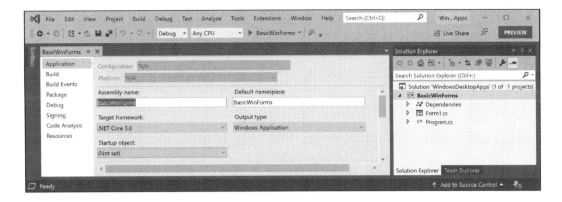

7. In **Solution Explorer**, double-click or right-click the `Form1.cs` and select **Open**, and note that at the time of writing in September 2019, the Windows Forms designer does not support .NET Core 3.0, as shown in the following screenshot:

 More Information: You can track the progress of the Windows Forms designer at the following link: `https://github.com/dotnet/winforms/blob/master/Documentation/winforms-designer.md`

8. Navigate to **Debug | Start Without Debugging** or press *Ctrl + F5*, note the resizable window with the title **Form1**, and then click the close button in its top-right corner to exit the application.

Reviewing a new Windows Forms application

Let's review the code in an empty Windows Forms application.

1. In **Solution Explorer**, open **Program.cs** and note that it is similar to a console app with a `Main` entry point method, and that it instantiates a `Form1` class and runs it, as shown in the following code with comments removed to save space:

```
static class Program
{
  [STAThread]
  static void Main()
  {
    Application.EnableVisualStyles();
    Application.SetCompatibleTextRenderingDefault(false);
    Application.Run(new Form1());
  }
}
```

2. In **Solution Explorer**, expand **Form1.cs**, open the **Form1** class, and note it is a partial class and the call to `InitializeComponent` in its constructor, as shown in the following code:

```
public partial class Form1 : Form
{
  public Form1()
  {
    InitializeComponent();
  }
}
```

3. In **Solution Explorer**, expand **Form1.cs**, open **Form1.Designer.cs**, expand the **Windows Form Designer generated code** section, and note that the code would be messy to understand and modify manually, as shown in the following code, which defines the button:

```
private void InitializeComponent()
{
  this.components = new System.ComponentModel.Container();
  this.AutoScaleMode = System.Windows.Forms.AutoScaleMode.Font;
  this.ClientSize = new System.Drawing.Size(800, 450);
  this.Text = "Form1";
}
```

4. Close any edit windows.

Migrating a legacy Windows Forms application

In this task, you will add a Windows Forms application for .NET Framework to the solution so that you can use the Windows Forms visual designer, and then migrate it to .NET Core 3.0.

1. In Visual Studio 2019, navigate to **File** | **Add** | **New Project...**

2. In the search box, enter `windows forms` and select **Windows Forms App (.NET Framework)**, as shown in the following screenshot:

3. Click **Next**.

4. For **Project name**, enter `LegacyWinForms` and click **Create**.

5. Navigate to **View** | **Toolbox** or press *Ctrl + W, X* and then pin the Toolbox. Note that you might have different key bindings. If so, then you can navigate to **Tools** | **Import and Export Settings** and reset your settings to **Visual C#** to use the same key bindings as the ones I have used in this chapter.

6. In **Toolbox**, expand **Common Controls**.

7. Drag and drop some controls, like **Button**, **MonthCalendar**, **Label**, and **TextBox** onto **Form1**, as shown in the following screenshot:

8. Navigate to **View** | **Properties Window** or press *Ctrl + W, P* or *F4*.

9. Select the button, change its **(Name)** property to `btnGoToChristmas`, and change its **Text** property to `Go to Christmas`.

10. Double-click the button, note that an event handler method is written for you, and enter statements to set the calendar to select Christmas Day 2019, as shown highlighted in the following code:

```
private void BtnGoToChristmas_Click(object sender, EventArgs e)
{
  DateTime christmas = new DateTime(2019, 12, 25);
  monthCalendar1.SelectionStart = christmas;
  monthCalendar1.SelectionEnd = christmas;
}
```

11. In **Solution Explorer**, right-click the solution and select **Set StartUp Projects...**

12. In the **Solution 'WindowsDesktopApps' Properties Pages** dialog box, for **Startup Project**, select **Current selection**, and then click **OK**.

13. In **Solution Explorer**, select the **LegacyWinForms** project and note its name becomes bold to indicate that it is the current selection.

14. Navigate to **Debug** | **Start Without Debugging** or press *Ctrl + F5*, click the button, and note the month calendar animates to select Christmas Day, and then click the close button in the top-right corner to exit the app.

Migrating a Windows Forms app

Now, we can migrate this to the .NET Core 3.0 project. Remember that we only need to do this as a temporary measure. Once the Windows Forms designer is ported to .NET Core 3.0 and is available in a future release of Visual Studio 2019, migrating won't be necessary.

1. Drag and drop `Form1` from the **LegacyWinForms** folder into the **BasicWinForms** folder, which will prompt you to overwrite the following files:
    ○ `Form1.cs`
    ○ `Form1.Designer.cs`
    ○ `Form1.resx`

2. In the `BasicWinForms` project, modify `Program.cs` to specific the legacy namespace when instantiating and running `Form1`, as shown in the following code:

```
Application.Run(new LegacyWinForms.Form1());
```

3. In **Solution Explorer**, select the **BasicWinForms** project.

4. Navigate to **Debug | Start Without Debugging** or press *Ctrl + F5*, click the button, note the month calendar animates to select Christmas Day, and then close the app.

5. Close the project and solution.

Migrating WPF apps to .NET Core 3.0

If you have existing WPF apps that need to move from .NET Framework to .NET Core 3.0, then like migrating Windows Forms, it is possible today, but tricky. This will improve over the next year or so, especially with future releases of Visual Studio 2019 and the release of .NET 5.0 in November 2020.

More Information: You can read more about migrating WPF apps to .NET Core 3.0 at the following link: `https://devblogs.microsoft.com/dotnet/migrating-a-sample-wpf-app-to-net-core-3-part-1/`

Migrating legacy apps using the Windows Compatibility Pack

Windows Compatibility Pack provides access to APIs that were previously available only for .NET Framework. It can be used from both .NET Core as well as .NET Standard.

More Information: You can read more about the Windows Compatibility Pack at the following link: `https://devblogs.microsoft.com/dotnet/announcing-the-windows-compatibility-pack-for-net-core/`

Understanding the modern Windows platform

Microsoft continues to improve their Windows platform, which includes technologies like Universal Windows Platform and Fluent Design System for building modern apps.

Understanding Universal Windows Platform

UWP is Microsoft's latest technology solution to build applications for its Windows suite of operating systems. It provides a guaranteed API layer across multiple device types. You can create a single app package that can be uploaded to a single store to be distributed to reach all the device types your app can run on. These devices include Windows 10 desktops, laptops, and tablets, the Xbox One and later video game systems, and Mixed Reality Headsets like Microsoft HoloLens.

UWP provides standard mechanisms to detect the capabilities of the current device and then activate additional features of your app to fully take advantage of them.

UWP with XAML provides layout panels that adapt how they display their child controls to make the most of the device they are currently running on. It is the Windows app equivalent of web page responsive design. They also provide visual state triggers to alter the layout based on dynamic changes, such as the horizontal or vertical orientation of a tablet.

Understanding Fluent Design System

Microsoft's Fluent Design System will be delivered in multiple waves, rather than as a "Big Bang" all in one go, to help developers slowly migrate from traditional styles of user interface to more modern ones.

Wave 1, available in Windows 10 Fall Creators Update, released in October 2017 and refined in the subsequent waves as part of biannual Windows 10 updates, included the following features:

- Acrylic material
- Connected animations
- Parallax views
- Reveal lighting

Filling user interface elements with acrylic brushes

Acrylic material is a semi-transparent blur-effect brush that can be used to fill user interface elements to add depth and perspective to your apps. Acrylic can show through what is in the background behind the app, or elements within the app that are behind a pane. Acrylic material can be customized with varying colors and transparencies.

More Information: You can read more about how and when to use Acrylic material at the following link: `https://docs.microsoft.com/en-us/windows/uwp/design/style/acrylic`

Connecting user interface elements with animations

When navigating around a user interface, animating elements to draw connections between screens helps users to understand where they are and how to interact with your app.

More Information: You can read more about how and when to use connected animations at the following link: `https://docs.microsoft.com/en-us/windows/uwp/design/motion/connected-animation`

Parallax views and Reveal lighting

Parallax views are backgrounds, often images, that move at a slower rate than the foreground during scrolling to provide a feeling of depth and give your apps a modern feel.

More Information: You can read more about Parallax at the following link: `https://docs.microsoft.com/en-us/windows/uwp/design/motion/parallax`

Reveal lighting helps the user understand which of the visual elements in the user interface is an interactive element by *lighting up* as the user moves their mouse cursor over that element to draw their focus.

More Information: You can read more about how and when to use Reveal to bring focus to user interface elements at the following link: `https://docs.microsoft.com/en-us/windows/uwp/design/style/reveal`

Understanding XAML Standard

In 2006, Microsoft released WPF, which was the first technology to use XAML. Silverlight, for web and mobile apps, quickly followed, but it is no longer supported by Microsoft. WPF is still used today to create Windows desktop applications; for example, Microsoft Visual Studio 2019 is partially built using WPF.

XAML can be used to build parts of the following apps:

- **UWP apps** for Windows 10 devices, Xbox One, and Mixed Reality Headsets.
- **WPF apps** for the Windows desktop, including Windows 7 and later.
- **Xamarin apps** for mobile and desktop devices including Android, iOS, and macOS.

Like .NET, XAML has fragmented, with slight variations in capabilities between XAML for different platforms. So, just as .NET Standard is an initiative to bring various platforms of .NET together, XAML Standard was an initiative to do the same for XAML. Now that .NET will be unified in 2020, I expect the same to happen with XAML since Microsoft has not been active in the XAML Standard public GitHub repository.

More Information: You can read more about XAML Standard: a set of principles that drive XAML dialect alignment at the following link: `https://github.com/Microsoft/xaml-standard`

Simplifying code using XAML

XAML simplifies C# code, especially when building a user interface.

Imagine that you need two or more buttons laid out horizontally to create a toolbar. In C#, you might write this code:

```
var toolbar = new StackPanel();
toolbar.Orientation = Orientation.Horizontal;
var newButton = new Button();
newButton.Content = "New";
newButton.Background = new SolidColorBrush(Colors.Pink);
toolbar.Children.Add(newButton);
var openButton = new Button();
openButton.Content = "Open";
openButton.Background = new SolidColorBrush(Colors.Pink);
toolbar.Children.Add(openButton);
```

In XAML, this could be simplified to the following lines of code. When this XAML is processed, the equivalent properties are set, and methods are called to achieve the same goal as the preceding C# code:

```
<StackPanel Name="toolbar" Orientation="Horizontal">
  <Button Name="newButton" Background="Pink">New</Button>
  <Button Name="openButton" Background="Pink">Open</Button>
</StackPanel>
```

XAML is an alternative and better way of declaring and instantiating .NET types for use in a user interface.

Choosing common controls

There are lots of predefined controls that you can choose from for common user interface scenarios. Almost all versions of XAML support these controls:

Controls	Description
Button, Menu, Toolbar	Executing actions
CheckBox, RadioButton	Choosing options
Calendar, DatePicker	Choosing dates
ComboBox, ListBox, ListView, TreeView	Choosing items from lists and hierarchical trees
Canvas, DockPanel, Grid, StackPanel, WrapPanel	Layout containers that affect their children in different ways
Label, TextBlock	Displaying read-only text
RichTextBox, TextBox	Editing text
Image, MediaElement	Embedding images, videos, and audio files
DataGrid	Viewing and editing data as quickly and easily as possible
Scrollbar, Slider, StatusBar	Miscellaneous user interface elements

Understanding markup extensions

To support some advanced features, XAML uses markup extensions. Some of the most important enable element and data binding and reuse of resources, as shown in the following list:

- {Binding} links an element to a value from another element or a data source.
- {StaticResource} links an element to a shared resource.
- {ThemeResource} links an element to a shared resource defined in a theme.

You will see some practical examples of markup extensions throughout this chapter.

Creating a modern Windows app

We will start by creating a simple UWP app, with some common controls and modern features of Fluent Design like acrylic material.

Enabling developer mode

To be able to create apps for UWP, you must enable developer mode in Windows 10.

1. Navigate to **Start** | **Settings** | **Update & Security** | **For developers**, and then click on **Developer mode**.

2. Accept the warning about how it "could expose your device and personal data to security risk or harm your device," and then close the **Settings** app.

Creating a UWP project

Now you will add a new UWP app project to your solution.

1. In Visual Studio 2019, open the `WindowsDesktopApps` solution.

2. Navigate to **File** | **Add** | **New Project...**.

3. In the **Add a new project** dialog, enter uwp in search box, select the **Blank App (Universal Windows)** template for C#, and then click **Next**.

4. For the **Project name**, enter `FluentUwpApp` and then click on **Create**.

5. In the **New Universal Windows Platform Project** dialog, choose the latest version of Windows 10 for **Target Version** and **Minimum Version** and click on **OK**.

Good Practice: Since the Fluent Design System was first released with Window 10 Fall Creators Update (10.0; Build 16299) then you should be able to select that to support the features that we will cover in this chapter, but while you're learning, it's best to use the latest to avoid unexpected incompatibilities. Developers writing UWP apps for a general audience should choose one of the latest builds of Windows 10 for Minimum Version. Developers writing enterprise apps should choose an older Minimum Version. Build 10240 was released in July 2015 and is a good choice for maximum compatibility, but you will not have access to modern features such as Fluent Design System.

6. In **Solution Explorer**, double-click on the `MainPage.xaml` file to open it for editing. You will see the XAML design window showing a graphical view and a XAML view. You will be able to make the following observations:

   ○ The XAML designer is split horizontally, but you can toggle to a vertical split and collapse one side by clicking on the buttons on the right edge of the divider.

   ○ You can swap views by clicking on the double-arrow button in the divider.

   ○ You can scroll and zoom in both views.

7. For **Design** view, change the device to **13.3" Desktop (1280 x 720) 100% scale** and zoom to **100%**.

8. Navigate to **View** | **Toolbox** or press *Ctrl + W, X*. Note that the toolbox has sections for **Common XAML Controls**, **All XAML Controls**, and **General**.

9. At the top of the toolbox is a search box. Enter the letters bu, and then note that the list of controls is filtered.

10. Drag and drop the **Button** control from the toolbox onto the **Design** view.

11. Resize it by clicking, holding, and dragging any of the eight square-shape resize handles on each edge and in each corner.

Note that the button is given a fixed width and height, and fixed left (30 units) and top (40 units) margins, to position and size it absolutely inside the grid, as shown in the following screenshot:

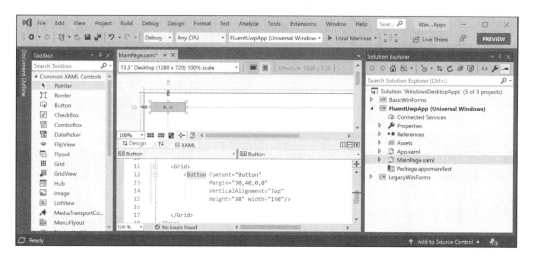

Although you can drag and drop controls, it is better to use the XAML view for layout so that you can position items relatively and implement more of a responsive design.

12. In the XAML view, find the `Button` element and delete it.

13. In the XAML view, inside the `Grid` element, enter the following markup:

```
<Button Margin="6" Padding="6" Name="ClickMeButton">
  Click Me
</Button>
```

14. Change the zoom to 50% and note that the button is automatically sized to its content, **Click Me**, aligned vertically in the center and aligned horizontally to the left, even if you toggle between vertical and horizontal phone layouts.

15. In the XAML view, delete the `Grid` element, and modify the XAML to wrap the `Button` element inside a horizontally-orientated `StackPanel` with a light gray background that is inside a vertically orientated (by default) `StackPanel`, and note the change in its layout to be in the top-left of the available space, as shown in the following code:

```
<StackPanel>
  <StackPanel Orientation="Horizontal" Padding="4"
              Background="LightGray" Name="toolbar">
    <Button Margin="6" Padding="6" Name="ClickMeButton">
      Click Me
    </Button>
  </StackPanel>
</StackPanel>
```

16. Modify the `Button` element to give it a new event handler for its `Click` event, as shown in the following screenshot:

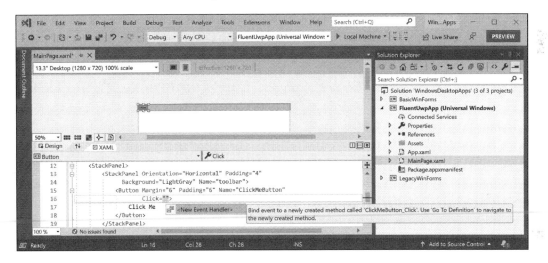

17. Right-click the event handler name and select **Go To Definition** or press *F12*.

18. Add a statement to the event handler method that sets the content of the button to the current time, as shown highlighted in the following code:

```
private void ClickMeButton_Click(object sender, RoutedEventArgs e)
{
  ClickMeButton.Content = DateTime.Now.ToString("hh:mm:ss");
}
```

19. Navigate to **Build | Configuration Manager...** for the **FluentUwpApp** project, select the **Build** and **Deploy** checkboxes, select **Platform** of **x64**, and then select **Close**, as shown in the following screenshot:

20. Run the application by navigating to **Debug | Start Without Debugging** or pressing *Ctrl + F5*.

21. Click on the **Click Me** button and note that every time you click on the button, the button's content changes to show the current time.

Exploring common controls and acrylic brushes

Now you will explore some common controls and painting with acrylic brushes.

1. Open `MainPage.xaml`, set the stack panel's background to use the acrylic system window brush, and add some elements to the stack panel after the button for the user to enter their name, as shown highlighted in the following markup:

```
<StackPanel
  Background="{ThemeResource SystemControlAcrylicWindowBrush}">
  <StackPanel Orientation="Horizontal" Padding="4"
            Background="LightGray" Name="toolbar">
    <Button Margin="6" Padding="6" Name="ClickMeButton"
          Click="ClickMeButton_Click">
      Click Me
    </Button>
    <TextBlock Text="First name:"
```

```
                VerticalAlignment="Center" Margin="4" />
        <TextBox PlaceholderText="Enter your name"
                VerticalAlignment="Center" Width="200" />
      </StackPanel>
    </StackPanel>
```

2. Run the application by navigating to **Debug | Start Without Debugging**, and note the tinted acrylic material showing the green tent and orange sunset over the mountains of one of the standard Windows 10 wallpapers through the app window background, as shown in the following screenshot:

Acrylic uses a lot of system resources, so if an app loses the focus, or your device is low on battery, then acrylic is disabled automatically.

Exploring Reveal

Reveal is built-in for some controls, such as `ListView` and `NavigationView`, that you will see later. For other controls, you can enable it by applying a theme style. First, we will add some XAML to define a calculator user interface made up of a grid of buttons. Then, we will add an event handler for the page's `Loaded` event so that we can apply the Reveal theme style and other properties by enumerating the buttons instead of having to manually set attributes for each one in XAML.

1. Open `MainPage.xaml`, add a new horizontal stack panel under the one used as a toolbar, and add a grid with buttons to define a calculator, as shown highlighted in the following markup:

```
<StackPanel
  Background="{ThemeResource SystemControlAcrylicWindowBrush}">
  <StackPanel Orientation="Horizontal" Padding="4"
```

```
                    Background="LightGray" Name="toolbar">
    <Button Margin="6" Padding="6" Name="ClickMeButton"
            Click="ClickMeButton_Click">
      Click Me
    </Button>
    <TextBlock Text="First name:"
      VerticalAlignment="Center" Margin="4" />
    <TextBox PlaceholderText="Enter your name"
      VerticalAlignment="Center" Width="200" />
  </StackPanel>
  <StackPanel Orientation="Horizontal">
    <Grid Background="DarkGray" Margin="10"
          Padding="5" Name="gridCalculator">
      <Grid.ColumnDefinitions>
        <ColumnDefinition/>
        <ColumnDefinition/>
        <ColumnDefinition/>
        <ColumnDefinition/>
      </Grid.ColumnDefinitions>
      <Grid.RowDefinitions>
        <RowDefinition/>
        <RowDefinition/>
        <RowDefinition/>
        <RowDefinition/>
      </Grid.RowDefinitions>
      <Button Grid.Row="0" Grid.Column="0" Content="X" />
      <Button Grid.Row="0" Grid.Column="1" Content="/" />
      <Button Grid.Row="0" Grid.Column="2" Content="+" />
      <Button Grid.Row="0" Grid.Column="3" Content="-" />
      <Button Grid.Row="1" Grid.Column="0" Content="7" />
      <Button Grid.Row="1" Grid.Column="1" Content="8" />
      <Button Grid.Row="1" Grid.Column="2" Content="9" />
      <Button Grid.Row="1" Grid.Column="3" Content="0" />
      <Button Grid.Row="2" Grid.Column="0" Content="4" />
      <Button Grid.Row="2" Grid.Column="1" Content="5" />
      <Button Grid.Row="2" Grid.Column="2" Content="6" />
      <Button Grid.Row="2" Grid.Column="3" Content="." />
      <Button Grid.Row="3" Grid.Column="0" Content="1" />
      <Button Grid.Row="3" Grid.Column="1" Content="2" />
      <Button Grid.Row="3" Grid.Column="2" Content="3" />
      <Button Grid.Row="3" Grid.Column="3" Content="=" />
    </Grid>
  </StackPanel>
</StackPanel>
```

2. In the Page element, add a new event handler for Loaded, as shown highlighted in the following markup:

```
<Page
  ...
```

```
Background="{ThemeResource ApplicationPageBackgroundThemeBrush}"
Loaded="Page_Loaded">
```

3. Right-click `Page_Loaded` and select **Go To Definition** or press *F12*.

4. Add statements to the `Page_Loaded` method to loop through all of the calculator buttons, setting them to be the same size, and apply the Reveal style, as shown in the following code:

```
private void Page_Loaded(object sender, RoutedEventArgs e)
{
    Style reveal = Resources.ThemeDictionaries[
      "ButtonRevealStyle"] as Style;

    foreach (Button b in gridCalculator.Children.OfType<Button>())
    {
        b.FontSize = 24;
        b.Width = 54;
        b.Height = 54;
        b.Style = reveal;
    }
}
```

5. Run the application by navigating to **Debug | Start Without Debugging**, and note the calculator buttons start with a flat gray user interface.

6. When the user moves their mouse pointer over the bottom-right corner of the 8 button, we see that Reveal lights it up, and parts of the surrounding buttons light up too, as shown in the following screenshot:

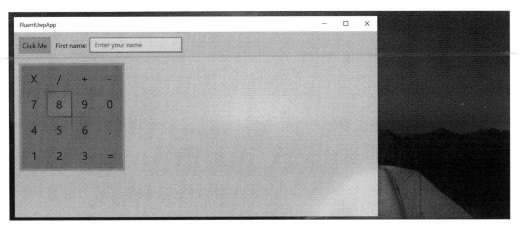

7. Close the app.

The implementation of the Reveal effect has subtlety changed over the recent biannual updates to Windows 10, so the effect in your app may look slightly different.

Installing more controls

In addition to dozens of built-in controls, you can install additional ones as NuGet packages and one of the best is the **UWP Community Toolkit**.

More Information: You can read more about the UWP Community Toolkit at the following link: `http://www.uwpcommunitytoolkit.com/`

One of the toolkit controls is an editor for Markdown.

More Information: You can read about the Markdown project at the following link: `https://daringfireball.net/projects/markdown/`

Let's install the UWP Community Toolkit now and explore some of its controls.

1. In the **FluentUwpApp** project, right-click on **References**, and select **Manage NuGet Packages....**
2. Click **Browse**, search for `Microsoft.Toolkit.Uwp.UI.Controls`, and click on **Install**, as shown in the following screenshot:

3. Review the changes and accept the license agreement.
4. Navigate to **Build | Build FluentUwpApp**. This will restore packages.

5. Open `MainPage.xaml`, and in the `Page` element, import the toolkit namespace as a prefix named `kit`, as shown highlighted in the following markup:

```
<Page
  ...
  xmlns:kit="using:Microsoft.Toolkit.Uwp.UI.Controls"
  mc:Ignorable="d"
  Background="{ThemeResource ApplicationPageBackgroundThemeBrush}"
  Loaded="Page_Loaded">
```

6. Inside the second horizontal stack panel and after the calculator grid, add a textbox and a markdown text block that are data bound together so that the text in the textbox becomes the source of the markdown control, as shown highlighted in the following markup:

```
<StackPanel Orientation="Horizontal">
  <Grid Background="DarkGray" Margin="10"
        Padding="5" Name="gridCalculator">
  ...
  </Grid>
  <TextBox Name="markdownSource" Text="# Welcome"
           Header="Enter some Markdown text:"
           VerticalAlignment="Stretch" Margin="5"
           AcceptsReturn="True" />
  <kit:MarkdownTextBlock Margin="5"
     Text="{Binding ElementName=markdownSource, Path=Text}"
     VerticalAlignment="Stretch" HorizontalAlignment="Stretch" />
</StackPanel>
```

7. Run the application by navigating to **Debug | Start Without Debugging** and note that the user can enter Markdown syntax in the textbox, and it is rendered in the Markdown text block, as shown in the following screenshot:

Using resources and templates

When building graphical user interfaces, you will often want to use a resource, such as a brush to paint the background of controls or an instance of a class to perform custom conversions. These resources can be defined in a single place and shared throughout the app.

Sharing resources

A good place to define shared resources is at the app level, so let's see how to do that.

1. In **Solution Explorer**, open the `App.xaml` file.

2. Add the following markup inside the existing `Application` element to define a linear gradient brush with a key of `rainbow`, as shown highlighted in the following markup:

```
<Application
    x:Class="FluentUwpApp.App"
    xmlns="http://schemas.microsoft.com/winfx/2006/xaml/
presentation"
    xmlns:x="http://schemas.microsoft.com/winfx/2006/xaml"
    xmlns:local="using:FluentUwpApp">

  <Application.Resources>
    <LinearGradientBrush x:Key="rainbow">
      <GradientStop Color="Red" Offset="0" />
      <GradientStop Color="Orange" Offset="0.1" />
      <GradientStop Color="Yellow" Offset="0.3" />
      <GradientStop Color="Green" Offset="0.5" />
      <GradientStop Color="Blue" Offset="0.7" />
      <GradientStop Color="Indigo" Offset="0.9" />
     <GradientStop Color="Violet" Offset="1" />
    </LinearGradientBrush>
  </Application.Resources>

</Application>
```

3. Navigate to **Build | Build FluentUwpApp**.

4. In `MainPage.xaml`, modify the `StackPanel` element named `toolbar` to change its background from `LightGray` to the static resource `rainbow` brush, as shown in the following markup:

```
<StackPanel Orientation="Horizontal" Padding="4"
            Background="{StaticResource rainbow}" Name="toolbar">
```

5. As you enter the reference to a static resource, IntelliSense will show your `rainbow` resource and the built-in resources, as shown in the following screenshot:

 Good Practice: A resource can be an instance of any object. To share it within an application, define it in the `App.xaml` file and give it a unique key. To set an element's property with a resource, use `{StaticResource key}`.

Resources can be defined and stored inside any element of XAML, not just at the app level. For example, if a resource is only needed on `MainPage`, then it can be defined there. You can also dynamically load XAML files at runtime.

 More Information: You can read more about the Resource Management System at the following link: `https://docs.microsoft.com/en-us/windows/uwp/app-resources/`

Replacing a control template

You can redefine how a control looks by replacing its default template. The default control template for a button is flat and transparent.

One of the most common resources is a style that can set multiple properties at once. If a style has a unique key then it must be explicitly set, like we did earlier with the linear gradient. If it doesn't have a key, then it will be automatically applied based on the `TargetType` property.

1. In `App.xaml`, define a control template inside the `Application.Resources` element and note that the `Style` element will automatically set the `Template` property of all controls that are `TargetType`, that is, buttons, to use the defined control template, as shown highlighted in the following markup:

```
<Application.Resources>

  <LinearGradientBrush x:Key="rainbow">
  ...
  </LinearGradientBrush>

  <ControlTemplate x:Key="DarkGlassButton"
                   TargetType="Button">
    <Border BorderBrush="#FFFFFFFF"
            BorderThickness="1,1,1,1" CornerRadius="4,4,4,4">
      <Border x:Name="border" Background="#7F000000"
              BorderBrush="#FF000000"
              BorderThickness="1,1,1,1"
              CornerRadius="4,4,4,4">
        <Grid>
          <Grid.RowDefinitions>
            <RowDefinition Height="*"/>
            <RowDefinition Height="*"/>
          </Grid.RowDefinitions>
          <Border Opacity="0"
                  HorizontalAlignment="Stretch" x:Name="glow"
                  Width="Auto" Grid.RowSpan="2"
                  CornerRadius="4,4,4,4">
          </Border>
          <ContentPresenter HorizontalAlignment="Center"
                            VerticalAlignment="Center"
                            Width="Auto"
                            Grid.RowSpan="2" Padding="4"/>
          <Border HorizontalAlignment="Stretch" Margin="0,0,0,0"
                  x:Name="shine" Width="Auto"
                  CornerRadius="4,4,0,0">
            <Border.Background>
              <LinearGradientBrush EndPoint="0.5,0.9"
                                   StartPoint="0.5,0.03">
                <GradientStop Color="#99FFFFFF" Offset="0"/>
                <GradientStop Color="#33FFFFFF" Offset="1"/>
              </LinearGradientBrush>
            </Border.Background>
          </Border>
```

```
          </Grid>
        </Border>
      </Border>
  </ControlTemplate>

  <Style TargetType="Button">
    <Setter Property="Template"
            Value="{StaticResource DarkGlassButton}" />
    <Setter Property="Foreground" Value="White" />
  </Style>

</Application.Resources>
```

2. Run the application and note the black glass effect on the button in the toolbar.

The calculator buttons are not affected at runtime by this black glass effect because we replace their styles using code after the page has loaded.

Using data binding

When building graphical user interfaces, you will often want to bind a property of one control to another, or to some data.

Binding to elements

The simplest type of binding is between elements.

1. In `MainPage.xaml`, after the second horizontal stack panel and inside the outer vertical stack panel, add a text block for instructions, a slider for selecting a rotation, a grid containing stack panel and text blocks to show the selected rotation in degrees, a radial gauge from the UWP Community Toolkit, and a red square to rotate, as shown highlighted in the following markup:

```
<kit:MarkdownTextBlock Margin="5"
  Text="{Binding ElementName=markdownSource, Path=Text}"
  VerticalAlignment="Stretch"
  HorizontalAlignment="Stretch" />
</StackPanel>

<TextBlock Grid.ColumnSpan="2" Margin="10">
  Use the slider to rotate the square:
</TextBlock>
```

```xml
        <Slider Value="180" Minimum="0" Maximum="360"
                Name="sliderRotation" Margin="10,0" />

        <Grid>
          <Grid.ColumnDefinitions>
            <ColumnDefinition/>
            <ColumnDefinition/>
            <ColumnDefinition/>
          </Grid.ColumnDefinitions>
          <StackPanel Orientation="Horizontal"
                      VerticalAlignment="Center"
                      HorizontalAlignment="Center">
            <TextBlock FontSize="30"
              Text="{Binding ElementName=sliderRotation, Path=Value}"
  />
            <TextBlock Text="degrees" FontSize="30" Margin="10,0" />
          </StackPanel>
          <kit:RadialGauge Grid.Column="1" Minimum="0" Maximum="360"
            Value="{Binding ElementName=sliderRotation, Path=Value}"
            Height="200" Width="200" />
          <Rectangle Grid.Column="2" Height="100" Width="100"
  Fill="Red">
              <Rectangle.RenderTransform>
                <RotateTransform
                  Angle="{Binding ElementName=sliderRotation,
  Path=Value}" />
              </Rectangle.RenderTransform>
          </Rectangle>
        </Grid>

    </StackPanel>
  </Page>
```

2. Note that the text of the text block, the value of the radial gauge, and the angle of the rotation transform are all bound to the slider's value using the {Binding} markup extension that's specific the name of the element and the name, also known as the path, of a property to bind to.

3. Run the app and then click, hold, and drag the slider to rotate the red square, as shown in the following screenshot:

Creating an HTTP service to bind to

To illustrate binding to data sources, we will create an app for the Northwind database that shows categories and products. We will start by adding two controllers to the `NorthwindService` that you created in *Chapter 18, Building and Consuming Web Services*.

1. In Visual Studio Code, open the `PracticalApps` workspace.

2. In the **NorthwindService** project, in the **Controllers** folder, add a file, and name it `CategoriesController.cs`.

3. Write statements to define a Web API controller class with two action methods that respond to HTTP GET requests that use the Northwind database context to retrieve all categories, or a single category using its ID, as shown in the following code:

```
using Microsoft.AspNetCore.Mvc;
using Packt.Shared;
using System.Collections.Generic;
using System.Linq;

namespace NorthwindService.Controllers
{
    [Route("api/[controller]")]
```

```
    [ApiController]
    public class CategoriesController : ControllerBase
    {
      private readonly Northwind db;

      public CategoriesController(Northwind db)
      {
        this.db = db;
      }

      // GET: api/categories
      [HttpGet]
      [ProducesResponseType(200, Type =
  typeof(IEnumerable<Category>))]
      public IEnumerable<Category> Get()
      {
        var categories = db.Categories.ToArray();
        return categories;
      }

      // GET api/categories/5
      [HttpGet("{id}" , Name = nameof(GetCategory))]
      [ProducesResponseType(200, Type = typeof(Category))]
      [ProducesResponseType(404)]
      public Category GetCategory(int id)
      {
        var category = db.Categories.Find(id);
        return category;
      }
    }
}
```

4. In the `Controllers` folder, add a file, and name it `ProductsController.cs`.

5. Write statements to define a Web API controller class with two action methods that respond to HTTP GET requests that use the Northwind database context to retrieve all products, or a list of products for a category ID, as shown in the following code:

```
using Microsoft.AspNetCore.Mvc;
using Packt.Shared;
using System.Collections.Generic;
using System.Linq;

namespace NorthwindService.Controllers
{
  [Route("api/[controller]")]
  [ApiController]
```

```
public class ProductsController : ControllerBase
{
  private readonly Northwind db;

  public ProductsController(Northwind db)
  {
    this.db = db;
  }

  // GET: api/products
  [HttpGet]
  [ProducesResponseType(200,
    Type = typeof(IEnumerable<Product>))]
  public IEnumerable<Product> Get()
  {
    var products = db.Products.ToArray();
    return products;
  }

  // GET api/products/5
  [HttpGet("{id}", Name = nameof(GetProductsByCategoryID))]
  [ProducesResponseType(200,
    Type = typeof(IEnumerable<Product>))]
  public IEnumerable<Product> GetProductsByCategoryID(int id)
  {
    var products = db.Products.Where(
        product => product.CategoryID == id)
        .ToArray();

    return products;
  }
 }
}
```

6. Navigate to **Terminal | New Terminal** and select **NorthwindService**.

7. In **Terminal**, restore packages and compile by entering the following command: `dotnet build`.

8. Test `NorthwindService` by starting the Web API service using `dotnet run`.

9. Start Chrome, navigate to `https://localhost:5001/api/products/1` and ensure the service returns only products in category 1, that is, beverages, as shown in the following screenshot:

[{"productID":1,"productName":"Chai","supplierID":1,"categoryID":1,"quantityPerUnit":"10 boxes x 20 bags","unitPrice":18,"unitsInStock":39,"unitsOnOrder":0,"reorderLevel":10,"discontinued":false,"category":null,"supplier":null},
{"productID":2,"productName":"Chang","supplierID":1,"categoryID":1,"quantityPerUnit":"24 - 12 oz bottles","unitPrice":19,"unitsInStock":17,"unitsOnOrder":40,"reorderLevel":25,"discontinued":false,"category":null,"supplier":null},
{"productID":24,"productName":"Guaran\u00E1 Fant\u00E1stica","supplierID":10,"categoryID":1,"quantityPerUnit":"12 - 355 ml cans","unitPrice":4.5,"unitsInStock":20,"unitsOnOrder":0,"reorderLevel":0,"discontinued":true,"category":null,"supplier":null},
{"productID":34,"productName":"Sasquatch Ale","supplierID":16,"categoryID":1,"quantityPerUnit":"24 - 12 oz bottles","unitPrice":14,"unitsInStock":111,"unitsOnOrder":0,"reorderLevel":15,"discontinued":false,"category":null,"supplier":null},
{"productID":35,"productName":"Steeleye Stout","supplierID":16,"categoryID":1,"quantityPerUnit":"24 - 12 oz bottles","unitPrice":18,"unitsInStock":20,"unitsOnOrder":0,"reorderLevel":15,"discontinued":false,"category":null,"supplier":null},
{"productID":38,"productName":"C\u00F4te de Blaye","supplierID":18,"categoryID":1,"quantityPerUnit":"12 - 75 cl bottles","unitPrice":263.5,"unitsInStock":17,"unitsOnOrder":0,"reorderLevel":15,"discontinued":false,"category":null,"supplier":null},
{"productID":39,"productName":"Chartreuse verte","supplierID":18,"categoryID":1,"quantityPerUnit":"750 cc per bottle","unitPrice":18,"unitsInStock":69,"unitsOnOrder":0,"reorderLevel":5,"discontinued":false,"category":null,"supplier":null},
{"productID":43,"productName":"Ipoh Coffee","supplierID":20,"categoryID":1,"quantityPerUnit":"16 - 500 g tins","unitPrice":46,"unitsInStock":17,"unitsOnOrder":10,"reorderLevel":25,"discontinued":false,"category":null,"supplier":null},
{"productID":67,"productName":"Laughing Lumberjack Lager","supplierID":16,"categoryID":1,"quantityPerUnit":"24 - 12 oz bottles","unitPrice":14,"unitsInStock":52,"unitsOnOrder":0,"reorderLevel":10,"discontinued":false,"category":null,"supplier":null},
{"productID":70,"productName":"Outback Lager","supplierID":7,"categoryID":1,"quantityPerUnit":"24 - 355 ml bottles","unitPrice":15,"unitsInStock":15,"unitsOnOrder":10,"reorderLevel":30,"discontinued":false,"category":null,"supplier":null},
{"productID":75,"productName":"Rh\u00F6nbr\u00E4u Klosterbier","supplierID":12,"categoryID":1,"quantityPerUnit":"24 - 0.5 1 bottles","unitPrice":7.75,"unitsInStock":125,"unitsOnOrder":0,"reorderLevel":25,"discontinued":false,"category":null,"supplier":null},
{"productID":76,"productName":"Lakkalik\u00F6\u00F6ri","supplierID":23,"categoryID":1,"quantityPerUnit":"500 ml","unitPrice":18,"unitsInStock":57,"unitsOnOrder":0,"reorderLevel":20,"discontinued":false,"category":null,"supplier":null}]

Downloading the web service's certificate

To call this web service from a Windows app, we need the SSL certificate that it uses to encrypt communication over HTTPS. We will use Chrome to do this.

1. In Chrome, click the padlock to the left of the `https` in the address bar, and then click **Certificate (Valid)**.

2. Click the **Details** tab, and then click **Copy To File…**.

3. In the **Export Certificate Wizard**, click **Next**.

4. In the **Export File Format** step, select **DER encoded binary X.509 (.CER)** and click **Next**, as shown in the following screenshot:

5. Click **Browse**, navigate to the
    `C:\Code\PracticalApps\WindowsDesktopApps` folder, and then create a
    new `Certificates` folder.

6. Open the `Certificates` folder, enter the filename `selfcertlocalhost.cer`,
    and click **Save**.

7. Click **Next**, review the summary, and then click **Finish**.

8. Close the browser.

We exported the localhost self-signed certificate so that we can import it into the
UWP app that you will now create so that it can call the HTTP service securely.

 Good Practice: When deploying a web service and its UWP app into
production, you should register an appropriate certificate for your
organization and use it for web services and any apps that call them.

Binding to data from a secure HTTP service

We will now create a UWP app to consume categories and products from
`NorthwindService` that uses that certificate to securely communicate with the web
service.

1. If necessary, start Visual Studio 2019 and open the `WindowsDesktopApps`
    solution.

2. Navigate to **File | Add | New Project....**

3. In the **Add a new project** dialog, in the **Recent project templates** list, select **Blank App (Universal Windows)**, and then click **Next**.

4. For the **Project name**, enter NorthwindFluent, and then click **Create**.

5. Select the latest Windows 10 build for both **Target Version** and **Minimum Version**.

6. In the **NorthwindFluent** project, open Package.appxmanifest.

7. Navigate to the **Declarations** tab.

8. In **Available Declarations**, select **Certificates** and then click **Add**.

9. In **Certificates**, click **Add New**.

10. For **Store name**, select **Trusted Root Certificate Authorities**, and for **Content**, select the path to the selfcertlocalhost.cer file, as shown in the following screenshot:

11. Save the changes to the Package.appxmanifest file.

Creating the user interface to call the HTTP service

Now we can create a user interface to call the web service.

1. In the **NorthwindFluent** project, navigate to **Project | Add New Item**, and add a **Blank Page** project item named `NotImplementedPage`. This will be used for parts of the app that we will not implement yet.

2. Inside the existing `Grid` element, add a text block saying, "Not yet implemented.", centered on the page, as shown in the following markup:

```
<TextBlock Text="Not yet implemented."
          VerticalAlignment="Center" HorizontalAlignment="Center"
          FontSize="20" />
```

3. Navigate to **File | Add | Existing Project...**.

4. Navigate to the `C:\Code\PracticalApps\NorthwindEntityLib` folder and select `NorthwindEntityLib.csproj`.

5. In the `NorthwindFluent` project, right-click **References** and select **Add Reference...**.

6. In **Projects**, select the check box for the `NorthwindEntitiesLib` project, and then click **OK**. Note that we do not need to reference the data context library.

7. In the `NorthwindFluent` project, add default and small size images for each of the eight categories to the `Assets` folder, named `category1.jpeg`, `category1-small.jpeg`, `category2.jpeg`, `category2-small.jpeg`, and so on.

> **More Information**: You can download suitable images at the following link: `https://github.com/markjprice/cs8dotnetcore3/tree/master/Assets`

8. If you drag and drop the images into the `Assets` folder then they will be included in the project automatically. If you just copy the files in the filesystem then the project does not know to include them. In **Solution Explorer**, toggle **Show All Files**, select the images, right-click, and select **Include In Project**.

9. In the `NorthwindFluent` project, add a class named `CategoriesViewModel` and import the `Packt.Shared`, `System.Collections.ObjectModel`, `System.Net.Http`, and `System.Runtime.Serialization.Json` namespaces.

10. Define a property to store an observable collection of categories and populate its `Categories` property by calling the HTTP service and deserializing the response, as shown in the following code:

```
using Packt.Shared;
using System;
using System.Collections.Generic;
using System.Collections.ObjectModel;
using System.Linq;
using System.Net.Http;
using System.Runtime.Serialization.Json;

namespace NorthwindFluent
{
  public class CategoriesViewModel
  {
    public class CategoryJson
    {
      public int categoryID;
      public string categoryName;
      public string description;
    }

    public ObservableCollection<Category> Categories { get; set; }

    public CategoriesViewModel()
    {
      using (var http = new HttpClient())
      {
        http.BaseAddress = new Uri("https://localhost:5001/");

        var serializer = new DataContractJsonSerializer(
          typeof(List<CategoryJson>));

        var stream = http.GetStreamAsync("api/categories").Result;

        var cats = serializer.ReadObject(stream)
          as List<CategoryJson>;

        var categories = cats.Select(c =>
          new Category
          {
            CategoryID = c.categoryID,
            CategoryName = c.categoryName,
            Description = c.description
          });

        Categories = new ObservableCollection
```

```
          <Category>(categories);
        }
      }
    }
  }
}
```

We had to define a class named `CategoryJson` because the `DataContractJsonSerializer` class is not smart enough to understand the camel casing used in JSON and convert automatically to the title casing used in C#. The simplest solution is to do the conversion manually using LINQ projection.

An alternative would be to use a class like `JsonObject`, but it is fairly low-level to work with and would also require mapping between types, or a third-party library, but I wanted to use built-in types.

 More Information: You can read about `JsonObject` at the following link: `https://docs.microsoft.com/en-us/uwp/api/windows.data.json.jsonobject`

Converting numbers to images

Each category has an ID, 1 to 8. We have images that include the category ID in their filename. To make it easy to map category ID values to category images, we will create a custom converter by implementing the `IValueConverter` interface. `IValueConverter` implementations do not have to implement two-way conversions if the app will only convert one way as ours will, from an `int` to a `BitmapImage`.

1. In the `NorthwindFluent` project, add a class named `CategoryIDToImageConverter`.

2. Implement the `IValueConverter` interface, and convert the integer value for the category ID into a valid path to the appropriate image file, as shown in the following code:

```
using System;
using Windows.UI.Xaml.Data;
using Windows.UI.Xaml.Media.Imaging;

namespace NorthwindFluent
{
  public class CategoryIDToImageConverter : IValueConverter
  {
    public object Convert(object value, Type targetType,
      object parameter, string language)
    {
      int number = (int)value;
```

```
      string path = string.Format(
        format: "{0}/Assets/category{1}-small.jpeg",
        arg0: Environment.CurrentDirectory,
        arg1: number);

      var image = new BitmapImage(new Uri(path));

      return image;
    }

    public object ConvertBack(object value, Type targetType,
      object parameter, string language)
    {
      throw new NotImplementedException();
    }
  }
}
```

3. Navigate to **Build | Build NorthwindFluent**.

4. In the `NorthwindFluent` project, add a **Blank Page** item named `CategoriesPage`.

5. Open `CategoriesPage.xaml.cs`, and add statements to define a `ViewModel` property, and then set it in the constructor, as shown highlighted in the following code:

```
public sealed partial class CategoriesPage : Page
{
  public CategoriesViewModel ViewModel { get; set; }

  public CategoriesPage()
  {
    this.InitializeComponent();
    ViewModel = new CategoriesViewModel();
  }
}
```

6. Open `CategoriesPage.xaml`, import the `Packt.Shared` namespace as `nw`, define a page resource to instantiate a `CategoryIDToImageConverter`, and add elements to make a user interface for categories, as shown highlighted in the following markup:

```
<Page
  x:Class="NorthwindFluent.CategoriesPage"
  xmlns="http://schemas.microsoft.com/winfx/2006/xaml/
presentation"
  xmlns:x="http://schemas.microsoft.com/winfx/2006/xaml"
  xmlns:local="using:NorthwindFluent"
  xmlns:nw="using:Packt.Shared"
  xmlns:d="http://schemas.microsoft.com/expression/blend/2008"
```

```xml
  xmlns:mc="http://schemas.openxmlformats.org/markup-
compatibility/2006"
  mc:Ignorable="d"
  Background="{ThemeResource ApplicationPageBackgroundThemeBrush}">
  <Page.Resources>
    <local:CategoryIDToImageConverter x:Key="id2image" />
  </Page.Resources>
  <Grid>
  <ParallaxView Source="{x:Bind ForegroundElement}"
VerticalShift="50">
    <Image x:Name="BackgroundImage"
           Source="Assets/categories.jpeg"
           Stretch="UniformToFill"/>
  </ParallaxView>

  <ListView x:Name="ForegroundElement"
            ItemsSource="{x:Bind ViewModel.Categories}">
    <ListView.Header>
      <Grid Padding="20"
        Background="{ThemeResource
SystemControlAcrylicElementBrush}">
        <TextBlock Style="{StaticResource TitleTextBlockStyle}"
                   FontSize="24" VerticalAlignment="Center"
                   Margin="12,0" Text="Categories"/>
      </Grid>
    </ListView.Header>

    <ListView.ItemTemplate>
      <DataTemplate x:DataType="nw:Category">
        <Grid Margin="4">
          <Grid.ColumnDefinitions>
            <ColumnDefinition />
            <ColumnDefinition />
          </Grid.ColumnDefinitions>
          <Image
Source="{x:Bind CategoryID, Converter={StaticResource id2image}}"
             Stretch="UniformToFill" Height="200" Width="300" />

          <StackPanel Padding="10" Grid.Column="1" Background=
   "{ThemeResource SystemControlAcrylicElementMediumHighBrush}">
            <TextBlock Text="{x:Bind CategoryName}" FontSize="20"
/>
            <TextBlock Text="{x:Bind Description}" FontSize="16"
/>
          </StackPanel>
        </Grid>
      </DataTemplate>
    </ListView.ItemTemplate>
  </ListView>
  </Grid>
</Page>
```

Note that the code does the following:

- ° Imports the `Packt.Shared` namespace using `nw` as the element prefix.
- ° Defines a page resource that instantiates a converter from category IDs to images.
- ° Uses a `ParallaxView` to provide a large image as a scrolling background for the foreground element, which is the list view of categories, so when the list scrolls, the large background image moves slightly too.
- ° Binds the list view to the view model's `Categories` collection.
- ° Gives the list view an in-app acrylic header.
- ° Gives the list view an item template for rendering each category using its name, description, and an image by converting its ID into an image asset path.

7. Open `MainPage.xaml` and replace the `Grid` with elements to define a navigation view that automatically uses Acrylic material and Reveal highlight in its pane, as shown in the following markup:

```xml
<Page
  x:Class="NorthwindFluent.MainPage"
  xmlns="http://schemas.microsoft.com/winfx/2006/xaml/
presentation"
  xmlns:x="http://schemas.microsoft.com/winfx/2006/xaml"
  xmlns:local="using:NorthwindFluent"
  xmlns:d="http://schemas.microsoft.com/expression/blend/2008"
  xmlns:mc="http://schemas.openxmlformats.org/markup-
compatibility/2006"
  mc:Ignorable="d"
  Background="{ThemeResource ApplicationPageBackgroundThemeBrush}">

  <NavigationView x:Name="NavView"
                  ItemInvoked="NavView_ItemInvoked"
                  Loaded="NavView_Loaded">

    <NavigationView.AutoSuggestBox>
      <AutoSuggestBox x:Name="ASB" QueryIcon="Find"/>
    </NavigationView.AutoSuggestBox>

    <NavigationView.HeaderTemplate>
      <DataTemplate>
        <Grid>
          <Grid.ColumnDefinitions>
            <ColumnDefinition Width="Auto"/>
            <ColumnDefinition/>
          </Grid.ColumnDefinitions>
          <TextBlock Style="{StaticResource TitleTextBlockStyle}"
```

```
                        FontSize="28"
                        VerticalAlignment="Center" Margin="12,0"
                        Text="Northwind Fluent"/>
              <CommandBar Grid.Column="1"
                        HorizontalAlignment="Right"
                        DefaultLabelPosition="Right"
        Background="{ThemeResource
    SystemControlBackgroundAltHighBrush}">
                <AppBarButton Label="Refresh" Icon="Refresh"
                        Name="RefreshButton"
                        Click="RefreshButton_Click"/>
              </CommandBar>
            </Grid>
          </DataTemplate>
        </NavigationView.HeaderTemplate>

        <Frame x:Name="ContentFrame">
          <Frame.ContentTransitions>
            <TransitionCollection>
              <NavigationThemeTransition/>
            </TransitionCollection>
          </Frame.ContentTransitions>
        </Frame>
      </NavigationView>
    </Page>
```

8. Open `MainPage.xaml.cs` and modify its contents, as shown in the following code:

```
using System;
using Windows.UI.Xaml;
using Windows.UI.Xaml.Controls;

namespace NorthwindFluent
{
  public sealed partial class MainPage : Page
  {
    public MainPage()
    {
      this.InitializeComponent();
    }

    private void NavView_Loaded(object sender, RoutedEventArgs e)
    {
      NavView.MenuItems.Add(new NavigationViewItem
      {
        Content = "Categories",
        Icon = new SymbolIcon(Symbol.BrowsePhotos),
```

```
      Tag = "categories"
    });

    NavView.MenuItems.Add(new NavigationViewItem
    {
      Content = "Products",
      Icon = new SymbolIcon(Symbol.AllApps),
      Tag = "products"
    });

    NavView.MenuItems.Add(new NavigationViewItem
    {
      Content = "Suppliers",
      Icon = new SymbolIcon(Symbol.Contact2),
      Tag = "suppliers"
    });

    NavView.MenuItems.Add(new NavigationViewItemSeparator());

    NavView.MenuItems.Add(new NavigationViewItem
    {
      Content = "Customers",
      Icon = new SymbolIcon(Symbol.People),
      Tag = "customers"
    });

    NavView.MenuItems.Add(new NavigationViewItem
    {
      Content = "Orders",
      Icon = new SymbolIcon(Symbol.PhoneBook),
      Tag = "orders"
    });

    NavView.MenuItems.Add(new NavigationViewItem
    {
      Content = "Shippers",
      Icon = new SymbolIcon(Symbol.PostUpdate),
      Tag = "shippers"
    });
}

private void NavView_ItemInvoked(NavigationView sender,
  NavigationViewItemInvokedEventArgs args)
{
  switch (args.InvokedItem.ToString())
  {
    case "Categories":
      ContentFrame.Navigate(typeof(CategoriesPage));
      break;
    default:
```

```
            ContentFrame.Navigate(typeof(NotImplementedPage));
            break;
        }
    }

    private async void RefreshButton_Click(
      object sender, RoutedEventArgs e)
    {
      var notImplementedDialog = new ContentDialog
      {
        Title = "Not implemented",
        Content =
"The Refresh functionality has not yet been implemented.",
        CloseButtonText = "OK"
      };

      ContentDialogResult result =
        await notImplementedDialog.ShowAsync();
    }
  }
}
```

Note that the code does the following:

- ° When the NavView loads, we add menu items to it to show lists of: **Categories**, **Products**, **Suppliers**, **Customers**, **Orders**, and **Shippers**.

- ° Only **Categories** will be implemented at first, so in the event handler for clicking a NavView menu item, we navigate to its page. For all other menu items, we show NotImplementedPage.

- ° The **Refresh** button has not yet been implemented, so we show a pop-up dialog box instead. Like most APIs in UWP, the method to show a dialog is asynchronous. We can use the await keyword for any Task. This means that the main thread will not be blocked while we wait, but it will remember its current position within the statements so that, once the Task has completed, the main thread continues executing from that same point. To use the await keyword, we must mark the method with the async keyword. They always work as a pair. This allows us to write code that looks as simple as synchronous, but underneath it is much more complex. Internally, await creates a state machine to manage the complexity of passing state between any worker threads and the user interface thread.

Testing the HTTP service data binding

Now we can test the UWP app calling the HTTP service.

1. In Visual Studio Code, make sure that the NorthwindService project is running.

2. In Visual Studio 2019, navigate to **Build | Configuration Manager**, and then set the NorthwindFluent app to build and deploy for the **x64** platform.

3. Navigate to **Debug | Start Without Debugging** or press *Ctrl + F5*.

4. Resize the window to show its responsive design, as explained in the following bullets:

    ° When wide, as on a laptop-size device, the full navigation shows with icons and text.

    ° When half-width, as when put side-by-side on a tablet, the navigation is thin and only shows the icons.

    ° When narrow, as on a phone-size device, the navigation hides and the user must click on the hamburger menu to show the navigation pane.

5. As you move your mouse over the navigation, note the Reveal lighting, and when you click on a menu item, such as **Orders**, the highlight bar stretches and animates as it moves, and the **Not yet implemented** message appears, as shown in the following screenshot:

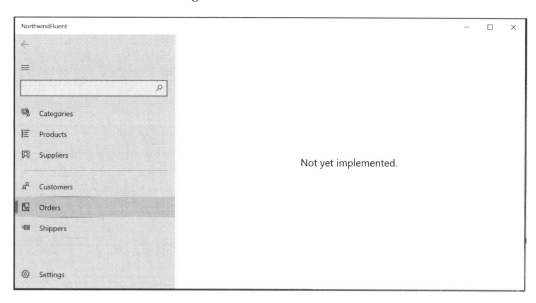

`NavView` adds the search box at the top and the **Settings** menu item at the bottom.

6. Click **Categories** and note the in-app acrylic of the **Categories** header and the Parallax effect on the background image when scrolling up and down the list of categories, and then click on the hamburger menu to collapse the navigation view and give more space for the categories list, as shown in the following screenshot:

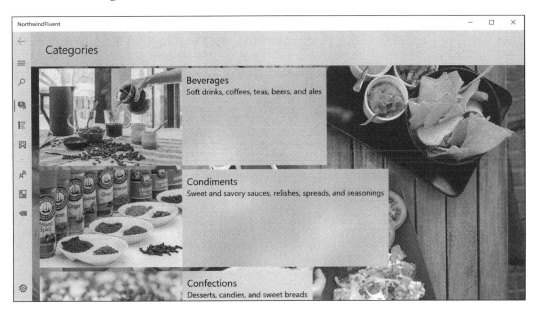

7. Close the app.

I will leave it as an optional exercise for the reader to implement a page for products that is shown when a user clicks on each category that only shows products in that category, or on the Products menu item that shows all 77 products.

Practicing and exploring

Test your knowledge and understanding by answering some questions, get some hands-on practice, and explore this chapter's topics with deeper research.

Exercise 20.1 – Test your knowledge

Answer the following questions:

1. .NET Core 3.0 is cross-platform. Windows Forms and WPF apps can run on .NET Core 3.0. Can those apps therefore run on macOS and Linux?

2. How does a Windows Forms app define its user interface and why is this a problem?

3. How can a WPF or UWP app define its user interface and why is this good for developers?

4. List five layout containers and how their child elements are positioned within them.

5. What is the difference between `Margin` and `Padding` for an element like a `Button`?

6. How are event handlers attached to an object using XAML?

7. What do XAML styles do?

8. Where can you define resources?

9. How can you bind the property of one element to a property on another element?

10. Why might you implement `IValueConverter`?

Exercise 20.2 – Explore topics

Use the following links to read more about this chapter's topics.

- **Enable your device for development**: https://docs.microsoft.com/en-us/windows/uwp/get-started/enable-your-device-for-development

- **Get started with Windows 10 apps**: https://docs.microsoft.com/en-us/windows/uwp/get-started/

- **Getting Started with the Windows Community Toolkit**: https://docs.microsoft.com/en-us/windows/communitytoolkit/getting-started

- **Design and code Windows apps**: https://docs.microsoft.com/en-us/windows/uwp/design/

- **Develop UWP apps**: https://docs.microsoft.com/en-us/windows/uwp/develop/

Summary

In this chapter, you learned that .NET Core 3.0 supports older technologies for building Windows desktop applications including Windows Forms and WPF.

You learned how to build a graphical user interface using XAML and the new Fluent Design System, including features such as Acrylic material, Reveal lighting, and Parallax view.

You also learned how to share resources in an app, how to replace a control's template, how to bind to data and controls, and how to prevent thread blocking with multitasking and the C# `async` and `await` keywords.

In the next chapter, you will learn how to build mobile apps using Xamarin.Forms.

Chapter 21

Building Cross-Platform Mobile Apps Using Xamarin.Forms

This chapter is about learning how to take C# mobile by building a cross-platform mobile app for iOS and Android. The mobile app will allow the listing and management of customers in the Northwind database.

Apart from UWP apps in *Chapter 20, Building Windows Desktop Apps*, this is the only chapter that does not use .NET Core 3.0. But by 2020, with the release of .NET 5.0, all app models, including mobile, will share the same unified .NET platform.

Mobile development cannot be learned in a single chapter, but like web development, mobile development is so important these days that I wanted to introduce you to some of what is possible. Think of this chapter as a bonus. This chapter will give you a taste to inspire you, and then you can learn more from a book dedicated to mobile development.

More Information: For examples of mobile projects that you could build, you could read *Xamarin.Forms Projects*, available at the following link: `https://www.packtpub.com/application-development/xamarinforms-projects`

The mobile app that you create will call the Northwind service that you built using ASP.NET Core Web API in *Chapter 18, Building and Consuming Web Services*. If you have not built the Northwind service, please go back and build it now or download it from the GitHub repository for this book at the following link:

`https://github.com/markjprice/cs8dotnetcore3`

You will need a computer with macOS, Xcode, and Visual Studio for Mac to complete this chapter. The client-side Xamarin.Forms mobile app will be written using **Visual Studio for Mac**.

In this chapter, we will cover the following topics:

- Understanding Xamarin and Xamarin.Forms
- Building mobile apps using Xamarin.Forms
- Consuming a web service from a mobile app

Understanding Xamarin and Xamarin.Forms

To create a mobile app that only needs to run on iPhones, you might choose to build it with Objective-C or Swift and UIKit using Xcode.

To create a mobile app that only needs to run on Android phones, you might choose to build it with Java or Kotlin and Android SDK using Android Studio.

 More Information: In 2019, iPhone and Android have a combined global smartphone market share of 99.6%. What about the other 0.4%? Xamarin supports creating Tizen mobile apps for Samsung devices. You can read about **Tizen .NET** at the following link: `https://docs.microsoft.com/en-us/xamarin/xamarin-forms/platform/other/tizen`

But what if you need to create a mobile app that can run on iPhones *and* Android phones? And what if you only want to create that mobile app once using a programming language and development platform that you are already familiar with? **Xamarin** enables developers to build cross-platform mobile apps for Apple iOS (iPhone and iPad), macOS, and Google Android using C# and .NET, which are then compiled to native APIs and run on native phone platforms. It is based on the open source implementation of .NET known as **Mono**.

Business logic layer code can be written once and shared between all mobile platforms. User interface interactions and APIs are different on various mobile platforms, so the user interface layer is often custom for each platform. But even here, there is a technology that can ease development.

How Xamarin.Forms extends Xamarin

Xamarin.Forms extends Xamarin to make cross-platform mobile development even easier by sharing most of the user interface layer, as well as the business logic layer.

Like WPF and UWP apps, Xamarin.Forms uses XAML to define the user interface once for all platforms using abstractions of platform-specific user interface components. Applications built with Xamarin.Forms draw the user interface using native platform widgets, so the app's look-and-feel fits naturally with the target mobile platform.

A user experience built using Xamarin.Forms will never perfectly fit a specific platform like one custom built with Xamarin, but for enterprise mobile apps, it is more than good enough.

Mobile first, cloud first

Mobile apps are often supported by services in the cloud. Satya Nadella, CEO of Microsoft, famously said this:

> *To me, when we say mobile first, it's not the mobility of the device, it's actually the mobility of the individual experience. [...] The only way you are going to be able to orchestrate the mobility of these applications and data is through the cloud.*

As you have seen earlier in this book, to create an ASP.NET Core Web API service to support a mobile app, we can use Visual Studio Code. To create Xamarin. Forms apps, developers can use either Visual Studio 2019 or Visual Studio for Mac. To compile iOS apps, you will require a Mac and Xcode.

 More Information: If you want to use Visual Studio 2019 to create a mobile app, then you can read how to connect to a Mac build host at the following link: https://docs.microsoft. com/en-us/xamarin/ios/get-started/installation/ windows/connecting-to-mac/

Market share numbers should be taken in the context that iOS users engage far more with their devices, which is important for monetizing mobile apps, either through up-front sales, in-app purchases, or advertising. Recent analyst reports show that iPhone apps tend to generate at least 60% more revenue than Android apps, but do your own research here as the mobile world moves fast.

A summary of which coding tool can be used on its own to build which type of app is shown in the following table:

	iOS	Android	ASP.NET Core Web API
Visual Studio Code	No	No	Yes
Visual Studio for Mac	Yes	Yes	Yes
Visual Studio 2019	No	Yes	Yes

 More Information: You can read about the pros and cons of the two major mobile platforms based on aspects such as revenue generation and user engagement at the following link: `https://fueled.com/blog/app-store-vs-google-play/`

Understanding additional functionality

We will build a mobile app that uses a lot of the skills and knowledge that you learned in previous chapters. We will also use some functionality that you have not seen before.

Understanding the INotificationPropertyChanged interface

The `INotifyPropertyChanged` interface enables a model class to support two-way data binding. It works by forcing the class to have an event named `PropertyChanged`, as shown in the following code:

```
using System.ComponentModel;

public interface INotifyPropertyChanged
{
   event PropertyChangedEventHandler PropertyChanged;
}
```

Inside each property in the class, when setting a new value, you must raise the event (if it is not `null`) with an instance of `PropertyChangedEventArgs` containing the name of the property as a `string` value, as shown in the following code:

```
private string companyName;

public string CompanyName
{
  get => companyName;
  set
  {
    companyName = value; // store the new value being set

    PropertyChanged?.Invoke(this,
      new PropertyChangedEventArgs(nameof(CompanyName)));
  }
}
```

When a user interface control is data-bound to the property, it will automatically update to show the new value when it changes.

This interface is not just for mobile apps. It can also be used in other graphical user interfaces such as Windows desktop apps.

Understanding dependency services

Mobile platforms such as iOS and Android implement common features in different ways, so we need a way to get a platform-native implementation of common features. We can do that using dependency services. It works like this:

- Define an interface for the common feature, for example, `IDialer` for a phone number dialer.

- Implement the interface for all the mobile platforms that you need to support, for example, iOS and Android, and register the implementations with an attribute, as shown in the following code:

```
[assembly: Dependency(typeof(PhoneDialer))]
namespace NorthwindMobile.iOS
{
   public class PhoneDialer : IDialer
```

- In the common mobile project, get the platform-native implementation of an interface by using the dependency service, as shown in the following code:

```
var dialer = DependencyService.Get<IDialer>();
```

 More Information: You can read more about Xamarin dependency services at the following link: `https://docs.microsoft.com/en-us/xamarin/xamarin-forms/app-fundamentals/dependency-service/introduction`

Understanding Xamarin.Forms user interface components

Xamarin.Forms includes some specialized controls for building mobile user interfaces. They are divided into four categories:

- **Pages**: represent cross-platform mobile application screens, for example, `ContentPage`, `NavigationPage`, and `CarouselPage`.

- **Layouts**: represent the structure of a combination of other user interface components, for example, `StackLayout`, `RelativeLayout`, and `FlexLayout`.

- **Views**: represent a single user interface component, for example, Label, Entry, Editor, and Button.
- **Cells**: represent a single item in a list or table view, for example, TextCell, ImageCell, SwitchCell, and EntryCell.

Understanding the ContentPage view

The ContentPage view is for simple user interfaces.

It has a ToolbarItems property that shows actions the user can perform in a platform-native way. Each ToolbarItem can have an icon and text.

```
<ContentPage.ToolbarItems>
  <ToolbarItem Text="Add" Activated="Add_Activated"
               Order="Primary" Priority="0" />
</ContentPage.ToolbarItems>
```

More Information: You can read more about Xamarin.Forms Pages at the following link: https://docs.microsoft.com/en-us/xamarin/xamarin-forms/user-interface/controls/pages

Understanding the Entry and Editor controls

The Entry and Editor controls are used for editing text values and are often data-bound to an entity model property, as shown in the following markup:

```
<Editor Text="{Binding CompanyName, Mode=TwoWay}" />
```

Use Entry for a single line of text.

More Information: You can read about the Entry control at the following link: https://docs.microsoft.com/en-us/xamarin/xamarin-forms/user-interface/text/entry

Use Editor for multiple lines of text.

More Information: You can read about the Editor control at the following link: https://docs.microsoft.com/en-us/xamarin/xamarin-forms/user-interface/text/editor

Understanding the ListView control

The `ListView` control is used for long lists of data-bound values of the same type. It can have headers and footers and its list items can be grouped.

It has cells to contain each list item. There are two built-in cell types: text and image. Developers can define custom cell types.

Cells can have context actions that appear when the cell is swiped on iPhone or long pressed on Android. A context action that is destructive can be shown in red, as shown in the following markup:

```
<TextCell Text="{Binding CompanyName}"
          Detail="{Binding Location}">
  <TextCell.ContextActions>
    <MenuItem Clicked="Customer_Phoned" Text="Phone" />
    <MenuItem Clicked="Customer_Deleted" Text="Delete"
              IsDestructive="True" />
  </TextCell.ContextActions>
</TextCell>
```

More Information: You can read more about the `ListView` control at the following link: `https://docs.microsoft.com/en-us/xamarin/xamarin-forms/user-interface/listview/`

Building mobile apps using Xamarin.Forms

We will build a mobile app that runs on either iOS or Android for managing customers in Northwind.

Good Practice: If you have never run Xcode, run it now to see the Start window to ensure that all its required components are installed and registered. If you do not run Xcode, then you might get errors with your projects later in Visual Studio for Mac.

Adding Android SDKs

To target Android, you must install at least one Android SDK. A default installation of Visual Studio for Mac already includes one Android SDK, but it is often an older version to support as many Android devices as possible.

To use the latest features of Xamarin.Forms, you must install a more recent Android SDK:

1. Start Visual Studio for Mac and navigate to **Visual Studio | Preferences**.

2. In **Preferences**, navigate to **Projects | SDK Locations | Android**, and select the **Android Platform SDK** and **System Image** that you want, for example, **Android 10.0 - Q**. When installing an Android SDK, you must select at least one **System Image** to use as a virtual machine emulator for testing.

3. Select or clear checkboxes to decide what to install or remove, or click the **Updates Available** button to update existing selections and then click **Install Updates**, as shown in the following screenshot:

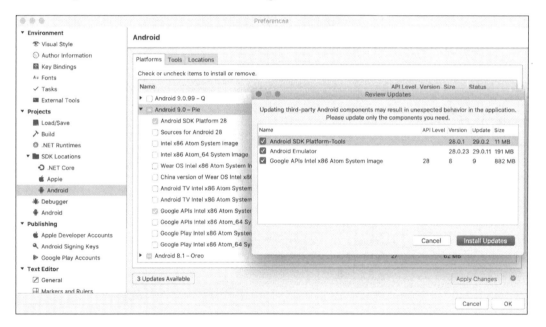

You might also have to set the paths on the **Locations** tab.

Creating a Xamarin.Forms solution

We will now create a solution with projects for a cross-platform mobile app:

1. Either click **New** in the Start window, navigate to **File | New Solution...** or press *Shift + Command + N*.

2. In the **New Project** dialog, select **Multiplatform | App** in the left-hand column, and select **Xamarin.Forms | Blank Forms App** using C# in the middle column, and then click on **Next**.

3. Enter **App Name** as `NorthwindMobile`, **Organization Identifier** as `com.packt`, and select **Shared Code** to **Use Shared Library**, as shown in the following screenshot:

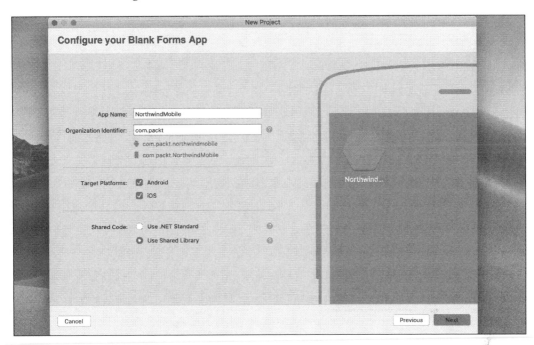

4. Click on **Next**.

5. Change **Location** to `/Users/[user_folder]/Code/PracticalApps`, and then click **Create**. After a few moments, the solution and three projects will be created, as shown in the following list:

    1. `NorthwindMobile`: Components shared cross-device, including XAML files defining the user interface.

    2. `NorthwindMobile.Android`: Components specific to Android.

    3. `NorthwindMobile.iOS`: Components specific to iOS.

6. NuGet packages should be automatically restored, but if not, then right-click on the `NorthwindMobile` solution, choose **Update NuGet Packages**, and accept any license agreements.

7. Navigate to **Build | Build All** and wait for the solution to build the projects, as shown in the following screenshot:

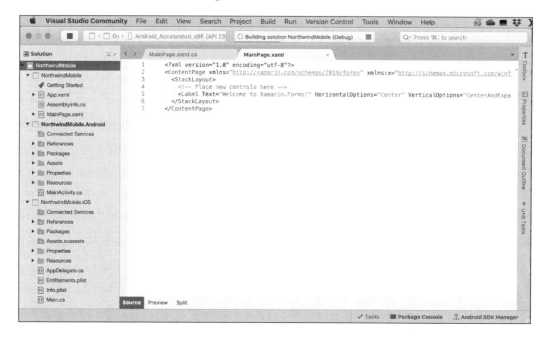

Creating an entity model with two-way data binding

Although we could reuse the .NET Standard entity data model library that you created in *Chapter 14, Practical Applications of C# and .NET*, we need the entities to implement two-way data binding, so we will create a new `Customer` entity class and it can be put in the project shared by both iOS and Android:

1. Right-click on the project named `NorthwindMobile`, go to **Add | New Folder**, and name it `Models`.

2. Right-click on the `Models` folder and go to **Add | New File...**

3. In the **New File** dialog, go to **General | Empty Class**, enter the name `Customer`, and click **New**.

4. Modify the statements to define a `Customer` class that implements the `INotifyPropertyChanged` interface and has six properties, as shown in the following code:

```
using System.Collections.Generic;
using System.Collections.ObjectModel;
using System.ComponentModel;
```

```csharp
using System.Runtime.CompilerServices;

namespace NorthwindMobile.Models
{
  public class Customer : INotifyPropertyChanged
  {
    public static IList<Customer> Customers;

    static Customer()
    {
      Customers = new ObservableCollection<Customer>();
    }

    public event PropertyChangedEventHandler
      PropertyChanged;

    private string customerID;
    private string companyName;
    private string contactName;
    private string city;
    private string country;
    private string phone;

    // this attribute sets the propertyName parameter
    // using the context in which this method is called
    private void NotifyPropertyChanged(
      [CallerMemberName] string propertyName = "")
    {
      // if an event handler has been set then invoke
      // the delegate and pass the name of the property
      PropertyChanged?.Invoke(this,
        new PropertyChangedEventArgs(propertyName));
    }

    public string CustomerID
    {
      get => customerID;
      set
      {
        customerID = value;
        NotifyPropertyChanged();
      }
    }

    public string CompanyName
    {
      get => companyName;
      set
      {
        companyName = value;
        NotifyPropertyChanged();
      }
```

```
    }

    public string ContactName
    {
      get => contactName;
      set
      {
        contactName = value;
        NotifyPropertyChanged();
      }
    }

    public string City
    {
      get => city;
      set
      {
        city = value;
        NotifyPropertyChanged();
      }
    }

    public string Country
    {
      get => country;
      set
      {
        country = value;
        NotifyPropertyChanged();
      }
    }

    public string Phone
    {
      get => phone;
      set
      {
        phone = value;
        NotifyPropertyChanged();
      }
    }

    public string Location
    {
      get => $"{City}, {Country}";
    }

    // for testing before calling web service
    public static void AddSampleData()
    {
      Customers.Add(new Customer
      {
```

```
            CustomerID = "ALFKI",
            CompanyName = "Alfreds Futterkiste",
            ContactName = "Maria Anders",
            City = "Berlin",
            Country = "Germany",
            Phone = "030-0074321"
        });

        Customers.Add(new Customer
        {
            CustomerID = "FRANK",
            CompanyName = "Frankenversand",
            ContactName = "Peter Franken",
            City = "München",
            Country = "Germany",
            Phone = "089-0877310"
        });

        Customers.Add(new Customer
        {
            CustomerID = "SEVES",
            CompanyName = "Seven Seas Imports",
            ContactName = "Hari Kumar",
            City = "London",
            Country = "UK",
            Phone = "(171) 555-1717"
        });
    }
  }
}
```

Note the following:

- The class implements `INotifyPropertyChanged`, so a two-way bound user interface component such as `Editor` will update the property and vice versa. There is a `PropertyChanged` event that is raised whenever one of the properties is modified using a `NotifyPropertyChanged` private method to simplify the implementation.

- After loading from the service, which will be implemented later in this chapter, the customers are cached locally using `ObservableCollection`. This supports notifications to any bound user interface components, such as `ListView` so that the user interface can redraw itself when the underlying data adds or removes items from the collection.

- In addition to properties for storing values retrieved from the HTTP service, the class defines a read-only `Location` property. This will be bound to a summary list of customers to show the location of each one.

- For testing purposes, when the HTTP service is not available, there is a method to populate three sample customers.

Creating a component for dialing phone numbers

To show an example of a component that is specific to Android and iOS, you will define and then implement a phone dialer component:

1. Right-click on the `NorthwindMobile` folder and choose **Add | New File...**.

2. Go to **General | Empty Interface**, name the file `IDialer`, and click **New**.

3. Modify the `IDialer` contents, as shown in the following code:

```
namespace NorthwindMobile
{
  public interface IDialer
  {
    bool Dial(string number);
  }
}
```

4. Right-click on the `NorthwindMobile.iOS` folder and choose **Add | New File...**.

5. Go to **General | Empty Class**, name the file `PhoneDialer`, and click **New**.

6. Modify its contents, as shown in the following code:

```
using Foundation;
using NorthwindMobile.iOS;
using UIKit;
using Xamarin.Forms;

[assembly: Dependency(typeof(PhoneDialer))]
namespace NorthwindMobile.iOS
{
  public class PhoneDialer : IDialer
  {
    public bool Dial(string number)
    {
      return UIApplication.SharedApplication.OpenUrl(
        new NSUrl("tel:" + number));
    }
  }
}
```

7. Right-click the `Packages` folder in the `NorthwindMobile.Android` project and choose **Add NuGet Packages...**.

8. Search for `Plugin.CurrentActivity` and click **Add Package**.

9. Open `MainActivity.cs` and import the `Plugin.CurrentActivity` namespace.

10. In the `OnCreate` method, add a statement to initialize the current activity, as shown in the following code:

```
CrossCurrentActivity.Current.Init(
  this, savedInstanceState);
```

11. Right-click the `NorthwindMobile.Android` folder and choose **Add** | **New File...**.

12. Choose **General** | **Empty Class**, name the file `PhoneDialer`, and click **New**.

13. Modify its contents, as shown in the following code:

```
using Android.Content;
using Android.Telephony;
using NorthwindMobile.Droid;
using Plugin.CurrentActivity;
using System.Linq;
using Xamarin.Forms;
using Uri = Android.Net.Uri;

[assembly: Dependency(typeof(PhoneDialer))]
namespace NorthwindMobile.Droid
{
  public class PhoneDialer : IDialer
  {
    public bool Dial(string number)
    {
      var context = CrossCurrentActivity.Current.Activity;

      if (context == null) return false;

      var intent = new Intent(Intent.ActionCall);
      intent.SetData(Uri.Parse("tel:" + number));

      if (IsIntentAvailable(context, intent))
      {
        context.StartActivity(intent); return true;
      }

      return false;
    }

    public static bool IsIntentAvailable(
      Context context, Intent intent)
    {
      var packageManager = context.PackageManager;

      var list = packageManager
        .QueryIntentServices(intent, 0)
        .Union(packageManager
```

```
        .QueryIntentActivities(intent, 0));

    if (list.Any()) return true;

    var manager = TelephonyManager.FromContext(context);
    return manager.PhoneType != PhoneType.None;
  }
 }
}
```

14. In the `NorthwindMobile.Android` project, expand **Properties**, and open `AndroidManifest.xml`.

15. In **Required permissions**, check the **CallPhone** permission, as shown in the following screenshot:

Creating views for the customers list and customer details

You will now replace the existing `MainPage` with a view to show a list of customers and a view to show the details for a customer:

1. In the `NorthwindMobile` project, right-click `MainPage.xaml`, select **Remove**, and then click **Remove from Project**.

2. Right-click the `NorthwindMobile` project, select **Add | New Folder**, and name the new folder `Views`.

3. Right-click the `Views` folder, choose **Add | New File...**, and then select **Forms | Forms ContentPage XAML**.

4. Name the file `CustomersList` and click **New**.

5. Right-click the `Views` folder, choose **Add | New File...**, and then select **Forms | Forms ContentPage XAML**.

6. Name the file `CustomerDetails` and click **New**.

Implementing the customer list view

First, we will implement the list of customers:

1. Open `CustomersList.xaml` and modify its contents, as shown highlighted in the following markup:

```xml
<?xml version="1.0" encoding="UTF-8"?>
<ContentPage
  xmlns="http://xamarin.com/schemas/2014/forms"
  xmlns:x="http://schemas.microsoft.com/winfx/2009/xaml"
  x:Class="NorthwindMobile.Views.CustomersList"
  Title="List">

  <ContentPage.Content>
    <ListView ItemsSource="{Binding .}"
              VerticalOptions="Center"
              HorizontalOptions="Center"
              IsPullToRefreshEnabled="True"
              ItemTapped="Customer_Tapped"
              Refreshing="Customers_Refreshing">
      <ListView.Header>
        <Label Text="Northwind Customers"
               BackgroundColor="Silver" />
      </ListView.Header>
      <ListView.ItemTemplate>
        <DataTemplate>
          <TextCell Text="{Binding CompanyName}"
                    Detail="{Binding Location}">
            <TextCell.ContextActions>
              <MenuItem Clicked="Customer_Phoned"
                        Text="Phone" />
              <MenuItem Clicked="Customer_Deleted"
                        Text="Delete"
                        IsDestructive="True" />
            </TextCell.ContextActions>
          </TextCell>
        </DataTemplate>
      </ListView.ItemTemplate>
    </ListView>
  </ContentPage.Content>

  <ContentPage.ToolbarItems>
```

```
    <ToolbarItem Text="Add" Activated="Add_Activated"
                 Order="Primary" Priority="0" />
  </ContentPage.ToolbarItems>

</ContentPage>
```

Note the following:

- ° `ContentPage` has had its `Title` attribute set to `List`.
- ° `ListView` has its `IsPullToRefreshEnabled` set to `true`.
- ° Handlers have been written for the following events:

  `Customer_Tapped`: A customer being tapped to show their details.

  `Customers_Refreshing`: The list being pulled down to refresh its items.

  `Customer_Phoned`: A cell being swiped left on iPhone or long pressed on Android and then tapping **Phone**.

  `Customer_Deleted`: A cell being swiped left on iPhone or long pressed on Android and then tapping **Delete**.

  `Add_Activated`: The **Add** button being tapped.

- ° A data template defines how to display each customer: large text for the company name and smaller text for the location underneath.
- ° An **Add** button is displayed so that users can navigate to a detail view to add a new customer.

2. Open `CustomersList.xaml.cs` and modify the contents, as shown highlighted in the following code:

```
using System;
using System.Threading.Tasks;
using NorthwindMobile.Models;
using Xamarin.Forms;

namespace NorthwindMobile.Views
{
  public partial class CustomersList : ContentPage
  {
    public CustomersList()
    {
      InitializeComponent();
      Customer.Customers.Clear();
      Customer.AddSampleData();
      BindingContext = Customer.Customers;
    }

    async void Customer_Tapped(
      object sender, ItemTappedEventArgs e)
```

```
  {
    var c = e.Item as Customer;
    if (c == null) return;

    // navigate to the detail view and show the tapped customer
    await Navigation.PushAsync(new CustomerDetails(c));
  }

  async void Customers_Refreshing(object sender, EventArgs e)
  {
    var listView = sender as ListView;
    listView.IsRefreshing = true;

    // simulate a refresh
    await Task.Delay(1500);

    listView.IsRefreshing = false;
  }

  void Customer_Deleted(object sender, EventArgs e)
  {
    var menuItem = sender as MenuItem;
    Customer c = menuItem.BindingContext as Customer;
    Customer.Customers.Remove(c);
  }

  async void Customer_Phoned(object sender, EventArgs e)
  {
    var menuItem = sender as MenuItem;
    var c = menuItem.BindingContext as Customer;

    if (await this.DisplayAlert("Dial a Number",
      "Would you like to call " + c.Phone + "?",
      "Yes", "No"))
    {
      var dialer = DependencyService.Get<IDialer>();
      if (dialer != null) dialer.Dial(c.Phone);
    }
  }

  async void Add_Activated(object sender, EventArgs e)
  {
    await Navigation.PushAsync(new CustomerDetails());
  }
  }
  }
}
```

Note the following:

- ° `BindingContext` is set to the sample list of `Customers` in the constructor of the page.

- ° When a customer in the list view is tapped, the user is taken to a details view (which you will create in the next step).

- ○ When the list view is pulled down, it triggers a simulated refresh that takes 1.5 seconds.

- ○ When a customer is deleted in the list view, they are removed from the bound collection of customers.

- ○ When a customer in the list view is swiped, and the **Phone** button is tapped, a dialog prompts the user as to whether they want to dial the number, and if so, the platform-native implementation will be retrieved using the dependency resolver and then used to dial the number.

- ○ When the **Add** button is tapped, the user is taken to the customer detail page to enter details for a new customer.

Implementing the customer detail view

Next, we will implement the customer detail view:

1. Open `CustomerDetails.xaml` and modify its contents, as shown highlighted in the following markup, and note the following:

   - ○ `Title` of `ContentPage` has been set to `Edit`.

   - ○ A customer `Grid` with two columns and six rows is used for the layout. This is the same `Grid` element that was introduced in *Chapter 20, Building Windows Desktop Apps*.

   - ○ `Entry` views are two-way data bound to properties of the `Customer` class.

   - ○ `InsertButton` has an event handler to execute code to add a new customer.

```xml
<?xml version="1.0" encoding="UTF-8"?>
<ContentPage
  xmlns="http://xamarin.com/schemas/2014/forms"
  xmlns:x="http://schemas.microsoft.com/winfx/2009/xaml"
  x:Class="NorthwindMobile.Views.CustomerDetails"
  Title="Edit">

  <ContentPage.Content>
    <StackLayout VerticalOptions="Fill"
                 HorizontalOptions="Fill">
      <Grid BackgroundColor="Silver">
        <Grid.ColumnDefinitions>
          <ColumnDefinition/>
          <ColumnDefinition/>
        </Grid.ColumnDefinitions>
        <Grid.RowDefinitions>
          <RowDefinition/>
```

```xml
                    <RowDefinition/>
                    <RowDefinition/>
                    <RowDefinition/>
                    <RowDefinition/>
                    <RowDefinition/>
                </Grid.RowDefinitions>
                <Label Text="Customer ID" VerticalOptions="Center"
                        Margin="6" />
                <Entry Text="{Binding CustomerID, Mode=TwoWay}"
                        Grid.Column="1" />
                <Label Text="Company Name" Grid.Row="1"
                        VerticalOptions="Center" Margin="6" />
                <Entry Text="{Binding CompanyName, Mode=TwoWay}"
                        Grid.Column="1" Grid.Row="1" />
                <Label Text="Contact Name" Grid.Row="2"
                        VerticalOptions="Center" Margin="6" />
                <Entry Text="{Binding ContactName, Mode=TwoWay}"
                        Grid.Column="1" Grid.Row="2" />
                <Label Text="City" Grid.Row="3"
                        VerticalOptions="Center" Margin="6" />
                <Entry Text="{Binding City, Mode=TwoWay}"
                        Grid.Column="1" Grid.Row="3" />
                <Label Text="Country" Grid.Row="4"
                        VerticalOptions="Center" Margin="6" />
                <Entry Text="{Binding Country, Mode=TwoWay}"
                        Grid.Column="1" Grid.Row="4" />
                <Label Text="Phone" Grid.Row="5"
                        VerticalOptions="Center" Margin="6" />
                <Entry Text="{Binding Phone, Mode=TwoWay}"
                        Grid.Column="1" Grid.Row="5" />
            </Grid>
            <Button x:Name="InsertButton" Text="Insert Customer"
                    Clicked="InsertButton_Clicked" />
        </StackLayout>
    </ContentPage.Content>
</ContentPage>
```

2. Open `CustomerDetails.xaml.cs` and modify its contents, as shown in the following code:

```csharp
using System;
using NorthwindMobile.Models;
using Xamarin.Forms;

namespace NorthwindMobile.Views
{
  public partial class CustomerDetails : ContentPage
  {
    public CustomerDetails()
    {
      InitializeComponent();
      BindingContext = new Customer();
      Title = "Add Customer";
    }
```

```
public CustomerDetails(Customer customer)
{
  InitializeComponent();
  BindingContext = customer;
  InsertButton.IsVisible = false;
}

async void InsertButton_Clicked(object sender, EventArgs e)
{
  Customer.Customers.Add((Customer)BindingContext);
  await Navigation.PopAsync(animated: true);
}
  }
}
```

Note the following:

- The default constructor sets the binding context to a new `customer` instance and the view title is changed to `Add Customer`.

- The constructor with a `customer` parameter sets the binding context to that instance and hides the **Insert** button because it is not needed when editing an existing customer due to two-way data binding.

- When **Insert** is tapped, the new customer is added to the collection and the navigation is moved back to the previous view asynchronously.

Setting the main page for the mobile app

Finally, we need to modify the mobile app to use our customer list wrapped in a navigation page as the main page instead of the old one that we deleted, which was created by the project template:

1. Open `App.xaml.cs`.

2. Import the `NorthwindMobile.Views` namespace.

3. Modify the statement that sets `MainPage` to create an instance of `CustomersList` wrapped in an instance of `NavigationPage`, as shown in the following code:

```
MainPage = new NavigationPage(new CustomersList());
```

Testing the mobile app

We will now test the mobile app using an iPhone emulator:

1. In Visual Studio for Mac, to the right of the **Run** button in the toolbar, select the **NorthwindMobile.iOS** project, select **Debug**, and select **iPhone XR iOS 12.4** (or later), as shown in the following screenshot:

2. Click on the **Run** button in the toolbar or navigate to **Run | Start Debugging**. The project will build, and then after a few moments, **Simulator** will appear, your running mobile app, as shown in the following screenshot:

3. Click **Seven Seas Imports** and modify its **Company Name**, as shown in the following screenshot of the customer details page:

4. Click **List** to return to the list of customers and note that the company name has been updated due to the two-way data binding.

5. Click **Add**, and then fill in the fields for a new customer, as shown in the following screenshot:

6. Click **Insert Customer** and note that the new customer has been added to the bottom of the list.

7. Slide one of the customers to the left to reveal two action buttons, **Phone** and **Delete**, as shown in the following screenshot:

8. Click **Phone** and note the pop-up prompt to the user to dial the number of that customer with **Yes** and **No** buttons.

9. Click **No**.

10. Slide one of the customers to the left to reveal two action buttons, **Phone** and **Delete**, and then click on **Delete**, and note that the customer is removed.

11. Click, hold, and drag the list down and then release, and note the animation effect for refreshing the list, but remember that we did not implement this feature, so the list does not change.

12. Navigate to **Simulator | Quit Simulator** or press *Cmd* + *Q*.

We will now make the mobile app call `NorthwindService` to get the list of customers.

Consuming a web service from a mobile app

Apple's **App Transport Security (ATS)** forces developers to use good practice, including secure connections between an app and a web service. ATS is enabled by default and your mobile apps will throw an exception if they do not connect securely.

 More Information: You can read more about ATS at the following link: `https://docs.microsoft.com/en-us/xamarin/ios/app-fundamentals/ats`

If you need to call a web service that is secured with a self-signed certificate like our `NorthwindService` is, it is possible but complicated.

 More Information: You can read more about handling self-signed certificates at the following link: `https://docs.remotingsdk.com/Clients/Tasks/HandlingSelfSignedCertificates/NET/`

For simplicity, we will allow insecure connections to the web service and disable the security checks in the mobile app.

Configuring the web service to allow insecure requests

First, we will enable the web service to handle insecure connections at a new URL:

1. Start Visual Studio Code and open the `NorthwindService` project.
2. Open `Startup.cs`, and in the `Configure` method, comment out the HTTPS redirection, as shown highlighted in the following code:

```
public void Configure(IApplicationBuilder app,
   IWebHostEnvironment env)
{
   if (env.IsDevelopment())
   {
     app.UseDeveloperExceptionPage();
   }

   // app.UseHttpsRedirection();

   app.UseRouting();
```

3. Open `Program.cs`, and in the `CreateHostBuilder` method, add the insecure URL, as shown highlighted in the following code:

```
public static IHostBuilder CreateHostBuilder(
  string[] args) =>
  Host.CreateDefaultBuilder(args)
    .ConfigureWebHostDefaults(webBuilder =>
    {
      webBuilder.UseStartup<Startup>();
      webBuilder.UseUrls(
        "https://localhost:5001", // for MVC
        "http://localhost:5003"   // for iOS
      );
    });
```

4. Navigate to **Terminal | New Terminal** and select `NorthwindService`.

5. In **Terminal**, start the web service by entering the following command:
```
dotnet run
```

6. Start Chrome and test that the web service is returning customers as JSON by navigating to the following URL: `http://localhost:5003/api/customers/`

7. Close Chrome.

Configuring the iOS app to allow insecure connections

Now you will configure the `NorthwindMobile.iOS` project to disable ATS to allow insecure HTTP requests to the web service:

1. In the `NorthwindMobile.iOS` project, open **Info.plist**.

2. Click the **Source** tab, add a new entry named `NSAppTransportSecurity`, and set its **Type** to **Dictionary**.

3. In the dictionary, add a new entry named `NSAllowsArbitraryLoads` and set its **Type** to **Boolean** with a value of **Yes**, as shown in the following screenshot:

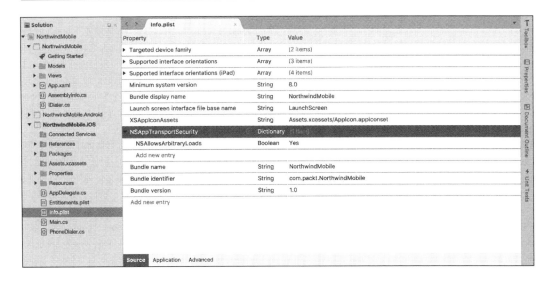

Adding NuGet packages for consuming a web service

Next, we must add some NuGet packages to each of the platform-specific projects to enable HTTP requests and process the JSON responses:

1. In the `NorthwindMobile.iOS` project, right-click on the folder named `Packages` and choose **Add NuGet Packages...**.

2. In the **Add Packages** dialog, in the **Search** box, enter `System.Net.Http`.

3. Select the package named **System.Net.Http** and then click **Add Package**.

4. In the **License Acceptance** dialog, click **Accept**.

5. In the `NorthwindMobile.iOS`, right-click on the folder named `Packages` and choose **Add NuGet Packages...**.

6. In the **Add Packages** dialog, in the **Search** box, enter `Newtonsoft.Json`.

7. Select the package named **Newtonsoft.Json** and then click **Add Package**.

8. Repeat the previous steps, 1 to 7, to add the same two NuGet packages to the project named `NorthwindMobile.Android`.

Getting customers from the web service

Now, we can modify the customers list page to get its list of customers from the web service instead of using sample data:

1. In the `NorthwindMobile` project, open `Views\CustomersList.xaml.cs`.

2. Import the following namespaces:

```
using System;
using System.Collections.Generic;
using System.Linq;
using System.Net.Http;
using System.Net.Http.Headers;
using System.Threading.Tasks;
using Newtonsoft.Json;
using NorthwindMobile.Models;
using Xamarin.Forms;
```

3. Modify the `CustomersList` constructor to load the list of customers using the service proxy instead of the `AddSampleData` method, as shown in the following code:

```
public CustomersList()
{
  InitializeComponent();

  Customer.Customers.Clear();
  // Customer.AddSampleData();

  var client = new HttpClient
  {
    BaseAddress = new Uri("http://localhost:5003/")
  };

  client.DefaultRequestHeaders.Accept.Add(
    new MediaTypeWithQualityHeaderValue(
    "application/json"));

  HttpResponseMessage response = client
    .GetAsync("api/customers").Result;

  response.EnsureSuccessStatusCode();

  string content = response.Content
    .ReadAsStringAsync().Result;

  var customersFromService = JsonConvert
    .DeserializeObject<IEnumerable<Customer>>(content);

  foreach (Customer c in customersFromService
    .OrderBy(customer => customer.CompanyName))
  {
    Customer.Customers.Add(c);
```

```
    }

    BindingContext = Customer.Customers;
}
```

4. Navigate to **Build | Clean All**. Changes to `Info.plist` like allowing insecure connections sometimes requires a clean build.

5. Navigate to **Build | Build All**.

6. Run the `NorthwindMobile` project and note that 91 customers are loaded from the web service, as shown in the following screenshot:

7. Navigate to **Simulator | Quit Simulator** or press *Cmd + Q*.

Practicing and exploring

Test your knowledge and understanding by answering some questions, get some hands-on practice, and explore this chapter's topics with more in-depth research.

Exercise 21.1 – Test your knowledge

Answer the following questions:

1. What is the difference between Xamarin and Xamarin.Forms?

2. What are the four categories of Xamarin.Forms user interface components and what do they represent?

3. List four types of cell.

4. How can you enable a user to perform an action on a cell in a list view?

5. How do you define a dependency service to implement platform-specific functionality?

6. When would you use an `Entry` instead of an `Editor`?

7. What is the effect of setting `IsDestructive` to `true` for a menu item in a cell's context actions?

8. When would you call the methods `PushAsync` and `PopAsync` in a Xamarin. Forms mobile app?

9. How do you show a pop-up modal message with simple button choices like Yes or No?

10. What is Apple's ATS and why is it important?

Exercise 21.2 - Explore topics

Use the following links to read more about this chapter's topics:

- **Xamarin.Forms documentation**: https://docs.microsoft.com/en-us/xamarin/xamarin-forms/

- **Xamarin.Essentials provides developers with cross-platform APIs for their mobile applications**: https://docs.microsoft.com/en-us/xamarin/essentials/

- **Self Signed iOS Certifcates and Certificate Pinning in a Xamarin. Forms application**: https://nicksnettravels.builttoroam.com/ios-certificate/

- **Protecting your users with certificate pinning**: https://basdecort.com/2018/07/18/protecting-your-users-with-certificate-pinning/

- **HttpClient and SSL/TLS implementation selector for iOS/macOS**: https://docs.microsoft.com/en-gb/xamarin/cross-platform/macios/http-stack

Summary

In this chapter, you learned how to build a mobile app using Xamarin.Forms, which is cross-platform for iOS and Android (and potentially other platforms) and consumes data from a web service using the `System.Net.Http` and `Newtonsoft.Json` NuGet packages.

Epilogue

I wanted this book to be different from the others on the market. I hope that you found it to be a brisk, fun read, packed with practical hands-on walk-throughs of each subject.

For subjects that you wanted to learn more about, I hope that the **More Information** notes and links that I provided pointed you in the right direction.

I have already started work on the fifth edition, which we plan to publish soon after the release of .NET 5.0 in November 2020. If you have suggestions for subjects that you would like to see covered, or you spot mistakes that need fixing in the book or code, please let me know via my GitHub account at the following link:

```
https://github.com/markjprice/
```

I wish you the best of luck with all your C# and .NET projects!

Other Books You May Enjoy

If you enjoyed this book, you may be interested in these other books by Packt:

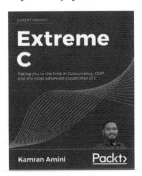

Extreme C

Kamran Amini

ISBN: 978-1-78934-362-5

- Build advanced C knowledge on strong foundations, rooted in first principles
- Memory structures, compiler pipelines. This book will help you understand how they work, and how to make the most of them
- Apply object-oriented design principles to your procedural C code
- Write low-level code that's close to the hardware and squeezes maximum performance out of a computer system
- Master concurrency, multithreading, multiprocessing, and integration with other languages
- Testing and debugging, packaging and delivery, inter-process communication, and enterprise architecture for C program

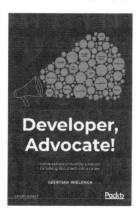

Developer, Advocate!

Geertjan Wielenga

ISBN: 978-1-78913-874-0

Expert opinions on:

- Discover how developer advocates are putting developer interests at the heart of the software industry in companies including Microsoft and Google

- Gain the confidence to use your voice in the tech community

- Immerse yourself in developer advocacy techniques

- Understand and overcome the challenges and obstacles facing developer advocates today

- Hear predictions from the people at the cutting edge of tech

- Explore your career options in developer advocacy

Leave a review - let other readers know what you think

Please share your thoughts on this book with others by leaving a review on the site that you bought it from. If you purchased the book from Amazon, please leave us an honest review on this book's Amazon page. This is vital so that other potential readers can see and use your unbiased opinion to make purchasing decisions, we can understand what our customers think about our products, and our authors can see your feedback on the title that they have worked with Packt to create. It will only take a few minutes of your time, but is valuable to other potential customers, our authors, and Packt. Thank you!

Index

B

bags
working with, LINQ used 404-406
Base Class Library (BCL) 7
big integers
working with 254
binary arithmetic operators 73, 74
binary classification 654
binary number system 42
binary object
converting, to string 95, 96
binary shift operators 77, 78
bitwise operators 77, 78
Blazor
about 464
reference link 466
blog archive page type
reviewing 585
book solution code repository
cloning 18
Booleans
storing 47
Bootstrap
URL 490
Bootstrap grid system
reference link 582
braces
using, with if statements 81
breakpoint
customizing 125, 126
setting 121, 122
Brotli algorithm
used, for compressing 310, 312
byte arrays
strings, encoding as 314, 315, 316

C

C# 1.0 to C# 8.0 26-28
cache busting, via params
reference link 527
casting
between, types 89
within inheritance hierarchies 213
casting exceptions
avoiding 214, 215
catch blocks

await keyword, using 454
C# basics 31
C# compiler versions
discovering 29, 30
enabling 30
reference link 29
C# grammar
about 32
blocks 33
comments 32
statements 32
checked statement
overflow exceptions, throwing with 102, 103
child task 444
circular reference, solving
reference link 228
C# keywords
relating, to .NET types 231-233
classes
extending 208
inheritance, preventing 211
inheriting from 207
members, hiding 209, 210
members, overriding 210
overriding, preventing 211
splitting, with partial 171, 172
classic ASP.NET
versus modern ASP.NET Core 483, 484
class, instantiating
about 147
assembly, referencing 147
namespace, importing 147, 148
class libraries
building 144
class, defining 145, 146
class, initiating 147
creating 145
creating, for Northwind database
context 473, 476
creating, for Northwind entity models 468-472
creating, that needs testing 136, 137
inheriting, from System.Object 149
members 146
multiple files, managing 148
objects 148
setting up 179-181

D

data binding
between elements 707, 708
HTTP service, creating 709
HTTP service data binding, testing 724, 725
numbers, converting to images 717-723
to data, from secure HTTP service 713, 714
user interface, creating to call
       HTTP service 715-717
using 707

data manipulation, with EF Core
about 387
entities, deleting 390, 391
entities, inserting 387-389
entities, updating 389, 390

data protection
block sizes 331
IVs 331
IVs, generating 332
keys, generating 332
key sizes 330
keys, using 330
salts 331
techniques 329

data protection, techniques
authentication 330
authorization 330
encryption and decryption 329
hashes 329
signatures 330

data science 651

data seeding
about 368
reference link 368

dates
strings, parsing to 96, 97

deadlocks
avoiding 448, 449

Debug
instrumenting with 129
reference link 129

debugging
during, development 120

decimal number system
using 42

decimal types
versus double types 45-47

deconstruct method
about 205
reference link 166

deep learning 655

default implementations
interfaces, defining with 195-198

default rounding rules 93

default trace listener
writing 130

default values
obtaining, for types 51, 52

delegates
defining 188, 189
handling 188, 189
used, for calling methods 186, 187

dependency injection (DI) design pattern
reference link 516

dependency services 733

dependent assemblies 228

destructor 205

development environment
setting up 2
tools, recommendation 3

dictionaries
about 268, 269
working with 271

Dictionary Attacks
reference link 331

Digital Signature Algorithm (DSA)
about 333
versus RSA 342

directories
managing 294-296

Dispose method 207

DNS
working with 277, 278

Document Database Providers, for Entity
       Framework Core
reference link 360

do statement
looping with 87

dotnet CLI
used, for compiling code 17
used, for running code 17

dotnet command
about 236
project, creating 236
project, managing 237

types, converting to 94, 95
string formatting 259
strings
  building efficiently 260
  encodings, as byte arrays 314-316
  parsing, to dates 96, 97
  parsing, to number 96, 97
  parsing, to times 96, 97
struct types
  working with 203, 204
Structured Query Language (SQL) 396
supervised classification 654
supplier model
  enabling, to insert entities 500, 501
Support Vector Machine (SVM) 657
Swagger
  enabling 627, 631, 632
  reference link 631, 632
Swagger UI
  about 631
  used, for testing requests 632-637
switch expressions
  used, for simplifying switch statements 85
  using 114
switch statement
  branching with 82
  pattern matching with 84, 85
  using 114
  simplifying, with switch expressions 85
symbols 262
synchronization types
  applying 451
syntactic sugar
  used, for Sweetening LINQ syntax 417
syntax
  of regular expression 262
System.Convert type
  converting with 92
System.IO.FileSystem
  reference link 231
System.Text.Json APIs
  reference link 323

T

tasks
  about 429, 430
  child tasks 444

nested tasks 444
  pros and cons, reference link 441
  running, asynchronously 437
  used, for running multiple actions
        asynchronously 439-441
  waiting for 441, 442
  working 444
Task.WaitAll(Task[]) method 441
Task.WaitAny(Task[]) method 441
templates
  control template, replacing 705
  defining 583
  using 704
test controller logic
  reference link 520
Test Driven Development (TDD)
  about 135
  reference link 135
testing dataset 653
text
  decoding 313
  decoding, in files 316
  digits entered, checking as 261
  encoding 313
  encoding, in files 316
  storing 40
  working with 255
text encodings
  ANSI/ISO encodings 314
  ASCI 314
  UTF-7 314
  UTF-8 314
  UTF-16 314
  UTF-32 314
text input
  obtaining, from user 61
text streams
  writing to 303, 304
ThenBy method
  used, for sorting entities by single
        property 402
thread 429, 430
thread pool
  reference link 430
Trace
  instrumenting with 129
trace levels
  switching 132-135

Made in the USA
Middletown, DE
01 September 2020

18079508R00453